Mental Health
and
Mental Illness

FIFTH EDITION

Mental Health
and
Mental Illness

■■■■■

FIFTH EDITION

Patricia D. Barry, R.N., Ph.D., C.S.
*Clinical Nurse Specialist
in Consultation/Liaison Psychiatry
Psychotherapist in Private Practice
Nursing Consultant
Hartford, Connecticut*

J.B. Lippincott Company
Philadelphia

Acquisitions Editor: **Margaret Belcher**
Sponsoring Editor: **Ellen Campbell**
Project Editor: **Barbara Ryalls**
Indexer: **Lynne Mahan**
Art Director: **Susan Hermansen**
Text Designer: **Holly Reid McLaughlin**
Cover Designer: **Larry Pezzato**
Production Manager: **Helen Ewan**
Production Coordinator: **Kathryn Rule**
Compositor: **Bi-Comp, Inc.**
Printer/Binder: **R. R. Donnelly & Sons Company**

5th Edition

Library of Congress Cataloging-in-Publication Data

Barry, Patricia D.
 Mental health and mental illness / Patricia D. Barry. — 5th ed.
  p.   cm.
 Includes bibliographical references and index.
 ISBN 0-397-55013-8
 1. Psychiatry. 2. Mental health. 3. Psychiatric nursing.
 I. Title.
  [DNLM: 1. Mental Disorders—nurses' instruction. 2. Mental
 Health—nurses' instruction. 3. Psychiatric Nursing. WY 160 B281m
 1994]
 RC454.4B372   1994
 616.89—dc20
 DNLM/DLC   93-1743
 for Library of Congress   CIP

Any procedure or practice described in this book should be applied by the health care practitioner under appropriate supervision in accordance with professional standards of care used with regard to the unique circumstances that apply in each practice situation. Care has been taken to confirm the accuracy of information presented and to describe generally accepted practices. However, the authors, editors, and publisher cannot accept any responsibility for errors or omissions or for any consequences from application of the information in this book and make no warranty, express or implied, with respect to the contents of the book.

Every effort has been made to ensure drug selections and dosages are in accordance with current recommendations and practice. Because of ongoing research, changes in government regulations, and the constant flow of information on drug therapy, reactions, and interactions, the reader is cautioned to check the package insert for each drug for indications, dosages, warnings, and precautions, particularly if the drug is new or infrequently used.

To my family, and to nurses and their clients

■■■■■
Preface

It is a pleasure to present the fifth edition of **Mental Health and Mental Illness.**

The changes in mental health care in the United States during the past decade have markedly altered the way in which nurses plan and deliver care to clients with mental disorders. The financial constraints imposed by rapidly escalating health care costs require that the care of such clients have an essential focus on delivering therapeutic care in much shorter periods of time.

The urgency of this "time-effective" requirement has caused a refinement of the role of nursing in mental health care delivery. The roles that nurses perform in mental health settings contribute significantly to restabilizing clients who are learning to cope with their life circumstances in new ways. In fact, some would say that the primary reason for hospital admission is to provide an environment of nursing care in which to stabilize an individual's health status, and to provide health care teaching so that effective health self-care is possible when discharge occurs.

Consequently, this edition includes a new unit on the field of mental health as it is impacted by the mental health care needs of a changing population. Economic patterns forcing this change include the prevalence of homeless persons, many of whom are psychiatrically disabled, and governmental and insurance industry cost containment.

The most widely utilized classification of mental disorders that describes the different types of mental illness is published by the American Psychiatric Association (APA) in a book titled *The Diagnostic and Statistical Manual of Mental Disoders* (DSM), which is reviewed and updated every 5 to 7 years. Committees of psychiatrists, psychologists, nurses, and social workers meet in every region of the United States to discuss revisions to the previous list. The most recent revision of the categories of mental disorders was the *Third Edition, Revised* (DSM-III-R), published in 1987. The APA will publish the *Fourth Edition* (DSM-IV) in early 1994; during the preparation of this fifth edition of **Mental Health and Mental Illness,** a preliminary working draft of the DSM-IV list of mental disorders was published. There-

vii

fore, Unit VI Categories of Mental Disorders have been updated to reflect the changes that are expected to appear in DSM-IV.

The text continues to expand on the knowledge base of nursing process and nursing diagnosis as the conceptual framework for mental health nursing. A new unit on "Nursing the Client with a Mental Disorder" includes chapters on the use of nursing diagnosis and nursing care planning in the mental health setting. The chapter on nursing care planning provides nursing care guidelines for clients with the altered mental states most commonly seen in inpatient settings (including psychosis, depression, mania, anxiety, confusional state, and violence), using a case study format that consists of a clinical history followed by nursing diagnosis and care planning recommendations.

These guidelines provide simple and appropriate nursing actions that implement the nursing diagnoses for specific altered mental states. They can also provide nurses with a framework of intervention when caring for clients who may have a specific DSM-IV mental disorder *diagnosis* but who present with two or three different types of mental *states*. Nursing care recommendations for each of the specific types of mental disorders are also included in the chapters in Unit VI, Categories of Mental Disorders.

The fifth edition continues to expand on the knowledge of stress adaptation theory. All chapters have been revised to integrate the concepts of effective coping in the theoretical base of mental health theory. In addition, the role of ineffective coping has been emphasized to assist the student in understanding the continuum of maladaptive behaviors that may be encountered in mental illness.

At the end of each unit, the reader will find exercises for developing critical thinking skills, which include a case study and discussion questions. These exercises are based on a hypothetical situation that pertains to the content of the unit. The discussion questions related to each case study are designed to prompt students to examine their own responses to the circumstances described. This new material can give students and faculty the opportunity to examine and increase their understanding of the personal vulnerability, sensibility, and individual value systems that are an important foundation of mental health nursing and that have a significant influence on the quality of mental health nursing care.

As *Mental Health and Mental Illness* enters its next stage of development, I want to thank those faculty members who generously gave of their time and expertise to evaluate and provide feedback about this edition. In the book's early planning stages, I wanted to know the specific content that would be most useful to include to meet the changing needs of mental health nursing faculty members and their students. Accordingly, Lippincott developed a questionnaire that was mailed to a number of faculty members who use this text. Nursing educators, representing all regions of the country, were asked to describe the content that would be most valuable to add or expand upon in this edition.

Psychiatric nursing faculty responded by sending thoughtful, well-analyzed, and organized comments about the content of the previous edition and the ways in which new content could be useful in their faculty positions in mental health nursing. These recommendations formed the foundation of planning for this, the fifth edition.

I would also like to thank the nursing faculty who select this text for their students; I hope that it will meet your needs and theirs as we all work to provide compassionate nursing care to individuals whose quality of life is deeply affected by mental illness.

I want to say thank-you also to two Lippincott editors. I met initially with Ellen Campbell (who developed the questionnaire) to integrate the faculty recommendations into the outline of the new edition. It has been a pleasure to know and work with Ellen for several years. Margaret Belcher subsequently became the book's editor and has been a remarkable godmother as the plan of the book went through several stages of development. Margaret's vision of the overall goals of this revision as they related to the identified needs of faculty was unwavering. I have developed a strong appreciation for her keen intellect, as well as her understanding of the scope of nursing education in today's mental health care environment.

Nancy Jeresak, a clinical nurse specialist at the Institute of Living in Hartford, Connecticut, provided expert clinical consultation for the case material described in Chapter 19, Nursing Care Planning with Specific Types of Disordered Mental States. It is important to note that each mental state description includes a composite of hypothetical clinical information. In no case is the clinical material descriptive of an actual client in the Institute of Living. Judy Logan provided valuable library assistance in the research of information and references used in the new and revised chapters in this edition. She also contributed significantly to the updating of chapter bibliographies.

Very importantly, the excellent assistance of Judy Bierly in preparing, reviewing, and organizing all aspects of the manuscript preparation was essential to the successful completion of this revision. I am deeply indebted to her for her editorial assistance and overview of the project.

Patricia D. Barry, R.N., Ph.D., C.S.
Hartford, Connecticut
May 1993

■■■■■
Contents

Unit II
Concepts of Psychiatric/Mental Health Nursing

Unit V
Nursing the Client with a Mental Disorder
157

Unit **VII**
Interventions and Treatment of
Mental Disorders

Mental Health
and
Mental Illness

FIFTH EDITION

Unit I

Patterns of Mental Health Care

Chapter 1

■■■■■

Current and Evolving Patterns of Mental Health Care

Behavioral Objectives

After reading this chapter the student will be able to:

Name the three major forces that have caused changes in mental health care since the 1940s.

Explain how each of the above forces is continuing to cause changes in mental health care services.

Explain the shift from inpatient to community-based mental health services which began in the late 1950s.

Describe the current economic factors that have affected the availability of mental health care services.

List three of the major plans designed to decrease mental health care costs.

The treatment of mental disorders has gone through many stages of development during the past 100 years. The guiding principle throughout has been to move the mentally disordered person from his or her normal family, social, and community surroundings to a sheltered environment. During the past 20 years the sheltered environment has shifted from one that was primarily custodial to one that is dynamically oriented toward rehabilitation of the person with a mental disorder. This philosophic change in treatment is evident from the preadmission to active treatment and postdischarge phases of mental health care.

■ Changes in Inpatient Mental Health Treatment

There are many forces that have shaped these changes. The most significant forces have been:

1. The development of medications that significantly decrease the major symptoms of psychiatric disorders, psychosis, and depression. These medications, when properly used, can allow persons who formerly required long-term institutionalization to return to outpatient community care.
2. Economic forces that do not support long-term psychiatric care. Funding emphasis has shifted from chronic inpatient care to community models of outpatient care.
3. The advent of a variety of mental health disciplines that train individuals to work with different aspects of a mental health client's psychological and social functioning in both inpatient and community care settings. With their combined skills, these individuals comprise a treatment team that provides a comprehensive mental health care approach.

A discussion of the medications used to treat various symptoms of mental disorders can be found in Unit VII, Interventions and Treatment of Mental Disorders (Chapter 31, Psychopharmacology and Electroshock Treatment of Mental Disorders). The economic forces that are shaping the changing patterns of mental health care in the United States will be addressed in this chapter. The mental health treatment team and its approaches to therapeutic care will be presented in Chapter 3, Inpatient Hospitalization: The Mental Health Treatment Team and the Therapeutic Milieu.

■ History of the Shift from Inpatient to Community-Based Mental Health Services

The transfer from inpatient to outpatient care of seriously mentally disordered individuals began in the late 1950s and early 1960s. This change was the result of a number of factors:

1. Research on psychiatric disorders was increasingly demonstrating that environmental and social factors contributed strongly to the development of mental illness.
2. An increase in the incidence of mental illness in the community can be inferred by the incidence of mental disorders in inductees into the Armed Services. During the pre-induction process of U.S. citizens in World War II, 1,875,000 men were found to be emotionally unfit for service and 850,000 (40% of *all* discharges) were released from active service because of mental illness.
3. The introduction of phenothiazines (the major tranquilizers) in the mid-1950s reduced the incidence of active psychotic episodes in persons with schizophrenia and other types of psychotic mental disorders.
4. Studies in state mental institutions revealed that the conditions under which patients lived were poor.

The outcome of these findings was that many government agencies were eager to develop community-based programs in which formerly state-supported mental patients could receive care as outpatients in their home communities. During the early 1960s there was momentum in this country to develop the "Great Society." Many social programs were started as a result of legislation passed during the Kennedy and Johnson administrations.

The premise of community psychiatry is that custodial, institution-based care should be reserved only for acutely ill individuals. People formerly treated in long-term residential care centers should be returned to their home environments. Its focus also is on prevention, using community-based programs.

■■■■■■■■■

"It is based on the assumption that sociocultural conditions significantly influence the definition, manifestation, and course of mental illness.
It studies the role of the social environment in mental illness.

■ ■ ■ ■ ■ ■ ■ ■ ■   *continued*

It is concerned with the organization and delivery of mental health services.

It uses social and environmental measures to prevent mental illness and to treat and care for those who develop mental disorders.

It supplies treatment and care as close as possible to the patient's residence or workplace.

It utilizes community resources to extend services beyond the more conventional treatment programs."*

* Community Psychiatry: A Reappraisal. New York, Mental Health Materials Center 1983

■ The Importance of Economic Factors in Decision-Making About Mental Health Treatment

As pointed out above, the availability of new medications that significantly decreased dangerous levels of psychosis and depression caused health care and economic strategists to call for major changes in the treatment of mental illness. During the 1950s, mentally disordered individuals who were previously dangerous to themselves or others could be treated with medications and were able to return safely to their communities.

During the 1980s, the cost of health care in the United States increased at a greater rate than any other cost in our national economy. These costs have been addressed in both the public and private sectors. The result has been strategic planning to reduce costs. Mental health care costs have been targeted in the following areas:

1. Deinstitutionalization in public-funded mental health care.
2. Changes in payment mechanisms by private insurers for both inpatient and outpatient care.
3. The use of diagnostic related groups (DRGs) by federal and state funding agencies to create guidelines for lengths of hospital stay.
4. Quality assurance programs mandated by public and private agencies to ensure the quality of health care to all persons, regardless of whether their care is paid by the individual, public funding, or insurance.

These factors have brought about many changes in current mental health treatment and will continue to be important forces in the future. The reasons are described below.

Deinstitutionalization. Rather than serving as centers for chronic care, federal and state-funded, long-term psychiatric care institutions have adapted to treat persons in crisis or with serious mental disorders requiring acute (14 days or less) and mid-term (usually up to 60 days) treatment. The effects of deinstitutionalization on mental health care will be discussed in Chapter 2, Community Treatment Settings for Mental Disorders. Alternative, community-based mental health treatment programs are intended to provide ongoing treatment for the chronically mentally ill individual.

Changes in payment mechanisms used by private insurers for mental health care. Because mental health care costs have escalated faster than general physical health care costs, stringent limits have been set for both inpatient and outpatient mental health treatment. The limit on inpatient care costs has resulted in a more aggressive treatment process during acute "crisis" admissions, usually 14 days or less in duration. Longer-term admissions are becoming increasingly rare because of the stringent criteria used to justify inpatient hospitalization.

The emphasis on short lengths of inpatient admissions is being driven by a policy known as "capping." Capping is the practice of allowing a limited dollar amount for lifetime psychiatric care. For example, an insurance company may set a limit of $50,000 on the amount that it will reimburse to a person during his or her lifetime for any type of psychiatric care, whether in the hospital or in the community. A person with a chronic psychiatric disorder such as schizophrenia can use the "lifetime" psychiatric benefit before the age of 30.

Use of diagnostic related groups (DRGs) by federal and state funding agencies. In another effort to reduce unnecessary hospital costs, DRGs are being used to establish guidelines for appropriate lengths of stay. Using these guidelines, hospitals are permitted to charge for a specific number of days of treatment. The approved number of days can be extended only when there are unusual complications that meet previously defined criteria. Payments for Medicaid and Medicare admissions cut off after the DRG deadline is reached. Accordingly, short-term aggressive treatment that discharges clients as soon as they are reasonably able to leave the hospital is rewarded. On the other hand, if hospitals lag in discharging a significant number of their clients, they can quickly encounter major financial difficulties.

Quality assurance programs mandated by public and private agencies. These programs are designed to monitor the quality of health care delivered in the hospital and the community. All health care providers, including nurses, are reviewed, whether in inpatient or outpatient settings and public or privately funded health care. Using quality assurance guidelines, the following aspects of health care are evaluated:

1. Assessment
2. Accuracy of diagnosis
3. Rationale for diagnostic testing
4. Effectiveness of care planning
5. Evaluation of outcomes

The quality assurance programs in hospitals actively review the care planning of nurses in the psychiatric setting. Good quality inpatient and outpatient mental health care is strongly dependent on the effective use of the nursing process by psychiatric nurses. The nursing process will be described in Unit II, Concepts of Psychiatric/Mental Health Nursing.

CHAPTER 1 QUESTIONS

1. What single treatment mode, when properly used, can allow persons who formerly required long-term institutionalization to return to outpatient community care?

2. Name the cost factor that increased at a greater rate than any other in the United States during the 1980s.

3. Define "capping."

4. What are two aspects of health care that are evaluated using quality assurance guidelines?

BIBLIOGRAPHY

Burgess, A.W. (1990). *Psychiatric nursing in the hospital and the community* (5th ed.). Norwalk, CT: Appleton & Lange.

Johnson, B. (1993). *Psychiatric Mental Health Nursing* (3rd ed.). Philadelphia: J.B. Lippincott.

McFarland, G.K., Wasli, E.L., & Gerety, E.K. (1992). *Nursing diagnosis and process in psychiatric mental health nursing* (2nd ed.). Philadelphia: J.B. Lippincott.

McFarland, G.K., Thomas, M.D. (1991). *Psychiatric mental health nursing: Application of the nursing process*. Philadelphia: J.B. Lippincott.

Riesdorph-Ostrow, W. (1989). Deinstitutionalization: a public policy perspective. *Journal of Psychosocial Nursing & Mental Health Services, 27,* 4–8.

Shives, L.R. (Ed.). (1990). *Basic concepts of psychiatric mental health nursing* (2nd ed.). Philadelphia: J.B. Lippincott.

Stuart, G.W., & Sundeen, S.J. (Eds.). (1991). *Principles and practice of psychiatric nursing* (4th ed.). St. Louis: Mosby–Year Book.

Wilson, H.S., & Kneisl, C.R. (1992). *Psychiatric nursing*. Redwood City, CA: Addison-Wesley Health Sciences Division.

Chapter 2

■■■■■

Community Treatment Settings for Mental Disorders

Behavioral Objectives

After reading this chapter the student will be able to:

Name three different groups of individuals who are outpatient mental health care consumers.

List the different types of payment mechanisms that are used for community mental health services.

Describe the five basic mental health services of a community mental health center.

Name the three most common problems of the homeless mentally ill.

Describe the differences between the services offered by community mental health centers and the assertive community treatment model of mental health care.

Mental Health and Mental Illness,
Fifth Edition, by Patricia D. Barry.
J.B. Lippincott Company, Philadelphia © 1994.

In order to decrease all health care costs, pressure is being actively exerted to treat persons with mental disorders in their home environments. There are three major populations of individuals who may be home-based or outpatient mental health care consumers:

1. *The physically disabled or elderly infirm who require home services for mental health care.* These individuals use a variety of payment options that affect the quality and duration of their care at home: Medicare or Medicaid, private health insurance, health maintenance organizations, self-pay, or indigent with no available funds. The clinical options open to these individuals include contracting for mental health services from visiting nurse associations, other public or private mental health care-giver groups, or private practitioners.

2. *Individuals with nondisabling mental disorders who are able to continue working and fulfilling their normal social roles.* The ability of such individuals to continue their normal roles is supported by the use of psychotropic medications. Psychotropic medications are ones that alter the neurochemistry of the brain so that brain chemistry approaches more normal levels. Disabling mental symptoms are reduced to more comfortable levels. Pharmacotherapy is augmented by outpatient individual or outpatient group therapy. Funding options for outpatient therapy and medications include partial funding by private health insurance, limited numbers of therapy sessions funded by health maintenance organizations, very restricted numbers of sessions funded by Medicaid and Medicare, or self-payment by persons who have adequate resources. The individual who lacks financial or insurance resources will most often function at a borderline disabled level. This type of disabled mental functioning usually increases the risks not only to the individual, but also to his or her family members.

3. *Individuals who are psychiatrically disabled.* Because of the decreasing public and private support for mental health services, there is a growing percentage of persons with chronic, disabling mental disorders. It is this segment of the population that is particularly affected by the current crisis in health care costs. The Community Mental Health Act was originally designed to provide a range of mental health care options to all persons. Inadequate funding and lack of comprehensive policy planning left woeful gaps in care, particularly when accompanied by the national trend in deinstitutionalizing chronically mentally disabled per-

sons. Currently, the most commonly used treatment option open to chronically mentally ill persons is the community mental health center.

■ Community Mental Health Centers (CMHCs)

The Community Mental Health Act, passed in 1964, states that a community health center should be accessible to the community it serves and that it should provide five basic services:

1. Inpatient treatment
2. Outpatient treatment
3. Partial hospitalization (day or night programs)
4. Emergency services on a 24-hour-a-day basis
5. Consultation and education services to community agencies, groups, and individuals

Several other services, while not mandatory, are desirable in order to assist in the functioning, implementation, and continuity of these five basic services:

6. Diagnostic services
7. Rehabilitation
8. Precare and aftercare
9. Training programs for professionals and nonprofessionals
10. Research and evaluation

When a center has all 10 of these services and they are fully operational, the center is known as a **comprehensive community mental health center.**

The Community Mental Health Act specifies that such a center must serve a specific area with a population between 75,000 and 200,000. This geographic area is known as a **catchment area.** In a densely populated urban area, such a maximum population may be found in less than 100 square blocks; in some remote rural areas, the minimum population may be scattered over hundreds of square miles. Thus, the community mental health center is not always in close proximity to area residents wanting or needing services. Ideally, though, travel time to the center should not exceed 1 hour.

Of the delivery modalities within the community mental health system, two have enjoyed outstanding growth and appear to have permanently changed the face of psychiatric practice. They are crisis intervention and the partial hospital or day-treatment programs. Almost all private and public mental hospitals have begun both partial hospitalization and crisis intervention services.

■ The Homeless and Mental Illness

The political decision-making to deinstitutionalize persons with chronic mental illness began with the advent of phenothiazine medications. These medications dramatically reduced the psychosis-induced instability of many individuals with serious mental disorders. Legislators at both the state and federal levels looked at the high cost of long-term psychiatric hospitalization. Social scientists assured them that community-based care would be in the best interests of all concerned: the mentally ill and the general, tax-paying public.

It was believed that chronically mentally ill persons who were institutionalized developed a social breakdown syndrome. This syndrome included the following characteristics: lack of initiative, submission to authority, withdrawal, and excessive dependence on the institution.

While deinstitutionalization was humane in its original philosophy, the actual implementation of the concept has been seriously undermined by the lack of good community alternatives. It has been widely recognized that the largest group of users of public community mental health services are the poor. At this time a large proportion of the individuals utilizing community mental health treatment services are the "homeless" poor. Of the homeless, nearly half are chronically mentally ill. These individuals are often alienated from their families and are socially isolated. They avoid contact with social structures such as community mental health treatment centers. Because of these factors they often discontinue their medications, become psychotic and disorganized, and begin to live on the street.

As noted above, community-based crisis intervention and partial hospitalization programs are the most important deterrents to inpatient hospitalization. These two types of outpatient care are currently being offered by two intervention models: community mental health centers and assertive community treatment.

■ Assertive Community Treatment (ACT)

During the 1980s, community mental health professionals recognized that the use of assertive, active outreach to the homeless mentally ill and others who avoided coming to community mental health centers was an important intervention model. Table 2-1 compares the differences in approach.

Early research on the cost-effectiveness of these two programs indicates that clients who are participating in ACT programs have fewer hospitalizations on an annual basis than persons using CMHCs. The cost of the ACT program is higher on a per-client basis than that of

Table 2-1. Comparison of Characteristics of Assertive Community Treatment (ACT) and Community Mental Health Center (CMHC) Programs

Characteristic	ACT	CMHC
Treatment base	Predominately in the community	In the community, but predominantly in the clinic
Staffing	Clinical staff-to-client ratio of around 1 to 10	Clinical staff-to-client ratio of around 1 to 30 to 50
Frequency of contact	Daily in most cases	Usually once every one or two weeks
Frequency of contact with family or support structure	Average of once a week	Occasional
Medication	Responsibility of staff; can be administered by staff daily if needed	Responsibility of client or family
Physical health	Monitored by program staff	Therapist and case manager encourage a healthy life-style
After-hours service	Monitored by program staff; team on call	Provided by therapist or case manager during day hours, emergency room or mobile team otherwise
Occupational rehabilitation	Actual job placement or volunteer job	Psychosocial programs
Housing arrangements	Responsibility of staff	Varies, but usually responsibility of client and family
Continuity of care	Team follows case through hospitalization; maintains legal, health system, and other contacts	Responsibility of therapist and case manager
Staff structure	Team structure: integration of clinical and case management roles	Individual staff model: therapist and case manager are different individuals

Hospital and Community Psychiatry, 41(6), p. 643, 1990. Copyright 1990, the American Psychiatric Association. Reprinted by permission.

the CMHC. The higher cost is offset by the higher psychiatric hospitalization patterns of CMHC clients or, more important, the higher psychiatric hospitalization patterns of the mentally ill who do not customarily use the CMHC services.

In contrast to the CMHC model, which requires that clients seek out services at the mental health center, the direct searching out of mentally ill persons in the community ensures that a larger percentage of potential clients are reached. Additionally, the ACT model uses a case manager who oversees all aspects of support, including direct mental health services, housing, physical care, and so on. The case manager is also the clinician providing direct care. The case load of the case manager is usually around 10 to 12 clients and allows for more active support of the client during precrisis periods.

An important component of this model is ongoing training in activities of daily living, such as communication, problem-solving, and coping skills. Other important aspects of the case manager approach are medication overview and support regarding adequate housing and physical care. More detailed research on the ACT model can support its use and increased availability to the chronically mentally ill, who are the primary users of community psychiatry services.

■ **General Hospital Emergency Room Treatment of Psychiatric Emergencies Among the Homeless**

When community programs are unsuccessful in averting psychiatric hospital admission, the triage of psychiatric clients in the emergency rooms of general hospitals is instituted. The term *triage* describes the way that the care of persons with mental or physical health problems is prioritized. Persons who are most acutely ill with a prognosis of surviving their current illness are prioritized at the highest level. Health care resources are apportioned according to the priority of care assigned to a specific health problem.

In the current health care environment there are large numbers of homeless or unemployed persons with no health insurance. Particularly during the past decade, the use of the general hospital emergency room has markedly increased as the initial care setting. Many homeless individuals suffer from chronic mental disorders such as schizophrenia, substance abuse, or cognitive mental disorders. Sometimes they are diagnosed with all three disorders concurrently. Adding to their psychiatric distress is their noncompliance in taking the medications that could stabilize their mental conditions.

Changes in the law have allowed law enforcement agencies to

involuntarily admit mentally disturbed, antisocial, or dangerous individuals to general hospital emergency rooms for crisis assessment and intervention services. Inner city hospitals have shown an increase of nearly 100% in the number of admissions of mentally ill persons to their emergency rooms during the past decade.

Because of deinstitutionalization, transfer of these individuals to mental institutions has been severely restricted by sharp decreases in mental hospital bed capacities. Accordingly, emergency rooms may have to hold these individuals in cramped, inadequate quarters for several days before discharging them to the street or to a mental institution. The use of a triage evaluation system prioritizes rapid transfer to the general hospital inpatient unit or mental institution. Those individuals who are not stabilized within 4 hours by psychotropic medication or who pose a high risk of danger to themselves, staff members, or other emergency room clients will most likely be transferred.

CHAPTER 2 QUESTIONS

1. What is the largest group of users of public community mental health services?

2. Name the three payment methods used for community mental health services.

3. Describe the two delivery modalities within the community mental health system that are the most important deterrents to inpatient hospitalizations.

4. Explain three advantages of the assertive community treatment (ACT) model of community mental health care.

BIBLIOGRAPHY

Bedell, J., & Ward, J.C. (1989). An intensive community-based treatment alternative to state hospitalization. *Hospital & Community Psychiatry, 40,* 533–535.

Cohen, N.L. (Ed.). (1991). *Psychiatric outreach to the mentally ill.* San Francisco: Jossey-Bass.

Community psychiatry: a reappraisal. (1983). New York: Mental Health Materials Center.

Goldberg, K. (Ed.). (1988). *Differing approaches to partial hospitalization.* San Francisco: Jossey-Bass.

Harvard Mental Health Letter. (1992). *9,* 5–6.

Junginger, J. (1990). Psychiatric hospitalization and community-based program attendance. *Psychiatric Quarterly, 61,* 251–259.

Lazare, A. (Ed.). (1989). *Outpatient psychiatry: Diagnosis and treatment* (2nd ed.). Baltimore: Williams & Wilkins.

Lewis, J.A., & Lewis, M.D. (1990). *Community counseling.* Pacific Grove, CA: Brooks-Cole.

Pittman, D.C., Parsons, R., & Peterson, R.W. (1990). Easing the way: A multifaceted approach to day treatment. *Journal of Psychosocial Nursing & Mental Health Services, 28,* 6–11.

Prior, L. (1991). Community versus hospital care: the crisis in psychiatric provision. *Social Science & Medicine, 32,* 483–489.

Taube, C.A., Morlock, L., Burns, B.J., & Santos, A.B. (1990). New directions in research on assertive community treatment. *Hospital & Community Psychiatry, 41,* 642–647.

Chapter 3

■ ■ ■ ■ ■

Inpatient Hospitalization: The Mental Health Treatment Team and the Therapeutic Milieu

Behavioral Objectives

After reading this chapter the student will be able to:

Name the conditions that precede admission to an inpatient mental health treatment setting.

Describe six members of the inpatient mental health treatment team and the clinical roles they fill.

List three characteristics that contribute to effective mental health team communication.

Describe the meaning of the concept **therapeutic milieu**.

List the characteristics of a therapeutic environment.

Describe the objectives of a therapeutic treatment team.

Mental Health and Mental Illness,
Fifth Edition, by Patricia D. Barry.
J.B. Lippincott Company, Philadelphia © 1994.

Inpatient hospitalization of persons with a mental disorder becomes necessary when one or more of the following conditions is present:

1. There is a change in mental status that increases the risk of harm to self or other so that safety must be provided. Admission can be voluntary or court ordered.
2. The normal social environment of the individual is not able to continue the emotional, physical, or financial support of the vulnerable, mentally disabled person.
3. There is a self-perception that the emotionally vulnerable individual is unable to cope effectively. The mental status of the individual must then meet the admission criteria of an inpatient psychiatric unit.

Because of stringent mental health care reimbursement mechanisms, inpatient hospitalization is planned in an aggressive manner designed to restore a person's effective coping ability as soon as possible. Such an objective requires rapid preadmission assessment; this includes selection of the appropriate inpatient setting to meet the particular needs of the person with a mental disorder. For example, a person with a substance abuse disorder can sometimes be effectively treated in a partial hospitalization drug program. Certain characteristics of the client's history may indicate that he or she would be better suited to inpatient hospitalization in a local drug treatment center, whereas another person would be recommended to a residential drug treatment program in a different location.

■ Preliminary Care Planning in the Inpatient Treatment Setting

Care planning for a newly admitted person with a mental disorder ideally begins before he or she is admitted. Consultation between the clinical director, usually a physician, and the head nurse or unit manager can assist in assigning an incoming client to a particular location on the unit that will provide him or her with a proper level of safety. In addition, the newly admitted person is often preassigned by the clinical director to a particular treatment team. The clinical leader of the team is called the **team leader**. He or she will usually begin to consider treatment options before the newly admitted person arrives on the unit.

■ The Mental Health Treatment Team

The ability to provide rapid and aggressive assessment and treatment in the inpatient setting requires a cohesive team of clinicians with comprehensive skills in assessing and treating mental disorders in a secure and supportive environment. These team members are named below with a brief description of their roles.

The **clinical director** is usually a psychiatrist. The care of inpatients is his or her ultimate responsibility. In addition to the clinical director there usually are other inpatient staff psychiatrists who assist in the care of clients by providing overall direction in assessment and care planning, provision of safety, and prescription of appropriate medications to ensure a therapeutic treatment outcome.

The **head nurse or unit manager**, usually a registered nurse, manages the physical environment and resources of the unit. He or she also supervises other registered nurses and nursing personnel on the unit.

The **registered nurse** in the psychiatric setting uses the nursing process to plan and implement the care of his or her assigned clients. The philosophy and scope of practice of psychiatric nursing will be presented in Chapter 5, Person-Centered Nursing. The nursing process will be presented in Chapter 17, The Nursing Process in the Mental Health Setting. The role of the registered nurse on the mental health team is to assess collaboratively the client's current problems and personal resources and develop a nursing care plan that provides for the client's safety and hygiene needs, as well as the safety and hygiene needs of other inpatients and the mental health team. The safety of all individuals on the unit, whether clients or staff members, is a major priority in nursing care. The administration of medications is a nursing function on most psychiatric units. Some units, however, have **medication technicians**, supervised by hospital pharmacists, who prepare and deliver medications to clients.

Other functions in the nursing role will be dependent on a client's specific symptoms, the level of expertise of the nurse, and the particular norms of the unit regarding the functions of nurses. Other nursing personnel that work under the direction of the registered nurse include the licensed practical nurse, the psychiatric aide, and the orderly.

The role of the **licensed practical nurse** is to assist in the implementation of the nursing care plan, including assessing, implementing, and evaluating the client's current status. These observations are reported to the registered nurse, who uses the new data to evaluate the current nursing plan and modify nursing interventions to achieve the desired outcomes. Licensed practical nurses may also be asked to prepare and deliver medication on psychiatric units.

The **psychiatric aide** is a member of the therapeutic team who receives his or her training in programs developed by the psychiatric institution. Usually this job category is found in large psychiatric institutions. Typically, general hospital psychiatric units do not have the in-service training capability to develop such a position. The psychiatric aide in most instances develops good assessment and intervention skills and is a valuable asset to the nursing team.

The **orderly** may be a permanently assigned member of the psychiatric team depending on the size and resources of the psychiatric unit. This individual's presence is most important during critical incidents on the unit, when numbers of physically strong personnel are needed as a deterrent to loss of control in a client or group of clients.

Another member of the mental health team is the **clinical psychologist**. He or she is trained to administer psychological tests that can identify the specific causes of a person's mental dysfunction. Such information can be used to design strategic, symptom-related intervention. In addition, the targeting of the cause of symptoms can usually assist physicians in selecting appropriate medications for reducing these symptoms.

Another important member of the mental health treatment team is the **psychiatric social worker**. He or she brings knowledge of community resources that can assist in the recovery of the person with mental illness. A psychiatric social worker is knowledgeable about the effect of family on the development, course, and treatment of mental disorders. He or she meets with family members during periods of hospitalization to obtain information about the client's family history and context of the client's current need for hospitalization.

Expressive therapists are trained to use a special medium, such as art, music, drama, or other creative modalities, to allow expression of the emotional conflict that has caused the client's need for hospitalization. The client may be able to express the underlying conflict using one of these modalities, even though he or she may not have an intellectual understanding of the cause of his or her conflict. By using the insights gained through expressive work, therapists can assist clients in reaching a deeper understanding of why they became ill and how they can address the resulting problems.

The **occupational therapist** is another important contributor to the treatment team. He or she designs activities in conjunction with clients that provide structured outlets for emotional or physical tensions. These activities also test the client's abilities to solve problems, set goals, maintain concentration, and perform purposeful tasks. The inability to participate in one or more of these functions can provide information to the team about the client's current clinical status and rate of improvement.

■ Communication Within the Treatment Team

The goal of in-hospital treatment is to identify rapidly the symptoms that caused the need for hospitalization, develop a treatment plan that will modify the symptoms, and identify the effective coping behaviors that are necessary to meet discharge requirements.

Skilled mental health clinicians work as a team to assess and intervene in the comprehensive range of ineffective client behaviors that indicate mental disorder. The inherent factor that contributes to cohesive teamwork is mutual trust. Mutual trust can occur in an environment where there is general respect for the unique role and skills of each clinical discipline.

Team communication is the essence of effective care planning. Each discipline includes skills that evaluate specific aspects of behavior and functioning: mental status, social skills, cognitive status, vocational capacities, and so on. When the observations and identified client care goals of each discipline are discussed, the result can be a comprehensive plan designed to meet the unique and specific needs of each client.

An important consideration in team communication is that the unit management and members of the team recognize the value of ongoing evaluation of the team communication process. For example, does the team take time to discuss and evaluate its own communication patterns? Does it recognize conflict? Does it provide a mechanism to work through the conflict? Does it take time away from the unit for a "day away" or "retreat" to evaluate its current status, ongoing goals, and deterrents to achieving those goals. Most teams find that prioritizing such questions allows for a higher level of professional performance and job satisfaction for each member of the team. Effective communication within the team supports the concept of the therapeutic milieu.

■ The Therapeutic Milieu

The term **milieu** is derived from the French words *ma*, meaning "my," and *lieu*, meaning "place." The phrase "my place" signifies a trusted environment where one can be real and authentic and respected for his or her realness and authenticity. The concept of the therapeutic milieu is based on the premise that the current, "here and now" behavior of an individual is a reflection of his or her current reality and normal social interactions. This reflection offers insights about why the individual is having difficulty in his or her internal reality or social interactions with others. The treatment team can be most effective by assessing these "here and now" behaviors and designing interventions to modify them so that therapeutic client insights and outcomes can be realized.

Several characteristics of a therapeutic milieu have been identified by Jack (1989). They are as follows:

1. Every interaction is an opportunity for therapeutic intervention.
2. Clients must assume responsibility for their own behavior.
3. Problem solving is achieved by discussion, negotiation, and consensus, rather than by a few authority figures.
4. Community meetings exist to discuss information and interactions that apply to all staff and clients.
5. Peer pressure is a useful and powerful tool.
6. Inappropriate behaviors are dealt with as they occur.
7. Communication is open and direct between the staff and the clients.
8. Clients are encouraged to participate actively in their own treatment and in decision making on the unit.
9. The unit remains in close contact with the community, and there is frequent communication with family and significant members of the client's social network.
10. Usually the unit's door is open, and the clients have access to areas beyond the unit (p. 70).

■ Therapeutic Team Treatment

By using these "here and now" therapeutic milieu concepts, the treatment team is able to develop a comprehensive list of the mental status symptoms, social interactive style, and behaviors that caused the client to be hospitalized. Therapeutic team treatment includes the following objectives:

1. Developing a team treatment plan to modify specific ineffective coping and social behaviors.
2. Naming the objectives or goals of inpatient treatment for each of these ineffective behaviors.

3. Describing the intervention plan for each member of the mental health treatment team with the client.
4. Listing the mental status and coping criteria necessary for discharge.
5. Describing the outpatient discharge recommendations of the team.

The most therapeutic inpatient hospitalizations are ensured when team planning occurs as described above. Well-synchronized team planning is the result of good clinical leadership and professional participation by each member of the team. Such planning and therapeutic outcomes can be a significant contributor to the ongoing job satisfaction of each team member.

CHAPTER 3 QUESTIONS

1. When does care planning for a newly admitted person with a mental disorder ideally begin?

2. Which member of the mental health treatment team generally assesses client problems, develops a care plan that provides for client's safety and hygiene needs, and administers medications?

3. What inherent factor contributes to cohesive team work on the mental health treatment team?

4. On what premise is the concept of the therapeutic milieu based?

BIBLIOGRAPHY

Cumming, J. (1990). The community as milieu–a memoir. *Community Mental Health Journal, 26,* 15–25.
Emrich, K. (1989). Helping or hurting? Interacting in the psychiatric milieu. *Journal of Psychosocial Nursing & Mental Health Services, 27,* 26–29.

Harsch, H.H., Koran, L.M., & Young, L.D. (1991). A profile of academic medical-psychiatric units. *General Hospital Psychiatry, 13,* 291–295.

Jack, L.W. (1989). Use of milieu as a problem-solving strategy in addiction treatment. *Nursing Clinics of North America, 24,* 69–80.

Kahn, E.M., & Fredrick, N. (1988). Milieu-oriented management strategies on acute care units for the chronically mentally ill. *Archives of Psychiatric Nursing, 2,* 134–140.

Moore, N.S. (1990). A team approach to psychiatric care. *Nursing Management, 21,* 52–53.

Yoest, M.A. (1989). The clinical nurse specialist on the psychiatric team. *Journal of Psychosocial Nursing & Mental Health Services, 27,* 27–32.

Yurkovich, E. (1990). Patient and nurse roles in the therapeutic community. *Perspectives in Psychiatric Care, 25,* 18–22.

Chapter 4

■■■■■

Legal and Ethical Issues in Mental Health Nursing

Behavioral Objectives

After reading this chapter the student will be able to:

Summarize the ethical codes for nurses.

Define the following terms: **socialization, values, ethics**.

Describe the following rights of mentally ill people who are hospitalized:
    a. Right to treatment
    b. Confidentiality
    c. Habeas corpus
    d. Right to refuse treatment

Explain the following legal terms:
    a. **Competency**
    b. **"Dangerousness"** as it pertains to the mentally ill person
    c. **Involuntary commitment**

Mental Health and Mental Illness,
Fifth Edition, by Patricia D. Barry.
J.B. Lippincott Company, Philadelphia © 1994.

■ The Code of Nursing

The role of nurses is to safeguard the well-being of people entrusted to their care. The Code of Nursing, revised by the American Nurses Association in 1985, describes the ways in which a nurse should carry out this role:

1. The nurse provides services with respect for human dignity and the uniqueness of the client unrestricted by considerations of social or economic status, personal attributes, or the nature of health problems.
2. The nurse safeguards the client's right to privacy by judiciously protecting information of a confidential nature.
3. The nurse acts to safeguard the client and the public when health care and safety are affected by the incompetent, unethical, or illegal practice of any person.
4. The nurse assumes responsibility and accountability for individual nursing judgments and actions.
5. The nurse maintains competence in nursing.
6. The nurse exercises informed judgment and uses individual competence and qualifications as criteria in seeking consultation, accepting responsibilities, and delegating nursing activities to others.
7. The nurse participates in activities that contribute to the ongoing development of the profession's body of knowledge.
8. The nurse participates in the profession's efforts to implement and improve standards of nursing.
9. The nurse participates in the profession's efforts to establish and maintain conditions of employment conducive to high-quality nursing care.
10. The nurse participates in the profession's efforts to protect the public from misinformation and misrepresentation and to maintain the integrity of nursing.
11. The nurse collaborates with members of the health professions and other citizens in promoting community and national efforts to meet the health needs of the public.

The code is based on the assumption that a nurse has a well-formulated sense of ethics and legal responsibilities. The field of mental health nursing involves working with people who have varying levels of mental competence or judgment. Accordingly, it becomes essential that mental health nurses be aware of ethics within their scope of practice. **Ethics** is defined as the knowledge of the principles of good and evil. When the ethics of a particular field or discipline are discussed, it is expected that the individual within that field possesses a basic set of ethical values about his or her conduct individually and in interpersonal relationships. Professional ethics are then built on the basic personal ethics foundation.

The Social Policy Statement issued by the American Nurses Association has become the basis of the Nursing Practice Acts in many states. It defines nursing as "the diagnosis and treatment of the human response to illness." This broad definition of nursing practice encompasses a very wide range of nursing care functions. It implies that the nurse is aware of the moral obligations of his or her care of clients.

Personal ethics are formed as a person is socialized. **Socialization** is a developmental process during which the young child gains acceptance from his or her parents and other authority figures by conforming to their rules. These rules are the "dos and don'ts" that are gradually internalized to form the child's value system. A **value** is a basic internal guideline that causes an emotional response in a person.

These values or personal guides develop and evolve throughout one's lifetime. They form the basis, either consciously or unconsciously, of a person's decisions and actions. Values, which are at the core of a person's selfhood, do not change easily or quickly. Ideally they are dynamic and are subject to modification and change as a person matures and acquires more wisdom and knowledge about himself or herself and others. When this does not happen the outcome is an inflexible personality. This type of inflexibility is the result of insecurity and the need to avoid anxiety.

■ The Ethics of Nursing

Because the primary function of mental health nursing is relating with people, it is important to review the way in which nursing "care" occurs. Richards has examined the concepts of "caring for" versus "caring about." When a person "cares for" another, the implication is that the other is like a child and is incapable of caring for himself or herself; he or she is dependent and cannot make any contributions to his or her own well-being. "Caring about," on the other hand, demonstrates respect for the other as a full human being. Although a client may be temporarily incapacitated (to a greater or lesser degree), the nurse should continually relate to him or her in a manner that promotes self-acceptance, ability to care for self, and ultimate restoration of health.

It can be very helpful for us to review our own philosophies of client care to determine which approach we use in our practices. A nurse who consistently uses the first approach described above does not contribute to the ultimate well-being of his or her clients.

The Code of Nursing Practice listed in the beginning of the chapter describes the ethical relationship that should exist between a nurse and a mental health client. These ethical codes, although clearly stated, can sometimes create conflicts within us. Because it deals with all aspects of human existence, nursing practice cannot consist of circumstances that fit within perfect guidelines. In actual practice, we may find ourselves caught between a personal belief, a professional ethic, or a law that causes strong disagreement and consternation. If this occurs and the dilemma seems unresolvable, it can be helpful to seek the counsel of someone in the profession who is knowledgeable about the issues involved.

■ Legal Aspects of Mental Health Nursing

Physically or mentally ill persons are in a dependent position when hospitalized. Accordingly, the legal systems in various states have instituted laws designed to safeguard their well-being. Laws regarding mentally ill people differ from state to state, so it is important that nurses obtain specific information about the statutes affecting their delivery of care during orientation programs in their respective institutions or agencies. Laws are developed by a society as an outcome of personal and professional values and ethics. A single instance of violation of another's well-being does not usually result in a law designed to forbid its recurrence. Instead, repetition of similar types of violations causes people to respond with indignation and call for a law to control and punish its continued occurrence.

Right to Treatment

All people who are hospitalized for mental illness have the right to treatment. As the result of lawsuits brought to court during the 1960s and 1970s, mental health professionals are increasingly aware of their legal responsibilities to clients. A court decision of the mid-1960s (*Rouse v Cameron*) (373 F. 2d 451 [D.C. Cir. 1966]) declared that a mentally ill person has the following rights to treatment:

1. A treatment plan that is continuously reviewed by a qualified mental health professional and modified, if necessary
2. A mental examination and review of a client's care plan every 90 days by a qualified mental health professional other than the professional responsible for supervising and implementing the plan
3. A statement of client problems and needs
4. A statement of the least restrictive treatment conditions necessary
5. Intermediate and long-range goals and a timetable for implementing them
6. A statement of rationale for the plan
7. A description of proposed staff involvement
8. Criteria for release to a less restrictive environment and discharge
9. Notation of therapeutic tasks to be performed by the client

Confidentiality

The client in the mental health setting has many rights to safeguard his or her well-being. These include the right to confidentiality. **Confidentiality** requires that the nurse's knowledge of all aspects of the client's condition belong, in essence, to the client. The nurse cannot reveal this information publicly without the informed consent of the client. Obviously, the nurse's documentation of information revealed in the nurse-client relationship falls within this guideline.

In the nurse-client relationship the client may share sensitive or potentially damaging information with the nurse. It is important that the nurse be aware of the specific guidelines regarding documentation or verbal reporting of this information developed by the institution in which he or she is working. A wise rule is that, if you are in doubt, you should not chart this material until the situation is discussed with a supervisor. It is also important to remember that a client's chart can be used at any time in a legal proceeding. The client's chart should contain accurate documentation using guidelines established by the institution in which the nurse is working. Upon changing institutions, it is important for the nurse to determine what information is recorded in what manner in the new setting. Guidelines can vary among different institutions. If it should be necessary to change any charted material, the following recommendations should be closely followed:

1. The record should never be erased.
2. A line should be drawn through the erroneous material in the chart and the corrected version substituted.
3. The correction should be dated and initialed.
4. A chart should never be altered after material has been subpoenaed in a lawsuit. This may be considered tampering with evidence and could result in a serious penalty.

Another important aspect of confidentiality or privacy is the disclosure of information by a client who requests that the nurse not share it with anyone else. It is unwise for the nurse to agree to such a request. Because the nurse is a member of a treatment team, such information should be shared verbally with the director of the team, whose clinical judgment forms the basis of the decisions about whether and how this information should be shared with the team. Inexperienced students or nurses sometimes may want to maintain this requested confidentiality, but it can sometimes have tragic consequences if the information would have averted danger to the client or others. In addition, a request for confidentiality is often an attempt by the client, conscious or otherwise, to split the members of the health care team.

Informed Consent and Competency

Consent is a person's agreement to an act that will affect his or her body or to disclosure of information about himself or herself. There are four general types of consent. **Informed consent** is the agreement by a competent person who has been given the information necessary to weigh the advantages and disadvantages of the treatment that is being proposed to him or her. **Implied consent** is the consent a person gives when allowing himself or herself to undergo routine laboratory work or x-rays, or to take medications administered by a caregiver. **Presumed consent** comes into play when an unconscious person is given life-saving treatment in a life-threatening situation. **Vicarious consent** is given by parents, guardians, or conservators when a person is incapable of deciding for himself or herself.

In addition to decisions regarding treatment, another type of informed consent (particularly important to a person with past or present mental illness) refers to the release of information about a client's outpatient treatment or hospitalization. Such consent is usually sought so that health care insurance firms, future employers, or the legal system can obtain information about the client. Because such information can be potentially damaging to a client, he or she has the right to know exactly what information will be given and why it is needed. The person explaining the informed consent procedure should be knowledgeable and serve as a client advocate.

Competency is a person's mental status that renders him or her capable of sound decision-making and management of his or her own life circumstances. The concept of competency is subject to different legal definitions, depending on circumstances and the particular state in which a person lives.

The decision to obtain a court decision on mental competency is usually made when family members or care-givers have serious concerns about a person's judgment and ability to handle his or her own affairs. If sufficient data is presented to the judge, he or she can order that a guardian, conservator, or committee be appointed to make and implement decisions that will safeguard all aspects of the client's well-being.

The case described below is one that can cloud an interpretation of competency.

> *Mary is a 52-year-old, single schoolteacher who was diagnosed with acute leukemia 3 years ago. Since that time she has undergone two rounds of chemotherapy, which caused excessive nausea, fatigue, and alopecia (baldness). Although her mental status has not deteriorated, she was physically weakened. Following the second round of chemotherapy she had to resign her teaching position, which she loved. Because of other medications she is receiving, her bones have become brittle. She has broken her collarbone, femur, and humerus in falls in her home. She is excessively frail and lives in near isolation.*

It is possible that a physician could attempt to treat this client with a third round of chemotherapy. The client could refuse, choosing instead to allow the natural evolution of death.

What is your reaction to this example?

Do you believe the client has the right to refuse treatment?

In some medical-surgical care settings, the rule of maintaining life, no matter what the cost to the mental health or quality of life of the client and his or her family, is the only factor considered in making treatment decisions. In such hospitals, when a terminally ill, but mentally competent, client refuses to undergo prolonged or painful treatment, the physicians may try to obtain a legal ruling of mental incompetence in order to give the clients these treatments.

Values in our society are gradually shifting to include consideration of quality of life in the decision about radical treatment. As a result, the medical and legal systems are more often responding with sensitive and thoughtful decisions that support the needs of clients and their families.

It is important to know that the client has a right to review his or her own chart. It is recommended and required in many institutions that such a request by a client be forwarded to his or her physician. It is wise for the physician to be present when the client is reading the chart in order to answer any questions and clarify any misunderstandings.

Involuntary Commitment

Most people who are mentally ill recognize their need for treatment and are relieved when they are hospitalized. Others, whose sense of reality and judgment are markedly altered, do not submit to hospitalization. When lack of treatment poses a danger to the client or others, it is often necessary to obtain a court order for commitment. The state is empowered by law to fulfill its obligation to protect its citizens.

The states have adopted different definitions of the mental state that constitutes **dangerousness.** Generally, it is a serious mental condition that has existed during the previous 30 days. The person must be examined by a psychiatrist when commitment is believed necessary. If suicide, homicide, serious bodily harm to self or others, or neglect that can lead to harm of self or others is believed by the examining psychiatrist to be a potential outcome, emergency commitment can be carried out immediately. The case must be reviewed by a judge with strong supporting evidence submitted for a continued court-ordered hospitalization.

Habeas Corpus

If a person is being held in a hospital against his or her will, he or she may apply for a writ of habeas corpus. A writ of **habeas corpus** has the purpose of requiring an immediate court hearing to determine a person's sanity. If the person is declared sane, then he or she must be released from the institution immediately.

Right to Refuse Treatment

Most of the rights of clients have been established because of legal precedents that were determined when former mental clients went to court to sue former care-givers for denial of their rights when they were hospitalized. Two of the most common treatments that have potentially negative side effects are electroshock treatment (EST) and all psychotropic medications. Phenothiazine medications have been specifically identified in lawsuits because of the permanent side effect called tardive dyskinesia, described in Chapter 31, Psychopharmacology and Electroshock Treatment of Mental Disorders. Mentally ill hospitalized clients, whether voluntarily or involuntarily admitted, have the right to information about these treatments and the right to refuse them.

In conclusion, the knowledge regarding ethics and legal issues in mental health nursing is expanding rapidly. As the issue of client rights became more urgent, nurses began to review their own ethical responsibilities to clients. One of the major reasons for the increase in knowledge of legal issues was consumer awareness that their needs were not being adequately met by the mental health care system. Lawsuits that mandated change in particular states often had effects beyond the boundaries of those states. Other states, in viewing the outcomes of these lawsuits, began to review and revise some of their own questionable practices.

CHAPTER 4 QUESTIONS

1. What is the difference between "caring for" and "caring about" a client?

2. Why have laws been instituted to safeguard the well-being of the physically and mentally ill?

3. What does it mean to have the right to a writ of habeas corpus?

4. How would you define the legal term "competency"?

BIBLIOGRAPHY

Bandman, E.L., & Bandman, B. (1990). *Nursing ethics across the life span.* Norwalk, CT: Appleton & Lange.
Cassidy, V.R. (1991). Ethical responsibilities in nursing: Research findings and issues. *Journal of Professional Nursing, 7,* 112–118.

Coletta, S. (1978). Values clarification in nursing: Why? *American Journal of Nursing, 78,* 2057.

Fowler, M.D. (1989). Ethical decision making in clinical practice. *Nursing Clinics of North America, 24,* 955–965.

Johnstone, M.J. (1989). Law, professional ethics and the problem of conflict with personal values. *International Nursing Review, 36,* 83–89.

Ketefian, S., & Ormond, I. (1988). *Moral reasoning and ethical practice in nursing: An integrative review.* New York: National League for Nursing.

McCloskey, J.C., & Grace, H.K. (Eds.). (1990). *Current issues in nursing.* St. Louis, MO: Mosby–Year Book.

McFarland, G.K., Thomas, M.D. (1991). *Psychiatric mental health nursing: Application of the nursing process.* Philadelphia: J.B. Lippincott.

Nursing: A social policy statement. (1980). Kansas City: American Nurses Association.

Pence, T., & Cantrall, J. (Eds.). (1990). *Ethics in nursing: An anthology.* New York: National League for Nursing.

Penticuff, J.H. (1991). Conceptual issues in nursing ethics research. *Journal of Medicine & Philosophy, 16,* 235–258.

Richards, F. (1975). Do you care for, or care about? *AORN Journal, 22,* 792–798.

Sadoff, R.L. (1992). *Psychiatric malpractice: Cases and comments for clinicians.* Washington, DC: American Psychiatric Press.

Developing Critical Thinking Skills Through Class Discussion

UNIT I Case Study
Patterns of Mental Health Care

Alice is a 26-year-old woman who was diagnosed with schizophrenia, a chronic mental illness, when she was 16 years old. She lives with her widowed mother, Ann Price, who has chronic emphysema. Because of her chronic illness Mrs. Price is unable to work. She and her daughter live on the meager income from their Social Security payments.

As her own physical condition has deteriorated, Mrs. Price has lacked the energy and motivation to be involved in the care of her daughter's mental illness. Alice has been noncompliant in taking her antipsychotic medication since her original diagnosis. She has been hospitalized seven times in the past 10 years as her psychoses have become severe.

She is being treated by the outpatient department of psychiatry at her local hospital, approximately 4 miles from her apartment. Because of her poor motivation and lack of interest in treatment, she has been assigned to a chronic schizophrenic medication group led by a clinical nurse specialist in psychiatry. She does not attend the group nor does she take her medication on a regular basis.

DISCUSSION QUESTIONS

1. As you hear the story of Alice, what are your major concerns?

2. What types of intervention from community resources could assist Alice to become more responsible for her own care while she is living with her mother?

36

3. What can happen to Alice if her mother becomes too ill to maintain her apartment?

4. Can Alice live alone? Why?

5. What are the significant risks to Alice's safety if she is no longer able to live with her mother?

6. If you were Alice's cousin, what would you do to investigate possible housing options for her? Health care options?

▪▪▪▪▪
Unit II

Concepts of Psychiatric/Mental Health Nursing

Chapter 5

■■■■■

Person-Centered Nursing

Behavioral Objectives

After reading this chapter the student will be able to:

Explain the concepts of nursing.

List and define the four themes of nursing practice.

Define the terms **psychopathology**, **psychosocial adaptation**, and **psychosocial maladaptation**.

Describe the nurse's role in treating a mentally ill individual.

The essence of nursing practice is to provide care to a person who is experiencing physical or mental distress. The goal of nursing is to restore the person to his or her highest potential for quality of life.

■ Concepts of Nursing Practice

Nursing is an art and a science that combines and integrates the theories and practices of many different fields: social sciences, such as psychology and sociology; basic sciences, such as anatomy, physiology, microbiology, and biochemistry; and medical science, the diagnosing and treating of illness. Nursing is a biopsychosocial science—

Mental Health and Mental Illness,
Fifth Edition, by Patricia D. Barry.
J.B. Lippincott Company, Philadelphia © 1994.

that is, in assessing and planning care for the human responses to illness, it draws on knowledge of human biology, psychology, and the human social systems of family, friends, and community as the foundations of its practice. This approach to assessment is called a **holistic** model of care.

Many nursing scientists have developed theoretical models about the concepts of nursing practice. As a whole, nursing models generally address four critical aspects or themes of nursing. These themes are:

1. Person
2. Nursing
3. Environment
4. Health

Person is viewed by the nurse as a human being comprised of biologic, psychological, and social functions or domains. These functions or domains are blended in a complex system that results in a unique individual.

Nursing is a role that includes the following dimensions of person-centered care: comfort, including physical and emotional care, and the monitoring and maintenance of safety and hygiene.

Environment includes all the internal and external forces that affect the well-being of the person. These forces include biologic, psychological, and social dynamics, as well as the external physical surroundings.

Health is a state of physical and mental functioning. It can exist in a continuum that ranges from wellness to death.

The concept of what constitutes health can be affected by a person's value judgments. What is subjectively viewed as "good" or "bad" health by one person may be viewed differently by another. The perception of what constitutes good health by health care professionals may depend on the professional discipline of the care-giver, for example, nursing, medicine, psychology, or social work.

■ The Role of Nursing in Addressing Psychosocial Needs

According to the prior definition of nursing practice, the nurse assesses the whole person using knowledge of normal and pathologic physical, psychological, and social functioning. In psychiatric/mental health nursing the whole-person focus continues, so that all aspects of a client's functioning are being assessed. The primary cause of admission to a mental health setting, however, is some form of mental disorder or psychopathology that has caused a temporary incapacity in the client's ability to function in his or her normal social environment. **Psychopathology** is defined as disease of the mind. The medical approach to care-giving is based on a model of curing pathology or disease, whether physical or mental. Using this approach, there is usually a specific focus on curing the identified disease.

Nursing, on the other hand, views the disease process as the cause of distress to the whole person. The distress resulting from disease affects the person's overall sense of well-being—physical, mental, and social. Nursing care involves assessing each of these functional domains. Care planning intervenes directly with the disease process using physicians' orders when necessary, as well as the guiding principles of nursing practice described above. In addition, the nurse assesses, plans, and implements care and continuously evaluates the outcomes of care as measured by client responses in the physical, mental, and social domains. This assessment process uses the same holistic principles whether the person has a mental or physical disorder.

In the mental health setting the primary focus is on the cause of the admission. The client has a mental disorder that has changed his or her mental functioning. When mental functioning is disordered, it results in behavioral changes that affect social relationships. The major goals of nursing care planning and intervention are to work collaboratively with other mental health disciplines to set a cohesive set of therapeutic goals that support the client's recovery and return to psychosocial adaptation.

■ Biopsychosocial Responses to Stress

Psychosocial adaptation is the ability of the human being to perceive reality and respond to it in a way that supports his or her own emotional and physical well-being and that of others in the social environment. When some aspect of mental functioning is disordered, it can result in misperceptions of reality and misjudgments that alter effective decision-making. When effective decision-making is altered, healthy coping processes deteriorate.

Psychosocial maladaptation is the result of ineffective coping. When maladaptation occurs it is the symptom of disordered perception or cognitive processes. The result of maladaptation is tension and distress in those persons who share the client's social environment.

In-hospital admission occurs when the client or members of his or her social environment determine that the level of distress requires professional intervention that is not available in the home, outpatient, or community mental health care system. It is important to note that the clinical role of nursing, that of assessing the whole-person response to illness, is a unique care-giving perspective. In contrast, other disciplines focus on specific aspects of functioning in their treatment models.

The nurse has the most intimate ongoing contact with the client. Accordingly, he or she can observe the subtle clinical changes that indicate improvement or deterioration in the client's condition. These changes can be the first indicators that the treatment plan is working or needs modification. The role of nursing is to implement the nursing care plan, and also to be the first observer of clinical changes for the treatment team. The reporting of clinical observations can alert the treatment team about the effectiveness of the team assessment and treatment plan. The nursing role is a critical factor in the successful treatment of mental disorders.

CHAPTER 5 QUESTIONS

1. What is the goal of nursing?

2. Define psychosocial adaptation.

3. What is the clinical role of nursing?

4. Describe the nurse's approach to care-giving of an individual with mental disease.

BIBLIOGRAPHY

Barry, P.D. (1989). *Psychosocial nursing: Assessment and intervention* (2nd ed.). Philadelphia: J.B. Lippincott.

Bayne, R., & Nicolson, P. (1993). *Counselling and psychology for health professionals.* New York: Chapman & Hall.

Bulechek, G.M., & McCloskey, J.C. (1992). *Nursing interventions.* Philadelphia: W.B. Saunders.

Friedman, M.M. (1992). *Family nursing: Theory and practice* (3rd ed.). Norwalk, CT: Appleton & Lange.

Kozier, B., Erb, G., & Olivieri, R. (1991). *Fundamentals of nursing: concepts, process, and practice* (4th ed.). Redwood City, CA: Addison-Wesley, Health Sciences Division.

Leininger, M.M. (Ed.). (1991). *Culture care diversity and universality: A theory of nursing.* New York: National League for Nursing.

Leino-Kilpi, H. (1991). Good nursing care—the relationship between client and nurse. *Hoitotiede, 3,* 200–207.

McFarland, G.K., Thomas, M.D. (1991). *Psychiatric mental health nursing: Application of the nursing process.* Philadelphia: J.B. Lippincott.

Pike, A.W. (1990). On the nature and place of empathy in clinical nursing practice. *Journal of Professional Nursing, 6,* 235–240.

Chapter 6
■■■■■

Establishing the Therapeutic Nursing Environment

Behavioral Objectives

After reading this chapter the student will be able to:

Define empathic care and list four characteristics of empathic caring.

Explain the concept of acceptance and describe why it is an important part of the therapeutic relationship.

Describe why explanations are important to the person with mental illness.

Define trust.

Explain the difference between empathy and sympathy and give an example of each.

Describe why limit setting is important in the treatment of the mentally ill person.

Define reality and explain why the ego may alter a person's awareness of reality.

Mental Health and Mental Illness,
Fifth Edition, by Patricia D. Barry.
J.B. Lippincott Company, Philadelphia © 1994.

■ Caring

There are many qualities that support therapeutic nursing practice. Regardless of the pattern of behavior that may characterize a client's illness, certain general principles apply to the care of all who show behavior disorders. Everyone has certain basic and psychosocial needs that must be met, no matter how different the surface behavior may be. Caring is a distinguishing characteristic of nursing practice. This characteristic of nursing practice and of nurses themselves has been studied by Dr. Patricia Benner. Benner says that nurses have the potential to provide skilled, empathic, and effective care. She describes the heart of caring as the ability to be empathic. Empathy is placing oneself within the experience of another without losing one's own sense of identity. Other abilities that expand one's empathy are "being there" and understanding the meaning of illness to the client; touching; listening; communicating verbally and nonverbally so that the client feels that he or she is understood; and demonstrating technical competence.

■ Acceptance

The client needs to be accepted exactly as he or she is, as a person of worth and dignity. An emotionally ill person cannot be expected to meet normal standards of behavior, nor should he or she be rewarded or punished as his or her behavior approaches or recedes from such standards.* Each of us has certain standards of conduct that we strive to maintain. When others fail to meet our standards, we tend to pass judgment upon them and to punish them in one way or another for their transgressions. This is acceptable behavior for normal individuals, but an emotionally ill person needs a *very low-pressure social environment* in which he or she can learn to live again with others, in much the same manner that a person who has been paralyzed must learn to walk again.

To accept a client as he or she is does not mean we sanction or approve of his or her behavior, but neither do we judge or punish him or her for it. Do not call attention to defects, nor show by word, action, attitude, or expression that you disapprove of him or her. You

---

* When a behavior modification program (see Chapter 29) is in operation, however, this tenet no longer holds. The behavior modification contract will describe the acceptable and unacceptable behavior on which staff interventions will be based.

must show an interest in a client as a human being—as an individual possessed of dignity and worth.

Acceptance often starts out as one sided. Frequently, the client wants no part of you or other staff members, nor of your help. He or she may be fearful of any closeness and suspicious of your intentions. If many of his or her previous interpersonal experiences have convinced the client that he or she is not acceptable to others, it may be difficult to change this self-concept. However, you must convey to the client that he or she is a worthwhile person, and that even though some behavior may be unacceptable, he or she—as a person—is acceptable. By setting limits on behavior in order to help the client behave more appropriately, and warmly supporting him or her all the while, he or she will slowly begin to feel accepted and viewed as a worthwhile person.

The mentally ill person may need to test the sincerity of the therapeutic relationship over and over again before his or her fears and doubts are all swept away. Acceptance is a way of expressing belief in the fundamental worth of another person. We all have a need for acceptance; the mentally ill have a very great need for it.

■ Explanations

Routines and procedures should always be explained at the client's level of understanding. Most of us like to be informed about what to expect in any given situation. Mentally ill clients are no exception. Always explain what is being done and why it is being done in such a way that full allowance is made for the client's symptom-imposed limitations. A client with a limited attention span needs a brief, clear, pointed explanation; an apprehensive client needs a firm explanation that assumes he or she will accept the procedure; and an indecisive client needs us to make his or her decisions for him or her and to outline procedures so that the client is not faced with the necessity of deciding. The purpose behind an explanation is to reduce anxiety whenever possible by preparing the client for what is to come.

■ Expression of Feelings

The client needs to be able to ventilate feelings without fear of retaliation. Encourage him or her to express his or her feelings. This allows the client to lower his or her own frustration level, and it assists you to assess real feelings and the motivation for his or her behavior. Talk and *actively listen* to the client. Conversation should center on the client—on his or her needs, wants, and interests—not on those of the listener. Allow the client to express emotions such as anxiety, fear, hostility, hatred, and anger.

A client's ability to express a negative emotion can be a very healthy sign, for strong emotions, bottled up, are potentially explosive and dangerous. Strange as it may seem, we can frequently be more help to a psychiatric client if we are the objects of his or her hostility rather than if the client likes us. Our quiet acceptance of his or her dislike permits him or her to discharge emotion without retaliation. One of the real dangers of hatred and hostility to the person who feels these emotions is the fear of retribution they carry. Therefore, the client needs an atmosphere in which his or her behavior is calmly accepted.

■ Mutual Trust

Like the need for acceptance, the need for mutual trust is vital to a therapeutic relationship. If we find our world a friendly and trustworthy place in which to live, we will bring this ability to trust to our work. If the client has suffered from a series of experiences that have convinced him or her that he or she cannot trust others, we must start at the beginning to establish a basis for trust, building slowly and carefully. Honesty, integrity, and consistency are all building blocks in laying such a foundation.

Explain in clear, simple language what you intend to do with and for your clients and let nothing interfere with carrying out your contract or pact. If you promise to visit a client daily, arrive at the appointed time, stay the length of time promised, and leave when time is up. Should something unavoidably cause a delay or prevent a visit, notify the client. This is the way to build trust.

If you tell a client that he or she may discuss problems, it is important to sit quietly and listen openly. The following chapter discusses counseling techniques that are helpful in this process. If the client's behavior becomes unacceptable, it is important to set reasonable limits so he or she can express his or her emotions constructively, not destructively.

■ Understanding

When we as staff personnel increase our own self-understanding, we are better able to understand client behavior. We each need to analyze our own feelings and motivations and usually need some help in developing skills in interpersonal relationships. Group discussions on emotions and their effects are very valuable in deepening self-awareness. We can become comfortable in our relationships with clients only when we feel secure about our ability to respond appropriately to client behavior.

When we are able to understand a client's behavior and find the underlying motivation, then and only then can we organize these findings into a truly therapeutic care plan designed to meet his or her needs. We must then constantly evaluate the client's behavior to see if his or her needs are being effectively met. This is what is called using the **dynamic approach.** Using professional knowledge and skill in such a manner that is constructive to the well-being of the client leads to a **therapeutic relationship.** Place yourself in the client's position to understand whatever he or she is experiencing. At the same time make efforts to establish and improve communication, especially in the field of active listening.

■ Empathy and Sympathy

As discussed at the beginning of the chapter, one of the important qualities in a helping relationship is **empathy.** Empathy is the ability to hear what another person is saying and be able to borrow temporarily the other person's feelings but still maintain our own feelings. When we are with a client we need to be able to maintain our objectivity in order to assess accurately the client's mental functioning. If we lose our objectivity by adopting the same feelings as the client, then we are experiencing **sympathy** and will not be able to assess the client's status. For example, if we are in a boat with someone who falls overboard we can throw them a life preserver and pull them to safety (comparable to an empathetic therapeutic intervention) or jump in after them when we don't know how to swim (comparable to sympathy).

■ Consistency

Consistency is a measure that contributes much to client security. All mentally ill clients are insecure and uncertain. Not knowing what to expect produces anxiety. Consistency in all areas of experience is valuable to the psychiatric client, for it builds into his or her environment something to depend on. A consistent hospital routine with firm limit setting is tremendously important to the client. It reduces the number of decisions he or she must make daily, and he or she learns what to expect from the environment. The attitude of the entire hospital staff toward the client likewise must be consistent; this consistency in attitude should extend from person to person and from shift to shift. When he or she is continuously exposed to an atmosphere of quiet understanding, the client's anxiety lessens, and he or she becomes increasingly aware of the acceptance of the staff.

■ Setting Limits

We have been stressing the acceptance of client behavior and the value of a permissive, therapeutic atmosphere. However, permissiveness must have a limit. The client cannot be allowed to do exactly as he or she pleases. The actual limitations on a client's behavior should be determined by the entire team to whom he or she is assigned, and those limitations should be consistently enforced by everyone who comes in contact with him or her.

If, through suspiciousness, a client refuses food and tries to starve himself or herself, do not permit it; if a client tries to take his or her life or the life of another on the ward, prevent it; if a client is overactive, do not allow him or her to become exhausted. We accept the fact that the client has a right to feel the way he or she feels, but limitations must be drawn and his or her behavior kept within these limits. If these limits are enforced in a consistent, quiet, matter-of-fact way, they contribute to the client's security.

Avoid physical and verbal force if possible. Force always traumatizes. None of us likes being forced to comply with the wishes of another, but in spite of every precaution, occasions may arise in which the use of force cannot be avoided. When it must be used, adequate help should be secured and the action carried out quickly and efficiently. When employing force, never show annoyance or anger toward client. Self-control in this situation is very important.

■ Reality

The ego, in an attempt to protect itself from intrapsychic or environmental awareness that is potentially anxiety-provoking, may use defense mechanisms that alter the person's perception of what is really happening. **Reality** is a person's accurate perception of what is really happening intrapsychically or environmentally.

The ability to differentiate between reality and unreality is often seriously affected in a mentally ill person. What he or she observes and hears may be very distorted. If a client is hallucinating, what he or she hears and sees may cause him or her to respond to his or her own unconscious motivation, and, because of this faulty perception, he or she may interpret and respond to the behavior of others in a very inappropriate way. If you can gain the trust and acceptance of such a client you will be in a position to help him or her validate his or her concepts of reality and to bring him or her back gently and slowly into the real world. While making the assessment, always try to establish the approximate degree of the client's distortion and of his or her ability or inability to respond to reality.

■ Reassurance

All of us need reassurance occasionally; the psychiatric client needs it constantly. Make every effort to see a situation as the client sees it. Reassurance is effective only if it does not contradict a false concept that the client holds (i.e., a concept or defense mechanism to protect his or her ego). The best way to reassure a client, in addition to well-placed verbal assurance, is by giving attention to matters that are important to him or her and by doing things for and with the client without asking anything in return, such as showing appreciation for an improvement in his or her behavior.

We do not change a client's behavior by reasoning with him or her. Simply telling why he or she ought to do something is not an effective way of getting cooperation, especially when he or she has emotional difficulties. The client has developed a pattern of behavior to defend himself or herself from anxiety-producing stress, and he or she uses what reason he or she is capable of using to bolster defensive patterns of thinking. If a false belief is based on strong emotional needs, the more we challenge it, the more the client will defend it. Work at helping to develop emotional security. With an improvement in this area, he or she will tend to develop slowly some insight into his or her behavior and the forces behind it. However, insight can be a threat as well as a help to the emotionally disturbed client. Thus, behavior should only be interpreted when the client is ready for it, secure enough to tolerate it, and able to apply it to alter his or her behavior. This help is best left in the hands of the psychiatrist.

Do not try to meet your own emotional needs through your client. Be trained and prepared to understand his or her needs and to meet them, with no thought of return for yourself other than to see your clients recover. Whenever we find ourselves evaluating a client's behavior in terms of right or wrong, or criticizing a client or defending or justifying ourselves, we are in danger of letting our own emotional needs take precedence over those of the client.

CHAPTER 6 QUESTIONS

1. Patricia Benner says the heart of caring is the ability to be empathic. What is empathy?

2. Why are explanations important to the mentally ill person?

3. How does limit setting help the mentally ill individual?

4. Why does the ego alter a person's perception of what is really happening?

BIBLIOGRAPHY

Barry, P.D. (1989). *Psychosocial nursing: Assessment and intervention* (2nd ed.). Philadelphia: J.B. Lippincott.

Benner, P.E. (1991). The role of experience, narrative, and community in skilled ethical comportment. *ANS—Advances in Nursing Science, 14,* 1–21.

Benner, P.E. (1984). *From novice to expert: Excellence and power in clinical nursing practice.* Menlo Park, CA: Addison-Wesley.

Benner, P.E., & Wrubel, J. (1991). The dialogue concerning caring. *Image—the Journal of Nursing Scholarship, 23,* 264–265.

Benner, P.E., & Wrubel, J. (1988). Caring comes first. *American Journal of Nursing, 88,* 1072–1075.

Benner, P.E., & Wrubel, J. (1988). *The primacy of caring: Stress and coping in health and illness.* Menlo Park, CA: Addison-Wesley.

Bulechek, G.M., & McCloskey, J.C. (1992). Nursing interventions. *Nursing Clinics of North America, 27,* Philadelphia: W.B. Saunders.

Kaplan, H., & Sadock, B. (1991). *Synopsis of psychiatry: Behavioral sciences, clinical psychiatry* (6th ed.). Baltimore: Williams & Wilkins.

Lewis, S. (1989). *Manual of psychosocial nursing interventions: Promoting mental health in medical-surgical settings.* Philadelphia: W.B. Saunders.

Litwack, L., Litwack, J., & Ballou, M. (1980). *Health counseling.* New York: Appleton-Century-Crofts.

Magnan, M.A., & Benner, P.E. (1989). Listening with care. *American Journal of Nursing, 89,* 219–221.

McFarland, G.K., Thomas, M.D. (1991). *Psychiatric mental health nursing: Application of the nursing process.* Philadelphia: J.B. Lippincott.

Orlick, S., & Benner, P.E. (1988). The primacy of caring. *American Journal of Nursing, 88,* 318–319.

Chapter 7

■■■■■

Building a Therapeutic Nurse–Client Relationship

Behavioral Objectives

After reading this chapter the student will be able to:

Name the important personal qualities in a therapeutic relationship.

Describe the two main types of communication.

Discuss the differences between open-ended and close-ended questioning.

Explain why contracting is important to both the nurse and the client.

Describe why termination of the counseling relationship is a dynamic that is important to the client's well-being after discharge.

Mental Health and Mental Illness,
Fifth Edition, by Patricia D. Barry.
J.B. Lippincott Company, Philadelphia © 1994.

The previous chapter presented many general concepts that form the basis of beginning a therapeutic relationship. This chapter covers the various counseling techniques that promote a therapeutic relationship.

■ Important Personal Qualities in a Therapeutic Relationship

In order to establish a helping relationship with a client, be aware of the personal qualities of a care-giver that help the client to establish trust. They are described by Carl Rogers and listed below:

1. **Unconditional positive regard**. Accept the client without negative judgment of his or her basic worth.
2. **Empathic understanding of the client's internal frame of reference.** Be aware of and have the capacity to empathize with the client's situation and the various dynamics that are contributing to it. Another word for the circumstances that led up to his or her current difficulty is **context**.
3. **Authenticity**. Allow yourself to be known to others (also called **transparency** or **genuineness**.

■ Communication Patterns in the Counseling Relationship

Chapter 6 (Establishing the Therapeutic Nursing Environment) discussed general concepts of communication with persons who are mentally ill. This chapter discusses specific counseling approaches that can ease conversations with a client and contribute toward a therapeutic outcome for him or her.

Nonverbal Communication in the Counseling Setting

The essence of a helping relationship is the communication or message that is relayed from the helper to the client *and* from the client to the helper. There are two types of messages: verbal and nonverbal. In the field of psychiatry, the way that we communicate nonverbally is very important. Psychiatric clients are particularly sensitive to the many nonverbal messages they receive from care-givers. They know whether they are liked, respected, distrusted, or considered a nuisance. We give off messages, usually without being aware of them. Clients give the same messages to us.

The means with which we tell clients how we are feeling about them are our eyes, posture, and gestures. The ability to maintain consistent eye contact is a strong indicator of relationship potential. When a person frequently looks away or keeps his or her eyes in a downcast position, we know that he or she is not comfortable. Posture is another indication of what a person's true feelings are about a given situation. A person who is standing or sitting erect is usually interested in what he or she is doing or who he or she is with. Conversely, one who is slouched and half turned away is saying "I really don't want to be here." Finally, gestures that we unconsciously make can be important nonverbal signs. For example, a quick movement by a care-giver in the presence of a markedly paranoid client can trigger a defensive reaction. A depressed client would meet the same movement with hardly a glance.

Verbal Communication in the Counseling Setting

When we are talking with a client we are essentially inviting him or her to join in verbal communication. The words we speak may prompt him or her to engage in a discussion or to "shut down" and not respond. The various methods of leading the client into discussion are as follows:

Indirect statements	Questioning
Direct statements	Advice-giving
Focusing	Summarizing

An **indirect leading statement** is purposely general and nonspecific, such as "Tell me about when you were growing up?" A **direct leading statement** is more specific: "You said your mother died when you were 6 years old?" **Focusing** is a helpful technique when you have explored a broad range of subjects and have a general idea about the client's circumstances. When you focus, you pay particular attention to a topic that seems especially sensitive for him or her. For example, you might ask, "Do you remember how you felt when your mother died?"

Questioning, particularly when **open-ended questions** are used, is a helpful way to encourage the client's insights into his or her difficulties. An open-ended question invites the client to give as much information as he or she wants. For example, you could ask, "You told me earlier you went to live with your aunt when your mother died. How was it for you to live with her?" In contrast, a **close-ended question** is one that frequently requires a one-word answer that ultimately closes off further discussion. You might say, "John, are you sad today?" If John answers "no" it shuts off further therapeutic discussion. Instead say, "John, how are you feeling today?" His answer to this will make it easier to explore how he is feeling.

Advice-giving is a counseling technique that *rarely* should be used in the counseling or psychiatric setting. Advice is actually "the easy way out" that can encourage the client's dependence and delay his or her rehabilitation. When a client asks for advice, gently turn the question back to him or her. The response, "John, what would you like to do?" for example, allows him to explore his options out loud with a caring, but impartial, person. Often, clients learn to form their own conclusions and trust their own judgments when this process is implemented.

If the client is in crisis or experiencing severe anxiety this approach is not helpful. Before responding to such a client, check with the client's primary nurse, who knows the client well and may be able to recommend alternate approaches to use with him or her.

Summarizing is a skilled form of verbal communication that occurs at the end of a session in which the nurse and the client have explored a number of issues. The helper briefly describes the affective and intellectual experiences that occurred during their time together. The use of summarizing leaves the client with the feeling that he or she accomplished something during the interview.

■ Other Aspects of the Therapeutic Relationship

Contract

Whenever we tell someone that we will do something, we are entering into a contract. In a therapeutic relationship, a **contract** is an agreement, direct or indirect, with another person. A **direct contract** is one that involves setting formal appointment times with a client or entering a primary nurse–client type of commitment. An **indirect contract** is less formal. Here you can commit to see the client at some time during a working shift. But remember, the client will come to depend on you. It promotes his or her trust in you and his or her sense of security, both important aspects of returning to good mental health. For example, if you will be off the next day, or working a different shift, let your client know when he or she can expect to see you next. Keep clients informed of your schedules; this indicates your respect for them and your regard for their needs and feelings.

Termination of Relationship

The therapeutic relationship is a very close, delicate, and intimate relationship between two people. During the course of interaction, if the client fully accepts the nurse or health care professional and cooperates toward an improved mental health goal, he or she tends to become quite dependent on and emotionally attached to the nurse. It is not easy to terminate an emotional dependency. It is usually quite traumatic for the client, and it may also be hard for us as staff members. If we give deeply of our professional skills, we will terminate those relationships with genuine regret and loss.

It is not easy to determine, at the start of a therapeutic relationship, just how long it may take to help a client back to a level where he or she may gain enough insight to be able to manage his or her feelings and behavior in an acceptable way. Ideally, you can indicate, both at the initiation of the relationship and at intervals during it, that hopefully the day will arrive when the client will no longer need specific help, when he or she will reach a plateau of emotional stability that will enable him or her to handle his or her own problems without your intervention.

The client is often fearful of his or her inability to make decisions and to act responsibly. He or she may fear the approaching time of return to family and job, concerned that he or she may not be well enough yet to carry on his or her work and family responsibilities. He or she may be fearful about acceptance by family and friends. He or she may wonder on whom to call for help if he or she needs it. The client may feel quite threatened by the withdrawal of your help—you have earned his or her trust and helped him or her face personal needs and adjust behavior to an acceptable level.

In anticipation of these fears, discuss them long before the relationship is terminated. Find ways to handle the client's fears. Slowly include other members of the treatment team to prepare him or her for discharge or for further therapy in or out of the hospital, as his or her needs may indicate. As you slowly withdraw from the relationship, include other clients on the ward in an enlarging circle to help promote the client's ability to socialize with others.

To make termination easier, assure the client that you would like to hear from him or her to know how he or she is and that he or she can come back to visit you in the hospital from time to time. The invitation to maintain contact is rarely abused by clients. Instead, such assurances, during the period before discharge when his or her anxiety about independence is high, will enhance his or her sense of security. In addition, during the immediate postdischarge period, the knowledge that he or she can call you often provides security without his or her ever actually placing a telephone call.

CHAPTER 7 QUESTIONS

1. What are two nonverbal ways that communicate the care-giver's interest in being with the client?

2. Why is an open-ended question more effective than a close-ended question as a counseling technique?

3. Why is contracting important to the mental health client?

4. How can the care-giver help prepare the client for termination of the counseling relationship?

BIBLIOGRAPHY

Barry, P.D. (1989). *Psychosocial nursing: Assessment and intervention* (2nd ed.). Philadelphia: J.B. Lippincott.

Brooke Army Medical Center. (1973). *Interpersonal skills.* (Videocassette). Fort Sam Houston, TX: Academy of Health Sciences.

Kaplan, H., & Sadock, B. (1991). *Synopsis of psychiatry: behavioral sciences, clinical psychiatry.* (6th ed.). Baltimore: Williams & Wilkins.

Keane, E. (1989). Listening and the counselling process. *Nursing Standard, 4,* 34–36.

Kirsch, I. (1990). *Changing expectations: A key to effective psychotherapy.* Pacific Grove, CA: Brooks-Cole.

Lewis, J.A., & Lewis, M.D. (1990). *Community counseling.* Pacific Grove, CA: Brooks/Cole.

Litwack, L., Litwack, J., & Ballou, M. (1980). *Health counseling.* New York: Appleton-Century-Crofts.

McFarland, G.K., Thomas, M.D. (1991). *Psychiatric mental health nursing: Application of the nursing process*. Philadelphia: J.B. Lippincott.

Richards, D., & Deale, A. (1991). Psychiatric nursing: Using behavioural psychotherapy skills. *Nursing Standard, 5*, 37–39.

Wilson, H.S., & Kneisl, C.R. (1992). *Psychiatric nursing* (4th ed.). Redwood City, CA: Addison-Wesley.

Developing Critical Thinking Skills Through Class Discussion

UNIT II Case Study
Concepts of Psychiatric/Mental Health Nursing

Gloria is 28 years old. She and her husband, Tom, have a 1-month-old infant. Almost as soon as Gloria arrived home from the hospital she began to have difficulty coping with her baby. She became acutely suicidally depressed and had frequent waves of anxiety about taking care of her baby. She was referred by her obstetrician to a psychiatrist, who admitted her to the hospital inpatient psychiatric unit.

DISCUSSION QUESTIONS

1. What are your personal reactions as you hear about Gloria and her circumstances?

2. Would you describe your reactions as sympathetic or empathic? Why? What are the differences between sympathy and empathy?

3. What difference does it make to the nurse whether he or she is responding to a client's distress with sympathy or empathy? And what difference can it make to the client?

4. If you wanted to ask Gloria why she was admitted to the hospital so that you could determine her own understanding and insight about why her doctor decided to admit her, how would you phrase the question?

5. What are the nonverbal cues that you can give to Gloria to indicate your caring for her well-being?

6. How can you tell if Gloria trusts you?

Unit III

Basic Concepts of Mental Health

Chapter 8

■■■■■

Human Growth and Development

Behavioral Objectives

After reading this chapter the student will be able to:

Identify the physical and mental characteristics that constitute a person's heredity.

Name three forces that influence the development of personality.

Explain the process of identification and how it influences personality development.

Describe the four steps involved in learning.

Explain the role of reinforcement in the learning process.

■ Heredity

When a sperm and an ovum unite to form a new life, each germ cell contributes 23 chromosomes on which a vast number of genes or genetic factors are arranged. These genes determine the type of body build the child will have, his or her skin and hair texture, eye color, general intellectual capacity and abilities, talents, and many other physical and mental characteristics. In short, they constitute the child's heredity.

Part of an infant's heredity includes the makeup of his or her neurologic system. **Neurotransmitters** are the biochemical substances that send messages from the central nervous system to the body tissues. These substances include adrenaline (epinephrine), noradrenaline (norepinephrine), and serotonin, to name a few of the many that are present in the body. Theorists believe these neurotransmitters strongly influence the level of drive a person has, as well as his or her emotions and the way he or she tolerates stress.

After 9 months of sheltered prenatal life, when every need of the growing fetus is supplied by the mother's body, the baby emerges from the uterus into a world that immediately begins to make demands on him or her and will continue to do so throughout his or her life. However, if the child has developed normally, he or she is well designed to live in and adapt to this world.

Babies come into the world with basic temperaments or personality dispositions. For example, some infants are more placid than others. In addition, the temperaments of the baby's parents can be similar or quite unlike that of their newborn. Depending on the compatibility of the baby's inborn disposition and those of his or her parents, the environment may hold varying degrees of conflict for the developing child.

Certain inborn personality characteristics have been identified by Terry Brazelton, a pediatrician who researches the development of newborns. These personality characteristics include 26 behaviors and 20 reflexes that can be observed and rated. The most easily observable of these appear in the following list.

General State Observations

Alertness	Motor maturity
General physical tone	Tremulousness
Cuddliness	Activity

Irritability

Startle reflex during
   examination

Lability of skin color

Lability of states

Self-quieting activity

Hand-to-mouth facility

Smiles

Response to light

Response to rattle

Response to bell

Response to pinprick

Orientation to various auditory
   and visual stimuli

Defensive movements

Consolability with intervention

Peak of excitement

Buildup of excitement

Pull to sit

■ Environment

The child's environment is a limited world—one reflected by his or her parents and their home—and it causes him or her to react to a multitude of new situations and to other human beings. The child's personality forms as the result of interaction between environment and heredity.

One important effect of environmental influences is the child's acquisition of values. **Values** are deeply held beliefs the child acquires during his or her formative years as the result of exposure to people who are important to him or her. In the desire to be accepted and to avoid disapproval, the child gradually takes on their values and beliefs. Conversely, he or she will also develop a value system based on exposure to individuals who displease him or her, forming values unlike theirs in order to be different from them. Values are the basis of much of our adult behavior and decision making.

■ Developmental Stages

Just as bodies go through successive stages of physical development until they reach adulthood, so, too, personalities normally undergo developmental stages until they reach maturity. Harmful influences may interfere with the normal physical growth and functioning of a tissue, an organ, or the entire body. Similarly, disturbing early experiences and unsatisfied emotional needs may lead to an arrest or **fixation** of the normal growth pattern of the personality and can result in personality distortions and immaturities.

Psychologists consider a wholesome mother-child relationship to be essential for the normal growth and personality development of the child. The child must feel wanted, loved, and enjoyed by his or her parents, and especially by his or her mother or the mother-figure.

If the child feels loved and cared for, a desirable sense of security will follow. If, on the other hand, the child experiences rejection, harshness, and frustration, his or her personality will often be characterized by anxiety, insecurity, and depression. He or she may develop hostile and aggressive tendencies. The emotional experiences of early years leave permanent imprints on the personality, although they may no longer be a part of the individual's consciousness.

One of the most important processes in influencing personality development is called **identification.** Through this process, the child, because of his or her love for and wish to be like the parent, particularly the parent of the same sex, molds himself or herself after that parent and adopts the parent's characteristics and attitudes. This is not a conscious imitation; it is automatic. If the parent is emotionally mature and well adjusted, this process of identification can greatly contribute to the development of similar characteristics in the child's personality.

As the personality continues to grow, it is influenced and molded by many factors. Some of the child's experiences will stimulate personality growth; others will block or distort its development. If the child experiences difficulties with the issues of security, love, aggression, and dependence, he or she may develop emotional problems. As the child begins to strive for independence, he or she will find it difficult to meet the new responsibilities that independence entails. Growth brings new problems and contradictory urges. Such challenges may sometimes result in emotional turmoil and sometimes in healthy, adaptive behavior.

Emotional development often progresses on an uneven course; but, if early identifications have been healthy and if most conflicts have been successfully resolved, eventually a mature, adult personality should emerge. Someone with a mature personality is one who has achieved a harmonious adjustment to his or her environment and can meet life's inevitable stresses realistically and effectively.

In order to understand deviant personality, it is important to understand how a normal personality develops. For our purposes, personality does not mean personal charm and distinction; rather, it is the total of all individual tendencies—including strengths and weaknesses, attributes, aspirations, and drives—that determines a person's adjustments to his or her material and social environment. Personality has been referred to as the internal psychophysiologic organization of an individual as he or she interacts with the external organization of the environment.

Personality is always in a state of flux. It is always in the process of becoming something else, yet ordinarily it retains an identifiable continuity from situation to situation, from year to year, and from birth to death.

Although definitions of personality vary greatly, most theorists agree on the following six points:

1. Personality is a relatively enduring organization of patterns of behavior characteristic of the individual.
2. Personality results from the complex interactions of heredity and environment. (Theorists do not agree whether biologic forces or psychosocial factors are more important.)
3. Dynamic forces, including psychobiologic drives produced by neurotransmitters, cause behavior.
4. Some of these dynamic forces are unknown to the individual; that is, unconscious causes of behavior do exist.
5. Childhood is an important time for forming and organizing relatively enduring patterns of behavioral characteristics of an individual.
6. Behavior, both in its outward and inward manifestations, is a function or expression of personality.

■ Personality Development and Learning

Few subjects have been as fully studied as the field of animal and human learning. Yet much remains to be understood about how learning occurs. Psychologists studying the process of learning have organized it into four steps:

1. First a person must want something (the drive, the **need,** or the motivation).
2. The person must then notice something that will satisfy his or her need (the **stimulus,** or the cue).
3. The person must then act on the stimulation (the **response**).
4. He or she must then get something (the reward, the **reinforcement,** or the need reduction).

These four steps of learning are, of course, much oversimplified. Learning is a process; each step can be infinitely elaborated. For example: A newborn baby becomes hungry, and needs impel him or her to restless activity. Mother offers food; the baby sucks, and the hunger pangs subside. The baby becomes comfortable and drowsy. Here are all the ingredients of a learning situation—a need (hunger), a stimulus (the feel of a nipple in the baby's mouth), a response (sucking), and reinforcement (relief from hunger). Accordingly, learning takes place.

At birth, a baby will actively seek the nipple, turning his or her head from side to side and making sucking responses if his or her cheek is stroked when he or she is hungry. The baby then learns that food (nipple plus sucking) brings relief. After a few weeks, the learning extends to include other elements of this sequence. Now the baby may stop crying from hunger when he or she is picked up. New cues have been tied in or associated with the food-brings-comfort pattern. Soon baby will smile when mother bends over him or her, even when he or she is not hungry, which indicates that the original food-brings-comfort learning has been elaborated into "mother is something good." The baby may learn to associate the feel of his or her mother's body with nursing, and he or she will wiggle with anticipation. **Reinforcement** is the process by which behavior is learned. A reinforcer is anything that causes behavior to be repeated. The greater the reinforcement, the stronger the learning. The reinforcement may have to come in succeeding episodes, or, if strong enough, a single reinforcement may result in fixing the pattern of learning. For instance, toilet training or learning to eat with fingers and later with a spoon becomes effective only after repeated efforts followed by the reinforcement. For example, reinforcement of eating behavior can be the pleasant feeling of satiety, a smile from mother, or the feeling of accomplishment from feeding oneself.

On the other hand, a single experience that is very painful or surprising, such as a burnt finger or tumbling down several stairs, will usually result in a clearly remembered learning experience. The baby will avoid the hot object and refuse, even when coaxed, to try the stairs again until his or her coordination is much better.

When the pattern of learning no longer serves the need, reinforcement ceases to operate. When this happens, the learning process progressively decreases and finally ceases altogether. This is called **extinction,** or in ordinary language, forgetting. Although lack of reinforcement is just one cause of forgetting, it is the chief one. Many things that are important to a child lose importance as the child matures, and lack of reinforcement causes a progressive decrease in the sharpness of the mental image, until memory finally ceases.

However, something well-learned once is never fully forgotten. We store it in our subconscious mind, and it can be brought back to immediate awareness. Sometimes remembrance is immediate; sometimes we must concentrate quite a bit before a dim memory emerges clearly to view. Learning of many activities, such as learning to play the piano, to type, or to tie an intricate knot, improves with reinforcement but will fade away or become extinct if the activity is not used. However, relearning a once-acquired skill is usually accomplished with a little practice.

CHAPTER 8 QUESTIONS

1. What are neurotransmitters and what role do they appear to play in personality?

2. How would you describe **identification** and the role it plays in personality development?

3. What are the four steps involved in learning?

4. Why does extinction of learning occur?

BIBLIOGRAPHY

Brazelton, T. (1991). What we can learn from the status of the newborn. *NIDA Research Monograph, 114,* 93–105.

Brazelton, T., & Yogman, M. (1986). *Affective development in infancy.* Norwood, NJ: Ablex Publishing.

Herson, M., Kazdin, A.E., & Bellack, A.S. (Eds.). (1991). *The clinical psychology handbook* (2nd ed.). New York: Pergamon Press.

Hurrelman, K. (1989). *Human development and health.* New York: Springer-Verlag.

Kaplan, H., & Sadock, B. (1991). *Synopsis of psychiatry: Behavioral sciences, clinical psychiatry* (6th ed.). Baltimore: Williams & Wilkins.

Murray, R.B., & Zentner, J.P. (1989). *Nursing assessment and health promotion strategies through the life span* (4th ed.). Norwalk, CT: Appleton & Lange.

Pfafflin, S.M. (Ed.). (1990). Psychology: Perspectives and practice. *Annals of the New York Academy of Sciences.*

Plotnick, R. (1993). *Introduction to psychology* (3rd ed.). Pacific Grove, CA: Brooks-Cole.

Sameroff, A.J., & Emde, R.N. (Eds.). (1989). *Relationship disturbances in early childhood: A development approach.* New York: Basic Books.

Chapter 9

■■■■■

Influence of Family and Social Environment on the Individual

Behavioral Objectives

After reading this chapter the student will be able to:

Describe the concept of personality disposition.

Define **maladaptation**.

Explain the concepts of **system**, **subsystem**, and **supersystem**.

Describe the term **dynamic** and explain the dynamics in a closed versus an open family.

Explain how the dynamics of a family are altered when one of its members is treated for mental illness.

Explain why sibling position in a family can have an effect on personality development.

Describe homeostasis in the family.

The family is the first social group experienced by a developing infant. The comfort of an individual with any social group during childhood and adulthood is shaped by his or her relationships with mother, father, siblings, and the extended family. The extended family includes grandparents, aunts, uncles, and cousins. Because of today's mobile society, some of the important roles usually performed by family members may be filled by friends, neighbors, teachers, ministers, and so on.

As described in the previous chapter, an infant is a unique being who is born with a certain disposition or temperament that is determined by his or her physical inheritance. For example, he or she may have a quiet, easy-going disposition, be irritable and difficult to please, or be very alert and inquisitive.

Just as the infant has his or her own unique disposition, so too do parents. Depending on the fit in disposition between a child and his or her parents, there may be a higher capacity for trust or for anxiety-producing tension or conflict. As an example, consider the experience of a cranky, irritable infant who is born to a frequently anxious mother versus an easy-going, confident mother. The psychological "fit" between a parent and child can be an important factor in the development of a child's self-esteem.

A family is a very complex social structure. There are countless factors that shape its development and that of each of its members. The term **family system** is used in the field of mental health as it describes maladaptive family patterns of communication that contribute to mental illness.

Maladaptation is the result of chronic ineffective coping on the part of one or both parents that starts dysfunctional patterns of responses to stress within one or more family members. These social and communication patterns are usually acquired by children in their socialization within the family. **Socialization** is the shaping of an individual to the communication style, beliefs, and emotional patterns of a social group. The growth and development of a child in the family is shaped by the internal and external stresses and forces that affect the child, the family, both parents, and every child in the family. Most of these family forces, stresses, and dynamics have been examined in order to understand the causes of mental illness.

Personality theorists generally believe that the usual cause of mental illness is the result of two factors: genetic physiological inheritance and the effect of the family environment during infancy and childhood. In order to understand the importance of the multiple forces and dynamics that occur in families, mental health theorists turned to the scientific field to find the terminology to describe family processes. From the field of biology general systems theory has been adopted to explain family processes and their effects on personality development.

■ General Systems Theory

General systems theory is a concept that is helpful to nurses in the care of clients. The original concept of systems theory was developed by von Bertalanffy in the 1920s. In his field of biology, he was constantly impressed by the organization of organisms and the dependence of biologic systems on one another. The metabolism and growth of one organism depends on another; for example, photosynthesis by trees requires carbon dioxide given off as a waste product by human metabolism. Conversely, humans use oxygen given off as a waste product by trees in their metabolic process.

As scientists from other fields began to apply von Bertalanffy's general systems concept to their own disciplines, they began to see that there was, indeed, an interdependence of one system on another. This concept can be applied to the smallest microscopic life form or to the solar system and the interactions of the planets.

This idea of interdependence applies very well to the fields of psychiatry and psychology. No human being exists in complete isolation from all others. The infant, for example, depends on others for his or her physical care and nurturing. His or her personality is formed as the result of interactions, primarily with immediate family and later with teachers, peers, and others.

■ Systems, Subsystems, and Supersystems

What is a system? A **system** is actually a collection of working parts that, when combined together, make up a more complex working object or abstract entity. These smaller components are called subsystems. They are essential to the overall functioning of a system. A **subsystem** is a concrete or abstract, essential part of a larger system and relates in specific ways with all parts of the larger entity. Without the subsystem, the system cannot function.

The human psyche is an example of an abstract system. It is made up of three major parts or subsystems. They are the id, ego, and superego. If one or more of these subsystems is not present, the psyche is unable to function. The cardiovascular system is another example. It is made up of several working subsystems—the heart, the arteries, veins, and so on.

The body itself is a very complex entity made up of a large number of systems. When a number of systems are essential for an entity to function, then it is called a supersystem. A **supersystem** is a large complex made up of many systems. A state's department of mental health is also a supersystem; it consists of many hospitals, departments, and groups of workers that are essential to its functioning.

Man as a System

Man is a system made up of two main subsystems, the physiological and the psychological. The physiologic subsystem includes many smaller subsystems, such as cardiovascular, neurologic, and musculoskeletal. If one of these subsystems fails, the result is that all the other subsystems will ultimately fail, and death will occur. Man's psychological subsystem includes the id, ego, and superego subsystems.

As suggested above, a human is part of larger systems that can be called supersystems. A person belongs to several social supersystems. His or her primary social system is the family. It is in the family that he or she acquires basic values, self-image, and the capacity for relating with others throughout his or her lifetime. In addition, a person belongs to social systems through school and work. A person is also a part of the ecologic supersystem; in the environment he or she lives interdependently with other animals, plants, gases, and water.

Systems Theory and Mental Illness

The concept of systems is important for our purposes. It allows us to look for the cause of mental illness somewhere within one of a human's subsystems or supersystems. Identification of the cause, when possible, allows us to plan therapeutic interventions.

■ Major Concepts in Family System Functioning

Family System Terminology

The immediate family into which a child is born is called the **nuclear family.** It is made up of mother, father, and siblings and is also known as the **family of origin.** The family members not in the nuclear family—grandparents, aunts, uncles, cousins, and so on—are known as the **extended family.**

Dynamics

A **dynamic** is a constantly operating force within a system that results in some type of action or observable result. If, for example, a person was orphaned as a young child or was born with a major handicap, it can be said that these factors lying deep within the experience of a person have a constantly operating effect on him or her. Dynamics are usually operating in all of us without our conscious awareness.

There are dynamics that occur within a person's psyche, such as unconscious impulses or drives of the id. In addition, there are social system dynamics that operate in families. These can include defensive avoidance of a family member with an explosive temper or schizophrenia.

Open and Closed Family Systems

Depending on the openness or closedness of the family, a child's needs will or will not be shaped or formed in such a way that is healthy and supports his or her continuing social and psychological development.

An **open family** is one in which the members, especially the parents, have had the opportunity to develop as healthy, active, members of society with positive self-esteem. They not only contribute to the society and to their families, but they are able to recognize their needs and have them met by others, when necessary. In other words, they know how to receive or to take from others, in a socially responsible manner, whatever they need to develop as actualized human beings. An open family allows for flexibility in the roles of its members.

A **closed family,** on the other hand, is rigid and allows little change in the roles and patterns in the family. Usually one of the parents (frequently both) has moderate to high levels of psychopathology. The climate in the home does not support the development and ultimate healthy separation of the child from the family when he or she reaches adulthood.

The majority of persons we work with in psychiatric settings come from the latter type of family. The dynamics in the closed family frequently contribute toward inadequate or pathologic personality development in the developing child. These traits evolve into the adult's personality. Remember that an individual's personality has been shaped over a long period of time. This usually happens to meet the family's needs but without their conscious awareness.

■ Effects of Mental Illness on Family Dynamics

Accordingly, when this family member becomes mentally ill it is a worsening of a mental state to which the family has become accustomed. If the person is treated in a mental health setting and his or her normally dysfunctional pattern is eliminated, the family's dynamics are changed significantly. A simple example of this is a woman who has a violent temper even when she is only mildly angry. Her family unconsciously knows her boiling point. They relate as a family in a way that will not upset her. Conversely, when the family is upset about something, she expresses the emotion that others feel, and it helps to clear the air. For this particular family this is their normal communication style. Equilibrium in the family is maintained by the dynamic of the mother's anger. If her boiling point were to change permanently to a better, healthier level, it would dramatically change the way the family members interact. The other family members would unconsciously work to restore the communications to their former normal style.

All families, open or closed, relate in a way that maintains their normal communication patterns. When the behavior of one person is changed, it disrupts these patterns and causes increased anxiety in all the other members. Accordingly, if people admitted to a mental health facility are treated with no attention to the family, their chances for long-term recovery are diminished. Family patterns that may have contributed to the development of the client's dysfunctional symptoms must be examined and, if necessary, modified. This requires that the family meet with a family therapist, usually one or more times weekly, during the client's hospitalization. The types of patterns and dynamics that exist in families are described below.

Sibling Position in Family of Origin

Studies of all types of families have found that birth order strongly influences the way a person communicates and behaves in a family. In addition, a person carries these interpersonal traits into adulthood, and they become part of the way he or she relates in any social setting. Generally, the oldest child is more responsive to criticism, is more responsible, achieves consistently, and functions behaviorally in a more rigid manner than younger brothers or sisters. These traits result from the parents' tendencies to demand more of oldest children and expect them to assist with the care of younger siblings.

The youngest child is frequently more dependent, less achievement-oriented, and often quite charming. This results from the love and attention received by the youngest child. If his or her needs were easily met, he or she did not learn to tolerate frustration in pursuit of goals.

The middle child, because of his or her position between the oldest and youngest children, frequently is more flexible and more independent. He or she also tends to be more easy-going than the oldest or youngest child. A client's interaction style in the hospital setting, both with care-givers and other clients, frequently reflects his or her sibling position.

Family Rules

Family rules are the unwritten expectations about what types of roles or behavior will be acceptable or unacceptable to the family. Remember that most people behave in ways that will ensure approval by those they care about. As we grow older we tend to conform to the expectations of others in order to maintain their love and acceptance. These rules are often based on the value system that each partner brings into a marriage. Remember that we inherit many of our values from our families. Most people tend to marry individuals with similar values or expectations. It is in this way that family patterns, rules, and expectations tend to remain somewhat similar from one generation to the next.

Boundaries

Within a family system **boundaries** are the rules that keep the role of one family member separate from another. Staying within one's role in the family is often the key to acceptance in the family. Boundaries develop as the result of family rules. For example, if women in a family have traditionally been passive, a daughter from such a family may be passive as well. She will most likely marry a man who enjoys his role as sole decision maker. This type of family pattern of relationships teaches the children to go to the father automatically when a decision needs to be made. If the mother uncharacteristically makes a major decision, conflict usually will result. She has, in effect, overstepped her customary boundary and altered her normal role in the family.

When a mentally ill person is successfully treated and reenters the family, the role he or she filled before treatment is changed. Accordingly, his or her normal boundaries of functioning are also different. A family therapy process, in conjunction with inpatient psychiatric hospitalization, is designed to renegotiate and reestablish boundaries and role patterns so that the newly discharged person's different (and more healthy) style of functioning will not be reshaped by the family to his or her preadmission family role.

Homeostasis

The concept of a system is helpful when we look at homeostasis or equilibrium within a family. It can be helpful to visualize a mobile with a number of objects hanging from it as a symbol of homeostasis. Compare the mobile to a family system. When it is in balance it maintains perfect equilibrium. If one of the objects is tapped what happens? All the other objects are affected and jostled. If one object is removed what happens? There is an even stronger effect. The entire mobile loses its balance.

Homeostasis is a dynamic, ever-changing state in which a system constantly works to maintain balance. As one subsystem or person changes, the other members alter their patterns of communication or behavior to maintain the balance of the family. When a person becomes mentally ill, the family struggles to counter the effects of his or her worsening symptoms. If admission to the hospital becomes necessary, it triggers a crisis. The removal of the person from the family can allow the family to work toward equilibrium or homeostasis. Remember, however, that without the return of the ill member to the family, true family homeostasis is disrupted.

The concept of general systems theory applies to all systems. It encourages us to view physically or mentally ill clients holistically. We are aware of the interaction of physical illness on the psyche, and conversely, of the psyche on physical illness. It also allows us to evaluate the interaction of the overall social system and family on the etiology, diagnosis, and treatment of illness.

CHAPTER 9 QUESTIONS

1. What might be the effect of a good psychological "fit" in disposition between parent and child?

2. How would you define socialization?

3. What is a dynamic? How do the dynamics in a closed family contribute to inadequate or pathologic personality development?

4. Explain homeostasis as it relates to the family.

BIBLIOGRAPHY

Barry, P.D. (1989). *Psychosocial nursing: Assessment and intervention* (2nd ed.). Philadelphia: J.B. Lippincott.

Combrinck-Graham, L. (1990). Developments in family systems theory and research. *Journal of the American Academy of Child & Adolescent Psychiatry*, 29, 501–512.

Kaplan, H., & Sadock, B. (1991). *Synopsis of psychiatry: Behavioral sciences, clinical psychiatry* (6th ed.). Baltimore: Williams & Wilkins.

Minuchin, S. (1974). *Families and family therapy*. Cambridge, MA: Harvard University Press.

Pervin, L.A. (Ed.). (1990). *Handbook of personality: Theory and research*. New York: Guilford Press.

Pine, F. (1990). *Drive, ego, object and self: A synthesis for clinical work*. New York: Basic Books.

Ramsey, C.N. (Ed.). (1989). *Family systems in medicine*. New York: Guilford Press.

Schultz, D.P. (1990). *Theories of personality* (4th ed.). Pacific Grove, CA: Brooks-Cole.

Toman, W. (1976). *Family constellation: Its effects on personality and social behavior* (3rd ed.). New York: Springer.

Wilson, H.S., & Kneisl, C.R. (1992). *Psychiatric nursing* (4th ed.). Redwood City, CA: Addison-Wesley.

Chapter 10

■■■■■

The Needs of a Human Being

Behavioral Objectives

After reading this chapter the student will be able to:

List the five childhood experiences that are very important to development.

Explain the concept of a hierarchy of human needs described by Maslow.

Name and describe the five levels of human needs identified by Maslow.

Discuss the differences in moral development and decision making between males and females identified by Gilligan.

Describe the concept of the ego ideal.

■ Development of Needs

The newborn infant shows a generalized response to all stimuli. Emotions develop as the baby reacts to his or her environment. For the infant, life is first of all a biologic fact. He or she responds physiologically to the unpleasantness of hunger and cold and to the need to move his or her muscles. It soon becomes necessary for the infant to react to a multitude of new situations and to other human beings.

84

Mental Health and Mental Illness, Fifth Edition, by Patricia D. Barry. J.B. Lippincott Company, Philadelphia © 1994.

One ability the infant possesses is highly significant—the inexplicable power to communicate emotional feeling tones (the power of **empathy**). The baby is able to sense and respond to feelings of approval and disapproval from the mother or mother-figure. Feelings of approval increase the newborn's sense of well-being, and the opposite feelings cause discomfort. This happens long before the baby is capable of understanding the meaning of either feeling.

Although all experiences are planted forever in the mind, at this time the infant only vaguely associates them with the mother-figure. Satisfactions are achieved with the first magic tool, crying, and comfort and discomfort are known but not understood. The baby's responses to comfort and discomfort begin to form a patterned behavior.

Experiences in childhood that are particularly important in future development are as follows:

Availability of a consistent, concerned care-giver

The feeding situation in early infancy (including weaning)

Toilet and cleanliness training

Early sex training

Training for control of anger and aggression

Adjusting to these situations can be quite upsetting to the child, and it takes patience and understanding on the part of the parents to help him or her accept social rules and regulations. If the parents approve of him or her as a person, even when they may disapprove of his or her actions, the child will usually accept their rules and values as his or her own and build them into a growing personality.

■ Hierarchy of Human Needs

Abraham Maslow, a psychologist, is one of the founders of the field of humanistic psychology. He believes that humans have levels of needs that must be met before each can develop into a psychologically mature person. He calls these the hierarchy of human needs:

1. Physiologic needs
2. Safety needs
3. Love and belonging needs
4. Esteem needs
5. Self-actualization needs

According to Maslow, it is impossible to progress from one stage of psychological development to the next higher stage until the needs at the lower level are met. For example, until a person has obtained the basic physiologic needs of the first level, it is impossible for him or her to move to the level of feeling safe and secure. Accordingly, until a person has a safe and secure environment, he or she will be unable to continue the process of feeling loved and accepted in his or her social environment.

Physiologic Needs

The growing child has many needs; some are physiologic and some are psychosocial. The physiologic needs are often called **basic** or **primary** needs because they are basic to physical survival. Six basic requirements are oxygen, food, water, sleep, protection from temperature extremes (clothing and shelter), and excretion. Extreme deprivation of any one will result in the person's death.

To these six should be added a seventh—sexual activity—not because deprivation of this activity would result in a person's death, but because, without it, the human race would become extinct. If these physiologic or biologic needs were humans' only concern, they would live on a very primitive level indeed. Brute force would determine survival.

Safety Needs

In order to develop in a psychologically healthy way, it is important that a person feel safe and secure from harm. This requires a predictable social and physical environment. Without feelings of safety, humans of any age, from infants to elderly adults, live with a chronic sense of fear that inhibits personal growth and fulfillment.

Love and Belonging Needs

Probably the deepest psychosocial need most of us have is the need for love or emotional security. Love is a complex feeling of trust, warmth, and understanding—of closeness, intimacy, and emotional give-and-take. From infancy, humans need to feel accepted. All babies need a sense of emotional security; they need to be "mothered" regularly—held against the mother's body, stroked, caressed, cuddled, spoken and sung to, and rocked. So deep is this need that some psychologists place it with the seven basic needs. Humans do not outgrow the need to love and be loved. They merely shift where they look for the need to be filled—from the parental figure to peers (persons of one's own age).

Esteem Needs

Until a person feels accepted and loved by others, it is difficult for him or her to love and accept himself or herself. The young child's sense of self-worth or self-esteem forms the basis of his or her supply of self-esteem in adulthood. Self-esteem is a feeling of self-acceptance and positive self-image. Esteem needs have two main parts: a sense of competence about oneself and the need for recognition and a good reputation. If these needs are not fully met, the person lacks the feelings of confidence and competence necessary to move to the next and highest level of human needs.

Within the esteem level of human needs is the need for status and recognition. Status is a person's particular place in society; this place is allotted to him or her by virtue of age, sex, abilities, vocation or profession, his or her parents' status, and his or her socioeconomic standing. Recognition is the approval or acceptance given the individual by society as he or she performs in keeping with the role society has accorded. The esteem of others nourishes and supports an individual's self-esteem.

Although in the United States we have a so-called classless society—that is, one without aristocratic titles—we do have criteria, such as success and money, that substitute for aristocracy and help to determine status. The pressure to succeed, to achieve, and to excel begins very early in our lives. Power and possessions are two very important symbols of success. The need for status and recognition is probably related directly to our need to belong—the need for approval and acceptance—first by the family, and then by the group.

Self-Actualization Needs

Finally, there is the need to achieve—the need to accomplish and do. Maslow believes that the need to self-actualize or fully develop one's potential is a constant driving force in all persons, regardless of age. When adults feel vague discontent with their lives, it is often because they have not fully developed their potentials. This usually occurs because a person is limiting his or her own capacity to further develop himself or herself, either personally, educationally, or in the working environment. It also can happen when a person's attempts at full personal development are thwarted by another person, financial circumstances, or other environmental factors. Full actualization requires that these self-created or other-created obstacles be overcome.

If the child's struggle to crawl, stand, walk, talk, and master his or her environment is rewarded by the approval of the significant figures in his or her life, he or she will learn the satisfaction of accomplishment and will build a healthy concept of himself or herself as a "doer of deeds," a success. If the child fails to earn the approval of those around him or her, if small achievements are ignored, or worse yet, criticized severely, he or she will build a picture of himself or herself as "one who fails." His or her pride diminished, the child may lose the ambition or drive to develop his or her potential as he or she reaches adulthood. His or her rights and limits should be clearly defined and respected by the family. Accordingly, the child will grow to respect his or her own rights, as well as the rights of others.

Self-development in the child is vital. He or she must gradually acquire a concept of *who* he or she is, *what* he or she is, and *what he or she can do*. By the time the child is 4 or 5 years old, he or she tends to have an exaggerated self-concept. He or she feels able to do anything, but the lessons slowly learned from the environment tend to level off this concept to a more realistic one. Some self-idealization continues in most adults. They have a strong tendency to see themselves much closer to perfection than they really are. This is the **ego ideal** Freud speaks of in relation to his concept of personality development. It is a strong motivation for continued growth.

■ Differing Needs of Men and Women

Carol Gilligan, a psychologist interested in the differences in the social development of males and females, has found that the sexes have somewhat different values underlying their relationship potential, as well as their moral development. She has found in her research that the basic need of women is to maintain relationships. They promote communication as a means of keeping relationships intact. Women tend to feel strong responsibility in relationships. Men, on the other hand, tend to shy away from relationships and instead seek achievement as their basic need. The need for achievement, according to Gilligan, is a strong factor in male decision making and ethical considerations.

CHAPTER 10 QUESTIONS

1. What are three experiences in childhood that are important in future development?

2. According to Maslow, when is it possible for a person to progress from one stage of psychological development to the next higher stage?

3. When does a person become psychologically mature, according to Maslow's hierarchy of human needs?

BIBLIOGRAPHY

Biernat, M. (1991). Gender stereotypes and the relationship between masculinity and femininity: A developmental analysis. *Journal of Personality & Social Psychology, 61*, 351–365.

Gilligan, C. (1982). *In a different voice.* Cambridge, MA: Harvard University Press.

Jacklin, C.N. (1989). Female and male: Issues of gender. *American Psychologist, 44*, 127–133.

Kaplan, H., & Sadock, B. (1991). *Synopsis of psychiatry: Behavioral sciences, clinical psychiatry* (6th ed.). Baltimore: Williams & Wilkins.

Lowry, R.J. (Ed.). (1973). *Dominance, self-esteem, self-actualization: Germinal papers of A.H. Maslow.* Monterey, CA: Brooks-Cole.

Mahler, M. (1974). Symbiosis and individuation: The psychological birth of the infant. *Psychoanalytic Study of the Child, 29*, 89.

Maslow, A. (1970). *Motivation and personality.* New York: Harper & Row.

McFarland, G.K., Thomas, M.D. (1991). *Psychiatric mental health nursing: Application of the nursing process.* Philadelphia: J.B. Lippincott.

Spitz, R. (1965). *The first year of life.* New York: International Universities Press.

Chapter 11

■■■■■

The Structure of Personality

Behavioral Objectives

After reading this chapter the student will be able to:

Name the three abstract structures of the personality identified by Freud and briefly describe the function of each.

Identify and define the three levels of consciousness in the mind described by Freud.

Name three causes of conflict in the personality.

■ Structural Theory of Personality

According to Freud, the personality is formed by the interaction of environment and heredity. The personality consists of three abstract structures: the **id,** the **ego,** and the **superego.** He called these the abstract structures of personality. It is the conflict among these parts and the resulting balance that produce behavior.

The Id

At birth, the child is all id. The id, therefore, is that part of the personality we are born with; it is ruled only by the **pleasure princi-**

Mental Health and Mental Illness,
Fifth Edition, by Patricia D. Barry.
J.B. Lippincott Company, Philadelphia © 1994.

ple—the concept that humans instinctually seek to avoid pain and discomfort and strive for gratification and pleasure. The id is the raw stuff of personality, consisting of the body's primitive, biologic drives, which strive only for satisfaction and pleasure.

Shortly after birth the baby is frustrated because his or her needs are not immediately satisfied. He or she cries to be fed, moved, or held, or to have his or her diaper changed, but finds he or she must often wait for a while. Crying is the baby's first form of protest; it is used as a tool to achieve needs. And so the second component of personality comes into being—the **ego** or **reality principle.**

The ego encompasses a large variety of functions that are essential to mental and physical well-being. They include the following:

Consciousness	Regulation and control of
Mastery of motor skills	emotions and impulses
Mobility	Object relations
Perception	Memory
Judgment	Thinking
Sense of reality	Defense mechanisms

The Ego

The ego is the part of the self that is most closely in touch with reality. Its job is to mediate between the urges of the id and the demands of the environment and to satisfy both in a way that coincides with physical and social reality. It is roughly equivalent to the terms "conscious awareness," or "the self." As it develops, the reality principle, or ego, overrules or operates in concert with the id, or pleasure principle, in guiding behavior.

By the time the average child is 3 years old, he or she has learned that there are many things he or she may not do and other things that he or she must do. The child is also learning to defer immediate satisfactions for anticipated or delayed satisfactions. For example, he or she will stop doing something that feels good in order to obtain his or her mother's approval. During this time, the child has learned to accept the attributes and standards of his or her parents as his or her own. The child is not yet able to understand the reasons behind behavior, but readily accepts his or her parents' judgment about what is right or wrong to do or say. He or she tends to idealize and view himself or herself as close to perfection. Thus his or her ego ideal is formed. The **ego ideal** is a high standard within the ego that motivates the individual to continued growth and self-actualization.

The Superego

Slowly, the child begins to make his or her own judgments about the rightness or wrongness of things and to regulate his or her conduct on the basis of these judgments. By the time the child is 7 years old, this judgment process should be fairly well integrated into the personality. Freud calls the judgment process the **superego** and labels it as being social or cultural in origin. The superego is roughly equivalent to what we call our **conscience**—the inner voice that tells us whether our thoughts and actions are good or bad.

The id, ego, and superego are involved in constant conflicts. These conflicts and frustrations give rise to our behavior and result in emotional growth. Without conflict and frustration, there would be no personality growth. Some conflicts are apparent to us; we are aware of some, consciously involved in many, but unaware of other conflicts. Because the conflicts that are unknown to us function at a deeper level, we cannot resolve them. Nevertheless, they act as strong motivators of our behavior.

■ Levels of Consciousness

One of Freud's greatest contributions to an understanding of human behavior was his concept of the **unconscious.** He saw the mind as consisting of three overlapping parts. These he labeled, from the one we are most aware of to the one we are least aware of, the **conscious mind,** the **subconscious mind,** and the **unconscious mind,** likening them to the parts of an iceberg.

The **conscious mind** refers to that part of the mind that is focused in a here-and-now awareness (the part of the iceberg that is above the water level, freely visible). The **subconscious mind** refers to that part of the mind just below immediate awareness—the storehouse for memories. These memories are either those that have ceased to be important to us or those that we suppressed because they are mildly uncomfortable. They can be brought back into awareness at will. (This is the part of the iceberg below the water level that can be seen by peering down into the water.) The **unconscious mind** refers to that part of the mind that is closed to immediate awareness. It is that vast reservoir of memories, experiences, and emotions that cannot be recalled. (This is the part of the iceberg that cannot be seen at all and may extend a great distance down into the water, completely unknown to the observers above it.)

■ Conflict

Conflicts among the three parts of the personality may result in behavior that is wholly conscious, partly conscious, wholly subconscious, or wholly unconscious. *The important aspect of behavior is that it usually resolves conflict.* Faced with an upsetting situation, people ordinarily do one of three things: (1) They become aggressive and oppose the situation. (2) They flee from it. (3) They compromise with it. This last way of handling a situation seems to be the most realistic one and the one most likely to resolve the conflict or anxiety.

Conflicts are resolved through the use of certain methods of thinking and acting that either eliminate the conflict or reduce its severity. These methods, commonly called **defense mechanisms** or **mental mechanisms,** are not always clear cut; in fact, they often overlap or may be used simultaneously. Many defense mechanisms have been identified; they will be described in Chapter 16, Ineffective Coping and Defense Mechanisms.

CHAPTER 11 QUESTIONS

1. How did Freud define the superego?

2. What did Freud call the part of the mind that is just below immediate awareness?

3. What are the three ways that people usually resolve conflicts?

BIBLIOGRAPHY

Barry, P.D. (1989). *Psychosocial nursing: Assessment and intervention* (2nd ed.). Philadelphia: J.B. Lippincott.

Combrinck-Graham, L. (1990). Developments in family systems theory and research. *Journal of the American Academy of Child & Adolescent Psychiatry, 29,* 501–512.

Goldstein, G., & Hersen, M. (Eds.). (1990). *Handbook of psychological assessment* (2nd ed.). New York: Pergamon Press.

Goodyer, I.M. (1990). *Life experiences, development, and childhood psychopathology*. New York: Wiley.

Hurrelmann, K. (1989). *Human development and health*. New York: Springer-Verlag.

Kaplan, H., & Sadock, B. (1991). *Synopsis of psychiatry: Behavioral sciences, clinical psychiatry* (6th ed.). Baltimore: Williams & Wilkins.

Pervin, L.A. (1990). *Handbook of personality: Theory and research*. New York: Guilford Press.

Schultz, D.P. (1990). *Theories of personality* (4th ed.). Pacific Grove, CA: Brooks-Cole.

Chapter 12

■ ■ ■ ■ ■

Theories of Personality Development

Behavioral Objectives

After reading this chapter the student will be able to:

List several factors that can influence a child's personality.

Name six people who have developed theories of personality.

List the six stages of personality development described by Freud. Indicate the age ranges of each.

Define sibling rivalry and give three examples that describe it.

List the eight stages of personality development described by Erik Erikson.

Explain the developmental tasks and challenges of each of the Erikson stages of personality development.

Why do people seem so different? Why is one person angry, aggressive, and ready to fight at the slightest provocation, while another is passive and gentle, always willing to compromise and bend in order to seek a peaceful solution?

The differences in basic personality style and energy level are apparent in any newborn nursery. One-day-old infants vary greatly in their amount of movement, crying vigor, sucking strength, and tolerance for discomfort. Any mother with more than one child will readily admit that each child exhibited definite differences throughout the neonatal period and infancy. One child was weaned more easily, another was more difficult to toilet train, and so forth.

■ Factors in Personality Development

One can observe that even with the same parents, the genetic makeup of each sibling is different. One may "take after" his or her mother and the other "lean to the father's side of the family." One child may be significantly brighter than another. Literature is full of references to "the beautiful sister" and "the ugly sister," to the son who is "the dreamer" and the son who is "the doer."

The order of birth also plays a role in personality development. The first child is born into a home where childbearing is a new experience for the parents. Not only is the infant new at the job of being an infant, but the parents are new at the job of being parents. The second child is born into a different situation. His or her parents have had some experience at being parents. They may be practiced at limit setting. They have, perhaps, made the house more childproof so that the second child is less likely to break valuable possessions or stray into situations of physical danger.

The first child is an only child until his or her brother or sister is born. He or she has the parents' full attention until suddenly the parents have a new baby, and he or she is an only child no longer. The second child is never an only child.

Although they often deny it, parents have preferences among their children. The father may like boys or more aggressive children, while the mother may prefer quiet, obedient children. Often the reverse is true, the mother favoring her sons and the father favoring his daughters.

With all of these variables, it is little wonder that a great number of theories (also referred to as **belief systems**) have evolved regarding the issue of how personality development occurs. That genetic factors play a part is virtually beyond dispute. The most universally accepted belief about heredity is that it is the background, the set, on which environmental factors play to form the personality.

For example, it is believed by some, although by no means proved, that an infant with a genetic predisposition to schizophrenia may develop in one family as a quiet, sensitive, artistic youth; in another as a person with schizoid personality (see Chapter 27, Personality Disorders); and in still another family as an acute schizophrenic (see Chapter 23, Schizophrenia and Other Psychotic Disorders) with a clearly defined psychosis. Studies on identical twins, who have identical genetic structures, show that there is a very high likelihood of each twin developing the same mental disorder even when they are separated at birth and reared in different families.

Related to the heredity-as-cause belief system, but containing some of its own special concepts, is the biochemical (or neurotransmitter) theory. There are subtle, but distinct, biochemical differences between persons with no mental disorder and persons with major mental illnesses. Which comes first, the biochemical disorder or the mental disorder, is still under dispute, but this area of investigation is among the most promising in psychiatric research today.

■ Theories of Personality Development

Most belief systems, however, have little to do with heredity or biochemistry. They are concerned with one or another facet of the individual person's development from birth on. They focus on the various forces that impinge on the child, such as the father, mother, siblings, family, or society; or the intrinsic developmental forces, such as the child's initial dependence and growth toward independence, the development of language, the development of motor skills, and bowel and bladder control.

It should be well-understood by the student at the outset that no theory is entirely and absolutely correct. At the same time, there is no place for a negative attitude that says, "since nobody knows, there's no reason for listening to anybody." Each theory has some element of truth in it.

Carl Jung emphasized concepts of the collective unconscious, individuation (becoming an individual), and introversion and extroversion.

Harry Stack Sullivan believed that the individual could be studied only in relation to his or her social interactions with others. Sullivan developed four basic postulates that underlie his theories:

1. The *Biological Postulate*, which states that man (as an animal) differs from all other animals in his cultural interdependence.
2. *Man's Essentially Human Mode of Functioning*, which refers to those characteristics that distinguish man from all other animal life.
3. *Significance of Anxiety*, which refers to the central role of anxiety in human development.
4. The *Tenderness Postulate*, in which Sullivan states that "the activity of an infant which arises from the tension of his needs produces tension in the mothering one which is felt by her as tenderness." Man has a growing capacity for tenderness.

Gertrude Mahler described the important psychological development that occurs in children during the first 2½ years of life. She believes that the availability of a consistent, loving care-giver, ideally the mother, is essential if the child is to avoid feeling abandoned and insecure during later life.

Erich Fromm's theories reflect the orientation of the social scientist. He emphasizes the role of society in mental disorders rather than the role of the individual, which is the classic psychoanalyst's concern. Fromm believes that "self-love" is really self-affirmation, which is the basis of the capacity to love others.

Alfred Adler influenced child psychiatry a great deal with his early considerations of organ inferiority and nervous character. He later became preoccupied with educational, social, and political issues as the causes of mental illness.

Karen Horney believed that specific cultural values and beliefs cause disturbances in human relationships leading to neuroses.

Jean Baker Miller describes the psychological development of women as a process in which they learn the value of being subordinate in order to gain acceptance from the larger social system, which includes men and authority figures. She also identifies several important traditional roles of women: the giver of care; the mediator, who avoids and mediates conflicts; and the avoider of power. She believes that these roles undermine women's ability to develop their full potential as human beings.

Wilhelm Reich made a valuable contribution to the understanding of how the character or personality style evident in adulthood is developed.

Otto Rank was primarily concerned with the application of psychoanalysis to mythology and literature.

Eugen Bleuler published a comprehensive study of schizophrenia (a term he coined).

Hermann Rorschach, who developed the ink blot test, was a pioneer in the elaboration of projective psychological testing.

Carl Rogers' theory of personality states that the values of a society and of a person living within that society may differ. If a person replaces his or her own values and choices regarding self-actualization with those of the social environment in order to gain acceptance and approval, conflict occurs in the form of anxiety.

■ Freud's Concept of Personality Development

Sigmund Freud (1856–1939) was a Viennese physician who made important contributions to our understanding of personality development. The contributions are a part of the system of psychology he named **psychoanalysis.** The word is obtained from the term *psyche,* or mind, and the process that Freud developed to analyze the way the mind works.

Freud emphasized an aspect of the personality that he termed **sexuality.** His selection of this term to express the pleasure-seeking component of the personality is unfortunate because it erroneously carries the implication that all forms of pleasure seeking are associated with genital sexuality and pleasure. Bear in mind that Freud's use of the term sexuality is quite broad and traces a step-by-step development of the psychosexual aspect of the personality from its earliest expression in the baby to maturity.

Freud divided the growth and development of the human body into phases, or stages. From birth to adulthood, he listed them as: (1) the oral stage; (2) the anal stage; (3) the phallic stage; (4) the latent stage; (5) the genital stage; and (6) adulthood.

The Oral Stage

The first stage of psychosexual development lasts from birth until about the end of the first year. It terminates in weaning. Before birth, the infant is fed through the maternal bloodstream and never experiences the pleasure provided by the gratification of this first instinctual need. With birth, however, a biologic need for food arises, and the infant receives satisfaction through nursing. Not only is the discomfort from hunger relieved by sucking but, as other tensions arise, the infant may turn to the most available substitute as a source of security and satisfaction—sucking his or her thumb. The mouth becomes the part of the body in which interests, sensation, and activities are centered and through which gratification is secured. If a baby is seldom held or loved, if he or she is left lying untended for long periods of time, often uncomfortable at not being turned or changed, or if he or she is consistently allowed to go hungry beyond the first hunger pangs, he or she will probably enter childhood and, ultimately, adulthood with a disturbed capacity to trust in all relationships.

The Anal-Expulsive Stage

This phase starts toward the end of the first year. At that time, the mouth begins to share its pleasure-giving role with the organs of elimination. The child becomes as interested in discovering his or her excretory functions as the mother is in controlling them. This period covers the toilet training stage and usually terminates early in the third year. The small child does not have the same feeling of revulsion for urine and feces that an adult has. To him or her the process of elimination is pleasure giving.

In our culture, toilet training is often begun early and is usually rigidly enforced. Usually toilet training is not possible until the necessary development of the nervous system has taken place (around the age of 2 years) and until the child has acquired a sign language to communicate his or her wants. When harsh parental expectations and/or punishment occur during this period, the child may develop anxiety that persists into adulthood, primarily around the issue of control.

The Phallic Stage

This phase is characterized by the child's growing awareness of the differences between the male and the female body. This stage usually extends from late in the third or early in the fourth year until the sixth year. At this stage of personality development, there is increasing interest in the genitals, and the child discovers that he or she achieves a pleasurable sensation when the genitals are handled or rubbed. As the child fondles himself or herself, he or she is not at all aware that he or she is doing something socially unacceptable—masturbating—and it is only when parents express displeasure in his or her actions that it assumes an abnormal significance to the child.

Masturbation is not physically harmful in any way, but it does pose an emotional problem when conflicts set in. If the child's unhappiness intensifies, he or she will resort to masturbation in secret, and this will increase his or her guilt feeling and isolate him or her even further from his or her parents. Obsessive masturbation can be avoided by a wise and tolerant attitude on the part of the mother and father. Parents should try to spend more time with the child during this period. A wholesome attitude in the home toward the human body will help the child pass through this phase with a minimum of difficulty.

Another problem that is frequently seen in children between 3 and 7 years of age (although this problem can also occur earlier and later in a child's life) is **sibling rivalry.** A sibling is a brother or a sister who is the offspring of the same parents. The phenomenon can also be observed in children with half-brothers or sisters, as well as adopted or step-siblings. The problem is most noticeable when a new brother or sister is born. At that time the older child is bound to feel dislodged from his or her previously secure position in the family circle. Because the parents, especially the mother, must spend extra time with the newborn, the older child feels neglected, unwanted, and jealous. He or she may actively hate the newcomer, or may even try to get rid of the baby. He or she resents his or her mother's limited attention and will try all kinds of attention-getting devices. If these fail, the child may resort to infantile behavior, such as thumb sucking or bed wetting. He or she may develop stuttering, or may lose his or her appetite. The child often misbehaves in the presence of guests. If parents perceive these difficulties appearing in their children and understand the causes, they can be sure to give each child his or her full share of attention and praise and divide their love equally among them.

The Latent Stage

The **latent** phase refers to the child's 7th through 12th years. The term latent suggests that this is a quiet time in which little development is occurring. Actually, it is a time when the personality traits, sex role mannerisms, and values that will accompany children into adulthood are deeply ingrained.

The Genital Stage

The genital stage is marked by the beginning of **puberty.** Puberty usually begins during the 12th year. The first stage of the genital phase, also known as **adolescence,** is characterized by profound physical changes combined with growing awareness of sex and sexual attraction toward others. This is a significant time for girls, because menstruation begins. The secondary sex characteristics start to appear, and sexual urges arise. Children need the close support of their parents during this time, and they especially need a full and frank explanation about the many changes taking place in their bodies and in their emotions. Explanations of sexual functioning and assurances that sexual feelings are normal help to decrease their anxieties and fears of being abnormal.

This final phase of transition from childhood to adulthood occurs by about the 18th year. As a rule, adolescence manifests itself later in boys than in girls. It is an acute period of transition that includes many physical and emotional strains. Caught between the dependency of childhood and the independence of adulthood, the teenager is strongly ambivalent in his or her desires and emotions. He or she is torn between desire for emancipation from parental controls and fear of the consequences of his or her own actions and judgments.

In addition to severing the parental bonds, the adolescent must seek a satisfactory relation with the opposite sex. He or she must also choose a vocation and start preparing for it, and must develop a sense of mature responsibility for self and others.

■ Erikson's Concept of Personality Development

Erik Erikson's concept of personality development does not stress the psychosexual aspect of the stages of development as Freud's does. Erikson compares the evolution of the personality to the evolution of tissues in the early stages of embryonic development. He believes that there is a timetable inherent in the development of various specialized tissues, organs, and systems in the physical body. Erikson proposes that during each stage of development there is a **developmental task** to be accomplished, and that each developmental task not only contributes some vital attribute of personality but lays the groundwork for the next task.

The stages of psychosocial development identified by Erikson and the developmental challenges of each stage are listed below:

1. Early infancy (birth to 1 year): Trust vs. mistrust
2. Later infancy (1 to 3 years): Autonomy vs. shame and doubt
3. Early childhood (4 to 5 years): Initiative vs. guilt
4. Later childhood (6 to 11 years): Industry vs. inferiority
5. Puberty and adolescence (12 to 20 years): Ego identity vs. role confusion
6. Early adulthood (20 to 40 years): Intimacy vs. isolation
7. Middle adulthood (40 to 60 years): Generality vs. stagnation
8. Late adulthood (60 years and older): Ego integrity vs. despair

Upon this concept he builds the theory that a whole or partial failure at one step means that the personality will be deficient in the trait that should have arisen at that particular time. If succeeding stages are developed on too weak a foundation, the total personality may suffer as a result. Erikson points out that these successive stages of personality development should not be thought of as arising at exact time periods but, rather, at approximate age levels, with considerable individual variation, and that the developmental tasks of each stage overlap. According to Erikson, if a developmental task is not fully mastered during a particular stage of development, it is possible for the unresolved issues of that stage to be worked through during later stages. Following is a brief description of Erikson's stages of psychosocial development.

Early Infancy

This period is characterized by **basic trust.** The child is completely helpless and at the mercy of adults. If he or she is warmly accepted, wanted, and loved, the child comes to know the world as a nice place and the people in it as friendly and helpful. He or she develops a cheerful confidence that his or her needs will be met. If, on the other hand, the baby feels unloved and unaccepted, he or she will develop a diffuse anxiety, a distrust of his or her small world. The baby may become preoccupied with his or her own needs as a result of uncertainty over whether they will be met. Because the baby is given so little opportunity to respond positively to others, he or she is likely to become demanding, fearful, hostile, or simply cold and withdrawn.

Basic trust is the necessary foundation for the capacity to love. The histories of people with schizophrenia, the largest group of mentally ill individuals, all have a remarkable sameness; they felt unloved and unwanted in childhood, so unloved that they failed to develop the basic trust that enables them to build binding ties with other human beings. The schizophrenic is afraid to love, afraid to invest affection in others. Thus, he or she lives in a world of isolation.

Later Infancy

This period is characterized by **autonomy.** Between the ages of 2 and 4 years, the young child comes into contact with increasing restrictions. He or she must adapt to the family and its practices. He or she must learn to adjust to social and moral norms. The child becomes fiercely rebellious at all these restrictions. His or her favorite word is no. He or she is impatient with routines and regulations, but because the child is still dependent on the very adults he or she defies, and because he or she desires their love and approval, the child usually will build a fine, but precarious, balance between independence and conformity.

Early Childhood

This period is characterized by **initiative** and occurs during the fourth and fifth years. As trust represents the first phase and independence the second, so the third is characterized by an outstanding attribute of personality—initiative. Early childhood is the period during which the child expands his or her imagination. He or she starts trying on, or identifying with, the role of the same-sex parent. The boy unconsciously adopts the mannerisms and attitudes of his father, while the girl adopts those of her mother. The underlying dynamic in the child who attempts new situations is positive self-esteem. Positive self-esteem is the internalization of the acceptance and approval he or she received from his or her parents during the first years of life.

Later Childhood

This period is characterized by **industry** and **accomplishment.** It is equivalent to the **latent** stage in Freud's classification. Children between 6 and 11 years of age have much energy that needs channeling into constructive accomplishments. The child is in school, and he or she learns to compete with peers in many areas. Pride in achievement develops as a result of praise and attention to his or her efforts. Group projects become absorbing; interests develop into hobbies. These are the joyous, exciting years of childhood, when the child learns to work beside and with others, when he or she begins to learn the skills, both intellectual and mechanical, necessary for a future role as a citizen in a complex society. It is the lull before the turbulent years of adolescence. Parents can assist the child's transition during latency by being actively involved in his or her activities and supporting his or her self-esteem.

Adolescence

This period can be a stormy one, characterized by a search for **identity.** The young boy or girl is usually ill-prepared for the great physiological changes that must occur before the body becomes ready for reproduction. During the same period, emotions must stabilize in preparation for assuming the responsibility of a family. An adolescent's new surge of sexual feelings, striving for independence from family restrictions, self-doubt about his or her abilities, and a strong sense of ambivalence can cause confusion.

The teenager needs to choose a vocation or career but often has qualms about the selection of a life's work. He or she may be bewildered by the vast array of possibilities and uncertain about what course he or she really wishes to follow. Sympathetic and understanding parents and teachers can do much to lighten the emotional burdens of the adolescent. They must understand his or her need to reject their standards and ideals temporarily. He or she finds security in identifying with peers in their mannerisms, dress, speech, and activities. If the teenager feels loved and knows his or her parents stand as safe ports in a storm where he or she can retire temporarily when the going gets too rough, he or she will emerge from the turmoil with a renewed sense of identity and with good, fundamental human values intact. His or her redefined identity is founded on inner integrity—a conviction that he or she is truly himself or herself, a person worthy of respect in the adult world.

Young Adulthood

The developmental challenge of the young adult between 20 and 40 years of age is to be capable of **intimacy.** Intimacy is the capacity to trust another in a deep and committed relationship. The challenge is to know and be known by another. This includes accepting one's own foibles, as well as those of another. Intimacy in a long-term sexual relationship is marked by love, concern, compassion, and commitment to the well-being of the other. A capacity for intimacy is also an essential characteristic of long-lasting, deep friendships. When a person is incapable of intimacy, he or she is aloof and isolated, shunning closeness with others.

Middle Adulthood

The middle-aged adult between 40 and 60 years is engaged in developing and guiding the next generation, be it children, grandchildren, coworkers, or young people in various types of social groups. The psychologically mature adult is productive rather than stagnant. The person who does not master this developmental hurdle is preoccupied with himself or herself to the exclusion of others' needs. The immature adult also exhibits a tendency toward hypochondriacal sickliness and general dissatisfaction with life.

Late Adulthood

This period is characterized by **integrity.** To Erikson, integrity sums up our ability to live out the later portion of our life with dignity and an assured sense of order and meaning in the total scheme of life. The facets of integrity are serenity, continual joy in living, a sense of accomplishment, and anticipation of worthwhile endeavors yet to be accomplished. These traits contrast with the despair that eventually develops in elderly adults who are unable to resolve the losses of later life or master this last stage of psychosocial development.

CHAPTER 12 QUESTIONS

1. What area of investigation is among the most promising in psychiatric research today?

2. Whose theory of personality development stated the belief that "self-love" is the basis of the capacity to love others?

3. According to Freud's theory of personality development, what characteristics might a child display if he or she suffered harsh parental expectations and/or punishment during toilet training?

4. According to Erikson's concept of personality development, what developmental challenge is faced in the period of puberty and adolescence (12 to 20 years)?

BIBLIOGRAPHY

Barry, P.D. (1989). *Psychosocial nursing: Assessment and intervention* (2nd ed.). Philadelphia: J.B. Lippincott.

Erikson, E. (1987). A way of looking at things. In S. Schlein, (Ed.). *Selected papers from 1930 to 1980.* New York: Norton.

Erikson, E. (1963). *Childhood and society* (2nd ed.). New York: Norton.

Freud, S. (1914). On the history of the psychoanalytic movement. In Freud, S. (1959). *Collected papers* (Vol. 1). New York: Basic Books. (*The ego and the id.* [1927]. London: Hogarth Press.)

Goodyer, I.M. (1990). *Life experiences, development, and childhood psychopathology.* Chichester, NY: Wiley.

Hurrelman, K. (1989). *Human development and health*. New York: Springer-Verlag.

Kaplan, H., & Sadock, B. (1991). *Synopsis of psychiatry: Behavioral sciences, clinical psychiatry* (6th ed.). Baltimore: Williams & Wilkins.

Pervin, L.A. (1990). *Handbook of personality: Theory and research*. New York: Guilford Press.

Schultz, D.P. (1990). *Theories of personality* (4th ed.). Pacific Grove, CA: Brooks-Cole.

Stelmack, R.M. (1991). Advances in personality theory and research. *Journal of Psychiatry & Neuroscience, 16*, 131–138.

Developing Critical Thinking Skills Through Class Discussion

UNIT III Case Study
Basic Concepts of Mental Health

Pablo is an 8-year-old who lives with his mother and father and five siblings in an inner-city housing project. When he was 2 years old his mother left him in the care of his aunt while she returned to Puerto Rico for a 1-week visit with her family. While there, Pablo's mother became seriously ill and did not return to this country for 7 months.

Pablo's father was overwhelmed by the demands of being a single parent and was rarely able to visit his son at the aunt's home. Pablo had been separated from his siblings because he was a "nervous" and "high-strung" youngster.

DISCUSSION QUESTIONS

1. What do you think it was like for Pablo to be separated from his mother when he was 2 years old?

2. Based on the readings in this unit, what do you think would have been the most supportive emotional environment for him when his mother became ill?

3. What would you tell Pablo about his mother's absence?

4. How could you reassure him during the long absence?

5. What are some of the changes that might occur in the family as a response to the mother's illness and absence?

6. What emotional effects of his mother's absence would you expect to see in Pablo at his current age?

7. Is it possible that his self-esteem would be altered by the event of his mother's absence? How so?

Unit IV

Mental Health and Mental Disorder

Chapter 13

■■■■■

Human Emotions

Behavioral Objectives

After reading this chapter the student will be able to:

Describe the physiologic changes caused by emotions such as anger and fear and explain what is meant by the "fight or flight" syndrome.

Explain three ways that a child may handle or repress his or her unacceptable feelings.

Describe anxiety and tell where in the mind it is experienced.

Describe how a small child expresses aggression and how he or she learns to control this feeling.

Identify the ways aggression can be expressed outwardly and inwardly.

List several types of behavior that are forms of self-destruction.

Describe the differences among the experiences of control, powerlessness, and hopelessness.

Mental Health and Mental Illness,
Fifth Edition, by Patricia D. Barry.
J.B. Lippincott Company, Philadelphia © 1994.

Emotions are **feeling states** that involve both physiologic and psychological changes. If a need is satisfied, the resulting emotion tends to be pleasant. For example, when babies are hungry, they make their needs known. When they are fed, they relax in satisfied, contented emotional states. Conversely, if a need is blocked, or ungratified, the resulting emotions are unpleasant. Thus, if babies are not fed when they make their needs known, they become tense and frustrated, usually showing their frames of mind by loud, angry crying.

■ Physiologic Response

Emotional stress, whether it is pleasantly or unpleasantly experienced, is often accompanied by physical changes. When persons are angry, heart and pulse rates speed up, faces flush, breathing quickens, and hands tremble. When struck by fear, some of the above symptoms may occur as may blanching or turning pale; in addition, mouths may become dry, lips may tremble, pupils may dilate, breath holding may happen, digestive tracts may slow down (peristalsis may actually reverse itself), and small hairs on the body may stand erect. Even a feeling of delight tends to produce physiologic changes, although they are not usually as intense as those evoked by anger, hatred, fear, or anxiety.

In the "fight or flight" syndrome, the physical reactions that accompany the emotions of anger and fear are readying the person and his or her body for active aggression or for escape from what is feared (hence, the name "fight or flight" syndrome). The adrenal glands pour out adrenaline into the bloodstream, and extra strength or power is available for quick action.

All people feel both pleasant and unpleasant emotions. Humans have needs they want filled; when the need is met they feel good, but an unmet need brings unpleasant emotions. Humans are creatures torn among many conflicting emotions. They run the range between the extremes of love and hate, childlike trust and paranoid suspiciousness, self-sacrificing bravery and lowly cowardice. Emotions are powerful motivators of behavior.

■ Control of Emotions

One of every person's major struggles is learning to control his or her emotions. Even in early childhood, one learns ways to express emotions or repress them. Some emotions are acceptable in a social group;

others are not. Each culture defines its own standards of behavior, and to be socially accepted, its citizens must conform to these standards.

Some cultures impose more control over emotions than others do. As an example of this, contrast the lack of emotionalism that is a valued personality characteristic in some ethnic groups with one that embraces a rich range of emotional responses. For example, a child raised in the former culture described above may be taught to repress expression of emotion, to become stoic. This is not to say that he or she is unemotional. He or she has the same strong urges to express joy, love, hatred, and fear as any other human being, but social acceptance by the immediate and extended family may depend in part on whether expression of emotion is controlled. Family custom may demand a deadpan facial expression even when experiencing intense fear, joy, or pain.

The child raised in an emotionally open culture may grow up in a highly charged atmosphere. He or she is encouraged to express his or her likes and dislikes freely; he or she is highly verbal, and laughter and tears may succeed each other quickly. Surging anger often results in aggressive behavior.

All too often, a child learns that the expression of some emotions is unacceptable. Since he or she feels these emotions, such as jealousy, hatred, anger, and fear, and since punishment may occur for showing them, repression may occur in one way or another. Repression is a defense mechanism that pushes unpleasant thoughts or feelings into the unconscious (see Chapter 16, Ineffective Coping and Defense Mechanisms).

Although a child may no longer be consciously aware of these repressed feelings, they can strongly influence his or her conscious choices. These buried feelings may cause a person to experience guilt, depression, hostility, or other negative feelings that are unexplainable. The child may displace these feelings onto toys, pets, or belongings; for example, he or she may break or destroy his or her possessions or mistreat a pet.

Mature, enlightened parents should encourage their children to feel their emotions fully and to verbalize their feelings when it is appropriate. They should help them find ways of expressing their feelings that damage neither society nor the child.

■ Commonly Experienced Emotional States

The following list includes many of the emotional states experienced by human beings.

As you are reading the names of each of the states below, notice if you experience the feeling associated with it. Where in your body do you experience the feeling? Is it in your mind or in your chest, stomach, or some other part? Feeling or emotion is usually experienced in the body, rather than in the mind. Feelings are very much intertwined with the body and somatic sensations, rather than in the thinking or head realm. Other names for feelings are **affect** and **mood**. Affect and mood are the internal or subjective feeling states. Affect is also used to describe the feeling state that can be seen by an observer making an objective assessment.

Aggression	Hate
Anger	Homesickness
Anxiety	Hopefulness
Bitterness	Hopelessness
Boredom	Jealousy
Complacency	Joy
Curiosity	Love
Cynicism	Peace
Depression	Powerlessness
Despair	Relief
Disillusionment	Resignation
Elation	Reverence
Enthusiasm	Shame
Envy	Shyness
Fear	Smugness
Fury	Spiritual Distress
Grief	Trust
Guilt	Wistfulness

Anxiety

Anxiety is a vague and unpleasant feeling that produces many somatic effects or physical sensations in the body: tenseness, tremors, cardiovascular excitation, gastrointestinal tightening, restlessness. It causes feelings of apprehension, helplessness, and general distress. Anxiety differs from the emotion of fear, in which there is a specific, identified cause of the fear. When a person is anxious, he or she is not able to identify the focus or reason for the emotional distress. Until the cause of anxiety is identified, the feeling will continue as an unspecific and unpleasant physical and mental state.

Fear

Fear is a feeling of dread associated with a specific cause that is identifiable. The feeling is accompanied by a subjective experience of psychological distress. If the fear is acute, normal problem-solving abilities are often diminished. A person may feel overwhelmed about being able to engage in problem solving to address the cause of the fear and to modify or change the contributing conditions.

The physiologic responses to fear include an increase in heart rate and blood pressure; dilation of pupils; vasoconstriction of peripheral blood vessels, resulting in whitening or blanching of the skin accompanied by a decrease in skin temperature. With acute fear the person's neuromuscular responses may be "frozen" or disorganized or uncoordinated. The change in body coordination and organization is matched by a mental state of disorganization.

Anger

Anger is an inborn emotional reaction to loss. In its most basic response, it stimulates the individual to retrieve or recover what was lost or to obtain what he or she wants to have. This can include the newborn infant who "loses" the nipple while nursing; the 6-month-old infant who drops his or her toy; the 2-year-old who wants a cookie; the adolescent who is angry about not being trusted to borrow the family car; the family that must go on welfare; or the individual who is forced into early retirement.

The physiologic responses to the emotion depend on the type of anger being experienced. There are two predominant patterns of anger: active, organized anger and helpless anger. Active anger is a physical and mental state in which the individual feels energized to use the angry feeling to correct the "wrong" or to retrieve what was lost. The person experiences the loss as a challenge that he or she has the power or strength to address. During the state of active or organized anger a person feels that he or she is in mental control, there is a heightening of skin color, respirations become fuller, and the blood pressure and pulse are decreased.

Helpless anger, on the other hand, is a distressing feeling. The individual perceives that he or she is unable to address the cause of his or her anger and feels disempowered. This experience is similar to that of powerlessness described below. In the state of helpless anger, the individual feels emotionally overwhelmed and disorganized. Breathing becomes rapid and shallow; the pupils dilate; systolic and diastolic blood pressure is elevated; and skin temperature is decreased due to vasoconstriction of the peripheral capillaries, hence the person appears pale.

Aggression

Just what is aggression? Karl Menninger, in his book, *Man Against Himself,* defines aggression as an emotion compounded of frustration and hate or rage. It is an emotion deeply rooted in every one of us, a vital part of our emotional being that must be either projected outward on the environment or directed inward, destructively, on the self. Freud, in attempting to explain the dual emotions of love and hate, postulated that there exist in every human being from the beginning of life dual impulses toward self-preservation and self-destruction. He called the constructive impulse **Eros** (love or life) and the destructive impulse **Thanatos** (hate or death). He conceived these forces as ever antagonistic, ever present, and ever striving. He said that we do not truly live until we love; that in the end we are undone by our own hate; and that Thanatos wins because death is the final end for all of us.

Karl Menninger likens hate to an ugly, gray stone wall that is softened in time by love. Love is compared to a creeping mantle of green ivy that covers the ugly starkness of the stone, turning it into a thing of beauty. He postulates that hate and frustration appear first in personality growth, followed by the appearance of love as we mature. Hate never completely disappears, however. It shows itself in various aggressive disguises and even, on occasion, in frankness when our controls slip.

Aggression becomes apparent in the infant shortly after birth. In the child's prenatal life, all of its needs are met, but with the advent of birth, its comfort is violently shattered. It is this birth trauma that supposedly sets the pattern for all subsequent frustration anxieties. As the infant becomes hungry, cold, wet, and uncomfortable, he or she exhibits rage by crying, stiffening, and contracting muscles. His or her skin flushes a deep red color, and he or she may hold his or her breath. As the baby grows older, he or she exhibits increasing rage when needs are not met. He or she may have temper tantrums, scream, hold his or her breath, scratch, strike out, throw and smash toys and other articles within reach, bite, pinch, kick, whine, and refuse to comply with instructions or admonitions. Still later, he or she may run away, use angry or abusive language, spit, or soil himself or herself intentionally. The child is narcissistic and wants his or her own way. This is common, frequently encountered behavior in the normal small child. It is a display of frank, uninhibited aggression.

The ego begins to defend itself by using defense mechanisms that operate at an unconscious level to control the unpleasant feelings of anxiety and anger. Depending on the developing ego strength of the child, these mechanisms can either help or hinder further personality development.

Outward Aggression

Progressively, these manifestations of aggression will be met by environmental controls, such as parents, other family members, and caregivers who start curbing temper tantrums and destructive behavior. The child resents restrictions and demands and his or her hostility builds. This feeling of hostility is accompanied by, or followed by, a deep feeling of guilt.

In addition to guilt feelings, he or she fears the loss of love and approval of the persons who are significant to him or her. Additionally, the child expects to be punished when he or she is disobedient. The small child learns to modify his or her behavior to conform to the demands of family and, later, to conform to the expected norms of society. Slowly he or she learns to build up his or her own inner controls (**ego strength**), and as a self-punishing system (**superego** or **conscience**) develops in the child, he or she learns to differentiate between right and wrong.

Because social laws deny permission to commit bodily assault on other persons or to wantonly destroy their property, we learn to channel aggression into sports, games, politics, business, hobbies, wit and humor, and other forms of socially acceptable activity. We may also displace it on nonretaliative objects or sublimate it. Hate and violence, whether controlled or not, remain as strong catalysts in the personality balance throughout life. Sometimes we manage to bury hate deeply, but often, when we least expect it, our controls slip and we demonstrate our rage in a very frank manner, if only for a few brief seconds, and then often to our great dismay!

The child, then, as he or she matures and his or her ego becomes stronger, learns to control emotions. Slowly, but steadily, his or her behavior can turn from a frank expression of anger to more veiled forms of aggression such as lying, stealing, defacing property, forgetting, denial, sarcasm, silence, rejection, truancy, bullying, swearing, or refusing to work up to potential.

Up to this point we have been discussing the outward expression of hostility: the directing of a person's wrath upon the environment. We have divided it into frank, overt, or direct aggression, and into veiled, covert, or indirect aggression. Now we will speak of another form of aggression, that which is inwardly directed upon the self.

Inward Aggression

The turning of aggression upon oneself appears in many forms and is a strong underlying force in many forms of self-destructive behavior. Suicide is, of course, the final form of self-destruction, but there are many degrees, or levels, of self-destruction before this final, violent form.

In medical practice, physicians are becoming increasingly aware of and interested in self-directed aggression as being a causative factor in physical or organic diseases. The part it plays in various types of mental disorders has long been known, but the line between physical diseases and psychosomatic diseases is becoming difficult to assess.

The fear of and wish for punishment is prominent in many people. Self-destruction tends to have both psychological and physical expression. When people have uncontrollable and, at the same time, inadmissible hate, they tend to develop physical symptoms as well as psychological ones. Love and hate are very often combined in the feelings people have about each other (ambivalence). Hopefully, the need to love and to be loved will become sufficiently well developed in most of us that it will dominate our relationships with our families and our friends.

But because people so often hate the people they also love and because they cannot bear to acknowledge this hate, even to themselves, and fear to expose it to others, attempts are made to deny it. The ego often succeeds in repressing it into the unconscious mind.

Inwardly directed aggression is primarily based on strong guilt feelings that are inadmissible to the ego. When hate is turned inward, life instincts must battle self-destructive tendencies and arrive at some form of compromise. These compromises, while often severely handicapping to the personality, do prevent the crude and immediate self-destructive impulse of suicide.

Pathologic Forms of Aggression

In some mental disorders, the effects of inwardly directed aggression appear in the wish to suffer. The extraordinary fact that a person should enjoy suffering or should prefer pain to pleasure is difficult for the average, normal person to accept. Yet, the neurotic enjoys ill health. The masochist frequently does violence to his or her body.

The psychologist sees alcohol and drug addictions as forms of self-destruction caused by a need for punishment from a sense of guilt related to aggressiveness. It is, in a sense, self-destruction accomplished by means of the very device used by the sufferer to relieve pain and a sense of inadequacy.

Criminality, antisocial behavior, and sexual perversion are all based on self-destructive tendencies. Frigidity and sexual impotence are very common forms of self-directed aggression. Self-mutilation, malingering, compulsive polysurgery, and unconsciously purposeful accidents are all forms of self-destruction. Biting fingernails, fingers, hands, arms, and legs; scratching and digging flesh; plucking out hair; rubbing skin to the inflammation point; banging the head; slapping or pounding oneself—these are all commonly seen forms of self-mutilation.

The unmet psychological needs for love and acceptance seem to be the chief causes of self-mutilation. Contributing factors of mechanical, physical, and chemical pathologies may also be present. The treatment of emotionally deprived persons must be based in part on our abilities as care-givers to convince them that they are wanted and loved. For an individual overwhelmed by his or her own hostility and other emotional conflicts, even the assurance that somebody loves him or her enough to listen to him or her and to try to help is, of itself, very supportive. Self-punishers must first learn to trust and hope in personal relationships before any other therapy can be effective. The importance of personal relationships is suggested in this quote from Freud: "A strong egoism is a protection against disease, but, in the last resort, we must begin to love in order that we may not fall ill, and must fall ill if, in consequence of frustration, we cannot love."

Hopelessness

Hopelessness is a self-perception in which individuals believe that they have no choices or alternatives in their current life situations. The belief that they are helpless to meet their own needs and change their circumstances continues to support the experience of hopelessness.

One of the adaptive needs of human beings is to feel that they have some measure of control over their own feelings as well as their functioning in the environment in which they live. Hopelessness is a state of perceiving that one has no control. It becomes a very limiting factor in having the energy to change or the belief that change from the current state is possible.

It is normal for all individuals to occasionally experience feelings of hopelessness. Usually, however, the perception serves to motivate the person to view the current experience from a different perspective. The ability to change the perspective in most cases will increase the level of energy to change, as well as the belief that change is possible.

When a feeling of hopelessness persists beyond 2 weeks, depression often results. The symptoms of depression are described in Chapter 24, Mood Disorders. Many of the factors described in the experience of hopelessness are also present in the state of powerlessness described below.

Powerlessness

Powerlessness is a self-perception that results in the belief that one's own actions cannot change the outcome of a current negative life situation. Usually a person can recognize that change is needed, but he or she feels incapable of making it happen. The feeling is often accompanied by a physical and mental experience of lacking the energy or strength to create a different outcome.

The differences between the subjective states of hopelessness and powerlessness are examined below showing the continuum from the experiences of control to powerlessness and hopelessness.

Perceptions of Control
In Control
The perception that one has choices and is able to create change in his or her psychological state or current life circumstances.

Powerlessness
The perception that one's actions cannot effect changes in outcome.

Hopelessness
The perception that one's needs have no potential to be met.

Spiritual Distress

Spiritual distress is a fundamental distress within the self that questions the meaning of one's life. As with other forms of emotional distress, this type of deep personal questioning is a normal human response. Personal growth and development are often motivated by this type of personal introspection. When the process consumes a significant amount of one's day and persists for a period beyond a few weeks, it is possible that it can undermine effective coping and lead to prolonged spiritual distress.

When spiritual distress occurs, a person expresses concern about the meaning of one's life, for example, the presence or absence of a belief in God, the meaning of suffering and pain, or the value of living. The normal religious practices that may previously have been valuable and meaningful may now be perceived as meaningless.

Prolonged spiritual distress that does not gradually move to deeper understanding or acceptance can eventually lead to the experience of hopelessness, described above. As with hopelessness, if the experience of spiritual distress does not lead to a different level of understanding or insight, depression can occur.

CHAPTER 13 QUESTIONS

1. Explain the "fight or flight" syndrome.

2. What is the difference between the emotions of fear and anxiety?

3. Describe active, organized anger.

4. Name the term that means a self-perception in which an individual believes that he or she has no choices or alternatives in his or her current life situation.

BIBLIOGRAPHY

Ballenger, J.C. (Ed.). (1990). *Clinical aspects of panic disorder.* New York: Wiley-Liss.

Barry, P.D. (1991). *An investigation of cardiovascular, respiratory, and skin temperature changes during relaxation and anger inductions.* Unpublished doctoral dissertation, The Union Institute, Cincinnati, OH.

Barry, P.D. (1989). *Psychosocial nursing: Assessment and intervention* (2nd ed.). Philadelphia: J.B. Lippincott.

Coryell, W., & Winokur, G. (Eds.). (1991). *The clinical management of anxiety disorders.* New York: Oxford University Press.

Cowles, K.V., & Rodgers, B.L. (1991). The concept of grief: A foundation for nursing research and practice. *Research in Nursing and Health, 14,* 119–127.

Freud, S. (1914). On the history of the psychoanalytic movement. In Freud, S. (1959). *Collected papers,* Vol. 1. New York: Basic Books. (*The ego and the id.* [1927]. London: Hogarth Press.)

Hall, R.C.W. (1990). *Anxiety and panic disorders: Their diagnosis and management.* Longwood, FL: Ryandic Publishing.

Kaplan, H., & Sadock, B. (1991). *Synopsis of psychiatry: Behavioral sciences, clinical psychiatry* (6th ed.) Baltimore: Williams & Wilkins.

Kubler-Ross, E. (1981). *Living with death and dying.* New York: Macmillan.

Plutchik, R., & Kellerman, H. (Eds.). (1990). *Emotion, psychopathology, and psychotherapy.* San Diego: Academic Press.

Taxonomy I with official nursing diagnoses. (1990). St. Louis, MO: North American Nursing Diagnosis Association.

Chapter 14

■ ■ ■ ■ ■

Mental Status Exam

Behavioral Objectives

After reading this chapter the student will be able to:

List the categories of mental status functioning.

Name the three spheres of **orientation.**

Describe three types of facial expressions, posture, and dress.

Define **apraxia**, **akathisia**, **akinesia**, and dyskinesia.

Name four categories of affect and give an example of one emotion in each category.

Define thinking.

Describe the differences between **thought content** and **thought process**.

Name and define five types of **thought disorders.**

Define perception.

Name and define two types of perception disorders.

Define **judgment.**

Mental Health and Mental Illness,
Fifth Edition, by Patricia D. Barry.
J.B. Lippincott Company, Philadelphia © 1994.

In order to work with persons who are mentally ill it is important to understand the various ways in which the psyche can dysfunction and to be able to identify the specific symptoms that the client is displaying. First, the symptoms of mental dysfunctioning must be recognized; only then is it possible to determine the category of mental illness the client is displaying. The treatment plan of persons with mental disorders will be based on interventions designed to reduce or eliminate the specific symptoms described in this chapter.

A person displays his or her mental state or status in many ways. In our normal dealings with people, when we notice something unusual about their behavior, we are actually seeing symptoms of an abnormal mental state. For example, if a person's speech is slow and unclear, his or her eyes do not focus, his or her clothes are dirty and disheveled, and his or her thoughts confused, we know that something is wrong. If a person smells like alcohol, then we may begin to form an opinion about the cause of his or her abnormal mental status. If, on the other hand, there is no such odor, then we can eliminate it from a wide range of other possible causes of the person's behavior. In the psychiatric setting it is important to view mental functioning as comprising many different categories of behavior. **Behavior** is the observable or objective sign of mental functioning. The categories of mental functioning are listed below.

Categories of Mental Status Functioning

Level of awareness and orientation

Appearance and behavior

Speech and communication

Mood or affect

Thinking

Perception

Memory

Judgment

■ Level of Awareness and Orientation

Level of awareness describes the client's wakefulness or consciousness. The levels of awareness range on a continuum from unconsciousness/coma → drowsiness/somnolence → normal alertness → hyperalertness → suspiciousness → mania.

Orientation is closely related to level of awareness. Depending on a client's level of awareness, he or she may be more or less oriented. Orientation is the person's ability to identify *who* he or she is, *where* he or she is, and the date and approximate time. These three categories of orientation are known as "orientation to time, person, and place" and are often abbreviated to "oriented × 3" to describe the person who is oriented.

■ Appearance and Behavior

This category includes observable characteristics of a person, which can also be termed objective data. These include **facies** or facial expression, posture, dress, physical characteristics, motor activity, and reaction to care-giver.

Facies or facial expression includes the following types of characteristics. Pay close attention to whether or not the facies matches the emotions and content expressed by the client during his or her interactions with others. The most common types of facial expressions are as follows:

Animated

Fixed and immobile (also called masked)

Sad or depressed

Angry

Pale or reddened, and so on (coloration of face)

Gestures are the subtle physical cues that can indicate what a person is feeling. These can include a flick of a finger or hand that can indicate annoyance, anger, discouragement, and so on; a shrug of the shoulders; a firm shake of the head; and other signs that signify meaning to the observer.

Posture is the way a person holds his or her body, and it often indicates how he or she is feeling. Some posture characteristics include the following:

Relaxed

Tense

Erect

Slouching, leaning away from the care-giver

Sitting, lying, and so on

Dress refers to the way a person clothes and cares for himself or herself. The way the person dresses usually reflects the appropriateness of his or her social judgment. Some dress characteristics include the following:

Neat

Careless

Eccentric

Foul-smelling, soiled, and so on

Physical characteristics, especially the unusual appearance of any part of the body, should be described. For example, the person may have had his or her foot amputated and may have long, unkempt hair and a beard.

Motor activity, the way in which a person moves his or her body, is another important indication of mental status. The various types of movement include the following:

Agitation, restlessness, and so on

Tremors

Motor retardation (slow movement)

Apraxia, or inability to carry out purposeful movement to achieve a goal

Abnormal movement
  Akathisia: extreme restlessness
  Akinesia: complete or partial loss of muscle movement
  Dyskinesia: excessive movement of mouth, protruding tongue, facial grimacing (a common side effect of the major tranquilizers)
  Parkinsonian movement: fine tremor accompanied by muscular rigidity

Reaction to care-giver includes the way that a client relates with or responds to a care-giver. Descriptions can include:
  Friendly
  Hostile
  Suspicious

■ Speech and Communication

In this category we are evaluating *how* the client is communicating, rather than *what* he or she is telling us. What the client is telling us is actually a reflection of his or her thinking process, which is described below. The ways in which a person's speech should be evaluated are as follows:

Rate—usually consistent with overall psychomotor status

Volume—quietness or loudness

Modulation and flow—lively or dispirited

Production—ability to produce words

Also included in this section are nonverbal forms of communication. These include facial expression, gesture, and posture, described in the previous section. It is a matter of choice whether they are described under communication or behavior.

■ Mood or Affect

Affect refers to a person's display of emotion or feelings he or she is experiencing. **Mood** is the subjective way a client explains his or her feelings. Actually, the two words can be used interchangeably to describe the feelings associated with thoughts about situations. The following list with accompanying descriptions includes only those emotional states that are considered beyond the normal range.

A. Inappropriate affects
1. Unexpected responses to a given situation
2. Discussion content that does not fit with accompanying emotions
B. Pleasurable affects
1. **Euphoria**—excessive and inappropriate feeling of well-being
2. **Exaltation**—intense elation accompanied by feelings of grandeur
C. Unpleasurable affects (**dysphoria**)
1. **Depression**—hopeless feeling of sadness; grief or mourning; prolonged and excessive sadness associated with a loss
2. **Anxiety**—feeling of apprehension that is caused by conflicts of which the client is not aware
3. **Fear**—excessive fright of consciously recognized danger
4. **Agitation**—anxiety associated with severe motor restlessness

5. **Ambivalence**—alternating and opposite feelings occurring in the same person about the same object

6. **Aggression**—rage, anger, or hostility that is excessive or seems unrelated to a person's current situation

7. **Mood swings** (also called **lability**)—alternating periods of elation and depression or anxiety in the same person within a limited time period

D. Lack of affect

1. **Blunted** or **flat affect**—normal range of emotions is missing; commonly seen in persons with depression, some forms of schizophrenia, and some types of organic brain syndrome; can be seen in persons whose personalities are tightly controlled and is termed **constricted** to describe both feeling and the whole personality

E. **La belle indifference**—of French derivation, meaning "the beautiful lack of concern" and used to describe lack of worry in a difficult situation that ordinarily warrants it

■ Thinking

A person's thinking ability is the way he or she functions intellectually. It is his or her process or way of thinking; his or her analysis of the world; his or her way of connecting or associating thoughts; and his or her overall organization of thoughts. Some of the major disorders in thinking are outlined below.

A. Disturbance in thought process (how a person thinks)

1. **Loose associations**—poorly connected or poorly organized thoughts

   a. **Circumstantiality**—frequent digressions on the way to eventual conclusion

   b. **Tangentiality**—frequent digression until initial reason for beginning a discussion is forgotten

2. **Flight of ideas**—rapid speaking with quick changes from one thought to another connected thought; frequently seen in manic clients

3. **Perseveration**—repetition of the same word in reply to different questions

4. **Blocking**—cessation of thought production for no apparent reason

B. Disturbance in thought content (what a client is thinking)
 1. **Delusion**—inaccurate belief that cannot be corrected by reasoning
    a. **Delusion of grandeur**—exaggerated belief about own abilities or importance
    b. **Delusion of reference**—client's false belief that he or she is the center of others' attention and discussion
    c. **Delusion of persecution**—client's false belief that others are seeking to hurt or in some other way damage him or her either physically or by insinuation
 2. **Preoccupation of thought**—connecting all occurrences and experiences to a central thought, usually one with strong emotional overtones
 3. **Obsessive thought**—unwelcome idea, emotion, or urge that repeatedly enters the consciousness
 4. **Phobia**—strong fear of a particular situation
    a. **Claustrophobia**—fear of being in an enclosed place
    b. **Agoraphobia**—fear of being in an open place, such as outdoors or on a highway
    c. **Acrophobia**—fear of high places
 5. Other disturbances of thought, or memory impairment—any type of change in ability to recall thoughts from the unconscious into consciousness in an accurate manner
    a. **Amnesia**—complete or partial inability to recall past experiences
    b. **Confabulation**—filling in gaps in memory with statements that are untrue
    c. **Dèja vu**—feeling of having experienced a new situation on a previous occasion (Note: this can normally occur in all individuals when they are fatigued or stressed.)

■ Perception

Perception is the way that a person experiences his or her environment and how he or she perceives his or her frame of reference within that environment. It is equivalent to the person's sense of reality. Perception derives from the senses of vision, hearing, touch, smell, and taste. The information perceived through the senses is monitored by the ego and its defenses. Dysfunction in the ego results in distortion of reality that can range from mild to severe.

A hallucination is the result of serious ego dysfunctioning. **Halluci-**

nations are false sensory perceptions that do not exist in reality. The most common types of hallucinations are as follows:

1. **Visual hallucination**—seeing object(s) not present in reality
2. **Auditory hallucination**—hearing sounds not present in reality
3. **Hypnagogic hallucination**—sensing any type of false sensory perception during the twilight period between being awake and falling asleep

There is another type of sensory dysfunction called an **illusion.** An illusion is a misinterpretation or distortion (by the ego) of an actual stimulus. Two other terms relating to perception of self or the environment are used to describe mental status dysfunctioning:

1. **Depersonalization**—feeling detached from one's surroundings
2. **Derealization**—ranging from a mild sense of unreality to a frank loss of reality about one's environment

■ Memory

Memory is the ability of the mind to recall earlier events. The two types of memory are **recent,** for events that happened during the previous few days, and **remote,** for events that occurred from the first recollections of childhood through adolescence, adulthood, and up until the current week.

Memory loss is one of the most important signs of cognitive impairment disorders. The two types of cognitive impairment disorders are delirium and dementia. Memory loss occurs both in delirium, which is an acute brain disorder that is usually reversible, and in dementia, a chronic, usually irreversible brain disease (see Chapter 21, Delirium, Dementia, and Other Cognitive Disorders).

■ Judgment

Judgment is the final outcome of the processes described above. It is a person's ability to form conclusions and behave in a socially appropriate manner. If the psyche is functioning properly in the thinking and feeling spheres and a person has good awareness of his or her surroundings, then he or she will form valid conclusions about appropriate conduct.

CHAPTER 14 QUESTIONS

1. What are the three spheres of orientation?

2. Define apraxia.

3. What do we call the emotional state of a person experiencing anxiety associated with severe motor restlessness?

4. What is an illusion?

5. What term is defined as a person's ability to form conclusions and behave in a socially appropriate manner?

BIBLIOGRAPHY

Barry, P.D. (1989). *Psychosocial nursing: Assessment and intervention* (2nd ed.). Philadelphia: J.B. Lippincott.

Bauer, J., Roberts, M.R., & Reisdorff, E.J. (1991). Evaluation of behavioral and cognitive changes: The mental status examination. *Emergency Medicine Clinics of North America, 9,* 1–12.

Kaplan, H., & Sadock, B. (1991). *Synopsis of psychiatry: Behavioral sciences, clinical psychiatry* (6th ed.). Baltimore: Williams & Wilkins.

McFarland, G.K., Thomas, M.D. (1991). *Psychiatric mental health nursing: Application of the nursing process.* Philadelphia: J.B. Lippincott.

Rosenthal, M.J. (1989). Towards selective and improved performance of the mental status examination. *Acta Psychiatrica Scandinavica, 80,* 207–215.

Standage, K. (1989). Structured interviews and the diagnosis of personality disorders. *Canadian Journal of Psychiatry, 34,* 906–912.

Stuart, G.W., & Sundeen, S.J. (Eds.). (1991). *Principles and practice of psychiatric nursing* (4th ed.) St. Louis, MO: Mosby–Year Book.

Wilson, H.S., & Kneisl, C.R. (1992). *Psychiatric nursing* (4th ed.). Redwood City, CA: Addison-Wesley.

Chapter 15

■■■■■

Stress, Effective Coping, and Adaptation

Behavioral Objectives

After reading this chapter the student will be able to:

Define the words **stress** and **stressor**.

Define coping and name the three stages of the coping process described by Lazarus.

List the three ways the mind judges events or occurrences in its monitoring process.

Describe the action of neurotransmitters as they relate to stress.

Describe the three major realms of psychological functioning that are affected by stress and name five responses under each.

Define **adaptation.**

Explain why an event that causes a change in a person's life causes stress.

Mental Health and Mental Illness,
Fifth Edition, by Patricia D. Barry.
J.B. Lippincott Company, Philadelphia © 1994.

Stress is a word in common use today. Many people believe that the world is becoming increasingly stressful. Indeed, it seems that the rapid changes in the world have had a strong impact on social systems and the individuals they comprise. **Stress** is a word that is used in two ways. The first refers to the subjective feeling of tension experienced in the physiological, intellectual, and emotional realms as a response to environmental events that are perceived as threatening. The second usage of the word commonly refers to those environmental events that result in internal feelings of stress. Actually, the correct word to use when describing a threatening environmental event is **stressor**.

■ The Coping Process

Psychological Stress

Coping refers to the way the mind responds to awarenesses that are threatening. It is important to be aware that an event that is perceived as threatening by one person may not be perceived as such by another. For example, an experienced pilot does not usually experience psychological distress when sitting at the controls. A neophyte student of flying may feel a high level of psychological distress when the time to solo arrives. It is the difference in threat to these two individuals that causes the differences in their responses. In addition to the psychological uniqueness of the meaning of flying a plane to the two pilots, there are differences in their physiologic responses to the event of piloting. These differences create an internal subjective reaction that can never be identical for any two people.

Because of the different subjective experiences of stress, it follows that coping responses are also uniquely different. Coping is the result of the exquisite interplay of perceptions of stressful events, the psychological meaning that is attributed to them, and the physiologic response associated with that meaning.

At the same time that the mind is monitoring all of these external and internal awarenesses, it gradually uses a variety of mechanisms to adapt to the stress associated with them. Some of these are unconscious devices, called defense mechanisms; they operate automatically. (Defense mechanisms are described in Chapter 16.) The person also engages in active, conscious problem solving about the distress. These solutions, usually ones that have worked in the past, are called coping devices.

As a person adapts to his or her internal feelings of stress, the mind modifies its awareness of both internal and external steps that make up the coping process. The mind constantly monitors the environ-ment in order to provide safety. Another word for monitoring is appraising.

Richard Lazarus has described the steps involved in the appraisal process. The three possible outcomes of **primary appraisal** are as follows:

1. The event is unimportant and can be ignored.
2. The event is good and contains no threat.
3. The event is potentially or already threatening due to one or more causes:
   a. It is harming the psyche or has resulted in a significant change in self-esteem, relationships, role, or physical health.
   b. It contains a threat that one of the events described in (a) above could occur.
   c. It may be a challenging rather than a threatening event if mastery results in a positive outcome.

The next step in this process is called **secondary appraisal.** During this stage, the mind decides whether it is OK or in trouble. If the mind experiences anxiety about the situation, it will automatically use defense mechanisms to regulate the unpleasant emotion associated with the awareness. In addition, during this state the individual can ask, "What can I do to help myself?" This is the time when conscious coping strategies are used by the person. For example, a college fresh-man feeling overwhelmed by all the new experiences may decide on any one of several options to reduce stress—to begin jogging, drop one difficult course, talk it out with his or her parents over the tele-phone, or any number of other stress-relieving activities.

The mind is continuously evaluating the outcome of its coping efforts and is ready to develop new strategies if those currently in use are not working. This is called **reappraisal.**

Physiologic Stress

Adaptation involves both a psychological and physiologic state of well-being. With increased research on the effects of neurotransmit-ters on the body, scientists are rapidly learning that it is impossible to separate the mind and body in assessing a person's health status. The most commonly known neurotransmitter is adrenaline. Think for a moment about what effects adrenaline causes in the body during an extremely angry moment or close call while driving. Awareness of the danger of a near-accident is experienced through the perceptual sphere of our psychological system. Anger is experienced through the emotional sphere of our psychological system. Both experiences, however, have strong physiologic effects. They include elevations in pulse and respirations, slowing of digestion, and so on.

Neurotransmitters are the bridge between the mind and body. They are biochemical substances released in the central nervous system that send messages through the sympathetic nervous system to all body organs and muscles. Researchers in the field of neurobiochemistry have currently identified more than 100 such substances, all having different effects within the body. Scientists expect they will increasingly be recognized as significant players in the mediation of stress and the development of many, if not most, physical illnesses.

General Adaptation Syndrome

When coping efforts are not successful, the result is a subjective feeling of anxiety and concurrent physiological symptoms of stress. These physical symptoms occur as the result of neurotransmitter stimulation described above. Hans Selye has described the physiologic response to stress in a concept called the **general adaptation syndrome** (GAS). The GAS includes the following three stages:

1. The alarm reaction—the body responds to a stressor with a strong defensive response stimulated by hormones from the adrenal cortex. This decreases to a steady and consistent physiological stress response. If the stressor is not withdrawn the body moves to the next stage.
2. The state of resistance—the body maintains resistance to the stressor until it disappears. If the stressor does not disappear the body moves to the next stage.
3. The stage of exhaustion—the effects of the continuing stressor cause the body's resistance ability to fail. Ultimately, without medical intervention, death will occur.

The human psyche and body are well-designed to endure the effects of stress. Realistically, however, they are limited in their ability to tolerate severe, unremitting stress. Eventually a point arrives at which either the mind or the body is unable to continue providing resistance to either environmental or intrapsychic stress. When this happens the person can become physically or mentally ill.

Table 15-1 presents the many responses that normal individuals experience when they are under stress. When people are under acute stress they often feel as though they are out of control. This is because normal functioning is altered in the many ways described below.

Table 15-1.   Responses to Stress

Type of Response	Manifestation	
Physiologic	Increased heart rate	Diarrhea
	Elevated blood pressure	Nausea and/or vomiting
	Tightness of chest	Sleep disturbance
	Difficulty in breathing	Anorexia
	Sweaty palms	Sneezing
	Trembling, tics, or twitching	Constant state of fatigue
		Accident proneness
	Tightness of neck or back muscles	Susceptibility to minor illness
		Slumped posture
	Headache	
	Urinary frequency	
Emotional	Irritability	Diminished initiative
	Angry outbursts	Tendency to cry
	Feeling of worthlessness	Sobbing without tears
	Depression	Reduction of personal involvement with others
	Suspiciousness	
	Jealousy	Tendency to blame others
	Restlessness	Critical of self and others
	Anxiousness	Self-deprecating
	Withdrawal	
	Lack of interest	
Intellectual	Forgetfulness	Lack of attention to details
	Preoccupation	Past oriented rather than present or future oriented
	Rumination	
	Mathematical and grammatical errors	Lack of awareness of external stimuli
	Errors in judging distance	Reduction in creativity
	Blocking	Diminished productivity
	Diminished fantasy life	
	Lack of concentration	
	Reduction in interest	

Editorial. (1977). *The American Nurse, 9,* 4.

■ The Effects of Coping on Mental and Physical Health

As nursing examines the effects of stress on physical and mental disease processes, coping has been identified as a critical factor that influences the potential for wellness or disease. Coping is the response to a demand or threat.

In 1980, the American Nurses Association described nursing as "the diagnosis and treatment of human responses to actual or potential health problems." The word "response" is a term that encompasses the concept of coping. Ideally, when a person is challenged or threatened by environmental stressors, he or she will have a variety of resources present that support healthy, effective coping. The resources that assist in an effective coping response include:

1. Good problem-solving ability
2. Prior experience with the stressor
3. Adequate knowledge about the cause of the stressor
4. Available support system, such as family, friends, and so on
5. Adequate sleep, nutrition, and physical hygiene to support normal mental and physical functioning.

If an individual is challenged or threatened by a stressful event and is unable to cope, he or she experiences psychological stress. If the stressful feeling is severe, it is possible that a mental disorder can occur. The primary cause of many types of mental disorders is ineffective coping.

When mental or physical disease is present the demands on an individual are greater. Effective coping becomes yet another demand on a person who is already weakened by the mental or physical condition. The role of a mental health nurse is to provide support that assists with effective immediate and long-term coping.

Adaptation

Adaptation is the process of coping effectively with one's social environment so that growth and development proceeds in a way that supports healthy social relationships, good self-esteem, and ongoing positive challenge. Psychosocial adaptation, as described in Chapter 5, Person-Centered Nursing, is the ability of an individual to perceive reality and respond to it in a way that supports his or her own emotional and physical well-being and that of others in the environment. All of these characteristics of adaptation are built on the foundation of

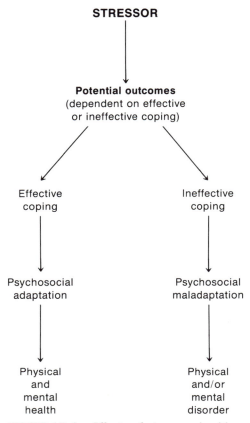

FIGURE 15-1. Effects of stress on health.

effective coping. When ineffective coping occurs it is the foundation of psychosocial maladaptation. Concepts relating to ineffective coping will be addressed in Chapter 16, Ineffective Coping and Defense Mechanisms. The relationship between stress, coping, and adaptation can be seen in Figure 15-1.

■ Life Events That Cause Stress

An important factor in the level of stress a person feels is the number of events in his or her life that are causing change. If a person's life is more or less routine and his or her personal and working lives are stable and without change or conflict, he or she undergoes relatively low levels of stress. In the current world of frequent change in the structure of the family and the workplace, very few people find this to be so. In fact, it is not uncommon to find that one life change often precipitates other life changes.

With the knowledge that stress is experienced in direct relationship to the number of life changes one is undergoing, it is possible to understand that an accumulating series of changes can intensify until one more new change becomes "the straw that breaks the camel's back." For example, if a woman is promoted to a new position in another city, she will usually encounter the following changes:

Leaving a workplace where she is secure and has many acquaintances

Moving to a new workplace where she must take on new responsibilities, usually before she is fully oriented and before she knows her new supervisors, peers, or subordinates

Leaving a home that she may need to sell or breaking a lease

Hunting for a new home, which is usually more costly

Moving her possessions

Leaving her friends and moving to a new area with no immediate support persons

Arranging for new telephone installation, changes of addresses to all friends, creditors, magazines, and so on

Can you see that what initially sounds like a positive event can actually cause an individual to experience increasing levels of stress? Holmes and Rahe, researchers in the field of stress, developed an assessment scale on which they established point values for the specific events the study participants reported as most stressful. The events and the points assigned to each appear in Table 15-2. The researchers found that when the study participants' stress points totaled more than 300, they frequently developed physical or mental illness.*

* Although unvalidated, my own finding in using this scale in stress workshops is that many people today experience stress at the 300-point level without developing physical or mental illness. This may be due to general adaptation to the increasing levels of stressors in our society during the 20 years since the original studies of Holmes and Rahe. A word of caution, however. Individuals who are experiencing stress at 300 or at a higher level should become familiar with events listed on the Holmes and Rahe scale. They would be wise to review future decisions carefully in order to reduce or delay current or anticipated changes that could introduce further stress and seriously compromise coping abilities.

Table 15-2. Social Readjustment Rating Scale

Item Number	Life Event (Item Value)*
1	Death of spouse (100)
2	Divorce (73)
3	Marital separation (65)
4	Jail term (63)
5	Death of close family member (63)
6	Personal injury or illness (53)
7	Marriage (50)
8	Fired at work (47)
9	Marital reconciliation (45)
10	Retirement (45)
11	Change in health of a family member (44)
12	Pregnancy (40)
13	Sex difficulties (39)
14	Gain of a new family member (39)
15	Business readjustment (39)
16	Change in financial state (39)
17	Death of a close friend (37)
18	Change to a different line of work (36)
19	Change in number of arguments with spouse (35)
20	Mortgage over $10,000 (31)
21	Foreclosure of mortgage or loan (30)
22	Change in responsibilities at work (29)
23	Son or daughter leaving home (29)
24	Trouble with in-laws (29)
25	Outstanding personal achievement (28)
26	Spouse begins or stops work (26)
27	Begin or end of school (26)
28	Change in living conditions (25)
29	Revision of personal habits (24)
30	Trouble with boss (23)
31	Change in work hours or conditions (20)
32	Change in residence (20)
33	Change in schools (20)
34	Change in recreation (19)
35	Change in church activities (19)
36	Change in social activities (18)
37	Mortgage or loan less than $10,000 (17)
38	Change in sleeping habits (16)
39	Change in number of family gatherings (15)
40	Change in eating habits (15)
41	Vacation (13)
42	Christmas (12)
43	Minor violations of the law (11)

* Signifies the numerical point value assigned to each stressor.

Holmes, R., Rahe R.H. (1967). The social readjustments rating scale. *Journal of Psychosomatic Research 11,* 213–218.

■ Effective Coping Techniques

There are a number of effective coping factors that coping researchers have identified. They will be described below. The use of nursing skills that draw on these factors can be helpful to clients with mental disorders.

The value of "worry." The experience of "worrying" about an upcoming threatening event can often be a trigger to effective coping. The important factor is how much worrying. A moderate level of worry is usually adaptive. For example, a person who is not worried about an upcoming serious event, such as coronary bypass surgery, may not be adequately prepared psychologically and may be overwhelmed just prior to surgery or during the immediate postoperative period.

The moderately worried person, on the other hand, engages in a variety of adaptive activities to decrease his or her mental distress. They include asking questions of the physician, talking with others who have had the surgery, problem solving about how to cope, and expressing concern about the surgery to family members and friends. Accordingly, they receive extra social support. The highly worried person is usually overwhelmed with anxiety to the point that he or she does few or none of the steps described above.

Focusing on the objective, concrete aspects of a current or anticipated threatening event. Usually when a person is undergoing a difficult time it is helpful for him or her to gather as much information as possible about what to expect. The information includes specific elements, for example, answers to specific questions such as: How long will this last? What will be going on around me? What will I see, hear, taste, smell, and so on? What is causing this to happen? What do other people do to cope with this situation?

Generally, it can be helpful for the person to obtain objective, concrete, realistic answers to these questions. Long, involved answers are not necessary. Complicated answers sometimes can generate more anxiety. Brief answers that provide specific elements of information can regulate emotional responses or stimulate problem solving.

The nurse can provide information so that an individual can judge how well he or she can perform or respond to specific types of events. When individuals have information about how to take care of themselves, they usually feel more able to cope with new types of situations. Realistically, in new situations most people don't know what they don't know! Accordingly, an empathic care-giver may be able to anticipate the specific aspects of the new situation that are likely to be anxiety provoking and share that information.

Effective coping is essential to good health, both physically and mentally. The next chapter describes information about what happens when normal coping efforts are not successful.

CHAPTER 15 QUESTIONS

1. Define the function of the mind called "reappraisal."

2. What are neurotransmitters?

3. How does the ANA describe nursing?

4. What does adaptation mean?

BIBLIOGRAPHY

The American Nurse (Editorial). (1977). *9*, 4.

Barnfather, J.S., Swain, M.A., & Erickson, H.C. (1989). Construct validity of an aspect of the coping process: Potential adaptation to stress. *Issues in Mental Health Nursing, 10,* 23–40.

Barry, P.D. (1989). *Psychosocial nursing: Assessment and intervention* (2nd ed.). Philadelphia: J.B. Lippincott.

Coyne, J.C., & Downey, G. (1991). Social factors and psychopathology: Stress, social support, and coping processes. *Annual Review of Psychology, 42,* 401–25.

Edwards, J.R., & Cooper, C.L. (1988). Research in stress, coping, and health: Theoretical and methodological issues. *Psychological Medicine, 18,* 15–20.

Friedhoff, A.J., & Simkowitz, P. (1989). A new conception of the relationship between psychological coping mechanisms and biological stress buffering systems. *British Journal of Psychiatry—Supplement, 4,* 61–66.

Holmes, R. & Rahe, R. (1967). The social adjustment rating scale. *Journal of Psychosomatic Research, 11,* 13.

Johnson, J.E., & Lauver, D.R. (1989). Alternative explanations of coping with stressful experiences associated with physical illness. *ANS—Advances in Nursing Science, 11,* 39–52.

Jones, P.S. (1991). Adaptability: A personal resource for health. *Scholarly Inquiry For Nursing Practice, 5,* 95–108.

Kaplan, H., & Sadock, B. (1991). *Synopsis of psychiatry: Behavioral sciences, clinical psychiatry* (6th ed.). Baltimore: Williams & Wilkins.

Nursing: A social policy statement. (1980). Kansas City, MO: American Nurses Association.

Ostell, A. (1991). Coping, problem solving and stress: A framework for intervention strategies. *British Journal of Medical Psychology, 64,* 11–24.

Puglisi-Allegra, S., & Oliverio, A. (1990). *Psychobiology of stress.* Boston: Kluwer Academic Publishers.

Standards for nursing practice. (1973). Kansas City, MO: American Nurses Association.

Sutherland, J.E. (1991). The link between stress and illness. Do our coping methods influence our health? *Postgraduate Medicine, 89,* 159–164.

Taxonomy I with official nursing diagnoses. (1990). St. Louis, MO: North American Nursing Diagnosis Association.

Chapter 16

■ ■ ■ ■ ■

Ineffective Coping and Defense Mechanisms

Behavioral Objectives

After reading this chapter the student will be able to:

Explain the American Nurses Association's definition of nursing practice.

Describe the role of ineffective coping in the list of nursing diagnosis categories.

Name the feeling that triggers the use of defense mechanisms.

List the four levels of defense mechanisms and the names of two defense mechanisms within each category.

Explain the use of denial and give an example of ineffective denial.

Describe the differences and similarities between repression and suppression.

Mental Health and Mental Illness,
Fifth Edition, by Patricia D. Barry.
J.B. Lippincott Company, Philadelphia © 1994.

The American Nurses Association has described nursing practice as the diagnosis and treatment of the human response to illness. The term **response** can be described as a reaction to a stimulus. It can also be generalized to include the concept of coping as a response to a stimulus or event. Effective coping has been identified as a factor that is essential to mental and physical health.

During the 1970s a group of nurses met to develop a list of the types of health problems that nurses are prepared to diagnose and treat in their clinical practices. The list they created was named the Taxonomy of Nursing Diagnosis. The nursing group, called the North American Nursing Diagnosis Association (NANDA), meets every 2 years to review the list and to add new diagnostic categories. Currently, the list includes 110 conditions. More than half of these conditions are psychosocial in nature. Most of the psychosocial category titles are very specific. They include such names as Social Isolation, Altered Parenting, Self-Esteem Disturbance, and so on. There are additional categories that include psychosocial factors, for example, Sleep Pattern Disturbance, Altered Health Maintenance, and Altered Sexuality Patterns.

In all the NANDA categories that involve a problem with psychosocial adaptation, ineffective coping is occurring. Indeed, ineffective coping is an umbrella term or comprehensive concept that is a fundamental factor in all mental disorders and all psychosocial-related nursing diagnoses.

Coping is the combination of conscious problem-solving strategies and unconscious defense mechanisms that result in the cognitive and behavioral responses to demanding or threatening events. The factors that comprise effective coping were described in the previous chapter.

■ The Use and Purpose of Defense Mechanisms

The use of defense mechanisms by the mind is an unconscious process; that is, the mind automatically activates them when the conscious coping techniques are unable to manage the anxiety of the threatening event.

Because adaptation is a fundamental characteristic of life, it is not strange that humans have developed unconscious defense mechanisms that increase their sense of security, protect their self-esteem, and solve their emotional dilemmas. The self-conscious personality, with its intense need for security and self-esteem, evokes protective mental defenses as instinctively as self-preservation prompts protection against physical harm. Anxiety is part of life from the cradle to the grave. Everyone, to a greater or lesser degree, employs defense mechanisms to supply comfort and defend against anxiety. A study of these mechanisms is essential to understanding human behavior and should lead to a clearer recognition of the forces operating in the psyche.

Some defense mechanisms, if employed within certain limits, may help to promote a sound personality. If used excessively, however, they may lead to a personality distortion. When properly used, these defense mechanisms are considered adaptive. Other mechanisms can be maladaptive; they progressively disorganize the personality.

Defense mechanisms are mental maneuvers performed by the ego in order to decrease the unpleasant feeling of anxiety. These mechanisms begin operating in early childhood. Different mechanisms appear as the child matures. These mechanisms are used automatically by a healthy ego. Depending on the level of stress a person is experiencing, the ego will shut out all or part of a painful awareness. Generally speaking, the defense mechanisms that develop early in life are used by adults only when severe stress occurs or when a person has a low tolerance for stress. The higher-level, more mature mechanisms develop as the personality matures. They are used when the level of stress being experienced is low to moderate.

■ Types of Defense Mechanisms

Defense mechanisms are classified by the age at which they appear in the child, the amount of reality they block, and the level of pathology they can cause. In this section the defenses seen most commonly in the mental health care setting will be discussed. In addition, examples of maladaptive use of these defenses will be given to illustrate their effect on personality and their potential to cause mental disorder.

Narcissistic Defense Mechanisms (Birth to 3 Years)

The term **narcissistic** is used to refer to a person who is self-centered in a very immature way. The word is derived from the Greek myth about Narcissus, a very handsome young man who fell in love with the reflection of his face in a pond. It is normal for toddlers and young children to be self-centered, but as the child develops, he or she should gradually develop the capacity to be aware of others as well as himself. Narcissistic defense mechanisms are the earliest defense mechanisms used by the ego. They are employed by the healthy adult ego only during periods of extreme stress. When used routinely, they cause severe forms of mental disorders, such as schizophrenia.

Denial is the first defense used in infancy. It remains available in the ego as the strongest defense for shutting out painful awareness in the environment. The person sees, hears, or perceives an event but the ego refuses to recognize it consciously. Denial and the other two defenses in this category are used when the ego senses a severe threat.

Tom is a married 53-year-old man with a high-level position in a large organization. He is told by the company president that his job will be ending in 2 months. He refused to discuss the matter further. Four weeks later he was continuing to refuse discussion of his termination with his boss. He became increasingly withdrawn. He did not disclose his situation to his wife and family.

Distortion is a defense mechanism that the ego uses to reshape external reality to reduce anxiety and restore a feeling of emotional comfort. It is the basis for hallucinations and nonparanoid types of delusions.

To continue with the story of Tom, he has not had a regular savings program and has few monetary savings. During his career he continuously told himself that he could never lose his job and would receive a plentiful monetary settlement when he retired. In essence, he deluded himself with a belief that was untrue.

Delusional projection is a mechanism by which the ego forms conclusions and beliefs that are not based on reality. These beliefs, when firmly rooted, form the basis of paranoid delusions, in which a person believes that someone is out to get him or her.

*After several weeks of using denial and distortion to quiet his unconscious psychological terror about his circumstances, the mental pressure is causing yet another serious defense mechanism to occur. While at work Tom increasingly believes that people at work are plotting against him and plan to injure him and eventually kill him to get rid of him. Incorrect beliefs that someone is going to purposely injure another is called **paranoia**.*

The effect of chronic use of narcissistic defense mechanisms to shut out reality is often a serious mental disorder. This disorder may require hospitalization when outpatient mental health intervention either does not occur or is not successful.

Immature Defense Mechanisms (Ages 2 to 4 Years)

The immature defenses develop during the toddler stage and are used by healthy adults under moderate to severe stress and by persons with all types of personality disorders. **Acting out** is the behavioral outcome of conflict between an unconscious need to express anger and a conscious need to deny it.

> *Ann is a 19-year-old college student who is living away from home for the first time. She has a high level of unconscious anger about emotional abuse she experienced from her mother. In relationships with women authority figures at her school, such as her freshman advisor, one of her instructors, and the dormitory monitor, she is aggressive and unreasonable. She is acting out or expressing the anger she feels towards her mother but does not consciously acknowledge.*

Avoidance causes a person unconsciously to stay away from any person, situation, or place that might cause unwanted sexual or aggressive feelings to occur.

> *Because of Ann's unresolved conflict with her mother she unconsciously avoids close relationships with all women. As a result Ann is increasingly isolated in her new college environment.*

Projection is a less pathologic form of delusional projection, described above. It occurs when a person is unable to acknowledge his or her own thoughts or feelings and attributes them to others.

> *When Ann's freshman adviser asks to meet with her, Ann is quiet and sullen. When her adviser asks what is wrong, Ann looks at her and angrily says, "I know you don't like me."*

Regression occurs when the ego is unable to tolerate severe intrapsychic or environmental stress. As a way of reducing anxiety, a person's psychosocial functioning returns to an earlier developmental stage.

> *In her family Ann was very dependent on her father and frequently acted child-like when she was with him. Now that she is away at college she has begun to visit a senior male student from her home town. He is becoming irritated with her frequent unexpected visits and her requests for assistance and counsel.*

The chronic use of immature defense mechanisms, while not as seriously maladaptive as narcissistic defenses, indicates major developmental and adaptation problems. Without modification of the defenses that Ann is using, she is at risk for depression, anxiety disorder, or other types of mental disorder that could require hospitalization.

Neurotic Defense Mechanisms

Neurotic defenses can cause a significant level of psychological distress, but usually do not result in the need for psychiatric hospitalization. If neurotic defenses cause some form of ineffective coping with a significant life event, it is possible that major forms of depression or anxiety may result in a brief hospitalization. Descriptions of neurotic defenses appear below.

Displacement occurs when feelings about a person or thing are shifted to another, safer object. Although the feelings are shifted, their original cause remains the same. For example, when a person is angry at his or her boss he or she may go home and become angry with his or her significant other or play an extra hard game of tennis. **Identification** is a defense mechanism that results in a person taking on the thoughts, feelings, or particular circumstances of another person as if they were his or her own. For example, an expectant father may develop symptoms of morning sickness similar to those of his pregnant wife.

Isolation is a defense mechanism that separates the emotion associated with a thought. The emotion is repressed, however. For example, a nurse may be working closely with a dying client and be able to acknowledge that the person's symptoms indicate he or she is near death. Although very attached to the client, the nurse may not experience the grief associated with this awareness until a later time. Other names for isolation are **intellectualization** and **rationalization.**

Reaction formation is a defense mechanism that is also known as **compensation.** It is used when a thought, feeling, or impulse is unacceptable to the ego. As a result, the ego causes the person to behave in the exact opposite manner. A person who has had an amputation, for example, may feel deep rage toward the surgeon, but when the doctor enters the room, the client is very cordial to him or her. **Repression** is sometimes considered to be one of the most important defense mechanisms. It causes the anxiety associated with any distressing internal awareness to be stored away in the unconscious. Without the capacity to repress painful thoughts, feelings, and memories, our ego could be overwhelmed by them.

Mature Defense Mechanisms

These defense mechanisms are used by the healthy, mature ego when it is under minimal stress. They have a larger conscious component than the defense mechanisms described in the lower levels.

Because of their conscious component, mature individuals often use them as conscious coping devices when they recognize they are experiencing stress. These mechanisms develop during the middle and later years of childhood. They include **altruism,** which is a defense that channels the desire to satisfy one's own needs into the wish to meet the needs of others. **Anticipation** is a defense by which the ego intellectually and emotionally acknowledges an upcoming situation that is expected to provoke anxiety. By acknowledging it and working through some of the anxiety in advance, the event will be less stressful when it occurs.

Humor is a defense used by the ego when it cannot fully tolerate a difficult situation. It is used without expense to the self or another person. Humor differs from **wit,** in which the actual anxiety-provoking subject is avoided. **Sublimation** operates in association with the defense of repression. In sublimation, repressed urge or desire is expressed in a socially acceptable or useful way. **Suppression** is a defense that is similar to repression, though unlike repression, which stores memories, thoughts, or feelings in the unconscious, suppression keeps memories, thoughts, or feelings in the subconscious or preconscious realm where they can be quickly retrieved.

Conversion—An Unclassified Defense Mechanism

Be aware of another defense mechanism that is actually a combination of elements of other defense mechanisms. **Conversion** is a mechanism by which the ego channels emotional conflicts into physical illness. An example is when an individual develops chronic diarrhea or constipation as the result of emotional conflict. In conversion, the symptoms are very real. Doctors are baffled, however, to explain the cause. When a physiological basis cannot be found despite good diagnostic workup, it is important to assess the psychological stress the client has been and is currently experiencing. The interaction between mind and body is increasingly being recognized as an important etiology in the development of physical illness. The field of **liaison psychiatry** addresses the emotional outcomes of physical illness.

■ Types of Behavior

Maladaptive Behavior

Maladaptive behavior is the result of ineffective coping and psychosocial maladaptation. When ineffective coping is caused by chronic use of narcissistic or immature defenses, there can be serious problems with behavior. Maladaptive behavior usually causes severe strain in family and social relationships. Consider, for example, the behavior of Ann, discussed earlier in the chapter.

Psychotic Behavior

Psychotic behavior is the most severe manifestation of ineffective coping. It is caused by psychosis. **Psychosis** is the mental state caused by a loss of contact with reality. Usually psychosis occurs when the actual external reality is too threatening or anxiety provoking to be acknowledged. The mind unconsciously uses every defense possible to deny, distort, and avoid reality when it does not have the strength to cope consciously and problem solve about the actual problem or sets of problems that are occurring. The story of Tom illustrates the potential for psychotic behavior because of his need to shut out totally the reality about his job loss. His behavior moves into the psychotic range when he begins to fear that his coworkers are plotting against him.

The cause of mental disorder is usually related to ineffective coping. The reason why persons with mental disorders are admitted to the hospital is to provide an environment that supports effective coping. The primary purpose of nursing care is to provide an environment where individuals can be restored to their prior effective coping level, receive medications that support coping, or learn new coping methods. The next unit describes how the nursing process in mental health care can assist clients to return to states of mental health.

CHAPTER 16 QUESTIONS

1. Define the term **coping**.

2. Do defense mechanisms contribute to a healthy personality? Explain how.

3. What category of defense mechanisms develops first in a child's life?

4. To what category of defense does repression belong? How does it operate?

BIBLIOGRAPHY

Barry, P.D. (1989). *Psychosocial nursing: Assessment and intervention* (2nd ed.). Philadelphia: J.B. Lippincott.

Brooke Army Medical Center. (1973). *Interpersonal skills* [Videocassette]. Fort Sam Houston, TX: Academy of Health Sciences.

Coyne, J.C., & Downey, G. (1991). Social factors and psychopathology: Stress, social support, and coping processes. *Annual Review of Psychology, 42*, 401–425.

Kaplan, H., & Sadock, B. (1991). *Synopsis of psychiatry: Behavioral sciences, clinical psychiatry* (6th ed.). Baltimore: Williams & Wilkins.

McFarland, G.K., Thomas, M.D. (1991). *Psychiatric mental health nursing: Application of the nursing process.* Philadelphia: J.B. Lippincott.

Nursing: A social policy statement. (1980). Kansas City, MO: American Nurses Association.

Ostell, A. (1991). Coping, problem solving and stress: A framework for intervention strategies. *British Journal of Medical Psychology, 64*, 11–24.

Sutherland, J.E. (1991). The link between stress and illness. Do our coping methods influence our health? *Postgraduate Medicine, 89*, 159–164.

Developing Critical Thinking Skills Through Class Discussion

UNIT IV Case Study
Mental Health and Mental Disorder

John is a 48-year-old engineer whose job has been eliminated in the aerospace industry. He does not believe he can locate another position in his geographic area. He also believes that his boss "had it out for him" and that is why his position was eliminated. He is married and has two children, ages 19 and 17. His family is accustomed to a comfortable middle-class lifestyle. His wife does not cope well with stress. His 19-year-old son is a sophomore in college. His 17-year-old daughter has already submitted college applications to five private universities. John is angry and bitter.

DISCUSSION QUESTIONS

1. What are some of the emotions that John may be experiencing at this time?

2. Since John is experiencing anger at this time, what is the likelihood that he is feeling helpless anger? Why?

3. If John's coping patterns are ineffective, what types of symptoms would you expect him to manifest?

(continued)

4. What would you identify as the causative factors in his ineffective coping?

5. What types of activities would you encourage John to engage in at this time in order to support effective coping?

6. Can you describe the different categories of mental status you would expect to see in John 1 week after his job termination?

Unit V

Nursing the Client with a Mental Disorder

Chapter 17

■■■■■

The Nursing Process in the Mental Health Setting

Behavioral Objectives

After reading this chapter the student will be able to:

Name the four steps of the nursing process.

List the different questions that are asked in collecting data for use in developing a nursing care plan.

Describe how problem solving is used in the second step of the nursing process.

Explain why contracting with the client is a part of the nursing care plan.

Use systems theory to explain why a nursing care plan is essential to a therapeutic outcome for the client.

Tell why the last step of the nursing process is important.

Mental Health and Mental Illness,
Fifth Edition, by Patricia D. Barry.
J.B. Lippincott Company, Philadelphia © 1994.

Interacting therapeutically with clients demands a capacity for relating well with people. In addition, the nurse must understand nursing theories, physical and psychosocial assessment, and specific nursing tasks. Nurses must also possess the cognitive skills of analyzing, decision making, and evaluating—indeed, a nearly limitless number and range of skills. Caring for clients is a complex process.

It is important to give structure to this process in order to be able to practice nursing skills in an organized manner. The term **nursing process** has been coined as a title for the steps involved in organizing and implementing client care. The four steps are as follows:

1. Assessment and diagnosis
2. Planning
3. Implementation/intervention
4. Evaluation

■ Assessment

Assessment is the first step of the process. It includes gathering all the information needed to diagnose the specific problems that require nursing care and to develop a care plan. The care plan is specifically designed to meet the client's unique needs and will result in a therapeutic outcome. This type of information seeking includes an initial interview session with the client in which the information listed below should be obtained. Frequently it may take more than one session to complete the collection of data. Depending on the information given in response to questions, additional questions might be useful in order to reach a good comprehension of the client's situation. In addition, while talking, the areas of mental functioning described earlier (see Chapter 14, Mental Status Exam) can be observed. The evaluation of mental status should be included under this section. The types of questions to be asked are listed below:

1. *Tell me what was going on that caused you to come into the hospital.* This information helps the nurse to understand the client's perception of his or her problem. A client commonly misinterprets the actual reason for admission and will relate his or her problem differently.
2. *Was there something specific that caused things to come to a crisis?* Frequently, the client's level of emotional stress has been in-

creasing for a number of days, weeks, or months. There has been an accompanying deterioration in his or her ability to cope with this stress. There is usually a precipitating event that causes the client to go into crisis (see Chapter 28, Crisis Intervention).

3. *With whom do you live?* This information describes the person's immediate support system or lack of it. He or she could be living with family or friends or may live alone. Watch emotional response as the question is answered; it can give clues as to the quality of his or her living situation. If a quick answer is given and eye contact is avoided, it could be an indication to explore this subject to obtain more information.

4. *How have things been for you with them?* One of the greatest factors in successful coping is the availability of a support system. Frequently, the members of the client's support system, whether family, friends, or some other type of support person or group, have been under stress or, for some reason, have been unavailable during the critical period before his or her crisis.

5. *What type of work do you do?* The answer to this question can give many types of information including his or her capacity for role functioning in a job, psychosocial status, and level of education.

6. *Have you been working up until this admission?* If the answer is no, then determine how recently he or she was able to work and what happened to lead him or her to stop working.

7. *Have you and your family (or whomever he or she lives with) been under any unusual stress during the past year?* Describe the type of stress being asked about. For example, *Has anyone in the family died? Been very sick? Has there been a divorce in the family?* Review the life-change events in the Holmes and Rahe scale that appears in Chapter 15, Stress, Effective Coping, and Adaptation, in order to be aware of the significant events that impose stress on individuals.

8. *When you are under stress, what do you usually do to help yourself?* This indicates the client's level of coping ability, as well as his or her problem-solving capacity and current reality orientation.

The answers to these questions will provide an understanding of the issues concerning the client. Other important sources of information during the assessment step are family members, current and former charts, and the reported observations of care-givers from nursing and other disciplines.

■ Nursing Diagnosis as the Final Step in Nursing Assessment

When an adequate amount of data has been collected it can be used to formulate nursing diagnoses as the basis for the planning of care. The use of nursing diagnoses in planning care has been defined as an essential part of the practice of nursing by the American Nurses Association Social Policy Statement. It has also been included in nurse practice acts written into law in many states. One of the implicit expectations of the diagnostic and treatment process is that the goal of the specific interventions designed in the planning stage must be identified so that a basis for evaluating nursing care outcomes is established.

The formal selection of a nursing diagnosis is done by a registered nurse, using the criteria developed by the institution in which he or she works. The information gathered by members of the nursing care team can be given to the registered nurse to further expand the information known about the client. Effective care planning depends on a reliable data base and on proper identification of problems appropriate for nursing intervention. These nursing problems are then classified into nursing diagnoses. The process of selecting and using nursing diagnosis in the mental health setting is described in Chapter 18, Nursing Diagnosis in the Mental Health Setting.

The most frequently used classification of diagnoses has been developed by the North American Nursing Diagnosis Association (NANDA). The list of classifications appears in Chapter 18, page 168. They are classified by the categories of normal human functioning.

■ Planning

The planning stage involves a problem-solving process. The steps are as follows:

1. Analyze the data.
2. Identify and rank the significant problems (stated in Nursing Diagnosis terminology).
3. Examine the possible causes of each.
4. Consider the possible interventions for each.
5. Rule out the interventions that are not possible to implement.
6. Consider the possible outcome of each of the possible interventions.

7. Choose one or more interventions for the identified nursing diagnosis. The identified problems and the interventions that will help resolve the client's problem are then discussed with the client. Usually he or she will agree with the plan. The client may also request that the plan be modified. In either case, the nurse and client should agree about the final plan. This is also known as a contract.

A written nursing care plan that is based on nursing diagnosis of client problems is the guide used by all members of the nursing staff so that the client receives consistent care. The use of such a plan ensures that all nursing members of the multidisciplinary team are working toward common goals on a full 24-hour basis. The plan can also indicate the direction of the therapeutic plan of nursing to the other clinical team members from psychiatry, social work, psychology, and so on. The development of a nursing care plan is described in Chapter 19, Nursing Care Planning with Specific Types of Disordered Mental States.

■ Implementation/Intervention

In this step, the nursing care plan is put into practice. It is the *action* part of the nursing process in which interventions are begun. The goal is to decrease or eliminate the symptoms of the specific problems that have been identified. A critical aspect of the implementing step is that the care plan should be used consistently by all members of the nursing care team. If not, the client's progress toward wellness will be undermined by inconsistent care approaches.

Another important aspect of the implementing stage is that ongoing assessment of the client's problem(s) should be part of daily nursing care. In addition, the data base can be further refined by obtaining more detailed information about the client's life, relationships, experiences, and so on. As more specific information about the client's problem is gathered, it may be necessary to alter the plan and at the same time notify other nursing colleagues about the change in approach and the new knowledge leading to the modification in the care plan.

In order to promote a systems approach, the care plan should be shared with the other members of the nursing staff and, in most instances, with the family. If a family therapist is working with the family, review the plan with him or her in case there are differences in the care approaches of nursing and the family therapist. The family therapist is usually aware of complex family dynamics that may have been detrimental to the hospitalized family member. When clients and family members receive conflicting messages from two different care disciplines they become confused. Accordingly, they may be noncompliant with the recommendations they receive. Ultimately, the client may lose the social support that could contribute toward more rapid resolution of his or her problems. When the nursing care plan is shared with the family, they experience a greater sense of security about their family member's prognosis. In addition, it is an opportunity to explain the interventions designed to support their loved one's mental disorder and to model a beneficial type of care-giving behavior. Specific interventions for the various psychiatric disorders are described in Unit 6, Categories of Mental Disorders.

■ Evaluation

Evaluation is the final step of the nursing process. During and after the intervention step, the outcome of nursing care can usually be observed. Is there a decrease in the symptoms that originally caused the plan to be implemented?

Evaluating involves obtaining feedback, verbal or nonverbal, from the client about the results of interventions. Verbal feedback is also known as subjective information; the client is directly describing how he or she feels. Nonverbal feedback includes those clues the client is giving, frequently without his or her awareness. These include facial or body gestures and observable emotional states, such as tenseness, anger, sadness, depression, and so on. This type of information is called objective; in a way, the client is the object being observed. The nurse's objective observations can, on occasion, differ from the subjective comments the client makes about himself or herself. For example, the client may say that he or she is feeling much better and more cheerful. On several occasions throughout the day, however, he or she may be observed sitting alone, silently weeping.

The evaluation stage is actually similar to the original step in the nursing process. The final step of the nursing process involves collecting data that will determine whether the goals of the nursing care plan were achieved. When an evaluation of any type of intervention process occurs, it is important to base the evaluation on criteria or standards that determine whether the goal was reached. This means that the symptoms of the problems originally identified should be decreased or entirely relieved. When the evaluation determines that some or all of the symptoms remain, the nursing process should be reinitiated. A reassessment of the *current* symptoms should occur, and a new or modified care plan should be instituted.

CHAPTER 17 QUESTIONS

1. Describe what is meant by the "nursing process."

2. What are the nurse's sources of information as he or she makes an assessment of a client in order to develop a care plan?

3. What is the name of the "action" part of the nursing process in which interventions are begun?

4. Why is goal setting important in planning specific interventions in the diagnostic and treatment process?

5. What must be done if the evaluation phase of the nursing process determines that some or all of the client's original symptoms remain?

BIBLIOGRAPHY

Alfaro, R. (1990). *Applying nursing diagnosis and nursing process: A step by step guide* (2nd ed.). Philadelphia: J.B. Lippincott.

Carpenito, L.J. (1991). *Nursing care plans and documentation: Nursing diagnosis and collaborative problems.* Philadelphia: J.B. Lippincott.

Johnson, B. (1993). *Psychiatric Mental Health Nursing* (3rd ed.). Philadelphia: J.B. Lippincott.

McFarland, G.K., Wasli, E.L., & Gerety, E.K. (1992). *Nursing diagnoses and process in psychiatric mental health nursing* (2nd ed.). Philadelphia: J.B. Lippincott.

McFarland, G.K., Thomas, M.D. (1991). *Psychiatric mental health nursing: Application of the nursing process.* Philadelphia: J.B. Lippincott.

Stuart, G.W., & Sundeen, S.J. (Eds.). (1991). *Principles and practice of psychiatric nursing* (4th ed.). St. Louis, MO: Mosby–Year Book.

Taxonomy II. (1992). St. Louis, MO: North American Nursing Diagnosis Association.

Ulrich, S.P., Canale, S.W., & Wendell, S.A. (1990). *Nursing care planning guides: A nursing diagnosis approach* (2nd ed.). Philadelphia: W.B. Saunders.

Chapter *18*

■ ■ ■ ■ ■

Nursing Diagnosis in the Mental Health Setting

Behavioral Objectives

After reading this chapter the student will be able to:

Name the number of nursing diagnoses identified by the North American Nursing Diagnosis Association.

Name three reasons why the use of nursing diagnoses in clinical practice was developed.

Describe why the use of a formal assessment tool is important in reviewing the range of potential health problems of a newly admitted client.

Describe five of the patterns of human functioning that are used in assessing and diagnosing clinical problems that nursing is prepared to diagnose and treat.

Explain why the assessment review of these patterns can assist the nurse in developing a comprehensive care plan.

In 1973 a group of nurses met in St. Louis in order to identify the types of health problems that nurses are clinically prepared to diagnose and treat. Their guiding principles in selecting a list of nursing diagnoses included the following:

1. Identify all clinical problems that nurses identify and diagnose in clients.
2. Develop specific and consistent names for the different problems that nursing care can address.
3. Classify the different diagnoses into groups and subgroups in order to study the relationships between the different diagnoses, as well as the specific patterns that contribute to the clinical problem.
4. Develop a numeric code for the various diagnoses, groups, and subgroups of diagnoses so that the codes can be used in computer systems data entry.

The original number of nurses that met in 1973 has expanded to include an international group of nurses from clinical, academic, and research settings. They meet every 2 years to review, analyze, and add to the list of nursing diagnoses. The list of approved nursing diagnoses is called Taxonomy I—Revised. Taxonomy is a word that describes the laws and principles covering the classification of items into natural and related groups.

■ Categories of Nursing Diagnosis

The most recent meeting of the North American Nursing Diagnosis Association (NANDA) was held in 1992. The approved list of 110 nursing diagnosis categories appears below. The nursing diagnosis categories that are most commonly seen in mental health settings are preceded by an asterisk (*).

■■■■■■■■■

North American Nursing Diagnosis Association (NANDA) List of Approved Nursing Diagnoses

Activity Intolerance
Activity Intolerance, High Risk for
*Adjustment, Impaired

■■■■■■■■■ *continued*

Airway Clearance, Ineffective
*Anxiety
Aspiration, High Risk for
*Body Image Disturbance
Body Temperature, High Risk for Altered
Breastfeeding, Effective
Breastfeeding, Ineffective
Breastfeeding, Interrupted
Breathing Pattern, Ineffective
*Caregiver Role Strain
*Caregiver Role Strain, High Risk for
Communication, Impaired Verbal
Constipation
Constipation, Colonic
Constipation, Perceived
*Decisional Conflict (Specify)
Decreased Cardiac Output
*Defensive Coping
*Denial, Ineffective
Diarrhea
Disuse Syndrome, High Risk for
Diversional Activity Deficit
Dysreflexia
*Family Coping: Compromised, Ineffective
*Family Coping: Disabling, Ineffective
*Family Coping: Potential for Growth
*Family Processes, Altered
*Fatigue
*Fear
Fluid Volume Deficit
Fluid Volume Deficit, Potential
Fluid Volume Excess
Gas Exchange, Impaired
*Grieving, Anticipatory
*Grieving, Dysfunctional
Growth and Development, Altered
*Health Maintenance, Altered
*Health-Seeking Behaviors (Specify)
*Home Maintenance Management, Impaired
*Hopelessness
Hyperthermia

■ ■ ■ ■ ■ ■ ■ ■ ■ *continued*

Hypothermia
Incontinence, Bowel
Incontinence, Functional
Incontinence, Reflex
Incontinence, Stress
Incontinence, Total
Incontinence, Urge
*Individual Coping, Ineffective
Infant Feeding Pattern, Ineffective
Infection, High Risk for
*Injury, High Risk for
*Knowledge Deficit (Specify)
*Noncompliance (Specify)
Nutrition, Altered: Less Than Body Requirements
Nutrition, Altered: More Than Body Requirements
Nutrition, Altered: Potential for More Than Body Requirements
Oral Mucous Membrane, Altered
Pain
Pain, Chronic
*Parental Role Conflict
*Parenting, Altered
*Parenting, High Risk for Altered
Peripheral Neurovascular Dysfunction, High Risk for
*Personal Identity Disturbance
Physical Mobility, Impaired
Poisoning, High Risk for
*Post-Trauma Response
*Powerlessness
Protection, Altered
*Rape Trauma Syndrome
*Rape Trauma Syndrome: Compound Reaction
*Rape Trauma Syndrome: Silent Reaction
*Relocation Stress Syndrome
*Role Performance, Altered
Self-Care Deficit
    Bathing/Hygiene
    Feeding
    Dressing/Grooming
    Toileting
*Self-Esteem, Chronic Low
*Self-Esteem, Situational Low

■■■■■■■■ *continued*

*Self-Esteem, Disturbance
*Self-Mutilation, High Risk for
*Sensory-Perceptual Alterations (Specify)
    (visual, auditory, kinesthetic, gustatory, tactile, olfactory)
*Sexual Dysfunction
*Sexuality Patterns, Altered
 Skin Integrity, High Risk for Impaired
 Skin Integrity, Impaired
*Sleep Pattern Disturbance
*Social Interaction, Impaired
*Social Isolation
*Spiritual Distress
 Suffocation, High Risk for
 Swallowing, Impaired
 Therapeutic Regimen, Ineffective Management of
 Thermoregulation, Ineffective
*Thought Processes, Altered
 Tissue Integrity, Impaired
 Tissue Perfused, Altered (Specify Type)
    (Renal, cerebral, cardiopulmonary, gastrointestinal,
    peripheral)
*Trauma, High Risk for
 Unilateral Neglect
 Urinary Elimination, Altered
 Urinary Retention
 Ventilation, Inability to Sustain Spontaneous
 Ventilatory Weaning Response, Dysfunctional
*Violence, High Risk for: Self-directed or directed at others

North American Nursing Diagnosis Association. (1993). *Classification of Nursing Diagnosis: Proceedings of the Tenth Conference.* Philadelphia: J. B. Lippincott.

The assessment of a newly admitted mental health client leads to the formation of nursing diagnoses. The process is illustrated in Figure 18-1.

■ Patterns of Human Responses

Whenever nursing assessment occurs and a nursing diagnosis assessment model is used, there are specific patterns of human functioning

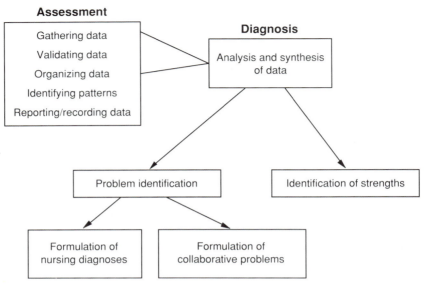

FIGURE 18-1. The Diagnostic Process. (In Alfaro-Lefevre, R. (1989). *Applying nursing diagnosis and nursing process: A step-by-step guide* (2nd ed.). Philadelphia: J.B. Lippincott. Used with permission.)

that are evaluated. They include:

1. **Exchanging**—This pattern includes the clinical problems present when normal physical functioning is altered.
2. **Communicating**—This pattern includes the clinical problems present when the capacity for verbal communication is altered.
3. **Relating**—This pattern includes the clinical problems present when normal, effective interpersonal processes are altered.
4. **Valuing**—This pattern includes the clinical problems associated with the meaning of significant personal events such as illness and death.
5. **Choosing**—This pattern includes the clinical problems present when there is ineffective coping, compliance, decision-making, or health-seeking behavior.
6. **Moving**—This pattern includes the clinical problems present when health status is altered by changes in physical mobility or body coordination.
7. **Perceiving**—This pattern includes the clinical problems present when perception of the self or the environment is altered due to acute or chronic psychological or physical distress.

8. **Knowing**—This pattern includes the clinical problems present when cognitive processes are altered due to a psychiatric disorder, organic brain deficits, knowledge deficit in an otherwise well-functioning individual, or knowledge deficit due to below-normal intellectual functioning.
9. **Feeling**—This pattern includes the clinical problems present when distressing affect or mood results in ineffective coping.

These patterns can be assessed by using a questionnaire format that covers a broad range of psychosocial and physical functions. The Barry Psychosocial Assessment Interview Schedule in Appendix A demonstrates the types of questions that provide adequate assessment data.

■ How Nursing Diagnoses Are Chosen

The nursing diagnosis categories are described in a manual published by NANDA. Information about the categories can also be found in a variety of nursing textbooks. Some of these are listed in the bibliography at the end of the chapter.

Definitions accompany each of the nursing diagnoses. These definitions have been developed and researched in clinical practice by nurses across the United States and Canada. Each nursing diagnosis category contains sections that describe the elements of the nursing problem/diagnosis. These sections are the **etiologic contributing risk factors** and the diagnosis' **defining characteristics.**

The **etiologic risk factors** of an actual nursing diagnosis such as Ineffective Individual Coping may be losing a job, getting a divorce, or moving to new city. These same risk factors may *potentially* place the person under increased stress and require psychosocial nursing interventions.

The **defining characteristics** of a nursing diagnosis are the signs or symptoms that the person is manifesting or describing related to the nursing problem. There are two categories of criteria that must be met for the diagnostic label to be applied. **Major** signs or symptoms *must* be present in order to use a particular nursing diagnosis. For example, for the nursing diagnosis Impaired Adjustment, at least one major defining characteristic must be present in order for the diagnostic criteria to be met: "verbalization of nonacceptance of health status change or inability to be involved in problem-solving or goal-setting."

Minor signs or symptoms *may* be present. In the diagnosis of Impaired Adjustment, minor defining characteristics are "lack of movement toward independence; extended period of shock, disbelief, or anger regarding health status change; lack of future-oriented thinking."

■ The Development of a Nursing Diagnosis

Following the assessment step of the nursing process, the assessment data are analyzed by the nurse and a nursing diagnosis statement is developed. The statement describes the specific clinical problem that can be addressed by nursing intervention. Usually a client will have at least three specific problems. A nursing diagnosis statement also includes the cause of the problem. This statement then guides the nursing care plan for all members of the nursing staff on a 24-hour basis.

The following are examples of nursing diagnosis statements that may be seen in the mental health setting. The actual nursing diagnosis category will be printed in italics. It is followed by the words "related to." The causative factor, which can be different for different clients, is indicated in bold type. The sample diagnoses are:

Social isolation related to **death of father and beginning college away from home.**

Sensory perceptual alterations: auditory hallucinations related to **psychosis.**

Impaired social interaction related to **hallucinations.**

Noncompliance related to **not taking psychotropic medication.**

The diagnosis states the problem and primary cause around which nursing care planning and interventions will be developed. It is important that the nursing diagnosis and resulting care plan are in agreement with the client's admitting diagnosis and the therapeutic goals of the multidisciplinary mental health team. The use of nursing diagnosis in care planning is described in Chapter 19, Nursing Care Planning with Specific Types of Disordered Mental States.

■ Collaborative Problems

The nursing diagnosis is always developed in conjunction with a medical diagnosis and related treatment plan. The nursing diagnosis rounds out and completes the care ordered by a physician. In psychiatric settings the diagnostic codes developed by the American Psychiatric Association are used to describe the condition for which a client is admitted to the inpatient setting. These are the same codes used in outpatient mental health care. All nursing diagnoses should be developed in conjunction with the identified mental disorder admitting diagnosis. These diagnostic codes are published in the *Diagnostic and Statistical Manual of Mental Disorders,* fourth edition (DSM-IV).

The nursing care plan is always developed to address the specific nursing diagnosis, as well as the added nursing interventions that are standard accepted nursing roles in the mental health setting. These include nursing assessment for physical safety, administration of medications, and so on.

The nursing diagnosis statements are presented in the multidisciplinary team meetings attended by all members of the unit clinical staff. By discussing the nursing diagnoses in these meetings, all members of the team are aware of the specific problems that nursing will be addressing that are unique for each client on the unit. The use of nursing diagnoses assists the nurse in organizing the nursing care plan so that therapeutic and time-effective nursing care is ensured. The nursing diagnosis step of the nursing process is essential to therapeutic nursing care. Properly selected nursing diagnoses provide the foundation of stating client problems so that therapeutic clinical outcomes can be achieved.

CHAPTER 18 QUESTIONS

1. Name five patterns of human functioning that are evaluated in the course of nursing assessment.

2. Describe the "defining characteristics" of a nursing diagnosis.

3. Name the components of a nursing diagnosis statement.

4. How many nursing diagnoses have been identified by the North American Nursing Diagnosis Association?

BIBLIOGRAPHY

Alfaro, R. (1990). *Applying nursing diagnosis and nursing process: A step by step guide* (2nd ed.). Philadelphia: J.B. Lippincott.

Carpenito, L.J. (1993). *Handbook of nursing diagnosis* (5th ed.). Philadelphia: J.B. Lippincott.

Carpenito, L.J. (1993). *Nursing diagnoses: Application to clinical practice* (5th ed.). Philadelphia: J.B. Lippincott.

McFarland, G.K., Wasli, E.L., & Gerety, E.K. (1992). *Nursing diagnoses and process in psychiatric mental health nursing* (2nd ed.). Philadelphia: J.B. Lippincott.

North American Nursing Diagnosis Association. (1993). *Classification of Nursing Diagnosis: Proceedings of the Tenth Conference.* Philadelphia, J.B. Lippincott.

Regan-Kubinski, M.J. (1991). A model of clinical judgment processes in psychiatric nursing. *Archives of Psychiatric Nursing, 5,* 262–270.

Taxonomy II. (1992). St. Louis, MO: North American Nursing Diagnosis Association.

Ulrich, S.P., Canale, S.W., & Wendell, S.A. (1990). *Nursing care planning guides: A nursing diagnosis approach* (2nd ed.). Philadelphia: W.B. Saunders.

Chapter 19

■■■■■

Nursing Care Planning with Specific Types of Disordered Mental States

Behavioral Objectives

After reading this chapter the student will be able to:

Name the three preliminary steps to effective nursing care planning.

Describe the five elements of a nursing care plan.

Explain the association between a nursing goal and the interventions designed to address the nursing diagnoses.

Give one example of a nursing intervention used with clients who demonstrate the following mental states: psychotic, depressed, manic, anxious, confused, or violent.

The nursing process is a way of organizing nursing care that provides a comprehensive overview of the mental health problems that contribute to the need for hospitalization. The planning of inpatient nursing care in mental health nursing is based on three preliminary steps:

1. Admission to an inpatient psychiatric setting with a diagnosed mental disorder selected from the *Diagnostic and Statistical Manual of Mental Disorders*, fourth edition (DSM-IV).
2. Nursing assessment of all mental and physical patterns so that specific problematic and/or illness patterns can be identified that are within the diagnostic and intervention scope of nursing practice.
3. Development of nursing diagnosis statements to describe the unique ineffective coping patterns that are causing the client's current problem(s).

This chapter includes information on how to develop a nursing care plan using a consistent care planning format. Many types of care planning formats are currently in use in this country. The most important criterion for selection of a specific format is that the client receives therapeutic care. Other important criteria for selection of a nursing care planning format include its ease of communication and comprehension by all nurses involved in the ongoing 24-hour client care.*

■ Mental States Requiring Specific Types of Nursing Planning

Most clients who are admitted to inpatient mental settings are diagnosed with a particular type of mental disorder prior to their admission. For example, a person may have a diagnosis of Major Depressive Disorder, Recurrent. A nurse can expect that this client will demonstrate symptoms of this disorder as described in the DSM-IV. The nurse can prepare to assess and treat these symptoms of depression. It is possible, however, that there may be a variety of other mental states that are also subtypes of behavior associated with depression; for example, there could also be anxiety and confusion that require different types of nursing assessment and care planning.

In order to assist in comprehensive care planning for the most

---

* This chapter, including the hypothetical cases, was prepared in consultation with Nancy Jarasek, a clinical nurse specialist at the Institute of Living in Hartford, CT.

frequently seen mental states in psychiatric care settings, this chapter will present a nursing care planning format with clinical case presentations based on the following mental states:

1. Psychosis
2. Depression
3. Mania
4. Anxiety
5. Confusional State
6. Violence

These mental states will be presented in association with a case description in which the mental state is prominent. The nursing care planning format presented below uses fundamental concepts in presenting the nursing care problems and their associated nursing diagnosis with each of the mental states. The format includes the following components:

Nursing Diagnosis—A statement of a nursing problem selected from the 1992 list of North American Nursing Diagnosis Association (NANDA)–Approved Nursing Diagnoses. The nursing diagnosis also includes a brief statement about the cause of the nursing problem.

Nursing Goal or Priority—A statement about the expected measurable client behavior that will demonstrate that the original clinical problem has been resolved or is decreased so that discharge is possible.

Nursing Intervention—A statement about the nursing behavior/action that can alter the client's clinical problem and achieve the nursing goal or priority.

Nursing Rationale—A statement developed in conjunction with each nursing intervention that provides the reasoning to support the nursing plan for each diagnosis.

Evaluation—A statement that describes the change in behavior that can be used as a measure of whether the nursing intervention is effective.

The nursing care plan format can be structured as shown in Table 19-1.

It should be noted that the care plan examples used in this chapter are not complete. A partial listing of nursing diagnoses associated with Care Plans #1 and #2 are included so that the student can learn

Table 19-1. Nursing Care Plan Format

Nursing Diagnosis:

Nursing Goal:

Nursing Interventions	Rationale
1.	1a.
2.	2a.
3.	3a.
4.	4a.
5.	5a.
6. etc.	6a. etc.

Evaluation:

---

about how nursing diagnoses are phrased. The care plan for each diagnosis is specifically related to that diagnosis only. Following the first two case examples, only one nursing diagnosis and care plan are developed for each case example. The diagnosis and accompanying care plan are based on a clinical problem that commonly accompanies that type of mental state.

Care Planning For a Psychotic Client

Anna is a 30-year-old single female. She is a chronic schizophrenic whose first schizophrenic episode occurred when she was a college sophomore. Since that time her social development has been markedly affected by her ongoing schizophrenia. In the past, she frequently did not take her medication; her noncompliance with medications resulted in frequent hospitalizations. She eventually became a homeless person.

During the past year she has taken her medication on a regular schedule, as demonstrated by laboratory blood testing of medication levels. Despite her compliance with medication, attendance at a medication group, and blood testing, her mental condition has deteriorated. She is admitted in order to (1) begin a new medication regimen on a new form of medication that requires close supervision of potentially health-threatening side effects and (2) restore reality testing. Her DSM-IV diagnosis is schizophrenia. The nursing diagnoses should be listed by highest priority first.

Nursing Diagnosis #1
Sensory-Perceptual Alteration (Auditory) related to schizophrenia.

Nursing Goal
To monitor effects of psychotropic medication for therapeutic effects on mental and physical state.

Nursing Interventions	Rationale
1. Assess and report level of symptoms, including changes in mental state and physical responses.	1a. If symptoms do not decrease, medication level may be reassessed.
2. Decrease social stimulation until paranoid symptoms subside.	2a. Overstimulation can result in more severe symptoms, as well as possible risk of violence to self and others.
3. Document mental state responses, every 2 hours.	3a. Shift-to-shift monitoring will be easier to perform.

Evaluation
Documentation will describe decrease in auditory hallucinations and paranoid symptoms.

(*continued*)

Care Planning For a Psychotic Client (continued)

Nursing Diagnosis #2
Social Interaction, Impaired related to schizophrenia with paranoid ideation. Violence, Moderate, Risk for: Self-directed or directed toward others related to schizophrenic with paranoid ideation

Nursing Goal
To protect client from mental or physical injury to self or others because of her paranoid and aggressive behavior.

Nursing Interventions	Rationale
1. Restrict client to own room rather than have her participate in group activities until paranoid behavior decreases.	1a. Client could injure others or be injured because of her severe suspiciousness of others.
2. Monitor client in room every ½ hour.	2a. Determine if medication effects are sedating her activity level and paranoid ideation.
3. Spend brief periods of time (2–3 minutes) interacting with client to assess current mental status.	3a. Excessive interaction with client will stimulate paranoid ideation.

Evaluation
Aggressive behavior is nonexistent or minimal without causing interpersonal confrontation.

Nursing Diagnosis #3
Thermoregulation, Ineffective related to being newly medicated with clozapine.

Nursing Goal
To maintain body temperature below 100°F.

Nursing Interventions	Rationale
1. Take body temperature using noninvasive technique every hour.	1a. Elevated temperature can occur rapidly as negative side effect of clozapine drug therapy.
2. Record body temperature and report a temperature in excess of 100°F.	2a. Immediate action is necessary to prevent hyperthermia crisis.

(continued)

Care Planning For a Psychotic Client (continued)

Evaluation
Temperature is regulated below 100°F.

Nursing Diagnosis #4
Self-Care Deficit (Feeding).

Nursing Goal
To provide adequate nutrition to maintain admission body weight.

Nursing Interventions	Rationale
1. Review diet choices on daily hospital menu.	1a. Give client choice and control over food choices.
2. Obtain list of favorite foods.	2a. Client will be more likely to eat favorite foods.
3. Monitor client briefly while eating and record observations.	3a. Client may be throwing away food because of paranoid ideation about poisoned food.
4. Observe and record percentage of ingested food from tray.	4a. See 3a.
5. Request consultation for client with dietitian if meals are not 60% eaten.	5a. Dietitian is experienced in consulting regarding paranoid food ideations.

Evaluation
Weight will not decrease below current level. Client will gain 2 pounds per week during hospital admission period.

Care Planning For a Depressed Client

Tom is a 21-year-old college junior who is a music major in a local college. The precipitating event of this admission is the break-up of a 2-year relationship with his girlfriend. The relationship had begun at the same time his parents divorced. He has not yet addressed the emotional issues regarding the divorce. In addition, he is experiencing increased academic stress because final exams are 1 week away. He is sleep deprived because of extra hours spent completing term papers and studying for finals.

Nursing Diagnosis #1
Grieving, Dysfunctional related to break-up with girlfriend, as well as the ending of his parents' marriage.

Nursing Goal
To monitor effects of verbalization about loss of girlfriend, as well as adjustment to parents' divorce.

Nursing Interventions	Rationale
1. Encourage discussion of loss of girlfriend and parents' divorce in individual and group sessions.	1a. Discussion can allow release of painful emotion and support the development of insight.
2. Observe family visits and recommend discussion about feelings with family members.	2a. Increased communication with family can potentially increase his experience of support and decrease his feelings of isolation.

Evaluation
Documentation will record summary of his discussions about loss. In addition, family visits and follow-up comments will be recorded. Comments will reflect increased insight about his responses and his choices.

Nursing Diagnosis #2
Individual Coping, Ineffective related to approaching final exams.

Nursing Goal
To problem-solve with Tom about effective study habits while hospitalized; to provide a suitable environment for studying.

(continued)

Care Planning For a Depressed Client (continued)

Nursing Interventions	Rationale
1. Meet with Tom in morning to decide study plans for the day.	1a. Tom's coping ability is decreased because of the crisis that precipitated his admission. Accordingly, his problem-solving skills are decreased.
2. Provide quiet, suitable environment for effective study skills.	2a. Tom's level of concentration is decreased due to admission crisis.
3. Encourage Tom to invite fellow students to study with him on unit.	3a. Companionship can increase Tom's social support, decrease isolation, and maintain his interest in studying.

Evaluation

Tom's study times will be documented. He will study at least 3 hours a day.

Nursing Diagnosis #3

Sleep Pattern Disturbance related to difficulty falling asleep associated with depression.

Nursing Goal

To stabilize sleep patterns so that 6 hours minimum of sleep is obtained.

Nursing Interventions	Rationale
1. Observe and report sleep patterns.	1a. The documentation of evening and night staff regarding sleep patterns can assist selection of effective interventions.
2. Teach effective sleep hygiene, e.g. no caffeine, no TV/radio, no conversation for ½ hour before bedtime.	2a. The reduction of stimulants and stimulation can provide assistance in returning to predepression sleep patterns.

Evaluation

Day, evening, and night staff will document teaching, as well as hours of recorded sleep. Six hours of apparent sleep will be recorded.

Care Planning For a Manic Client

Barbara is a 30-year-old single female. She has had a bipolar disorder since age 21. She is currently living in a homeless shelter. She has a mental status that includes flight of ideas, religious delusions, loose associations, and grandiosity. She is admitted for stabilization of her thought disorder.

Nursing Diagnosis
Thought Processes, Altered related to mania phase of bipolar disorder.

Nursing Goal
To reduce the behavioral responses associated with the client's altered thought processes.

Nursing Interventions	Rationale
1. Reduce external stimuli, e.g. limit presence and participation in unit activities, as well as access to radio and TV.	1a. Excessive stimulation will enhance the content of the delusions.
2. Maintain consistent caregivers.	2a. Exacerbation of thought disorder and excitability can occur with excessive clinician interactions.
3. Assess and record thought content and behavior every 2 hours.	3a. Effectiveness of medications can be more closely monitored on a shift-to-shift basis.
4. Maintain fair but firm limit-setting, e.g. schedule 2 hours' time in room, ½ hour out of room.	4a. A consistent set of limits will increase the client's sense of control.

Evaluation
Documentation will demonstrate a reduction in behavioral responses to altered thought processes.

Angie is a 24-year-old female who has been married for 4 years. She is employed as a computer programmer. She is the adult child of an alcoholic father. Within the last week she saw a made-for-TV movie on incest that resulted in nightmares of being raped. Within the past 2 days she has begun to have memory flashbacks of smelling alcohol and being sexually abused by her father. She was admitted to the hospital because of acute anxiety accompanied by frequent episodes of tachycardia (rapid heartbeat) and hyperventilation (rapid breathing).

Nursing Diagnosis
Post Trauma Response related to remembering of childhood sexual abuse by father.

Nursing Goal
To provide client with safe, nonjudgmental environment while memories of incest are entering into conscious awareness.

Nursing Interventions	Rationale
1. Remove client from daily responsibilities at home and work.	1a. Allow client to re-experience memories in quiet, nondemanding environment.
2. Ask client to record flashbacks and dreams of trauma memories.	2a. Recording by client can assist with reality testing and problem solving about responses.
3. Assess level of anxiety and record.	3a. Recording by staff will document the progression of trauma symptoms.
4. Intervene when anxiety symptoms are moderate to severe.	
a. Hyperventilation: Ask client to breathe into paper bag.	4a. Acidosis will decrease.
b. Tachycardia: Encourage client to talk then exercise.	4b. Ventilation can reduce anxiety symptoms. Exercise reduces the physical causes of tachycardia caused by anxiety.
c. Agitation	4c. Same as 4b.
d. Check on availability of medication.	4d. Medication can effectively reduce all symptoms discussed above.

Evaluation
Documentation will describe that anxiety responses will decrease each day.

Anthony is an 84-year-old male who was the head of his own construction business. His wife died 1 month ago. He was found yesterday wandering in traffic. He was confused and dressed in his pajamas. Apparently his wife compensated for his failing mental state. Since her death, his four children have avoided facing the reality of his dementia. His safety is severely compromised by his living alone.

Nursing Diagnosis
Family Coping: Disabling, Ineffective related to father's dementia.

Nursing Goal
To increase reality testing and problem-solving with family to ensure Anthony's safety.

Nursing Interventions	Rationale
1. Meet with all children and their spouses to discuss father's condition.	1a. Meeting with only one child can increase potential for conflict in family if other members continue to deny the reality of parent's condition.
2. Ask family to select one member who will serve as liaison between family and nurse.	2a. Communication and decision making can be severely compromised by multiple, independent decision makers.
3. Contact liaison person every day with update on father's condition.	3a. Reality testing of family will be increased.
4. Report evidence of family dissension to mental health team leader.	4a. Administrative intervention may be necessary if family denial persists.
5. Discuss and assess current plans of family for father's care following consultation with Social Service.	5a. Level of denial vs. effective problem solving can be assessed.

Evaluation
Discharge plan that supports father's physical, mental, and spiritual well-being will be developed with family liaison person.

Discharge plan will be communicated to family in conjunction with nursing and Social Service.

Family will demonstrate agreement to coordinate this plan of care during planning meeting.

Roles of responsible family members will be clarified.

Communication plan for case coordinator and care-givers will be developed by consensus in family.

David is a 26-year-old male with an explosive, angry personality. He has had repeated hospitalizations. This hospitalization was necessary because he was angry with his parents because of their pending divorce. He became suicidal and took an overdose of antidepressants. After hospitalization and following a visit from his mother, he became violently angry, threw a chair in the day room, and threatened the staff when they attempted to subdue him.

Nursing Diagnosis

Violence, High Risk for: Self directed and directed toward others related to explosive personality.

Nursing Goal

To reduce risk of injury to self or staff.

Nursing Interventions	Rationale
1. Maintain client's and staff members' safety.	
*a. Four-point restraints for 24 hours using following method:	Each arm and leg must be restrained before safety of other clients and the staff is ensured.
1. Check cuffs for pressure every 15 minutes.	Injury to client can occur if cuffs prevent normal blood flow.
2. Release alternate links once an hour and do range-of-motion exercises.	Injury to client can occur when stationary position is enforced.
3. Examine skin for evidence of chafing, edema, or other signs of distress.	Decreases risk of injury from restraints.
b. Document status of client every 15 minutes.	Legally required.
c. One-to-one staff: client monitoring at all times.	Decreases risk of injury to self.
d. Discuss with client when he is subdued why he is on restraint and what he plans to do when the restraints are removed.	Increases reality testing and allows client to problem solve regarding his options.

* Restraint methods should follow specific institutional requirements that adhere to legal restraint guidelines.

Evaluation

At the time of discharge, no injury has occurred to client or staff as a result of client's violence.

CHAPTER 19 QUESTIONS

1. Name the three steps of the nursing care planning process in mental health nursing.

2. What are the written elements of a nursing care plan?

3. In the nursing care planning process, what is the rationale for decreasing the social stimulation of a person with a severe mental disorder?

4. What is the importance of documentation of nursing assessments and interventions?

BIBLIOGRAPHY

Carpenito, L.J. (1991). *Nursing care plans and documentation: Nursing diagnosis and collaborative problems.* Philadelphia: J.B. Lippincott.

Johnson, B. (1993). *Psychiatric Mental Health Nursing* (3rd ed.). Philadelphia: J.B. Lippincott.

McFarland G.K., Wasli, E.L., & Gerety, E.K. (1992). *Nursing diagnosis and process in psychiatric mental health nursing* (2nd ed.). Philadelphia: J.B. Lippincott.

McFarland, G.K., Thomas, M.D. (1991). *Psychiatric mental health nursing: Application of the nursing process.* Philadelphia: J.B. Lippincott.

Savage, P. (1991). Patient assessment in psychiatric nursing. *Journal of Advanced Nursing, 16,* 311–316.

Schultz, J.M., & Dark, S.L. (1990). *Manual of psychiatric nursing care plans* (3rd ed.). Philadelphia: J.B. Lippincott.

Ulrich, S.P., Canale, S.W., & Wendell, S.A. (1990). *Nursing care planning guides: A nursing diagnosis approach* (2nd ed.). Philadelphia: W.B. Saunders.

Developing Critical Thinking Skills Through Class Discussion

UNIT V Case Study
Nursing the Client With a Mental Disorder

Peter is a 79-year-old widower who has early dementia related to Alzheimer's disease. Since the death of his wife 2 years ago, he has been living with his 82-year-old brother, Andrew. Andrew, who had been in good health, died suddenly 3 days ago of a cerebral vascular accident. Andrew's daughter, Marilyn, lives in the same community and is the only relative within a several hundred mile radius. She is divorced, works full time, and has four children, aged 11 to 17.

DISCUSSION QUESTIONS

1. Using Maslow's Hierarchy of Human Needs in Chapter 10 as a guide, can you determine and prioritize Peter's needs during the next week?

2. Discuss the reasons for your priorities.

3. Can you name the different types of challenges to a family when suddenly confronted with the care of a mentally disordered loved one.

(continued)

4. If you were Marilyn, how would you begin to examine your options for Peter's care?

5. Can you select five nursing diagnoses that you might expect Peter to experience as the result of the sudden loss of his caregiver and home environment? Why?

6. Can you name five nursing diagnoses that may occur in Marilyn or in her family as a response to the loss of her father and the sudden care burden of her uncle. Why?

7. If you were Marilyn's friend, what are some methods you would use to give her emotional support during this period of time.

■■■■■
Unit VI

Categories of Mental Disorders

As human beings begin to experience changes in mental state and behavior on the continuum from mental health to mental disorder, a cluster of unusual mental symptoms usually occurs. This cluster of mental symptoms frequently falls into certain patterns that fit a specific type of mental disorder. Such clusters of mental symptoms and patterns of mental changes are described in lists of the various categories of mental disorders that are published in a book by the American Psychiatric Association (APA) titled *The Diagnostic and Statistical Manual of Mental Disorders,* more commonly known as the DSM.

In early 1994, the APA will publish the categories of mental disorders, fourth edition (DMV-IV), to replace the third edition, revised (DSM-III-R). All chapter headings in this unit reflect the changes that are expected to appear in the DSM-IV according to the DSM-IV working draft, which was published in 1993. Diagnostic criteria of mental disorders are based on the DSM-III-R.

Chapter 20

■■■■■

Disorders Usually First Diagnosed in Infancy, Childhood, or Adolescence

Behavioral Objectives

After reading this chapter the student will be able to:

Name five major categories of mental disorders first evident in infancy, childhood, or adolescence.

List two conditions in each category.

Explain five possible causes of mental retardation.

Name the four categories of mental retardation and the IQ levels of each.

Describe the differences between socialized non-aggressive conduct disorder, avoidant disorder of childhood or adolescence, and schizoid disorder of childhood or adolescence.

This chapter presents the clinical symptoms manifest in a variety of disorders that are primarily developmental in etiology. These conditions usually are evident during infancy, childhood, or adolescence and may diminish as the child matures or as the result of therapeutic intervention with the child and his or her family.

Often, however, these disorders continue to manifest themselves in the adult personality. Usually they are of a mild nature, so that the adult is able to engage in the normal roles of adulthood. When severe, they contribute toward lifelong difficulties that decrease the person's quality of life and that of his or her family. Such disorders, if not treated early, become deeply ingrained and are difficult, if not impossible, to reverse.

A wide variety of conditions are included in this category of mental disorders. Most are rarely seen in inpatient psychiatric facilities because the preferred method of treatment is in the outpatient setting. Accordingly, the nursing care of each condition is not included here. Exceptions are the sections on mental retardation and pervasive developmental disorders. The specific care recommended for each condition can be found in textbooks written about the disorders.

■ Mental Retardation

The most universally accepted definition of mental retardation in use today is that adopted by the American Association on Mental Deficiency.

The terms **idiot, imbecile,** and **moron** are still in common use in Europe. **Feeblemindedness** was used in the past in the United States to refer to the mild forms of mental retardation and continues to be used in Great Britain. **Oligophrenia** is still commonly used in the Soviet Union and some other Western European countries. None of these terms is currently popular in the United States.

Approximately 3% of the population of the United States (nearly 7 million people) are said to be mentally retarded. The vast majority (87%) of the mentally retarded are classified as borderline or mildly retarded, while the remainder (13%) are classified as moderate, severe, or profound (Table 20-1). Only about 60,000 to 90,000 of the mentally retarded population, those in the severe or profound categories, require lifetime custodial care. A disproportionately large number of the mildly retarded group of nearly 6 million come from the lower socioeconomic levels of society.

Table 20-1. Developmental Characteristics of the Mentally Retarded

Degree of Mental Retardation	Preschool Age 0–5 Maturation and Development	School Age 6–20 Training and Education	Adults 21 and Over Social and Vocational Adequacy
Profound IQ 0–25	Gross retardation; minimal capacity for functioning in sensorimotor areas; needs nursing care	Some motor development present; may respond to minimal or limited training in self-help	Some motor and speech development; may achieve very limited self-care; needs nursing care
Severe IQ 20–40	Poor motor development; minimal speech; generally unable to profit from training in self-help; little or no communication skills	Can talk or learn to communicate; can be trained in elemental health habits; profits from systematic habit training	May contribute partially to self-maintenance under complete supervision; can develop self-protection skills to a minimal useful level in controlled environment
Moderate IQ 35–55	Can talk or learn to communicate; poor social awareness; fair motor development; profits from training in self-help; can be managed with moderate supervision	Can profit from training in social and occupational skills; unlikely to progress beyond second grade level in academic subjects; may learn to travel alone in familiar places	May achieve self-maintenance in unskilled or semi-skilled work under sheltered conditions; needs supervision and guidance when under mild social or economic stress
Mild IQ 50–70	Can develop social and communication skills; minimal retardation in sensorimotor areas; often not distinguished from normal until later age	Can learn academic skills up to approximately sixth grade level by late teens; can be guided toward social conformity	Can usually achieve social and vocational skills adequate to minimal self-support but may need guidance and assistance when under unusual social or economic stress

Adapted from *Mental Retardation Activities of the U.S. Department of Health, Education, and Welfare.* Washington, DC, U.S. Government Printing Office, and *Diagnostic and Statistical Manual* III-R (1987). Washington, DC: American Psychiatric Association.

Causes of Retardation

Retardation may be present at birth or it may begin during childhood. Its causes are many and in some cases as yet unknown. Some forms are familial or genetic (i.e., they are transmitted through parental genes from generation to generation, or parental genes may become damaged or rearranged by accident or radiation). Other forms are thought to be caused by damage to the embryo's developing nervous system while in the mother's uterus. This damage may result from a variety of causes.

It is also possible that the stress of birth causes some types of retardation. The baby's head molds under great pressure as it advances through the birth canal, and considerable damage can occur to the delicate blood vessels in the brain. Anoxia, or lack of sufficient oxygen to the brain, can cause retardation. This oxygen starvation can occur prenatally, perinatally, or postnatally.

Childhood diseases with high fever and toxicity can result in brain damage, especially in the very young; glandular imbalances may prevent normal central nervous system growth; chemical imbalances in the blood may result in brain damage; and accidents and falls may seriously injure the brain.

Many of the most common causes of mental retardation can be ascribed to social, cultural, and economic factors. These are classed as environmental factors; we are becoming more aware of the impact the environment has on our learning processes. If a child is functioning at a lower level than normal, and it is due to cultural deprivation, it is possible for him or her to achieve normal intellectual growth, provided he or she receives early and adequate help. Other forms of

Table 20-2.   Nursing Care Needs of the Mentally Retarded

Level of Retardation	Nursing Care Needs
Mildly retarded	Coping skills are limited during periods of moderate to heavy stress, needs extra support; preventive health care teaching should be developed to meet the level of understanding
Moderately retarded	Dependent on care-givers for assistance with activities of daily living; can follow simple instructions
Severely retarded	Constant supervision is required due to level of functioning at the infant or early childhood level
Profoundly retarded	Complete care is required

retardation, however, appear to be self-limiting; it is possible to develop a mind to its full potential, but it is not possible to change its innate intelligence level.

Nursing Care of the Mentally Retarded

It is unusual to see mentally retarded persons in the psychiatric setting unless they also have a psychiatric disorder. In such cases the nursing care plan for the specific psychiatric disorder can be modified to meet the needs of the person based on the degree of mental retardation. Table 20-2 explains the nursing care needs based on level of retardation.

■ Pervasive Developmental Disorders: Autistic Disorder

One of the most profound mental disorders in a person of any age is autistic disorder. This is a condition that most commonly manifests itself in infancy but may begin as late as 36 months of age. It usually does not change significantly over the life span. Individuals with this disorder are usually institutionalized in long-term facilities. The autistic person is markedly dysfunctional in most realms of human functioning. The aspects of impaired functioning are:

1. Interpersonal relations
   a. Lack of awareness of the presence of other persons; lack of awareness of others' emotions or their need for privacy
   b. No comfort-seeking when distressed
   c. Limited or no imitation, social play, or capacity to form peer friendships
2. Verbal and nonverbal communication
   a. Abnormal eye-to-eye contact
   b. Abnormal speech patterns
   c. Abnormal conversational ability
3. Activity level and interests
   a. Repetitive body movements
   b. Preoccupation with objects
   c. Very low range of interests

Nursing Care of Autistic Disorders

The care of an autistic person requires nearly 24-hour monitoring. Accordingly, they are most often institutionalized in long-term facilities. They usually cannot be left alone because of their lack of judgment. Depending on the level of impairment they may require full assistance with all the normal activities of daily living—bathing, eating, dressing, toileting, and so on. Their environments should be secure to ensure safety. They may become combative and can pose a safety risk to themselves and others. Accordingly, a high level of nursing vigilance is necessary.

■ Specific Developmental Disorders

Academic Skills Disorders

These disorders include three educational areas in which children may have problems:

1. Developmental arithmetic disorder
2. Developmental expressive writing disorder
3. Developmental reading disorder

These conditions fall into the functional developmental disorder categories when the skill level within one or all of these domains is markedly below the individual's normal expected level of performance. This is determined by standardized, individual testing. The deficit causes interference in the child's or adult's normal activities of daily living that require the skill(s). These deficits are not due to a defect in hearing or vision or to a neurologic disorder.

Language and Speech Disorders

These disorders include three types of dysfunctions. They are:

1. Developmental articulation disorder
2. Developmental expressive language disorder
3. Developmental receptive language disorder

The criteria that determine each of these categories include, for Category 1, a consistent failure to use developmentally expected speech sounds. In all three of these disorders the symptoms are not due to a pervasive developmental disorder.

Category 2 includes the criterion of lack of correlation between a standardized test of expressive language and the person's nonverbal IQ, determined by an individually administered test; the expressive language score is substantially lower than the IQ score. In addition, the disturbance significantly interferes with academic achievement and/or activities of daily living (ADL).

Category 3 includes the criterion that the score received on a standardized test of receptive language does not correlate with a standardized, individually administered IQ test. The deficit also interferes significantly with academic achievement and/or ADL.

Motor Skills Disorder

The disorder in this category is **developmental coordination disorder.** In this condition, the person is significantly unable to perform academic functions or ADL requiring motor coordination at a level similar to other children or adults of his or her age. This condition is not caused by a physical disorder, such as cerebral palsy, hemiplegia, or muscular dystrophy.

Disruptive Behavior Disorders

The categories under this major classification include:

1. Attention deficit hyperactivity disorder
2. Conduct disorder, group type
3. Conduct disorder, solitary aggressive type
4. Conduct disorder, undifferentiated type
5. Oppositional defiant disorder

The child with **attention deficit disorder** displays a majority of the behaviors listed below. They occur more frequently than in other children in the same age group. They are fidgeting; difficulty remaining seated; distractibility; difficulty waiting turn, following instructions, sustaining attention, remaining task-focused, and playing quietly; blurting out answers prematurely; excessive talking; interrupting; inattention; excessively losing things; and engaging in dangerous activities. In addition, these behaviors begin to manifest themselves before age 7 and they are not related to a pervasive personality disorder. The various diagnostic categories can be further classified as mild, moderate, or severe.

The conduct disorders all have the same potential list of diagnostic criteria; the differences between them are related to the situations in which they occur. In the **group type** the conduct problems occur primarily in a group activity with peers. In the **solitary aggressive type** there is aggressive physical activity directed primarily toward adults and peers. The **undifferentiated type** can contain a mixture of symptoms of the other categories within this classification.

The diagnostic criteria for the conduct disorders require that at least three of the following symptoms be present. The person:

1. Has stolen or forged (without confrontation of a victim) on more than one occasion
2. Has run away from home at least twice
3. Lies
4. Has deliberately set fires
5. Has been truant frequently
6. Has broken into someone else's home, building, or car
7. Has deliberately destroyed others' property
8. Has been physically cruel to animals
9. Has forced someone into sexual activity
10. Has used a weapon in more than one fight
11. Often initiates physical fights
12. Has stolen with confrontation of a victim
13. Has been physically cruel to people*

The conduct disorders can be further classified as mild, moderate, or severe.

The **oppositional defiant disorder** is a disturbance that has been present for at least 6 months. The symptoms used as criteria should be present more frequently than they are in other children of the same age. The symptoms include frequent episodes of loss of temper, arguing with adults, defying or refusing adult's requests or rules, deliberately annoying others, blaming others for own mistakes, becoming easily aggravated, becoming resentful or angry, swearing, and being angry. This category is further classified as mild, moderate, or severe.

■ Anxiety Disorders of Childhood and Adolescence

Marked anxiety is the presenting symptom for all three of the diagnostic subgroups in this category. (For more detailed information on the phenomenon of anxiety refer to Chapter 25, Anxiety and Somatoform Disorders.) The three subcategories are as follows:

1. Separation anxiety disorder
2. Avoidant disorder of childhood or adolescence
3. Overanxious disorder

*Adapted from *Desk Reference to the Diagnostic Criteria from DSM-III-R.* (1987). Washington, DC: American Psychiatric Association, p. 58.

The youngster with a **separation anxiety disorder** experiences anxiety at or near the panic level when he or she is separated from a major attachment figure, such as a parent, sibling, and so on. The reaction exceeds what would be expected of a child of his or her age. The child demonstrates clinging behavior and is unable or finds it difficult to be away from home independently, at camp or on school outings, for instance. Physical signs of anxiety appear in anticipation of separation. These include stomach aches, nausea, vomiting, diarrhea, headaches, and so on. Cardiovascular symptoms such as dizziness and palpitations may occur in older children and adolescents. Their separation from significant others may cause morbid fears about death or accidents that might happen to themselves or their parents.

Avoidant disorder of childhood or adolescence involves the young person avoiding or pulling away from relationships with others, while maintaining warm relationships with family members. Excessive timidity and refusal to talk with others is also demonstrated. In adolescents, lack of normal sexual development and interest may occur.

Overanxious disorder includes behavior that indicates constant worrying and fearfulness. The worrying is not associated with a specific event, such as separation. Rather, the child projects his or her terror into new situations or new acquaintances.

■ Eating Disorders

This category of disorders includes major disturbances in eating behavior. Increasingly, some of these conditions are seen in adults, but the patterns leading to the adult behavior were present in childhood or adolescence. These disorders include the following:

1. Anorexia nervosa
2. Bulimia nervosa
3. Pica
4. Rumination disorder of infancy
5. Atypical eating disorder

Anorexia nervosa is a condition that is seen primarily in females (95%) between 12 and 18 years of age. The young woman develops a strong fear of becoming obese; this fear does not decrease as weight loss occurs. She has a distorted body image and views herself as being fat, even when she is emaciated. The diagnosis of anorexia nervosa is made when the weight loss is more than 15% of ideal body weight for height, body build, and age, and there is no physical cause for the weight loss. If not reversed, this condition can be fatal.

Bulimia is an eating disorder that occurs predominately in adolescent or young adult females. The person indulges in eating binges of high-calorie food. She is aware of the abnormal eating pattern. The binge eating may be pleasurable, but it is followed by a depressed mood. The binge episode ends abruptly with abdominal pain, self-induced vomiting, or sleep. The young woman repeatedly attempts to lose weight by self-induced vomiting, laxatives or diuretics, or severely restrictive diets. She also has rapidly fluctuating weight changes of over 10 pounds due to the alternating dieting and binging. She is fearful that she will not be able to stop eating voluntarily.

Pica is an eating disorder seen most frequently in toddlers between 12 and 24 months of age. The youngster persistently eats nonnutritive substances such as paint, sand, plaster, and so on. It usually disappears spontaneously.

Rumination disorder of infancy is a condition in which an infant, usually between 3 and 12 months of age, repeatedly regurgitates partially digested food without nausea or other gastrointestinal illness. In order to meet the criteria for this diagnosis, the condition must follow a period of normal functioning and occur for 1 month. The infant experiences weight loss or fails to gain weight at a normal rate for his or her age.

Atypical eating disorder is a category for eating disorders that do not meet the criteria of the conditions described above. For example, if a person experiences severe emotional trauma that involves some aspect of eating, such as a child who is unreasonably disciplined for not completely eating all the food on the plate, he or she may demonstrate some aberration of normal eating behavior at the time or during a later stage of development.

■ Gender Identity Disorders

These disorders include conditions in which a person feels emotional distress about his or her sexual identity. The categories include:

1. Gender identity disorder of childhood
2. Transsexualism
3. Gender identity disorder of adolescence or adulthood, non-transsexual type.

In the first category a prepubertal girl experiences and describes intense distress about being a girl. She avoids feminine clothing and prefers to dress like a boy. She repudiates her feminine anatomy and may express a desire for a penis, reject urinating in a sitting position, or state that she does not want to grow breasts or menstruate.

A prepubertal boy with the same condition wishes to dress and act like a girl and resists his masculine anatomy by stating that he wants to become a woman, be rid of his penis or testes, or prefers that he not have them.

Category 2 includes postpubertal symptoms of persistent discomfort with one's sex accompanied by at least a 2-year desire to be rid of one's sexual organs and secondary sex characteristics and to have those of the opposite sex. Classification in this category includes further description of type: **asexual, homosexual, heterosexual,** or **unspecified**.

Category 3 includes frequent or persistent postpubertal discomfort with one's own sex, persistent or recurrent cross-dressing, but without the goal of sexual excitement (as in **transvestic fetishism,** which will be described under the sexual dysfunctions in a later chapter). This person has no wish to be rid of his or her sexual organs or secondary sexual characteristics.

■ Tic Disorders

The disorders included in this category all include an abnormality of gross motor movement called tics. A **tic** is a rapid involuntary movement of a related group of muscles or the involuntary production of words or noises.

The subcategories of this classification are:

1. Tourette's disorder
2. Chronic motor or vocal tic disorder
3. Transient tic disorder
4. Atypical tic disorder
5. Atypical movement disorder

Tourette's disorder occurs before the age of 21 and usually has a chronic lifelong course. The person experiences multiple vocal and motor (body) tics in many muscle groups. The intensity of the symptoms varies over months and the condition is present over 1 year in order to be diagnosed as Tourette's disorder.

Chronic motor or vocal tic disorder includes the presence of either motor or vocal tics, but not both in someone under age 21. They occur very frequently for a period of over a year. There is no other neurologic condition causing the tics.

■ Elimination Disorders

Functional encopresis is a disorder in which a child over 4 years of age passes feces voluntarily or involuntarily in socially inappropriate places at least once a month. Approximately 1% of 5-year-olds demonstrate this behavior. There are two other subclassifications of this disorder: the **primary type**, in which there was no period of fecal incontinence for a period of 1 year before the disturbance; and the **secondary type**, in which there was a full year of fecal incontinence before the dysfunction.

Functional enuresis is a condition in which a child under 5, and over a socially accepted age for toilet training, voids involuntarily during the daytime or nighttime. The child has at least two events per month between 5 and 6 years of age and one event per month for older children.

Approximately 10% of all 5-year-old children experience this condition. It usually disappears as the child matures physically and mentally. It is not caused by a physical disease. This condition has the similar subclassifications of primary and secondary types described above, with the same criteria, substituting urinary incontinence for fecal incontinence. Within this category it is important to specify the pattern of enuresis: **nocturnal only** (at night), **diurnal only** (during the daytime), or **nocturnal and diurnal.**

■ Speech Disorders Not Elsewhere Classified

Cluttering is a speech disorder that involves both the rhythm and rate of speech. It results in a form of speech that is not understandable. **Stuttering** is a speech disorder that disrupts fluency by repetitions or prolongation of syllables.

■ Other Disorders of Infancy and Childhood

This category includes a variety of unrelated conditions:

1. Elective mutism
2. Identity disorder
3. Reactive attachment disorder of infancy or early childhood
4. Stereotype/habit disorder
5. Undifferentiated attention-deficit disorder

Elective mutism is a condition in which a person has the ability to speak and understand language but refuses to talk in one or more major social situations.

Identity disorder is a condition in which a person experiences distress about a number of identity issues, such as at least three of the following:

1. Long-term goals
2. Career choice
3. Friendship patterns
4. Sexual orientation and behavior
5. Religious identification
6. Moral value systems
7. Group loyalties*

In addition, the following symptom is present: decreased functioning in work or social situations for at least 3 months as a result of the symptoms listed above. The symptoms are known to be unrelated to any other mental disorder and are not severe enough to be classified as a **borderline personality disorder.**

Reactive attachment disorder of infancy or early childhood is a condition that affects a child's ability to bond with or attach to others in a trusting manner. The child either is aloof and uninterested in social relations or is inappropriately familiar with unknown persons. These symptoms are unrelated to mental retardation or to a pervasive developmental disorder.

The child has been improperly cared for with a history of persistent lack of concern about the child's basic emotional needs for comfort, stimulation, and protection; continual disregard of the child's basic physical needs including adequate housing, nutrition, and protection from danger; or continuous change of primary care-giver reducing the potential for attachment. The course of the disorder usually begins with improper care, leading to the incapacity to form attachments.

Stereotype/habit disorder involves repetitive intentional behaviors such as head banging, body weaving, and hand shaking. The activity either causes or risks physical injury or interferes with normal ADL.

Undifferentiated attention-deficit disorder has the primary symptom of inattention that is developmentally inappropriate. It is a different disorder whose underlying causes are unlike those of attention

Desk Reference to the Diagnostic Criteria from DSM-III-R. (1987). Washington, DC: American Psychiatric Association, pp. 72–73.

deficit hyperactivity disorder, in which the child's excessive activity results in poor concentration or an unstable and chaotic environment. In the latter situation the child's inattention is caused by his or her disruptive environment.

CHAPTER 20 QUESTIONS

1. Name the profound mental disorder that commonly manifests itself in infancy and leaves a person markedly dysfunctional in most realms of human functioning.

2. Describe **avoidant disorder of childhood or adolescence**.

3. What are five eating disorders of childhood and adolescence?

4. What is **Tourette's syndrome**?

BIBLIOGRAPHY

American Psychiatric Association. (1991). *DSM-IV options book*. Washington, DC: American Psychiatric Press.

American Psychiatric Association. (1987). *Diagnostic and statistical manual of mental disorders* (3rd ed., rev.). Washington, DC: American Psychiatric Press.

Clunn, P. (Ed.). (1991). *Child psychiatric nursing*. St. Louis, MO: Mosby–Year Book.

Lewis, M.L. (Ed.). (1991). *Child and adolescent psychiatry: A comprehensive textbook*. Baltimore: Williams & Wilkins.

McFarland, G.K, Thomas, M.D. (1991). *Psychiatric mental health nursing: Application of the nursing process*. Philadelphia: J.B. Lippincott.

Rew, L. (1991). Intuition in psychiatric-mental health nursing. *Journal of Child & Adolescent Psychiatric & Mental Health Nursing, 4,* 110–115.

Stuart, G.W., & Sundeen, S.J. (Eds.). (1991). *Principles and practice of psychiatric nursing* (4th ed.). St. Louis, MO: Mosby–Year Book.

Verhulst, F.C., & Koot, H.M. (1991). *Child psychiatric epidemiology: Concepts, methods, and findings*. Newbury Park, CA: Sage Publications.

Chapter 21

■■■■■

Delirium, Dementia, and Other Cognitive Disorders

Behavioral Objectives

After reading this chapter the student will be able to:

List the causes of cognitive impairment disorders and describe one condition under each category.

Define **psychosis, delirium,** and **dementia.**

Describe the nursing care of clients with delirium.

Describe the nursing care of clients with dementia.

Identify the basic causes that underlie cognitive impairment disorders.

Explain the difference between acute organic psychoses and chronic organic psychoses.

Describe the symptoms of senile and presenile dementia and note the age difference for each type of dementia.

List the symptoms associated with the following forms of alcoholic psychoses: delirium tremens and Korsakoff's psychosis.

Mental Health and Mental Illness,
Fifth Edition, by Patricia D. Barry.
J.B. Lippincott Company, Philadelphia © 1994.

Cognitive impairment disorders are caused by dysfunctions in brain anatomy or physiology. They can result in a severe disruption of mental status called **psychosis.**

A psychosis is the most serious form of mental disorder. A person who is psychotic temporarily loses contact with reality. There are two main types of organic psychosis: delirium and dementia. Generally, delirium is an acute condition that develops rapidly and subsides spontaneously or when the underlying physical cause is treated. Dementia is caused by a chronic, irreversible physical deterioration of anatomic parts of the brain. Accordingly, dementia usually cannot be reversed. Delirium and dementia will be discussed later in this chapter.

Psychoses that are caused by cognitive impairment disorders are different from functional psychoses such as those caused by schizophrenia. Functional psychoses are not associated with any known physical abnormality (although researchers in the field of neuropsychiatry believe that there is a basic defect in the biochemistry of the brain that causes functional psychoses). Cognitive psychotic conditions have a variety of causes or etiologies. The following "mend a mind" mnemonic aid helps you to recall the various possible causes of cognitive impairment disorders:

M Metabolic disorder	**M** Mechanical disease
E Electrical disorder	**I** Infectious disease
N Neoplastic disease	**N** Nutritional disease
D Degenerative disease	**D** Drug toxicity
A Arterial disease	

The types of conditions that belong to the various categories are outlined below.

■ ■ ■ ■ ■ ■ ■ ■ ■

Metabolic
  Endocrine gland disorders
  Electrolyte imbalances

■ ■ ■ ■ ■ ■ ■ ■ ■ *continued*

Electrical
  Epileptic disorders
Neoplastic
  Benign or malignant tumors of the brain or elsewhere
Degenerative
  Alzheimer's disease
  Huntington's chorea
Arterial
  Cerebrovascular accident (CVA)
  Degenerative changes of cerebral arteries
  Multiple infarct dementia
Mechanical
  Head injury
Infectious
  Encephalitis
  Meningitis
  Cerebral abscess
  General systemic infections
Nutritional
  Nicotinic acid
  Vitamin B_{12}
  Thiamine
  Folic acid
Drugs
  Alcohol
  Prescribed medications

The conditions listed above can produce a variety of acute psychiatric symptoms including acute confusion, hallucinations, and delusions. Generally speaking, one of the differences in the psychotic
episodes of people with cognitive impairment disorders, contrasted
with those of people with functional psychiatric illness, is that the
hallucinations of the client with cognitive impairment disorder tend
to be primarily visual, while those of the functionally ill client are
usually auditory. Some of the conditions, for example, epileptic disorders, do not routinely cause psychiatric disturbance. On occasion,
depending on the types of neurologic dysfunction in the different
parts of the brain, psychiatric symptoms of various types and severity
may occur. In addition, the neurologic disorder can also cause the

basic personality tendencies of the person to be magnified. For example, a person who has always been mildly suspicious may become paranoid.

Table 21-1 presents the symptoms seen in delirium and dementia. Development of a nursing care plan for the client with a cognitive impairment disorder should include nursing assessment of the mental status categories in this chart. The planning and intervention steps of the nursing process can be developed more easily when the specific types and symptoms of mental dysfunction are identified.

Table 21-1. Symptoms of the Two Types of Cognitive Impairment Disorders

Categories	Delirium	Dementia
Onset	Usually rapid: waxes and wanes abruptly	Usually slow: 1 month or more
Level of awareness	Increased or decreased	Normal or decreased
Orientation	Disoriented	Usually not affected until late in course
Appearance and behavior	May be semicomatose; agitated	Usually slowed responses
Speech and communication	Incoherent; degree of change based on severity of delirium	Usually slowed because of cognitive deficits
Mood	Labile; anxiety or panic common	Constricted affect or depression
Thinking process	Markedly altered	Mildly altered decreased intellectual ability
Memory	Partial or full loss of recent memory; remote memory intact	Partial loss of both recent and remote memory
Perception	Usually markedly altered	Usually intact or mildly affected
Abstract thinking and judgment	Markedly decreased	Mildly decreased
Sleep-wake cycle	Disrupted	Not affected
Treatment	Identify and remove underlying cause; symptomatic treatment	Symptomatic treatment
Prognosis	Reversible in most cases	Usually irreversible

Kaplan H., Sadock, B. (1985); Lishman (1978). In Barry, P. (1984) *Psychosocial Nursing Assessment and Intervention*. Philadelphia: J.B. Lippincott.

■ Delirium

Delirium usually is an acute cognitive impairment disorder that produces a marked change in mental status. A toxic condition related to one of the categories described in the mnemonic above causes delirium. To determine its cause and prevent its occurrence an immediate assessment of physiologic status is needed: a physical examination, diagnostic workup including laboratory tests and other tests as indicated, and review of all medications. Once the underlying cause is diagnosed and treated, the person usually returns to his or her previously existing mental status and personality style.

Nursing Care of Clients With Delirium

A client who is developing a toxic cognitive impairment disorder, whether he or she is on a psychiatric, medical, or surgical unit, often demonstrates symptoms of his or her changing mental status before full-blown delirium occurs. Regardless of mental status on admission, he or she becomes more restless and agitated. There may be physiological changes such as increased temperature, blood pressure and pulse, and facial flushing. Such changes indicate that the client's status is changing: you should check on this client frequently to determine how quickly his or her mental or physical state is deteriorating. Notify the physician as soon as you determine the specific changes. Ideally, a delirious episode can be avoided if a diagnostic evaluation is performed with little delay and proper medication is ordered.

The drug of choice for many clients with cognitive impairment disorder is haloperidol (Haldol). It is a major tranquilizer of the butyrophenone group, which is chosen over the major tranquilizers of the phenothiazine group because it has fewer anticholinergic effects on the other body systems. Remember that a client with an organic brain syndrome suffers from an illness in one or more of the many physiological systems; therefore, you do not want to give this client a medication with anticholinergic effects, since it likely will further disrupt the body's homeostasis. One of the side effects of haloperidol (Haldol) is the risk of tardive dyskinesia (see Chapter 31, Psychopharmacology and Electroshock Treatment of Mental Disorders). Because of this risk, it is wise to discontinue this medication as soon as the acute delirious episode has passed. If one of your clients continues to be on this medication, double check with the charge nurse to be sure that it is still indicated. Generally speaking, once the underlying physical cause of the cognitive impairment disorder is treated, and if the client has had no prior history of major psychiatric illness, the medication can be discontinued or replaced by a minor tranquilizer that has fewer toxic effects.

Caring for a client experiencing a delirious episode can be frightening. Maintain your own composure during the time you are with him or her. The client with cognitive impairment disorder, although out of control, will remember what happened. Avoid saying or doing anything that could further alarm him or her or cause him or her to remember you in an unpleasant light. Caring firmness and honesty are the most therapeutic behaviors you can display.

Restraints
Safeguard the client's safety during such an episode. If he or she is totally out of control, use whatever mechanism your hospital has devised to gather enough people to restrain the client. Remember, these may include nonnursing personnel who are afraid and may use stronger restraint than absolutely necessary. Your composure and quiet directions can calm them and strongly affect their handling of the client. Watch that their physical restraint does not unnecessarily injure the client.

Do not leave the client alone during an acute psychotic episode. Restraints may or may not be used depending on the policies of the institution, the orders of the physician, and the circumstances of the client's cognitive impairment disorder. Although medication decreases the acute state, it may still be necessary to restrain the client for his or her own safety.

Restraints are frightening to a client who is confused as the result of delirium. They should be used only after careful assessment of the client's problem. The need for restraints should be explained quietly to the client, even if he or she does not appear to be able to understand. It is important to obtain the order of a physician or to know what the *written* policy of the institution states about the use of restraints. The use of restraints and their abuse is an important legal issue for nurses. Liability can result in lawsuits if the nurse using restraints is not legally covered by such a policy.

The types of restraints available include wrist and ankle restraints and camisoles. Make sure the wrist and ankle restraints are properly padded to safeguard the integrity of the skin. Restraints should be released at least every 2 hours to allow for freedom of movement and to check the condition of the skin. Also check that good body positioning is maintained when restraints are used.

Another important point to remember when you are caring for a client who has had a delirious episode is that the terror he or she experienced while he or she was delirious remains repressed in his or her unconscious. He or she may demonstrate increased levels of anxiety or experience frightening nightmares after the psychotic episode. If you gently ask what he or she remembers feeling and thinking while it was happening, the client may be relieved to describe it to you. As the painful thoughts and feelings are released, anxiety and nightmares should diminish. Your caring and knowledge in listening to his or her experience can comfort and reassure the client.

■ Dementia

Dementia is a change in mental status that is due to physical changes in the brain. It usually is a chronic condition that progresses slowly and is not reversible. Dementia is frequently associated with the elderly and is often incorrectly assumed to be a part of the aging process. Actually, many elderly people retain their intellectual functioning into their 80s and 90s. Important factors determining whether dementia occurs are genetic predisposition, family history, nutritional status, and general level of health.

Nursing Care of Clients With Dementia

Often people who are hospitalized in nursing homes have varying levels of dementia, as do elderly people in the acute hospital setting. Table 21-1 can help you identify the various symptoms of dementia the client is experiencing. Chart the severity of these symptoms and take them into consideration as you develop the nursing care plan. The participation of family members, whenever possible, is valuable, because the client's altered mental status, including impaired memory, may result in an inaccurate or incomplete data base. The following should be considered when completing the remaining steps of the nursing process.

Give good basic physical care.

Give simple verbal directions in a calm voice.

Avoid sensory overload.

Provide a regular toileting schedule. Clients may forget to void and are embarrassed by their incontinence.

Monitor and document bowel activity.

Monitor and document nutritional intake.

Maintain reality orientation by mentioning the day of the week and discussing seasonal and current events.

Provide night light. Clients with cognitive impairment disorders are susceptible to **sundowning,** a decrease in orientation at night.

Provide some type of enjoyable activity.

Avoid using physical restraints unless indicated.

Avoid placing intravenous lines in lower arm. They are often displaced by the confused client.

Elderly people who are mildly confused, forgetful, and listless should not automatically be assumed to have dementia. Remember that elderly people have experienced a profound number of losses, and they may be acutely depressed. Nutritional deprivation, a possible cause of cognitive impairment disorder, can also cause depression. The symptoms of acute depression and mild dementia can appear similar. If you suspect depression, obtain a psychiatric consultation if the client is in a nonpsychiatric institution.

■ Other Cognitive Impairment Disorders

All of the following mental disorders have an organic etiology, which can be discovered in the client's history, physical exam, or laboratory tests, but they do not meet the specific criteria of delirium and dementia.

Amnestic syndrome is a cognitive impairment disorder in which the level of consciousness is not affected as it is in other organic brain disorders. Short-term and long-term memory are impaired, and the client is in an amnestic state. It is a rare condition.

Organic delusional syndrome is a mental disorder in which the main symptom is a predominant delusion that occurs with no change in level of consciousness, no significant loss of intellectual abilities, and no hallucinations.

Organic hallucinosis is a mental disorder in which the client experiences hallucinations. There are no changes in level of consciousness, intellectual abilities, or mood; nor are there delusions accompanying the hallucinations.

Organic mood syndrome is a change in mental status marked by two of the symptoms listed under manic or major depressive episode (see Chapter 25). There are no changes in level of consciousness or in intellectual abilities. There are no hallucinations or delusions.

Organic anxiety syndrome is a mental disorder characterized by active, recurrent panic attacks or generalized anxiety.

Organic personality syndrome is a major change in a person's personality style, including at least one of the following:

Emotional swings (lability) or sudden flaring of emotions such as crying, angry outbursts

Decrease in impulse control, for example, shoplifting, poor social or sexual judgment

Suspiciousness or paranoid ideation

Apathy and decreased interest in normal pursuits of life

Intoxication is a separate syndrome unlike those caused by other cognitive impairment disorders. It is caused by recent intake of one or more psychoactive substances. The result is abnormal behavior, such as impairment of judgment, occupational functioning, or social functioning. These behavioral changes are due to the effects of the substance on the central nervous system.

Withdrawal is a separate syndrome unlike the other cognitive impairment disorders that is caused by the reduction or cessation of ingestion of a psychoactive substance following its regular use.

This section will concentrate on the most frequently seen substance-related mental disorders in the clinical setting. In the event that you are caring for a client whose condition is not described in this section it may be helpful to refer to the *Diagnostic and Statistical Manual of Mental Disorder*, fourth edition (DSM-IV) on your clinical unit or in the library. It will describe the specific symptoms of the condition.

DSM-IV categories of substance-induced cognitive impairment disorders include a large number of syndromes. These conditions present a wide variety of symptoms. The full presentation of symptoms for all conditions can be found in the DSM-IV. In this section, the symptoms of intoxication and withdrawal are described for each of the major drug-induced cognitive impairment disorders. In each case, none of the physical or mental symptoms is caused by any other type of medical condition. The names of other conditions that can develop with prolonged drug use appear under each major drug abuse group.

■ Substance-Induced Delirium

Alcohol-Induced Cognitive Impairment Disorders

Alcohol intoxication is a condition in which recent ingestion of alcohol causes negative behavioral effects, including at least one of the following signs: slurred speech, uncoordination, unsteady walking, nystagmus, or flushed face. In addition, at least one of the following psychological symptoms appears: mood change, irritability, excessive talking, or impaired attention.

Uncomplicated alcohol withdrawal occurs when there is a decrease or cessation of heavy, prolonged use of alcohol. It is followed within several hours by coarse tremors of the hands, tongue, and eyelids. In addition, at least one of the following symptoms appears: nausea and vomiting; weakness or malaise; anxiety; depressed or irritable mood; autonomic hyperactivity, such as tachycardia, sweating, and elevated blood pressure; or orthostatic hypotension.

When alcohol withdrawal is accompanied by delirium it is called **alcohol withdrawal delirium.** Another name for this condition is **delirium tremens,** an acute psychosis that may be precipitated in the alcoholic by such factors as fever, infection, and exposure. As the name suggests, delirium and tremor (especially of the hands) are two outstanding symptoms. The delirium is preceded by an aversion for food and by restlessness, irritability, and disturbed sleep.

Amphetamine (or Similarly Acting Sympathomimetic)-Induced Cognitive Impairment Disorder

The drugs included in this category are those of the substituted phenethylamine: amphetamine, dextroamphetamine, and methamphetamine (speed). Other differing drugs such as methylphenidate or appetite suppressants (diet pills) are also included. Intoxication in this category includes the same physical and psychological symptoms as those of cocaine intoxication. Abrupt or gradual withdrawal from the drug induces depression and two or more of the following symptoms: increase in dreaming, disturbed sleep, and fatigue. Those who abuse these drugs can also develop delirium and delusional disorders.

Cannabis-Induced Cognitive Impairment Disorder

The symptoms in cannabis (marijuana, hashish, or THC) intoxication are tachycardia and at least one of the following psychological symptoms that occur shortly after use: perception of slowed time, intensified subjective perceptions, apathy, and elation. In addition, one or more of the following physical symptoms appear: dry mouth, increase in appetite, and redness of the eyes. Disruption in social and occupational functioning and suspiciousness can result. A more severe form of cannabis-related mental disorder is cannabis delusional disorder. There are no changes in level of consciousness and intellectual abilities, no major symptoms of depression, and no hallucinations or delusions.

Cocaine-Induced Cognitive Impairment Disorder

Cocaine intoxication occurs within 1 hour of using the drug and includes at least two of the following psychological symptoms: euphoria, grandiosity, excessive wordiness, excessive vigilance, and psychomotor agitation. In addition, at least two of the following physiological conditions are present: dilated pupils, elevated blood pressure, tachycardia, nausea and vomiting, and chills or perspiration. There also are symptoms of antisocial behavior.

Hallucinogen-Induced Cognitive Impairment Disorder

The drugs included in this category are substances related to 5-hydroxytryptamine (for example, LSD), dimethyltryptamine (DMT), and substances related to catecholamine (for example, mescaline). The hallucinogenic drugs are not categorized by intoxication or withdrawal. Rather, they markedly alter the mental status of those who use them and can cause hallucinosis, delusional disorder, and affective disorder.

Inhalant-Induced Cognitive Impairment Disorder

Inhalant intoxication follows the use of an inhalant that results in abnormal changes in behavior such as assaultiveness, impaired judgment, belligerence, and/or impaired occupational or social functioning. At least two of the following signs must be present: dizziness, nystagmus, uncoordination, slurred speech, unsteady gait, lethargy, depressed reflexes, psychomotor retardation, tremor, generalized muscle weakness, blurred vision, stupor or coma, and/or euphoria.

Opioid-Induced Cognitive Impairment Disorder

The drugs included in this category are heroin, morphine, and the morphine-like drugs, such as meperidine (Demerol) and methadone. The diagnostic criteria for **opioid intoxication** are recent use of an opioid; constriction of pupils, or dilatation if there is a major overdose; and the presence of one or more emotional or neurologic signs: euphoria, dysphoria, apathy, or psychomotor retardation.

Symptoms of **opioid withdrawal** include at least four of the following signs: tachycardia, mild hypertension, fever, lacrimation, dilated pupils, rhinorrhea (running nose), piloerection (hairs of skin standing on end), sweating, diarrhea, and yawning.

Phencyclidine (PCP)-Induced Cognitive Impairment Disorder

The most common drugs in this category are known by the following names: Ketalar, TCP, PCP, angel dust, THC, crystal, and peace pill. These substances are usually ingested by inhaling or smoking. The symptoms of intoxication shortly following ingestion include at least two of the following physiological symptoms: decreased pain response, tachycardia and elevated blood pressure, dysarthria, decrease in voluntary muscle coordination, and horizontal or vertical nystagmus. In addition, there should be at least two of the following psychological symptoms: severe anxiety, mood swings, elation, grandiosity, psychomotor agitation, and sensation experienced in a different part of the body than where pressure is applied. Abuses of this class of drugs can also cause delirium and mixed mental disorder.

Sedative—Hypnotic-Induced Cognitive Impairment Disorder

Intoxication within this category can be caused by any of the following drugs: sedatives, including pentobarbital sodium (Nembutal), secobarbital (Seconal), and a combination of secobarbital sodium and amobarbital sodium (Tuinal); the minor tranquilizers, benzodiazepines, including chlordiazepoxide (Librium), diazepam (Valium), and oxazepam (Serax). The common hypnotics are ethchlorvynol (Placidyl), flurazepam hydrochloride (Dalmane), glutethimide (Doriden), methyprylon (Noludar), chloral hydrate, and methaqualone. The symptoms of intoxication are the same as those for alcohol. Any differences are due to differences in basic personality structures of different people.

Withdrawal symptoms following prolonged, heavy use of the drug are also similar to alcohol withdrawal symptoms. At least three of the following physical symptoms are present in this brain syndrome:

Coarse tremors of the hands, eyelids, and tongue

Nausea and vomiting

Malaise or weakness

Autonomic hyperactivity

Anxiety

Depressed or irritable mood

Orthostatic hypotension

Other syndromes that can develop in abusers of this family of drugs are withdrawal delirium and amnestic disorder.

■ Physical Conditions That Can Cause Mental Disorders

The physical conditions that can cause mental disorders follow our "mend a mind" mnemonic. The following section has been added to this chapter, although it is not one of the DSM-III-R classifications. Its purpose is to familiarize you with physical conditions that can disrupt the anatomy or physiology of the brain. Such disruption can cause changes in mental status.

Psychosis Associated With Metabolic Disorders

This category of cognitive impairment disorders includes those caused by endocrine disorders: complications of diabetes (other than cerebral arteriosclerosis) and disorders of the thyroid, pituitary, adrenals, and other endocrine glands.

Hyperactivity or hypoactivity of the thyroid gland often results in mental disturbances. If the secretion of the gland is insufficient, a condition known as **myxedema** develops. In addition to a well-known syndrome of physical symptoms (lowered blood pressure, temperature, pulse rate, and respiration rate; chilliness of the body, especially cold hands and feet; slowed down physical activity; and dullness of facial expression) such clients become slow in their thinking and in their ability to grasp ideas. Their memory becomes impaired, and their speech become slow and listless. Some are irritable, fretful, fault-finding, or even paranoid in their ideas and attitudes. Congenital insufficiency of the thyroid gland results in a condition called **cretinism,** in which there are both mental and physical defects.

An overactive thyroid gives rise to a condition known as **exophthalmic goiter** or **Graves' disease.** The client's symptoms are the exact opposite of those suffering from insufficient thyroxine. The client is nervous, high strung, irritable, very active, anxious, and apprehensive. In acute thyroid intoxication, he or she may go into acute delirium, accompanied by incoherence, hallucinations, and great restlessness. This intoxication may lead to coma and death.

An undersecretion of the islands of Langerhans in the pancreas causes **diabetes mellitus.** Diabetes is characterized by a hyperglycemia (or excessive amount of sugar in the blood) due to a deficiency of insulin that helps the cells burn up sugars. When the hyperglycemia mounts too high, the client goes into diabetic coma. He or she becomes irritable, anxious, and confused; he or she hallucinates and may even become delirious before reaching the convulsion state. Without treatment, coma usually results.

In addition to the disorders of the endocrine system, another type of metabolic disturbance is related to electrolyte imbalance. The brain is accustomed to functioning in homeostatic balance. Due to illness or other factors, the body's electrolytes may be out of balance. Sensitive brain tissue that is bathed in the body fluids of blood and cerebrospinal fluid is affected by excessively high or low levels of electrolytes. Table 21-2 lists the electrolytes and their generally accepted normal ranges as a guideline for recognizing electrolyte imbalance as the cause for mental status changes in a general hospital client.

Be aware, however, that when clients have been chronically physically ill, their body tissues have had a gradual period of time to adjust to altered electrolyte levels. Accordingly, their electrolyte levels may extend above or below the ranges shown above with no toxic effects on brain tissue.

Psychosis Associated With Electrical Disorders

In certain clients with idiopathic epilepsy, the epileptic attack may take the form of an episode of excitement with hallucinations, fears, and violent outbreaks. Most commonly, clouding of consciousness occurs before or after a convulsive attack, or instead of a convulsion, the client may show only dazed reaction with deep confusion, bewil-

Table 21-2.   Electrolytes That Can Alter Mental Status

Electrolyte	Normal Range	Abnormal Levels
Calcium	8.5–10.5	Hypocalcemia, hypercalcemia
Sodium	135–145 MEq/liter	Hyponatremia, hypernatremia
Phosphorus	2.6–4.5	Hypophosphatemia, hyperphosphatemia
Potassium	3.5–5.0 MEq/liter	Hypokalemia, hyperkalemia
Base bicarbonate	Blood pH 7.38–7.42 Bicarb level 24 MEq/liter	Acidosis, alkalosis

derment and anxiety. There are no psychiatric disorders directly related to epilepsy, however, and this type of occurrence is relatively rare.

Psychosis Associated With Neoplastic Disorders

Tumors that develop in the brain can produce psychotic reactions. Such tumors may be benign or malignant. The benign tumors are usually encapsulated. If diagnosed before their growing pressure has done much damage and if located in an area where surgery is feasible, they are often successfully removed. Angiomas, or blood tumors, although benign, do not lend themselves well to surgical removal. Malignant tumors spread rapidly and usually result in severe mental imbalance. Surgery is of little avail, and although radiation therapy is usually tried, it merely slows down the spreading of the tumor. Chemotherapy may or may not help. An additional type of neoplasm that frequently results in acute depression is carcinoma of the pancreas. The cause of this acute change in mental state is not known.

Psychosis Associated With Degenerative Disorders

Alzheimer's disease is the most common degenerative condition that results in significant dementia. It is a condition that begins with gradual decrease in memory, emotional stability, and general functioning. The initial symptoms usually appear between the ages of 40 and 60. Intellectual ability and personality functioning gradually decrease. Memory fails markedly. There are muscular and gait changes. Within a year, profound dementia accompanied by hallucinations and delusions usually occurs. Complete nursing care is required.

Another example of this type of disorder is **Huntington's chorea,** a hereditary, sex-linked form of psychosis. It appears chiefly in men, usually in their early 30s, and progresses rapidly so that the client ages mentally in a very short time and becomes helplessly psychotic in a few years.

Psychosis Associated With Arterial Disorders

The brain must receive a rich supply of oxygen in order to function normally. Anoxia, from whatever cause, can seriously affect the nervous tissue and result in brain damage. **Cerebral arteriosclerosis** (hardening of the arteries of the brain) is a frequent cognitive impairment disorder. The number of clients admitted to public mental hospitals with this disorder is exceeded only by schizophrenics. The onset of arteriosclerotic mental disorder varies widely but, in general, may appear between the years of 50 and 65. Among the early symptoms are headaches, dizziness, inability to sustain concentration, short attention span, emotional instability, memory impairment, and episodes of confusion. Some clients develop paranoid delusions; some develop epileptiform convulsions; others show fluctuations in orientation and memory.

When this disease becomes advanced, small thromboses may form in small intracranial blood vessels, and the client will have a series of minor strokes. Following the rupture of such a vessel and until the small blood clot is absorbed again, the client will be confused and have difficulties in speech, memory will ramble back into youth, and perhaps he or she will show some small degree of muscular paralysis. This is called **multi-infarct dementia.**

Also included in this category are circulatory disturbances such as cerebral thrombosis, cerebral embolism, arterial hypertension, cardiorenal disease, and cardiac disease (particularly in decompensation). When a large blood vessel becomes occluded by a large clot, or ruptures, the symptoms are much more severe, and we say the client has had a **stroke** or a **cerebrovascular accident** (CVA).

In about half of these vascular accidents, consciousness is either lost or greatly disturbed. If a coma develops, it may range from a brief episode or may terminate in death. Paralysis of the muscles on the opposite side of the body from the site of the cerebral hemorrhage usually results (**hemiplegia**), or there may be **monoplegia** (paralysis of just one extremity), **paraplegia** (paralysis of both legs), or **quadriplegia** (paralysis of all four extremities or the entire body). **Aphasia** (the inability to correctly say the words one is thinking) is frequently present, swallowing may be difficult or impossible, and bladder and bowel control may be lost.

Psychosis Associated With Mechanical Disorders

These disorders include injury or trauma to the brain from an external force. Oddly enough, relatively few head injuries result in permanent brain damage. The brain tissue, although extremely delicate, is very well protected by its meningeal coverings and the bony case of the cranium. However, some injuries *do* result in extensive brain damage. In this event, scar tissue usually develops in the injured area.

Three types of acute psychoses due to trauma are **concussion, traumatic coma,** and **traumatic delirium.** Concussion very commonly results from a head injury. Its symptoms are amnesia (the client will have a memory loss from just before the time of the accident up until awakening from unconsciousness), unconsciousness (which may be momentary or continue for several hours), and nausea (the client may vomit as he or she regains consciousness). He or she may regain consciousness suddenly, or may pass through a variable period of clouded consciousness and confusion. He or she usually recovers fully in a short time, but if the brain damage is more pronounced, coma may develop or the concussion may be followed by a chronic state of deterioration, personality change, or chronic emotional invalidism.

Traumatic delirium may follow emergence from a traumatic coma or stupor. If the delirium is mild, the client acts more or less bewildered, irritable, and restless. If it is severe, he or she may be noisy, belligerent, demanding, and verbally abusive. Delirium or coma of more than a month's duration usually indicates severe brain damage.

In the event the client does not recover from his or her concussion (i.e., the brain damage becomes chronic), he or she may show mental enfeeblement accompanied by epileptic seizures, paralyses, and other neurologic disturbances. He or she may develop a definite personality change, becoming unstable, aggressive, quarrelsome, and destructive; or he or she may become depressed, apprehensive, easily fatigued, in short, a chronic, complaining invalid.

Psychosis Associated With Infectious Disorders

Intracranial infections, such as encephalitis, meningitis, and cerebral abscess, can result in hallucinations, delusions, and other psychotic symptoms. Once the acute episode has passed, there usually are no ongoing psychiatric side effects. On occasion, there can be some ongoing changes in personality traits, such as increased stubbornness, that become part of a person's permanent personality style.

In addition, systemic infections (pneumonia, typhoid, malaria, acute rheumatic fever) are very often associated with acute mental disturbances. Toxins produced by viral and bacterial invasion of the bloodstream may involve the central nervous system, and delirium is frequently seen. The higher the fever, usually the more intense is the delirium.

Psychosis Associated With Nutritional Disorders

Certain vitamins are essential to a well-functioning neurologic system. Often, inadequate nutrition can result in deterioration of neurologic functioning within the tissues of the brain. When this occurs, psychiatric symptoms may develop. Deficiencies in several B vitamins can cause these changes in mental status. The vitamins are nicotinic acid, B_{12}, thiamine, and folic acid.

While **pellagra** is not common today, it may occur in the chronic alcoholic whose diet has consisted chiefly of alcohol over a period of several months, in poverty areas where residents are very restricted in their choice of foods, and in people suffering from intestinal diseases that prevent the absorption of food. Advanced pellagra exhibits symptoms of mental confusion and delirious states. Irritability, distrust, anxiety, and depression are also common. The disorder is due to a lack of vitamin B (especially the nicotinic acid factor).

Pernicious anemia, while seldom reaching the frank psychotic state, does exhibit the milder symptoms of mental fatigue, memory loss, irritability, depression, and apprehension.

Thiamine deficiency can result in Wernicke's encephalopathy, most commonly seen in chronic alcoholic clients. It also may be present in clients with carcinomas of the digestive tract, tuberculosis, or toxemia.

Folic acid deficiency is an important *and* reversible cause of dementia symptoms in the elderly. The symptoms are progressive dementia, depression, and in some cases, epilepsy. When given therapeutic doses of folic acid, the client's mental status improves in many cases. It can take several months, however, for improvement to occur.

Psychosis Associated With Drug Side Effects

A significant cause of drug-related cognitive impairment disorders are the side effects of medications used in physical illness. Many cardiac drugs cause psychiatric symptoms, such as anxiety, depression, short-term memory loss, disorientation, emotional lability, and hallucinations. In addition, synergistic effects of two or more medications may result in a toxic level of medication that affects neurophysiological functioning. **Synergism** is the effect of separate entities that when combined have a greater effect than the sum of their individual actions. It is similar to a 1 + 1 = 3 result. Any good drug reference lists the reported psychiatric side effects that can occur with use of specific medications.

CHAPTER 21 QUESTIONS

1. Define psychosis.

2. What is dementia?

3. What syndrome results in a major change in a person's personality style?

4. Name the two syndromes caused by the ingestion and cessation of ingestion of psychoactive substances.

5. Name four nutritional deficiencies that can cause changes in mental status.

BIBLIOGRAPHY

American Psychiatric Association. (1991). *DSM-IV options book.* Washington, DC: American Psychiatric Press.

American Psychiatric Association. (1987). *Diagnostic and statistical manual of mental disorders* (3rd ed., rev.). Washington, DC: American Psychiatric Press.

Kaplan, H., & Sadock, B. (1991). *Synopsis of psychiatry: Behavioral sciences, clinical psychiatry* (6th ed.). Baltimore: Williams & Wilkins.

McFarland, G.K, Thomas, M.D. (1991). *Psychiatric mental health nursing: Application of the nursing process.* Philadelphia: J.B. Lippincott.

Stuart, G.W., & Sundeen, S.J. (Eds.). (1991). *Principles and practice of psychiatric nursing* (4th ed.). St. Louis, MO: Mosby–Year Book.

Wilson, H.S., & Kneisl, C.R. (1992). *Psychiatric nursing* (4th ed.). Redwood City, CA: Addison-Wesley.

Chapter 22

■■■■■

Substance-Related Disorders

Behavioral Objectives

After reading this chapter the student will be able to:

Draw up an outline using the following drug or drug categories: opioids; barbiturates, sedatives, tranquilizers, or other hypnotics; amphetamines; cannabis. Under each of these drug headings, list the following information:
1. The names of the most commonly used forms of the drug.
2. The basic physical effects of each.
3. The withdrawal symptoms.
4. The treatment and nursing care for withdrawing the client from the drug.

The diagnosis substance-related disorder is now used in place of **psychoactive substance-use disorder** and the term **drug addiction.** It is used for clients whose mental states are altered by alcohol, drugs, tobacco, and ordinary caffeine-containing beverages. Included are changes in mental status caused by the side effects of medically prescribed drugs taken as medically indicated.

This chapter includes information on the behavioral aspects of the maladaptive use of substances. The changes in mental status caused by such use are described in the previous chapter on cognitive impairment disorders.

228

Mental Health and Mental Illness,
Fifth Edition, by Patricia D. Barry.
J.B. Lippincott Company, Philadelphia © 1994.

There are 12 major categories of substances that are abused under this classification.

Alcohol

Amphetamine or similarly acting sympathomimetic

Caffeine

Cannabis

Cocaine

Hallucinogen

Inhalant

Nicotine

Opioid

Phencyclidine (PCP) or similarly acting arylcyclohexylamine

Sedative, hypnotic, or anxiolytic

Polysubstance abuse

Other substance related disorders (includes changes in mental state caused by side effects of medications prescribed for medical conditions).

■ Substance Dependence and Substance Abuse

The diagnostic criteria for each of these disorders fall under two terms: **substance dependence** and **substance abuse.**

Substance dependence describes a condition in which the individual's symptoms (listed below) have persisted for at least 1 month or occurred frequently over a longer period of time. The individual must manifest three of the following symptoms:

Increasing amounts of the substance are ingested more frequently than the person intended.

Excessive time is spent obtaining the substance.

Important occupational, social, or recreational pursuits are decreased or ceased because of the substance use.

One or more unsuccessful efforts to cut down or control the substance use has been tried, but persistent desire continues.

Frequent intoxication or withdrawal symptoms affect occupational, social, or recreational role obligations.

Use of the substance continues despite difficulties it presents in role functioning or physical problems it causes.

Tolerance for the drug markedly increases (at least a 50% increase in dose is needed to sustain the effects of the drug).

Characteristic withdrawal symptoms occur.

Substance is taken frequently to avoid withdrawal symptoms.

Psychoactive **substance abuse** is a more severe form of substance abuse than psychoactive substance dependence. It is rated according to severity. The categories are:

Mild: The person meets the three symptoms that qualify him or her for the condition, but has few of the remaining symptoms. His or her role obligations are minimally affected.

Moderate: The impairment is between the criteria for mild or severe.

Severe: Multiple symptoms in excess of the three required for diagnosis. Marked impairment of various role obligations.

In partial remission: During a 6-month period symptoms of dependence and some substance use have occurred.

In full remission: For 6 months there has been no substance use nor symptoms of dependence.

The criteria for psychoactive substance abuse are:

1. A maladaptive pattern of psychoactive substance use as manifested by one of the following:
   a. Ongoing use of the substance despite a continued problem with role functioning or a physical condition caused by the use of the substance; or,
   b. Continued use of the substance despite its potential for creating a physically hazardous situation.
2. Some symptoms of the disorder have been present for over a month.
3. The individual does not meet the criteria for substance dependence.

■ Alcohol Abuse

Alcohol substance-use disorder includes the two categories of substance abuse and substance dependence. The criteria for alcohol substance abuse follow:

1. A pattern of pathologic alcohol use is noted.
   a. Daily use of alcohol is necessary to function.
   b. Person is unable to cut down or stop drinking.
   c. Binges last longer than 2 days.
   d. Person occasionally consumes as much as a fifth of liquor per day.
   e. Amnesia occurs during periods of intoxication (blackouts).
2. Social or occupational functioning is impaired.
3. Disturbance lasts longer than 1 month.

Alcohol dependence includes either a pattern of pathologic alcohol use or impairment in social or occupational functioning. In addition there is evidence of tolerance or withdrawal symptoms.

Treatment Approaches to Alcoholism

Before treatment can begin, the client's body must be detoxified of alcohol. With the physiologic dependency that results from alcoholism, detoxification usually must be medically supervised to ensure the client's physical and mental well-being. This most frequently takes place in a general hospital medical-surgical setting or in an alcohol rehabilitation center, not on a general psychiatric unit. Refer to any standard text on alcoholism treatment for specific information about the treatment and nursing care of this complex physiological condition. Once detoxification is completed, three major treatment options are most frequently presented to recovering alcoholics—Alcoholics Anonymous, aversive therapy with disulfiram (Antabuse), or an inpatient rehabilitation treatment program.

Alcoholics Anonymous

Alcoholics Anonymous (AA) is a peer-support, self-help program that has helped millions of recovering alcoholics to achieve a life of sobriety. It was begun in 1935 by two recovering alcoholics who banded together to help each other. They were Bill Wilson, a stockbroker, and Dr. Bob Smith, a physician. By supporting each other as peers, they were able to remain sober. They decided to share this support with others. In this way AA was founded. They developed a series of steps to help the alcoholic recover.

AA is an organization that exists on a worldwide basis in most communities. Its simple, free approach has brought hope to millions of alcoholics and their families. AA has also developed a related organization for the families of alcoholics called Al-Anon. There is also a group available for adolescent children of alcoholics called Alateen.

Antabuse

Disulfiram or Antabuse therapy is considered a useful adjunct treatment for some types of alcoholics. It is a form of behavior therapy (see Chapter 29) that uses learning principles to cause the client to associate the thought of drinking with an unpleasant stimulus; in this way the client can be motivated to avoid drinking.

Disulfiram (Antabuse) is a drug that causes the metabolism of alcohol to be blocked. The result is a buildup of acetaldehyde, which is a toxic by-product of alcohol metabolism in the body. Acetaldehyde produces a variety of very unpleasant physical symptoms, such as flushing, sweating, palpitations, dyspnea, hyperventilation, tachycardia, hypotension, nausea, and vomiting.

The body's reaction to even a small amount of alcohol can be violent and, indeed, can be physiologically threatening to the body's homeostasis. Accordingly, this treatment should be used only with a compliant, motivated individual in order to avoid serious complications.

Inpatient Treatment Programs

Some people with alcoholism and other types of substance use disorders have need for more structure in their return to sobriety. A treatment program that has met with increasing success is an inpatient treatment approach in which a therapeutic environment (see Chapter 29, Milieu Therapy and Behavior Modification) is utilized. In many institutions alcohol and drug abuse clients are treated in the same setting. Following the detoxification period, there is intensive emphasis on individual, group, and family therapy. Counselors in the individual and group therapy sessions frequently are recovered substance abusers. Many of these programs include intensive education and behavior modification to teach new coping skills to these individuals who have previously turned to alcohol because of their inability to cope. The major emphasis of this teaching is on communication skills and stress management.

Nursing Care of Clients With Alcoholism

Nursing care planning includes prioritizing the areas of functioning that are most threatening to the client's physical or mental well-being. For example, during episodes of acute cognitive impairment disorder, such as intoxication, withdrawal, or withdrawal delirium, follow the guidelines presented under the nursing care of clients with delirium in Chapter 21, Delirium, Dementia, and Other Cognitive Disorders.

Treatment with the benzodiazepines (minor tranquilizers) or barbiturates is effective in managing the life-threatening and distressing effects of alcohol withdrawal during detoxification. If the drug is administered and its effects are monitored and titrated (balanced) carefully, the nurse can maintain the client in a calm and wakeful state. The sedative usually needs to be administered over a 24- to 48-hour period and is reduced to smaller doses over 2 to 3 days until it is discontinued.

Maintain adequate fluid and nutritional needs. The client, because of nutritional deprivation, usually has inadequate electrolyte and vitamin levels.

Once the acute detoxification stage is over, the client's long-term needs should be more actively addressed in the nursing care plan. Alcoholic people are at risk for many types of dysfunction. Evaluate the potential risks in the following list in assessing your client and planning your nursing intervention. Base your plans, including counseling and preventive teaching, on positive findings in any of the areas described below.

■■■■■■■■■

Physical State

Increased susceptibility to infection
Altered nutritional status
Interference with sleep activity
Interference with sexual activity
Impairment of vital organs
Diminished energy
Increased risk of accident and injury
Substantial reduction in life span
Insufficient exercise

Psychosocial State

Low self-concept
Feelings of alienation, guilt, depression, anger
Increased risk of suicide
Increased consumption of other drugs that interact with alcohol
Interferences with interpersonal relationships, including family,
    friends, co-workers
Lack of creative diversion such as hobbies, recreational activities
Thwarted personal growth, learning, and maturity
Delayed development of potential
Lack of philosophical or spiritual pursuits

■■■■■■■■■ *continued*

Economic State

Possible loss of job or demotion
Indebtedness

Legal Entanglements

Increased incidence of arrest for driving while intoxicated (DWI)
or for assaults, including child abuse, spouse battering, and
tavern fights
Increased likelihood of divorce, and difficulties surrounding cus-
tody of children

Factors Associated with the Diagnosis of Alcoholism

Social stigma with regard to alcoholism
Lack of acceptance of the diagnosis by all involved

Adapted from Estes, N., Smith-DiJulio K., Heinemann, M. (1980). *Nursing diagnosis of the alcoholic person.* St. Louis, MO: C.V. Mosby, pp 2, 3.

■ Amphetamine Abuse

The drugs included in this category of drug disorder are amphetamines, dextroamphetamine sulfate (Dexedrine), methamphetamine
(speed), and others that have amphetamine-like action, such as
methylphenidate or other substances used as appetite suppressants
(diet pills). The abuse and dependence subcategories include the
symptoms listed earlier in this chapter. In addition, there is a frequent
drug use pattern of taking the drug for 10 to 14 days at a time.

Amphetamines are frequently used to treat obesity; they are used
by students to stay alert and study, by truck drivers to stay awake,
and by soldiers to decrease fatigue and increase aggression. Evidence
today suggests that amphetamines *are* addicting, tolerance *does* develop to their use, they produce both dependency and withdrawal
states, and they are clearly among the most dangerous drugs pres-
ently available. In the most mentally stable person amphetamines are
able to produce a toxic psychosis that is clinically indistinguishable
from paranoid schizophrenia. Death from overdosage is usually associated with hyperpyrexia, convulsions, and cardiovascular shock.
The intravenous use of these drugs since the 1960s has resulted fairly
often in cases of severe serum hepatitis, lung abscess, and endocardi-
tis. In 1970, necrotizing angiitis was first reported as a result of intra-

venous amphetamine abuse. Necrotizing angiitis is the destruction of the lining of blood vessels due to a toxic substance.

In most cases, amphetamine psychosis clears in a matter of days or weeks following withdrawal of the drug, differentiating it from paranoid schizophrenia. Antipsychotic agents (phenothiazines or haloperidol) often help. The withdrawal depression, which may reach suicidal proportions, may be treated with tricyclic antidepressants.

■ Cannabis Abuse

The substances included in this category are marijuana, hashish, and occasionally, purified delta-9-tetrahydrocannabinol (THC). Marijuana is the most commonly used substance in this category. It has been a subject of controversy since 500 BC in China. During the 19th century cannabis was widely prescribed for a variety of ailments and discomforts (coughing, fatigue, migraine, asthma, delirium tremens, etc.). It remained in the U.S. *Pharmacopoeia* until 1941.

Its ability to cause euphoria has been of principal interest throughout history. The effects from smoking marijuana last 2 to 4 hours, and from ingestion of the drug, 5 to 12 hours. Marijuana also has a tendency to produce sedation. There is no substantial evidence in the world literature, however, that cannabis induces either mental or physical deterioration, at least not in well-integrated, stable people.

Adverse reactions to cannabis appear to be dose related and depend on the setting in which the drug is used. Although rare, anxiety states, with or without paranoid thinking, panic states, and toxic psychosis have been reported.

An amotivational syndrome has been discussed in association with cannabis use, but careful studies fail to prove that this syndrome does, in fact, follow the use of the drug. It may be a sociocultural phenomenon that happens to coincide with the regular use of marijuana.

■ Cocaine Abuse

The cocaine abuse category includes the general symptoms of drug abuse listed earlier in the chapter. In addition, during periods of intoxication, there are delusions and hallucinations with an otherwise clear sensorium.

Cocaine is an alkaloid derived from the leaf of the plant *Erythoxylon coca*, a shrub indigenous to Bolivia and Peru. Its leaves have been chewed by natives of these countries for many years, producing central nervous system stimulation. The "high" is similar to that achieved by amphetamines (i.e., euphoria, exhilaration, and a powerful sense of well-being and confidence).

Cocaine abuse is a problem of almost epidemic proportions in our society today. The pattern of cocaine use has altered from snorting the cocaine intranasally to intravenous injection or smoking. There has also been a change in the form of cocaine to "freebase." Freebase is available in a product called "crack." Crack is an inexpensive, very potent, and readily available substance. It has significantly increased the number of cocaine abusers. Cocaine intoxication is marked by excitement, euphoria, restlessness, stereotyped movement, and gnashing, grinding, or clenching the teeth.

Tolerance develops, as does physical dependency. Acute toxic effects may be treated with a short-acting barbiturate administered intravenously. A toxic psychosis with visual, auditory, and tactile hallucinations and a paranoid delusional system may develop as with amphetamines. When psychosis develops, it is classified as a cocaine psychiatric disorder.

■ Hallucinogen Abuse

This subcategory includes abuse of substances structurally related to 5-hydroxytryptamine. These are lysergic acid diethylamine (LSD), dimethyltryptamine (DMT), and substances related to catecholamines (for example, mescaline). The abuse symptoms are those described earlier. In addition, episodes of hallucinogen affective disorder can occur at unpredictable times for years following termination of the drug.

■ Nicotine Abuse

Tobacco use continues in this country despite widespread knowledge that it is an important factor in the development of cardiovascular disease, cancer, and severe forms of lung disease. In severe cases of tobacco dependence, several signs of tobacco withdrawal symptoms include the following:

Craving for tobacco	Gastrointestinal disturbance
Anxiety	Drowsiness
Irritability	Headache
Restlessness	

■ Opioid Abuse

The client with an opioid use disorder experiences the same symptoms as described for barbiturates. Taken in normal, medically supervised doses, the barbiturates and opioids mildly depress the action of the nerves, skeletal muscles, and the heart muscle. They slow down heart rate and breathing and lower blood pressure. In higher doses, however, the effects resemble alcoholic drunkenness, with confusion, slurred speech, and staggering. The ability to think, to concentrate, and to work is difficult, and emotional control is weakened. Users may become irritable and angry and want to fight someone. Sometimes, they fall into a deep sleep from which it is difficult to arouse them. In addition, in the abuse category clients experience episodes of intoxication that involve impairments of respiration and consciousness. The opioid drugs include heroin, morphine, and synthetics with morphine-like action, such as meperidine (Demerol) and methadone.

References to opium smoking can be found so far back in Oriental history that we do not know the date of its first use as a producer of pleasant dreams. It is still smoked in some areas in Asiatic countries, but in Western countries, the alkaloids of opium are preferred. Morphine is one of the main alkaloids of opium, and heroin is a derivative of morphine. **Heroin** is the narcotic most widely used by addicts today. Because of its strong addictive power, it has been outlawed in the United States and cannot be made, imported, or sold legally.

When a person becomes dependent on heroin his or her body craves repeated and larger doses of the drug. Once the habit starts, larger and larger doses are required to get the same effects. This happens because the body develops a tolerance for the drug.

One of the signs of heroin addiction is **withdrawal sickness.** When the user stops the drug, he or she sweats, shakes, gets chills and diarrhea, vomits, and suffers sharp stomach pain. In addition to physical dependence on narcotics, there is also a strong psychological dependence.

Typically, the first emotional reaction to heroin is an erasing of fears and a relief from worry. This is usually followed by a state of inactivity bordering on stupor. Heroin, which is a fine white powder, is usually mixed into a liquid solution and injected into a vein. It tends to dull the edges of reality. Addicts report that heroin "makes troubles roll off the mind," and makes them feel more sure of themselves. This drug also reduces feelings of pain.

The drug depresses certain areas of the brain and reduces hunger, thirst, and the sex drive. Because addicts do not usually feel hungry, they must usually be treated for malnutrition when hospitalized.

■ Phencyclidine (PCP) Abuse

Drugs included in this category are ketamine (Ketalar) and the thiopene analogue of phencylidine (TCP). This subcategory includes the general symptoms of abuse referred to earlier. In addition, in the abuse subcategory the person experiences delirium associated with the drug or a mixed cognitive impairment disorder.

■ Sedative-Hypnotic Abuse

The drugs that are most commonly abused in this category are the anxiolytic drugs, including chlordiazepoxide (Librium), diazepam (Valium), and oxazepam (Serax). The sedatives that are regularly abused are pentobarbital sodium (Nembutal), secobarbital (Seconal), phenobarbital (Luminal), and amobarbital (Amytal). Commonly abused hypnotics are ethchlorvynol (Placidyl), flurazepam (Dalmane), glutethimide (Doriden), methyprylon (Noludar), chloral hydrate, paraldehyde, and methaqualone.

Barbiturates

The sedative category includes **barbiturates,** which belong to a large family of drugs manufactured for the purpose of relaxing (depressing) the central nervous system. They are synthetic drugs made from barbituric acid (a coal-tar product). Doctors prescribe these drugs widely to treat insomnia, high blood pressure, and epilepsy. They are occasionally used in the treatment of mental illness and to sedate clients before and during surgery. They are often used in combination with other drugs to treat many other types of illness and medical conditions. The symptoms of barbiturates have been discussed in the section on opioid abuse.

Often barbiturates are obtained illegally. Because doctors prescribe these drugs so frequently, many people consider them safe to use freely. They are not safe drugs. Overdoses can cause death. They are a leading cause of accidental poisoning deaths in the United States. These drugs distort the way that people see things and slow down their reactions and responses. They are an important cause of automobile accidents. When taken with alcohol, they tend to potentiate (enhance) the effects of the alcohol.

Because they are so easily obtained and produce sleep readily, barbiturates are frequently used in suicide attempts. Barbiturates range from the short-acting but fast-starting pentobarbital sodium

(Nembutal) and secobarbital (Seconal) to the long-acting but slow-starting phenobarbital (Luminal), amobarbital (Amytal), and butabarbital (Butisol). The short-acting preparations are the ones most commonly abused. In the doses ordinarily taken by the drug abuser, barbiturates produce mood shifts, restlessness, euphoria, excitement, and in some individuals, hallucinations. The users become confused and may be unable to walk or perform tasks requiring muscular activity.

The barbiturates are physically addictive. The body needs increasingly higher doses to feel the effects. True addiction, however, requires taking large doses of the drug for more than a few weeks.

Sudden withdrawal of barbiturates from someone dependent on them is extremely dangerous because it may result in death. A physician will hospitalize the addict and withdraw the drug slowly in order to alleviate the cramps, nausea, delirium, and convulsions that attend withdrawal. Some experts consider barbiturate addiction more difficult to cure than a narcotic dependency. It takes several months for a barbiturate user's body chemistry to return to normal.

Methaqualone

A nonbarbiturate sedative-hypnotic, methaqualone (Quaalude), was first introduced in the United States in 1966. Marketed as having little potential for abuse and no effect on dream-stage sleep, it rapidly became used as a recreation chemical. It was found, however, to suppress REM sleep (rapid-eye-movement associated with dreaming). Tolerance to the drug may develop. It is capable of producing both considerable psychological and physical dependence.

A withdrawal syndrome has been observed in people using over 600 mg per day for prolonged periods of time. The withdrawal syndrome begins within 24 hours of cessation of use of the drug, persists for 2 to 3 days, and consists of insomnia, headache, abdominal cramps, anorexia, nausea, irritability, and anxiety. Hallucinations and nightmares have also been reported.

The symptoms of the abuse and dependence subcategories are listed earlier in the chapter. The person with this disorder uses the equivalent of 600 mg or more of secobarbital (Seconal) or 60 mg or more of diazepam and experiences amnestic periods during intoxification. The person in the dependence category experiences an increasing need or withdrawal symptoms of cognitive impairment disorder occur.

The nursing care of this client and clients with the other substance use disorders in this chapter is essentially the same as for the alcoholic client described earlier. The side effects of drug withdrawal that are most threatening to health and require the greatest vigilance occur during the detoxification period. The cognitive impairment disorders and the nursing care required during withdrawal and detoxification are described in Chapter 21.

Benzodiazepines

Chlordiazepoxide (Librium) and diazepam (Valium) are widely used as minor tranquilizers for the control of anxiety. They produce less euphoria than the preceding two hypnotics, but a withdrawal syndrome may occur when large doses (several hundred milligrams per day) are abruptly stopped. Convulsions may be delayed by several weeks and are managed as with meprobamate withdrawal described below.

Meprobamate

Introduced as an antianxiety drug in 1954, meprobamate's therapeutic usefulness is in considerable doubt, but it is still widely prescribed and popular. Tolerance develops, and withdrawal symptoms can occur. Abrupt withdrawal causes tremors, ataxia, headache, insomnia, and gastrointestinal disturbances lasting for several days. Occasionally, convulsions occur (usually upon withdrawal from 3 g or more daily). A delirium tremens-like state may occur in 36 to 48 hours. Diphenylhydantoin sodium (phenytoin) IV is useful in controlling convulsions.

CHAPTER 22 QUESTIONS

1. How does substance dependence differ from substance abuse?

2. Once detoxification is complete, what are three major treatment options most frequently presented to recovering alcoholics?

3. What type of drug use is able to produce a toxic psychosis that is clinically indistinguishable from paranoid schizophrenia?

4. Name four signs of tobacco withdrawal symptoms in severe cases of tobacco dependence.

BIBLIOGRAPHY

American Psychiatric Association. (1991). *DSM-IV options book.* Washington, DC: American Psychiatric Press.

American Psychiatric Association. (1987). *Diagnostic and statistical manual of mental disorders* (3rd ed., rev.). Washington, DC: American Psychiatric Press.

Estes, N., Smith DiJulio, K., & Heinemann, M. (1980). *Nursing diagnosis of the alcoholic person.* St. Louis, MO: Mosby.

Kaplan, H., & Sadock, B. (1991). *Synopsis of psychiatry: Behavioral sciences, clinical psychiatry* (6th ed.). Baltimore: Williams & Wilkins.

McFarland, G.K., Thomas, M.D. (1991). *Psychiatric mental health nursing: Application of the nursing process.* Philadelphia: J.B. Lippincott.

Stuart, G.W., & Sundeen, S.J. (Eds.). (1991). *Principles and practice of psychiatric nursing* (4th ed.). St. Louis, MO: Mosby–Year Book.

Wilson, H.S., & Kneisl, C.R. (1992). *Psychiatric nursing* (4th ed.). Redwood City, CA: Addison-Wesley.

Chapter 23

■■■■■

Schizophrenia and Other Psychotic Disorders

Behavioral Objectives

After reading this chapter the student will be able to:

List five major criteria necessary for a diagnosis of schizophrenia and describe them.

Name the five types of schizophrenia and explain the main characteristic of each.

Define the terms **hallucination, delusion,** and **loosening of associations.**

Describe the possible causes of schizophrenia using the psychoanalytic theory and the physiological theory.

The functional group of psychoses, of which schizophrenia is the most prevalent, is divided into five types: schizophrenia, major mood disorders, paranoid states, other nonorganic psychoses (primarily psychotic depressive reaction), and psychoses with origin specific to childhood (see Chapter 20, Disorders Usually First Diagnosed in Infancy, Childhood, or Adolescence). The term **dysfunctional mental states** describes the specific mental states that occur in each of these conditions.

Mental Health and Mental Illness,
Fifth Edition, by Patricia D. Barry.
J.B. Lippincott Company, Philadelphia © 1994.

A person's basic type of personality will be the predisposing factor as to which form of psychosis he or she will develop. It occasionally happens that a person with recurrent psychosis *may* show a different form than the one he or she evidenced earlier. As a rule, however, if psychosis occurs several times in the life of a person, it tends to follow the same behavioral pattern each time.

■ Schizophrenic Disorders

The behavioral patterns of **schizophrenic** clients are characterized by much disorganization and discord of the personality. Schizophrenia comes from two Greek words—one meaning *to split,* and the other, *mind.* Schizophrenia includes a large group of disorders characterized by disturbances of thinking, mood, and behavior. Disturbances of thinking are shown by changes in concept formation that often lead to misinterpretation of reality and, on occasion, to delusions and hallucinations. These delusions and hallucinations often appear to be psychologically self-protective.

Accompanying mood changes may include ambivalent, constricted, and inappropriate emotional responsiveness and loss of empathy with others. Behavior may be withdrawn, regressive, and bizarre. In the schizophrenias, the mental status is primarily due to a thought disorder. These states must be distinguished from the major affective disorders, which are disorders of mood. In paranoid states psychotic symptoms, other than a narrow but deep distortion of reality, are absent.

Theories of Causes of Schizophrenia

Today's researchers are probing into body and brain chemistry to see if there is, perhaps, some chemical substance affecting the nervous tissues of these disorganized people. The biochemical substances released in the brain are known as neurotransmitters. The purpose of the neurotransmitters is, as their name implies, to transmit or send messages within the brain or between the brain and various parts of the body. There are many known neurotransmitter substances in the brain, and perhaps others that have not yet been identified by neurobiologists. The neurotransmitter that is most frequently mentioned as a possible factor in the development of schizophrenia is dopamine. Research has demonstrated that there is a possible association between the behavioral symptoms of schizophrenia and the presence of elevated levels of dopamine in schizophrenic clients.

One of the factors that contributed to the research into the relationship between neurotransmitters and schizophrenia was the recognition that the mental status that resulted from the use of lysergic acid diethylamine (LSD) was similar in many ways to the mental status changes experienced by people with schizophrenic illness.

Should research bear out the theory that perhaps the schizophrenic has a chemical or physiological basis for his or her psychosis, we shall have to classify this large group of psychoses as organic rather than functional. Or perhaps it will be found that the schizophrenic has both a physiological and a psychological cause for his or her psychotic state.

According to psychoanalytic theory, the schizophrenic person appears to have a childhood deprived of meaningful relationships with the important people in his or her family circle. An outstanding fact is that most of these people have felt that as children they were unloved, unwanted, and unimportant to their families. This lack of good, firm interpersonal relationships at an early age results in immature adult personalities that find it difficult to adjust socially or to relate intimately with other people.

Symptoms of Schizophrenia

Thought disorder is evidenced by behavior or spoken thoughts that are disorderly, unrealistic, and often irrational. **Autism** is common.* People with thought disorders disregard external reality to a large extent. When expressing thought in words, the schizophrenic shows a loss of orderly progression of thought by using unconnected words. This is termed **fragmentation,** or **word salad.** He or she may also coin new words that have no meaning to the listener. We call these new words **neologisms.** His or her speech lacks unity, clearness, and coherence, reflecting the confusion of his or her mind.

The schizophrenic is often given to eccentric, unexplained, and sudden activities. Undirected restlessness, fitful behavior, and impulsive, apparently unpremeditated acts are frequent. To sum up his or her behavior, it is **autistic** (i.e., actions, thoughts, feelings, ideas, and experiences are inappropriate, distorted, and not easily understood by other people). He or she may laugh or show pleasure as the result of a painful experience, or may weep when the occasion would call for laughter (inappropriate emotional responses).

---

* Autism is a mental state in which a person seems unaware of external reality.

A **lack of affect,** or emotional **blunting,** is coldness of emotional response to others. The client fails to relate to others in a meaningful way. He or she is emotionally shallow, and whatever emotion he or she does evidence is often inappropriate.

Withdrawal is a progressive shutting out of the world. There is reduction in interest, initiative, and spontaneity. Many clients seem to have withdrawn behind barriers, which if they could be penetrated, would reveal loneliness, hopelessness, hatred, and fear. The client may defend himself or herself by building a shell of indifference around himself or herself. The withdrawal may vary from a mild degree of isolation to one so profound that the client seems to be completely unaware of his or her surroundings. However, these severely withdrawn people, in spite of appearances, are sometimes acutely aware of all that goes on in the environment.

Regression varies in degree from slight to profound. There is a tendency for the schizophrenic client to retreat to a more primitive and infantile level of thinking and behaving.

A **delusion** is a fixed, false belief based on a misinterpretation of fact. Since the ideas, or mental content, of the schizophrenic are so often delusional, and since the needs of the client are so often disguised by symbolism, his or her thought content often appears complicated and difficult to understand. His or her delusions tend to center around themes of persecution, grandiosity, sex, and religion. He or she dramatizes problems, strivings, and conflicts in fantastic delusional beliefs.

Another common symptom of schizophrenia is **hallucinations.** Hallucinations are sensory perceptions that have no basis in fact. They come, instead, from troublesome material from the client's inner life. They are very real to him or her. Sometimes they are terrifying, sometimes accusing, sometimes pleasurable.

Diagnostic Criteria of Schizophrenia

When unresolved anxiety mounts too high, the schizophrenic person tends to meet problems by turning away from the real world and withdrawing into a dream world of his or her own that is produced through fantasy, projection, delusions, and hallucinations. In other words, he or she becomes psychotic.

Although there are five major subdivisions of schizophrenia, each with distinguishing characteristics, there are several overall characteristics possessed by all subgroups.

■■■■■■■■■

Schizophrenia*

A. Presence of characteristic psychotic symptoms in the active phase: either (1), (2), or (3) for at least 1 week (unless the symptoms are successfully treated):
1. two of the following:
   a. delusions
   b. prominent hallucinations (throughout the day for several days or several times a week for several weeks, each hallucinatory experience not being limited to a few brief moments)
   c. incoherence or marked loosening of associations
   d. catatonic behavior
   e. flat or grossly inappropriate affect
2. bizarre delusions (i.e., involving a phenomenon that the person's culture would regard as totally implausible, e.g., thought broadcasting, being controlled by a dead person)
3. prominent hallucinations (as defined in [1b] above) of a voice with content having no apparent relation to depression or elation, or a voice keeping up a running commentary on the person's behavior or thoughts, or two or more voices conversing with each other
B. During the course of the disturbance, functioning in such areas as work, social relations, and self-care is markedly below the highest level achieved before onset of the disturbance (or, when the onset is in childhood or adolescence, failure to achieve expected level of social development).
C. Schizoaffective Disorder and Mood Disorder with Psychotic Features have been ruled out, i.e., if a Major Depressive or Manic Syndrome has ever been present during an active phase of the disturbance, or the total duration of all episodes of a mood syndrome has been brief relative to the total duration of the active and residual phases of the disturbance.
D. Continuous signs of the disturbance for at least 6 months. The 6-month period must include an active phase (of at least 1 week, or less if symptoms have been successfully treated) during which there were psychotic symptoms characteristic of Schizophrenia (symptoms in A), with or without a prodromal or residual phase, as defined below.

* Desk Reference to the Diagnostic Criteria of the DSM-III-R (1987). pp. 113–116.

■■■■■■■■■ *continued*

Prodromal phase: A clear deterioration in functioning before the active phase of the disturbance that is not due to a disturbance in mood or to a Psychoactive Substance Use Disorder and that involves at least two of the symptoms listed below.

Residual phase: Following the active phase of the disturbance, persistence of at least two of the symptoms noted below, these not being due to a disturbance in mood or to a Psychoactive Substance Use Disorder.

Prodromal or Residual Symptoms:

1. marked social isolation or withdrawal
2. marked impairment in role functioning as wage-earner, student, or homemaker.
3. markedly peculiar behavior (e.g., collecting garbage, talking to self in public, hoarding food)
4. marked impairment in personal hygiene and grooming
5. blunted or inappropriate affect
6. digressive, vague, overelaborate, or circumstantial speech, or poverty of content of speech
7. odd beliefs or magical thinking, influencing behavior and inconsistent with cultural norms, e.g., superstitiousness, belief in clairvoyance, telepathy, "sixth sense," "others can feel my feelings," overvalued ideas, ideas of reference
8. unusual perceptual experiences, e.g., recurrent illusions, sensing the presence of a force or person not actually present
9. marked lack of initiative, interests, or energy. . . .

E. It cannot be established that an organic factor initiated and maintained the disturbance
F. If there is a history of Autistic Disorder, the additional diagnosis of Schizophrenia is made only if prominent delusions or hallucinations are also present.

Classification of Course. The Course of the Disturbance is Coded in the Fifth Digit:

1. Subchronic. The time from the beginning of the disturbance, when the person first began to show signs of the disturbance (including prodromal, active, and residual phases) more or less continuously, is less than 2 years, but at least 6 months.
2. Chronic. Same as above, but more than 2 years.
3. Subchronic with Acute Exacerbation. Re-emergence of prominent psychotic symptoms in a person with a subchronic course who has been in the residual phase of the disturbance.
4. Chronic with Acute Exacerbation. Reemergence of prominent psychotic symptoms in a person with a chronic course who has been in the residual phase of the disturbance.

■ ■ ■ ■ ■ ■ ■ ■ ■ *continued*

5. In Remission. When a person with a history of Schizophrenia is free of all signs of the disturbance (whether or not on medication), "in Remission" should be coded. Differentiating Schizophrenia in Remission from No Mental Disorder requires consideration of overall level of functioning, length of time since the last episode of disturbance, total duration of the disturbance, and whether prophylactic treatment is being given.
0. Unspecified.

Major Categories of Schizophrenia

The major types of schizophrenia are:

Catatonic   Undifferentiated
Disorganized   Residual
Paranoid

Catatonic Type

The **catatonic type** appears primarily in two major forms. One form is characterized by apparent stupor, immobility, mutism, and negativism; the other phase is characterized by unorganized, excessive, impulsive, and sometimes destructive behavior. The diagnosis can be made if any of the symptoms described below are present.

In **catatonic stupor,** or withdrawal, the client shows no interest in his or her environment. The client's facial expression is vacant, he or she stares into space, his or her head is usually bowed, and he or she may lie, sit, or stand very still for long periods of time. The client often must be tube fed and given complete physical care when in this state. While apparently unheeding and insensible, the client's consciousness is actually very clear, and after recovery he or she will often relate minute details of what went on about him or her. He or she lives in an unreal world and seems oblivious to external environment. Occasionally, he or she may be seen whispering and smiling slightly to himself or herself; at other times, he or she may use odd mannerisms and strange positioning of head and extremities.

If someone raises his or her arm into an upright position, he or she will maintain this position an amazingly long time. The term **waxy flexibility** is used to describe this phenomenon. Two other peculiar mannerisms are occasionally seen: **echolalia,** in which the client repeats all words or phrases directed toward him or her but offers no conversation of his or her own, and **echopraxia,** in which the client mimics all actions of the person who is addressing him or her, but makes no answer at all.

Catatonic negativism is marked by resistance to instructions of others or to purposeful action. **Catatonic rigidity** is the holding of a particular posture for long periods of time and resistance to being moved.

In **catatonic excitement,** the client's behavior is characterized by impulsive and stereotyped activities, poorly coordinated, and often lacking apparent purpose. Hostility and feelings of resentment are common; unprovoked outbursts of violence and destructiveness may occur; hallucinations are frequent. The flow of speech may vary from mutism to a rapid speech, also known as pressured speech, suggesting flight of ideas. Some excitements are in the form of short panic reactions.

The characteristic symptoms of catatonia are withdrawal, regression, repetitive stereotyped actions, odd mannerisms, strange positioning of parts of the body, waxy flexibility, mutism, and hallucinations.

Disorganized Type
The **disorganized type,** formerly known as the **hebephrenic type,** has an insidious onset that usually begins in adolescence. The client's emotions become shallow and inappropriate. He or she withdraws from social contacts, appears preoccupied, smiles and giggles frequently in a silly manner, and his or her speech becomes badly fragmented, often to the point of incoherence. Bizarre delusions and hallucinations, often of a pleasant type, if present, are transient and not well-organized. Hypochondriacal complaints are frequent. There is more disorganization of personality and habits in the disorganized type than in any of the other types of schizophrenia, but it is rarely seen today because of early intervention, the use of the powerful phenothiazine drugs, and the end of the era of long-term institutionalization of clients.

Paranoid Type
The **paranoid schizophrenic** adds suspiciousness, projection, and delusions of persecution to his or her other basic schizophrenic traits. Delusions occupy a prominent place in his or her mental concepts, and hallucinations are tied in with these delusions.

Voices command him or her from the air or out of the walls; he or she may refuse medications or food for fear of being poisoned. He or she is usually highly verbal and will tell you about the detectives who are following him or her everywhere, or about unseen instruments that are reading his or her mind. At times, he or she may become quite aggressive and even combative. His or her utterances may become disconnected and fragmentary.

The paranoid schizophrenic does not demonstrate the following traits normally associated with other forms of schizophrenia: incoherence, marked loosening of associations, catatonic behavior, grossly disorganized behavior, or flat or very inappropriate affect.

Undifferentiated and Residual Types
Schizophrenia, undifferentiated type refers to less severe psychotic symptoms that cannot be classified in the types described above or to symptoms that meet the criteria for more than one of the other schizophrenia categories.

Schizophrenia, residual type is a classification used when the client has had at least one episode of schizophrenia but does not display acute psychotic symptoms. Other symptoms of schizophrenia are present, however. They include the following:

Eccentric behavior	Social withdrawal
Emotional blunting or blunted affect	Disordered thinking
	Loosening of associations

Loosening of associations is a type of thinking in which the normal connectedness between ideas or thoughts seems haphazard. The thinking process does not flow in a normal pattern.

Nursing Care of Clients With Schizophrenic Disorders

The schizophrenic client admitted to a psychiatric institution is out of control. His or her thoughts and feelings are bizarre. He or she may be terrified or overwhelmed with grief or rage, or may seem to be falling apart psychologically (also known as **disintegrating**). **Disintegration** is the disruption of the normal influence of the ego on combining our thoughts, feelings, memories, and perceptions into a realistic view of ourselves and our environment. When the ego loses its ability to maintain these psychological functions in balance, the client feels as though he or she really is falling apart.

To a nurse observing a client who is experiencing an acute schizophrenic episode, it appears that he or she has indeed lost his or her ability to function psychologically. For nurses new to the psychiatric setting, this can be a frightening experience. Seeing a fellow human in his or her rawest emotional state touches our own vulnerability as human beings. Our own safety can be threatened. In addition, we may wonder whether this could ever happen to us. As a result, we can be flooded with anxiety as we imagine the terror of losing control.

You may have a family member or friend who has experienced a psychotic disorder. Memories associated with their psychotic episodes may also create fear, anxiety, or sadness in you. It is important to realize that these feelings are common in all people new to the psychiatric unit, regardless of their care-giving discipline: nursing, medicine, social work, and so on. As you learn more about the nature of the illness, its treatment, and prognosis, and discuss your feelings with peers, supervisors, or instructors, these feelings can gradually diminish.

Assessment

A basic rule governs those who work with psychiatric clients: a consistent nurse should be assigned to the care of each client. This is essential, especially for the psychotic client whose level of functioning is, in some way, severely regressed. As a young child benefits from the security of a consistent care-giver and is disturbed by frequent changes in care-givers, so, too, is the client with a psychotic disorder.

The assessment of the newly admitted, schizophrenic client is a slow process that requires obtaining information from many people, including the client. Despite the psychotic episodes he or she is experiencing, he or she may have periods when he or she can give reliable information. The family or friends of the client are important because they can often give facts that validate the client's statements or fill in the many gaps of knowledge that are important in understanding the client's current illness. It is also possible to discern maladaptive family relationship patterns that may have contributed to the person's current disorder. In addition, if these dynamics are not addressed in the treatment setting, they can undermine his or her ability to function independently once he or she is discharged from the hospital.

When talking with the client early in his or her admission, always remember his or her need for safety. Accordingly, maintain a non-threatening, calm communication style, observing for signs of increasing anxiety and agitation. Rather than continuing an interview with an increasingly anxious psychotic client, tell him or her gently you will return later. The types of questions you can ask appear in Chapter 7, Building a Therapeutic Nurse-Client Relationship. They should be modified to accommodate the client's level of functioning.

The assessment of the psychotic client will include the data obtained by members of other disciplines on the treatment team. Depending on the particular treatment philosophy of the institution in which you are working, this information may be pooled and used in a unified team approach to provide a positive therapeutic care plan. The nursing diagnoses that are determined in reviewing the data will form the basis of the planning step. Essentially, the symptoms or problems the client demonstrates should ultimately diminish during the treatment process.

Planning

The planning step of the nursing process should be integrated with the overall plan of the multidisciplinary treatment team as developed by the client's primary therapist. The recommendations in Chapter 19, Nursing Care Planning with Specific Types of Disordered Mental States, should be used in developing the care plan according to the nursing process model. The discussion on the nursing care of the psychotic client will be limited to specific recommendations for interventions with this type of client. It is important to remember that the treatment process of the psychotic client may be lengthy. Accordingly, planning should include both short-term and long-term goals. In this way the client and care-givers will have realistic, achievable goals to minimize discouragement if progress is slow.

Implementation

First, be concerned with the client's safety and physical well-being. The psychotic client who experiences loss of contact with reality is at particular risk of self-harm and the harm of others. The assessment process should include this major consideration. Intervention includes active steps to ensure the safety of the client and all others with whom he or she comes in contact. This includes careful monitoring of the environment by the nurse. It may be necessary for the high-risk client to be secluded until medication reduces the level of risk. Limits and controls that you carry out in a therapeutic and supportive manner promote the client's sense of control and security. These should be outlined carefully in the nursing care plan so that they are carried out in a consistent manner by other nurses in your absence.

The psychotic client is often unable to care for himself or herself. Nursing intervention includes ensuring that bathing, dressing, eating, and toileting are adequately maintained. If you need to encourage the client to care for himself or herself or you must provide assistance in self-care, make sure your attitude and actions will preserve the client's self-esteem and dignity.

Know how to intervene therapeutically when the client is experiencing hallucinations or delusions. These periods can be very frightening to the client. One aspect of his or her ego is aware that he or she has lost contact with reality, and he or she becomes highly anxious. When a nurse sits quietly, accepting and understanding the client's distress, the client's sense of trust can slowly develop. As the nurse gradually understands the cause of the client's emotional distress, he or she can respond to the client's statements about his or her perceptions, thoughts, or feelings in ways that can gently restore a stronger sense of reality.

Do not agree with nor in any way enter into the client's misperceptions. Rather, repeat the client's statements so that he or she knows he or she is being heard, and then gently tell him or her that you do not hear the same voices or feel the same things that he or she is describing. Reality-based discussions by the client can be validated, and the nurse can encourage reality orientation by the nature of questioning used in discussion with the client.

It is especially important with the families of schizophrenic clients to use a family therapy approach. Nurses can sometimes actively participate in this process. Attend treatment team meetings in which the family patterns are discussed so that, regardless of your level of involvement, you will understand the issues that the client has faced and will continue to face in his or her family. Your interventions should be supportive to the overall family system of which the client is an integral member.

Evaluation
Evaluation of the nursing intervention should be based on whether or not there is a decrease in the original symptoms observed in the assessment process. Evaluation of both short-term and long-term goals should be an ongoing process. When revision is indicated, the nursing process should be reinstituted.

■ Delusional (Paranoid) Disorders

The behavioral pattern in paranoia is characterized by a firm, fixed system of delusion in an otherwise well-balanced personality. This delusional system centers around feelings of persecution and grandiosity. The major areas of activity most frequently involved are those of religion, politics, or another person. The delusional system slowly develops after a false interpretation of an actual occurrence. There are no hallucinations. The client simply becomes convinced that a certain thing or situation is true, and he or she will accept no proof, regardless of how convincing it is, that he or she has a wrong concept of the thing or situation.

The types of delusional (paranoid) disorders are:

Erotomanic   Persecutory

Grandiose   Somatic

Jealous   Unspecified

In the **erotomanic** disorder the individual believes that someone, usually of higher status than he or she, is in love with him or her. In the **grandiose** type the person has an inflated sense of self-worth, power, identity, knowledge, or special relationship to a famous person or to God. In the **jealous** form the individual believes incorrectly that his or her sexual partner is unfaithful.

In the **persecutory** type, the person becomes increasingly suspicious of people and situations. He or she feels that people are spying on him or her with intentions of harming him or her. He or she develops ideas of reference in which he or she assumes anything other people are talking about concerns him or her. As his or her persecution complex enlarges, so does his or her opinion of himself or herself; he or she becomes grandiose. This self-importance is reflected in statements such as "a foreign government is after me," or "an international ring is pursuing me."

In the **somatic** type the individual believes he or she has some physical disease, disorder, or defect. The **unspecified** type does not fit any of the previous categories, but does have a general delusion(s) that is not grounded in reality.

Nursing Care of Clients With Delusional (Paranoid) Disorders

The general nursing care principles of the client with schizophrenia should be employed with the delusional client. Depending on the level and type of delusion he or she can be a risk to himself or herself and to others. His or her delusions will continue until the effects of medication and hospitalization gradually diminish the level of psychosis. Until that time, you must frequently monitor the client and, if indicated, use physical and pharmacologic restraints to ensure his or her safety and that of others.

When institutionalized, suspiciousness often involves food and medications, and persuading him or her to eat or take medications often poses a real problem. The unusual aspect of a paranoid person is that he or she is well oriented to person, place, and time, and that outside of his or her special delusional system, he or she thinks, speaks, and acts rationally. Thus, he or she frequently is able to convince acquaintances that his or her "idea" is true and may be able to gather a group around him or her who become convinced that he or she is a great reformer, leader, or prophet, until finally the fallacy of his or her claims becomes clearly evident to them and they turn away in disillusionment.

The outstanding symptoms of paranoia are a well-developed delusional system involving feelings of persecution and grandiosity, strong projection, and suspiciousness; there are no hallucinations. These people may become dangerous. So great is their fear of being harmed by others that they may strike out first in self-defense. Therapy has not been especially effective in changing these delusional concepts. Phenothiazine medication and/or electroconvulsive therapy (ECT) may be helpful.

■ Other Psychotic Disorders

This category includes the following disorders:

Brief reactive psychosis
Schizophreniform disorder
Schizoaffective disorder
Induced psychotic disorder
Atypical psychosis

Brief reactive psychosis is a condition that can occur as the result of an acutely stressful episode before which the person functioned normally and had no other type of physical or mental disorder. The person experiences severe emotional distress and one or more of the following signs of psychosis: delusions, hallucinations, loose associations or incoherence, and severely catatonic or disorganized behavior. The symptoms disappear within 1 month, and the individual returns to his or her previous level of functioning.

Schizophreniform disorder meets some of the criteria of schizophrenia, however, the condition lasts less than 6 months, disallowing the schizophrenia diagnosis. There are 2 subclassifications of this type: the first is labelled **with good prognostic features.** These features include: no flat affect; good pre-illness social and work role functioning; onset of psychotic symptoms within 4 weeks of the first noted changes in normal behavior or functioning. The second subcategory is **without good prognostic features.** It includes the classic schizophrenia symptoms.

Schizoaffective disorder is a condition that manifests a mixture of symptoms of a major depressive disorder or the manic phase of bipolar disorder, as well as some of the symptoms that meet the criteria of schizophrenia. There is a history of delusions or hallucinations during the period of the disturbance, but no permanent mood symptoms. The disorder does not meet all the criteria for schizophrenia. It is unknown whether there is an underlying organic cause.

Induced psychotic disorder (shared paranoid disorder) is a condition in which a second person takes on a delusion similar to that of another who has a delusional (paranoid) disorder. The affected individual has no prior history of psychosis or schizophrenia.

Atypical psychosis is a category for those conditions that involve the symptoms of psychosis, but do not meet the full range of criteria of the other categories of functional psychotic mental disorders.

CHAPTER 23 QUESTIONS

1. What neurotransmitter is most frequently mentioned as a possible factor in the development of schizophrenia?

2. What are the five major types of schizophrenia?

3. What is a basic rule governing the care of psychiatric clients?

4. Describe the behavioral pattern in paranoia.

BIBLIOGRAPHY

American Psychiatric Association. (1991). *DSM-IV options book.* Washington, DC: American Psychiatric Press.

American Psychiatric Association. (1987). *Diagnostic and statistical manual of mental disorders* (3rd ed., rev.). Washington, DC: American Psychiatric Press.

Kaplan, H., & Sadock, B. (1991). *Synopsis of psychiatry: Behavioral sciences, clinical psychiatry* (6th ed.). Baltimore: Williams & Wilkins.

McFarland, G.K., Thomas, M.D. (1991). *Psychiatric mental health nursing: Application of the nursing process*. Philadelphia: J.B. Lippincott.

Stuart, G.W., & Sundeen, S.J. (Eds.). (1991). *Principles and practice of psychiatric nursing* (4th ed.). St. Louis, MO: Mosby–Year Book.

Wilson, H.S., & Kneisl, C.R. (1992). *Psychiatric nursing* (4th ed.) Redwood City, CA: Addison-Wesley.

Chapter 24

■■■■■

Mood Disorders

Behavioral Objectives

After reading this chapter the student will be able to:

List six major symptoms of the client with a major depressive disorder.

Tell the difference between the symptoms of a person with a bipolar and a person with a cyclo-thymic disorder.

Name the medication most commonly prescribed for people with a bipolar mental disorder.

Describe three of the common abnormal mental states of the person with a manic type of bipolar disorder.

Describe five symptoms of a person who is acutely suicidal.

The affective mental disorders include those mental conditions that cause a change in a person's mood (also known as affect) or emotional state for a prolonged period of time. The changed emotional state may be either depression or elation, or a combination occurring in alternative cycles. These conditions are not caused by another physical or mental disorder. It is important to note that a variety of physical illnesses or disorders and side effects of medication can result in

Mental Health and Mental Illness, Fifth Edition, by Patricia D. Barry. J.B. Lippincott Company, Philadelphia © 1994.

depressive symptoms. Such physiologically induced conditions are not included in this category; rather, they are classified under the cognitive impairment disorders category (see Chapter 21, Delirium, Dementia, and Other Cognitive Disorders).

The two major categories of disorder under this classification are **bipolar disorders** and **depressive disorders**. They include the following major categories:

I. Bipolar Disorders
   A. Bipolar disorder
   B. Cyclothymia
II. Depressive Disorders
   A. Major depression
   B. Dysthymia

■ Bipolar Disorder

The person with bipolar disorder demonstrates strong, exaggerated, and cyclic mood swings. All normal people are subject to a moderate degree of mood swing (*see* Figure 24-1). The form found in this type of mental illness is, however, a very exaggerated form lasting for weeks

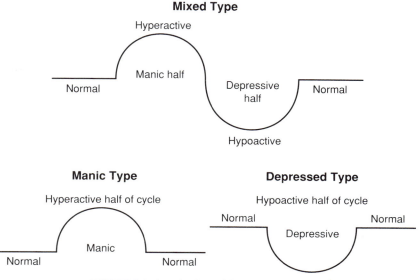

FIGURE 24-1. Cycles of bipolar disorder.

or months at a time. There is a slow but steady increase in mood elevation and hyperactivity up to a climax of frenzy, then a slow decrease in activity down to normal behavior again. Then, as a rule, the client will start into the opposite cycle of hypoactivity, accompanied by depression, only to swing slowly through this cycle and back to balance once more.

These episodes tend to recur several times within the client's lifetime. It is not unusual for a client to experience only one half of the cycle, i.e., only the hyperactive (manic) phase of behavior or recurrent episodes of hypoactive (depressive) behavior. Whether he or she shows the entire cycle or only half of it, he or she will, even without treatment, return to normal and may be normal for several years, then repeat the cycle (or half-cycle) again. Modern therapy helps speed up the rate of recovery greatly.

Manic Phase or Type

As the client enters a hyperactive, or manic, phase of the cycle, his or her physical appearance becomes increasingly disheveled as he or she speeds up physically, intellectually, and emotionally. The client becomes increasingly restless and aggressive. The id seems to take over, and the superego loses all control over the self. The client's thoughts speed up so that he or she becomes easily distractable. This gives rise to flight of ideas, as the client's mind darts from subject to subject, and accelerated speech flits from one idea to another. His or her mood becomes euphoric, then shifts into exaltation, and finally, at the peak of the half-cycle, into frenzy. The client in this state sleeps and eats very little, losing weight rapidly. He or she frequently smashes or breaks things unintentionally. If prevented from doing something he or she wishes to do, he or she may become angry.

Because the client is so easily distracted, however, he or she can usually be managed fairly well. As a matter of fact, he or she is usually happy-go-lucky, friendly, bossy, and highly verbal. He or she has delusions of grandeur and feels possessed of great charm, power, abilities, and wealth. If one or two of these hyperactive people are placed on a ward with a group of hypoactive clients, they actually have a stimulating effect on the latter by causing them to interact better. However, they also tend to offend other clients on the ward, since their language and actions are often coarse, lewd, and suggestive. With the gradual subsiding of their hyperactivity, moral values again settle into place, and behavior becomes more and more acceptable.

Depressed Phase or Type

The hypoactive phase, or half-cycle, which usually follows the manic phase, gradually slows the entire personality. Speech becomes slow, halting, and anxious as the superego takes over, and the client becomes increasingly self-accusative. He or she paces slowly, later sits on a chair, rocking his or her body back and forth and moaning dejectedly. Finally, he or she takes to bed or the floor, where he or she slowly and restlessly moves in a small, circumscribed area. He or she is very dejected, has a fixation about his or her worthlessness, the magnitude of his or her sins, and the need for punishment. The client is directing all aggression inward and eventually blames himself or herself for all the sins and crimes in the world. His or her misery is very great. Just before, or immediately after reaching the bottom of this cycle, the client may attempt suicide. (When the client's activity reaches its very lowest ebb, he or she is usually too inert to carry out such a desire.) The client must be watched carefully during this period of self-destructive desire. Slowly he or she will return to normal balance again, acquiring more and more interest in life and in its daily activities. It may be many years before another manic-depressive cycle occurs, but it does tend to occur. The symptoms in the depressed phase of bipolar disorder are the same as those of major depressive disorder (described later in this chapter).

■ Cyclothymic Disorder

A person with this personality type tends to swing between moods of exhilaration and depression, but not to pathologic extremes. However, it is this personality type that may develop manic-depressive psychosis in stressful life situations or, in some cases, for no apparent reason. (Changes in brain chemistry have been postulated.) Two subforms are often seen, in which the person shows one of the moods much more than the other. If the client shows exhilaration much of the time, he or she is classified as a hypomanic person. He or she is usually outgoing, cheerful, and thoroughly enjoys life. He or she is vivacious, buoyant, confident, aggressive, and optimistic. His or her energy level is high, and he or she is gregarious. He or she has few inhibitions. Sometimes he or she is too easily swayed by new impressions. He or she usually makes an excellent salesperson. A few of this type are blustering, argumentative, and hypercritical. They all seem to have ready excuses for their failures and can usually talk themselves out of their difficulties. When these people become psychotic, they tend to become manic.

If a client shows a depressed pattern, he or she is classified as a melancholic person. He or she is the cyclothymic personality at the opposite pole from the hypomanic. The client tends to be easily depressed, though he or she is often kindly, quiet, sympathetic, and even-tempered. He or she is seldom eccentric. In moody periods, the client is a lonely person, solemn, submissive, gloomy, and self-deprecating. He or she often has feelings of inadequacy and hopelessness; he or she becomes discouraged easily, suffers in silence, and weeps easily, though not in the presence of others. He or she tends to be overly meticulous, conscientious, and preoccupied with work. He or she is fearful of disapproval and feels responsibility keenly. It is hard for him or her to make up his or her mind, and indecision and caution indicate his or her feeling of insecurity. Under stress he or she tends to develop a psychotic depression of the manic-depressive type.

The following criteria have been developed by the American Psychiatric Association for the manic and depressed phases of bipolar disorder:

■■■■■■■■■

Manic Episode

Note: A **manic syndrome** is defined as including criteria A, B, and C below. A **hypomanic syndrome** is defined as including criteria A and B, but no C, that is, no marked impairment.

A. A distinct period of abnormally and persistently elevated, expansive, or irritable mood.
B. During the period of mood disturbance, at least three of the following symptoms have persisted (four if the mood is only irritable) and have been present to a significant degree:
   1. inflated self-esteem or grandiosity
   2. decreased need for sleep, e.g., feels rested after only 3 hours sleep
   3. more talkative than usual or pressure to keep talking
   4. flight of ideas or subjective experience that thoughts are racing
   5. distractibility, i.e., attention too easily drawn to unimportant or irrelevant external stimuli
   6. increase in goal-directed activity (either socially, at work or school, or sexually) or psychomotor agitation

■ ■ ■ ■ ■ ■ ■ ■ ■   *continued*

7. excessive involvement in pleasurable activities that have a high potential for painful consequences, e.g., the person engages in unrestrained buying sprees, sexual indiscretions, or foolish business investments

C. Mood disturbance sufficiently severe to cause marked impairment in occupational functioning or in usual social activities or relationships with others, or to necessitate hospitalization to prevent harm to self or others.

D. Not due to the direct effects of a substance (e.g., drugs of abuse, medication) or a general medical condition (e.g., hyperthyroidism).

E. Not superimposed on Schizophrenia, Schizophreniform Disorder, Delusional Disorder, or Psychotic Disorder NOS.

F. Cannot be established that an organic factor initiated and maintained the disturbance.

Note: Somatic antidepressant treatment (e.g., drugs) that apparently precipitates a mood disturbance should not be considered an etiologic organic factor.

Manic Episode Codes: Fifth-digit Code Numbers and Criteria for Severity of Current State of Bipolar Disorder, Manic or Mixed:

1. Mild: Meets minimum symptom criteria for a Manic Episode (or almost meets symptom criteria if there has been a previous Manic Episode).
2. Moderate: Extreme increase in activity or impairment in judgment.
3. Severe, without Psychotic Features: Almost continual supervision required in order to prevent physical harm to self or others.
4. With Psychotic Features: Delusions, or catatonic symptoms. If possible, specify whether the psychotic features are mood-congruent or mood-incongruent.

    Mood-congruent Psychotic Features: Delusions or hallucinations whose contents is entirely consistent with the typical manic themes of inflated worth, power, knowledge, identity, or special relationship to a deity or famous person.

    Mood-incongruent Psychotic Features: Either (a) or (b):

    a. Delusions or hallucinations whose content does not involve the typical manic themes of inflated worth, power, knowledge, identity, or special relationship to a deity or famous person. Included are such symptoms as persecutory delusions (not directly related to grandiose ideas or themes), thought insertion, and delusions of being controlled.

    b. Catatonic symptoms, e.g., stupor, mutism, negativism, posturing.

■■■■■■■■ *continued*

5. In Partial Remission: Full criteria were previously, but are not currently, met; some signs or symptoms of the disturbance have persisted.
6. In Full Remission: Full criteria were previously met, but there have been no significant signs or symptoms of the disturbance for at least 6 months.
7. Unspecified.

Major Depressive Episode

Note: A **major depressive syndrome** is defined as criterion A below.

A. At least five of the following symptoms have been present during the same 2-week period and represent a change from previous functioning; at least one of the symptoms is either (1) depressed mood or (2) loss of interest or pleasure. (Do not include symptoms that are clearly due to a physical condition, mood-incongruent delusions or hallucinations, incoherence, or marked loosening of associations.)
   1. depressed mood (or can be irritable mood in children and adolescents) most of the day, nearly every day, as indicated either by subjective account or observation by others
   2. markedly diminished interest or pleasure in all, or almost all, activities most of the day, nearly every day (as indicated either by subjective account or observation by others of apathy most of the time)
   3. significant weight loss or weight gain when not dieting (e.g., more than 5% of body weight in a month), or decrease or increase in appetite nearly every day (in children, consider failure to make expected weight gains)
   4. insomnia or hypersomnia nearly every day
   5. psychomotor agitation or retardation nearly every day (observable by others, not merely subjective feelings of restlessness or being slowed down)
   6. fatigue or loss of energy nearly every day
   7. feelings of worthlessness or excessive or inappropriate guilt (which may be delusional) nearly every day (not merely self-reproach or guilt about being sick)
   8. diminished ability to think or concentrate or indecisiveness, nearly every day (either by subjective account or as observed by others)

■ ■ ■ ■ ■ ■ ■ ■ ■ *continued*

9. recurrent thoughts of death (not just of dying), recurrent suicidal ideation without a specific plan, or suicide attempt or a specific plan for committing suicide

B. 1. It cannot be established that an organic factor initiated and maintained the disturbance.

   2. The disturbance is not a normal reaction to the death of a loved one (Uncomplicated Bereavement).

Note: Morbid preoccupation with worthlessness, suicidal ideation, marked functional impairment or psychomotor retardation, or prolonged duration suggest bereavement complicated by Major Depression

C. At no time during the disturbance have there been delusions or hallucinations for as long as 2 weeks in the absence of prominent mood symptoms (i.e., before the mood symptoms developed or after they have remitted).

D. Not superimposed on Schizophrenia, Schizophreniform Disorder, Delusional Disorder, or Psychotic Disorder NOS.

Major Depressive Episode Codes: Fifth-digit Code Numbers and Criteria for Severity of Current State of Bipolar Disorder, Depressed, or Major Depression

1. Mild: Few, if any, symptoms in excess of those required to make the diagnosis, and symptoms result in only minor impairment in occupational functioning or in usual social activities or relationships with others.

2. Moderate: Symptoms or functional impairment between "mild" and "severe".

3. Severe, without Psychotic: Several symptoms in excess of those required to make the diagnosis, and symptoms markedly interfere with occupational functioning or with usual social activities or relationships with others.

4. With Psychotic Features: Delusions or hallucinations. If possible, specify whether the psychotic features are mood-congruent or mood-incongruent.

    Mood-congruent psychotic features: Delusions or hallucinations whose content is entirely consistent with the typical depressive themes of personal inadequacy, guilt, disease, death, nihilism, or deserved punishment. Included here are such symptoms as persecutory delusions (not directly related to depressive themes), thought insertion, thought broadcasting, and delusions of control.

■■■■■■■■■ *continued*

5. In Partial Remission: Intermediate between "In Full Remission" and "Mild," and no previous Dysthymia. (If Major Depressive Episode was superimposed on Dysthymia, the diagnosis of Dysthymia alone is given once the full criteria for a Major Depressive Episode are no longer met.)
6. In Full Remission: During the past 6 months no significant signs or symptoms of the disturbance.
0. Unspecified

Specify chronic if current episode has lasted 2 consecutive years without a period of 2 months or longer during which there were no significant depressive symptoms.

Specify if current episode is Melancholic Type.

Diagnostic criteria for Melancholic Type

The presence of at least five of the following:
1. loss of interest or pleasure in all, or almost all, activities
2. lack of reactivity to usually pleasurable stimuli (does not feel much better, even temporarily, when something good happens)
3. depression regularly worse in the morning
4. early morning awakening (at least 2 hours before usual time of awakening)
5. psychomotor retardation or agitation (not merely subjective complaints)
6. significant anorexia or weight loss (e.g., more than 5% of body weight in a month)
7. no significant personality disturbance before first major depressive episode
8. one or more previous major depressive episodes followed by complete, or nearly complete, recovery
9. previous good response to specific and adequate somatic antidepressant therapy, e.g., tricyclics, ECT, MAOI, lithium

Diagnostic Criteria for Seasonal Pattern Mood Disorder
A. There has been a regular temporal relationship between the onset of an episode of Bipolar Disorder (including Bipolar Disorder NOS) or Recurrent Major Depression (including Depressive Disorder NOS) and a particular 60-day period of the year (e.g., regular appearance of depression between the beginning of October and the end of November). Note: Do not include cases in which there is an obvious effect of seasonally related psychosocial stressors, e.g., regularly being unemployed every winter.

■■■■■■■■■ *continued*

B. Full remissions (or a change from depression to mania or hypomania) also occurred within a particular 60-day period of the year (e.g., depression disappears from mid-February to mid-April).
C. There have been at least three episodes of mood disturbance in 3 separate years that demonstrated the temporal seasonal relationship defined in A and B; at least 2 of the years were consecutive.
D. Seasonal episodes of mood disturbance, as described above, outnumbered any nonseasonal episodes of such disturbance that may have occurred by more than three to one.

Desk Reference to the Diagnostic Criteria of the DSM-III-R, pp 125–132, 1987.

■ Major Depressive Disorder

The person with major depressive illness demonstrates a variety of symptoms. These symptoms may be present in lesser form in all people who experience depression of any type. The person described in this section displays these symptoms in a more severe form. The symptoms are as follows:

1. Sad and dysphoric mood, including loss of pleasure in normal activities
2. Four of the following symptoms present for 2 weeks or more:
   a. Decrease or increase in appetite accompanied by weight loss or gain
   b. Changed sleep patterns, such as difficulty in falling asleep or early morning awakening
   c. Increased fatigue or agitation
   d. Increase or decrease in normal activity level, or decreased enjoyment of life and sexual drive
   e. Feelings of guilt and worthlessness
   f. Decrease in memory, concentration, and thinking ability
   g. Repeated thoughts of death, suicidal ideation, or planning of suicide
3. No display of hallucinations or delusions (other than those he or she may possibly experience about his or her own value or fault)

4. Unrelated to cognitive impairment disorders or uncomplicated bereavement; not a complication of schizophrenia or the other psychotic disorders

■ Dysthymic Disorder

In past editions of the *Diagnostic and Statistical Manual of Mental Disorders* (DSM), this condition was called depressive neurosis or neurotic depression. This condition is marked by feelings of depression that have existed for at least 2 years for adults and 1 year for children and adolescents. The symptoms are not as severe, however, as those of a major depressive episode. At least three of the following symptoms of depression are present: low energy level, insomnia or excessive sleeping, feelings or worthlessness, loss of pleasure in normally pleasurable activities, psychomotor slowing, sadness, pessimism about the future, or recurring thoughts of suicide.

■ Nursing Care of Clients With Mood Disorders

Bipolar Disorder, Manic Phase

The client with manic-depressive illness may be seen in the hospital during either an acute manic or depressive episode. During the manic phase of the illness, the client openly and sometimes aggressively tests the limits imposed by the therapeutic milieu and by specific caregivers. His or her critical tendencies and fault finding challenge the vulnerable aspects and the self-esteem of others. Although many of the mental status changes of the manic client may be similar to those of clients with schizophrenia, the personality traits of each have different qualities. The manic client is generally more engaging and warm than the schizophrenic client, who is detached and emotionally cold. Ideally, a primary nursing approach should be implemented.

Major areas of assessment and intervention include attention to the client's hyperactive state and monitoring of medication. Additional nursing interventions should be based on the client's mental status and physical and nutritional needs. The energy level of the manic client is almost limitless. The strain on his or her physical well-being, if not appropriately managed, is severe. The major tranquilizers are frequently used to decrease hyperactive status and to reduce the delusions, hallucinations, and disorientation that accompany the peak of manic excitement.

In addition to the major tranquilizers, lithium carbonate therapy is used to reduce the cyclic effects of the disorder. It is very effective in the treatment of manic-depressive illness. The drug will be described in more detail in Chapter 31, Psychopharmacology and Electroshock Treatment of Mental Disorders. Of particular importance to the client's treatment is the monitoring of serum lithium levels and titration of dosage, based on mental status and physical symptoms. Lithium promotes a therapeutic response in 6 to 10 days. Accurate and descriptive charting of the client's mental and physical signs is important in arranging the dose of lithium at an optimum therapeutic level. While the medication is gradually decreasing the frantic activity level of the client, other nursing measures can assist in maintaining his or her well-being.

Limit-setting, when reasonable, increases the client's sense of control and trust in the care-giving system. Note the specific approach to limit-setting in the nursing care plan so that all care-givers will be consistent and effective. Communication with other members of the care team about nursing interventions can assist in the overall therapeutic effectiveness of your plan. The client needs frequent showering because hyperactivity will increase perspiration. He or she will be motivated to eat if you provide him or her with foods that can be eaten while standing or moving. Ideally, the environment should not further stimulate the client's level of excitement. Keep noise and light levels low. Provide opportunities for physical activity so he or she will have an outlet and purpose for his or her hyperactivity.

Bipolar Disorder, Depressed Phase or Major Depressive Disorder

The depressed client feels hopeless and helpless. He or she is vulnerable and views himself or herself and his or her actions as worthless. He or she lacks the mental or physical energy to restore himself or herself or to feel hope for the future. Because of these factors, he or she is dependent on the nurse for a number of needs. It is important to prioritize these needs in the assessment and intervention process.

Assessment for Suicide Risk
If the client is acutely depressed, suicide risk should be constantly monitored. According to Dubin, the following populations have been found to have higher risk of suicide:

Older, single, divorced, or widowed males

Caucasians

Protestants

Unemployed people

People in poor physical health

People living alone

People with an anniversary of death or loss

People with sudden changes in life situation

People who leave suicide notes

Older homosexual men

Table 24-1 shows the assessment of suicidal risk factors that can be determined by a comprehensive psychiatric history.

When talking with a client admitted for acute depression or who appears acutely depressed, assess the degree of hopelessness they are feeling with a question such as, "Tom, you seem very discouraged today. Can you tell me how you feel?" If he acknowledges feeling very depressed or in any way raises your concerns about suicide potential, ask him, "Tom, when things seem so difficult for you, do you ever wonder about ending your life?" When a person is having suicidal thoughts it can be a relief to acknowledge them. If he or she acknowledges suicidal thoughts, report it immediately to the nurse in charge or to his or her physician. Follow the policy of your nursing unit regarding suicide precautions. If a client acknowledges suicidal thinking, other questions may further determine suicidal risk: "Have you thought about how you would end your life?" If he or she has developed a suicide plan, he or she is at increased risk. Another question that can help to determine increased risk is, "Tom, are there any reasons keeping you from going ahead with your plan?" The client who has no reason for staying alive may see suicide as the easiest way out of his or her situation.

The actively suicidal client must be monitored at all times. Keep his or her room free of any items that he or she could use to injure himself or herself or others. Items such as eating utensils, belts, and nail files, which you would not normally think of as dangerous, can be dangerous in the hands of a severely depressed client.

When a person is acutely depressed he or she usually demonstrates slowed thought processes, speech, movement, and so on. He or she may not be able to engage in conversation. Therapeutic intervention may simply involve just sitting quietly with him or her. Your presence may be very supportive.

When the client is able to talk with you, allow his or her statements and answers to your earlier questions to be the guide as to what he or she wants to talk about. Ask further questions based on his or her

Table 24-1. Assessing the Degree of Suicidal Risk

Behavior or Symptom	Intensity of Risk		
	Low	*Moderate*	*High*
Anxiety	Mild	Moderate	High or panic state
Depression	Mild	Moderate	Severe
Isolation/ withdrawal	Vague feelings of depression; no withdrawal	Some feelings of helplessness, hopelessness, and withdrawal	Hopeless, helpless, withdrawn, and self-deprecating
Daily functioning	Fairly good in most activities	Moderately good in some activities	Not good in any activities
Resources	Several	Some	Few or none
Coping strategies/ devices being used	Generally constructive	Some that are constructive	Predominantly destructive
Significant others	Several who are available	Few or only one available	Only one, or none available
Psychiatric help in past	None, or positive attitude toward	Yes, and moderately satisfied with	Negative view of help received
Lifestyle	Stable	Moderately stable or unstable	Unstable
Alcohol/drug use	Infrequently to excess	Frequently to excess	Continual abuse
Previous suicide attempts	None, or of low lethality	None to one or more of moderate lethality	None to multiple attempts of high lethality
Disorientation/ disorganization	None	Some	Marked
Hostility	Little or none	Some	Marked
Suicidal plan	Vague, fleeting thoughts but no plan	Frequent thoughts, occasional ideas about a plan	Frequent or constant thought with a specific plan

Reproduced with permission from Hatton D., Valente S., Rink A. Assessment of suicide risk. In *Suicide Assessment and Intervention* (1977). New York: Appleton-Century Crofts. p 56.

previous statements. Avoid making reassuring comments that may seem superficial and cause him or her to feel even more alone.

Accurate Documentation of Mental Status
Another aspect of nursing care of the depressed client is accurate documentation of his or her mental and physical states. The antide-

pressant medications usually take about 2 to 3 weeks to elicit a therapeutic response. Some of them also have sedative and hypnotic effects, as well as physiologic side effects. By accurately charting the client's changes in mental and physical status, you will help the physician determine when a therapeutic level of medication is reached or when the medication regimen needs to be reevaluated.

CHAPTER 24 QUESTIONS

1. What are the two major categories of mood or affective mental disorders?

2. Characterize the person with bipolar disorder, mixed type.

3. What drug is used to reduce the cyclical effects of bipolar disorder?

4. In what kind of mental client should suicide risk be constantly monitored?

BIBLIOGRAPHY

American Psychiatric Association. (1991). *DSM-IV options book.* Washington, DC: American Psychiatric Press.
American Psychiatric Association. (1987). *Diagnostic and statistical manual of mental disorders* (3rd., rev.). Washington, DC: American Psychiatric Press.
Kaplan, H., & Sadock, B. (1991). *Synopsis of psychiatry: Behavioral sciences, clinical psychiatry* (6th ed.). Baltimore: Williams & Wilkins.
McFarland, G.K., Thomas, M.D. (1991). *Psychiatric mental health nursing: Application of the nursing process.* Philadelphia: J.B. Lippincott.
Stuart, G.W., & Sundeen, S.J. (Eds.). (1991). *Principles and practice of psychiatric nursing* (4th ed.). St. Louis, MO: Mosby–Year Book.
Wilson, H.S., & Kneisel, C.R. (1992). *Psychiatric nursing* (4th ed.). Redwood City, CA: Addison-Wesley.

Chapter 25

■■■■■

Anxiety and Somatoform Disorders

Behavioral Objectives

After reading this chapter the student will be able to:

Define **dysphoria** and **anxiety.**

Describe the difference between anxiety and fear.

List several possible causes of anxiety.

Name five subjective and five objective signs of anxiety.

List the four levels of anxiety and describe the mental state accompanying each of them.

Name three categories of anxiety disorders and describe one condition in each category.

Name three categories of somatoform disorders and describe the psychological process that is occurring in each type.

One of the most common dysphoric emotions known to mankind is anxiety. **Dysphoria,** or **dysphoric** feeling, is an unpleasant emotion that causes psychological distress or conflict. The Tenth National Conference on Nursing Diagnosis described anxiety as "a vague, uneasy feeling, the source of which is often unspecific or unknown to the individual." As described in Chapter 13, Human Emotions, anxiety is different from fear. Fear is an uneasy feeling due to a *known* cause. The basic cause of anxiety is an unconscious conflict between the psyche and the environment or within the psyche itself. Intrapsychic conflicts are related to conflict between two or more of the intrapsychic structures of id, ego, and superego. For example, the id may cause a person to feel sexually attracted to another. The superego may judge the desire to be immoral. If the desire continues, anxiety can result.

The following are some of the specific causes of anxiety, which have also been described in the nursing diagnosis category of anxiety: unconscious conflict about essential values or goals of life: threat to self-concept; threat of death; threat to or change in health status; threat to or change in role functioning; threat to or change in environment; threat to or change in interaction patterns; situational/maturational crises; interpersonal transmission/contagion; unmet needs.

Hildegard Peplau, a psychiatric nurse theorist, has proposed four levels of anxiety.

■■■■■■■■■

Mild

Person is hyperalert and is sharply aware of the environment. His or her perceptual abilities of vision, hearing, and smell are increased.

Moderate

Person's perceptual abilities are decreased. The person can maintain his or her concentration on one activity, however (selective inattention).

Severe

Person's perceptual abilities are markedly diminished. His or her attention span is scattered.

Panic

Person is either paralyzed or severely agitated. He or she is filled with terror. The object of anxiety is overwhelming in its intensity.

Peplau also describes the intellectual capacity of an individual to learn from anxiety and adapt his or her behavior accordingly. For people in the mild-to-moderate range, she believes that if individuals have well-developed coping abilities, they are able to observe the situation causing the anxiety, describe and analyze it, formulate meanings and relations, discuss it with another person to obtain feedback and validation, and benefit from the experience by adapting.

If a person has a severe anxiety (panic level), he or she is unable to apply the intellectual skills described above. Instead, he or she seeks immediate relief in the easiest way possible to reduce anxiety. His or her initially easy escape from anxiety may not prove adaptive in the more distant future, however.

The behavior the person exhibits during his or her flight from anxiety usually falls into four patterns:

"Acting out" behavior, for example, projecting anger and blame onto others

Somatization (converting the stress into actual, physical symptoms or illness)

Immobilization or paralysis, for example, depression or withdrawal

Use of energy generated by anxiety to seek other solutions

Peplau believes that anxiety is a normal part of the human condition. It is the necessary impetus to change and develop better coping skills. Her recommendations for nursing care of the client with anxiety appear later in this chapter.

The North American Nursing Diagnosis Association (NANDA) has described the characteristics of anxiety using two types of criteria: subjective, which includes symptoms described by the client; and objective, which lists the symptoms that can be observed by the nurse. They appear in Table 25-1.

■ Anxiety Disorders

Many of the categories of anxiety disorder were formerly called neuroses or neurotic disorders. The term **neurosis** was discontinued in the *Diagnostic and Statistical Manual of Mental Disorders*, third edition

Table 25-1 Symptoms Experienced by the Client With Anxiety

Subjective Symptoms	Objective Symptoms
1. Increased tension	1. Sympathetic stimulation cardiovascular excitation, superficial vasoconstriction, pupil dilatation
2. Apprehension	
3. Painful and persistent increased helplessness	
	2. Restlessness
4. Uncertainty	3. Insomnia
5. Fearful	4. Glancing about
6. Scared	5. Poor eye contact
7. Regretful	6. Trembling/hand tremors
8. Overexcited	7. Extraneous movement (foot shuffling, hand/arm movements)
9. Rattled	
10. Distressed	8. Facial tension
11. Jittery	9. Voice quivering
12. Feelings of inadequacy	10. Focus on "self"
13. Shakiness	11. Increased wariness
14. Fear of unspecific consequences	12. Increased perspiration
15. Expressed concerns re: change in life events	

(DSM-III-R), and the new category heading of **anxiety disorder** replaced it. The subcategories of anxiety disorder are as follows:

1. Panic disorder
   a. With agoraphobia
   b. Without agoraphobia
2. Agoraphobia without history of panic disorder
3. Social phobia
4. Simple phobia
5. Obsessive—compulsive disorder
6. Posttraumatic stress disorder
7. Generalized anxiety disorder
8. Anxiety order not otherwise specified

Panic Disorder

Panic disorders are conditions in which the person experiences intense fear or discomfort accompanied by at least four of the following symptoms:

Shaking or trembling

Faintness, dizziness, or unsteadiness

Smothering sensation or shortness of breath

Accelerated heart rate or palpitations

Nausea or abdominal distress

Choking

Sweating

Derealization or depersonalization

Flushes or chills

Tingling sensations (paresthesias) or numbness

Chest pain or discomfort

Fear of dying

Fear of losing control or of going crazy

The specific numbers and duration of attacks help to clarify the diagnosis. These can be referred to in the DSM-III-R manual. The subtypes of panic disorder are **with agoraphobia** and **without agoraphobia.** The latter subtype is self-explanatory. Panic disorder with agoraphobia describes a person who is fearful of being in open areas, public places, or being alone where escape is difficult or help is unavailable. He or she avoids the feared location(s). There are five categories of severity of agoraphobic avoidance ranging from **mild** to **severe** and including the descriptive labels of **in partial remission** and **in full remission.** The same five categories are used to describe the current severity of panic attacks.

The next category of panic disorder is without agoraphobia. A person with this condition meets the criteria for panic disorder but does not experience agoraphobia. Agoraphobia without history of panic disorder is the next category. An individual with this form of panic disorder experiences agoraphobic symptoms but has no history of panic symptoms.

The treatment for each type is individual psychotherapy in which the therapist and client gradually explore developmental experiences that may have contributed to the disorder. Frequently, these experiences have been repressed for many years. As the traumatizing events are uncovered, the symptoms gradually disappear. Special phobia clinics, operating in a number of metropolitan areas, report limited success treating the problem using behavior modification techniques.

Frequently, people with anxiety are given minor tranquilizers by well-intentioned medical physicians. Unless there is a specific, identifiable cause related to a major loss, such as threat of death or loss of job or some other stressful event, such medication only prolongs the client's difficulty. When chronic, persistent anxiety is undermining a person's ability to fulfill normal role functions, he or she should seek psychiatric or counseling assistance. These people, despite the disabling nature of their conditions, are rarely treated in the inpatient setting. However, nursing care of those who are hospitalized will be covered later in the chapter.

Social Phobia and Simple Phobia

Social phobia is a condition in which a person experiences excessive anxiety when exposed to the scrutiny of others—in a classroom, while speaking publicly, or in a social setting. **Simple phobia** is a condition in which a specific object, for instance, snakes or spiders, stimulates overwhelming anxiety.

Obsessive—Compulsive Disorder

The word **obsessive** refers to the repetitive thoughts that a person has. For example, a woman may have the intrusive and recurring thought that she wants to injure her mother. The word **compulsive** refers to the repetitive, stereotyped act that the person finds himself or herself unable to resist performing. In this example, the woman may need to wash her hands every time she thinks about hurting her mother in order to neutralize the obsession. This obsessive—compulsive client could find both the thoughts and the actions repugnant, but her attempts to stop the pattern result in extreme anxiety.

Some clients experience relief from this condition by taking antidepressant medication. Psychoanalytic psychotherapy, when started early in the neurotic process, may help. Treatment of fully developed obsessive-compulsive neurosis is quite difficult. An alternative treatment is behavior therapy (see Chapter 29, Milieu Therapy and Behavior Modification), which aims to stop the unwanted thoughts, urges, or actions of the client.

Posttraumatic Stress Disorders

A person with a posttraumatic stress disorder has experienced a catastrophic event—a plane crash, hurricane, or war—that anyone would perceive as very stressful. Although it is common for a person recovering from such an event to experience marital stress, illness, or difficulties functioning at work, a person who develops this disorder is unable to work through dysphoric feelings and unpleasant thoughts that follow the trauma, and instead suppresses them in his or her unconscious.

The person with this disorder continues to experience unpleasant feelings and fears about the catastrophe that do not diminish with the usual passing of time. He or she experiences decreased interest in relationships and external events; lack of control over distressing memories or dreams of the event; sudden sensations of the event beginning again; survival guilt; sleep disorder; or difficulties with memory or concentration. Some Vietnam veterans experience this disorder as do victims of childhood incest and abuse.

When symptoms persist for 6 months or longer, the disorder is considered to be chronic. When symptoms do not occur until 6 months after the event, it is a **delayed onset** posttraumatic stress disorder.

Generalized Anxiety and Other Anxiety Disorders

A generalized anxiety disorder is a condition in which a person experiences excessive and unrealistic worry and anxiety about two or more life circumstances for at least 6 months or longer. During the 6-month period the individual experiences more days of unrealistic worry than days without the worry. At least 6 of the following 18 symptoms are present when the person is anxious:

Motor tension
1. Trembling, twitching, or feeling shaky
2. Muscle tension, aches, or soreness
3. Restlessness
4. Easy fatigability

Autonomic hyperactivity
5. Shortness of breath or smothering sensations
6. Palpitations or accelerated heart rate (tachycardia)
7. Sweating or cold, clammy hands
8. Dry mouth
9. Dizziness or light-headedness
10. Nausea, diarrhea, or other abdominal distress
11. Flushes (hot flashes) or chills
12. Frequent urination
13. Trouble swallowing or lump in throat

Vigilance and scanning
14. Feeling keyed up or on edge
15. Exaggerated startle response

16. Difficulty concentrating or mind going blank because of anxiety
17. Trouble falling or staying asleep*

The category termed **anxiety disorder not otherwise specified** includes anxiety or phobic avoidance symptoms that do not fit the criteria of the anxiety disorders described above.

■ Nursing Care of Clients With Anxiety Disorders

When a person is hospitalized for anxiety, he or she initially is relieved to be in a safe environment. Because these clients do not customarily require hospitalization, their admission is an indication of how acutely they are terrorized by feeling out of control.

The nursing care of these clients should follow the treatment plan of the multidisciplinary care team. Hildegard Peplau has proposed that people with excessive anxiety lack the capacity to decrease it, because they do not possess the same abilities to cope that others have. She recommends incorporating into the nursing care plan a process that teaches these coping skills.

The person who has a mild to moderate level of anxiety continues to retain intellectual ability. During the counseling process this client can use intellectual skills to define the problem, analyze it, and begin the problem-solving process. Your role as nurse counselor is to listen actively to the client's statements and ask perceptive questions that will help him or her analyze and solve his or her problem. You should not recommend solutions, because that would ultimately take control away from the client and promote his or her dependence on you. The goal of hospitalization is to encourage independence.

The client whose anxiety is at the severe-to-panic level initially requires anxiety relief. A counseling approach that encourages intellectual reasoning may cause further anxiety. Instead, let him or her describe the "here and now" of what is happening. He or she may be so emotionally scattered that he or she cannot make simple decisions. Give him or her simple directions in a calm, reassuring manner. Do not touch him or her or give advice or encouragement about the future. Document observations about his or her fluctuating anxiety state so that appropriate medication management is ensured.

Antianxiety medication is an important aspect of caring for people

---

* *Desk Reference to the Diagnostic Criteria from DSM III-R.* (1987). Washington, DC: American Psychiatric Association. p. 149.

with high levels of anxiety. The minor tranquilizers listed in Chapter 31 are the drugs of choice when there are no symptoms of psychosis accompanying the anxiety. The major tranquilizers are used only when psychotic thinking is present. In both instances the dosage of these drugs should be gradually decreased and discontinued as soon as the person's anxiety becomes tolerable. Both classes of drugs can cause drug dependence.

■ Somatoform Disorders

Somatoform disorders are mental conditions that cause physiological symptoms. They occur through an unconscious mental process. The conditions in this category are as follows:

Body dysmorphic disorder

Conversion disorder

Hypochondriasis

Somatization disorder

Somatoform pain disorder

Undifferentiated somatoform disorder

Other somatoform disorders

Body Dysmorphic Disorder

Body dysmorphic disorder is a condition in which a normal-appearing person is preoccupied with an imagined defect. It can also occur in an individual who grossly exaggerates a slight physical defect. This disorder is not as severe as a delusional disorder, somatic type, which was described in Chapter 23, Schizophrenia and Other Psychotic Disorders.

Conversion Disorder

Conversion disorders frequently mimic neurologic disorders. The most common symptoms are paralysis of one or more body parts, anesthesia (loss of feeling) or paresthesia (abnormal sensations, such as tingling, numbness, or heightened sensation), blindness, and so on. Frequently, the body part affected is related to an inner psychological conflict that the client is experiencing. For example, a couple may have serious marital discord. The husband can possibly be denying his awareness of the difficulties, but may be experiencing deep hatred at an unconscious level and want to kill his wife. He could experience a paralysis of his right arm, without any idea of its cause. These people are usually seen initially by medical physicians; a very thorough diagnostic process should rule out any physical etiology before a psychogenic cause is suspected. There are two subcategories of this condition: single episode or recurrent.

A person with a severe conversion disorder develops a rigid denial defense; he or she has been denying his or her inner conflict most of his or her lifetime. When such a client is hospitalized, he or she requires special care. Attempts to crack through his or her denial will result in higher levels of denial and increased anxiety. Consult with the clinician in charge of directing the client's care to learn the exact approach he or she is using and to obtain specific recommendations about nursing interventions so that your efforts are not counterthera-peutic.

As the client's level of denial gradually diminishes, you will observe increased anxiety. When this occurs, follow the recommendations for nursing care of anxious clients that were described earlier in the chapter.

Hypochondriasis

People with **hypochondriasis** magnify mild, vague physical symptoms into more severe symptoms of potentially serious illnesses that persist for over 6 months. The person is preoccupied thinking about his or her imagined disease. Although physical examination finds no evidence of physical pathology, he or she remains preoccupied with his or her fears.

Somatization Disorder

Somatization disorder is a condition that usually strikes a person before the age of 30. The person has a history of vague symptoms related to a specific body system. These occur as chronic illnesses that cause him or her to see a variety of physicians. Often he or she is hospitalized for diagnostic workup and may also have a pattern of multiple surgeries. The most common symptom complexes are related to gastrointestinal, cardiopulmonary, female reproductive, and neurologic body systems. He or she may also have vague, unexplained pain in these organs, or in the back. Sexual dysfunction may also be present. Depression and anxiety frequently accompany these symptoms. No physical cause can be found for these conditions

Somatoform Pain Disorder

Somatoform pain disorder is a condition in which a client is consistently preoccupied with pain for a period over 6 months. Thorough physical examination reveals no physiological basis for the pain or finds that although there is some pathology, the pain is beyond what should normally be expected.

Other Somatoform Disorders

Conditions in this category fit the general criteria of somatoform disorders, but lack the distinct symptom presentation of the other disorders in this category. The undifferentiated type has a history of lasting over 6 months. The category labelled **not otherwise specified** has a history of less than 6 months.

■ Nursing Care of Clients With Somatoform Disorders

People with these disorders are rarely seen in inpatient psychiatric settings. Instead, they are much more commonly admitted to medical units where their persistent physical symptoms and lack of physical findings frustrate the medical and nursing staffs. These clients strongly resist understanding the psychological basis for their difficulties. When presented with the suggestion that there may be a psychogenic cause, they frequently become angry and change physicians, only to begin anew their search for care.

CHAPTER 25 QUESTIONS

1. Describe how anxiety can be adaptive.

2. What are the five subjective responses to anxiety?

3. What was the original name of the type of mental disorder known as anxiety disorder?

4. Name the anxiety disorder in which a person is afraid to be in public spaces or open areas.

BIBLIOGRAPHY

American Psychiatric Association. (1991). *DSM-IV options book.* Washington, DC: American Psychiatric Press.

American Psychiatric Association. (1987). *Diagnostic and statistical manual of mental disorders* (3rd ed., rev.). Washington, DC: American Psychiatric Press.

Kaplan, H., & Sadock, B. (1991). *Synopsis of psychiatry: Behavioral sciences, clinical psychiatry* (6th ed.). Baltimore: Williams & Wilkins.

McFarland, G.K., Thomas, M.D. (1991). *Psychiatric mental health nursing: Application of the nursing process.* Philadelphia: J.B. Lippincott.

Peplau, H. (1983). Living and learning [Lecture]. Hartford, CT: Institute of Living, October 28.

Stuart, G.W., & Sundeen, S.J. (Eds.). (1991). *Principles and practice of psychiatric nursing* (4th ed.). St. Louis, MO: Mosby–Year Book.

Wilson, H.S., & Kneisl, C.R. (1992). *Psychiatric nursing* (4th ed.). Redwood City, CA: Addison-Wesley.

Chapter 26

■■■■■

Dissociative, Sexual, and Other Disorders

Behavioral Objectives

After reading this chapter the student will be able to:

Define the terms **sexuality** and **ego-dystonic.**

List the developmental factors that affect adult psychosexual functioning.

Describe the condition of transsexualism.

Name and define three paraphilias and three psychosexual disorders.

Name one condition from each of the following categories and describe the symptoms it presents: (1) dissociative disorders; (2) factitious disorders; (3) disorders of impulse control not elsewhere classified; and (4) adjustment disorders.

Mental Health and Mental Illness,
Fifth Edition, by Patricia D. Barry.
J.B. Lippincott Company, Philadelphia © 1994.

■ Dissociative Disorders

A person with a **dissociative disorder** experiences a sudden loss of association and integration of self-identity, consciousness, or motor control. He or she is unaware that this change has occurred. These disorders are rare and, because of their profound and unpredictable nature, are traumatizing to families as well as the person involved. In all cases, the possibility of an organic or other type of mental disorder is ruled out. The disorders in this category include the following:

Multiple personality disorder

Psychogenic fugue

Psychogenic amnesia

Depersonalization disorder (or depersonalization neurosis)

Dissociative disorder not otherwise specified

Multiple personality is a complex mental state that was described in the novel by Corbett Thigpen and Hervey Cleckley, *The Three Faces of Eve.* The fictional character of Dr. Jekyll and Mr. Hyde described by Robert Louis Stevenson is another example of multiple personality. The condition exists in a person who assumes two or more completely distinct identities and personalities during alternating times. The original personality has no knowledge or awareness of the concurrently existing personalities. Its course may begin in late adolescence or early adulthood. One of the primary causes of this disorder is chronic physical, mental, and/or sexual abuse in childhood and adolescence. This condition differs from psychogenic amnesia and psychogenic fugue, which are usually brief episodes in contrast to the chronic nature of multiple personality.

Psychogenic fugue is a mental state that results in a person traveling to a new location and assuming a new identity. He or she is unable to recall his or her former identity. He or she experiences mild disorientation as the transition from one identity to the other is occurring, because he or she is unable to make any association with his or her former life. As the fugue state passes, the person resumes his or her former identity with no recollection of the interim fugue identity.

Psychogenic amnesia is a condition in which a person is unable to recall commonly known types of information about himself or herself.

Depersonalization disorder is a condition in which a person experiences periods of unreality about who he or she is or about various aspects of his or her body. At times, the person may seem as though he or she is removed from himself or herself and is observing from a distance. Such experiences may occur to a mild degree in anyone, for example, someone who is hypoglycemic (low in circulating blood sugar). However, in depersonalization disorder, the symptoms are severe enough to cause dysfunction in the person's normal role or occupation.

A **dissociative disorder not otherwise specified** is a condition that contains some of the symptoms of the other conditions in this category but does not meet the full criteria for any of them.

■ Nursing Care of Clients With Dissociative Disorders

Nursing care of these clients requires a strong and consistent team approach so that short-term goals are therapeutic and gradually lead to a better long-term outcome. Good collaboration is essential among all team members. When accompanying symptoms of depression or anxiety occur, it can be helpful to follow the guidelines for nursing care of clients with depression (Chapter 24, Mood Disorders) or with anxiety (Chapter 25, Anxiety and Somatoform Disorders).

■ Sexual Disorders

Sexuality is an aspect of personality and interpersonal functioning that cannot be separated from a person's basic feelings about himself or herself and relationships with others. **Sexuality** can be defined as those aspects of the personality determined by a person's view of his or her sexual functioning, body image, and relatedness with other people of the same or opposite sex. It is affected by factors such as self-esteem, value formation, and id, ego, and superego functioning. In a psychologically healthy adult, sexuality is integrated or blended into the self-image in a way that is ego-syntonic. **Ego-syntonic** is a term that describes thoughts, perceptions, or actions that are acceptable to the ego and do not cause it to experience conflict.

The sexuality of an adult is the result of a long developmental process that begins at birth. Studies have found that parents and other authority figures relate differently with female infants than with male infants. Parents respond favorably to baby girls when they are sweet and verbal and to baby boys when they are physically active and aggressive. Children have a firm sense of their sexual role by the time they are 1½ to 2 years of age.

A child's self-image is the result of his or her own uniqueness, which includes both an inherited physiological and neuroendocrine base and inherited personality characteristics. This unique self then interacts and is shaped by his or her interactions with parents and other people important to him or her, as well as by moral training, experiences in school and with peers, and the media and environment at large.

Essentially, the child is seeking acceptance from others. The way in which his or her view of himself or herself is formed will be strongly affected by the attitudes, beliefs, and psychological health of those people in his or her environment whose approval is important to him or her. Because of this complex process, it is possible for his or her sexual view of himself or herself to be altered in a way that does not fit expected social norms. **Norms** are society's expectations that a person should behave within limits that it considers to be "normal."

Ego-dystonic is a term that describes conflict within the ego. The conflict can be between the ego and the environment or within the psyche itself. When a person's sexual functioning is ego-dystonic, he or she feels mental distress and may seek psychiatric treatment.

It is also possible for a person's sexual behavior to be ego-syntonic, but it causes conflict in society at large. For example, he or she may be homosexual and be comfortable with himself or herself as a person. Ego-syntonic homosexuality is not considered to be a mental disorder.

Two major categories of psychosexual disorders are paraphilias and sexual dysfunctions. **Paraphilia** is a sexual disorder in which a person requires unusual or bizarre fantasies in order to be sexually aroused. A **sexual dysfunction** is a sexual arousal disorder that is negatively affected by some physical or emotional cause. The two categories include the following diagnostic groups:

A. Paraphilias
   1. Exhibitionism
   2. Fetishism
   3. Frotteurism
   4. Pedophilia
   5. Sexual masochism
   6. Sexual sadism
   7. Transvestic fetishism
   8. Voyeurism
   9. Paraphilia not otherwise specified

B. Sexual dysfunctions
1. Sexual desire disorders
   a. Hypoactive sexual desire disorder
   b. Sexual aversion disorder
2. Sexual arousal disorders
   a. Female sexual arousal disorder
   b. Male erectile disorder
3. Orgasm disorders
   a. Inhibited female orgasm
   b. Inhibited male orgasm
   c. Premature ejaculation
4. Sexual pain disorders
   a. Dyspareunia
   b. Vaginismus
5. Other sexual dysfunction not otherwise specified
C. Other sexual disorders not otherwise specified

Paraphilias

Exhibitionism is sometimes combined with pedophilia, but ordinarily the (often) male exhibitionist prefers to expose his genitals to more mature girls or women. This is a very common sexual disorder. These men rarely rape. They take their sexual enjoyment from exhibiting themselves sexually and may achieve orgasm at the height of this pleasure.

Fetishism is another sexual disorder that is more common in men than women. The fetishist becomes attached to some object or body part. Perhaps this can be compared with the fetishistic attachment of small children to a toy, blanket, or other object that will satisfy their love instincts in the absence of their mothers. Some theorists consider the fetishistic attachment to be an effort to gain ego identification with a substitute object. This object attains a highly exaggerated value, becomes the main source of erotic gratification, and relieves both psychic and sexual tension as contact with it leads to orgasm. **Frotteurism** is a sexual disorder that results in intense sexual urges and fantasies that involve touching or rubbing against a nonconsenting person.

Pedophilia is a disorder in which sexual strivings are directed toward children. This is almost exclusively a male disorder. It occurs largely in impotent and weak men. The pedophile seems to be functioning at an immature psychosexual level, and psychologists sometimes ascribe his actions to fear and doubt concerning his own maleness. Because he expects rejection of and failure in adult sexual advances, he expresses himself to children. He may actually rape children, but much more often he may fondle their sexual organs or expose his own to them with a request that they fondle his. **Child molestation** is very rarely homosexual. The usual case history involves an adult, adolescent, or mentally retarded male with a prepubescent female.

Sadism and **masochism** are, respectively, the desire to inflict upon and the desire to receive from the sexual partner physical or mental pain. In milder forms, these desires are entirely compatible with normal sexual foreplay. In extreme forms they act as a substitute for normal sex and are considered disorders.

Voyeurism is another common sexual disorder. Voyeurs are "peeping Toms" who find sexual pleasure in secretly looking at others undressing or engaging in sexual activity. When these pursuits cause the person discomfort or become an exclusive sexual outlet they are called disorders.

Orgasm Disorders

There are two types of inhibited orgasm—**inhibited female orgasm** and **inhibited male orgasm.** They occur when a person has sexual desire and normal physiological signs of sexual excitement but fails to experience orgasm as the culmination of sexual activity.

Premature ejaculation is a condition in which the male releases semen and experiences orgasm with little or no control in delaying its occurrence.

Sexual Pain Disorders

Functional dyspareunia occurs when intercourse is consistently accompanied by genital pain in either males or females. The disorder has no physical cause. **Functional vaginismus** is a condition in which the outer third of the vagina consistently develops spasms that prevent or interfere with intercourse. The last two categories of **unspecified sexual dysfunction** and **unspecified disorder** do not meet the criteria of the other categories.

■ Other Mental Disorders

These mental disorders do not usually require hospitalization. Their symptoms and course of illness are usually not as complex as other mental conditions previously described. An overview of the classification follows.

Sleep Disorders

Dyssomnias

Insomnia disorders include difficulty falling asleep, remaining asleep, or obtaining restful sleep at a rate of at least 3 times a week. These include **insomnia related to another mental disorder,** for example, sleep loss related to major depression or generalized anxiety. **Insomnia related to a known organic factor** has an underlying physical cause. **Primary insomnia** is sleep loss that causes mental distress but is not related to the two causes described above.

Hypersomnia disorder is a condition that causes excessive sleep or results in a prolonged transition to being fully awake after sleeping. The various types, whose causes are explained by their title, are **hypersomnia related to another mental disorder, hypersomnia related to a known organic factor,** and **primary hypersomnia.**

Sleep-Wake Schedule Disorder

Sleep-wake schedule disorder occurs when a person's internal sleep-wake schedule does not fit with the schedule of his or her environment. This results either in insomnia or hypersomnia.

Parasomnias

Parasomnia is any type of disordered sleep. There are a number of such parasomnias. **Dream anxiety disorder** is a condition in which a person experiences anxiety-provoking dreams that cause him or her to waken fearfully. He or she quickly becomes oriented. However, **sleep terror disorder** is a condition in which a person experiences extreme anxiety, wakens abruptly from sleep, is confused for several minutes, and cannot be comforted by others.

Sleepwalking disorder is a condition in which a person experiences episodes of walking during sleep. He or she is not aware of the presence of others during these episodes, can be awakened only with extreme difficulty, and does not remember the episode when awake.

Factitious Disorders

Factitious disorders are psychological states in which a person pretends that he or she is experiencing some form of distress. A **factitious disorder with physical symptoms** is one in which a person creates a physical problem or pretends that he or she has one in order to obtain the psychological benefit of the attention of others.

A **factitious disorder with psychological symptoms** is one in which a person pretends that he or she has psychological distress. **Secondary gain** is a term that describes the sense of psychological well-being derived by a person when he or she receives care and attention from others as a response to his or her problems. A factitious disorder not otherwise specified is one that does not fit into either category above.

Impulse Control Disorders

This category includes a number of psychological conditions, not classified elsewhere, in which a person experiences a loss of control of certain impulses or urges. He or she lacks the ability to inhibit these urges.

Intermittent explosive disorder is a condition in which a person loses control of his or her aggressive energy. He or she seriously assaults other people, animals, property, and so on. This loss of control is out of proportion to the original stressor. **Kleptomania** is a condition in which a person cannot control the impulse to steal. **Pathologic gambling** is a condition in which a person cannot control the impulse to gamble. He or she is preoccupied with acquiring the money to gamble. He or she gambles increasingly larger amounts of money creating financial hardship for himself or herself and his or her family. He or she is unsuccessful in stopping his or her gambling.

Pyromania is deliberate fire-setting on more than one occasion preceded by emotional tension or arousal. Extreme pleasure is experienced when lighting the fire or observing its aftermath. It is not associated with setting fires for monetary gain.

Trichotillomania is a condition in which a person pulls out his or her own hair. It is preceded by emotional tension before pulling out the hair and it is followed by emotional relief. **Impulse control disorder not otherwise specified** includes any impulse control disorder not described above.

Adjustment Disorders

Adjustment disorders are conditions that occur within 3 months after a known psychosocial stressor occurs. The emotional symptoms are more distressing than would normally be expected from such a stressor and they impair normal role functioning. The following list of adjustment disorders are named for the emotional distress associated with each.

Adjustment disorder with anxious mood

Adjustment disorder with depressed mood

Adjustment disorder with disturbance of conduct

Adjustment disorder with mixed disturbance of emotions and conduct

Adjustment disorder with mixed emotional features

Adjustment disorder with physical complaints

Adjustment disorder with withdrawal

Adjustment disorder with work or academic inhibition

Adjustment disorder not otherwise specified

Psychological Factors Affecting Physical Condition

Psychological factors affecting physical condition is a mental disorder in which environmental causes are temporarily related to the development or worsening of a specific physical disorder. An example would be a person who has an abnormal cardiac pattern that is aggravated by chronic anxiety.

CHAPTER 26 QUESTIONS

1. What are the symptoms of dissociative disorder?

2. What are the primary causes of multiple personality disorder?

3. What factors contribute to sexuality?

4. What is the principle definition of the term ego-dystonic?

BIBLIOGRAPHY

American Psychiatric Association. (1991). *DSM-IV options book*. Washington, DC: American Psychiatric Press.

American Psychiatric Association. (1987). *Diagnostic and statistical manual of mental disorders* (3rd ed., rev.). Washington, DC: American Psychiatric Press.

Kaplan, H., & Sadock, B. (1991). *Synopsis of psychiatry: Behavioral sciences, clinical psychiatry* (6th ed.). Baltimore: Williams & Wilkins.

McFarland, G.K, Thomas, M.D. (1991). *Psychiatric mental health nursing: Application of the nursing process*. Philadelphia: J.B. Lippincott.

Stuart, G.W., & Sundeen, S.J. (Eds.). (1991). *Principles and practice of psychiatric nursing* (4th ed.). St. Louis, MO: Mosby–Year Book.

Wilson, H.S., & Kneisl, C.R. (1992). *Psychiatric nursing* (4th ed.). Redwood City, CA: Addison-Wesley.

Chapter 27

■■■■■

Personality Disorders

Behavioral Objectives

After reading this chapter the student will be able to:

Explain the differences between people who have a mental illness and those who have a personality disorder.

List the 11 personality disorders discussed and identify the maladaptive characteristics of each.

Compare and contrast the antisocial and narcissistic borderline personalities.

In prior units human needs were discussed, including psychological needs for tenderness in infancy, participation with others in childhood activities, sharing experiences with peers in the juvenile period, and close friendships and relationships in adolescence. Chapter 16, Ineffective Coping and Defense Mechanisms, discusses how a person erects defenses against aggressive and sexual tendencies and experiences socially unacceptable feelings and attitudes about important people in his or her life, particularly during childhood. These adaptive defenses allow a person to channel excessive anxiety and balance his or her needs; this person will have a healthy personality.

However, if a person builds up too many such defenses, he or she cannot reduce tension and anxiety, and his or her personality may become rigid, narrow, and nonspontaneous. If a person's defenses

Mental Health and Mental Illness,
Fifth Edition, by Patricia D. Barry.
J.B. Lippincott Company, Philadelphia © 1994.

become pathologically exaggerated or disorganized, he or she can eventually develop a **personality disorder.**

A person's basic personality forms during the early years, depending largely on the way he or she learns to adjust to situations, and it tends to remain identifiable throughout life. If a person develops mental illness, his or her basic personality traits will be similar before, during, and after a psychotic episode, even though his or her behavior tends to be more bizarre during the period of mental illness. The kind of mental disorder a person tends to develop when coping mechanisms fail depends largely on the basic personality structure that developed during his or her childhood.

Up to this point, we have discussed mental health and mental illness in considerable detail. We will now look at the vast number of people who seem to fit between the classifications of mentally healthy and mentally ill. These are the people whose behavior indicates they have maladapted to life stressors. Because their ego functioning and reality testing remain intact, most of them can adapt socially. These people have personality (or character) disorders.

The disorders included in this category are as follows:

Paranoid	Narcissistic
Schizoid	Avoidant
Schizotypal	Dependent
Antisocial	Obsessive-compulsive
Borderline	Passive-aggressive
Histrionic	

■ Paranoid Personality

These people tend to be hypersensitive, rigid, suspicious, jealous, and envious. They may have an exaggerated sense of their own importance and generally tend to blame others and ascribe evil motives to them. These characteristics quite often interfere with their ability to maintain satisfactory interpersonal relationships.

■ Schizoid Personality

This behavior pattern manifests emotional coldness, sensitiveness, fearfulness, inability to socialize well with others, and a tendency to daydream and withdraw from reality. A wide range of behaviors is included in the schizoid group. Most people with a schizoid personality are very sensitive people who feel lonely, imperfectly understood, and isolated. Many of them are timid, shy, self-conscious, and dissatisfied with themselves; others are more secretive, suspicious, and sometimes stubborn. Their feelings are very easily hurt. A child of this type is often teased by his or her playmates who look upon him or her as strange or a sissy. He or she is shy, cries easily, seldom participates in rough play, talks little, and makes no close friendships. Under acute stress he or she may retreat into fantasy and become autistic.

In adolescence, many of these youngsters show patterns of willfulness, disobedience, moodiness, passive stubbornness, and resentfulness. They resent advice, supervision, or correction. Such youngsters are often loners who prefer to get along without strong ties to other people. Although they may be disobedient and moody, they tend to do superior work in school.

In the upper grades and in college, they usually do very well, but tend to be quiet and unsociable. Their love of books may be a substitute for human companionship. They are often imaginative and idealistic and frequently are interested in plans for bettering humanity. They study abstract or philosophic courses in preference to concrete or objective types. Some of these people become artists, poets, or musicians.

Others, while retaining an imaginative attitude toward life and its experiences, lack the fine sensitivity of the above group. These people, while kindly and honest, are unsociable, dull, and taciturn; their personalities lack color and sparkle.

Many people have schizoid personalities—the overly sensitive person, the extremely shy person, the recluse, and the dreamer. Often, a sensitive and tender nature hides beneath a cold and unresponsive exterior, or a deeply kind person hides behind a gruff, apparently hostile facade. These types, fearful of hurt and intrusion into their inner world, camouflage their innate tenderness and kindness by erecting barriers that hold people at a distance.

■ Schizotypal Personality Disorder

A person with this type of personality disorder demonstrates many symptoms related to those of schizophrenia but of a less severe nature. He or she tends to be a loner and has an unusual pattern of talking that is vague and abstract. His or her emotions often do not match the content of his or her discussion and seem inappropriate for the circumstances in which he or she is involved. This person may seem preoccupied by his or her thoughts and is superstitious. He or she may believe he or she can read the minds of others or that others are reading his or her mind. He or she may be suspicious or paranoid and is unusually sensitive to criticism.

■ Antisocial Personality Disorder

People with this disorder are unable to form any significant attachment or loyalty to other people, groups, or society. They are controlled by their ids and are given to immediate pleasures. They have no sense of responsibility, and in spite of punishment and repeated humiliations, they fail to learn to modify their behavior (i.e., they fail to learn by experience). They are lacking in social judgment and tend to turn their frustrations upon society. They are able to rationalize their antisocial actions and consider them warranted, reasonable, and justified. Their character traits seem to be fixed expressions of conflict, and there is a certain compulsiveness to their antisocial acts.

The defect in their character structures is their failure to develop a socialized superego and ego ideals; if these do exist, they are directed toward personal acquisition of money and material goods and the control of others for immediate pleasures and satisfactions. The factor, or factors, that produce such an individual are unknown.

As a group, these clients probably cause the most problems in society. They are frequently in trouble with the law, and might first be seen in psychiatric consultation on the recommendation of the court or probation office. They are unable to tolerate frustration, are easily enraged, and can act out violently without feeling remorse. They sometimes describe themselves as cold-blooded and are often described by others as such. They can be ruthless and vindictive and tend to blame others for their behavior.

Someone with an antisocial personality demands much and gives little. He or she is typically affectionless, selfish, ungrateful, and self-centered, and may be exhibitionistic. He or she is unable to judge his or her behavior from another's standpoint. Even though this person is inadequate and hostile from a social standpoint, he or she is quite satisfied with his or her behavior. To him or her, routine is intolerable. He or she shows few feelings of anxiety, guilt, or remorse. He or she demands immediate and instant gratification of his or her desires, with no concern for the feelings or interests of others. Some of these people use alcohol or drugs. They may react to alcohol poorly and when under its influence become noisy, quarrelsome, and destructive. Their behavior prevents psychosocial adjustment. The personality defect may be limited to a single form of misbehavior, such as stealing, running away, or promiscuity.

■ Borderline Personality Disorder

A person with a borderline personality disorder demonstrates unpredictability and instability in many areas of interpersonal and intrapsychic functioning. For instance, he or she may have intense interpersonal relationships that widely alternate between love, hate, and dependency. His or her emotional stability is also unpredictable. He or she is impulsive and displays major and inappropriate mood shifts. He or she can experience profound identity disturbances relating to self and body image, sexual identity, life goals, and the nature of relationships and others. In addition, he or she engages in self-harmful activities, such as fighting, self-mutilation, and suicidal gestures.

■ Histrionic Personality Disorder

This type of personality is characterized by traits of vanity, self-indulgence, and a flair for dramatization or exhibitionism. These people are immature, self-centered, often vain, and prone to emotional outbursts. Sexual behavior can be provocative and seductive. Actually, most of these people are fearful of sex. Their provocative, attention-getting behavior appears to overlie dependency that is demanding of others. There is reason to suspect that many of these people were spoiled and overprotected in early years. Although they are usually actively engaged in the social world, they respond badly to the frustrations of reality.

Although this disorder is more common in women, the "Don Juan" character represents this personality type in men. His drive for sexual conquest and exhibitionism often hides a feeling of masculine inadequacy. His repeated conquests prove his lack of satisfaction in each successive affair.

■ Narcissistic Personality Disorder

These people are egocentric. **Egocentricity** describes a person's attitude and inner feeling that the world exists to meet his or her needs.

He or she is grandiose in his or her view of self and requires constant attention. His or her self-esteem is actually poor. When his or her self-esteem is threatened, he or she responds with marked anger or feelings of shame. As could be expected, his or her interpersonal relationships are strongly affected by these personality traits. He or she tends to manipulate and exploit other people in order to meet his or her own needs. He or she lacks empathy to understand the feelings of others.

■ Avoidant Personality Disorder

People with this type of disorder are basically afraid of rejection. They consciously and unconsciously make choices that will help them avoid conflict, humiliation, or shame. They tend to avoid social situations, although they desire affection and close relationships that will enhance their sense of worth. They have the capacity to engage in close relationships, but these friendships require constant approval from the others.

■ Dependent Personality Disorder

A person with a dependent disorder has a very poor sense of self and demonstrates a low level of self-confidence. He or she cannot make independent decisions or function as a responsible adult. He or she consistently defers or represses his or her own needs in order to gain the acceptance and approval of others. Interactions with others are marked by passivity. He or she is socially limited because he or she finds it difficult, if not impossible, to travel alone and be self-reliant.

■ Obsessive-Compulsive Personality Disorder

This person demonstrates a limited or constricted range of emotions. Warmth, spontaneity, and a feeling of emotional "connectedness" with others seem lacking in his or her personality. He or she ceaselessly strives for perfection, and he or she is stubborn. Decision making is difficult for him or her; he or she overly attends to trivial details and is unable to carry through the decision-making process to form a conclusion. Compulsive people are frequently overinvolved with their work to the exclusion of normal pleasure and satisfaction in the workplace. They commonly spend excessive time at work and lose time with family and in normal recreational activities.

■ Passive-Aggressive Personality Disorder

People with this behavior pattern show both passivity and aggressiveness. The aggression may take the passive forms of sullenness, procrastination, inefficiency, and obstructionism. Often such a person has a history of hostility toward a parent who has been dominant, rigid, unapproachable, demanding, and difficult to please.

His or her aggression is seen in immature attitudes such as irritability, temper tantrums, and even destructive behavior. Many people of this type show open, active hostility. They are withholding, provocative, antagonistic, competitive, and ambitious. They manifest a chip-on-the-shoulder attitude. Their speech is often sharp, biting, and argumentative. They demand special attention and assume unwarranted authority. These people have usually shown open hostility to their fathers. But, despite their superficial air of aggression, beneath the surface lies a deep dependency. This type of aggression is referred to as a reaction formation.

■ Treatment of the Personality Disorders

People with personality disorders are rarely hospitalized. Their personality traits may cause difficulty in their relationships with others in the family, at work, or in social settings. If outpatient psychiatric care is sought, the most appropriate treatment mode is individual or group psychotherapy, depending on the severity of the disorder. There are no specific recommendations for nursing care, because these clients usually are not treated in inpatient settings.

CHAPTER 27 QUESTIONS

1. Describe how a personality disorder develops.

2. What is the determining factor in the type of mental disorder that occurs when there is chronic failure of coping mechanisms?

3. What are the characteristics of a paranoid personality?

4. What is the characteristic interpersonal relationship pattern in persons with borderline personality disorder?

BIBLIOGRAPHY

American Psychiatric Association. (1991). *DSM-IV options book.* Washington, DC: American Psychiatric Press.

American Psychiatric Association. (1987). *Diagnostic and statistical manual of mental disorders* (3rd ed., rev.). Washington, DC: American Psychiatric Press.

Kaplan, H., & Sadock, B. (1991). *Synopsis of psychiatry: Behavioral sciences, clinical psychiatry* (6th ed.). Baltimore: Williams & Wilkins.

McFarland, G.K, Thomas, M.D. (1991). *Psychiatric mental health nursing: Application of the nursing process.* Philadelphia: J.B. Lippincott.

Stuart, G.W., & Sundeen, S.J. (Eds.). (1991). *Principles and practice of psychiatric nursing* (4th ed.). St. Louis, MO: Mosby–Year Book.

Wilson, H.S., & Kneisl, C.R. (1992). *Psychiatric nursing* (4th ed.). Redwood City, CA: Addison-Wesley.

Developing Critical Thinking Skills Through Class Discussion

UNIT VI Case Study
Categories of Mental Disorder

Rhonda is a 45-year-old housewife who has a long-standing depressive disorder. She is married to a controlling and unsupportive partner. Over the past 20 years she has been admitted to the psychiatric unit on three occasions when she experienced suicidal despair. Her most recent admission occurred following the marriage of her last child, who had been living at home. Her symptoms include severe depression, suicidal ideation and plan, and poor response to a new antidepressant medication.

DISCUSSION QUESTIONS

1. What would it be like to sit with Rhonda on the day of her admission? How would you begin to talk with her? What would you say?

2. Name five nursing diagnoses that you might expect to see in Rhonda's chart. Using Maslow's Hierarchy of Human Needs in Chapter 10, can you prioritize the importance of the diagnoses and explain the reasons for your choices?

3. What normal activities of daily living most likely would be affected by depression? How would you begin to assess whether they are being carried out by Rhonda?

(continued)

4. Would it be appropriate if Rhonda's clinical treatment plan included family or couple therapy while she is hospitalized? Why?

5. Can you describe the personal and family developmental issues that may be additional contributing factors to Rhonda's depression?

6. Can you name one nursing diagnosis that pertains to one of these developmental factors? Can you think of a nursing intervention that would be included in addressing this diagnosis?

Unit VII

Intervention and Treatment of Mental Disorders

Chapter 28

■■■■■

Crisis Intervention

Behavioral Objectives

After reading this chapter the student will be able to:

Describe the ways in which events can lead to crisis.

List the sequence of developments after a critical event that can lead to crisis.

Explain the symptoms of maladaptation exhibited by a person after crisis.

List the main developmental stages and describe two major developmental issues under each.

Describe the five types of situational events that are most likely to cause crisis.

A crisis of some type usually causes the onset of mental illness. There may be a specific event that triggers a deteriorating capacity for mental functioning—for instance, a new situation with which the person has no previous experience. Accordingly, he or she has no specific automatic behaviors or coping responses available to respond to or relieve him or her of the anxiety associated with such an event. There may be a number of stressful life experiences, compounded by a new situation, which is often "the straw that breaks the camel's back." The person's coping abilities are already taxed and do not respond as well as they did to earlier difficulties. Finally, the crisis may be one that appears to have no known cause or identifiable **triggering** or **precipitating event.** In such cases, subtle changes in the client's perception of events often cause distorted or disoriented awarenesses that are stressful in and of themselves. These distorted awarenesses most often occur in schizophrenia, manic depressive illness, psychotic depression, and delirium or dementia due to a general medical condition or substance abuse.

■ Sequence of Developments Following a Critical Event

A number of factors determine whether an event has crisis potential:

1. The perception of the event by the person. His or her accurate perception of the event is strongly influenced by his or her:
   a. Value system (what is important to him or her)
   b. Normal personality style
   c. Normal ego strength
   d. Response to issues of trust, self-esteem, control, loss, guilt, intimacy
   e. Coping skills during normal stresses of living
   f. Level of stress in the past year
   g. Availability of support from family, friends, care-givers
2. The degree of threat, as perceived by the person, to his or her:
   a. Personal safety
   b. Life goals
   c. Normal role functioning
   d. Family stability
3. The person's coping style: effective coping versus ineffective coping

When a person is functioning well mentally, his or her ego is able to tolerate the stress of a difficult new event by developing an ever-expanding set of responses to decrease his or her anxiety. Eventually, the new relief behaviors or conscious coping strategies decrease his or her anxiety, and crisis is avoided. He or she has adapted to the new event or life change. When effective coping does not occur, a maladaptive response develops. At times maladaptation becomes chronic. Crisis does not occur, but there is a change in the quality of the individual's life and the life of his or her family. The quality of life changes are due to diminished capacity to function both psychologically and socially in the way that he or she did before the triggering event occurred.

Another possible outcome is that a maladaptive response results in a decreasing ability to deal with anxiety and the emotional, intellectual, and physiological stresses accompanying it. While this is occurring, the person feels increasingly out of control. His or her awareness of environmental stimuli is decreased. The two possible outcomes of this progressive deterioration are immobility or panic. In either case, the person's capacity to help himself or herself is temporarily lost. Crisis results.

A crisis occurs over a limited period of time. It can last anywhere from a few days to a few weeks. It either decreases, because the client's coping strength gradually returns and he or she has an available support system, or it causes the person's mental functioning to deteriorate to the point at which hospitalization is necessary to protect the client or others.

■ Categories of Crisis

Two main categories of circumstances can challenge a person's ability to cope and adapt. The potential outcomes are developmental crises and life change crises (also known as situational crises).

Developmental Crises

The normal stages of development include many issues that must be worked through and resolved to allow normal progression into the next stage. On occasion, individuals are unable to make the transition, and one or more of these issues are unresolved. When a large number of the issues proves too taxing to resolve, crisis can occur. Below are outlined the developmental stages and the outcomes that may occur if the issues are not resolved.

■■■■■■■■■

Developmental Stages

Infancy and Early Childhood (birth to 3 years)
Major issues (progressive from birth): trust, dependency, awareness of separateness from mother, development of autonomy

■■■■■■■■■   *continued*

When issues are not resolved: distrust, poor self-confidence, fusion of self with care-giver, poor self-control

Childhood (3–11 years)
Major issues: identification with significant elders, development of initiative, security, and acceptance within family and eventually within peer group, mastery of age-appropriate skills and intellectual challenges

When issues are not resolved: guilt, lack of direction and purpose, self-undermining behavior, feelings of inadequacy

Adolescence (12–20 years)
Major issues: reawakening of oedipal conflicts (see Chap. 11 Structure of Personality) idealization of significant others, resolution of loss of childhood, development of sexual identity, acceptance by peer group, psychological separation from family as adolescent develops his or her own perceptions of the world, physical separation usually occurs a few years later

When issues are not resolved: inability to separate from family and assume independence, sexual confusion, self-consciousness, inability to form relationship with person of opposite sex, poor object relations

Early Adulthood (20–30 years)
Major issues: ability to develop intimacy and commitment within a relationship, commitment to employment, exploration, and clarification of societal norms as they pertain to self

When issues are not resolved: superficiality in relationships with others, poor goal setting, drifting in and out of relationships and employment, lack of responsibility to self and others

Middle Adulthood (30–50 years)
Major issues: maintenance of life goals, creativity, and spontaneity, ability to maintain meaningful relationships, appropriate channeling of emotions

When issues are not resolved: inability to work or to feel pleasure, poor motivation, egocentrism in relationships and in goal setting

Late Adulthood (50 years and older)
Major issues: ability to resolve losses of aging and to integrate ongoing losses, maintenance of hope, acceptance of uncertain future

■■■■■■■■ *continued*

When issues are not resolved: continual wishing to relive past experiences, inability to take pleasure in the present, loss of hope, depression

Although aging from one decade to the next can stress the psyche, it is usually less disruptive than the significant development stages described above, and the person adjusts to a changed self-image. At times, however, self-esteem temporarily decreases until the person accommodates to the change.

Situational Crises

Life change events that can cause crisis include death, divorce, major illness, marriage, childbirth, loss of a job, and retirement. Many times a life change event occurs at the same time a person is adapting to a new developmental stage. When this happens the person is at greater risk for inadequate coping. The life change events and their accompanying effects are described below.

Death

Death of a loved one or one's own anticipated death is the most severe social stressor that most people encounter in their lives. The losses associated with a death are many. A relationship with a significant other person contains connections to innumerable ongoing experiences and memories, as well as irreplaceable loss of support and caring that the other person provided. In some cases, the relationship with the other person was permeated with conflict. In either a loving or conflicting relationship the loss results in the eruption of strong feelings of grief, anger, guilt, and fear.

Before a person dies there is often a period of months or years of physical decline that allows him or her and those who know him or her gradually to work through (at least partially) the anticipated death. When this occurs, the coping process commonly follows a pattern similar to that described by Elisabeth Kubler-Ross, including stages of denial, anger, bargaining, depression, and acceptance. The dying person and the various family members frequently progress through these stages at different times. One or more family members may deny the illness, express anger, and become depressed, thereby increasing the stress on the family system.

Sudden, unexpected death has even greater crisis potential because family members have had no time to develop their coping ability. Such a death suddenly disrupts their entire world without warning. Even a few days of critical illness allow a family time to adjust, at least minimally, to the imminent death. When sudden death of a loved one occurs, the bereavement process in one or more family members often lasts beyond the normal 1-year period.

Divorce

Divorce was second in the list of most disruptive events reported by persons in the Holmes and Rahe research study on life change stressors. Divorce, similar to death, results in multiple changes within the family. However, the dynamic of choice is involved for one or both members of the couple. This element increases the potential for anger, guilt, and loss in both partners. The children, regardless of their ages, can be profoundly affected as well. Increased levels of anxiety and decreased self-esteem and role-functioning ability frequently occur.

Major Illness

Major illness, mental or physical, presents a moderate to severe challenge for individuals and their family members. Usually, they have had no experience with illness in the past, and their ability to cope and adapt is severely challenged. The ongoing effects of psychiatric illnesses, such as schizophrenia and major depressive illness, and chronic physical illnesses, such as cancer and heart disease, pose threats to self-image, body image, self-esteem, loss of control, issues of dependence and trust, separation from family, and changes in role functioning. Just as the ill person is under increased psychological stress, so are his or her family members, because they must adapt to losses associated with the changed health status and role functioning of their loved one. Communication patterns in the family are often permanently altered as a means of coping with the many changes in the family created by the illness.

Marriage

Although marriage is usually a happy event for a person and his or her family, it often creates a number of stresses for the couple as well as for their families. These include the couple's anticipated role changes and a heightened sense of responsibility. Family members may or may not agree with their loved one's choice of spouse. Often, as the time of marriage approaches, there is a greater awareness of differences in values pertaining to family, tradition, religion, and so on, leading to increased potential for interpersonal and psychological conflict.

Marriage also creates many losses. It may involve the first time a young person has lived apart from his or her family. The anticipated separation is usually accompanied by feelings of sadness and fear in the person about to be married and in his or her parents and siblings. If a man has been excessively emotionally close to his family, he will be unable to reach independent decisions or to reach an agreement with his new wife, if her views differ from those of his family. The issue of emotional separation from one's own family is significant in the development of a healthy marital relationship.

Childbirth

The implications of raising children have become increasingly important to young people during the past 2 decades. The decision about whether to have children is an important one in the developing relationship between two young people who are contemplating marriage. The values and beliefs about pregnancy, childbirth, and child-rearing have strong potential for conflict and are best addressed during the courtship period.

The arrival of a child causes a major shift in the interpersonal dynamics between a husband and wife. Many couples find that the arrival of the first child is a crisis event. Regardless of their psychological preparation, it involves changes in their lives and normal roles that were not anticipated. In most instances, the crisis is short-lived. Within 4 to 6 weeks, adaptation begins to occur.

■ Use of Nursing Process With Clients in Crisis

When a client is admitted in crisis, begin the nursing process immediately. You can provide support while you are admitting the client. Such availability of support from other persons is a key factor in the resolution of crisis. The more you understand the frame of reference of a client, the less isolated he or she feels. Major exceptions to this approach are with the client who is suspicious or paranoid.

Assessment

In caring for a client who is not coping, remember that each human being perceives the world in a different way from every other person. The unique set of circumstances that each person encounters in his or her development from infancy to adulthood creates different personality dynamics. As a result, the way that one person copes with a given situation can be quite different from another.

For example, if you were a passenger in a race car in the Indianapolis 500 Race, traveling at 120 miles per hour around a curve, you might feel a high level of anxiety. The driver, on the other hand, thrives on the experience. The perceptions of the driver and passenger regarding the experience are quite different. It is the frame of reference of each that determines the overall response. Accordingly, the more you understand about what a particular event means to a person, the more complete will be the data on which you base your care plan.

Planning

Most likely a client in crisis that you are working with will have been hospitalized by the time you are planning his or her care. One of the most important elements in the client's ability to resolve the crisis will be the sense of support he or she feels in the treatment setting. One of the ways you can ensure this is to develop a team plan with members of the various disciplines who will be caring for him or her. This is also known as systems planning. The care-giving team is usually made up of a psychiatrist, psychologist, family therapist, nurse, occupational therapist, drama therapist, and members of whatever other disciplines your institution uses in the care of clients.

Without such teamwork, each of these care-givers might otherwise work toward opposite directions. The person who suffers is the client. He or she will not feel you are working to help him or her if all members of your treatment plan are not working toward similar goals.

For this reason it is important to attend a team conference and understand the treatment plan of the psychiatrist or psychologist in charge of caring for the client. You can ask questions at this conference to clarify your understanding of the client, and also to share any information you may have obtained from the client.

In the development of the care plan be attentive to the client's most active concerns. A short-range care plan can be developed with specific dates to attend to these concerns. A client who is in crisis feels overwhelmed and finds it difficult to think of the mid- or long-term future. During the planning stage, the short-term and intermediate plan should be reviewed in the team conference with the other care-givers so that all understand the nursing goals.

As the specific goals of the short-term care plan are developed, share them with the client and discuss his or her reaction to each. He or she will feel less alone and more secure. Even if his or her depression makes him or her unresponsive, share the plan with him or her; at the very least, he or she will be listening. If the client is psychotic or violent, wait until medication has increased his or her ability to participate in a discussion about a care plan before you share it.

Never assume that a mentally ill person is helpless; it is countertherapeutic. The more you promote a client's feeling of helplessness and dependency, the longer you are prolonging his or her illness. Accordingly, if he or she is able to participate, even in the most minimal way, in the planning of care, his or her sense of control and personal strength will increase.

Implementation

During this step of the nursing process you begin to undertake what you developed in the nursing care plan. As you implement your plan, watch and listen carefully to the client. His or her verbal and nonverbal responses can give you an indication about whether or not the nursing approach is therapeutic.

Evaluation

During the last step of the nursing process use the intermediate goals to review the client's response to nursing intervention. Usually, however, new information is obtained, the client's condition improves or worsens, new medication is begun, or some other factor intervenes that requires you to use new data to modify or change the original plan. In essence, you must reinstitute the nursing process of assessing, planning, implementing, and evaluating in order to develop a plan that adjusts to his or her changed condition.

CHAPTER 28 QUESTIONS

1. What is the most common cause of the development of a mental disorder?

2. What are the types of threat that can result in crisis?

3. What is one emotional result of a maladaptive psychological response?

4. What are the four different types of situational crises?

BIBLIOGRAPHY

Aguilera, D. (1990). *Crisis intervention: Theory and methodology* (6th ed.). St. Louis, MO: Mosby–Year Book.

Ashmore, R. (1991). Crisis intervention and psychiatric referral. *Nursing Times, 87,* 50–51.

Barry, P.D. (1989). *Psychosocial nursing: Assessment and intervention* (2nd ed.) Philadelphia: J.B. Lippincott.

Kaplan, H., & Sadock, B. (1992). *Synopsis of psychiatry: Behavioral sciences, clinical psychiatry* (6th ed.). Baltimore: Williams & Wilkins.

Kubler-Ross, E. (1975). *Death: The final stage of growth.* Englewood Cliffs, NJ: Prentice-Hall.

McFarland, G.K., Thomas, M.D. (1991). *Psychiatric mental health nursing: Application of the nursing process.* Philadelphia: J.B. Lippincott.

Merrett, C. (1992). Crisis management—a guide to survival. *Occupational Health—London, 44,* 10–11.

Mezzich, J.E., & Zimmer, B. (Eds.). (1990). *Emergency psychiatry.* Madison, CT: International Universities Press.

Chapter 29

■■■■■

Milieu Therapy and Behavior Modification

Behavioral Objectives

After reading this chapter the student will be able to:

Explain how tranquilizing drugs have helped change the manner of treating mentally ill clients.

Identify the members of the hospital team who deal with emotionally ill clients.

Describe the type of atmosphere and attitudes that help establish a therapeutic milieu.

List the eight aims of staff members working with clients who are hospitalized for mental illness.

Explain why counseling family members is important in the treatment of mentally ill clients.

Describe the role of halfway houses in the rehabilitation of clients with emotional problems.

Describe the ways that a client's behavior may be modified or changed by the techniques of relaxation and desensitization, condition avoidance, and operant conditioning (token economy).

Explain the limitations of behavior modification as a therapeutic modality.

Mental Health and Mental Illness,
Fifth Edition, by Patricia D. Barry.
J.B. Lippincott Company, Philadelphia © 1994.

■ History of Development of the Therapeutic Milieu Concept

Under the old concept of custodial care for the mentally ill, many clients regressed, relinquished their responsibilities, and were relegated to "back wards." Here, they were provided with minimal physical care, locked in, and essentially left alone. Most of their decisions were made for them. They were dehumanized, garbed in unattractive clothing, and placed on a rigid institutional routine. When they acted out their hostility, they were subdued with sedative drugs, harsh commands, and, at times, manhandling. If they did not respond to these methods they were put into restraints, such as strait jackets or hand and ankle cuffs. Even those living on the better wards had to submit to regimentation and locked doors and lost their personal belongings and freedom. The staff members who cared for these clients often had little, if any, training in psychology or psychotherapy. The attendants or guards were hired and placed on the wards without in-service training, and they learned to cope with the behavior of their clients to the best of their abilities.

The **milieutherapie** approach was introduced during the first 2 decades of the 1900s by Hermann Simon, a German psychiatrist. Although brief references in historic accounts acknowledge the importance of environment in the treatment of mental disorders, Simon's approach was the first use of the therapeutic milieu on a large scale. The major focus of this approach is that a client's social environment can be therapeutic for him or her. When all those around the client, staff members and other clients alike, are working to support his or her rehabilitation, their restoration to health can be more effectively ensured.

■ Acceptance of the Therapeutic Milieu Concept

The therapeutic milieu concept was not widely adopted in this country until the 1960s. A number of dynamics operating before that time supported its gradual acceptance. The introduction of the major tranquilizers during the mid-1900s had the greatest impact on treatment of the mentally ill client, adding another dimension to psychiatric therapy. They lowered the anxiety level, thus producing sustained relief of the symptoms of many disturbed mentally ill clients. As these drugs became more widely used, the amount of disturbed behavior on the nursing units decreased. The clients became less disorganized and more compliant. Their destructiveness decreased greatly. Accordingly, it became possible to improve the physical surroundings and to gain clients' cooperation in efforts being made for them.

While the severity of the clients' symptoms yielded to these tranquilizing drugs, great strides were also being made in the psychiatric field. Training was begun at all levels to teach hospital personnel the theory of psychiatric care. A client's behavior was regarded as an indication of his or her needs. The different care disciplines began to pool their knowledge and efforts to assess the needs of the client. Thus, the psychiatric team was born. It came to include all levels of professionals and paraprofessionals who had actual client contact. Today, in many hospitals, these teams include psychiatrists, psychologists, physicians, nurses, social workers, therapists for drama, art, recreation, and other therapies, teachers, counselors, pastors, and technicians.

When a new client is admitted, he or she is usually apprehensive, upset, and disturbed. This is a strange new world he or she is entering. Every effort is made to convey that he or she will be accepted as he or she is. No one will criticize, reprimand, or judge. His or her legal rights are explained. The client is evaluated physically, mentally, and emotionally during the first few days after arrival in order to determine his or her needs. On the basis of these evaluations, the team outlines a treatment program. If he or she is able to participate in this planning, the client is involved and aware of what forms of treatment are being scheduled and why.

■ The Treatment Model

Clients are encouraged to set up their own council and to form their own rules and regulations. When it is possible for them to do this, they are also expected to enforce these rules. When a resident breaks one of these rules or shows grossly unacceptable conduct, the entire ward then exerts social pressure on this person. This has proved much more effective in reshaping behavior than when the staff has enforced the hospital rules.

The client is encouraged to be answerable for himself or herself and his or her behavior as much as possible. He or she is not required to assume responsibility that he or she cannot handle. As he or she improves, more and more responsibilities are offered to the client. Clients should be encouraged to help other clients as much as possible in order to experience responsibility and satisfaction in tasks that hold real meaning.

Clients who tend to withdraw and isolate themselves socially should be placed in a unit that has as one of its primary goals the interaction of its members. The staff should continually reach out toward these withdrawn people and allow them plenty of time to respond. A one-to-one relationship is advisable.

In the past, staff members were cautioned not to become involved in the clients' problems. Their role was that of observing, recording, and controlling the clients' activities. A wide gulf existed between the controlled patient and the controlling staff. Today, emphasis is placed on the necessity of becoming involved with the client, of participating with him or her in order to positively influence the course of his or her illness. In this way, the client can feel accepted and learn to trust and feel that his or her rights as an individual are respected, that his or her treatment needs are being explored with him or her, that all efforts are directed toward helping him or her, and that there are genuine expectations of his or her improvement.

These changed attitudes, plus a realistic social setting on the units, add up to what is called a **therapeutic milieu** for the client. Milieu is a French word meaning a trusted environment. When the environment acts constructively to help the client function comfortably, encourages improved behavior and self-confidence, and enables him or her to assume responsibility and to socialize effectively, we say that a therapeutic milieu has been established (see Chapter 3).

One of the most important elements in the hospital environment is the nursing staff. Nurses are largely responsible for creating an environment that will be health-producing for the client. Of great importance are the interactions that exist among the clients and between the clients and you. The client must be the focus of interest and concern, so that you may help him or her to handle better stressful situations. Encourage him or her to become an active participant in all aspects of unit living. Give him or her the opportunity to discuss fears, problems, observations, successes, and failures openly and frankly with the staff and fellow clients. Group therapy sessions and informal, small, spontaneous interchanges are the best methods.

Each member of a therapeutic staff trained to understand the dynamics of behavior should reinforce the client's strengths and help him or her reduce his or her weaknesses. He or she often needs assistance in reestablishing contact with reality. Encourage him or her to participate in unit activities. Work and play can be used therapeutically, helping to work off pent-up emotions. The client can be encouraged to satisfy creative needs by making beautiful and useful objects. The social interchange on the unit tends to pull him or her back into reality.

Direct your efforts in the hospital to:

Convince the client that he or she is a person of worth and dignity.

Convince the client that you and the staff have realistic expectations that he or she can and will improve.

Provide the client with a therapeutic milieu that will act as a realistic social setting for his or her therapy.

Meet the client's physical, intellectual, and emotional needs as much as possible.

Emphasize and provide meaningful tasks and experiences for the client.

Reduce the social distance between you and the client.

Reduce the client's anxiety and fear.

Bring the client slowly but steadily closer to reality and to the community.

While the client is undergoing therapy in the hospital, his or her family should also enter family therapy. They should explore their own problems and anxieties in relation to their family members and each other. Since the client became ill within the family, work, and social settings, these settings should be examined and obvious areas of stress identified. Above all, family, friends, employer, and fellow workers should try to achieve a deeper understanding of the client's feelings and the reasons for his or her behavior if they are going to be able to accept and assist him or her when he or she returns from the hospital. As the client improves, he or she should be allowed short visits home to help reestablish emotional ties there and to help him or her progress toward eventual complete recovery.

If most of the emotional stress appears to develop within the family setting, complete rehabilitation in a halfway house may be advisable when he or she is well enough not to need around-the-clock care. He or she can live there for weeks until he or she is able to adjust better to the home setting. Some hospitals have special living units where clients may come and go daily to work. Some clients spend their evenings and nights at a halfway house and return daily to the hospital for therapy.

■ Behavior Modification

Behavior modification uses systems theory (see Chapter 9, Influence of Family and Social Environment on the Individual) to bring about change in the client. What the client *does* is the focus, rather than how he or she feels or why the client is as he or she is.

The field of behavior modification or behavior therapy is strongly based on the psychology of the learning process. Reports of treatment of behavioral disorders by this method or related forms of this method can be found throughout history. It was during the 1960s that behavioral therapy began to be used actively in the treatment of various types of mental disorders.

Behavior therapy differs from the traditional psychoanalytic approach to mental illness by focusing on the behavior of the person, rather than on an underlying cause. It is an appropriate therapeutic approach for certain types of mental disorders. Table 29-1 lists the conditions that have had positive response rates to specific behavioral therapy approaches. The therapy approach appears next to the condition.

The following terms describe the learning principles utilized in behavior modification or behavior therapy:

Operant conditioning—Conditioning or influencing behavior by rewarding a person for positive forms of behavior; also called **behavioral psychology** and **behavior modification**.

Positive reinforcement—When a person's behavior results in a positive response from others, he or she experiences a feeling of acceptance and internal pleasure; he or she is likely to repeat the same behavior.

Negative reinforcement—Rewarding a stoppage of an undesirable event or behavior.

Table 29-1 Behavior Therapy Approaches to Mental Disorders

Mental Disorder	Therapeutic Approach
Phobias or phobic disorders	Desensitization
Anxiety or chronic pain	Relaxation
	Biofeedback
Dependent or passive personality style	Assertiveness training
Alcoholism or smoking	Aversive conditioning
	Conditioned avoidance

Aversive stimulus—Any event that results in an unpleasant feeling.

Punishment—A type of reinforcement in which a negative behavior elicits a negative response from the environment. The outcome is a cessation or stopping of negative behavior.

Extinction—The complete inhibition of a conditioned reflex as a result of failure of the environment to reinforce it.

Behavioral modification involves modifying the environment of the client in such a way that desirable behaviors are rewarded and undesirable behaviors punished. An example of this is **operant conditioning** as seen in **token economy.** Here, each client on a small psychiatric inpatient unit or partial hospitalization unit has a **problem-oriented record,** on which problem behaviors are listed (such as pacing, excessive smoking, not socializing, talking to voices). A schedule is then drawn up to provide the client with tokens for desired behavior. For example, a client may be entitled to a token for every ½ hour in which he or she does not pace the floor, or for every 15-minute conversation he or she holds with another client. These tokens are used to purchase desired things. Perhaps the group is planning a picnic or a trip to an amusement park, and each client desiring to go will be charged 30 tokens. If a client does not have enough tokens, he or she is not permitted to go on the excursion. A token economy obviously takes a lot of staff and involves a lot of record keeping, but it does produce desired behaviors.

In a completely developed behavior modification program, the staff, too, may be rewarded for desired behavior (such as coming to work on time and getting the clients to cooperate). In this situation, there is usually a minimal base salary, and the staff can earn more if they produce more.

Another technique of behavior modification is termed **conditioned avoidance.** Here the habit pattern of the client is paired to an unpleasant stimulus so that the client learns to avoid both the stimulus and the habit. The classic example of this technique is the use of disulfiram (Antabuse) in the treatment of the alcoholic.

A classic use of behavior modification techniques is in the treatment of phobias by **relaxation** and **desensitization.** For example, if a client is afraid of flying, the therapist will compile a series of slides or photographs in hierarchical order from the most anxiety-provoking scenes to those that are completely neutral. Such a series may include: (1) a picture looking out of the window of an airplane on take-off (most anxiety-provoking), (2) a picture of the inside of the airplane, (3) the airport waiting room, (4) the airport ticket counter, (5) the airport parking lot, (6) the road to the airport, (7) the client's own car, (8) the client's driveway, and (9) the client's living room (least anxiety-provoking).

In an actual therapy situation there may be 20 or 30 items in the series. Then, the client is taught to relax by a method that is fairly similar to self-hypnosis. While the client is relaxed in the therapist's office, usually on a couch or in a lounge chair, the least anxiety-provoking scene is projected on a screen. The client learns to **pair** (associate) the feeling of relaxation and the picture he or she is viewing. Then the client works his or her way up the series of pictures until he or she comes to one that causes him or her to feel anxious. The series is then stopped, the client returned to a state of relaxation, and the series continued (going back a few pictures to a nonupsetting one). After many tries, the client will learn to pair the feeling of relaxation with what was formerly the most anxiety-provoking scene.

Following this **desensitization** procedure, the client will usually be taken on a field trip to the airport by the therapist. If at any time the client feels anxious, he or she is encouraged to practice relaxation, and the steps are retraced to a non-anxiety-provoking stage. Finally, when the client is ready, he or she may be taken for an actual airplane ride. However, the pattern of relaxation that occurs during the symbolic representation of the feared event usually generalizes to the real-life situation itself, making a field trip unnecessary.

The behavior treated in this example was the fear of flying. Using this therapeutic approach, it is not necessary for the client to ever know *why* he or she became afraid of flying. It is only required that the fear be stopped.

While these techniques appear to work on almost anyone, a client with a host of problem behaviors (e.g., a chronic paranoid schizophrenic) presents too formidable a task for any behavior therapist. The approach works best with phobias, some sexual disturbances, and some obsessive-compulsive neuroses.

CHAPTER 29 QUESTIONS

1. What is the central concept of milieu therapy?

2. What therapeutic interventions can assist clients in the therapeutic milieu?

3. What are the basic theoretical principles associated with behavior modification?

4. Which types of mental disorders are most appropriately treated with behavior modification therapy?

BIBLIOGRAPHY

Barry, P.D. (1989). *Psychosocial nursing: Assessment and intervention* (2nd ed.). Philadelphia: J.B. Lippincott.

Beck, A.T. (1991). Cognitive therapy. A 30-year retrospective. *American Psychologist, 46,* 368–375.

Freeman, A.M., Pretzer, J., Fleming, B., & Simon, K.M. (1990). *Clinical applications of cognitive therapy.* New York: Plenum Press.

Kaplan, H., & Sadock, B. (1991). *Synopsis of psychiatry: Behavioral sciences, clinical psychiatry* (6th ed.). Baltimore: Williams & Wilkins.

McFarland, G.K., Thomas, M.D. (1991). *Psychiatric mental health nursing: Application of the nursing process.* Philadelphia: J.B. Lippincott.

Mulvihill, D. (1989). Therapeutic relationships in milieu therapy. *Canadian Journal of Psychiatric Nursing, 30,* 21–22.

Sideleau, B. (1992). Activities of daily living. In J. Haber, P. Price-Hoskins, A. Leach McMahon, & B. Sideleau (Eds.). *Comprehensive psychiatric nursing* (4th ed.). St. Louis, MO: Mosby–Year Book.

Tuck, I., & Keels, M.C. (1992). Milieu therapy: A review of development of this concept and its implications for psychiatric nursing. *Issues in Mental Health Nursing, 13,* 51–58.

Chapter 30

■■■■■

Group Therapy

Behavioral Objectives

After reading this chapter the student will be able to:

List the three ways that group therapy can help clients with emotional problems.

Describe the differences between group therapy and psychotherapy and guidance therapy.

Describe the role of the leader in group therapy.

Explain why it can be helpful if the members of a therapy group share a degree of similarity in outlook and attitudes.

Indicate the method by which a qualified member of the health team would go about setting up a therapy group in the hospital.

There are many definitions and many concepts of **group therapy.** In fact, there are many concepts of just what constitutes a group, and just what therapy is. Actually, a well-functioning group may consist of as few as 4 people interacting together; the upper limit is 10 to 12.

We become members of many groups throughout our lives. At birth, we become members of the family group. Then come the play groups, groups in school, in church, and the important teenage peer group; then the social groups, business groups, political groups, and

Mental Health and Mental Illness,
Fifth Edition, by Patricia D. Barry.
J.B. Lippincott Company, Philadelphia © 1994.

parent groups. We remain in some of these groups temporarily, some permanently; some directly, and some indirectly; some voluntarily, and some involuntarily. But always, along life's way, we are involved in group activities.

We are told that our behavior is formed, influenced, and controlled by the dynamic forces existing within groups. If the child's first group—his or her family—fails to provide him or her with positive, gratifying interpersonal learning experiences, his or her psychosocial development may well become impaired. For instance, if the child has never learned how to get approval from his or her mother and father, he or she tends in later life to develop insecure relationships with authority figures, such as teachers and employers. If he or she fails to relate well with his or her peers in the latency period, and is unable to extract pleasure from association with them, he or she may have trouble in competition and with leadership skills, for it is during this period that leadership and the ability to compete are formed.

The concept of structured group interaction used to promote well-defined therapeutic objectives is based on the idea that people have a profound effect on one another, both constructive and destructive.

The word **therapy** indicates therapeutic treatment of some sort. **Therapeutic** refers to any form of treatment or relationship in which the actions, techniques, and practices are purposefully planned and directed toward goals that offer a beneficial effect to the client.

The first clients treated in groups in the United States were tubercular clients. Later, others with various psychosomatic conditions were treated; then the neurotic, the socially maladjusted, and the psychotic. In the early stages of group psychotherapy, it was considered necessary for the therapist to be a psychiatrist. Later, the clinical psychologist was considered sufficiently trained to conduct such sessions. Eventually nurses assumed this role.

■ The Nurse's Role in Group Therapy

Three types of groups most commonly have nurse leaders. One type is a **support group,** in which members explore feelings and thoughts related to a particular subject, such as women's issues or discharge from the hospital. The second is an **instructional group,** in which thoughts and feelings about particular needs related to discharge are discussed within the group. When appropriate, the group leader switches from a leadership role to a teaching role. In these first two groups the major role of the leader is to promote participation from the group members and clarify and paraphrase their statements. This means the leader repeats the statements of others in his or her own words. Such groups have a structure that is preestablished.

Interpretation and explanation of the causes of clients' conflicts are not undertaken in this setting. A registered nurse functioning as a staff nurse who has had previous group coleadership and group participation experience is qualified to lead such a group. He or she should discuss the content and process of the group with a supervisor. Ideally, the supervisor should be a certified clinical nurse specialist, a nurse who holds a master's degree in psychiatric/mental health nursing. It is helpful to receive supervision from a person prepared to understand the nursing perspective of client care. Occasionally, people from other disciplines, while skilled as mental health clinicians, lack the ability to integrate the concurrent nursing needs of the client into the group therapy process.

The third type of group, called **group therapy,** has less formal structure than the first two. In it, the members' thoughts and feelings are subject to the analysis and interpretation of the leader. This type of group requires a leader with advanced knowledge of intrapsychic and group dynamics. Customarily, group psychotherapy is led only by people prepared at the master's or doctoral level in one of the mental health disciplines. The nurse leader, when certified by the Psychiatric/Mental Health Division of the American Nurses Association, has met the following criteria:

1. Holds a master's degree in psychiatric/mental health nursing
2. Has 2 years post-master's experience working in a psychiatric setting
3. Has spent 100 hours in supervision with a board-certified mental health clinician from one of the following disciplines:
   a. Nursing
   b. Social work
   c. Psychology
   d. Psychiatry
4. Has passed a board examination prepared by the American Nurses Association, Division of Psychiatric/Mental Health Nursing

■ Types of Group Therapy

Group therapy is a method of treatment in which a number of clients with similar types of problems meet with the therapist in an organized, structured setting for the purpose of arriving at a better understanding of themselves and others, learning how to modify their behavior to a more socially acceptable form, and developing their ability to derive more satisfaction in their relationships with others.

Many varieties of therapy are included today under the general term of group therapy. Among those most commonly used are rehabilitation therapy, remotivation therapy, occupational therapy, physical therapy, play therapy (for children), work therapy, activity group therapy, psychodrama, art therapy, and the program of Alcoholics Anonymous, as well as therapy groups established for narcotic addicts, homosexuals, parents of cerebral palsy children, and parents of retarded children. There is no question that there can be some overlapping among these various therapies.

Codependence

One of the most therapeutic mental health concepts that has developed in the past 2 decades is called codependence. In most psychiatric inpatient units there will be one or more ongoing therapeutic groups whose purpose is to increase awareness about codependence and how it can affect coping and healthy communication.

Codependency is a cluster of personality traits and patterns that are identified by the chemical dependency field. It is believed that a family that is coping with an alcoholic member develops codependence as a way to cope with the illness. It is also possible that codependent traits are present in the majority of families as a result of the need to avoid emotional distress or conflict.

The characteristics of codependence can create psychological pain in individuals and all of their relationships. Some of the patterns seen in codependence include:

1. A strong compelling desire to solve other persons' problems.
2. Feeling other persons' feelings.
3. Taking responsibility for other persons' choices and actions.
4. Needing to deny one's own feelings.
5. Needing to please others.
6. Overcommiting one's time and energy.
7. Having low self-worth.
8. Feeling strong guilt and avoiding it by taking care of others.
9. Worrying frequently.
10. Feeling emotional turmoil.

There are a number of groups in clinical settings, as well as self-help groups in the community, that utilize the codependency concept in their therapeutic approach. These groups include Alcoholics Anonymous; Al-Anon, the group for spouses and loved ones of alcoholics; Adult Children of Alcoholics; similar groups for other types of chemical addiction; and general groups on codependency.

■ Formation of the Group

The leader should assume the responsibility for making all the arrangements for the group meeting. A treatment goal for the group should be established, as well as plans for its implementation. The nurse should then go to the treatment team and explain the plan for the group, asking for their cooperation in the project. The team members can help choose a balanced group of clients for these sessions, since they are usually quite familiar with the behavioral patterns of the clients under their care.

The next step is to involve the nurse specialist or staff psychiatrists (preferably the team psychiatrist whose clients are to be involved in the therapy) in the project, because supervision is essential to development of therapeutic leadership ability.

The leader should choose a room for the therapy that will accommodate the size of the group—one that is well lighted and ventilated and that is comfortably furnished. The chairs and couches should be arranged in a circle or semicircle.

When establishing a nurse-led group, the following suggestions can promote positive group process:

1. The nurse leader should interview potential group members to determine their appropriateness for the group.
2. The group should consist of 8 to 12 people.
3. The group can be homogeneous (people with similar problems, similar ages, and so on) or heterogeneous (people with a variety of backgrounds, mixed ages, and so on).
4. The group meetings in an inpatient setting are usually scheduled from twice weekly to once daily, depending on the purpose of the group.
5. The group should be relatively stable in order for the feeling of togetherness to develop. However, it can be "open-ended"; that is, when one or two members leave the group, another one or two can start with the group, so the majority of the group has not changed.
6. The length of the therapy is variable. In some instances, it goes on year after year with a few entering and leaving it from time to

time. In other instances, if the goal for which it was set up is reached, it may be disbanded.

7. The meetings should last from 1 to 1½ hours.

■ Leadership Style

The way in which a leader conducts a group can have an important effect on the way the group reaches its objective. The process is what is happening in the group—what dynamics are occurring and why.

Some group therapists may establish themselves as the authority figure in the group. This might be advisable if the group consists chiefly of withdrawn schizophrenics, where the primary goal would be to get them to interact with other members of the group and where a great deal of direct intervention might be needed.

However, the method becoming more and more popular is the method by which the group leader, or therapist, sits quietly in the background, controlling the interaction by indirect guidance, sometimes so indirect that it seems as though the clients are running the whole show. The leader invites the clients to share their situations and explain their problems to the entire group. On occasion he or she must quietly redirect the focus to a better solution of the problem, often saying only a word or two.

Unlike psychoanalysis, counseling, or guidance therapy, this form of client interaction does not aim to solve a single, specific situational problem. Rather, its aim is to bring people with similar problems together to help them ventilate their feelings to each other, explore common emotional problems, face their traumatic memories together, and face up to their unacceptable feelings. The leader rarely directs the conversation or suggests remedies for problems but, rather, acts as a catalyst, helping the ebb and flow of strong emotion, group approval, or group criticism that results from the discussions. The leader encourages clients to express their feelings about people and situations, about themselves and their families, their fears and hopes, their hospitalization, and their illness.

■ The Group Process

At times a client will express deep hostility toward society, toward a family member, an employer, a fellow worker, and even toward another member of the group. The other clients can realize, through this anger, that other people can hate and plot revenge and desire to kill, even as they do. They can identify with this destructive form of hate. By assuring the angry client that they, too, entertain similar "bad" emotions, these other clients help restore his or her self-confidence and help channel his or her destructive impulses without harm to others.

Sometimes a group member receives hostility from fellow members. They may tell him or her in no uncertain terms that his or her feeling, behavior, or thinking is wrong. This may result in a behavioral change or a changing concept in the person thus judged by his or her peers.

Slowly, a sense of belonging develops in the group. An increased sense of self-identity is noticeable in most of the participants. Eventually, the clients in the group start behaving like members of a strongly knit family. What threatens one, threatens all. When one member rejoices over a problem worked through there is a sense of elation in the entire group. This is truly a client-administered form of therapy—clients administer therapy to each other. This form of client-acting-on-client is therapy at its best, and it is a strong deterrent of unacceptable behavior and acting out.

Some people become very anxious as a result of the increased intimacy that such a group formation engenders. Some become overwhelmed and oppressed by shame when they yield to the invitation to disclose the disturbing facts in their past lives. Some cannot tolerate the criticism of their fellow members and may develop antagonism toward those who so criticize them.

On the whole, once a client joins such a therapy group, he or she usually perseveres in it, and very often, members of the group, working out their problems together, become deep friends and carry on these friendships after they leave the hospital.

CHAPTER 30 QUESTIONS

1. What is the acceptable size range for a therapy group?

2. What three types of client groups can nurses lead?

3. What is the difference between a homogeneous and a heterogeneous group?

4. What are the two most common types of leadership styles in the inpatient psychiatric setting?

BIBLIOGRAPHY

Barry, P.D. (1989). *Psychosocial nursing: Assessment and intervention* (2nd ed.). Philadelphia: J.B. Lippincott.

Beattie, M. (1987). *Codependent No More.* San Francisco: Harper Collins.

Hoge, M.A., & McLoughlin, K.A. (1991). Group psychotherapy in acute treatment settings: Theory and techniques. *Hospital & Community Psychiatry, 42,* 153–158.

Kaplan, H., & Sadock, B. (1991). *Synopsis of psychiatry: Behavioral sciences, clinical psychiatry* (6th ed.). Baltimore: Williams & Wilkins.

Long, P., & Leach McMahon, A. (1992). Working with groups. In J. Haber, P. Price-Hoskins, A. Leach McMahon, & B. Sideleau (Eds.). *Comprehensive psychiatric nursing* (4th ed.). St. Louis, MO: Mosby–Year Book.

McFarland, G.K., Thomas, M.D. (1991). *Psychiatric mental health nursing: Application of the nursing process.* Philadelphia: J.B. Lippincott.

Rutan, J.S. (1992). Psychodynamic group psychotherapy. *International Journal of Group Psychotherapy, 42,* 19–35.

Schaef, A.E. (1986). *Co-dependence: Misunderstood—mistreated.* San Francisco: Harper Collins.

Shaffer, J.B.P., & Galinsky, M.D. (1989). *Models of group therapy* (2nd ed.). Englewood Cliffs, NJ: Prentice-Hall.

Whitfield, C.L. (1991). *Co-dependence: Healing the human condition.* Deerfield Beach, FL: Health Communications, Inc.

Chapter 31

■ ■ ■ ■ ■

Psychopharmacology and Electroshock Treatment of Mental Disorders

Behavioral Objectives

After reading this chapter the student will be able to:

List the seven groups of antipsychotics, indicate the effects of each, and name one prominent drug under each category.

Identify the six major types of antidepressants and the physical side effects that may result from the use of each type.

List the two chemical families that constitute the antianxiety medications and indicate why their use should be limited.

Explain why antiparkinsonian agents are frequently prescribed along with antipsychotics.

Name the kind of mental disorder for which lithium carbonate may be prescribed.

Define electroshock therapy and describe the conditions under which it is used.

Mental Health and Mental Illness,
Fifth Edition, by Patricia D. Barry.
J.B. Lippincott Company, Philadelphia © 1994.

The treatment of mental disorders is increasingly being called biologic psychiatry. The name identifies the importance of diagnosing and treating the underlying physiological changes in the brain that contribute to mental disorders. The development of medications that restore brain chemistry to near-normal levels has markedly altered the treatment of mental illness. The availability of these medications has been the single most important contributing factor to the discharge of hundreds of thousands of chronically mentally ill individuals from long-term mental institutions.

The knowledge and clinical use of medications in psychiatry is called psychopharmacology; medications used in the treatment of mental disorders are most commonly called psychotropic drugs. Psychotropic medications are those that affect behavior, psychological or cognitive function, and/or the sensory experience.

■ General Considerations About Psychopharmacology

The role of the nurse and mental health worker in the administration of all medications is central and indisputable. Usually, they are the ones who first perceive the need for medication in a particular client or the need to change the drugs he or she is receiving. They may be the first to recognize side effects or adverse reactions and to call them to the physician's attention. The nurse instructs the client in precautions to observe with certain medications. The psychiatrist, working together with the other members of the mental health team in the area of psychopharmacology, delivers a safer, more comprehensive service to the client as a result of the information he or she receives from the nurse about the client's response to medication.

Importance of Client Consent

The drugs used to treat mental disorders have many side effects (these will be discussed later in the chapter). Physicians and nurses are required to discuss these with their clients, and in doing so, can learn about the client's past experiences with psychotropic medication. Clients have the right to refuse to take these medications. They also have the right to know about the side effects caused by these medications before agreeing to take them.

Major Drugs

There are seven groups of drugs that are used most frequently for clients with mental disorders. These groups and their general function are as follows:

Antipsychotics alleviate psychosis.

Antidepressants reduce depression.

Antianxiety agents lower anxiety levels.

Sedatives/hypnotics also lower anxiety levels.

Antiparkinsonian agents decrease the extrapyramidal symptoms that develop as a side effect of major antipsychotics.

Anticonvulsants lower the potential for convulsions.

Antimanic drugs (lithium) are used to treat acute manic episodes.

There are subtle differences in the action of various members of the antipsychotics: some are more "alerting," some more sedating; each has particular side effects; some are more likely than others to cause symptoms mimicking Parkinson's disease. However, in terms of drug choice, the client's individual reaction, particular situation, and preference almost always casts the deciding vote.

Most clients can remember difficulties with drugs. A man who has experienced disturbed sexual functioning on thioridazine (Mellaril) will ask for something else. The person who has a tendency toward pseudoparkinsonism as a medication side effect and has had great difficulty in this regard with haloperidol (Haldol) or fluphenazine (Prolixin) may fear the same reaction will occur with other drugs. If the client's last medication experience was as an inpatient, the doses he or she remembers may be out of line for outpatient care. Too much sedation could make traveling dangerous or might result in the client staying at home in bed.

Nonetheless, wherever possible, the client's wishes are honored, and comments about his or her drug experiences always listened to. If there is a clear contradiction to the client's drug or dose choice, or if the nurse/physician believes that there is great importance in using a different drug, all of the facts are explained to the client and his or her full cooperation is sought. Further discussion of ethical considerations in administering psychiatric medications can be found in Chapter 4, Legal and Ethical Issues in Mental Health Nursing.

When a client is started on psychotropic drugs *for the first time*, more caution is required, and a careful history of drug sensitivities in both the client and the family must be obtained. A family history of success with a particular psychotropic drug in a blood relative with similar disease is considered as presumptive evidence that the present client may do best with the medication. For example, it is known that amitriptyline (Elavil) is more sedating than imipramine (Tofranil), and usually is a better choice when depression is accompanied by considerable anxiety, agitation, or insomnia. However, if two sisters in a family developed agitated depressions within a few years of each other and the first did well on Tofranil and less well on Elavil, using Tofranil in the second sister should be considered from the beginning. Both constitutional factors and family suggestibility play a role in drug response. Accordingly, information about family drug experience is sought and valued.

■ Antipsychotics

These therapeutically important drugs, also called neuroleptic agents, are divided chemically into seven groups: phenothiazines, thioxanthenes, butyrophenones, diphenylbutylpiperidine, dihydroindolone, dibenzoxazepine, and dibenzodiazepine. Of these the phenothiazines are the largest and most important group. The incidence of side effects from the major tranquilizer group is very high. Table 31-1 lists the various drugs and their normal dosages. See Table 31-2 for a comprehensive list of these drugs and their common side effects.

Phenothiazines

The introduction of phenothiazines in 1955 resulted in major changes in the treatment of mental illness. Most antipsychotics fall into this group. The oldest and most widely used drug in this category is chlorpromazine (Thorazine). It also has the highest incidence of allergic reactions, affecting the liver, skin, and blood; however, these side effects can occur with any drug in the group. Promazine (Sparine) has a cross-sensitivity with chlorpromazine (allergy to one will occur with the other), but switching to other phenothiazines will usually diminish the allergic reaction. One of the most common side effects of these drugs is that the person develops parkinsonian symptoms. More information about these symptoms and their treatment appears later in this chapter.

The most serious liver complication is obstructive jaundice, usually reversible if it is noticed in time and the offending drug is withdrawn. The skin complications include hypersensitivity to sunlight and vari-

Table 31-1 Drug Therapy for Psychosis (Listed in order from the most to the least sedating)

Drug	Daily Intensive-Treatment Dose (mg)	Daily Maintenance Dose (mg)	Available Dosage Size (mg)
Chlorpromazine			10, 25, 50, 100, 200 (tablets)
(Thorazine)	150–500	50–100	30, 75, 150, 200, 300* (spansules)
Triflupromazine (Vesprin)	50–150	25–50	10, 25, 50
Thioridazine (Mellaril)	200–300	20–60	10, 25, 50, 100, 150, 200
Mesoridazine (Serentil)	50–100	10–25	10, 25, 50, 100
Chlorprothixene (Taractan)	50–100	25–50	10, 25, 50, 100
Loxapine succinate (Loxitane)	25–50	10–50	10, 24, 50
Promazine (Sparine)	200–600	50–100	10, 25, 50, 100, 200
Carphenazine (Proketazine)	50–100	25–50	25, 100
Thiopropazate (Dartal)	20–30	5–15	5, 10
Fluphenazine (Permitil, Prolixin)	2–8	1–4	1, 2.5, 5
Perphenazine (Trilafon)	4–16	2–8	2, 4, 8, 16
Prochlorperazine (Compazine)	50–150	25–50	10, 15, 30, 75
Trifluoperazine (Stelazine)	10–20	1–10	1, 2, 5, 10
Haloperidol (Haldol)	2–5	1–2	0.5, 1, 2, 5
Thiothixene (Navane)	10–20	5–10	1, 2, 5, 10
Clozapine (Clozaril)	300–900	300–450	25, 100

* Note: Most of these medications are available in tablet or spansule form; liquid concentrate (to prevent the client from holding the pill in his or her cheek); and IM injectable form.

ous skin eruptions and edema. Nurses who handle Thorazine concentrate, in particular, may develop a contact dermatitis, in which case further direct exposure of the chemical to the skin must be avoided. Blood dyscrasis are not strictly dose related and occur most frequently in white, elderly, debilitated women; the most serious form is agranulocytosis. Most of this reaction occurs very rapidly, usually in the 6th to 8th week of treatment. Symptoms are sore throat, fever, chills, and weakness. Treatment of agranulocytosis should take place in the hospital, and if not promptly undertaken, risk of death is considerable. Following recovery, clients should never again be given any phenothiazine, tricyclic drug (see antidepressants), or diphenylmethane derivatives (see minor tranquilizers). Be keenly aware of this most dangerous of all adverse reactions to psychoactive drugs and act quickly if sore throat or any other symptoms of infection occur, especially in the population at risk (elderly, debilitated, etc.).

Of the other phenothiazines, the one of exceptional value in the outpatient setting is fluphenazine enanthate (Prolixin enanthate) or fluphenazine decanoate, 0.25 to 2 mL IM every 6 hours. Given IM every 10 days to 2 weeks in a dose of 0.25 to 2 mL (25 mg/mL), this drug can effectively handle most psychotic symptomatology. It is widely used in outpatients when there is some question about whether the client will reliably take oral medication. Prolixin enanthate has a higher-than-average incidence of extrapyramidal reactions. Usually the client is instructed to take an antiparkinsonian agent by mouth concurrently and is warned about the possibility of such reactions. If the reaction is severe, 50 mg of diphenhydramine (Benadryl) or 1 to 2 mg of benztropine mestylate (Cogentin) can be given IM.

The other phenothiazines (Table 31-1) differ somewhat in dose and severity of adverse reactions—drowsiness, hypotension (especially postural), extrapyramidal reactions, appetite and weight increase, depression, atropine-like effects (dry mouth, blurred vision, amenorrhea), and allergic reactions (see chlorpromazine).

Thioxanthenes

This category includes chlorprothixene (Taractan) and thiothixene (Natvane). Navane appears to cause less drowsiness and more extrapyramidal effects than Taractan and also, like Thorazine, may produce lenticular pigmentation. Other side effects are similar to the other major tranquilizers.

Table 31-2 Side Effects and Dose Equivalents of
Antipsychotic Medications

Generic Drug Name (Trade name)	Side Effects*	Dosage Range† per 24-Hour Period (mg)	Chlorpromazine Oral Dose Equivalent (mg)
Aliphatic dimethylamine subgroup			
Chlorpromazine hydrochloride (Thorazine)	1–9, 11, 12–15, 23	300–1200	50
Triflupromazine (Vesprin)	1–12	60–150	12.5 to 15
Piperidine subgroup			
Thioridazine hydrochloride (Mellaril)	1–3, 6–7, 12–13, 17–19	30–800	50
Mesoridazine besylate (Serentil)	1–7, 13, 19, 21	100–400	25
Piperacetazine (Quide)	1, 6–7, 10–11, 19–20, 23, 29	20–160	5
Piperazine subgroup			
Acetophenazine dimaleate (Tindal)	1, 6	40–80	10
Carphenazine dimaleate (Proketazine)	1, 6, 8, 9	75–400	12.5 to 15
Fluphenazine hydrochloride (Permitil, Prolixin)	1–9, 11–12, 15, 18	1–20	1
Perphenazine (Trilafon)	1–9, 11–12	6–64	4
Prochlorperazine dimaleate (Compazine)	1–7, 9, 11–12, 15, 20	15–150	5–10
Trifluoperazine hydrochloride (Stelazine)	1–2, 4–9, 11–12, 15, 18	2–20	2
Tricyclic dibenzodiazepine subgroup			
Clozapine (Clozaril)	1–9, 14, 24–29	250–900	50

(continued)

Table 31-2 (Continued)

Generic Drug Name (Trade name)	Side Effects*	Dosage Ranget per 24-Hour Period (mg)	Chlorpromazine Oral Dose Equivalent (mg)
Thioxanthene subgroup			
Thiothixene hydrochloride (Navane)	1, 3, 5–7, 10, 12–14, 18, 23	6–60	2–4
Chlorprothixene (Taractan)	1–10, 14, 15, 18, 20, 21, 23	30–600	50
Butyrophenone subgroup			
Haloperidol, Haldol	1, 6	2–30	150–2250
Diphenylbutylpiperidine subgroup			
Pimozide, Ovap	1, 3–5, 7–8, 12, 28–29	1–2	75–150
Dihydroindolone subgroup			
Molindone, Moban	Similar to chlorpromazine hydrochloride (Thorazine)	50–200	100–400

* Side effects listed here are not intended to be a complete account of all possible adverse reactions reported.

† Drug dosage varies with the client's response and the severity of the disease.

Key to Side Effects

1. Sedation or sleep	16. Menstrual irregularities
2. Ataxia	17. Nausea and vomiting
3. Dry mouth	18. Edema
4. Constipation	19. Impotence
5. Dermatitis	20. Increased appetite
6. Extrapyramidal symptoms	21. Bradycardia
7. Orthostatic hypotension	22. Increased gastric secretions
8. Blood dyscrasia (usually agranulocytosis)	23. Photosensitivity
9. Jaundice	24. Dizziness
10. Convulsions	25. Insomnia
11. Antiemetic	26. Headache
12. Blurred vision	27. Seizures
13. Hypothermia	28. Amenorrhea
14. Tachycardia	29. Electrocardiogram changes
15. Nasal congestion	

Reprinted with permission from Hahn, A., Barkin, R., & Oestrich, S. (1982). *Pharmacology in nursing* (15th ed.). St. Louis, MO: C. V. Mosby.

Butyrophenones

Haloperidol (Haldol) is similar in effect and side reactions to the other major tranquilizers. It may, however, produce very severe extrapyramidal effects. It tends to cause less appetite increase and weight gain than the others.

Dibenzoxazepines

Loxapine succinate (Loxitane) is chemically related to the tricyclic antidepressants and is used for treatment of the symptoms of schizophrenia. It comes in three strengths—10 mg, 25 mg, and 50 mg. The starting dose ranges from 20 to 50 mg per day, with a maximum dose of 250 mg per day suggested. Twenty milligrams of Loxitane is roughly equivalent to 200 mg of Thorazine. In its sedating qualities, it is similar to Stelazine.

Tricyclic Dibenzodiazepines

A new type of medication has been introduced as an antipsychotic treatment for chronic psychotic mental disorders. The generic name of this drug is clozapine (Clozaril), and it belongs to a drug class called tricyclic dibenzodiazepines. It reduces the psychotic mental symptoms of schizophrenia with fewer side effects. The response of long-term chronic schizophrenics to clozapine has been very positive and more therapeutic than any other class of antipsychotic medications, including the phenothiazenes.

The starting dose is half of a 25-mg tablet every day. The dose is increased slowly by 25 to 50 mg daily until either adverse effects or the normal therapeutic range of 300 to 450 mg per day is reached. There are individuals who take up to 900 mg per day with therapeutic effects and no adverse effects. Side effects can include hypotension, seizures, and agranulocytosis. A baseline and weekly white blood cell count is required while a client is on this medication.

Diphenylbutylpiperidine

This category includes the generic medication pimozide (Orap) that is occasionally used to treat Tourette's disorder. The symptoms that respond to pimozide are facial, motor, and phonic tics. The normal daily dose is usually 1 to 5 mg. Side effects include extrapyramidal symptoms, as well as breast enlargement, blood dyscrasias, mood alterations, and tachycardia.

Dihydroindolone

This category is a new chemical class of antipsychotics. It includes molindone (Mobon). The normal daily range of medication is 100 to 200 mg. The effects of this medication are very similar to both the therapeutic and adverse effects of the phenothiazenes.

Other Pharmacology Adjuncts in the Treatment of Psychotic Disorders

Anticonvulsant medications are used to treat the psychotic symptoms associated with a rare form of complex epileptic seizure that results in bizarre behavioral effects and confusion.

Antianxiety agents are used in conjunction with the antipsychotic drugs when the psychotic episode is accompanied by severe anxiety. Sedatives and hypnotics are also used in conjunction with antipsychotic medications when normal sleep patterns are disrupted by the psychotic mental state. Antimanic agents are those drugs used during the manic phase of bipolar disorder; the manic phase is often accompanied by a psychotic mental state.

■ Antidepressants

Five chemical groups of drugs have marked effect on depressive syndromes. They are the dibenzazepines (the tricyclics), tetracyclics, bicyclics, triazolopyridines, aminoketones, and the monoamine oxidase inhibitors (MAOIs). The differences in these antidepressants and their effect can be seen in Table 31-3.

Antidepressant effects of these drugs are generally not noticed for 2 to 3 weeks, and the client must usually be encouraged to continue taking his or her medicine even though at first there is little improvement. Initially, the client's psychomotor retardation, often part of the depressive picture, may seem increased by the drowsiness that the medication causes.

Once his or her depressive symptomatology is relieved, the client tends to discontinue the medication prematurely. However, he or she should ordinarily continue on the antidepressant for 3 to 6 months, and then undergo gradual dosage reduction for up to a total of 1 to 1½ years.

Tricyclics and Tetracyclics

The **tricyclic antidepressants** include amitriptyline (Elavil), clomipramine (Anafranil), desipramine (Norpramin), doxepin (Adapin, Sinequan), imipramine (Trofranil), nortriptyline (Averntyl, Pamelor), protriptyline (Vivactil), and trimipramine (Surmontil).

The side effects of the tricyclics closely resemble those of the phenothiazines to which they are related. They frequently have toxic effects on many of the body's physical systems, notably the cardiovascular system. The section on adverse effects covers these side effects more clearly. Note the tendency to aggravate or precipitate narrow angle glaucoma. Before starting tricyclics ask the client whether he or she has this condition, if he or she has experienced eye

Table 31-3   Antidepressants

Generic Name	Trade Name	Usual Dosage per Day (mg)	*Side Effects
Tricyclics			
Amitriptylene	Elavil	50–100	1–17
Clomipramine	Anafranil	50–100	2–8, 10, 11, 14, 18–21
Desipramine	Norpromin	25–100	5–8, 11, 12, 14, 15, 18, 21–27
Doxepin	Sinequan, Adapin	75–100	1–9, 11–13, 16, 29
Imipramine	Tofranil	50–150	2–8, 10, 12, 14, 15, 16, 24, 27, 29
Nortriptyline	Pamelor	25–100	1–15, 22, 24, 26, 27
Protriptyline	Vivactil	15–30	1–9, 11–15, 17, 21
Trimipramine	Surmontil	50–100	1–12, 14, 15, 16, 25, 27, 29, 30
Tetracyclics			
Amoxapine	Asendin	150–400	1–9, 11–14, 18, 25, 29
Maprotiline	Ludiomil	100–200	1–16, 18, 25–27, 29
Bicyclics			
Fluoxetine hydrochloride	Prozac	20–40	1, 6, 8, 11–13, 18, 21, 22, 28, 31–39
Setraline	Zoloft	50–200	3, 6, 8, 11–13, 19, 21, 28, 34, 36, 37, 40–45

(continued)

Table 31-3 (Continued)

Generic Name	Trade Name	Usual Dosage per Day (mg)	*Side Effects
Triazolopridine			
Trazodone	Desyrel	50–300	1, 3, 6, 9–11, 13, 14, 18, 19, 21, 25, 36, 43, 46–49
Aminoketones			
Bupropion	Wellbutrin	100–300	2, 3, 6, 8, 11, 8, 21, 22, 28, 31

* Side effects

1. Sedation
2. Constipation
3. Dry mouth
4. Blurred vision
5. Urinary hesitancy
6. GI upset
7. Tachycardia
8. Weight gain
9. Fatigue
10. Blood dyscrasia
11. CNS stimulation
12. Rash
13. Headache
14. Hypotension
15. Hypertension
16. Photosensitivity
17. Changes in blood sugar
18. Seizures
19. Sexual dysfunction
20. Dyspepsia
21. Insomnia
22. Anxiety
23. Agitation
24. Allergic reactions
25. Extrapyramidal effects
26. Arrythmias
27. Jaundice
28. Weight loss
29. Edema
30. Heat or cold intolerance
31. Restlessness
32. Nightmares
33. Impaired motor performance
34. Tremor
35. Diaphoresis
36. Diarrhea
37. Manic episodes
38. Weakness
39. Pruritus
40. Dermatologic problems
41. Decrease in serum uric acid
42. Abdominal pain
43. Dizziness
44. Confusion
45. Chest pain
46. Malaise
47. Fainting
48. Hallucinations
49. Delusions

pain, or if he or she has seen halos around lights. The client should be examined for the presence of infected conjunctivae (reddened eyes). The hypotensive effect (as with the phenothiazines) is the most serious side effect in the elderly, and they should be told not to stand up too quickly. Tricyclics also tend to produce withdrawal symptoms upon abrupt discontinuation of a dose over 150 mg per day for 6 to 8 weeks. Withdrawal consists of nausea, vomiting, abdominal cramps, diarrhea, chills, insomnia, and anxiety. Withdrawal begins 4 to 5 days after discontinuation and last 3 to 5 days; it is avoided by gradual withdrawal over 3 to 4 weeks.

Tricyclics cause two types of toxic mental effects. The first consists of a shift from the original depression to a state of manic-like excitement, and the second resembles an organic brain syndrome, especially in the elderly, ranging anywhere from a transient defect in recent memory to delirium.

The **tetracyclic antidepressants** include amoxapine (Asendin), and maprofiline (Ludiomil). They are a more recent chemical class of antidepressants than the tricyclics. Their therapeutic and adverse effects are similar to those of the tricyclics.

The following conditions are contraindications for the use of tricyclic or tetracyclic antidepressants: agitation or overstimulation, alcoholism, angina pectoris, asthma, benign prostatic hypertrophy, blood disorders, congestive heart failure, epilepsy, glaucoma (narrow angle), hyperthyroidism, impaired liver function, kidney disease, myocardial infarct (within 1 year), paroxysmal tachycardia, pregnancy, preoperative status, and pyloric stenosis.

Bicyclics (Serotonin Reuptake Inhibitors)

An important new class of antidepressant drugs, called serotonin reuptake inhibitors, has been introduced to the treatment of depression during the past 5 years. These drugs alter the availability of serotonin, a neurochemical that is decreased in the brains of depressed people. The action of the new class of drugs is to increase the presence of serotonin in the brain structures involved in the regulation of emotion.

Because these antidepressant medications are chemically different from the tricyclic and tetracyclic antidepressants, their side effects are different. They can be reviewed in Table 31-4.

Triazolopyridine

This class of drug includes trazadone hydrochloride (Desyrel). This medication has high sedating properties; low cardiovascular toxicity, unlike the tricyclics and tetracyclics; and no anticholinergic properties. It can be a good drug of choice for use in the elderly.

Aminoketones

Another new antidepressant class includes bupropion (Wellburtrin). This medication has a stimulant effect, no anticholinergic effects, and low cardiovascular toxicity.

Table 31-4   Antianxiety Drugs

Drug Class	Drug Name	Side Effects
Benzodiazepines	Alprazolam (Xanax) Chlordiazepoxide (Librium) Chlorazepate (Tranxene) Diazepam (Valium) Flurazepam (Dalmane) Lorazepam (Ativan) Oxazepam (Serax) Prazepam (Centrax) Quazepam (Doral) Temazepam (Restoril) Triazolam (Halcion)	Sedation, dependence, decreased memory, hypotension, nausea, blood dyscrasias, vertigo, drowsiness, paradoxical agitation, slurred speech
Diphenylmethane derivatives	Hydroxyzine (Atarax, Vistaril)	Dry mouth, drowsiness, tremor convulsions, allergic reactions
Propanediols	Meprobamate (Equanil, Miltown) Tybamate (Solacen, Tybatran)	Same as benzodiazepines
Other	Buspirone hydrochloride (BuSpar)	Sedation, headache, nausea, increased nervousness, faintness

Monoamine Oxidase Inhibitors

The MAOIs can be useful in some clients not affected by the tricyclics. However, they cause potentially serious side effects. Accordingly, they are considered by some authorities to be unacceptable for general use in a community mental health setting. Be sure to caution the physician in cases where the client's reliability or ability to understand and follow directions is questionable. The dangers are two. Hypertensive crisis may occur in clients on MAOIs who eat foods that contain tyramine or dopa. Such foods include aged cheese, broad beans, yeast products, Chianti wine, pickled herring, chocolate, and chicken livers. The symptoms of such a crisis are sharp elevation in blood pressure, throbbing headache, nausea, vomiting, elevated temperature, sweating, and stiff neck. Chlorpromazine (50 to 100 mg IM) is often effective in aborting the episode. The second danger is potentiation of other drugs. The list is long and contains many drugs in common use in medical problems, such as central nervous system depressants, sympathomimetics, ganglion blocking and anticholinergic agents (used in peptic ulcer and other gastrointestinal conditions), antihistamines, opiates, diuretics, chloroquine, hypoglycemic drugs, corticosteroids, antirheumatic compounds, and the tricyclic antidepressants.

■ Antianxiety Drugs

These drugs can be divided into three chemical families: benzodiazepines, which include chlordiazepoxide (Librium), diazepam (Valium), and oxazepam (Serax); diphenylmethane derivatives, such as hydroxyzine (Atarax, Vistaril); and propanediols, which include meprobamate (Miltown) and tybamate (Solacen, Tybatran). Buspirone hydrochloride (Buspar) is a nonbenzodiazepine used in the treatment of anxiety disorders.

The antianxiety agents have limited usefulness in the outpatient setting, unless the anxiety is incapacitating. Anxiety normally accompanies growth and change and is an important ingredient in providing the motivation for most psychotherapeutic work. Most clients can tolerate a moderate level of anxiety without medication. They find that it rapidly diminishes as their energies are directed toward therapy and growth. Further, these drugs are more similar than not to the barbiturates and other CNS depressants. They have a high potential for habituation and addiction and carry the same danger on withdrawal (convulsions and delirium tremens) as the other CNS depressants. See Table 31-4 for a more complete description of the side effects of this family of drugs.

■ Sedatives and Hypnotics

Chemically, these CNS depressants are divided into barbiturates and nonbarbiturates. These drugs have a very limited but important place in psychiatry. They have withdrawal effects (e.g., convulsions) when discontinued abruptly, especially at high dosages. Withdrawal from severe abuse situations should always be carried out in a hospital. When severe sleep disturbances are a problem and cannot be handled by the sedating phenothiazines, either paraldehyde or chloral hydrate are recommended, since these drugs carry the least potential for abuse of the sedative/hypnotics. A list of popular sedatives is given here for completeness, not as a recommendation for use.

Barbiturates
>   amobarbital (Amytal)
>   butabarbital (Butisol)
>   phenobarbital (Nembutal)
>   phenobarbital (Eskapen, Eskabarb, Luminal)
>   secobarbital (Seconal)

Nonbarbiturates
>   chloral hydrate (Felsules, Rectules, Noctec)
>   ethchlorvynol (Placidyl)
>   ethinamate (Valmid)
>   flurazepam (Dalmane)
>   glutethimide (Doriden)
>   methyprylon (Noludar)
>   quazepam (Doral)
>   paraldehyde

■ Antiparkinsonian Agents

Benztropine (Cogentin), biperiden (Akineton), procyclidine (Kema-drin), and trihexyphenidyl (Artane) are used most frequently. If one does not work well enough after a trial, the client is switched to another. More and more physicians use these agents only after dystonic effects appear, while others prefer to start them simultaneously with the major tranquilizer. After accommodation to the tranquilizer (6 to 8 weeks), the antiparkinsonian dose can usually be lowered or a milder agent used (Cogentin is the most powerful). Some clients remain convinced, however, that the antiparkinsonian is the real tranquilizer and will not be without it. The atropine-like effect of these agents adds to the similar effect of the tranquilizers and causes blurred vision and dry mouth. If the vision is not improved with dosage reduction, dime-store reading glasses are recommended (especially for clients who must read). Hard candy is recommended for the dry mouth.

■ Anticonvulsants

Occasionally, seizures occur as a symptom with certain types of mental disorders, particularly those with mania. When they occur or are anticipated, there are two drugs of choice most often used in the psychiatric setting. They include carbamazapine (Tegretol), ordered at 200 mg intervals twice a day until symptoms are controlled. The second medication is divalproex (Depacote). The usual daily dose is 750 mg.

■ Antimanic Drugs

Lithium Carbonate

This drug (Eskalith, Lithonate, Lithane) is the treatment of choice in acute manic episodes, which it can terminate within 10 days in 90% of clients. Lithium is an essential pharmacologic agent in the treatment of bipolar disorders. A bipolar disorder can include acute episodes of psychosis during the manic phase and severe depression during the depressed phase. Often, it is necessary to use antipsychotic and antidepressant medications in conjunction with lithium.

It is also used with varying success in other forms of cyclic illness, whether or not there is a manic phase. Because the effective therapeutic dosage is fairly close to the toxic dosage, it is important to monitor the lithium blood level regularly. This is done with a laboratory test called a serum lithium level.

Six hundred to 1800 mg of lithium carbonate per day in divided doses usually produces a serum lithium level of 0.6 to 1.5 mEq/L. This is within the therapeutic range and not significantly toxic. Because lithium is excreted at far different rates in various people, a serum determination must be made frequently at the beginning to be sure the 1.5-mEq/L limit is not exceeded. In the presence of febrile illness or in any situation that causes a loss of fluids (including administration of diuretics), the lithium level must be closely watched.

Common side effects are nausea, occasional vomiting and mild abdominal pain, fatigue, and thirst. These gradually subside and later recurrence may signal impending intoxication. Intoxication generally occurs when serum levels exceed 2 mEq/L and it produces confusion, coarse tremor, muscle twitching, and difficult speech. More severe effects include ataxia, nystagmus, hyperreflexia, stupor, and coma. Fatalities are rare.

■ Adverse Effects of Psychotropic Medications

The most severe side effect of the major tranquilizers and tricyclic antidepressants is that the extrapyramidal tract of the CNS can develop mild to severe reactions to the drugs. The exact cause of this action is unknown. It is thought to be related to the medication's blockade of the dopamine-mediated response.

The extrapyramidal effects that the antiparkinsonian agents are used to treat can be produced by all the major tranquilizers in large enough doses. These drug-induced effects can be divided into four classes:

Dystonic effects, which occur the first day of treatment, up to 1 week

Akathisia, which begins during the 2nd week of treatment

Pseudoparkinsonism, which appears after 3 or 4 weeks of treatment

Dyskinesia

Dystonia manifests as muscle spasms of the head, neck, lips, and tongue and appears as torticollis (severe neck muscle spasms), retrocollis, opisthotonus (arched position of body caused by neurologic disorder), oculogyric crisis (eyeballs are fixed in upward position), trismus (lock jaw), slurred speech, dysphagia (difficult swallowing), and laryngospasm (which can be life-threatening).

Akathisia, or motor restlessness, is seen as constant pacing and inability to sit down.

Pseudoparkinsonism is characterized by a masked face (immobile) and shuffling gait with pill-rolling movements of hands, coarse tremor, drooling, and waxy skin. It is also seen as weakness, diminished drive, and muscular rigidity.

It may often be impossible to tell except by trial and error whether the akathisia seen is the result of anxiety, which would require more phenothiazine, or is an extrapyramidal effect, which would require less.

Tardive dyskinesia can occur with long-term treatment with some phenothiazines, especially in women, the elderly, and those with some brain damage. It is not relieved by antiparkinsonian drugs and is a permanent irreversible side effect. It is recognized by rhythmic facial and tongue movements. The problems with this side effect must be weighed against the problems of continuing psychosis in the population at risk.

Another major side effect is due to action of the major tranquilizers and tricyclic antidepressants on the autonomic nervous system. This results in anticholinergic, atropine-like effects such as dry mouth, constipation, and urinary retention. The autonomic effects also account for the hypotensive effects.

It is especially important to be aware of the more common adverse reactions or side effects of the psychotropic chemicals. Many of these have been discussed under the individual drug headings and in chart form for easy reference. Some drugs cause a sympathetic nervous system response (either fight or flight) and a group of symptoms related to this, such as tachycardia, high blood pressure, excitement, and hypomania. Others elicit a parasympathetic nervous system response (more vegetative) with a slowed pulse, hypotension, and drowsiness. Still others bring forth allergic responses and many cause primitive nervous system responses such as tremors and pseudo-parkinsonism.

Drugs within a certain group (such as the tricyclics) also vary one from another in the severity of the adverse effects they cause. Finally, the individual client's response can cause a great difference in both a drug's therapeutic effectiveness and the type and degree of adverse effect seen.

When these adverse effects are bothersome to the client the problem is often dose related, and it diminishes when the dose is reduced. It can usually be handled satisfactorily without discontinuing medication. However, these side effects are the most common reason that clients reduce or stop their medication. The nurse can question the client about these effects, reassure him or her, suggest measures to reduce the annoyance, and recognize and report the more serious and dangerous adverse reactions.

When there is a clear choice between having a nonpsychotic client with blurred vision and a dry mouth, or a psychotic client without these symptoms, almost everyone will opt for the former. Not every choice is clear; the nurse and psychiatrist must weigh the various choices until the best possible solution is found for the particular client at the particular time.

■ Nursing Responsibilities

What are your duties in administering and/or monitoring major and minor tranquilizers and mood-elevating drugs to clients? First, be well acquainted with their actions, dosages, forms, characteristics, and complications.* Use great care and caution in administering these drugs, observe the client closely, both for behavioral and physical reactions, and chart these observations. Record and report failure of

---

* In addition, the nurse should be aware of the legal and ethical issues of psychotropic drug administration. See Chapter 4.

the drug to produce the desired effect. Immediately report sensitivity or toxic reaction. Since the physician usually adjusts the dosage to the individual's physical and emotional requirements and since each person's tolerance or reaction to these drugs is specifically his or her own, you must judge whether the dosage is achieving the desired results. The physician must rely on these observations to decide whether the dosage should be maintained, decreased, or increased.

Realize that drugs, no matter how effective, are by no means the final answer to mental health problems, in spite of the excellent response of psychotic clients to modern therapy. Drugs cannot in themselves repair personality disorders, nor can they take the place of meeting sociologic needs. Their major contribution is symptom removal. This will enable the client to respond to other therapies more effectively.

■ Electroshock Therapy

One of the alternatives to psychopharmacology when a client does not respond to treatment for depression is **electroshock therapy** (EST). (Electroshock therapy and electroconvulsive therapy, ECT, are the same treatment.) It is reserved for specific types of mental disorders that cannot be treated by medication—most effectively in treating moderate to severe depression. Because it carries some physical risks, it should be used only when one or both of the following conditions exist:

The client cannot physically tolerate the many toxic physiological side effects of the tricyclic or MAOI antidepressants. This client usually has heart disease, allergies, or other types of physical disorders that would be aggravated by antidepressant medications.

The client has not responded favorably to treatment with antidepressant medication after a time period of several weeks, and continues to be moderately to severely depressed.

Administration of EST

A client receiving EST is placed on a stretcher and given a brief-acting general anesthetic. Next he or she is given a muscle relaxant such as succinylcholine (Anectine) to counteract the grand mal muscular contractions that accompany electric shock. He or she is also given a high concentration of oxygen by the anesthesiologist. Next, an electric current passes between two electrodes placed on the head and he or she receives a shock that results in a mild to moderate convulsive movement. Following the treatment, the client will become confused within the next 5 to 15 minutes. The confusion usually clears within a few hours; however, amnesia about the actual EST experience will remain indefinitely.

Theories About the Therapeutic Effects of EST

Researches have discovered that there are specific brain neurotransmitters that underlie man's basic emotions of rage, fear, and so on. As these neurochemical actions are researched, scientists theorize that EST causes a chemical reaction in the brain. This reaction results in a shift of the neurochemistry of depression. It is known, for example, that a chemical solution of any kind undergoes change when an electric shock passes through it. Now, however, psychobiologic research on the neurotransmitters, norepinephrine and serotonin, indicate that they are implicated in depression, but the effects of EST on these two neurotransmitters is not fully understood.

Nursing Care of Clients Receiving EST

EST is usually administered in a room adjacent to the psychiatric unit. During the procedure, a psychiatrist, anesthesiologist, and nurse are present. In order to ensure the client's safety, oxygen and suctioning apparatus, as well as emergency resuscitative drugs, are present. If needed, they are administered by the anesthesiologist. Nursing care involves obtaining the client's signature on the informed consent form and answering any questions the client may have. If it is the client's first EST treatment and if the client is unusually anxious or has not received an adequate explanation from the psychiatrist, you should ask the doctor to revisit the client before he or she is brought to the EST room. EST can be very frightening to clients, and because it is usually repeated 3 times a week for a total of 6 to 10 treatments, you should carefully prepare the client for his or her first treatment so he or she will not fear the remainder.

Bring the client to the EST room in loose-fitting clothing. Remove dentures and hairpins. While the electric shock is given to the client, hold his or her arms at his or her sides to prevent uncontrolled thrashing. Following the treatment, hold his or her head to the side to prevent aspiration of saliva.

Closely monitor the client's vital signs and airway while he or she is waking from the treatment. Ensure his or her safety in bed, so confusion following EST will not cause harm.

Confusion and memory loss regarding recent events are the two most common changes in mental state that result from EST. Orientation returns more rapidly than recall of recent events. The severity of these two changes often depends on the client's age and the number of treatments he or she has received. Often, the client feels frightened by these changes in mental state. Quietly reassure him or her that these are the expected effects of the EST and that they will pass in time.

CHAPTER 31 QUESTIONS

1. What factor has markedly altered the treatment of mental illness?

2. What is the largest and most important group of major tranquilizers?

3. What three chemical groups of drugs have a marked effect on depressive syndromes?

4. Which drug is the treatment of choice in acute manic episodes?

BIBLIOGRAPHY

Barry, P.D. (1989). *Psychosocial nursing: Assessment and intervention* (2nd ed.). Philadelphia: J. B. Lippincott.

Cooper, J., Bloom, F., & Roth, R. (1991). *The biochemical basis of neuropharmacology* (6th ed.). New York: Oxford University Press.

Facts and Comparisons. (1989). Philadelphia: J. B. Lippincott, *12*.

Harris, B. (1992). Psychopharmacology. In J. Haber, P. Price-Hoskins, A. Leach McMahon, & B. Sideleau (Eds.). *Comprehensive psychiatric nursing* (4th ed.). St. Louis, MO: Mosby–Year Book.

Janicak, P.G., & Davis, J.M. (Eds.). (1991). *A selective update on psychopharmacologic and somatic therapies in psychiatry-I*. Longwood, FL: Ryandic Publishing Inc. (Psychiatric Medicine, Vol. 9, No. 1.)

Janicak, P.G., & David, J.M. (Eds.). (1991). *A selective update on psychopharmacologic and somatic therapies in psychiatry-II*. Longwood, FL, Ryanadic Publishing Inc. (Psychiatric Medicine, Vol. 9, No. 2.)

Kaplan, H., & Sadock, B. (1991). *Synopsis of psychiatry: Behavioral sciences, clinical psychiatry* (6th ed.). Baltimore: Williams & Wilkins.

Klawans, H.L., Goetz, C.G., & Tanner, C.M. (1992). *Textbook of clinical neuropharmacology and therapeutics* (2nd ed.). New York: Raven Press.

McFarland, G.K., Thomas, M.D. (1991). *Psychiatric mental health nursing: Application of the nursing process.* Philadelphia: J.B. Lippincott.

McKenney, L., & Salerno, E. (Eds.). (1992). *Mosby's pharmacology in nursing.* St. Louis, MO: Mosby–Year Book.

Rosin, U., & Kohler, G.K. (1991). Psychodynamic aspects of psychopharmacology in functional somatic complaints. *Psychotherapy & Psychosomatics, 56,* 129–134.

Chapter 32

■■■■■

Nursing Care of the Older Adult With a Mental Disorder

Behavioral Objectives

After reading this chapter the student will be able to:

Name the percentage of older Americans who are institutionalized.

Describe why general systems theory is important in assessing the health status of the older adult.

List the types of losses older adults can experience.

Name the most common types of mental distress in the elderly and describe each condition and the types of nursing intervention that can reduce the distress.

Advances in health care and government involvement in ensuring adequate care for older adults have resulted in large numbers of people living into their 70s, 80s, and 90s. A great majority of the elderly are self-sufficient and live in their own homes. They are able to maintain an independent lifestyle, often with the involvement of family members who assist them in a variety of supportive ways.

Mental Health and Mental Illness,
Fifth Edition, by Patricia D. Barry.
J.B. Lippincott Company, Philadelphia © 1994.

Indeed, although there is a prevalent misconception that the majority of old people are institutionalized, it is not true. It is estimated that 11.7% of the U.S. population—25 million people—are over 65. The number of institutionalized Americans over age 65 is approximately 1,126,000, or only 0.4% of the total population. With few exceptions, the majority of those people were no longer able to live independently or with their families because their mental or physical condition was progressively worsening. The inability of the family system to continue coping with the increasing strain of the infirmity, rather than the severity of the infirmity, determines when institutionalization occurs in most cases.

In considering the nursing care of the elderly with mental disorders, we must remain constantly aware of general systems theory, discussed in Chapter 9, Influence of Family and Social Environment on the Individual. All aspects of our functioning are constantly interacting: physical, psychological, and social systems. In children and younger adults, the interactions of these three realms of our being are occurring at all times, although they may not be completely evident. In aged people, it is the effects of these interactions that create the difficulties that they encounter as time progresses.

The majority of older people remain intellectually aware and are capable of independent living until very old age. Despite the losses they encounter, they remain remarkably adaptable and resilient. Their long life experience has prepared them to flow with the currents of change that accompany aging rather than be overwhelmed by them.

■ Effects of Loss on the Older Adult

People of all ages experience losses brought about by physical illness and disabilities. The losses are accompanied by a grieving process in which a variety of mental changes occur as the grief is resolved. The grieving process can take up to 1 year when a significant loss occurs. For the elderly, the number of losses they experience can occur in a succession that does not allow them time to adequately resolve one loss before another occurs. Examples of losses frequently encountered in the aging process are as follows:

Loss of employment through retirement
Loss of self-image, if job was a strong source of self-gratification
Loss of physical health
Loss of good body image as a result of declining health

Loss of independence as infirmities increase

Loss of mobility

Loss of spouse, friends, or other family members owing to death

Loss of opportunities for social contact with others

Loss of home

Loss of income

Needless to say, these losses strain a person's coping abilities. The mastery of this strain requires well-functioning intellectual and emotional resources. But age slowly degenerates these resources.

As we age, our bodies, minds, and social systems begin to change at an increased rate. Brain tissue is not immune to these physiological changes that are occurring throughout the body. The changes in the brain affect our intellectual and emotional capabilities, including our abilities to cope.

■ The Most Common Psychosocial Disorders of the Aged

It is important to distinguish between the terms **psychiatric** and **psychosocial** when referring to mental disorders in the aged. In order to be termed a psychiatric disorder, a person's mental status must meet the criteria of the *Diagnostic and Statistical Manual of Mental Disorders,* fourth edition, revised (DSM-IV) categories of mental disorders (see Chapters 20 to 27). Many people who experience mental distress and emotional pain do not meet these formal criteria. The quality of their lives and that of their families can be severely disrupted, however, because of the impact of their decreasing mental abilities on their psychosocial functioning. The following are the most common types of mental distress in the elderly:

Depression

Insomnia

Cognitive impairment

Stress reactions

Decrease in social and daily living skills

■ Nursing Care of the Older Adult With Depression

The incidence of depression in the elderly has never been well- documented by research. The number of people of all ages with depression that meet the DSM-III-R criteria of major affective illness is approximately 4% to 6%. As described above, the elderly experience a number of losses as aging progresses. Because unresolved loss is a major factor in many depressive reactions, it is possible that the amount of depression in the elderly is higher than that in the general population.

Remember that two of the symptoms of depression are slowing of cognitive functioning and decrease in memory. These are also the symptoms of progressive dementia, a form of cognitive impairment disorder. Unfortunately primary health care-givers often do not take the time to obtain more information from their clients in order to differentiate between the possible causes of decreased intellectual functioning. Depression is treatable and reversible; generally, dementia is not. Too often, the symptoms of depression are assumed to be the signs of dementia; no treatment occurs, and the person's emotional discomfort continues. The symptoms that are present in older people who meet the criteria of depression are at least 2 weeks of experiencing the following symptoms:

Dysphoric feelings of sadness and hopelessness

Changes in appetite

Changes in sleep patterns

Loss of energy

Lack of interest or pleasure in normal activities

Increased feelings of guilt

Slowed or agitated physical activity

Decreased thinking, concentration, and memory

The most common treatments for depression in the elderly are psychotherapy and antidepressant medication.

The nursing care recommendations given in this chapter should be used as a basis for nursing care planning with depressed older adults. Another nursing care approach that can be considered is nurse-led support groups. This type of group is not the same as a psychotherapy group in which there is more intensive probing and interpretation of a person's statements. Rather, it is a group in which the depressed person has the opportunity to relate with other people who have similar problems.

Often, older people, whether living in their own home, with family members, or in institutions, are isolated from other people. The opportunity to engage in discussion with others in a formal group can provide them with a sense of support and understanding that may have been lacking in their lives. Caring family members, despite their best intentions, cannot provide for all of the psychosocial needs of their aging relative. The sharing of feelings and thoughts with others who are experiencing similar changes can be reassuring and fulfilling.

Nursing care of a depressed older person who is taking antidepressant medication also involves careful observation for the many physical side effects caused by antidepressants (see Chapter 31, Psychopharmacology and Electroshock Treatment of Mental Disorders). These medications can have negative effects on each of the body's major systems. If there is a previously existing physical disorder, these drugs could worsen it. Furthermore, these medications can cause physical symptoms that can be confused with newly emerging illnesses. Remember to document routinely mental and physical status, noting and reporting changes in either. This will assist the physician in evaluating the therapeutic effects of the medication.

■ Nursing Care of the Older Adult With Cognitive Impairment

Cognitive impairment is a decrease in the intellectual aspect of mental functioning; it includes a decrease in problem-solving ability, reasoning, judgment, concentration, and memory. The two most common causes (mentioned in the preceding section) are depression and cognitive impairment disorders.

Remember that some organic brain syndromes are reversible. Ideally, all people suspected of having a dementia type of cognitive impairment disorder should receive a thorough physical examination and laboratory tests to rule out any other physical condition that could cause a toxic brain syndrome and could be reversed with treatment (see Chapter 21, Delirium, Dementia, and Other Cognitive Disorders). Toxic brain syndromes can be caused by medication side effects, nutritional deficiencies, different types of physical illness such as metabolic disorders, infection, or trauma, and so on.

The clients should also be examined by a psychiatrist. Within the field of psychiatry a new subspecialty, geriatric psychiatry, has developed specifically to care for the older adult with mental disorders. Whenever possible, someone trained in this specialty, who has a systems perspective of the multiple causes of geriatric mental disorders, should perform the psychiatric evaluation.

People with cognitive impairment experience a number of other changes in mental functioning as an outcome of their decreased intellectual ability. Their capacity to cope with stress is decreased, because their ability to solve problems and think through the various events they are encountering is hampered. In addition, they experience a decrease in self-esteem because they can no longer rely on their minds. As a result, they may gradually withdraw from relationships and stop attending social functions, because they do not want others to notice their decreased mental functioning.

Stressful Effects on the Family of the Aged Person

Cognitive impairment in an elderly family member places a strain on the entire family system as its members try to adapt. For example, an elderly lady who lives alone may have a physician's appointment, which her son calls to remind her of on the morning of the appointment. When he arrives after a ½-hour drive to discover that his mother has forgotten about it and is not ready to leave, he may become frustrated and angry. As these types of events increase and concern rises about the safety of the aging person living alone, many families elect to bring the elderly relative into their home. The immediate solution can be positive for all concerned. If the cognitive impairment worsens, however, the level of strain on the family increases.

The children of the aging relative, sometimes called the "sandwich generation," experience increased stress as they attempt to balance the needs of their parents with those of their own children. Family communication in the immediate family can become rigid and closed as negative emotions are avoided. Communication in the extended family network of relatives can be equally affected if there is resentment by the person who assumes the caretaking role.

As the mental impairment of the older person increases, it is not unusual for the stress within the family to rise to a critical point, at which a decision is made to institutionalize the older adult rather than risk what feels like or actually is family disintegration.

Increasingly, support services are being developed in the community to assist families before they reach a crisis point. These include adult daycare programs or programs designed to relieve the primary care-giver. In addition, programs for the primary care-giver are beginning to include group or individual counseling, giving them a chance to relieve themselves of unpleasant feelings such as sadness, anger, or guilt that frequently accompany the care of a cognitively impaired person. Other helpful programs support coping by increasing knowledge of resources and problem-solving skills for both the older adult and his or her care-givers.

The nursing care of the institutionalized older adult with cognitive impairment is described in Chapter 21, Delirium, Dementia, and Other Cognitive Disorders, under the sections on dementia or delirium, depending on the cause of the mental disorder.

■ Nursing Care of the Older Adult With Insomnia

Another condition that causes mental distress for many elderly people is insomnia. **Insomnia** is a disturbance in a person's normal sleeping pattern. Insomnia can be due to many causes: pain caused by physical conditions, stimulant or diuretic medications, effects of excessive coffee or nicotine, sleeping at other times during the day, poor sleeping environment, or depression or anxiety.

Nearly one-fourth of healthy adults over 65 years report sleeping difficulties. In fact, many people overestimate their need for sleep. It should be noted that as a person ages, his or her metabolic rate declines, and his or her need for sleep decreases. In addition, as a person grows older, there are changes in brain wave activity during the various stages of sleep that contribute to his or her increased wakefulness.

Many times, people who experience sleep disturbances of varying levels of difficulty further contribute to the problem by worrying about not sleeping in advance of going to bed. Gradually, they condition themselves so that the thought of not sleeping is accompanied by anxiety.

Generally, it can be helpful to remember that the body maintains regulating mechanisms to ensure its own well-being. Sleep occurs when it is necessary to maintain physical and mental equilibrium. An important fact for nurses to know is that hypnotic medications—chronically overused in this country—are effective for no more than 2 weeks, in most cases.

The majority of people with insomnia are not in institutions and are not recipients of nursing care. Appropriate nursing intervention, regardless of the setting, includes sharing accurate information, providing an environment that is conducive to sleep, and using the therapeutic nursing approaches recommended in Chapter 26, Dissociative, Sexual, and Other Disorders.

■ Nursing Care of the Older Adult With Decrease in Social and Daily Living Skills

An aging person may experience a decrease in his or her normal relationship abilities and living skills. Often, this is the result of cognitive impairment, decreased opportunities for social relationships, and other types of deprivation. Accordingly, as he or she is less able to maintain relationships and to care adequately for his or her nutritional and hygiene needs, it becomes necessary for him or her to be cared for by relatives, agencies, or institutions.

An innovative program designed by clinicians at the Florida Mental Health Institute seeks to address the needs of two populations: institutionalized clients for whom the goal is discharge, and people who are not institutionalized, but whose poor self-care will soon lead to admission if there is no intervention.

The programs they designed are aimed at teaching skills—hygiene; self-maintenance skills, such as laundering, meal planning, and money management; normal communication skills; and so on.

Nurses can teach these skills to institutionalized people who lack them and can reinforce their accomplishments with warmth and approval. Also, nurse-led groups that address the topics discussed above are helpful in teaching social and daily living skills and promoting a supportive group environment in which skill acquisition can take place.

■ Nursing Care of the Older Adult With Stress Reactions

As described early in the chapter, biopsychosocial assessment of older people allows appropriate intervention to be developed. The number of life stressors experienced in old age is usually high. In most cases, adults maintain the same style of coping in old age that they have used throughout their lifetime, but now, a series of life stressors can pile up, undermining coping abilities and overloading coping strength.

A mild form of cognitive impairment, added to this scenario, can further reduce tolerance for stress. Coping strength is greatly dependent on a person's intellectual capacity. As it diminishes, so too can tolerance for stress.

The most important external factor in a person's capacity to deal with stress is the availability of support people. Ideally, this support is available from family members or friends. Community support services are hard-pressed to meet the needs of the ever-increasing number of elderly clients.

Some of the primary factors that determine an older person's stress tolerance are as follows:

1. Perception of the stressful incident. Does the person view this event as significantly threatening? Why?
2. History of other stressful incidents during the previous year. Is the current incident the "straw that breaks the camel's back"?
3. Degree of cognitive impairment due to organic causes.
4. Availability of support people.

Retirement

The level of stress tolerance for older adults is often related to the issue of retirement. The partner of the retired person can be equally affected. Reichard, Livson, and Peterson have proposed the following three basic personality types that adapt well to retirement:

1. The mature type. Emotionally well adjusted; life is satisfying for them.
2. The "rocking chair" type. Easygoing natures; relieved to be free of responsibilities of work and active family.
3. The "armored" type. Actively involved in life to avoid feelings of uselessness; probably have many type A personality characteristics; goal oriented.

They also believe that there are two personality types who may not cope well with retirement:

1. The angry type. Resentment about unfulfilled goals causes them to resist acceptance of retirement.
2. The self-hating type. Feelings of failure cause ongoing guilt and poor self-esteem.

Catastrophic Reaction

On occasion, if an older person is severely stressed, he or she may be subject to a catastrophic reaction. A **catastrophic reaction** occurs when there is a sudden, unexpected stressor, and the person's normal coping mechanisms fail. The result is severe anxiety accompanied by disruption of equilibrium in the physical, intellectual, and emotional realms (see Chapter 15, Stress, Effective Coping, and Adaptation). This response is also known as a panic reaction. Frequently it is due to organic impairment that decreases a person's intellectual capacity to think through and adapt to the stressor.

When an older person is demonstrating decreased tolerance for stress, it often is an indication that his or her problem-solving and decision-making capacities are decreased. Care-givers can help by reviewing the person's current life situation with him or her, with the intention of identifying situations that are problematic. In addition, it is wise to have him or her describe potentially stressful circumstances he or she is anticipating. Often, by using the following problem-solving process, solutions can be found that decrease the stress he or she is experiencing.

Problem-Solving Process

1. Identify the problem. Describe why it is a problem and what factors are feeding into it.
2. Describe the possible solutions.
3. Choose the best solution.
4. Implement it.
5. Evaluate the outcome. If not successful, analyze why, choose an alternative from item 2 above, and implement and evaluate it.

Often, this process relieves the person's distress because it gives him or her the opportunity to describe it. He or she has a stronger sense of mastery of the problem. Recommend the use of this process to the client's family, whether the client is in a hospital or living independently.

If the person is unable to actively participate in this process, it may be necessary to assume a more custodial role. Problem solving by the nurse, in consultation with the family, if available, can provide the client with a stronger sense of security.

Generally, it is unwise to routinely administer minor tranquilizers to institutionalized people experiencing chronic stress reactions due to organic impairment. Instead, whenever possible, control the environment to minimize the potential for such reactions.

For older people living independently and experiencing increasing amounts of stress, individual counseling is often helpful. This can assist them in identifying both causes and solutions for their stress. In addition, it can help to reduce their anxiety levels. Minor tranquilizers should be avoided, except in the transition period immediately following a severe stressor, such as the unexpected loss of a spouse.

Another stress reliever in the healthy adult is a regular exercise regimen, such as daily walking. The tension-relieving benefits of exercise can have therapeutic effects in chronically stressed individuals.

CHAPTER 32 QUESTIONS

1. What are five types of losses frequently experienced by older adults?

2. What are the most common psychosocial disorders of the aged?

3. Which two symptoms of depression are also symptoms of dementia?

4. What are three common signs of cognitive impairment?

BIBLIOGRAPHY

Barry, P.D. (1989). *Psychosocial nursing: Assessment and intervention* (2nd ed.). Philadelphia: J.B. Lippincott.

Bergener, M. (Ed.). (1991). *Challenges in aging.* New York: Academic Press.

Eliopoulos, C. *Health assessment of the older adult* (2nd ed.). Redwood City, CA: Addison-Wesley, Health Sciences Division.

Fopma-Loy, J. (1989). Geropsychiatric nursing: Focus and setting. *Archives of Psychiatric Nursing, 3,* 183–190.

Hogstel, M.O. (1991). Assessing mental status. *Journal of Gerontological Nursing, 17,* 42–43.

Hogstel, M.O. (Ed.). (1990). *Geropsychiatric nursing.* St. Louis, MO: Mosby–Year Book.

Hughes, C.P. (1992). Community psychiatric nursing and depression in elderly people. *Journal of Advanced Nursing, 17,* 34–42.

McFarland, G.K., Thomas, M.D. (1991). *Psychiatric mental health nursing: Application of the nursing process.* Philadelphia: J.B. Lippincott.

Reichard, S., Livson, F. & Peterson, P. (1980). In L. Stein (ed). *Aging and personality: A study of 87 older men.* Salem, NH: Ayer Company Publications.

Tillman-Jones, T.K. (1990). How to work with elderly patients on a general psychiatric unit. *Journal of Psychosocial Nursing & Mental Health Services, 28,* 27–31.

Developing Critical Thinking Skills
Through Class Discussion

UNIT VII Case Study
Interventions and Treatment
of Mental Disorders

Henry is a 59-year-old married man who has had a long-standing alcohol disorder. He was laid off from his construction job 3 years ago because of his poor attendance, fighting with co-workers, and poor attitude toward his supervisors. He has consistently refused to go into treatment. His wife, Susan, is a long-suffering person who makes excuses for him, buffers his difficult personality with their adult children, and works two jobs to meet family expenses. His children, while teenagers, encouraged their father to enter alcohol treatment. During their 20s, they actively encouraged their mother to leave the marriage, which she refused to do. One week ago Henry was driving while intoxicated; he struck and killed a pedestrian.

DISCUSSION QUESTIONS

1. As a result of the accident, this family is in crisis. The children are disgusted with their father. If you were a child in this family, how would you feel toward your father? Toward your mother?

2. Susan is in a state of exhaustion and shock. Using the list of crisis potential factors in the Sequence of Developments Following a Critical Event in Chapter 28, examine the current mental state, based on each of the factors, that Susan may be experiencing at this time.

3. If Susan continues to cope ineffectively with this crisis event, for what types of mental disorder described in Chapters 20–27 would she be at risk? Why?

4. When Susan has recovered from the acute effects of this crisis, with what types of activities could she be encouraged to become involved?

5. What would be the advantages of Susan attending a self-help type of group?

6. If Susan were to become involved in Al-Anon or a codependents type of self-help group, how could her attitude toward her husband's alcohol disorder be altered?

7. What are the potential outcomes or results for Susan, Henry, and their marriage if her attitude toward his condition is changed?

Answers to Chapter Questions

Chapter 1

1. medications
2. health care costs
3. **Capping** is the policy of insurance companies of allowing a certain dollar amount for lifetime psychiatric care.
4.
    1) assessment
    2) accuracy of diagnosis
    3) rationale for diagnostic testing
    4) effectiveness of care planning
    5) evaluation of outcomes

Chapter 2

1. the poor (could also answer, the chronically mental ill)
2. Medicare or Medicaid, private health services, health maintenance organizations, self-pay, or no available funds
3. crisis intervention and partial hospital or day-treatment programs
4.
    1) Clients participating in ACT programs have fewer hospitalizations on an annual basis than CMHCs.
    2) Direct searching out of mentally ill persons in the community ensures that a larger percentage of potential clients are reached.
    3) A case manager oversees all aspects of support including direct mental health services, housing, physical care, and so on, and provides ongoing training in activities of daily living. A small case load allows for more active support of the client during precrisis periods.

Chapter 3

1. before he or she is admitted
2. the registered nurse
3. mutual trust

4. that the current "here and now" behavior of an individual is a reflection of his or her current reality and normal social interactions

Chapter 4

1. When a person "cares for" another, the implication is that the other is like a child and is incapable of caring for himself or herself, is dependent, and cannot make a contribution to his or her own well-being. "Caring about" shows respect for the other person as a full human being and promotes self-respect and the ability to care for self.
2. Because the physically or mentally ill person is in a dependent position and may not be capable of safeguarding his or her own well-being.
3. If a person is held in a hospital against his or her will, that person may apply for a writ of habeas corpus. It requires an immediate court hearing to determine a person's sanity. If declared sane, the individual must be released from the institution.
4. Competency is a person's mental status that renders him or her capable of sound decision making and management of his or her own life circumstances. The exact legal definition varies with circumstances.

Chapter 5

1. The goal of nursing is to restore the person to his or her highest potential for quality of life.
2. Psychosocial adaptation is the ability of the human being to perceive reality and respond to it in a way that supports his or her own emotional and physical well-being and that of others in the social environment.
3. The clinical role of nursing is to assess the whole-person response to illness.
4. The nurse focuses on the whole person. He or she has the most intimate ongoing contact with the client and can observe subtle clinical changes. The nurse implements the nursing care plan, observes change, and alerts the treatment team of its effectiveness.

Chapter 6

1. Empathy is placing oneself within the experience of another without losing one's own sense of identity.

2. Explanations reduce anxiety in the client by preparing him or her for what is to come. The care-giver must explain things with full allowance for the client's limitations.
3. Though acceptance of client behavior and some permissiveness is important to the mentally ill client, there must be limits on his or her behavior. These limits should be determined by the treatment team. If limits are enforced in a consistent, quiet, matter-of-fact way, they contribute to client security.
4. The ego attempts to protect itself from intrapsychic or environmental awareness that may provoke anxiety.

Chapter 7

1. consistent eye contact and an erect sitting or standing posture
2. An open-ended question invites the client to give as much information as he or she desires and makes it easier to explore how he or she is feeling. A close-ended question generally requires only a one-word answer and closes off further discussion.
3. Contracting promotes trust in the care-giver and a sense of security, both important to returning to good mental health.
4. Speak of the time of termination at the start of counseling and at intervals during counseling. Discuss the client's termination fears. Include other members of the treatment team in preparation for discharge. Include other clients in circle to help client socialize with others. Invite client to visit and call.

Chapter 8

1. Neurotransmitters are biochemical substances that send messages from the central nervous system to the body tissues. Theorists believe they strongly influence the level of drive a person has, the emotions, and the way the person tolerates stress.
2. Identification is the process by which a child, because of love for and wish to be like the parent, particularly the parent of the same sex, molds himself or herself after that parent and adopts the parent's characteristics and attitude. If the parent is emotionally mature and well-adjusted, this process can greatly contribute to the development of similar characteristics in the child's personality.
3. need, stimulus, response, reinforcement
4. The learning process progressively decreases and finally ceases to become extinct when it no longer serves a need, and reinforcement ceases.

Chapter 9

1. a high capacity for trust and self-esteem in the child
2. Socialization is the shaping of an individual to the communication style, beliefs, and emotional patterns of a social group.
3. A dynamic is a constantly operating force within a system that results in some type of action or observable result.

   A closed family is rigid and allows little change in the roles and patterns in the family. Usually one or both parents have moderate to high levels of psychopathology. The home climate does not support the development and ultimate healthy separation of the child from the family.
4. Homeostasis is a dynamic, ever-changing state in which a system constantly works to maintain balance. As one person in a family changes, the other members alter their patterns of communication or behavior to maintain the balance of the family.

Chapter 10

1. availability of consistent, concerned care-giver; feeding situation in early infancy; toilet and cleanliness training; early sex training; training for control of anger and aggression
2. when the needs at the lower level are met
3. when he or she has self-actualized or fully developed his or her potential personally, educationally, and in the working environment

Chapter 11

1. Freud called it the judgment process and labeled it social and cultural in origin. It is roughly equivalent to the conscience.
2. the subconscious
3. They become aggressive and oppose the situation, flee from it, or compromise with it.

Chapter 12

1. the biochemical or neurotransmitter effect on mental disorders
2. Erich Fromm's

3. may develop anxiety that persists into adulthood, primarily around the issue of control
4. identity vs. role confusion

Chapter 13

1. The physical reactions that accompany the emotions of anger and fear are readying the person's body for active aggression or for escape from what is feared. The adrenal glands pour out adrenaline into the bloodstream, and extra strength or power is available for quick action.
2. With the emotion of fear there is a specific, identified cause of the fear. When a person is anxious, he or she cannot identify the reason for emotional distress.
3. a physical and mental state in which the individual feels energized to use the angry feeling to correct the "wrong" or retrieve what was lost. The person feels in mental control. There is a heightening of skin color, respirations become fuller, and the blood pressure and pulse are decreased.
4. hopelessness

Chapter 14

1. time, person, place
2. an inability to carry out purposeful movement to achieve a goal
3. agitation
4. An illusion is a type of sensory dysfunction—a misinterpretation or distortion (by the ego) of an actual stimulus.
5. judgment

Chapter 15

1. the continuous evaluation of the outcome of its coping efforts, and the readiness to develop new strategies if the current ones are not working
2. Neurotransmitters are biochemical substances released in the central nervous system that send messages through the sympathetic nervous system to all body organs and muscles. They are the link between mind and body.
3. as "the diagnosis and treatment of human responses to actual or potential health problems."

4. the process of coping effectively with one's social environment so that growth and development proceeds in a way that supports healthy social relationships, good self-esteem, and ongoing positive challenge

Chapter 16

1. Coping is the combination of conscious problem-solving strategies and unconscious defense mechanisms that results in cognitive or behavioral responses to demanding or threatening events.
2. Yes. They assist in normal adaptation and effective coping.
3. narcissistic defense mechanisms
4. neurotic defense mechanisms. Repression operates by storing anxiety in the unconscious.

Chapter 17

1. the term used for the steps involved in organizing and implementing client care
2. one or more interview sessions with the client in which the nurse listens to client responses to questions and observes the client's mental status; also, family members, current and former charts, observations of care-givers from nursing and other disciplines
3. implementation
4. provides basis for evaluating nursing care outcomes
5. nursing process must be reinstated, a reassessment made of client's current symptoms, and a new or modified care plan instituted

Chapter 18

1. exchanging, communicating, relating, valuing, choosing, moving, perceiving, knowing, feeling
2. the signs or symptoms that the person is manifesting or describing related to the nursing problem
3. a description of the specific clinical problem that can be addressed by nursing intervention, and the cause of the problem
4. 110

Chapter 19

1. admission to an inpatient psychiatric setting with a diagnosed mental disorder selected from the *Diagnostic and Statistical Manual of Mental Disorders;* nursing assessment of all mental and physical patterns so that nursing diagnoses and interventions can be planned; development of nursing diagnosis statements that describe the unique ineffective coping patterns that are causing the client's current problem(s)
2. nursing diagnoses; nursing goal or priority; nursing intervention(s); nursing rationale; evaluation
3. Overstimulation can result in more severe symptoms.
4. Shift-to-shift changes can be noted and changes in care plan can be developed to respond to client's changing mental state(s).

Chapter 20

1. autistic disorder
2. A young person with **avoidant disorder** avoids or pulls away from relationships with others, while maintaining warm relationships with family members. Excessive timidity and refusal to talk with others is also demonstrated, and in adolescents, lack of normal sexual development may occur.
3. anorexia nervosa, bulimia nervosa, pica, rumination disorder of infancy, atypical eating disorder
4. **Tourette's disorder** is a disorder in which a person experiences multiple vocal and motor (body) tics in many muscle groups. This disorder occurs before the age of 21 and usually has a chronic lifelong course. The intensity of symptoms varies over months

Chapter 21

1. Psychosis is a severe disruption of mental status. It is the most serious form of mental disorder. A psychotic person temporarily loses contact with reality.
2. Dementia is a change in mental status that is caused by physical changes in the brain. It is usually a chronic condition that progresses slowly and is not reversible.
3. organic personality syndrome
4. intoxication and withdrawal
5. nicotinic acid, B, thiamine, and folic acid

Chapter 22

1. Substance dependence is less severe.
2. Alcoholics Anonymous, aversive therapy with disulfiram (Antabuse), or inpatient rehabilitation treatment program
3. the abuse of amphetamines
4. craving for tobacco, anxiety, irritability, restlessness, gastrointestinal disturbance, drowsiness, headache

Chapter 23

1. dopamine
2. catatonic, disorganized, paranoid, undifferentiated, and residual
3. A consistent care-giver (nurse) should be assigned to each client.
4. Paranoia is characterized by a firm, fixed system of delusion in an otherwise well-balanced personalilty. This delusional system centers around feelings of persecution and grandiosity.

Chapter 24

1. bipolar disorders and depressive disorders
2. He or she demonstrates strong, exaggerated, and cyclic mood swings.
3. lithium carbonate
4. the acutely depressed client

Chapter 25

1. Anxiety can provide the impetus to change and to develop better coping skills.
2. increased tension, apprehension, painful and persistent feelings of helplessness, jitteriness, and unidentifiable cause of worry
3. neurosis
4. agoraphobia

Chapter 26

1. sudden loss of association and integration of self-identity, consciousness, or motor control (person is unaware that these changes have occurred)
2. childhood sexual, mental, or physical abuse
3. self-esteem, body image, value formation, and id, ego, and superego
4. Ego-dystonic is conflict within the ego, either between the person and his or her social environment or within himself or herself.

Chapter 27

1. A personality disorder can develop when a person builds up too many defenses against socially unacceptable feelings about important people in his or her life. When the tension and anxiety can't be controlled by the defenses, he or she may develop a personality that is rigid, narrow, and lacking in spontaneity.
2. the personality structure that developed in childhood
3. hypersensitivity, rigidity, suspiciousness, jealousy, envy, exaggerated sense of own importance, blaming of others, ascribing evil motives to others
4. intense interpersonal relationships that alternate widely between love, hate, and dependency

Chapter 28

1. a crisis of some type
2. personal safety, life goals, normal role functioning, family stability
3. a decreasing ability to cope with anxiety and the resulting emotional, intellectual, and physiologic stresses that accompany it
4. death, divorce, major illness, marriage, childbirth, loss of a job, retirement

Chapter 29

1. Milieu therapy uses the social system of the clinical unit to reshape the client's behavior.
2. Encourage client to become socially involved in the unit with other clients and staff members; assist client to express his or her fears, problems,

failures and important issues with staff and other clients; and support attendance at group therapy and therapeutic community meetings.
3. systems theory and theory of learning
4. phobias or phobic disorders, anxiety, chronic pain, dependent or passive personality style, alcoholism, smoking

Chapter 30

1. from 4 to 12 people
2. support groups, instructional groups, and group therapy
3. A homogeneous group contains similar types of individuals, for example, all women, all divorced people, or all schizophrenics.
4. direct authoritarian and indirect guidance

Chapter 31

1. the development of medication that restores brain chemistry to near-normal levels
2. phenothiazines
3. dibenzazepines, monoamine oxidase inhibitors, serotonin reuptake inhibitors
4. lithium carbonate

Chapter 32

1. loss of employment through retirement; loss of self-image, if job was an important source of self-gratification; loss of physical health; loss of good body image as result of declining health; and loss of independence as infirmities increase
2. depression, insomnia, cognitive impairment, stress reactions, and decrease in social and daily living skills
3. slowing of cognitive functioning and decrease in memory
4. decrease in problem-solving ability, decrease in coping ability, decrease in self-esteem, social isolation

Glossary

acting out. See *defense mechanisms, immature.*

adaptation. The process by which the ego uses unconscious coping strategies to adjust in a healthy manner to the stresses of life.

adjustment disorder. A mental disorder in which a person is unable to resolve a crisis that occurred at least 3 months previously.

affect. The mood or emotion an individual feels in response to a given situation or thought. Affect may be described, according to its expression, as blunted, blocked, flat, inappropriate, or displaced.

aggression. Excessive rage, anger, or hostility that is seemingly unrelated to a person's current situation.

agoraphobia. A mental condition that manifests itself in excessive fear of open spaces.

akathisia. Extreme restlessness.

akinesia. The complete or partial loss of muscle movement.

altruism. See *defense mechanisms, mature.*

ambivalence. The coexistence of two opposing feelings toward another person, object, or idea. (For example, feelings of love and hate, pleasure and pain, or liking and disliking may exist simultaneously.)

amnesia. Complete or partial inability to recall past experiences.

anorexia nervosa. An eating disorder that occurs primarily in young females and in which there is a strong fear of becoming obese.

anticipation. See *defense mechanisms, mature.*

anxiety. Apprehension, tension, or uneasiness due to an unknown cause. Primarily of intrapsychic origin, unlike fear, which is the emotional response to a consciously recognized and usually external threat or danger. Anxiety and fear are accompanied by physiologic changes. Anxiety is pathologic when present to such an extent that it interferes with effectiveness in living, achievement of desired goals or satisfactions, or reasonable emotional comfort.

anxiety disorder. A general category of mental illness found in DSM-III-R that is characterized by an excessively uneasy and tense mental state

380

with no explainable cause. Includes the following major categories: phobic disorders, anxiety states, and posttraumatic stress disorders.

anxiety disorder of childhood. A mental disorder that develops during early childhood or adolescence, in which excessive feelings of apprehension and tension occur as the result of an unknown cause. The categories include separation anxiety disorder, avoidance disorder of childhood or adolescence, and overanxious disorder. (See Index.)

aphasia. Partial or complete loss of the power of expression or the ability to understand either written or spoken language. The cause may be functional, organic, or both.

apraxia. The inability to carry out purposeful movement to achieve a goal.

autism. A mental state in which a person seems unaware of external reality; primarily seen in schizophrenia.

avoidance. See *defense mechanisms, immature.*

awareness. See *level of awareness.*

behavior. The visible or observable signs of a person's psychological response to his or her internal and external environments.

behavior modification. Changing a person's behavior by rewarding positive behavior and ignoring negative behavior. Also known as *behavioral psychology.*

blunted (or flat) affect. Lack of a normal range of emotions.

boundary. Within a family, the rules that keep the role of one family member separate from another.

bulimia. An eating disorder seen primarily in adolescent or young adult females. It involves eating binges of high-calorie food.

catastrophic reaction. Occurs when there is a sudden, unexpected stressor and the person's normal coping mechanisms fail.

catatonic. A certain type of schizophrenia in which a person appears to be in a stupor. Rigid posture is also common. In addition, the person may be mute and unable to speak.

circumstantiality. A speaking and thinking style in which the person frequently switches topics but eventually reaches a conclusion.

claustrophobia. Fear of being in an enclosed space.

closed family. A family in which rigidity allows for little change in family roles and patterns.

cognitive impairment. A decrease in the intellectual aspect of mental functioning.

compensation. See *defense mechanisms, neurotic.*

competency. In law, the mental status of a person who is capable of sound decision making and management of his or her own life circumstances.

compulsion. An act that a person finds himself or herself forced to do (generally against his or her wishes) in order to reduce anxiety. See also *obsession.*

conduct disorder. A mental disorder in which a person violates the rights of others. It includes the following categories: undersocialized type, socialized type, aggressive type, and nonaggressive type. (See Index.)

consent. A legal term for the agreement by a person to an act that will affect his or her body, or to disclose information about himself or herself.

consent, informed. In law, the agreement by a competent person who has been given the information necessary to weigh the advantages and disadvantages of what is being proposed.

consent, presumed. In law, the type of agreement that occurs when an unconscious person is given life-saving treatment in a life-threatening situation.

consent, vicarious. In law, the agreement given when a person is incapable of making decisions for himself or herself. Instead, parents guardians, or conservators make the decision.

constricted personality. A personality that is tightly controlled.

conversion. An ego defense by which emotional conflicts are channeled into physical illness.

coping. The way a person's psychological or intrapsychic system responds to external or internal awarenesses that are threatening.

covert. Implies secrecy, or hidden reasons for conscious actions or behavior.

crisis intervention therapy. A type of brief psychiatric treatment in which individuals (and/or families) are assisted in their efforts to cope and to solve problems in crisis situations. The treatment approach is immediate, supportive, and direct.

cyclothymic. Describes a person who has high and low mood swings that are not as pronounced as a person with manic-depressive bipolar disorder.

decompensation. The failure of the ego to use defense mechanisms.

defense mechanism. A mental maneuver performed by the ego to decrease the unpleasant feeling of anxiety. As the ego matures, it uses increasingly mature levels of defense mechanisms. The levels, starting with the most basic, are: 1) narcissistic, 2) immature, 3) neurotic, and 4) mature.
1. *narcissistic defense mechanisms.* The most basic of the defense mechanisms used by the ego. They develop during the first year and are used during childhood. In addition, they are used by healthy individuals under moderate to severe stress and routinely by individuals with severe forms of certain types of personality disorders.
   a. *denial.* The first defense used in infancy, it remains the strongest defense we have to shut out painful awareness in the environment.
   b. *delusional projection.* The ego forms conclusions and beliefs that are not based on reality.
   c. *distortion.* The ego reshapes external reality to reduce anxiety and restore a feeling of emotional comfort.
2. *immature defense mechanisms.* Second level of defense mechanisms, developed during the toddler state.
   a. *acting out.* The result of conflict caused by anxiety that the person cannot tolerate. He impulsively acts out the conflict.
   b. *avoidance.* The ego causes a person to unconsciously stay away

from any person, situation, or place that might cause unwanted sexual or aggressive feelings.

    c. *hypochondriasis*. The ego magnifies generally mild, vague physical symptoms into more severe symptoms of potentially serious illnesses.

    d. *projection*. A less pathologic form of delusional projection (defined above).

    e. *regression*. The ego is unable to tolerate severe intrapsychic or environmental stress, resulting in a behavioral retreat to an earlier stage of development.

3. *neurotic defense mechanisms*. The third level of defense mechanisms frequently used by all persons who are psychologically "healthy."

    a. *displacement*. The ego shifts unacceptable feelings about a person or thing to another object.

    b. *identification*. The ego causes a person to take on the thoughts, feelings, or particular circumstances of another person as if they were his or her own.

    c. *isolation*. The ego separates emotion from a thought. Also known as intellectualization or rationalization.

    d. *reaction formula*. A defense used by the ego when a thought, feeling, or impulse is unacceptable. See also *compensation*.

    e. *repression*. Considered one of the most important defense mechanisms, the ego causes anxiety associated with distressing internal awareness to be stored away in the unconscious.

4. *mature defense mechanisms*. The highest or fourth level of defense mechanisms used by the healthy, mature ego when it is under minimal stress.

    a. *altruism*. The ego channels the desire to satisfy one's own needs into meeting the needs of others.

    b. *anticipation*. The ego acknowledges both intellectually and emotionally an upcoming, anxiety-provoking situation.

    c. *humor*. A defense used by the ego when it cannot fully tolerate a difficult situation.

    d. *sublimation*. An ego defense in which unacceptable thoughts or feelings are channeled into more acceptable outlets.

    e. *suppression*. Differs from repression in that memories, thoughts, or feelings are quickly retrieved from the subconscious or preconscious rather than being deeply buried in the unconscious.

déjà vu.   A feeling that one has experienced a new situation on a previous occasion. (French for "already seen")

delirium.   An acute organic brain syndrome that usually is reversible.

delusion.   A false belief or opinion that is unreasonable and causes distortion in judgment.

delusional projection.   See *defense mechanisms, narcissistic*.

dementia.   Chronic organic brain syndrome that usually is irreversible.

denial.   See *defense mechanisms, narcissistic*.

depersonalization.   A mental state in which a person experiences periods of unreality about who he or she is or about various aspects of his or her body.

depression. A hopeless feeling of sadness, grief, or mourning associated with a loss. Also the depressed phase of bipolar disorder.

derealization. A neutral state that can range from a mild sense of unreality to a frank loss of reality about one's environment.

disintegration. The disruption of the normal influence of the ego on combining thoughts, feelings, memories, and perceptions into a realistic view of self and environment.

displacement. See *defense mechanisms, neurotic.*

dissociative disorder. A mental disorder in which a person experiences a sudden loss of self-identity and takes on the identity of another. It includes the following categories: psychogenic amnesia, psychogenic fugue, multiple personality, depersonalization disorder, and atypical dissociative disorder. (See Index.)

distortion. See *defense mechanisms, narcissistic.*

double-bind. A type of interaction, generally associated with schizophrenic families, in which one individual demands a response to a message containing mutually contradictory signals while the other is unable to respond or comment on the inconsistent and incongruous message. Best characterized by the "damned if you do, damned if you don't" situation.

dyad. Refers to the relationship between two people; dyadic pair can be husband and wife, parent and child, sibling and sibling.

dynamic. A constantly operating force within a system, such as a person's psyche, that results in some type of action or observable result.

dyskinesia. Excessive movement of mouth accompanied by protruding tongue. Seen most often in tardive dyskinesia—a permanent negative effect of phenothiazines.

dysphoria. Unpleasant emotion that causes psychological distress or conflict.

dystonia. Severely impaired muscle tone.

eating disorder. A mental disorder that includes major disturbances in eating behavior. The category includes: anorexia nervosa, bulimia, pica, rumination disorder of infancy and atypical eating disorder. (See Index.)

echolalia. The pathologic repetition or imitation of another's speech. Seen in some forms of schizophrenia.

echopraxia. The pathologic repetition or imitation of another's movements. Seen in some forms of schizophrenia.

ego. That part of the personality, according to Freudian theory, that mediates between the primitive, pleasure-seeking instinctual drives of the id and the self-critical, prohibitive, restraining forces of the superego. The compromises worked out on an unconscious level help to resolve intrapsychic conflict by keeping thoughts, interpretations, judgments, and behavior practical and efficient. The ego is directed by the reality principle, meaning it is in contact with the real world as well as the id and superego. The ego develops as the individual grows. See also *superego; id.*

ego ideal. A high standard within the ego that motivates the individual to continued growth and self-actualization.

ego-dystonic. Describes thoughts, perceptions, or actions that are unacceptable and conflict producing within the ego.

ego-syntonic. Describes thoughts, perceptions, or actions that are acceptable to the ego.

electroshock therapy (EST). A method of treatment in which an electric current is passed through the brain causing a grand-mal seizure. Useful in certain types of depressions. Also known as electroconvulsive therapy (ECT).

empathy. The ability to "feel with" another person while retaining one's own sense of objectivity.

encopresis, functional. A disorder in which feces are passed in socially inappropriate places.

eneuresis. Involuntary voiding by a child beyond an age that is socially acceptable.

ethics. The knowledge of the principles of good and evil.

euphoria. An excessive and inappropriate feeling of well-being.

exaltation. Intense elation accompanied by feelings of grandeur.

exhibitionism. A sexual disorder in which a person (usually make) obtains sexual pleasure in displaying the genitals in a public setting.

explosive disorder. A disorder that results in episodes of severe violence, rage, or destruction as the result of a stressor that would not be responded to in a similar manner by normal persons.

extended family. All family members other than mother, father, and siblings.

extinction. The process of eliminating particular types of behavior due to a lack of response to that behavior by persons in the environment.

extrapyramidal reaction. Refers to side effects of some major psychotropic drugs on the extrapyramidal system of the central nervous system. Characterized by a variety of physical signs and symptoms (similar to those seen in patients with Parkinson's disease) that include muscular rigidity, tremors, drooling, restlessness, shuffling gait, blurred vision, and other neurologic disturbances.

facies. Facial expressions.

factitious disorder. A mental disorder in which the person consciously pretends to have symptoms of a physical or mental disorder.

family of origin. See *nuclear family*.

family rules. Unwritten expectations about what types of roles or behavior will be acceptable or unacceptable to the family.

family therapy. Psychotherapeutic treatment of more than one member of a family. The treatment may be supportive, directive, or interpretive.

fear. Excessive fright of consciously recognized danger.

fetishism. A sexual disorder in which a person derives abnormal sexual pleasure from an object or a body part.

functional. Refers to mental disorders (disorders of functioning) in which no physical or organic cause is known.

general adaptation syndrome (GAS). Hans Selye's description of the physiologic response to stress.

gestalt psychology. The study of mental process and behavior with emphasis on a total perceptual configuration and the interrelation of component parts. Generally refers to the "whole person" approach to assessment and treatment of psychiatric clients.

grandiosity. An objective experience in which the person feels that he or she is very important and holds great power.

group therapy. Application by one or more therapists of psychotherapeutic techniques to a group of individuals who may have similar problems and are in reasonably good contact with reality. The optimal size of a group is six to ten members. As a therapy procedure, it is popular because it is a versatile, economical, and, for certain individuals, successful modality.

habeas corpus. Writ requiring an immediate court hearing to determine a person's sanity.

hallucination. An imagined sensory perception that occurs without an external stimulus; can be auditory, visual, or tactile; usually occurs in psychotic disorders, but can occur in both chronic and acute organic brain disorders.

heterosexuality. Sexual interest and behavior toward persons of the opposite sex.

homeostasis. A term borrowed from physiology; the self-regulating intrapsychic processes that are optimal for comfort and survival.

homosexuality. Sexual preference, attraction, and relationship between two people of the same sex.

homosexuality, ego-dystonic type. A condition in which a person who is sexually aroused by persons of the same sex experiences psychological distress as the result of his or her sexual preference.

humor. See *defense mechanisms, mature.*

hyperchondriasis. A mental condition in which the angry feelings that a person cannot express toward another are transferred into physical symptoms.

hypochondriasis. See *defense mechanisms, immature.*

id. In Freudian theory, the id is identified as the storage place of psychic energy. It is guided by the pleasure principle, curbed by the ego, and is unconscious. (See *ego, superego.*)

identification. See *defense mechanisms, neurotic.*

illusion. A misinterpreted sensory impression, usually auditory or visual; or false interpretation of an actual stimulus.

impotence. Condition in which there is sexual desire but the physiologic response is lacking or diminished.

impulse disorder. A mental disorder in which a person is unable to control urges related primarily to his or her aggressive drive. The categories include pathologic gambling, kleptomania, pyromania, intermittent explosive disorder, isolated explosive disorder, and atypical impulse control disorder. (See Index.)

insight. The ability of an individual to understand himself or herself and the basis for his or her attitudes and behavior.

insomnia. A disturbance in a person's normal sleeping pattern.

instructional group. A group in which persons learn and discuss new knowledge about a particular topic.

intellectualization. Another name for isolation. See also *defense mechanisms*.

intimacy. The capacity to trust another within a deep and committed relationship.

intrapsychic. Refers to all that takes place within the mind (psyche).

isolation. See *defense mechanisms, neurotic*.

judgment. The ability of a person to behave in a socially appropriate manner.

kleptomania. A condition in which a person spontaneously takes objects with no specific need for them.

la belle indifference. A lack of concern in a situation that would cause worry in a normal individual.

lability. Alternating periods of elation and depression; also known as mood swings.

latent. Adjective used to describe feelings, drives, and emotions that influence behaivor but remain repressed, outside of conscious thought.

lenticular pigmentation. A condition in which the normally clear lens in the eye becomes colored.

level of awareness. A description of the client's wakefulness or consciousness.

liaison psychiatry. A field that addresses the emotional stress of illness on the psyche.

major affective disorder. A serious mental disorder marked by a severe disturbance in emotional state.

maladaptation. An unhealthy outcome of an attempt by the ego to adapt to the stresses of life. The result is a decreased quality of life. See *adaptation*.

malingering. A condition in which a person pretends to be physically ill.

mania. A mental state accompanied by extreme excitement, restlessness, talkativeness, inflated self-esteem, and decreased need for sleep. The hyperactive phase of bipolar disorder.

masochism. A sexual disorder in which pleasure is obtained by having mental or physical pain inflicted by the sexual partner.

memory. The ability of a person to recall past events, both recent and remote.

mental mechanism. See *defense mechanisms*.

milieu. The immediate environment of persons, objects, and general surroundings.

mood. The internal feelings that a person experiences in response to a situation or thought.

motivation. Describes the individual's will and determination to persevere and succeed.

mutism. A condition in which a person is unable to communicate verbally.

narcissistic. Describes an extreme form of self-love in adults. This form of self-love is normal, however, in toddlers and young children.

narcissistic defense mechanism. The most basic level of defense mechanisms used by the ego. It is commonly used by normal children under 5 years of age, normal adults when under moderate to severe stress, and persons with certain types of personality disorders.

neologism.   A word that is invented or made up by condensing other words into a new one. Typical in schizophrenia.

neurotransmitter.   A biochemical substance (also known as catecholamine) that sends messages within the brain and from the central nervous system to the body.

norms.   The expectation that a society places on persons to behave in ways that it considers to be normal.

nosology.   The scientific classification of diseases.

nuclear family.   The immediate family into which a child is born.

nursing process.   The manner in which nursing care ideally occurs. It consists of the following four steps:

assessing. First step in nursing process; gathering data to aid in developing a care plane for the client.

planning. The second stage of the nursing process; the problem solving process results in a nursing care plan.

implementing. Putting into practice the nursing care plan.

evaluating. The final step of the nursing process. Observing and determining the outcome of nursing care.

nystagmus.   A condition in which there is constant movement of the eyeball.

obsession.   A persistent, recurring thought or urge occurring more or less against the person's wishes. Often leads to compulsive acts. See *compulsion.*

oculogyric crisis.   A condition in which the eyeballs are fixed in an upward position.

open family.   A family in which members, especially parents, have developed as healthy, active members of society. Communications within the family are honest and not avoided.

operant conditioning.   Conditioning or influencing behavior by rewarding a person for positive forms of behavior.

opisthotonos.   An arched position of the body caused by severe neurologic disorder.

organic.   Refers to disorders in which a physical, chemical, or structural cause is discernible.

organic brain syndrome (OBS).   Organic mental disorder. Mental status disorder caused by physiologic or anatomic changes in the brain.

overt.   Open, conscious and unhidden actions, behavior, and emotions.

panic disorders.   Cause symptoms of overwhelming anxiety that can include dizziness or feelings of faintness, difficult breathing, choking or smothering feelings, chest pain, palpitations, sweating, hot and cold flashes, tingling of the hands and feet, and trembling.

paranoid.   Used as an adjective to describe unwarranted suspiciousness and distrust of others.

paranoid state.   A mental disorder marked by psychotic suspicion.

paraphilia. Sexual perversion; any type of abnormal sex act that results in orgasm. It includes fetishism, transvestism, zoophilia, pedophilia, exhibitionism, voyeurism, sexual masochism, sexual sadism, and atypical paraphilia. (See Index.)

parkinsonian movement. A fine tremor accompanied by muscular rigidity.

pedophilia. A sexual disorder in which a child is the sexual choice of an adult.

perception. The way a person experiences his or her environment; includes his or her frame of reference about himself or herself.

personality. The characteristic way in which a person behaves. It is the deeply ingrained pattern of behavior that each person evolves, both consciously and unconsciously, as his or her style of life or way of being.

personality disorder. A mental disorder in which the ego overuses certain types of defense mechanisms that result in a variety of exaggerated personalilty or character traits. The category includes paranoid, schizoid, schizotypal, histrionic, narcissistic, antisocial, borderline, avoidant, dependent, compulsive, and passive-aggressive personality disorders. (See Index.)

phenothiazines. The major group of psychotropic drugs used in the treatment of mental illness, chiefly the psychoses. Their chemical action is on the central nervous system.

phobia or phobic disorder. An irrational, persistent, obsessive, intense fear of an object or situation that results in increased anxiety and tension and that interferes with the individual's normal functioning.

positive reinforcement. Occurs when a person's behavior results in a positive response from others.

precipitating event. The situation or event that causes a client to go into crisis.

preoccupation of thought. A thought process in which a person connects all experiences to a central thought, usually one with strong emotional overtones.

projection. See *defense mechanisms, immature.*

pseudoparkinsonism. A condition that mimics the symptoms of Parkinson's disease.

psyche. A term that refers to the mind. It is made up of the id, ego, and superego.

psychoanalysis. A form of psychotherapy developed by Freud, based on his theories of personality development and disorder, generally requiring basic commitments from the client (analysand) to the therapist (analyst) regarding time, money, and procedure. The technique of psychoanalysis involves an examination of the thoughts of a client and the interpretation of his or her dreams, emotions, and behavior. Its focus is mainly on the way the ego handles the id tensions. In psychoanalysis, success is measured by the degree of insight the client is able to gain into the unconscious motivations of his or her behavior.

psychodrama. A form of group psychotherapy in which clients dramatize their emotional problems. By assuming roles in order to act out their conflicts, they reveal repressed feelings that have been disturbing to them.

psychogenic. Implies that the causative factors of a symptom or illness are due to mental rather than organic factors.

psychosexual disorder. Includes a variety of conditions that pertain to a person's distress with his or her sexual functioning.

psychosis. A major mental illness characterized by any of the following symptoms: loss of contact with reality, bizarre thinking and behavior, delusions, hallucinations, regression, disorientation. Intrapsychically, it results from the unconscious becoming conscious and taking over control of the individual. In psychosis, the ego is overwhelmed by the id and the superego.

psychosocial. A term that describes the interrelationship between a person's psyche and his or her social system.

psychotherapy. The treatment of mental disorders or a psychosomatic condition by psychological methods using a variety of approaches including psychoanalysis, group therapy, family therapy, psychodrama, hypnotism, simple counseling, suggestion.

psychotic. Adjective describing a person experiencing psychosis.

pyromania. A condition in which a person sets fires for no specific reason.

rationalization. (Also known as isolation or intellectualization.) See *defense mechanisms, neurotic.*

reaction formation. See *defense mechanisms, neurotic.*

reality. The way things actually are.

reality-oriented therapy. Refers to any therapeutic approach the focus of which is on helping the client to define his or her reality, to improve his or her ability to adjust and to function productively and satisfactorily within his or her real situation.

regression. See *defense mechanisms, immature.*

reinforcement. An action that increases the likelihood of changing a person's behavior. It is used in behavior modification therapy.

repression. See *defense mechanisms, neurotic.*

sadism. A sexual disorder in which sexual pleasure is obtained by inflicting mental or physical pain on the sexual partner.

schizophrenia. A severe mental disorder accompanied by psychosis. It includes hallucinations, delusions, and disturbed mood. The categories of schizophrenia all share the preceding symptoms. Each category, however, has a unique symptom that is described as follows:

1. *disorganized type.* Inappropriate, usually silly, emotion.
2. *catatonic type.* A mute, negative, immobile stupor.
3. *paranoid type.* Extreme, delusional suspiciousness.
4. *undifferentiated type.* Mixed untypical symptoms.
5. *residual type.* Chronic symptoms of schizophrenia described above but not severe enough to require hospitalization.

schizophrenogenic. An adjective used to describe the object or situation that is believed to be causative in the development of schizophrenia.

sexuality. Those aspects of the personality determined by a person's view of his or her sexual functioning, body image, and relatedness with other persons of the same or opposite sex.

socialization. A developmental process during which the young child gains acceptance from his or her parents and other authority figures by conforming to their rules.

somatoform disorder. A mental condition that results in physiologic symptoms through an unconscious process. It includes the following categories: somatization disorder, conversion disorder, psychogenic pain disorder, hypochondriasis, and atypical somatoform disorder. (See Index.)

stereotyped movement disorder. A mental disorder that results in tics, which are involuntary movements or involuntary production of words. It includes the following categories: transient tic disorder, chronic motor tic disorder, Tourette's disorder, atypical tic disorder, and atypical movement disorder. (See Index.)

stimulus. An action or awareness that results in a response in a person.

stress. The internal feeling of tension that is a response to a stressor.

stressor. A threatening environmental event.

stuttering. A condition marked by disruption of a normal flow of speech.

sublimation. See *defense mechanisms, mature.*

substance abuse. A mental disorder in which a person uses drugs and becomes intoxicated, is unable to decrease use, experiences physical or mental complications because of the drug use, and experiences impairment of social functioning. Generally, a less severe form of drug use than substance dependence.

substance dependence. A severe form of drug abuse in which the person is physiologically dependent on the drug. Withdrawal from the drug would result in a toxic physiologic action. Generally, it is a more severe form of drug use disorder than is substance abuse.

subsystem. A concrete or abstract entity that belongs to a larger system and relates in specific ways with all parts of a larger system.

sundowning. A decrease in orientation at night; caused by organic brain syndrome.

superego. The third part of the Freudian personality theory; it guides and restrains, criticizes and punishes just as the parents did when the individual was a child. It is unconscious, and it is learned. Like the id, the superego also wants its own way. It is sometimes referred to as the conscience.

supersystem. A large complex made up of many systems, for example, a state department of mental health, made up of many hospitals and many different types of personnel.

support group. A group in which persons with similar concerns explore thoughts and feelings related to these concerns.

suppression. See *defense mechanisms, mature.*

sympathy. The taking on of the feelings and circumstances of other people. The helper loses his or her own separate identity.

synergism.   The combined result of separate entities that together have a greater effect than the sum of their individual actions.

system.   An assemblage or combination of parts (subsystems) that form a complex or unified whole.

tangentiality.   A symptom of thought disorder in which the person switches topics frequently and fails to complete discussion of any of them.

thought disorder.   A mental status that is the result of a disturbance in normal thinking. It is usually seen in schizophrenia and is evidenced by behavior or spoken words that are confused and irrational.

torticollis.   Severe spasm of the neck muscles on the side of the neck.

transactional analysis.   A psychodynamic approach that attempts to understand the interplay between individuals in terms of the roles they have been assigned, have assumed, or play in their transactions with others.

unconscious.   The storage place of those mental processes of which the individual is unaware. The repressed feelings and their energy are stored in the unconscious, and they directly influence the individual's behavior.

value.   An affective disposition or deeply held belief about a person, object, or idea.

voyeurism.   A sexual disorder in which sexual pleasure is obtained by observing other people undress or engage in sexual activity.

waxy flexibility.   A pathologic condition in which the body maintains the position in which it is placed. Seen in some forms of schizophrenia.

word salad.   A jumbled mixture of words and phrases that have no meaning and are illogical in their sequence. Seen most often in schizophrenia. (For example, ''Backter dyce tonked up snorfel blend.'')

ASSESSMENT TOOLS

Barry Psychosocial Assessment

This comprehensive assessment tool uses Gordon's functional health patterns to facilitate the data-gathering process and promote the identification of corresponding nursing diagnoses.

The assessment categories include the following patterns:
- Health perception–health management
- Nutritional-metabolic
- Elimination
- Activity-exercise
- Sleep-rest
- Cognitive-perceptual

- Self-perception–self-concept
- Role-relationship
- Sexuality-reproductive
- Coping–stress tolerance
- Value-belief

These categories help the nurse focus on specific aspects of assessment and identify problem areas. Problem areas are identified through a focused assessment.

Assess all boxed questions subjectively, rather than asked of the client directly. Bold italic statements advise the nurse how to proceed.

Admitting Information

Name_____ Age____ Date of admission_____

Marital status   S___ M___ W___ D___   How long?_____

Occupation_____ Years of education completed____

Date of assessment_____ Admitting diagnosis_____

HEALTH PERCEPTION–HEALTH MANAGEMENT
Patient's Perception of Illness

What was the original problem that caused you to come to the hospital?_____

On what date did you first become ill?_____
What caused this illness?_____
How do you feel about being in a hospital?_____

How can the physician's and nurses help you most?_____

How will this illness affect you when your are out of the hospital?_____

Do you think it will cause any changes in your life?_____
How will it affect your family?_____

Barry Psychosocial Assessment (continued)

Potential for noncompliance?   Yes _____   No _____   Possible _____

Related to: _____ Anxiety   _____ Unsatisfactory relationship
            _____ Negative side effects   with care-giving environ-
                  of prescribed treatment   ment or care-givers
                                                 _____ Other

Explain:

Potential for injury?   Yes _____   No _____   Possible _____

Explain:

NUTRITIONAL-METABOLIC

How does your current appetite compare with your normal appetite?

Same _____   Increased _____   Decreased _____

How long has it been different? _____

How your weight fluctuated by more than 5 lb in the last several weeks?

Yes _____   No _____   How many pounds? _____

What is you normal fluid intake per day? ml* _____   Your current intake? ml _____

Nurse can substitute estimate of milliliters for client's reported fluid intake.

Aspects of client's illness or condition that could contribute to organic mental
disorder?

No _____   Yes _____

Delirium type _____   Dementia type _____

Possible cause:

_____ Metabolic   _____ Infectious disease
_____ Electrolytes   _____ Neoplastic disease
_____ Other metabolic or endocrine   _____ Nutritional disease
      condition   _____ Degenerative (chronic) brain
_____ Arterial disease   disease
_____ Mechanical disease   _____ Drug toxicity
_____ Electrical disorder

ELIMINATION
What is your current pattern of bowel movements?

Constipated _____ Diarrhea _____ Incontinent _____

How does this compare to normal?

Same _____ Different _____

Explain:

What is your current pattern of urination? _____

How does this compare to normal?

Same _____ Different _____

Explain:

Possibility that emotional distress may be contributing to any change?

High _____ Moderate _____ Low _____

ACTIVITY-EXERCISE
What is your normal energy level?

High _____ Moderate _____ Low _____

Has it changed in the past 6 months? Yes _____ No _____

To what do you attribute the cause?_____
_____

How would you describe your normal activity level?

High _____ Moderate _____ Low _____

How may it change following this hospitalization?_____

What types of activities do you normally pursue outside the home?_____

What recreational activities do you enjoy?_____

Do you anticipate your ability to manage your home will be changed following your hospitalization?_____

Explain:

Barry Psychosocial Assessment (*continued*)

Current self-care deficits?

Feeding _____   Bathing _____   Dressing _____   Toileting _____

Anticipated deficits following hospitalization? _____

Current impairment in mobility? _____

Anticipated immobility following hospitalization? _____

Alterations in the following?

Airway clearance   How? _____

Breathing patterns   How? _____

Cardiac output   How? _____

Respiratory function   How? _____

Potential for altered tissue perfusion as manifested by altered

cognitive-perceptual patterns?

SLEEP-REST
Normal sleeping pattern

How many hours do you normally sleep per night?

From what hour to what hour? _____ to _____

Changes in normal sleeping pattern

Do you have difficulty falling asleep? _____

Do you awaken in the middle of night? _____

Do you awaken early in the morning? _____

Are you sleeping more or fewer hours than normal? _____   How many? _____

COGNITIVE-PERCEPTUAL

Are you feeling pain now? _____   How severe? _____   How often? _____

What relieves the pain? _____

What information does this client need to know to manage this illness or health state?

Ability to comprehend this information?

Good _____ Moderate _____ Poor _____

If poor, explain:

Mental Status Exam

Level of awareness and orientation _____

Appearance and behavior _____

Speech and communication _____

Affect (mood) _____

Thinking process _____

Related to: Inability to evaluate reality _____ Aging _____ Other _____

Explain:

If there is a distortion of the thought process, a focused assessment is indicated.

Perception _____

Abstract thinking _____

Social judgment _____

Memory _____

Impairment in short-term memory _____ Long-term _____

Is there evidence of unilateral neglect? Yes _____ No _____ Does not apply _____

Self-perception

Does the client describe feelings of anxiety or uneasiness? _____

Is he able to identify a cause? Yes _____ No _____

Cause? _____

If the client feels anxious but cannot identify a cause, assess for the major coping risks of physical illness below.

Barry Psychosocial Assessment (*continued*)

Is there anything you are frightened of during this hospitalization or illness?
Yes _____ No _____ What is it? _____
How will this illness affect your future plans? _____
Normally, do you believe that you control what happens to you (internal locus of control) or do you believe that other people or events control what happens (external locus of control)?

Internal locus of control _____
External locus of control _____

Will this illness affect the way you feel about yourself? _____
How? _____ About your body? _____

Psychosocial Risks of Illness
What are the major issues of this illness for this client? _____
For this family? _____
Use the following space to record client and family comments illustrating how they are coping with these issues.

Trust	Client _____
	Family _____
Self-esteem	Client _____
	Family _____
Body image	Client _____
	Family _____
Control	Client _____
	Family _____
Loss	Client _____
	Family _____
Guilt	Client _____
	Family _____
Intimacy	Client _____
	Family _____

Could one or more of these issues be contributing to feelings of anxiety, hopelessness, powerlessness, or disturbance in self-concept?
Yes _____ No _____ Possible _____
If so, explain which ones and proceed with a focused assessment.

ROLE-RELATIONSHIP

What is your occupation? _____

How many years have you been in this occupation? _____

Do you anticipate that this illness will have an effect on your ability to work?

Yes _____   No _____   How? _____

With whom do you live? _____ Are they supportive? _____

Who are the most important people in your life? _____

Do you ever feel socially isolated?   Yes _____   No _____

Explain:

Is there any indication in this history of social isolation or impaired social
interaction?

Yes _____   No _____

Explain:

Ability to communicate

Within normal limits _____   Impaired _____

Describe:

FAMILY HISTORY

Who are the members of your immediate family? What are their ages and how
are they related to you? Please include deceased members and when they died.

Name of family member _____

Relationship to you _____ Age _____ Date of death _____

Name of family member _____

Relationship to you _____ Age _____ Date of death _____

Name of family member _____

Relationship to you _____ Age _____ Date of death _____

Name of family member _____

Relationship to you _____ Age _____ Date of death _____

Name of family member _____

Relationship to you _____ Age _____ Date of death _____

What is your position in relation to your brothers and sisters? For example, are
you the second oldest, the youngest . . .? _____

How often do you see your immediate family members? _____

What goes on in your family when something bad happens? _____

What do most of the members do? _____

Barry Psychosocial Assessment (*continued*)

Have any of your relationships within your immediate and extended family changed recently? _____

Which ones? _____

How have they changed? _____

Is there any change in the way you parent your children?

Yes _____   No _____

Is so, to what do you attribute the cause?

_____ New baby

_____ Death of family member

_____ Illness in other family member

_____ Change in residence (describe reason for change)

_____ Other (describe)

What is your normal role within your family? _____

What role do the significant other people in your family play? _____

Potential for disruption of these roles by this illness? High _____

Moderate _____   Low _____

Explain:

While the client is describing the family, is there any indication of uncontrolled anger or rage?

Yes _____   No _____

Related to a specific issue or person?

Explain:

Open (trusting) or closed (untrusting) communication style in family? (Can be initially determined by statements and emotional expression of client.) _____

_____

Developmental stage of family

_____ Early married

_____ Married with no children

_____ Active childbearing

_____ Preschool or school-age
          children

_____ Adolescent children and
          children leaving home

_____ Middle-aged, children no
          longer at home

_____ Elderly, well-functioning

_____ Elderly, infirm

Is there any other aspect of your family or the way your family normally operates that you think should be added here? What is it?

If any item discussed in this section appears to be a current stressor for this client or family, it can be assessed using a focused approach with the other items under coping-stress tolerance pattern.

Interpersonal style

_____ Dependent	_____ Superior
_____ Controlled	_____ Uninvolved
_____ Dramatizing	_____ Mixed (usually two styles
_____ Suspicious	predominate)
_____ Self-sacrificing	_____ No predominant personality
	style

Write a brief sentence explaining your choice.

Response to you as the interviewer. Guarded? _____   Open? _____
Is the client able to maintain good eye contact?

SEXUALITY-REPRODUCTIVE

Have you experienced any recent change in your sexual functioning?
Yes _____   No _____
How? _____
For how long?_____
Do you associate your change in sexual functioning with some event in your life?
_____
Do you think this illness could change your normal pattern of sexual functioning?
_____
How? _____
_____

Is this change in sexuality patterns related to:
_____ Ineffective coping
_____ Change or loss of body part
_____ Prenatal or postpartum changes
Changes in neurovegetative functioning related to depression
Explain:

Use focus assessment if necessary.

Barry Psychosocial Assessment (continued)

COPING–STRESS TOLERANCE
Level of Stress During Year Before Admission

How long have you been out of work with this illness? _____

Have you experienced any recent change in your job? _____

Have you been under any unusual job stress during the past year? _____

What was the cause?

_____ Retirement	_____ Same job, but new boss or work-
_____ Fired	ing relationship
_____ Other. Explain:	_____ Promotion or demotion

Do you expect the stress will be present when you return to work? _____

The preceding questions should be adapted for students to a school situation.

Have there been changes in your family during the last 2 years?

Which family members are involved? Include dates.

Death _____

Was this someyou you were close to? _____

Divorce _____

Child leaving home _____

Cause? _____

Other _____

Has there been any other unusual stress during the last year that is still affecting you?

Describe:

Any unusual stress in your family?

Describe:

Normal Coping Ability

When you go through a very difficult time, how do you handle it?

_____ Talk it out with someone	_____ Get angry and yell
_____ Drink	_____ Get angry and clam up
_____ Ignore it	_____ Get angry and hit or throw some-
_____ Become anxious	thing
_____ Withdraw from others	_____ Other (explain)
_____ Become depressed	

How often do you experience feelings of depression? _____

In the past, what is the longest period of time this feeling has lasted? _____

Have you felt depressed during the past few weeks?   Yes _____   No _____
To what do you attribute the cause? _____

If rape trauma is the cause of this admission do not explore the psychological reaction with the client until reading the report of the rape crisis counselor, who should have met with the client within an hour of arrival at the emergency department. Either follow the recommendations on the report for ongoing assessment or proceed with gentle questioning about current feelings.

What is the most serious trauma you have experienced? _____
What was the most difficult time you have experienced in your life? _____
How long did it take you to get over it? _____
What did you do to cope with it? _____

Potential for Self-Harm
This part of the assessment should be included if moderate to severe depression is present.

Have you ever thought of committing suicide?   Yes _____   No _____
If yes, continue on.

What would you do to end your life?   No plan _____   Plan _____
Describe:

What would prevent you from committing suicide? _____

Substances That May Be Used as Stress-Relievers
Smoking history
Do you smoke? _____   How long have you been smoking? _____
How many packs per day? _____
Alcohol use history
Do you drink? _____   How often? _____   How much? _____
Is there a history of alcoholism in your family? _____   Who? _____
Drug use
What prescribed medications are you currently using?
Name of medications _____
Dose or schedule _____   Prescribing physician _____
Are you currently using any other drugs?   Yes _____   No _____
What are they? _____
How long have you been using them? _____
What is the usual amount? _____   How often? _____
Have you ever been treated for substance abuse? _____

VALUE-BELIEF
What is your religious affiliation? _____
Do you consider yourself active or inactive in practicing your religion?
Active _____   Inactive _____

Barry Psychosocial Assessment (continued)

Is your religious leader a supportive person?   Yes _____   No _____
Explain:

What does this illness mean to you? _____
Are you experiencing spiritual distress?   Yes _____   No _____
Explain:

What would you consider to be the primary cause of this spiritual distress (actual, possible, or potential)?
_____ Inability to practice spiritual rituals
_____ Conflict between religious, spiritual, or cultural beliefs and prescribed
         health regimen
_____ Crisis of illness, suffering, or death
_____ Other (explain)

Do you expect there will be any disparity in your care-givers' approach that could present a problem to you? _____
Any problems in the areas of
_____ Spiritual rituals   _____ Communication
_____ Cause of illness   _____ Problem solving
_____ Perception of illness and sick _____ Nutrition
         role   _____ Family response
_____ Health maintenance
Explain:

How has this illness affected your relationship with God or the supreme being of your religion?
Explain:

The 11 functional health patterns were named by Marjorie Gordon (1987) in *Nursing diagnosis: Process and application,* New York: McGraw-Hill.

From Barry, P.D. (1989). *Psychosocial nursing: Assessment and intervention.* (2nd ed.). Philadelphia: J.B. Lippincott. Used with permission.

Appendix *B:*

DSM-IV Classification: Draft Criteria

Note: These codes are preliminary and are subject to further updates and modifications after additional consultations.

Disorders Usually First Diagnosed in Infancy, Childhood, or Adolescence

Mental Retardation

317	Mild Mental Retardation
318.0	Moderate Retardation
318.1	Severe Mental Retardation
318.2	Profound Mental Retardation
319	Mental Retardation, Severity Unspecified

Learning Disorders (Academic Skills Disorder)

315.00	Reading Disorder (Developmental Reading Disorder)
315.1	Mathematics Disorder (Developmental Arithmetic Disorder)
315.2	Disorder of Written Expression (Developmental Expressive Writing Disorder)
315.9	Learning Disorder NOS

Motor Skills Disorder

315.4	Developmental Coordination Disorder

Pervasive Developmental Disorders

299.00	Autistic Disorder
299.80	Rett's Disorder
299.10	Childhood Disintegrative Disorder
	Asperger's Disorder (? placement)
299.80	Pervasive Developmental Disorder NOS (including Atypical Autism)

DSM-IV Classification: Draft Criteria (*continued*)

Disruptive Behavior and Attention-deficit Disorders

Attention-deficit/Hyperactivity Disorder
314.00	Predominantly Inattentive Type
314.01	Predominantly Hyperactive-impulsive Type
314.01	Combined type
314.9	Attention-deficit/Hyperactivity Disorder NOS
313.81	Oppositional Defiant Disorder
312.8	Conduct Disorder
312.9	Disruptive Behavior Disorder NOS

Feeding and Eating Disorders of Infancy or Early Childhood

307.52	Pica
307.53	Rumination Disorder
307.59	Feeding Disorder of Infancy or Early Childhood

Tic Disorders

307.23	Tourette's Disorder
307.22	Chronic Motor or Vocal Tic Disorder
307.21	Transient Tic Disorder
307.20	Tic Disorder NOS

Communication Disorders

315.31	Expressive Language Disorder (Developmental Expressive Language Disorder)
315.31	Mixed Receptive/Expressive Language Disorder (Developmental Receptive Language Disorder)
315.39	Phonological Disorder (Developmental Articulation Disorder)
307.0	Stuttering
315.39	Communication Disorder NOS

Elimination Disorders

307.7	Encopresis
307.6	Enuresis

Other Disorders of Infancy, Childhood, or Adolescence

309.21	Separation Anxiety Disorder
313.23	Selective Mutism (Elective Mutism)
313.89	Reactive Attachment Disorder of Infancy or Early Childhood
307.3	Stereotypic Movement Disorder (Stereotypy/Habit Disorder)
313.9	Disorder of Infancy, Childhood, or Adolescence NOS

Delirium, Dementia, Amnestic and Other Cognitive Disorders

Deliria

293.0	Delirium Due to a General Medical Condition
—.—	Substance-induced Delirium *(refer to specific substance for code)*
—.—	Delirium Due to Multiple Etiologies *(use multiple codes based on specific etiologies)*
293.89	Delirium NOS

Dementias

Dementia of the Alzheimer's Type

With Early Onset: If Onset at Age 65 or Below.
290.10	Uncomplicated
290.11	With Delirium
290.12	With Delusions
290.13	With Depressed Mood
290.14	With Hallucinations
290.15	With Perceptual Disturbance
290.16	With Behavioral Disturbance
290.17	With Communication Disturbance

With Late Onset: If Onset After Age 65.
290.00	Uncomplicated
290.30	With Delirium
290.20	With Delusions
290.21	With Depressed Mood
290.22	With Hallucinations
290.23	With Perceptual Disturbance
290.24	With Behavioral Disturbance
290.25	With Communication Disturbance

Vascular Dementia (D:9)
290.40	Uncomplicated
290.41	With Delirium
290.42	With Delusions
290.43	With Depressed Mood
290.44	With Hallucinations
290.45	With Perceptual Disturbance
290.46	With Behavioral Disturbance
290.47	With Communication Disturbance

DSM-IV Classification: Draft Criteria (*continued*)

Dementias Due to Other General Medical Conditions

294.9	Dementia Due to HIV Disease (*Code 043.1 on Axis III*)
294.1	Dementia Due to Head Trauma (*Code 905.0 on Axis III*)
294.1	Dementia Due to Parkinson's Disease (*Code 332.0 on Axis III*)
294.1	Dementia Due to Huntington's Disease (*Code 333.4 on Axis III*)
290.10	Dementia Due to Pick's Disease (*Code 333.1 on Axis III*)
290.10	Dementia Due to Creutzfeldt-Jakob Disease (*Code 046.1 on Axis III*)
294.1	Dementia Due to Other General Medical Condition
—.—	Substance-induced Persisting Dementia (*refer to specific substance for code*)
—.—	Delirium Due to Multiple Etiologies (*use multiple codes based on specific etiologies*)
294.8	Dementia NOS

Amnestic Disorders

294.0	Amnestic Disorder Due to a General Medical Condition
—.—	Substance-induced Persisting Amnestic Disorder (*refer to specific substance for code*)
294.8	Amnestic Disorder NOS

294.9   Cognitive Disorder NOS

Mental Disorders Due to a General Medical Condition Not Elsewhere Classified

293.89	Catatonic Disorder Due to a General Medical Condition
310.1	Personality Change Due to a General Medical Condition
293.9	Mental Disorder NOS Due to a General Medical Condition

Substance-Related Disorders

Alcohol Use Disorders

303.90	Alcohol Dependence
305.00	Alcohol Abuse
303.00	Alcohol Intoxication
291.8	Alcohol Withdrawal
291.0	Alcohol Delirium
291.2	Alcohol Persisting Dementia
291.1	Alcohol Persisting Amnestic Disorder

Alcohol Psychotic Disorder
291.5   With Delusions
291.3   With Hallucinations
291.8   Alcohol Mood Disorder
291.8   Alcohol Anxiety Disorder
292.8   Alcohol Sexual Dysfunction
292.89 Alcohol Sleep Disorder
291.9   Alcohol Use Disorder NOS

Amphetamine (or Related Substance) Use Disorders

304.40 Amphetamine (or Related Substance) Dependence
305.70 Amphetamine (or Related Substance) Abuse
305.70 Amphetamine (or Related Substance) Intoxication
292.0   Amphetamine (or Related Substance) Withdrawal
292.81 Amphetamine (or Related Substance) Delirium
        Amphetamine (or Related Substance) Psychotic Disorder
291.11 With Delusions
291.12 With Hallucinations
292.84 Amphetamine (or Related Substance) Mood Disorder
292.89 Amphetamine (or Related Substance) Anxiety Disorder
292.89 Amphetamine (or Related Substance) Sexual Dysfunction
292.89 Amphetamine (or Related Substance) Sleep Disorder
292.9   Amphetamine (or Related Substance) Use Disorder NOS

Caffeine Use Disorders

305.90 Caffeine Intoxication
292.84 Caffeine Anxiety Disorder
292.89 Caffeine Sleep Disorder
292.9   Caffeine Use Disorder NOS

Cannabis Use Disorders

304.30 Cannabis Dependence
305.20 Cannabis Abuse
305.20 Cannabis Intoxication
292.81 Cannabis Delirium
        Cannabis Psychotic Disorder
291.11 With Delusions
291.12 With Hallucinations
292.89 Cannabis Anxiety Disorder
292.9   Cannabis Use Disorder NOS

Cocaine Use Disorders

304.20 Cocaine Dependence
305.60 Cocaine Abuse

DSM-IV Classification: Draft Criteria (*continued*)

305.60	Cocaine Intoxication
292.0	Cocaine Withdrawal
292.81	Cocaine Delirium
	Cocaine Psychotic Disorder
291.11	With Delusions
291.12	With Hallucinations
292.84	Cocaine Mood Disorder
292.89	Cocaine Anxiety Disorder
292.89	Cocaine Sexual Dysfunction
292.89	Cocaine Sleep Disorder
292.9	Cocaine Use Disorder NOS

Hallucinogen Use Disorders

304.50	Hallucinogen Dependence
305.30	Hallucinogen Abuse
305.30	Hallucinogen Intoxication
292.89	Hallucinogen Persisting Perception Disorder
292.81	Hallucinogen Delirium
	Hallucinogen Psychotic Disorder
291.11	With Delusions
291.12	With Hallucinations
292.84	Hallucinogen Mood Disorder
292.89	Hallucinogen Anxiety Disorder
292.9	Hallucinogen Use Disorder NOS

Inhalant Use Disorders

304.60	Inhalant Dependence
305.90	Inhalant Abuse
305.90	Inhalant Intoxication
292.81	Inhalant Delirium
292.82	Inhalant Persisting Dementia
	Inhalant Psychotic Disorder
291.11	With Delusions
291.12	With Hallucinations
292.84	Inhalant Mood Disorder
292.89	Inhalant Anxiety Disorder
292.9	Inhalant Use Disorder NOS

Nicotine Use Disorders

305.10	Nicotine Dependence
292.0	Nicotine Withdrawal
292.9	Nicotine Use Disorder NOS

Opioid Use Disorders

304.00	Opioid Dependence
305.50	Opioid Abuse
305.50	Opioid Intoxication
292.0	Opioid Withdrawal
292.81	Opioid Delirium
	Opioid Psychotic Disorder
291.11	With Delusions
291.12	With Hallucinations
294.84	Opioid Mood Disorder
292.89	Opioid Sleep Disorder
292.89	Opioid Sexual Dysfunction
292.9	Opioid Use Disorder NOS

Phencyclidine (or Related Substance) Use Disorders

304.90	Phencyclidine (or Related Substance) Dependence
305.90	Phencyclidine (or Related Substance) Abuse
305.90	Phencyclidine (or Related Substance) Intoxication
292.81	Phencyclidine (or Related Substance) Delirium
	Phencyclidine (or Related Substance) Psychotic Disorder
291.11	With Delusions
291.12	With Hallucinations
292.84	Phencyclidine (or Related Substance) Mood Disorder
292.89	Phencyclidine (or Related Substance) Anxiety Disorder
292.9	Phencyclidine (or Related Substance) Use Disorder NOS

Sedative, Hypnotic, or Anxiolytic Substance Use Disorders

304.10	Sedative, Hypnotic, or Anxiolytic Dependence
305.40	Sedative, Hypnotic, or Anxiolytic Abuse
305.40	Sedative, Hypnotic, or Anxiolytic Intoxication
292.0	Sedative, Hypnotic, or Anxiolytic Withdrawal
292.81	Sedative, Hypnotic, or Anxiolytic Delirium
292.82	Sedative, Hypnotic, or Anxiolytic Persisting Dementia
292.83	Sedative, Hypnotic, or Anxiolytic Persisting Amnestic Disorder
	Sedative, Hypnotic, or Anxiolytic Psychotic Disorder
291.11	With Delusions
291.12	With Hallucinations
292.84	Sedative, Hypnotic, or Anxiolytic Mood Disorder
292.89	Sedative, Hypnotic, or Anxiolytic Anxiety Disorder
292.89	Sedative, Hypnotic, or Anxiolytic Sleep Disorder
292.89	Sedative, Hypnotic, or Anxiolytic Sexual Dysfunction
292.9	Sedative, Hypnotic, or Anxiolytic Use Disorder NOS

DSM-IV Classification: Draft Criteria (*continued*)

Polysubstance Use Disorder

304.80   Polysubstance Dependence (E:27)

Other (or Unknown) Substance Use Disorders

304.90	Other (or Unknown) Substance Dependence
305.90	Other (or Unknown) Substance Abuse
305.90	Other (or Unknown) Substance Intoxication
292.0	Other (or Unknown) Substance Withdrawal
292.81	Other (or Unknown) Substance Delirium
292.82	Other (or Unknown) Substance Persisting Dementia
292.83	Other (or Unknown) Substance Persisting Amnestic Disorder
	Other (or Unknown) Substance Psychotic Disorder
291.11	With Delusions
291.12	With Hallucinations
292.84	Other (or Unknown) Substance Mood Disorder
292.89	Other (or Unknown) Substance Anxiety Disorder
292.89	Other (or Unknown) Substance Sexual Dysfunction
292.89	Other (or Unknown) Substance Sleep Disorder
292.9	Other (or Unknown) Substance Use Disorder NOS

Schizophrenia and Other Psychotic Disorders

Schizophrenia

295.30	Paranoid Type
295.10	Disorganized Type
295.20	Catatonic Type
295.90	Undifferentiated Type
295.60	Residual Type
295.40	Schizophreniform Disorder
295.70	Schizoaffective Disorder
297.1	Delusional Disorder
298.8	Brief Psychotic Disorder
297.3	Shared Psychotic Disorder (Folle a Deux)
	Psychotic Disorder Due to a General Medical Condition
293.81	With Delusions
293.82	With Hallucinations
——.—	Substance-induced Psychotic Disorder (*refer to specific substances for codes*)
298.9	Psychotic Disorder NOS

Mood Disorders

Depressive Disorders

Major Depressive Disorder
   296.2x   Single Episode
   296.3x   Recurrent
   300.4   Dysthymic Disorder
   311   Depressive Disorder NOS

Bipolar Disorders

Bipolar I Disorder
   296.0x   Single Manic Episode
   296.4   Most Recent Episodic Hypomanic
   296.4x   Most Recent Episodic Manic
   296.6x   Most Recent Episode Mixed
   296.5x   Most Recent Episode Depressed
   296.7   Most Recent Episode Unspecified
   296.89   Bipolar II Disorder (Recurrent major depressive episodes with
               hypomania)
   301.13   Cyclothymic Disorder
   296.80   Bipolar Disorder NOS

293.83   Mood Disorder Due to a General Medical Condition

——.—   Substance-induced Mood Disorder *(refer to specific
            substances for codes)*

296.90   Mood Disorder NOS

Anxiety Disorders

Panic Disorder
   300.01   Without Agoraphobia
   300.21   With Agoraphobia
   300.22   Agoraphobia Without History of Panic Disorder
   300.29   Specific Phobia (Simple Phobia)
   300.23   Social Phobia (Social Anxiety Disorder)
   300.3   Obsessive-Compulsive Disorder
   309.81   Posttraumatic Stress Disorder
   300.3   Acute Stress Disorder

DSM-IV Classification: Draft Criteria (*continued*)

300.02	Generalized Anxiety Disorder (includes Overanxious Disorder of Childhood)
293.89	Anxiety Disorder Due to a General Medical Condition
---.-	Substance-induced Anxiety Disorder (*refer to specific substances for codes*)

300.00   Anxiety Disorder NOS

Somatoform Disorders

300.81	Somatization Disorder
300.11	Conversion Disorder
300.7	Hypochondriasis

300.71	*Body Dysmorphic Disorder*
	Pain Disorder
307.80	Associated with Psychological Factors
307.89	Associated with Both Psychological Factors and a General Medical Condition
300.82	Undifferentiated Somatoform Disorder
300.89	Somatoform Disorder NOS

Factitious Disorders

Factitious Disorder

300.16	With Predominantly Psychological Signs and Symptoms
300.17	With Predominantly Physical Signs and Symptoms
300.18	With Combined Psychological and Physical Signs and Symptoms

300.19   Factitious Disorder NOS

Dissociative Disorders

300.12	Dissociative Amnesia
300.13	Dissociative Fugue
300.14	Dissociative Identity Disorder (Multiple Personality Disorder)
300.6	Depersonalization Disorder
300.15	Dissociative Disorder NOS

Sexual and Gender Identity Disorders

Sexual Dysfunctions

Sexual Desire Disorders
302.71   Hypoactive Sexual Desire Disorder
?302.79   Sexual Aversion Disorder

Sexual Arousal Disorders
302.72   Female Sexual Arousal Disorder
302.72   Male Erectile Disorder

Orgasm Disorders
302.73   Female Orgasmic Disorder (Inhibited Female Orgasm)
302.74   Male Orgasmic Disorder (Inhibited Male Orgasm)
302.75   Premature Ejaculation

Sexual Pain Disorders
302.76   Dyspareunia
306.51   Vaginismus

Sexual Dysfunctions Due to a General Medical Condition
607.84   Male Erectile Disorder Due to a General Medical Condition
608.89   Male Dyspareunia Due to a General Medical Condition
625.0   Female Dyspareunia Due to a General Medical Condition
608.89   Male Hypoactive Sexual Desire Disorder Due to a General Medical Condition
625.8   Female Hypoactive Sexual Desire Disorder Due to a General Medical Condition
608.89   Other Male Sexual Dysfunction Due to a General Medical Condition
625.8   Other Female Sexual Dysfunction Due to a General Medical Condition
——.—   Substance-induced Sexual Dysfunction *(refer to specific substances for codes)*
302.70   ***Sexual Dysfunction NOS***

Paraphilias
302.4   Exhibitionism
302.81   Fetishism
?302.85   Frotteurism
302.2   Pedophilia
302.83   Sexual Masochism
302.84   Sexual Sadism
302.82   Voyeurism
302.3   Transvestic Fetishism

DSM-IV Classification: Draft Criteria (*continued*)

302.9	Paraphilia NOS
302.9	*Sexual Disorder NOS*

Gender Identity Disorders

Gender Identity Disorder
302.6	In Children
302.85	In Adolescents and Adults
302.6	Gender Identity Disorder NOS

Eating Disorder

307.1	Anorexia Nervosa
307.51	Bulimia Nervosa
307.50	Eating disorder NOS

Sleep Disorders

Primary Sleep Disorders

Dyssomnias
307.42	Primary Insomnia
307.44	Primary Hypersomnia
347	Narcolepsy
780.59	Breathing-Related Sleep Disorder
307.45	Circadian Rhythm Sleep Disorder (Sleep-Wake Schedule Disorder)
307.47	Dyssomnia NOS

Parasomnias
307.47	Nightmare Disorder (Dream Anxiety Disorder)
307.46	Sleep Terror Disorder
307.46	Sleepwalking Disorder
?307.47	Parasomnia NOS

Sleep Disorders Related to Another Mental Disorder

307.42	Insomnia Related to [Axis I or Axis II Disorder]
307.44	Hypersomnia Related to [Axis I or Axis II Disorder]

Other Sleep Disorders

Sleep Disorders Due to a General Medical Condition
780.52	Insomnia Type
780.54	Hypersomnia Type
780.59	Parasomnia Type
780.59	Mixed Type
—.—	Substance-induced Sleep Disorder *(refer to specific substances for codes)*

Impulse Control Disorders Not Elsewhere Classified

312.34	Intermittent Explosive Disorder
312.32	Kleptomania
312.33	Pyromania
312.31	Pathological Gambling
?312.39	Trichotillomania
312.30	Impulse Control NOS

Adjustment Disorders

Adjustment Disorder

309.24	With Anxiety
309.0	With Depressed Mood
309.3	With Disturbance of Conduct
309.4	With Mixed Disturbance of Emotions and Conduct
309.28	With Mixed Anxiety and Depressed Mood
309.9	Unspecified

Personality Disorders

301.0	Paranoid Personality Disorder
301.20	Schizoid Personality Disorder
301.22	Schizotypal Personality Disorder
301.7	Antisocial Personality Disorder
301.83	Borderline Personality Disorder
301.50	Histrionic Personality Disorder
301.81	Narcissistic Personality Disorder
301.82	Avoidant Personality Disorder
301.6	Dependent Personality Disorder
301.4	Obsessive-Compulsive Personality Disorder
301.9	Personality Disorder NOS

DSM-IV Classification: Draft Criteria (*continued*)

Other Conditions That May Be a Focus of Clinical Attention

(Psychological Factors) Affecting Medical Condition

Choose name based on nature of factors:

Mental Disorder Affecting Medical Condition
Psychological Symptoms Affecting Medical Condition
Personality Traits or Coping Style Affecting Medical Condition
Maladaptive Health Behaviors Affecting Medical Condition
Unspecified Psychological Factors Affecting Medical Condition

Medication-induced Movement Disorders

332.1	Neuroleptic-induced Parkinsonism
333.92	Neuroleptic Malignant Syndrome
333.7	Neuroleptic-induced Acute Dystonia
333.99	Neuroleptic-induced Acute Akathisia
333.82	Neuroleptic-induced Tardive Dyskinesia
333.1	Medication-induced Postural Tremor
333.90	Medication-induced Movement Disorder NOS

995.2   Adverse Effects of Medication NOS

Relational Problems

V61.9	Relational Problem Related to A Mental Disorder or General Medical Condition
V61.20	Parent-Child Relational Problem
V61.12	Partner Relational Problem
V61.8	Sibling Relational Problem
V62.81	Relational Problem NOS

Problems Related to Abuse or Neglect

V61.21	Physical Abuse of Child
V61.22	Sexual Abuse of Child
V61.21	Neglect of Child
V61.10	Physical Abuse of Adult
V61.11	Sexual Abuse of Adult

Additional Conditions That May Be a Focus of Clinical Attention

V62.82	Bereavement
V40.0	Borderline Intellectual Functioning
V62.3	Academic Problem
V62.2	Occupational Problem

V71.02	Childhood or Adolescent Antisocial Behavior
V71.01	Adult Antisocial Behavior
V65.2	Malingering
V62.89	Phase of Life Problem
V15.81	Noncompliance with Treatment for a Mental Disorder
313.82	Identity Problem
V62.61	Religious or Spiritual Problem
V62.4	Acculturation Problem
780.9	Age-Associated Memory Decline

Additional Codes

300.9	Unspecified Mental Disorder
V71.09	No Diagnosis or Condition on Axis 1
799.9	Diagnosis or Condition Deferred on Axis 1
V71.09	No Diagnosis on Axis II
799.9	Diagnosis Deferred on Axis II

DSM-IV Draft criteria (3/1/1993), Washington, DC: American Psychiatric Association.

Index

Page numbers followed by *f* indicate figures; *t* following a page number indicates tabular material.

MARVA COLLINS' WAY

MARVA COLLINS' WAY

Marva Collins and Civia Tamarkin

J. P. TARCHER, INC.
Los Angeles
Distributed by Houghton Mifflin Company
Boston

Library of Congress Cataloging in Publication Data

Collins, Marva.
   Marva Collins' way

   1. Collins, Marva. 2. Teachers–Illinois–Chicago–
Biography. I. Tamarkin, Civia. II. Title.
LA2317.C62A35   1982   372.11′092′4   82-10516
ISBN 0-87477-235-4

   J. P. Tarcher, Inc.
   9110 Sunset Blvd.
   Los Angeles, CA 90069

Design by Mike Yazzolino
Publishing consultant: Victoria Pasternack

Manufactured in the United States of America

S   10   9   8   7   6   5   4   3   2
First Edition

*To our children and all children,
may they find their own way.*

1	**2**	**3**	**4**
5	**6**	**7**	**8**
9	**10**	**11**	**12**
13	**14**	**15**	**16**

CONTENTS

Prologue

I first met Marva Collins in February 1980, when I was reporting a cover story on education for *Time* magazine. It was a period of upheaval in education. Everything that had been festering for years seemed to be coming to the surface. What was emerging was a major crisis, the result of a rash of school system bankruptcies, the politics of court-ordered busing, declining public school enrollments, low reading scores, and rampant teacher incompetence.

As a stringer in *Time*'s Midwest bureau, I had convinced the editors to take a hard look at what was going on in classrooms around the country. I was looking at the situation not only through the eyes of a journalist but also as a former teacher and as a parent who was dissatisfied with many of the teachers my daughter had had, first in the Chicago public schools and later in a private school. To find out what had gone wrong with American education and what could be done about it, I and other *Time* correspondents interviewed parents, teachers, students, school board members, and academics across the nation.

In my investigative odyssey, one of the teachers I talked to was Marva Collins, the brash, outspoken founder of Chicago's Westside Preparatory School. Marva had already been taken up by the media, hoisted onto an educational pedestal, and hailed as education's heroine. Scores of newspapers and magazine articles and several television features, including a segment of CBS's *60 Minutes*, had named her the miracle worker who had succeeded where other teachers had failed. Anxious to get her views on education and to find out if she was indeed different from other teachers, I accepted her invitation to come out to Garfield Park to see just what it was she was doing.

As I pulled off the expressway and entered the Garfield Park neighborhood, I could see it was a hazy vestige of its former self, a part of Chicago that stood forlornly like some dowdy spinster who had been jilted of her prime. The warren of streets and boulevards hugging the park's perimeter, four miles west of the city's downtown loop, was crowded with run-down greystones, six-flats, twelve-flats, and courtyard apartment buildings. Most of the stately old mansions along Hamlin Avenue had been abused, ignored, and haphazardly chopped up into apartments. Many of the front lawns were now dry dirt plots strewn with broken glass or covered with knee-high weed thickets. A Star of David carved over the doorway of the Morningstar Baptist Church, which used to be the Wilno Synagogue, was the only hint of the neighborhood's ethnic past.

On the corner of Springfield and Adams streets was Delano Grammar School. It had been one of the best schools in the Chicago system, and former graduates, now grandparents, still remembered teachers like Mrs. Wilson, who stayed an extra hour every day for a year, teaching her eighth-grade class to play Hohner harmonicas.

The school now loomed ingloriously, a clumsy, pathetic hodgepodge of mismatched building annexes sprouting from its side. Its playground—once the gathering place and training ground for such neighborhood celebrities as Tom Hayes, Sid Rosenthal, and Saul Farber, all-American basketball stars, and Saul's brother Eddie, who played professional baseball for the Cleveland Indians—was now buried beneath the annexes, so that all that remained were patches of gravel planted with rusted swings and slides.

If it hadn't been for Marva Collins, Garfield Park would have remained a forgotten neighborhood. But she had replaced all the old heroes. Marva Collins was a powerful force in that neighborhood. I found that out as soon as I pulled up in front of her house. Four young men in their middle to late teens were loitering across the street. One of them approached me as I got out of the car.

"You going to see Mrs. Collins' school?" he asked.

I nodded uncomfortably. After all, Garfield Park was the kind of place you drove through with your car doors locked and your windows rolled up.

"OK," he said. "You don't have to worry about anything. We'll watch your car for you."

I was struck by the respect they seemed to have for Marva. Later I related the incident to her and asked what her secret was.

"There's no secret," she answered. "I just deal honestly with children. They know I don't turn my nose down at them. They listen to me because I'm not some outsider who comes over here and talks down to them about what it is like to be poor. I'm right here working with them all the time. If everyone in the neighborhood treated these children with the same consistent interest, the children would do for them what they do for me."

What I eventually came to realize about Marva was that she was a teacher all the time, not just in the classroom. For her, being a teacher had turned into a fixed idea to which she obsessively referred all things and all experiences. If some found her single-mindedness overbearing, her students and the other children in the neighborhood saw it as a sign of her implacable devotion to them. And they, in turn, were fiercely loyal to her.

Meeting Marva, I was reminded of something Dr. Ralph Tyler, a former dean of social sciences at the University of Chicago, had once told me. "Teaching," he had said, "is not just a job. It is a human service, and it must be thought of as a mission." Marva seemed to see it that way. With an overwhelming dedication—which, I might add, could easily be mistaken for self-importance—she allowed teaching to consume her. As I got to know her, I saw that her life was so wrapped up in her teaching and in her students that she seldom needed anything else. She drew most of her pleasure and pain from her children. Oddly, people could accept that quality in a parent, but they had difficulty understanding it in a teacher. To many, Marva would often appear too good to be true.

When I first saw her in action in the classroom, she was every bit as impressive as the media had made her out to be. Actually, I had been wary of her miracle image, dismissing it as the stuff of media hype. But watching her perform, I suddenly understood how that image had come about. It was really a question of semantics. While Marva Collins didn't work "miracles," she was indeed a miraculous teacher. She had an exuberance, an energy about her that was both captivating and contagious.

The control and rapport she had with her students amazed me. From my own years as a high school English teacher, I knew that was no simple thing to achieve.

Marva's approach appeared so natural. There was a sense of maternalism about it. She was constantly in motion about the class, patting heads, touching shoulders, hugging and praising her students. There were more than thirty students in that room, yet no one seemed to be lost in the crowd. Somehow, during the course of the day, Marva managed to give each child personalized attention. She didn't just teach them, she nurtured them. And from the way the children responded, I could tell Marva wasn't merely putting on an act for a visitor. There was an incredible bond between her and her students.

Learning in Marva Collins' class was clearly an exciting, shared experience. The children were eager to learn. They waved their hands and jumped up and down in their seats, asking her to call on them. It had been a long time since I had seen a class work as well as this one. Many of the students were below average; some, in fact, had been tagged with learning disabilities. But their motivation was impressive.

Much of the media attention Marva Collins received focused on *what* she taught—on the fact that she had seven-, eight-, and nine-year-old ghetto children reading and reciting William Shakespeare and Geoffrey Chaucer. But I was more intrigued by *how* she taught and *why* her approach worked. There was a method there, but it was not readily definable. To understand it, I knew I would have to spend more than just one day in her classroom.

I wasn't naive enough to think Marva Collins had the

cure-all for the ailments of education. The problems were far too complex and chronic. Students' reading and other test scores had been declining since 1963. More than thirty million adult Americans were functional illiterates; some twenty million Americans over the age of eighteen could not read well enough to understand a want ad or a job application. The U.S. illiteracy rate was three times higher than that of the Soviet Union. American students were scoring lower on achievement tests than students from other industrially advanced nations, such as Germany, Japan, and Great Britain.

But after I watched Marva Collins and after I did all the interviews and research in connection with the *Time* story, one thing became clear: the teacher in the front of the classroom made the difference. For years educators had pointed an accusing finger at parents, at television, at the schools' lack of funds, at children's home lives and backgrounds, and at what the National Education Association described as "the distractions which characterized American life in the past decade or so." Now, suddenly and dramatically, the public was no longer willing to accept the blame. Instead, teachers themselves were coming under scrutiny.

The previous summer, headlines announced that half of the first-year teachers in the Dallas school system had failed to pass the Wesman Personnel Classification Test, an exam measuring verbal reasoning and mathematical abilities. The Houston Independent School District discovered that half its teacher applicants scored lower in math than the average high school senior, and about one-third scored just as poorly in language skills. And the situation wasn't limited to Texas. One-third of the teachers in Florida County flunked eighth-grade math tests and tenth-grade reading tests. And only half of the applicants for jobs in the Mobile, Alabama, schools passed the National Teacher Examination. A much-publicized study by W. Timothy Weaver of Boston University confirmed that college students majoring in education scored lower on the Scholastic Aptitude Test than majors in almost every other field.

The spotlight on school finances also underscored the deteriorating quality of American education. Faced with school closings, program cuts, teacher layoffs, and possible tax hikes, parents began to take a critical look at the kind of education their children were getting. In a number of instances across the country, parents sued school districts for malpractice. There was a renewed push for minimum competency testing of teachers as well as of students. State legislatures began passing bills requiring teachers be tested for their basic skills. Teacher colleges came under attack for seemingly handing out diplomas as though they were Green Stamps. Parents stormed school board meetings to demand teacher accountability. Others turned to private schools, and some even yanked their children out of the classroom altogether and taught them at home.

Marva Collins had come to the public's attention. From the ivy-covered walls of Princeton to the grade schools of Wyoming, educators clamored to attend her workshops, and they flocked to her classroom from as far away as Germany and Spain to observe her technique. Publishers were after her to endorse textbooks; manufacturers wanted her to advertise educational products. A Hollywood producer planned to make a movie about her, and a group of entrepreneurs tried to set up a franchise of Marva Collins schools. Distraught parents sought her advice, and politicians solicited her help. Weeks before I met her, she had been offered the post of Los Angeles County superintendent of schools as well as a seat on Chicago's Board of Education. Within the year, she would be invited by President Carter to a White House conference on education and be tapped for a cabinet spot in then President-elect Reagan's administration.

It was a celebrity status never before accorded a simple grade-school teacher. Everyone saw in Marva Collins what he or she wanted to see. Journalists viewed her as a maverick up against the system. Taxpayers, tired of subsidizing the growing cost of education, liked Marva's no-frills, no-gimmicks, basic approach to teaching, particularly when she was quoted as saying that more government spending was not the answer to the problems facing schools. Parents of low achievers looked to her as someone who offered hope to their children. Minority groups regarded her as a champion of equal opportunity. Conservatives seized upon her self-reliance, her traditionalism, and her insistence that old-fashioned values be taught in the classroom. And to liberals, she was a romantic idealist out to right the wrongs of society. Some teachers found her an inspirational model, while others saw her as a charlatan, a quitter who had gone outside the system, and even a threat to public education.

Perhaps no teacher deserved such attention. The headlines were calling her "super-teacher" and referring to what she did as "blackboard magic" and "miracle on Adams Street." Two years later she would make headlines of a different sort.

It took me more than a year of observing her teaching, of following her students' progress, and of talking to parents, psychologists, and other educators to separate the real Marva from her myth. She wasn't perfect, she wasn't a superwoman. For that matter, she was neither an academic, a scholar, nor the perfect grammarian. But what could not be disputed was that Marva Collins motivated children and made them want to achieve. That is what this book is about—a teacher teaching.

Civia Tamarkin

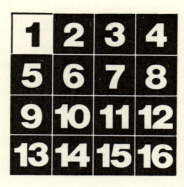

Marva Collins got Freddie Harris to take off his St. Louis Cardinals jacket and hang it on the back of his chair.

It was shortly after the bell rang on the first day of school, and teachers at Delano Elementary School on Chicago's Near West Side were being unusually tolerant of students because no one was up to a challenge so soon. In fact, short of a knock-down fight, teachers were overlooking just about everything as they shuffled class cards and gave out seat assignments. No one wanted to march a student into the principal's office and admit things had already gotten out of control just ten minutes into the new 1974–1975 school year.

It didn't seem particularly significant whether or not Freddie was wearing a jacket in class, until Marva noticed how defiantly his fists were shoved into the pockets. Actually her only concern was that it was too hot for him to sit in class all day wearing that jacket. The room was already choking in a late-summer heat that promised to get worse by midmorning. When she moved closer to him and saw how tightly his lips were pressed together and how his shoulders were hunched up around his neck, she realized that Freddie Harris was working hard at being tough.

Freddie expected his stay at Delano, and in particular this class, to be brief. At nine years old he was a repeater in second grade, a troublemaker whose file down in the office bulged with psychologists' reports and harsh evaluations from previous teachers. Last May he was suspended for the remainder of the school term for fighting. The time before, he was kicked out for throwing food in the lunchroom. Before that, he had cussed at a teacher. He was readmitted now for the new fall semester with the principal's warning that the next infraction would get him thrown out of Delano for good.

That suited Freddie just fine. He didn't like school, and he didn't like the other children any more than they liked him. The children his age thought he was a baby for being stuck in second grade, and the second-graders thought he was just big and dumb. Besides, he figured, once he was out of Delano, he would be finished with school. His old lady, he thought, wasn't going to pay for any private school, and she didn't like churches much so there was no chance of his being sent to a parochial school. All he had to do was get kicked out of this class and he could hang around all day and do what he wanted.

So when Marva asked him to take off his jacket, he just slumped further down in his seat, his fists stuffed into his pockets and his legs stretched out under the chair in front of him.

"Peach," Marva said softly, "you don't need to wear that jacket in class. Let's take it off and get out a pencil so we can do some work." She knew Freddie was trying to bait her, and her technique in this kind of situation was to be matter-of-fact. She was not sure yet how far Freddie would push it. Was he just introducing himself or trying for something more? She looked hard at him, wondering how many other teachers had fueled his fight.

Freddie turned his head away sharply, fixing his stare on the broken pane of glass in the third window.

"Sweetheart," said Marva, "it's so hot in here you're going to roast yourself."

He didn't move. She reached out and teasingly mussed his hair. "Besides," she said, "you're such a handsome, strong boy, I don't see why you want to cover up those big muscles of yours."

Marva thought she saw his mouth relax slightly, even hold back a smile, so she cupped his face in her hands and slowly drew him toward her. New children have such dull eyes, she thought, such sullen looks and empty expressions. At seven, eight, and nine years old they have already resigned themselves to failure.

Freddie refused to look up at her, though he allowed her to caress his face.

"Come on, peach, we have work to do," she said, standing straight and tall before him. Marva always stood tall, being easily six feet even without the high heels she liked to wear, never stooping under her height, not even when she was a long-armed and skinny-legged child with a size twelve shoe and the other children teased her that she could knock the roof off the church. "You can't just sit in a seat and grow smart," she said. Her eyes, which could turn dark and cold when she was angry, were soft on his face.

Then, because he hadn't jerked away from her touch, she let one hand fall to the collar of his jacket, and with the other she started to pull apart the front snap. His hand shot out of a pocket and locked tightly around her wrist.

"You are so very angry," she murmured gently, "but I know you're not angry with me, because I haven't done anything to you. We all have a good me and a bad me inside us, and I know that you have a good you. Will you help me find it? I'm your friend and I'm going to help you all the time and I'm going to love you all the time. I love you already, and I'm going to love you even when you don't love yourself."

She pulled him close to her, his head resting against her hip. Her long fingers kneaded the tension from his shoulders and stroked the back of his neck. Marva worked painstakingly to know each child, training herself to catch the gesture, look, or remark that would tell her what a child needed.

Freddie pushed back into his chair, sat up tall, and with quick, short pulls began popping apart the snaps on his jacket, slipping his arms out of the sleeves. Marva bent over him, balanced his chin on the crook of her finger, and tilted his head back so that he was looking straight at her. The subdued tone of her voice gave way suddenly to a new firmness. "I promise, you are going to *do,* you are going to *produce.* I am not going to let you fail."

Marva walked up to the front of the class. She had been teaching for fourteen and a half years—two at Monroe County

Training School in Beatrice, Alabama and twelve and a half in the Chicago public schools; and while she had grown to hate the teaching profession as a whole, she loved to teach. Septembers were always the same. She expected the anxiety would have worn off by now. It never did. She didn't sleep the night before school started, uneasy as a child going off for the first time.

With every new class there was so much to do. Somehow her room at Delano had become a way station for the castoffs the other teachers didn't want. There were always children like Freddie Harris, the discipline problems. Last year she had her hands full with James Thomas. James had acted up all through kindergarten and first grade, and most teachers couldn't stand him.

When James misbehaved in her class during the first week of school, Marva called him over to her.

"James, do you know how to spell your name?" she asked.

The child nodded that he did.

"Well, fine," Marva said, "you go over to the file cabinet, open the drawer, and see if you can find your cumulative record card and read it."

James took out the card, glanced at it, and brought it to Marva with a puzzled look on his face. School had just started and Marva had already given him a grade of "Good" in conduct.

"Do you think you deserve that grade?" asked Marva.

"No," he answered.

"Do you want that grade?"

"Uh huh," he whispered.

"Then you go back to your seat and earn it."

James Thomas was not a problem the rest of the year.

Besides the troublemakers, Marva had children like Bernette Miller, the heavy-set, slow-moving girl in the first row, whose drawn-out speech prompted a previous teacher to dismiss her as a child with a learning disability. And there were children like pigtailed Wanda Lewis, who had never learned how to spell her name or which side of the notebook paper to write on. She had been passed on to the next grade simply because she was so quiet.

Marva stopped beside Bernette Miller's desk. She said nothing, but the children instantly shuffled around in their seats and faced forward. She had a commanding authority, an almost hypnotic presence.

Marva was a striking woman with high cheekbones and strong angular features, which she inherited along with a love of jewelry from a great-grandmother who was a Choctaw Indian. Slender though not willowy, Marva was immediately discernible in a crowd—even without the visibility afforded by her height—for she had acquired a poise and sophistication that gave her appearance a deliberate style.

Marva would rarely wear slacks, and she never wore loose-fitting shifts or casually assembled blouses and skirts. Sloppy dressing showed disrespect for oneself, for the children, and for the profession. From the first day of class Marva was teaching that self-respect is the most important thing a person can have. For herself and for the children Marva dressed impeccably, favoring cashmere sweaters, suits, and herring-bone tweeds. Her clothing was tailored and stylishly simple, but she usually added an ornamental touch: a carved belt cinched over a sweater, a gold medallion on a chain, an organdy boutonniere, or perhaps a lace handkerchief fanned in pleats across a pocket and held in place by a beaded lion's-head brooch. In Marva's opinion, it was important to have a unique imprint. She felt she was different from most people and delighted in her difference. It was an attitude often mistaken for arrogance.

"I am a teacher," she said to the class on this first day. "A teacher is someone who leads. There is no magic here. Mrs. Collins is no miracle worker. I do not walk on water, I do not part the sea. I just love children and work harder than a lot of people, and so will you.

"I know most of you can't spell your name. You don't know the alphabet, you don't know how to read, you don't know homonyms or how to syllabicate. I promise you that you will. None of you has ever failed. School may have failed you. Well, goodbye to failure, children. Welcome to success. You will read hard books in here and understand what you read. You will write every day so that writing becomes second nature to you.

You will memorize a poem every week so that you can train your minds to remember things. It is useless for you to learn something in school if you are not going to remember it.

"But you must help me to help you. If you don't give anything, don't expect anything. Success is not coming to you, you must come to it."

The children looked puzzled. They were accustomed to warnings, threats, and rules of order on the first day of class. If nothing else, Marva vowed she would get through to these children because she was so determined. Or just plain stubborn. She was, in fact, more strong-willed than most, maybe even a bit too strong-willed for her own good. Over and over her mother used to warn her, "Marva, you'll never come to any good 'cause once your mind is set, there's no telling you what to do."

Marva Collins was not going to let any child make her a bad teacher.

"The first thing we are going to do in here, children," Marva told her class, "is an awful lot of believing in ourselves."

Freddie Harris decided to give this teacher a try 'cause she sure was different from all the other teachers he had messed with and 'cause it seemed like he was getting nowhere by acting up, at least, not for now. He finished helping Marva hand out excerpts from Emerson's "Self Reliance." Freddie and all the other children began riffling through the mimeographed pages, shaking their heads in disbelief at all the print, mumbling an occasional "Wow" or "No way, man."

"What are you all getting so worried about?" Marva said. "I don't expect you to know how to read this. I will read it to you, but you must listen to what it says."

She liked to begin the school year with "Self Reliance." Marva believed that it was one of the most important things a student, especially a black student, could ever learn.

"Now let's look at the title. The first thing you must always look at is the title. What is the first thing you must look at, children? The t——."

"Title," a sprinkling of voices offered shyly.

"Very good." Marva walked to the blackboard, picked up a piece of chalk, and printed "Self Reliance" across the newly washed surface. "The title is 'Self Reliance,' " she repeated, marking the vowel sounds with colored chalk. "These are called diacritical marks, and they show us how to pronounce vowel sounds. The *e* in *self* has the short sound *eh,* so we put a breve over it. The first *e* and the *i* in *reliance* have macrons, which tell us those vowel sounds are long; the vowels say their own names."

Marva moved down the aisle by the windows. "Now we are going to read an essay called 'Self Reliance.' What is the title?" Marva asked the boy in the fifth seat of the third row, who was rubbing his fingers along the edge of the desk. The boy lowered his head, chin resting against his chest, and moved his fingers up and down in a nervous rhythm, waiting for his turn to pass.

"What is the title, sweetheart? Don't just sit there with your mouth shut. If you don't know, then say, 'Mrs. Collins, I don't know.' Don't ever be afraid of making a mistake. If you can't make a mistake, you can't make anything."

She sidled around the desks until she was beside him, her hand resting on his shoulder. Then she asked the same question of the child behind him.

" 'Self Reliance,' " the girl answered.

"Very good," said Marva, unfastening the girl's barette and repositioning it to hold back a few stray strands of hair. "Let's keep the hair out of your eyes, pet, so you can see." Marva continued down the aisle, asking each child in that row to tell her the title, getting each child accustomed to speaking in class, and with each answer she said, "Very good," *"Très bien," "Laudo,"* or *"Sehr gut,"* explaining that she was praising them in French, Latin, and German.

"Now," she said, "self-reliance means to believe in yourself. What does self-reliance mean? To be———."

"To believe in yourself," echoed a few faint voices.

"Everybody, in big outdoor voices, what does it mean?"

"To believe in yourself," the children said, more boldly.

"Very, very good, children," Marva told them in a steady businesslike voice, her eyes looking down on the paper as she calmed their rising enthusiasm and signaled them on to the next thought. Marva could lead with her eyes and her voice, winning control by a look or an inflection. Now her tone seemed to belie the praise she had just uttered, as if she were warning the children not to be too satisfied with one small success but to remember how much more there was to learn.

"The author of 'Self Reliance' was a man named Ralph Waldo Emerson," she continued. "You must always read the author's name. If you like what an author writes, but you don't know the author's name, then you won't be able to find any more of his stories to read." She paused, gauging the children's interest. A few were wriggling in their seats. Wanda Lewis, in the back of the class, seemed lost in herself, staring out the window, tapping a pencil against her pudgy cheek.

"Darling," Marva motioned to Wanda, "if you just sit and look, you are going nowhere. Come up here beside me so we can keep track of one another." Marva helped the girl push her desk up the narrow aisle, manuevering it to the front of the row as the other children shuffled their desks aside.

"All right, children," she quieted the class. "Mr. Emerson was a writer, a poet, and a lecturer who lived in the 1800s. A lecturer is someone who talks before an audience or a class." Marva wrote the word on the board, underlining *lecture*. "The base word is *lecture*, which is a talk or a speech. Someone who gives the talk or speech is a *lecturer*. Freddie, what is a lecturer?"

"Someone who gives a speech to a lot of people," Freddie murmured, smiling.

"That's very, very good, sweetheart," Marva told him. "See, you're so used to being wrong, you're afraid to be right. But speak more loudly next time. When you whisper, it means 'I don't like myself. I don't believe what I say.' What you say is important. Each of you is the most important child in the world.

"Now, children, Mr. Emerson was born in Boston in 1803. Where is Boston?" She waited for a response. "Come on, children, think, think, shake your brains! James, come up here to the map and show us where Boston is."

A stocky boy with short-cropped hair walked hesitantly to the wall map. Marva straightened his collar, telling him what a handsome shirt it was. She put her arm around him. With her free hand she guided his index finger to the correct spot on the map.

"That's wonderful, James. Boston is the capital of Massachusetts. Thank you, James, you are just so bright," she told him as he sat down grinning. "Ralph Waldo Emerson was born in Boston, Massachusetts, and his father was a minister. Where was Mr. Emerson born, children?"

"Boston," they answered.

"Very good. Boston. Now when Ralph was not quite eight years old, as old as some of you, his father died. The family was so poor that Ralph and his brother had to share the same winter coat. Yet Ralph and all of his three brothers studied hard and they all went to Harvard College when they grew up."

She moved around the room as she spoke, patting a head or caressing an arm. "When he graduated, Ralph Waldo Emerson became a teacher for a while to help pay for his brother William's college education, and then he became a minister. Mr. Emerson was always questioning life, and he didn't always agree with the church or the other ministers. How many of you question life? How many of you wonder why things happen the way they do?"

Two students immediately raised their hands. The rest watched curiously, surprised by their classmates' willingness to respond.

"Do you mean to tell me that only a few of you question the way things are?" Marva asked, exaggerating her amazement. "Well, I guess most of you think life is wonderful. Everyone always has enough to eat, a good place to live. There is no suffering, no poverty . . ."

Her words were muffled by the children's groans and giggles.

"Of course, you don't," she continued slowly. "Every time you say 'That's not fair' or you wonder why something is the way it is, you are questioning life, just as Mr. Emerson did. He believed that every person has a free will and can choose to make his life what he wants it to be. I believe that. I believe that you can make your life anything you want it to be."

Marva read aloud passages from the essay. She felt the children's restlessness as she read. Their eyes were roving around the room. A few had their arms slung over the backs of their chairs, their feet swinging sideways into the aisles. But

Marva continued. When she finished, she sat on the edge of a child's desk and looked at the class.

She said in a lower voice, "So you think this work is too difficult for you? Well, do not expect to do baby work in here. School can teach you how to lead a good life. We all come here to make life better. And the knowledge you put in your heads is going to save whom? You, not me. Mr. Emerson is telling us to trust our own thoughts, to think for ourselves and not worry about what other people tell us to think. Tanya, what does Emerson tell us to do?"

"Trust ourselves," replied Tanya.

"Very, very good, Tanya," Marva said. "James, what does Emerson tell us to do?"

"Trust ourselves."

"Very good, James. You're so clever, but I don't want to see you put your head on the desk. If you are sleepy, you should be home. This is a classroom, not a hospital or a hotel. I don't ever want to see any of you napping in your seats or just sitting with your hands folded, doing nothing. This is not a prayer meeting. If I see your hands folded, I'm going to put a Bible in them."

The children giggled and Marva smiled. A bond was beginning to grow between them. What she said and did this first day would determine the rest of their year together. She left nothing to chance.

It was Marva Collins' attitude that made children learn. What she did was brainwash them into succeeding. She was forever saying "You can do it," convincing her students there wasn't anything they could not do. There were no excuses for a child's not learning. There was no point in fixing the blame on television, or parents, or a child's environment. The decisive factor was the teacher up in front of the class. If a child sensed a teacher didn't care, then all the textbooks and prepackaged lesson plans and audio-visual equipment and fancy, new, carpeted, air-conditioned building facilities weren't going to get that child to learn.

"Children," she began, "today will decide whether you succeed or fail tomorrow. I promise you, I won't let you fail. I care about you. I love you. You can pay people to teach, but not to care.

"Some teachers sit behind a big desk, like a king in a castle, and the children are like the poor peasants. The desk isolates them from the children. But I don't sit behind a big desk in front of the class. I walk up and down the rows of desks every day and I hug each of you every day.

"Have you ever been afraid to go up to the teacher's desk? Did you think someone would laugh at you if you made a mistake?"

Marva didn't wait for an answer. She knew each child was following her closely. "Tell me when I'm wrong. You must never be afraid to tell a teacher if she is wrong. I'm not God. My mouth is no prayerbook. We shall work together. How many of you have been afraid to ask other teachers questions?"

Hands immediately went up.

"Why were you afraid to ask, Michele?"

"I was afraid the teacher would holler."

"Why were you afraid, Jerome?"

"I was afraid I would get hit with a ruler," he said flatly, expecting the snickers that came from his classmates.

"When you were afraid of a teacher, Bernette, what were you afraid of?"

"I was afraid she would make everyone laugh at me. My other teacher used to act like she was perfect or something. She used to make me feel dumb."

"Sometimes I don't like other grown-ups very much because they think they know everything. I don't know everything," Marva said. "I can learn all the time."

There was excitement building and Marva worked the momentum, like an entertainer who felt the pulse of an audience. "Oh, I love to see your eyes dance," she said. "New children have such dull eyes, but yours are already coming alive." She continued more seriously. "How many times did you feel old enough or smart enough to do something and then some grown-up told you 'You don't know how to do that'? I never like to hear grown-ups say that to a child. I don't know what you know. I can't wriggle down inside your skin or get into your brains. I am just another human being who has lived longer than you. I'm not smarter. I'm not greater. I bleed when I'm hurt, and I'm tired when I don't get enough sleep. But I am always here, to what? To help you. Freddie, tell me what you learned from Mr. Emerson's essay."

Freddie looked attentively at Marva but didn't answer.

"You have a right to your opinion. You say what you think," Marva told him. "Don't care what anyone else thinks. What's inside of you is important."

"I learned about self-reliance," Freddie whispered.

"Speak in a big voice, peach. What does self-reliance mean? Believing in ———."

"Believing in yourself?"

"Of course it does, but say it with confidence so we all know you believe in what you're saying. Let us all know how bright you are," Marva said, nodding. "Chris, what did you learn from Mr. Emerson?"

"To trust my own thoughts."

"Very good, Chris. See how much you already know? Marcus, what did you learn?"

"If you don't think for yourself, other people will tell you what to think."

Marva's eyes glistened. She laughed, sweeping her arm dramatically to her brow as she held herself up against the window sill, feigning a swoon. "Oh, I just can't stand it. You're all so bright. You're all so sagacious. *Sagacious* means smart and wise. What does *sagacious* mean, children?"

"Smart and wise," they chanted.

"And who is sagacious?"

"We are," they shouted.

"You certainly are." Marva put a throaty emphasis on *certainly* as she walked the rows of desks ruffling hair, pinching a cheek, squeezing a shoulder.

It was a beginning. The skills would come later with the daily drills of sounds and words over and over until Marva was tired of the litany. First she had to convince the children she cared about them, convince them to trust her, and make them believe they could do anything they wanted to do.

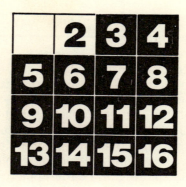

On the second day of school, Marva taught the English folk tale "The Little Red Hen and the Grain of Wheat." She had long believed that fairy tales and fables were effective in promoting emotional, intellectual, and social development. Most of the students were intrigued by the modulation of her voice and the changes in her face as she read aloud, shifting from one character to the next.

After the fourth round of quacking and squeaking and grunting "Not I," Marva noticed that Bernette Miller had taken off her locket and was looping the chain around her fingers, twisting it into a Cat's Cradle.

"You knew how to play with a chain when you came to school," Marva said. "Playing with a chain is a good way to get a job, isn't it? Put it away and listen to the story. I am not reading it just to entertain you. There is a lesson here. And we all better start paying attention to lessons like these, or this world we live in is surely headed for trouble."

Marva added, "I love you children all the time, even though I may correct you or disagree with you some of the time."

Marva finished the story. She closed the book, clasped it to her with one hand, and raised the other, index finger extended like a maestro's baton. Without losing the intensity delivered in the last line of the story, the discussion began.

"Do you think the little red hen was right in not sharing her bread with the duck, the mouse, and the pig?"

Heads nodded in agreement.

"Why was she right?" There were various demonstrations of squirming and fidgeting but no volunteers. After a while they would enjoy the heaping doses of teacher-student dialogue, but for now it was still a new and intimidating proposition. "Come on, come on," Marva said, "I am not going to leave you alone to become workbook idiots. You are not going to spend your time in here pasting and coloring and circling pictures. We're going to do some thinking in here. Now, why do you feel the hen was right?"

"She done it all. They was lazy," came a voice from the back.

"She *did* all what? She did all the work, didn't she? She had to sow and cut and thresh the wheat, and she had to carry it to the mill to be ground into flour, and she had to bake the loaf of bread. The other animals *were* lazy. They didn't want to help do any of the work. They only wanted to help eat the bread. What is the moral of this story? What lesson does it teach us? If we don't work, we don't eat. If we don't work, we don't ——?"

"Eat," came the unanimous reply. There was safety in numbers. Getting a child to take a chance and venture his or her own answer was another matter.

"Now, what would you say if I told you I think that hen was being selfish. She should have shared what she had with the other barnyard animals. What do you think about that?"

"No." They all shook their heads.

"Why not? Don't grown-ups always tell children that they should share their toys or their cookies or their candy? Freddie?"

"It ain't the same," he said.

"*Isn't,* sweetheart, it *isn't* the same. Children, listen to me for a moment. To succeed in this world, you must speak correctly. I don't want to hear any jive talk in here or any of this stuff about black English. You must not just think of yourselves as black children or ghetto children. You must become citizens of the world, like Socrates.

"Now, Freddie, why do you think there is a difference between the little red hen who did not share her bread and little children, who are always being told they should share their toys with others?"

"The hen had to work hard for the bread."

"That's wonderful, Freddie. You are absolutely right. The hen earned what she had. There is no comparison between the two situations. They are not analogous. You all know the word *same*. Let's try to learn some big words. *Analogous* means same or similar.

"Suppose I ask a child to help me do some chores, and when the chores are done I give the child some candy. Does that child have to share it with you because you say 'Give me some?' "

They shook their heads again.

"Of course not. You have a right to be rewarded for your work, for your efforts, and you also have a right to keep what you have earned. You don't have to give it away every time someone comes up to you with a hand out asking for something. A person who has his hand out today is going to have that hand out tomorrow. You are not going to solve his problem by giving him something free. He has to learn to solve his own problem. If you give another student in this class the answer to the homework, are you helping that student? No, you are cheating him out of learning how to find the answer himself.

"So the lesson of the story is one of the most important lessons you can learn. The person who does the work will be the one who has plenty of food, good clothes, and a fine house. The lazy person is always going to be standing there with his hand out. You have the choice, the right to choose which kind of person you want to be."

There it was. Marva had played her full hand. A teacher had to sell children on the idea of learning.

Oddly, Marva had not planned on becoming a teacher. She had not, in fact, given much thought to what she would do. As a child she had had the usual fleeting sort of girlish aspirations. One day she wanted to be a nurse, the next a secretary. With a child's fickleness she moved on to each new thing, her wishes shaped by a character in a book or a picture in a magazine. In that she was no different from other children. But what distinguished Marva's life from those around her—from the black children living in the wooden shanties with whom she went to school—was that she could entertain the vagaries of ambition beyond the age when others had to reconcile or surrender theirs. Necessity made no such demands on her. She grew up wealthy, pampered, and sheltered by small-town innocence and a doting protective father. She lived the freedom other people only dreamt.

★ ★ ★

I was born on August 31, 1936, in Monroeville, Alabama, about fifty miles north of Mobile. I grew up during the Depression, but while I can remember hearing the grown-ups talk about how times were hard and there was no money, none of that really affected my own life.

My father, Henry Knight, was one of the richest black men in Monroeville. We lived in a six-bedroom white clapboard house that had polished wood floors, store-bought furniture, and oriental rugs. Ours was one of the finest houses in the northern end of town, which was where all the blacks lived. People used to joke that our house was so fine you had to take your shoes off before going inside. My mother, Bessie, dressed me like a doll in ruffled, ribboned dresses and crisply pleated store-bought school dresses tied in back with an ironed sash. Because I looked so different from the other children, I had to put up with a lot of teasing. My schoolmates were mostly dressed in clothes their mothers made from the empty twenty-five-pound flour sacks they got from my father's grocery store.

There was determination in my family. We were always a family of doers and achievers. My mother's father, William Nettles, farmed all night and peddled meat door to door during the day, and he was the first black man in town to have a car, a crank-up Model T Ford. Everyone else rode around in mule-drawn wagons. My other grandfather, Henry Knight, Sr., owned a store and several houses and lived off his rental properties. He was a patient, thrifty man who always looked successful in a suit and tie, a gold watch chain, and well-shined shoes. I remember wondering why he always wore Sunday clothes.

I believed my father was the greatest man who ever lived. I would never meet anyone I admired more. He was the moving force in my life and we had a very special relationship. Of course, I loved my mother, but we weren't as close. My mother was very prim and proper, not as free with the hugs and kisses as my dad. She showed her love and concern for me by making sure I ate the right foods and wore the right clothes. I knew she loved me, but I missed hearing her tell me that she did. As an adult I have come to understand how important it is to be openly affectionate with a child, to be sensitive to a child's feelings. I couldn't talk things over with my mother, which was especially frustrating since I was the only child in the family until I was fourteen and always needed someone to talk to. My father was always there. I could say anything to him, even if it was silly, and he would patiently listen. I never felt I had to prove anything to him. I always knew where I stood. But I could never quite please my mother. I was not as ladylike or as well-behaved or as pretty as she wanted me to be. Parents don't realize how they can nag and pick away at a child until there is nothing left to pick. My dad was always supportive, constantly telling me how smart and pretty and special I was, even when I wasn't, so I felt good about myself. However, I did become an overachiever, and I attribute that to my mother saying I would never come to any good.

My father had only a fourth-grade education, but he was the smartest person I ever knew. He was a risk-taker with an instinct for business. Taking over his father's grocery store, he parlayed the assets into a thousand-acre cattle ranch and the town funeral parlor. He was a clever businessman, and even when he didn't have enough collateral, he somehow convinced people to go along with him on faith. When products were scarce on every grocery shelf during the Second World War, my father made a deal with an A & P down in Florida that could buy goods in larger quantities. He was the only merchant in Alabama—black or white—who had steaks, nylon stockings, chocolate, and chewing gum for his customers.

The black community in Monroeville existed apart from the white community. Blacks who were engaged in business were important and had a lot of influence. Since my father was the only black undertaker and the only black proprietor of a grocery store, he was a leader in the black community. The white businessmen respected him, and among blacks he was well respected though he was not particularly liked. Many people were envious of him. Sometimes people said they didn't want to shop in his store and make him any richer, yet those same people came to him when they didn't have money because they knew he would give them credit.

If someone got into trouble in town and was headed for jail, my father stood the bail bond. Not only blacks but many whites—some who owned the big stores downtown—would sneak into our house after dark to borrow money from my father. They didn't want anyone to know they were having anything to do with blacks, much less borrowing money. My father never chased me out of the room or said "This is none of your business," so I learned very early in life that white society was not the bright paradise other black children thought it was.

My father treated me the same as he would have treated a son, mainly, I guess, because I was always following him around. I didn't have a lot of playmates my own age because the other children had to work in the cotton fields after school and during vacations. I used to beg my parents to let me go to the cotton fields with the other children. Once my father let me go and I caught a bad cold. My father said he had to spend more money for the doctor than I earned in two days picking cotton, so he didn't let me go back. It was just as well because the foreman had told me not to come back to his field. He didn't like my bright ideas for making my cotton weigh more, such as putting stones in the bottom of the sack or pulling the whole cotton boll, branch and all. The other children took their job seriously because they had to.

Another reason I spent so much time with my father was that my mother constantly shooed me out of the house. She was a fastidious housekeeper, impatient with an awkward child who always seemed to spill and break things. "You can't keep a house in order," she would tell me. "I hope I live to see you grow up 'cause the buzzards are gonna fly over your house." My mother didn't try teaching me to cook and sew. She later said she realized it was a mistake because when I first married Clarence Collins, he had to take charge of the cooking and sewing. The funny thing is that I picked up my mother's housekeeping habits and I now find I have many of the same quirks.

From the time I was eight I woke at dawn and went with my father to open the grocery store. The people in town would buy bread before they set off to work in the fields. Late afternoons I helped him add the day's receipts. I counted the pennies and quarters and put them into rolls, and I helped haul out the empty cartons and sacks, which my father burned in a huge bonfire. Sometimes we'd roast potatoes or hotdogs over the flames. When my father slaughtered a cow in the large yard behind the house, I was out there with him, sprawled across the overhanging limb of the chinaberry tree.

Sometimes I sat there daydreaming about travel to exotic places. Or I imagined myself grown up and married with children of my own. For all my tomboyish ways—climbing the plum and chinaberry trees, throwing the hard green berries, playing in dark, cool caves—I was always sure I wanted to get married and have children with enchanting names like Chiquita Denise and Frenette René. Strangely, I ended up giving my children ordinary names—Eric, Patrick, and Cynthia.

At night when all the chores were finished, my father and I sat together and I would read aloud from *The Montgomery Advertiser* and *The Mobile Press* or *Aesop's Fables* or poetry books, until my mother waved me on to bed. And I would fall asleep thinking about the things I had read, pretending I was one of the characters in the stories.

On Saturdays I rode through town with my father, sitting next to him on the front seat of the new black Cadillac he bought each year for his funeral parlor. As we drove past the black men loitering in the town square, my father shook his head and said how undignified they looked. And when we saw black women carrying baskets of whitefolk's laundry on their heads, my father always said, "If I have to work all day and night, I'll never see my family doing other people's washing."

During the summer, from the time I was seven, I went on cattle-buying trips with my father. One day a week we would drive through the Alabama Black Belt, from county to county, through the rolling prairies filled with goldenrod and cane-brake. Sometimes we went to the livestock markets in Montgomery.

In the 1940s Alabama cattle auctions were segregated, like everything else. Although everyone bid on the same cattle, blacks and whites sat in separate buying sections. I grew up with that racism. You were always reminded you were black. You were always expected to know your place. Blacks had to use separate water fountains and rest rooms. We weren't served in restaurants. We had to go around to a back window if we wanted food. My father always said he would whip me within an inch of my life if he caught me getting food at a back counter. He also wouldn't let my mother or me go into a department store because white sales clerks gave black customers a hard time about trying on clothes. Black women had to put a piece of plastic on their heads before trying on hats. My father would not allow my mother or me to be humiliated. He did all the shopping and brought clothes home for us.

He was a proud man and a nonconformist. He did things that were unheard of in those days. He marched into the dentist's office through the front door, though blacks were supposed to come in through the back. And he got away with it. No one said anything. I guess his money made the difference.

At an auction he outbid the buyers from Swift and Cudahy, the big meat packing houses. Afterwards, at the cashier's window, the buyers were waiting for my father. They shouted at him, backed him into a corner, and warned him not to come back to the cattle sales again.

I watched, frightened. Though I lived with the day-to-day realities of segregation and was used to hearing the word *nigger,* I had never directly experienced the violence and horrors of racism. I only heard about it. The grown-ups still talked about the Scottsboro boys. Occasionally I would hear about lynchings, or about people who were beaten up by the sheriff and dragged off to jail in the middle of the night. None of that had ever touched my own family. The first time I saw race hatred up close was when those buyers surrounded my father.

He did not apologize. He was silent, his eyes firmly set, not a muscle in him moving. He stood there tall and distinguished-looking in his starched shirt and creased trousers with the Stacy Adams shoes he always wore. He looked the men straight in their eyes and said he'd be coming back to the next auction. If they were going to kill him, he'd take one of them with him when he died.

I thought the men would hurt him then. They hesitated, asking each other what to do about "that nigger." Just then two other white men came by and broke things up. The buyers shrugged and walked away. On the way home my father told me, "I made an honest bid. If you believe in what you do, then you don't ever have to fear anyone."

Every sale after that, my mother pleaded with my father not to go, but he said, "I'm not going to stay away. I can't die but once." That was the kind of determination I learned from him. He was a man of strong values and uncompromising beliefs. I always believed strength was passed on from one generation to the next. I guess I felt secure and confident, maybe because I was Henry Knight's daughter, but also because growing up in a small town like Monroeville, Alabama, I was sheltered and protected from a lot of things. We didn't have the kind of crime they had in the big cities. We didn't worry about rapes or muggings or drugs. If those things were happening somewhere else, we only learned about it from the newspapers, and by the time we got the news from Mobile it was already history.

I lived in a town where everyone seemed to know and trust everyone else. Just about everybody was cousin this or cousin that. Like the other children in Monroeville I was free to roam from yard to yard collecting pecans and figs in the autumn, free to roam through the pine forests searching for cones, free to play in the low red-clay hills, sliding down mud banks, wading in creeks, building dams along the shore. It was a happy, carefree childhood.

When I was twelve, my parents separated. My father remained in Monroeville, while my mother and I moved forty miles south to Atmore. I don't really know what went wrong between my parents. Maybe I have just blocked the whole thing out of my mind. But somehow I was able to cope with their separation. My father had already taught me to be a survivor. He taught me that whatever happens in life, a person has to go forward. Perhaps I forced myself to adjust so I could show my father I was just like him.

I remained close with my father, and he continued to be the strongest force in my life. I visited him summers, weekends, and sometimes during the week. He was never farther than a phone call or a short drive away. In the meantime Atmore became home. I spent my adolescence there with my mother, her new husband, and a new baby sister, Cynthia.

But the years in Monroeville were the great, great years of my childhood. Those were the years that made me what I am.

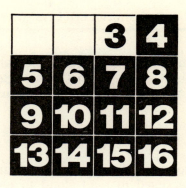

$\mathbf{M}$arva moved up and down the rows of desks. "I could just cry that you have no sounds," she said, "for sounds make up words, and words are thoughts. Ideas. And the thoughts and ideas in your heads make you what you are.

"Well, you will have the sounds. You will never have to guess at them. Sounds are like keys, opening the door to words. If you don't have the right key, you can't open the door to your house, can you? If you don't have the right sounds, you can't pronounce a word."

Marva twirled around to the board and wrote *The catamaran sailed around the ait*. "What does that mean?" she asked. The class looked lost. "All right, let's see what we have. Let's syllabicate *catamaran*. The first vowel sound is a short *a*, as in cat. The next two vowel sounds are *uh,* which we mark with this sign, called a German schwa. It looks like an upside-down *e,* but I don't ever want to hear any of you calling it an upside-down *e* sound. It is called a German schwa. All right, the last *a* also has a short vowel sound, *ran.* Catamaran. A catamaran is a kind of sailboat.

"The catamaran sailed around the ait. The vowels *a* and *i* make one sound, the sound of a long *a*. The rule is: when two vowels go walking, the first one does the talking; it says its name. Ait. An ait is a small island in the middle of a river or lake.

"So now you know that the sailboat sailed around the small island. See how you were lost in words? That will never happen to you again. You will learn all the rules so that words

will no longer be a mystery. You will be able to talk to anyone, no matter how smart, no matter how rich, no matter how
pretty. You are all clever bright children, and there's nothing
you can't do."

★   ★   ★

I learned to read before I was old enough to go to school.
My grandmother used to read aloud to me from her Bible,
sounding out words by syllables. She had learned to read and
spell by syllables when she was in school. By listening to her
and imitating what she said, I learned the letter sounds and
how to blend them together to read printed words. Once I discovered how to sound out words, I tried reading everything I
could get my hands on: labels on cans and boxes, the farmer's
almanac, newspapers, books of fairy tales and fables, and especially Grandma Annie Knight's huge black-leather Bible. My favorite was the story about Joseph and his brothers. I read it over
and over until my grandmother—"Mama-Dear," as I called
her—would shake her head and say, "Baby, you read so much
I'm afraid you're gonna lose your mind." The old people in the
South had a superstition that a child who was too studious—
prissy was their word for it—was headed for trouble.

My introduction to literature began with the Bible stories I
heard from my grandmother. Mama-Dear read her Bible every
day. Down South everyone was religious. I grew up during the
time of the big revival meetings when going to church was serious business. If you didn't go, you were an outcast. But Mama-
Dear was the most pious, prayerful person I ever saw. Every
morning and every night she got down on her knees beside her
high, four-poster bed and said her prayers. When Mama-Dear
wasn't praying or reading her Bible, she was walking around
the house singing "Precious Lord Take My Hand" and "What A
Friend We Have In Jesus." She was forever reciting proverbs.
Time and tide wait for no man. Good that comes too late is good
for nothing. "Baby," she would say to me, "a good name will go
farther than you will." I got so tired of hearing those proverbs
when I was a child. Now I use them all the time. Sometimes
they are the best way of saying what needs to be said. I teach

them to my students. I have a collection of proverbs for class discussions and writing assignments.

I spent a lot of time with Mama-Dear and Grandpa Daddy Henry. Some nights the three of us sat in front of the fireplace as the flames cast shadows that danced on the walls. The scent of burning pinecones floated lightly through the living room while Mama-Dear recited poems like "Hiawatha" or "Paul Revere's Ride." She had memorized them as a schoolgirl and was still proud of knowing them by heart.

I was smitten with poetry and literature. But there were no libraries for black children in Alabama. The only books I could get were the ones I bought, borrowed, or received as gifts. When my parents took me visiting to someone's house, I would disappear, rummaging through cabinets and shelves in search of books. A book was a treasure, and I lost myself in every one I found—a basic reader brought home from school, a *True Confessions* magazine, or even a dictionary. I read Nancy Drew mysteries, gothic romances, Richard Wright's *Black Boy* and *Native Son,* and Booker T. Washington, who I thought was the second greatest man next to my father. And I loved Erskine Caldwell's *God's Little Acre,* though my mother didn't approve of my reading such books. I bought half a dozen copies of *God's Little Acre* with the money I earned helping in the store. I hid them in different places as insurance. Every time my mother found the book and threw it away, I would take out another copy and continue reading.

It was Aunt Ruby Jones, my mother's sister, who introduced me to William Shakespeare. Aunt Ruby had gone back to high school after marrying and having two children. When I was at her house playing with my cousins, I would see her studying and reading from her schoolbooks. One night I overheard Aunt Ruby talking to Uncle Robert about someone named Lady Macbeth. Then she opened an old gray book and began reading:

She should have died hereafter;
There would have been a time for such a word.
Tomorrow, and tomorrow, and tomorrow,
Creeps in this petty pace from day to day. . . .

I was only nine at the time, but I was enthralled by the lines. For days after that I walked around with "Tomorrow, and tomorrow, and tomorrow" spinning in my head. The next visit to Aunt Ruby's, I asked if I could borrow that gray book. I read through *Macbeth,* and while I was not able to grasp its full meaning, I was fascinated by the action and the characters of the play. I thought it was such fun to say "Double, double, toil and trouble." My interest in Shakespeare wasn't encouraged until I reached high school. We never read Shakespeare in the lower grades. Most students still don't.

Along with the other black children in Monroeville I spent the primary grades at Bethlehem Academy, a clapboard building with unpainted walls and a woodburning stove in each room. There were two grades to a classroom. Books were in short supply, and most of our teachers had only a tenth grade education themselves.

Out of all the teachers at Bethlehem two left a strong impression. I got off to a bad start with my first teacher, a heavy-set woman who often wore a blue dress patterned with red, green, and yellow alphabet letters. In the first week of school when we were learning arabic numerals, I kept making the numeral 2 backwards. Each time I drew it wrong the teacher rapped my fingers with a ruler. I never understood why she kept hitting me. If I had known how to do it right, I would have. She acted as though I had made the mistake deliberately.

I never forgot that experience. It has influenced the teaching methods I use with my students. To me an error means a child needs help, not a reprimand or ridicule for doing it wrong. No child should ever be told "That's stupid" or "You can't do it" or "You don't know what you're doing." Adults should take a positive approach with children. The most important thing we can do as parents and teachers is build a child's self-confidence. Any child can learn if he or she has not already been taught too thoroughly that learning is impossible. Children need reassurance and encouragement. They have to be told that it is all right to make mistakes because mistakes are part of learning. I tell my students: "If you knew everything there is to know, then you wouldn't have to be in school."

Praise is essential in developing the right attitude toward learning and toward school. We all know this in theory. In practice we often forget the importance of praise in dealing with children. We forget how sensitive children can be and how fragile their egos are. It is painful for a child to be told "This is wrong." Rather than punishing, teachers and parents should encourage continued effort: "This is good. It's a wonderful try, but it is not quite right. Let's try correcting this together."

I praise every child's effort. I put every child's paper up on the wall or the bulletin board, not just the perfect ones. And I never put a failing grade or red marks all over a paper. That is a sure way to turn a child off of learning. Put yourself in the place of a child who is handed back a paper with a low grade while the other children have received high marks. Imagine how that child feels when everyone asks each other, as children always do, "What did you get on your paper?" That child wants to crumple the paper and throw it away. That child wants to get away from school. I write "very good" or "wonderful work" or make a smiling face on every paper. Then I handle errors by working individually with each child. We correct errors on a separate piece of paper, on an individual work sheet, or at the blackboard. I learned the value of blackboard practice from my fourth grade teacher, Mrs. McGants.

Mrs. McGants was a patient, good teacher. She had her students work at the blackboard so she could correct mistakes as quickly as they were made. Children need immediate feedback, especially in math and language where they need to master one skill before they can go on to the next. I do not wait days before returning papers. Errors will mean nothing to a child several days later when the class has moved on to something new. Delay in correcting errors only makes the child fall behind.

I find that children often understand a concept better when you take them to the blackboard rather than trying to show them at their seat. This practice helps the rest of the class at the same time, especially the shy child who will never come out and say that he or she does not understand. I draw a large part of my curriculum from these errors, not from the teaching guides. One child's errors become a lesson for the whole class. If one child is having trouble with something, it is likely that others are also, and all can benefit from a review.

My teaching methods evolved, in part, from my own experiences as a student. My first grade teacher was a model for what not to do. My fourth grade teacher showed me what to do. Miss Rolle, my tenth grade teacher at Escambia County Training School, was my favorite. She was probably not as beautiful as I then thought, but the way she walked and moved made her seem very sophisticated. I wanted to be just like her. Though Miss Rolle was from Alabama, she did not have a thick southern accent. I was so impressed by how articulate she was and how she enunciated her words that I practiced imitating her. I studied vocabulary from the dictionary all the time. Townsfolk used to tell my father, "The way that girl puts words together is like something out of the pages of a book." The white salesmen who came from Mobile to take purchasing orders for cans of beans and boxes of chickens would come into my dad's grocery store and ask, "Henry, where's your girl? I sure do like listening to the way she talks."

I suppose it is because of Miss Rolle that I stress proper speech and pronunciation with my own students. I try to get them in the habit of using correct grammar when they speak, and I have them read aloud every day so I can check pronunciation as well as comprehension. Having children read silently in class only allows their mistakes to go unnoticed. I have heard children read *capa-city* for *capacity, denny* instead of *deny,* or *doze* instead of *does,* treating the final *s* as though it pluralized the word *doe.* Children frequently reverse letters when they read. For example, they confuse *sacred* and *scared, diary* and *dairy, angel* and *angle.* If children read silently, they continue to make those mistakes.

Another reason for reading aloud is to build vocabulary. A child reading silently skips over big words he doesn't know. When I am there listening to a child read, I can interrupt to ask the meaning. The whole class benefits as we can look up the definition, the base word within the larger word, and the part of speech. I also have my students read aloud for tone, inflection, and punctuation. Reading aloud helps a child realize the difference between a comma, a period, a question mark, and an exclamation point. Children who are just learning to read tend to read individual words, not groups of words or phrases. That limits comprehension. I encourage my students to become idea readers, not word readers. By reading aloud children learn to understand words within the context of a sentence, and they see how words connect with each other to express an idea. This practice promotes not only good reading but good writing.

My students read everything orally—literature, science, social studies, and history. I even have them read their compositions aloud every day. It makes children more conscious of sentence structure, allows them to proofread for punctuation errors and word omissions, and helps them develop a certain presence and authority in front of an audience. Miss Rolle used to make us stand and read our papers to the class.

Except for Miss Rolle's and Mrs. McGants' classes, my schooling was typical of the separate and unequal education black children received in Alabama during the forties and fifties. Yet I found my own way around the inequities.

At Escambia County Training School—all high schools for black students were called training schools—girls did not graduate without taking home economics. I suppose it was the whitefolks way of saying all black women would never be anything more than homemakers or domestics. I refused to take it and signed up for a typing course instead. Shortly before graduation the principal called me into his office to say that unless I took the required course, I would not receive my diploma. I told him that I already knew enough about housekeeping. I didn't know what I was going to do when I went out into the world, but typing was going to be of more help than home economics. I never knew what made the principal change his mind. I was the only female student who ever graduated from Escambia County Training School without taking home economics.

From the day I became aware of what college was, I made up my mind I was going. My parents never stressed college degrees, not having had a high school education themselves, but they stressed learning.

I chose Clark College in Atlanta, an exclusive, all-black liberal arts school for girls. My father had no objection. He was proud of my being the first one in the family to go to college, and he believed it was his duty as a parent to make sure his child had the best. From the way the neighbors carried on, my father might have committed a cardinal sin. "What are you sending that girl to college for?" they asked him. "You'll never get your money back, 'cause that girl's never gonna do a thing for you."

Everything at Clark was very southern and very proper with a certain finishing-school mentality. How a student dressed was just as important as what she learned. My house-mother made certain I wore hats and white gloves, and she once sent me back to my room to change because I had made the "mistake" of wearing suede shoes with a leather jacket. To this day I am very conscious of clothes and appearance.

I don't believe I learned very much at college. It was my own fault. I went to college not really knowing what I wanted to do. At the last minute I decided to major in secretarial science. It seemed the practical thing to do. With a business sense picked up from my father and a knowledge of typing and book-keeping, I expected to get an office job upon graduating from Clark. I also took some education courses because they interested me, though I had no intention of becoming a teacher.

In June of 1957 I returned to Alabama with my degree and discovered that the only office positions available to blacks were civil service jobs. None of the private companies wanted to hire a black secretary. I filled out a civil service application. I turned down the one available job because it was in Montgomery and I wasn't ready to leave home again. Still, finding some kind of job was a matter of pride. After the way people had chided my father about paying my way to Clark, I was not about to let that degree collect dust.

I finally found a job teaching typing, shorthand, bookkeeping, and business law at Monroe County Training School, and considered myself fortunate. In those days teaching jobs were hard to come by in Alabama. Teachers seemed to live and die in their jobs. More than just a proper occupation for a woman, teaching was one of the only occupations at the time for an educated black woman. For all my attempts to be different, I finally had to settle for that. I had to accommodate myself to the realities of life in Alabama.

Some things are meant to be.

From the very first day, I felt comfortable teaching. With some experience conducting Sunday school classes at church, I was used to standing up and speaking before a group. I liked being around people, working with them and helping them understand things. I had always been fascinated with learning, with the *process* of discovering something new, and it was exciting to share in the discoveries made by my tenth, eleventh, and twelfth grade students at Monroe County Training School.

I didn't know anything about educational theory, and I have often thought that worked in my favor. Without preconceived ideas and not bound by rules, I was forced to deal with my students as individuals, to talk to them, listen to them, find out their needs. I wasn't trying to see how they fit into any learning patterns or educational models. I followed my instincts and taught according to what felt right. I brought my own experiences to the classroom, trying to figure out how I had learned as a student. I remembered what had bored me and what had interested me, which teachers I had liked and which ones I had disliked, and applied it all to my teaching.

Not having any formal theory or textbook methodology to follow made me receptive to new ideas. I was constantly learning along with my students, always looking for new ways to make a lesson more exciting. My colleagues were very helpful, offering suggestions and sharing their methods. They all seemed to care so much about their students. I may have been naive or too idealistic, but at the time the whole teaching profession seemed inspiring.

The principal at Monroe really taught me how to teach. He was especially hard on new teachers. He sat in my classroom every day for two months observing, shaking or nodding his head and taking notes. After class he would sit me down and lecture me as though I were one of the children. He told me to get to the point of a lesson more directly. He would say, "Well, you lost the boy in the third seat of the last row." He trained me to watch the students' faces, to see by their eyes if they understood. I learned that a good teacher knows the students, not just the subject.

After two years at Monroe I liked teaching but wasn't ready to commit myself. I was immature. Staying with my father on weekends and with my grandparents during the week, I was still too unsettled to dedicate myself fully to anything.

As a teacher I now try to teach children how to deal with life. More than reading, writing, and arithmetic, I want to give them a philosophy for living. But at twenty-one I was too sheltered and too protected to know how to deal with life myself. Though I earned a salary, my father continued to give me spending money—which I continued to accept—and he bought me expensive clothes, did everything for me. He even warmed up my car in the morning and filled the gas tank at the pump behind his store.

At some point my dependence on my father began to bother me. I felt constricted by small-town life. After four years in Atlanta I found Monroeville too confining. It was time to grow up and be on my own.

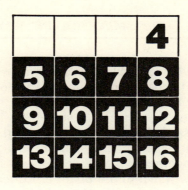

In June 1959, at the close of the school year, I left for Chicago to visit my grandmother's cousin, Annie Townsend, for a two month vacation. I did not plan on getting a job, finding a husband, starting a family, and settling down in Garfield Park.

After a few days in Chicago, I got tired of being a tourist. On an impulse I read through the want ads in the newspaper and applied for a job as a medical secretary at Mount Sinai Hospital. I was hired. I didn't know anything about medicine, but I began teaching myself Latin to understand the medical terms. The job was so exciting I decided to stay in Chicago. I took an apartment in a large, U-shaped courtyard building on Hamlin Avenue, overlooking Garfield Park. It was a small apartment with a Murphy bed and a sunny kitchen. It seemed elegant to me, but the best part was that this place was truly my own. My first apartment was close to the hospital, close to Cousin Annie, and close to Clarence Collins.

Clarence lived with his parents next door to Cousin Annie. I was first attracted to him by his devotion to his family. He was one of eleven children, eight boys and three girls, a close-knit family. When I met Clarence, he was working as a draftsman for the Sunbeam Appliance Company, a job he would keep for close to twenty years. While he did not have a college education and was not as well-read as I, he was just as determined. He was also more level-headed. And he was kind and gentle. All the neighborhood children gathered around him, and several went with us to Riverview Amusement Park on our first date. I knew that any man who could be so patient with someone else's children was bound to be a good father and a good husband. Within a year we were married.

I continued to work as a secretary, but soon I missed teaching. I missed the classroom. I missed the excitement of helping students discover the solution to a problem, of seeing the pieces fit together.

I went downtown to the Board of Education and filled out a teaching application. All I had to do was send for my college transcripts and my Alabama teaching credentials. Since I had not taken methodology courses, I was not eligible to take the certification exam. It didn't matter because teachers in the Chicago school system didn't have to be certified. There was a teacher shortage at that time, so as long as you had a college degree, you could teach. If you weren't certified, you worked as a full-time-basis substitute which meant you were assigned to a school but had no seniority and were not guaranteed permanent placement. Years later the Chicago Teachers' Union pressured the school board to grant automatic certification to those who had been in the school system for three years.

I received a letter telling me to report to Calhoun South Elementary School on Jackson Boulevard, where I was given a second grade class. I didn't have any experience teaching such young children, but I assumed the principles were the same as in teaching older students. I had to motivate the children, create a desire for learning. I had to make them understand why it was important to learn. And I had to make them feel worthwhile and confident.

I drew on my own childhood memories, recalling the things that had made me feel happy, sad, excited, hurt, or afraid, the things that made me want to laugh or cry. And I tried to be sensitive to those feelings in my students. I found that hugging and touching and saying "I love you" immediately made them feel secure and comfortable in the classroom, establishing a bond between us and also among the children.

Children are quick to mimic adults. If a teacher ridicules or picks on a child, chances are the children will pick on each other. And of course the reverse is true.

At first I followed the Board of Education curriculum.

Soon I thought the work was way below the children's ability. They could learn much more. So I expanded the curriculum. If a lesson called for the children to locate all the triangles on a page and color them in with crayons, I would tell the children to put a green capital *D* above the second triangle and to color the fourth triangle red and the seventh one blue. Then I would have them write the words *red* and *blue* above those triangles. The children were learning not only to recognize shapes but to follow directions, to think, to count, to distinguish colors, and to write. The group activity also kept them more attentive than they would have been if I had left them alone to work quietly by themselves.

After a few weeks my students were bored with the required second grade reader. I couldn't blame them. There were no real stories in those books, nothing to occupy a child's mind or stimulate thought. The pages were filled with pictures of boys and girls playing, and below the pictures were sentences like "Run, Pepper, run" and "See Pepper run." There was no reason for the children to bother reading the words. All they had to do was look at the pictures.

Never having taught second grade before, I didn't know very much about how to teach reading. I didn't know about the debate between advocates of the phonics method, in which children learn to decode vowel and consonant sounds in a word, and the look-say method, in which they identify words with pictures and build a "sight vocabulary" by reading sentences that use the same words over and over. It seemed to me that the natural thing to do was teach the children to sound out words. That was how I had learned to read, so that was what I taught my second graders. I disregarded the teaching guide, which followed the look-say method.

It seemed to me that the children would be more anxious to read if they were interested in what they were reading. I didn't have any expert studies to go by. It was just common sense. Why would a child want to put out the effort just to read "See Pepper run"? I stopped using the required reader and brought in books from the library and from bookstores. My children read from *Aesop's Fables*, *Grimm's Fairy Tales*, Hans Christian Andersen, La Fontaine's *Fables*, and Leo Tolstoy's

Fables and Fairytales. I chose those stories because they teach values and morals and lessons about life. Fairy tales and fables allow children to put things in perspective—greed, trouble, happiness, meanness, and joy. After reading those stories you have something to think over and discuss. More than anything, I wanted my students to be excited about reading. I wanted them to understand that reading is not an exercise in memorizing words but a way to bring ideas to light.

I had my students draw their own pictures to illustrate the stories. Sometimes we acted out the fables, or we made up our own ending. We even composed our own fables. I would start and then each child would add a sentence. I felt my way along, trying out new ideas and experimenting with different methods and lessons. And I loved it. I loved watching my students' faces when they discovered the solution to a math problem or recognized on their own the parallel between two stories. There was an effervescent quality to their excitement.

I taught at Calhoun for a year, leaving when I became pregnant with our first son, Eric. I knew I would go back to teaching.

While I was at Calhoun, Clarence and I bought a gray-stone two-flat at 3819 West Adams Street. It was down the street from Delano Elementary School and just around the corner from my apartment on Hamlin Avenue.

Garfield Park was a nice, respectable neighborhood of mostly Jewish, Italian, and Irish families. We were one of the first black families to move in. Looking back, I suppose I should have realized how fast the neighborhood was changing. The bank on Madison Street closed down. Steel grates appeared across some of the storefronts at night, and there were "For Rent" signs in many of the shop windows. At the time I didn't know anything about changing neighborhoods. I had grown up in a town where people mostly stayed in the same place all their lives.

In 1962, a year after we moved into the house, Eric was born. Three years later we had a second son, Patrick, and in 1968 our daughter Cynthia came along. By that time Garfield Park had turned into another Chicago ghetto. Prostitutes and street gangs staked out the area. There were razed lots, boarded-up windows, and vacant buildings. The worst destruction took place in April 1968 during the riots that followed Martin Luther King's death. People went crazy. They ran through the streets breaking windows, looting, and setting buildings on fire. It was terrifying. We locked ourselves in the house for days. When the rioting was over, there wasn't much of anything left in Garfield Park. All the stores were closed down. Clarence had to walk nearly a mile to get a gallon of milk.

With small children and a growing family Clarence and I simply could not afford to move away from Garfield Park. A lot of our friends began to move away. Maybe it was my rebel streak, but the more I saw people run off and forget about their old friends and neighbors, the more I resolved to stay, even later when we had enough money. I had put down roots in Garfield Park, and I wasn't going to give up that easily.

In the years since then I have been fighting an attitude, the apathy. No one seems to have any pride anymore. I don't understand what happens to people in urban areas like Garfield Park. In Alabama the poor blacks used to wash down every inch of their unpainted wooden shacks with Octagon Laundry Soap. They swept under their porches, even if they didn't have store-bought brooms. They cut down branches from trees and tied them together with rags or string to make brushbrooms. People in Alabama would shake their heads in disgust if they saw a dirty mop hanging out to dry on someone's porch railing, or greying sheets dangling from a clothesline. My mother used to say you can just look outside a person's house and tell what he is.

The one thing everyone in Alabama had was pride. That pride was a consistent part of a southern upbringing. The poor children came to school with neatly sewn patches on their clothes. Their clothes may have been old, but they were clean. If your children were dirty, you didn't belong anywhere in the social order of the town. If you had a dirty water bucket, you were a disgrace, and if you drank from the dipper instead of a glass, you were considered a heathen. If you didn't mow your lawn or clip your hedges, you were ostracized. When the neighbor next door saw you mowing your lawn, he would mow his. And on Sundays, after the church services, each family set out a picnic dinner and everyone saw who could have the best food. If your dinner didn't spread out well, you were disgraced.

Neighborhoods like Garfield Park are made up mostly of people from the South, like myself. I don't understand why my southern pride stuck while theirs didn't. Part of the problem is that people are looking for easy solutions. They have been led to believe that someone else is going to do things for them. Too many black people have fallen into the pattern of listening to the self-proclaimed leaders who find it in their own best interest to make people feel there are "free rides" in this world. If so many foreign immigrants could come to America and make it, so can people like those in Garfield Park. But unfortunately, so many blacks are waiting for white America to be their Messiah.

I don't think politicians are going to change things. And I don't think marching or violent protest accomplishes anything in the long run. I tell my students all the time: "If you raise your fist and yell at someone today, he may give you something because he feels sorry for you or is frightened of you, but what are you going to do tomorrow and the next day and ten years from now?"

I am convinced that the real solution is education. We have to teach children self-reliance and self-respect. We have to teach them the importance of learning, of developing skills, of doing for themselves. I am always reminding my students that if you give a man a fish, he will eat for only a day. If you teach him how to fish, he will feed himself for a lifetime. That's why I stay in Garfield Park. The legacy I want to leave behind is a generation of children who realize that you can't get something for nothing, who are proud and resourceful enough to take care of their own. In this messed up world, the only children who are going to make something of themselves are those who come from strong parents or those who have had a strong teacher. One or the other. Or both.

I went back to teaching in February 1963, when my son Eric was six months old. I didn't like leaving him with a baby-sitter all day. But I had to work. Without my salary, we had a hard time meeting the mortgage. Fortunately, I was assigned to Delano Elementary School, just down the street from my house. It enabled me to come home at lunchtime or in case of an emergency. I had a sixth grade class the first year, a second grade class the next, and later I settled in as a second grade teacher. Except for two brief maternity leaves when Patrick and Cindy were born, I stayed at Delano for several years. The job at Delano offered the best of all worlds. Eventually it turned into a nightmare, not because of the students but because of the other teachers.

When I started at Delano I was impressed by the principal, an older German man, a classical scholar who read the *Iliad* to students during lunchtime. He held faculty workshops where he recited Donne, Yeats, and Byron, stopping in the middle of a poem to ask his teachers to supply the next line. When they couldn't, he waved his hand with disgust and said, "Some of you aren't worth a Sam Hill." I learned a lot from him, and I began teaching poetry and classical literature to my students. Above all the principal taught me that a good teacher is one who continues to learn along with the students.

I got along well with most of the teachers at first, particularly the older ones whom I learned from. I used to sit at lunch with a woman from Arkansas and discuss ways to get children to like reading. Her advice to me was to involve the children in the story and never to let them stare passively at words on a page. She told me to have them take the place of one of the characters in a story and then ask them questions about what they thought and felt. She also suggested that I have the children write a letter to one of the characters. To this day I find these are excellent ways to get a child excited about a story.

Over the years the faculty at Delano changed. Some teachers retired, some transferred to other schools voluntarily, some were shifted around the city by the administrative bureaucracy. Their replacements were a different breed of teachers, people who really didn't care or know what they were doing. Several were young men who became teachers to avoid the draft and Vietnam. Many others were quick to admit they didn't really want to teach but couldn't think of anything else to do. All they wanted was to get by.

A new principal came to Delano. He didn't pay much attention to what went on in the classrooms, as long as things were quiet and orderly. Practically the only time he came into my room was to tell me the shades on the windows weren't even. He said it made a poor impression on people passing by the school. One time he interrupted a child reciting Robert Frost's "Fire and Ice" to tell me I had better get my class outside for the fire drill. It was the sixth fire drill in two days. On his way out the principal walked over to one of my girls and told her she could not sit in class with her shoes off. What do a child's shoes have to do with her brains? That child had created havoc in two other classrooms. Finally she had settled down to learn.

The longer I taught in the public school system, the more I came to think that schools were concerned with everything but teaching. Teaching was the last priority, something you were supposed to do after you collected the milk money, put up the bulletin boards—which must never display spring flowers in January or a leftover winter scene in March—straightened the shades and desks, filled out forms in triplicate, punched all the computer cards with pre-test and post-test scores, and charted all the reading levels so they could be shipped downtown to the Board of Education. Everybody was test crazy. It seemed as though the administrators only wanted to probe IQs and rank test scores. It didn't matter whether the children learned anything at all. Nothing was important except their performance on standardized tests. Teachers were supposed to teach skills specifically for those tests. The strange thing was that if a child didn't learn, no one held the teachers responsible. If an eighth-grader didn't know how to read, no one went back to that child's first, second, or third grade teacher to ask what went wrong. No, it was always the child's fault.

I couldn't stand all that. I couldn't stand the pretense that there was teaching going on, that children were getting an education. The children were merely being pushed ahead, unprepared, to make room for more failures. They couldn't read and they couldn't write, but they were passed along to the next grade anyway.

I became convinced that the many poor readers in the Chicago school system were casualties of the look-say method of teaching reading. The method was first used in the 1830s to teach deaf-mutes to read. Then some educators, including

Horace Mann, had the bright idea of introducing the look-say or whole-word or sight-reading method into the public schools, reasoning that if deaf children could learn to read by this, then surely it would make reading simpler for all children. By the 1920s sight-reading was adopted by many school systems and accepted nationwide. It has been popular ever since. Rudolf Flesch's 1955 classic *Why Johnny Can't Read* argued that the look-say method with its Dick-and-Jane books was producing generations of children who couldn't read, couldn't spell, and had no sense of grammar. His argument didn't dissuade many schools. Neither did the growing number of illiterate children.

I could never understand how anyone expected a child to learn to read by recognizing "sight" words. Take away the pictures that illustrate the words and the familiar word sequence, and reading turns into guesswork. With the look-say method a child is taught to memorize a controlled vocabulary. He or she isn't taught the rules for vowel and consonant sounds, so the child can't figure out new words independently. For example, learning the word *look* without learning the double *o* sound, the child is helpless when confronted with *took* or *book*. He or she has to wait to memorize those words later on.

Rather than have a child rely on a memorized vocabulary, I always thought it better to teach a child how to attack a word phonetically. Over the years I saw that children became better readers and spellers when they learned by phonics. But they had to learn intensive phonics—all the regular and irregular sound patterns in the English language—not some bootleg version for sounding out the first and last letters of a word. I saw that if a child knew the rules for vowel and consonant sounds and for syllabification, and the exceptions to the rules, then that child could pick up anything and read it.

So I didn't follow the look-say teaching guide. In fact I went beyond the required curriculum in many of my lessons. For example, I taught my students how to add and subtract, but I also taught them that *arithmetic* is a Greek word meaning to count and that numbers were called *digits* after the Latin word *digitus,* meaning finger, because people used to count on their fingers. I taught them about Pythagoras, who believed that mathematics made a pupil perfect and ready to meet the gods. I told them what Socrates said about straight thinking leading to straight living. I read aloud to them from *The Great Quotations* and *101 Famous Poems*. We talked about Emerson's "Self Reliance," Bacon's "On Education," and parts of Thoreau's *Walden*: "If a man does not keep pace with his companions, perhaps it is because he hears a different drummer."

But I did not teach my students these things to be pedantic. I hoped that what they read and learned would affect their whole lives, teaching them how to live. I tried to introduce my children to a world that extends beyond the ghetto of Garfield Park. Until you reveal a larger world to children, they don't realize there is anything to reach for.

My approach was to teach the total child. A teacher should help develop a child's character, help build a positive self-image. I was concerned about everything—attitudes, manners, grooming. I made sure my students' faces were clean, their hair combed, their shirts tucked in, and their socks pulled up. I told them to walk with their heads up and their shoulders back, to have dignity and confidence. And I cautioned them that what a person thinks of himself will determine his destiny. Those were the things my parents told me, and I still believe them.

I was brought up to follow my own convictions and not to change myself in order to please others. But because I did things my own way, the other teachers at Delano resented me. I faced that same kind of problem my whole life. My strong will always seemed to distance me from people, even when I was a child.

At Delano the hardest battle I ever fought was to be me. Somehow, everything I did annoyed my colleagues, from the way I dressed to the way I taught. As more criticism began to build up, they even questioned my intentions. I drew away from them, becoming completely absorbed in my teaching. However, my retreat only made things worse. When I kept to myself, the other teachers were offended by my standoffishness.

Each year, I became more discontented at Delano. Apart from the politics—the bickering and pettiness among teachers over who got which students, who got supplies, who was going to work recess or lunch duty—I was frustrated like so many teachers in so many schools by the bureaucracy, the record-keeping, the "Up the Down Staircase" syndrome. Where do they find all the minutia that keeps you from teaching?

The curriculum changed with the passing of each fad. And the textbooks changed. Somebody, somewhere decided to water them down. Textbooks were being written two years below the grade level they were intended for. Why? Because students couldn't read. Instead of challenging students with materials that might improve their skills, the new books made it easier, using more pictures and fewer words. And simpler words. One textbook that used *enormous* and *apprehension* in a story came out in a revised edition that replaced those words with *big* and *fear*. The standards fell lower and lower.

I never thought I'd look back to the 1860s with awe. I came across a *Rhetorical Reader* published in 1862 that included works by John Ruskin, Oliver Goldsmith, John Milton, and Leo Tolstoy. It was intended for children in elementary school. Today these classical works are considered too difficult. Even the vocabulary in first grade readers has been reduced. A first grade reader from 1920 introduced 345 new words. Today one of the most popular first grade readers introduces only fifty-three words for the entire year. Yet a child starting school at age five already has a vocabulary of about 4,000 words.

There is a lot of money to be made from miseducation, from the easy to read easy to learn textbooks, workbooks, teacher manuals, educational games and visual aids. The textbook business is more than a billion-dollar-a-year industry and some of its biggest profits come from "audio-visual aids"—flash cards, tape cassettes, and filmstrips. No wonder the education industry encourages schools to focus on surface education.

Quite a few of my Delano colleagues felt the same way I did about the school system, but most were apathetic and afraid to make waves. That included the principal. Principals by nature are forever looking for harmony. Often they only want to serve their stint in a school as peacefully and with as few complications as possible, aspiring to a job in the district office. They handle their faculty with kid gloves, afraid of giving unfavorable year-end evaluations and afraid of adding an extra student to a classroom. The last thing in the world any principal wants is trouble with the teachers' union.

All of this added to my frustrations. After a certain point I became more outspoken, which seemed to isolate me even further from the other teachers. If I complained about the textbooks and curriculum, they were annoyed. If I complained about the excessive number of fire drills or the dirty lunchroom conditions or the lack of toilet paper in the student washrooms, they chided me for wasting time at the faculty meetings. They told me to close the door to my classroom and forget about it. But I couldn't.

Eventually, the tension deepened. Whenever I walked into the teachers' lounge, there was an uncomfortable and mean silence. The other teachers, sitting on the sofas drinking coffee and swapping stories about their students, cut their conversations short the moment I entered. Though I have always felt pretty confident of myself, I wasn't immune to their coldness. I hated feeling like an outcast. It brought back the same pain I experienced as a child when my classmates poked fun at my fancy clothes or ridiculed me for being tall and awkward. I didn't know how to make peace with my colleagues. I just wasn't good at small talk. It bothered me to sit around talking about some boy who was repeating sixth grade for the third time or about a new transfer student who had been to seven other schools without learning how to write his name. Those things weren't funny to me. I used to hear some teachers say "I hate these damn kids." That comment would destroy me. As a mother I would hate to think I had gone through the trouble of getting my children dressed and fed and sent them off to a school where the teacher's attitude was "I hate these damn kids." No matter what it cost me personally, I couldn't be like that.

It was a depressing situation. Several times I thought about looking for a job in another school, but I didn't want to teach in another part of the city. I wanted to work with the children in my neighborhood. By September 1974 I had resolved to survive by concentrating on my students. The new semester got off to a great start, and by the sixth week of school my students were eager for learning. I felt it was going to be a terrific year.

Marva stood in the doorway welcoming the children as they squeezed past her into the classroom. "I love your sweater," she told one of the boys. "Hello, sweetheart," she said, her large hand cupping a girl's chin, "who fixed your hair in such beautiful braids?" She told a boy who tried to push ahead of the others, "What good-looking shoes you have. Tie the laces, darling, so you don't fall and hurt yourself." Marva made sure she found something to praise in each of the children every day, even if it was nothing more than the color of their socks, a new pencil, a bright smile, or a good job of washing the back of their neck.

The children scrambled to their seats and began rummaging through their desks, putting lunches inside and taking out papers and pencils. Four boys huddled in the back of the room making plans for after school. A girl in the front row was combing her hair. Passing the child on her way to the blackboard, Marva took the comb from the girl's hand.

"Darling, put the comb away. Do you see me combing my hair in class? Do what you see me do. We don't comb our hair in public. How would it look if I came to class with a wet washrag and starting wiping my face? Washing our faces and combing our hair and brushing our teeth are all the things we do in private."

Marva looked around the room, saw that everyone was present, and began. "Who can tell me what homonyms are?"

"The second bell didn't ring yet," complained Jerome.

Jerome was like a nagging conscience, forever calling Marva's attention to points of order—pinpointing where they had left off in a story the previous day, reminding Marva to collect homework, notifying her that it was five minutes before lunchtime and the class should start putting away their books.

"Do you need a bell to tell your brain to start working?" Marva asked. "There was a Russian scientist named Ivan Pavlov, P-a-v-l-o-v." Marva wrote the name on the board, pointing out the short vowel sounds. "Pavlov tried the experiment of ringing a bell every time food was given to a dog. Pretty soon the dog learned that a ringing bell meant he would get some food. The dog associated the bell with food. What did the dog do? The dog *associated* the bell with food."

She printed the word *associated* on the board with its phonetic spelling. "The base word is *associate*. German schwa sound on the *a*, then macron *o*, macron *e*, macron *a*. *Associate*. And what does *associate* mean?"

Marva directed her question at Jerome. "Baby, what does *associate* mean? The dog associated the bell with the food. The bell made the dog do what? Think about the———."

"Think about the food," Jerome answered.

"Very good. *Associate* means that one thing makes you think about something else. *Associate* means to connect or join together. We associate Halloween with pumpkins. We associate Santa Claus with Christmas.

"Now Dr. Pavlov's dog associated the bell with the food. It became such a habit that his mouth watered when he heard a bell, even if he was not given any food. The bell rang and the dog acted hungry. Jerome, you don't need a bell to tell you that you are hungry, do you? Of course you don't. You're bright enough to know that by yourself. You don't need a bell to tell you when to start thinking either."

In the past six weeks, since the semester had begun, Marva's students had become used to these digressions. She never reprimanded a saucy remark like the one Jerome had made. She saw it as a test, a personal challenge. She liked to think she could transform anything into a learning experience.

A boy who kicked a classmate while going out to recess

had to look up the etymology of the word *kick* and report his findings to the class. When Wanda Lewis was chewing bubble gum and popped an enormous bubble all over her chin and nose, Marva had her look up the history of gum chewing and tell the class all about chicle and sapodilla trees.

The incident sparked a classroom discussion of botany, geography, and international trade. Marva told her students that sapodilla trees are evergreens, which differ from deciduous trees like the maples, oaks, and elms that grow in Garfield Park, because evergreens don't lose their leaves in the autumn. She pulled down the large world map and showed her class Mexico, Central America, and the tropical areas of South America where the sapodillas grow. She went on to explain how these countries sell the chicle from the trees to the United States in exchange for goods they don't have—"The word we use is *export.*"

It was typical of the spontaneous lessons Marva treated her class to daily. Nothing was irrelevant if it could be used to pique a child's intellectual curiosity.

Just as quickly as she had begun it, Marva dropped the discussion of Pavlovian psychology and brought the class back to the lesson on homonyms.

"Homonyms are like twins, but they are not identical twins," she said. "They are words that sound alike but have different middle vowels and different meanings. Anthony, use the homonyms *meet* and *meat* in sentences."

"Meet you next week?" answered Anthony, a small quiet boy, the kind of child who is easily overlooked in a classroom.

"Use a complete sentence, sweetheart. We must always speak in complete sentences. Can I meet you, when?"

"Can I meet you next week, Mrs. Collins?" Anthony replied.

"Very, very good."

"Mrs. Collins, Mrs. Collins," Freddie Harris shouted, stretching his arm as high as he could and bouncing in his seat. "I've got one, I've got one."

"All right, Freddie," Marva said, "why don't you give us a sentence using the word *meat,* the homonym with *ea?*"

"Dr. Pavlov's dog eats meat," Freddie said, sitting back in his seat very pleased with himself.

"Oh, you are so bright, so bright," Marva told him. "I can't believe no one ever told you what a brilliant child you are."

Marva had guessed the story of Pavlov's dog would find its way into the lesson. That was her method, to pool as much information as possible, to bombard the children with names and facts and anecdotes they could draw upon later. Of course the children wouldn't remember everything. Exposure to knowledge was what mattered. Some of it would sink in.

The children were learning their sounds. Each day in unison, like yogis chanting their mantras, the children followed Marva's lead, repeating the vowel sounds, the consonants, and the consonant blends—*br, bl, tw, spr.*

To a beat of one-two, one-two-three, they worked on the long vowel sounds: *"a, e—i, o, u.* I like reading, how about you?" Next they did the short vowel sounds, which Marva believed were especially troublesome for black children to pronounce: *"at, et, it, ot, ut.* Let's push the last door shut."

To link the sounds with spelling Marva printed several example words on the board.

"The vowel sound is *a* and the word is *ate.* The vowel sound is *a* and the word is *tail.* The vowel sound is *a* and the word is *may.* The vowel sound is *a* and the word is *straight.* The vowel sound is *a* and the word is *eight.*"

The class picked up the rhythm of motion and sound, and soon the excitement of a revival meeting spread through the room. The chorus of voices rose and fell accompanied by bobbing heads and clapping hands. The energy was contagious.

"Play and *stay. Play* and *stay,"* they sang. "I see two vowels, one, two. I see two vowels, one, two. I see two vowels and the sound is *a.* The word is *play.*"

So it went through the long and the short vowel sounds and then the consonants, each with an associative key. The letter *b* was the heart beat sound; *c* and *k* were copycats, both sounding like cracking nuts; *d* was a knock on the door; *f* a fighting cat; *g* a croaking frog; *h* a running boy panting. They chanted down the list to *z*, a buzzing bee.

Heart beat, heart beat, bh, bh, bh
Cracking nut, cracking nut, ck, ck, ck
Knock on the door, knock on the door, dh, dh, dh

Fighting cat, fighting cat, fff, fff, fff
Croaking frog, croaking frog, gh, gh, gh
Running boy, running boy, huh, huh, huh

Marva clapped her hands to keep up the pace, sustaining the children's energy and excitement. When they had finished, Marva praised her children, reminding them, "If you know the vowel and consonant rules, you will be able to spell and read every word."

★ ★ ★

By November, I saw the daily regimen of phonics drills beginning to work. It was a tedious, repetitive method of teaching reading, tedious for me as well as for the children. But there was no substitute for its effectiveness. The rhythmic tapping and hand clapping relieved some of the monotony. Before long the children were almost as familiar with the chanting of vowel and consonant sounds as they were with the jingles on television commercials or the songs on the latest Stevie Wonder album. Once in a while, I would hear some of my students in the lunchroom or in the hallway singing their own jazzed up versions of "Cracking nut, cracking nut, ck, ck, ck. Buzzing bee, buzzing bee, zzz, zzz, zzz."

In class the children were now blending vowels and consonants and sounding out words. They were beginning to read, using the text *Reading Is Fun*, the first book in the phonics-first series published by Open Court Publishing Company. The former principal at Delano had ordered the books years before and had encouraged his teachers to experiment with them. Most of the teachers declined, feeling that the Open Court books were too hard for their children. When the new principal took over, the phonics-first readers were packed away in the storeroom.

I liked the Open Court series because the poetry and story selections aimed to teach values as well as vocabulary.

Say well and do well

End with the same letter.

To say well is fine,

To do well is better.

Like the old *McGuffey Reader,* the Open Court series taught a lot more than "Look, look. See me." So my students worked through poems, fables, and stories like "Dick Whitington and His Cat," in addition to the selections that I read aloud to them daily right after lunch. The children sponged up information as though they were on their way to a children's version of College Bowl. They knew that trolls and elves came from Scandinavia, pixies lived in England, leprechauns came from Ireland, goblins were found in France, and poltergeists were noisy little German spirits. They learned that there are 343 different versions of the Cinderella story and that the first was printed in China in the year 340.

The book you give to a child who is learning to read determines what he or she will read later on. If we give children the boring Dick-and-Jane type of stories, how can we spark their curiosity in further reading? Fairy tales and fables whet a child's appetite for more reading, and they are an excellent means for teaching the rudiments of literary analysis. In fairy tales there is always a conflict or problem, the forces of good poised against the forces of evil. I teach my students to identify the protagonist and the antagonist. I also point out that in fairy tales there are often elements of three—three bears, three pigs, three wishes, Cinderella's three nights at the ball. I explain that the number three is widely symbolic, representing many things. One example I usually give is the three parts to our personality—the id, the ego, and the super-ego. I tell the children that the id is the person we are when we are first born, before we learn anything. The ego is our present self, the person we think we are. And the super-ego is our conscience, the person we feel we should be.

Even young children love to analyze a story this way, working out a puzzle and seeing how all the pieces fit together. The children suggest other associations for the number three, such as three strikes to an out in baseball or three meals a day. The search for connections between what they read and what they see around them gets the children's minds clicking for classroom discussion, which is the heart of the lesson. I remind my students that they each have an opinion and that their opinions are important. I don't tell them what to think. I try to teach them how to think. It is useful in these discussions to introduce a question without a clear-cut answer, a question to stimulate critical thinking. Did Goldilocks have the right to go into someone's house without permission? Was she right to destroy the bears' beds and eat their food?

To limber up their minds, I put my students through warm-up exercises. During an arithmetic lesson, for example, I might ask, "If it takes me three minutes to boil one egg in a pot of water, how long will it take me to boil two eggs?" Someone usually pops up, "We don't know times yet." Another student might venture, "It'll take two times as long."

I say, "You're going to have overcooked eggs if you do that. Stop and think. If I'm putting an egg in some water and bringing that water to a boil, what difference will it make if I put in two eggs instead of one? It will take the same amount of time for the eggs to cook, won't it?" The object is to get children to think, use not only book knowledge but common sense. Sometimes, I give my students incomplete questions with facts deliberately omitted. I do this to teach them how to evaluate information and to get them to realize that not every question can be answered. They eventually learn to tell me there isn't enough information.

★ ★ ★

The progress being made by Marva's students became obvious, one day, during a discussion of "Jack and the Beanstalk."

"Well, what about Jack?" Marva asked. "What kind of character do you think Jack is?"

"That Jack, he was sure dumb," said Chris.

"Yeah," laughed Freddie, "messing with that old giant. He could of been dead for sure."

"So you don't think he should have taken the chance and gone to the giant's castle?" Marva asked.

"I think he shoulda gone 'cause he got his daddy back and his daddy's things," Bernette replied.

"Aw, all he was thinking about was swiping those things," Freddie argued. "How'd he know for sure the money and the hen with the eggs was his dad's?"

"*Were* his dad's, darling," Marva corrected.

"Yeah, they were his dad's."

"He was no good," agreed Jerome, sitting back in his chair with his arms crossed on his chest. "He was just lazy. He didn't want to do no work, see, so he's looking to get by. Like you always telling us, Mrs. Collins, he's the one with his hand out looking for something he don't earn."

"He went begging the lady giant for food," whispered Anthony. A second later he seemed startled to realize that he had answered in class.

"Anthony, aren't we getting so brilliant!" exclaimed Marva.

"Shoot, I still think Jack was dumb," burst out Chris, who had been shaking his head during the other comments. "You don't give away no cow for some beans some dude says is magic till you make him show you how they work. Man, that Jack was getting set up!"

Chris was raising a whole new issue from the story. There was no holding them back now.

The dedicated teacher knows that feeling of epiphany, when all the pulling and pushing and coaxing and laboring over lessons finally take effect and the children go on their own. Marva watched the children's eagerness, thinking what a long road it had been to bring them to this point of openness. That first day of school they were shells of children with toughened faces and glassed-over eyes, devoid of hope and joy. Now they had enthusiasm.

"I don't know what St. Peter has planned for me," she said, "but you children are giving me my heaven on earth."

★ ★ ★

Naturally my optimum goal was to get the children in this class to see the intrinsic value of an education, so that they would want to learn for the sake of learning. That would come eventually. They were still seven, eight, and nine years old. While I had no use for bribes, I strongly believed in rewards. Praise—every day for every task—was the main incentive. But every so often, when it was earned and unsolicited, a little something more didn't hurt.

My students had been working hard, so I arranged for them to visit a local fast-food restaurant. We had been studying a science unit on how man gets his food, and the field trip seemed to fit right in. The owner agreed to take the children on a behind-the-scenes tour of the restaurant, showing them how food was prepared and how the business was run, treating each of them afterward to lunch. I had already cleared everything with the principal, who said it was a fine idea. "Those kids are always eating that junk food," he laughed. "Maybe they'll get a chance to see what goes into it."

This franchise restaurant was using a clown in its advertising campaign, and at 11 A.M. the clown came to class to lead the children to the restaurant. They were all squeals and giggles as they left Delano, though they were trying awfully hard to act like mature ladies and gentlemen. Tripping and shoving were kept to a minimum as the children attempted to heed my reminder that they were all ambassadors of the school and must be on their best behavior.

Just as our procession was turning the corner, the principal came rushing down the sidewalk, calling to me to stop. He was clutching his suit jacket together to keep it from flapping. He looked more out of sorts than usual.

"Marva, you can't go," he said, panting. "You have to bring your class back to the building. I've got a lot of trouble with the other teachers. They're giving me a hard time about letting you go."

"But you already gave permission," I said.

"I know, I know, but I didn't expect it to cause such a fuss."

"Look at these children, look how excited they are. I am not going to disappoint them. When you make a promise to children, you keep it, or you don't promise in the first place."

So I continued on to the restaurant with my children. I had to pay dearly for that decision. The principal apparently went back and said he had not given me permission to take my class on the outing. From then on it was open warfare with the faculty.

Someone started the rumor that I beat my students into behaving. When my second-graders were studying a science unit about dinosaurs, I posted their papers on the bulletin board outside the class, and some teachers spread the word that I had made up those papers myself. They said it was impossible for my students to write about the brontosaurus and the pterodactyl and the tyrannosaurus when their own classes were still struggling with the first thirteen words in the basal reader.

The harrassment kept up. Twice I found hate notes in my school mailbox: "You think you're so great. We think you're nothing." They were signed "A Colleague."

Some days, standing at the blackboard, I felt dizzy. I began to have trouble sleeping at night. There was a pulsating pressure against the sides of my head. I would sit up suddenly unable to breathe, gasping and then exhaling in quick spurts. I felt like I was dying.

I spent most of my time wondering what it would be like if I quit teaching altogether. I knew I would have to find another job. Even with my teaching salary we had barely enough money. A lot of it went to pay for summer camps and private schools for Eric, Patrick, and Cindy. As it was, Clarence had to work two jobs, getting up at 2 A.M. to mix cement at a construction site before going to his regular job at Sunbeam. I often typed medical reports on Saturdays to bring in extra cash. It would have been much easier if I had enrolled my children at Delano, but by the time Eric was old enough for school I had already been teaching at Delano for more than four years, and I realized that that school would never provide the kind of education I wanted for my children.

I was sure there were other things besides teaching. I considered finding a job in an office, working for a textbook publisher, or writing for one of the newspapers. I wrote some letters of inquiry, but it was no use. Every time I had an idea, it was driven from my head by one prevailing thought—there was no way I could leave the children in my class. Not in the middle of the year. Not when they had just come alive. Continuity was so important for these children.

I didn't think I could endure the tension much longer. I was tired of no one talking to me. Tired of the whole world hating me. I was glad when Christmas vacation finally came.

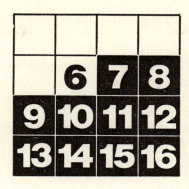

O ver the holidays, Clarence and the children did everything they could to cheer me up and get my mind off my problems at Delano. Without their support, I probably would have fallen apart completely. I've always had a quick temper and I often panicked about things. But Clarence, in his calm, comforting, common sense way, never failed to remain steady in a crisis. That was what I needed. Even my son Eric reassured me. "Now look, Mom," he said, "you're the one who's always telling us to be strong. Well, you've got to be strong yourself." He was only twelve at the time, but he already had a certain take-charge manner.

I wandered through the house trying to understand what was happening to me. For a few days I nursed self-pity. Then came the doubt, even guilt. Was I self-righteous? Too rigid? All my life I had been serious, too serious. I wished I could be more like everyone else. I even practiced being more casual about things, leaving the dinner dishes overnight in the sink. I ended up washing them before I went to sleep.

When I was sure I was right about something, I just couldn't back down or even compromise. As a teacher my sympathies were only with my students. Could I have done more to understand my colleagues? I was confused. The simplest values, things I had always understood, were now complicated.

After a while I began to see that it wasn't only the conflict with the faculty that had unleashed these emotions. It was everything about today's education. The indifference and the bureaucracy had made the daily struggle to educate children that much harder. I was also frustrated as a parent. I was having trouble finding a good school for my own children, getting them a decent education.

At the time I was sending my children to a Lutheran school miles away from Garfield Park, paying taxicabs and neighbors to drive the children there and pick them up again. Yet I wasn't pleased with the school. It was the fourth I had tried in less than seven years.

First I had sent Eric and Patrick to a Catholic school at the other end of the city. It cost $60 a month in tuition and more than $100 for a private cab to take them there. I thought it was worth it. They were getting a good basic education—Latin, grammar, and plenty of old-fashioned discipline instead of gimmicks and games.

From pre-school through first grade they had good teachers. By the time Eric was seven the school began opening up its curriculum to more "progressive" teaching methods and hiring lay teachers chiefly to attract more students. When I saw my sons doing word-picture games and coloring in workbooks rather than building their reading skills and vocabulary, I enrolled them in another school.

For all its prestige the private all-boys prep school quickly proved disappointing. Eric and Patrick were not learning phonics but were being drilled to memorize words on flash cards. They were reading from a basal text without classroom discussions, exercises, or questions to stimulate critical thinking. Worse, they were using look-say readers. Patrick, who was an eager reader when he transferred to the prep school in first grade, began to act as though a light bulb had clicked off inside. He stopped learning, he lost interest in reading, and the school tried to convince me that he needed a remedial class.

I met with the headmaster. I wanted to offer some assistance, not as an expert but as a concerned parent. I felt that if parents were willing to get involved—to help with more than fund-raising and chaperoning field trips—then maybe the children would start getting a better education. The headmaster appeared to be interested. In fact he asked me to draw up sample lesson plans and reading guides for teaching phonics. I did, though I had the feeling he was humoring me.

Nothing changed. At the end of fourth grade Eric was stumbling over words that he would have been able to sound out if he knew phonics. And Patrick was having problems reading. I worked with them in the evening, mostly trying to undo what they had done all day at school. So I told Clarence I didn't want the boys returning to the prep school the following semester. He found it difficult to comprehend my relentless pursuit of a good school. I think he believed that somewhere along the line a normal parental concern had become a cause célèbre. He assumed that as long as his sons were attending an expensive private school, they must be getting a solid education.

I understood how easily someone who was not in education, not in the classroom working with children, might think I was overreacting. Everyone thinks a school is a place where children learn. What else is a school for? People still believe in the tradition of dedicated, self-sacrificing school teachers. They don't know how the profession has changed.

The search for a school for my own three children opened my eyes: the public schools had no monopoly on poor education. Miseducation was a problem everywhere, a galloping epidemic that was infecting every school from the city to the suburbs whether public, parochial, or private. What was once the poor man's burden had become everyone's.

With this came another realization, that I couldn't escape the problem, as a teacher or as a mother. These parts of my life were inextricably interwoven; at Delano I was fighting for the kind of education I wanted for my own children. As a parent I tended to be protective, and I always felt that same driving concern as a teacher. I could never walk out of Delano at 3:15 and leave the school and the students entirely behind me. Were my students going home or would they wander the streets? Were their clothes warm enough? Would their stomachs be full tonight and would they have sheets on their beds?

During recess I watched from the doorway to make sure no child was being picked on by classmates or excluded from games. And when I saw anyone standing off alone, I took the child's hand, called the other children over, and began a new play circle. It was important to me that the children feel accepted in their group. I knew all too well what it felt like to be ostracized.

When I returned to Delano in January, I was more determined than ever to teach. Two weeks after school was back in session, everything came crashing down.

On a Friday afternoon the principal sent up a message saying he wanted to see me immediately in his office. I couldn't imagine what was so urgent that it couldn't wait until the end of the day. Did I forget to fill out some form? Was one of my students in trouble?

The principal was sitting behind his desk, looking very formal and very official. He was a short man; behind the desk he looked even smaller, swallowed up by filing cabinets and stacks of papers. He told me to sit down. I knew I wasn't going to like what he had to tell me.

He was taking my class away from me. Because of funding cuts, the school had lost some supervisory positions, so he had to put one of the master teachers back into the classroom. And he was giving her my class and switching me to another. She was retiring in June, he explained, after thirty years of teaching, and he wanted to make her last few months as easy as possible. I half-heard some backhanded compliments on how well my children were doing and how well behaved they were. She would have no problems.

What about the children? I flew upstairs to my class. My heart was pounding. I closed the door behind me, leaned against the wall, staring around the room cluttered with books, papers, posters, and plants. Some visitors might not have found it esthetically pleasing, but everything in it was for the children. My eyes went to the posters on the wall: *A Winner Never Quits and a Quitter Never Wins! Winners in Life Respond Positively to Pressure. If Life Gives You Lemons, Make Lemonade.* Each day the children repeated those sayings. Each day I proclaimed the message, driving home the importance of a positive attitude. I expected it of my students. Suddenly I no longer had it myself.

★　★　★

The children could see that Marva was upset.
"What's happening, Mrs. Collins?" Freddie asked.
"You okay, Mrs. Collins?" Anthony whispered, his brow furrowed. She rested her hands on his shoulders.
"Children, I have always been honest with you, so I'm not going to fool you now. The office is making some changes." Her grip tightened on Anthony's shoulders. "You are going to get another teacher, and I guess I am going to get another class."
She expected the moans, the chorus of noes, and the head shaking. Tears ran down Anthony's cheeks. Freddie slammed his hand against the side of his desk, shoving it against the wall.
"I'm never coming back here!" he shouted, his lips pursed tightly together, his arms and shoulders moving in quick angry jerks. "I'm gonna break every window in this place."
"Is that what my teaching has come to? Is that what I have been doing here all these months, teaching you how to break windows and slam desks? When you go looking for a job, some employer is sure to say, 'My, my, look at this young man. He certainly is qualified for the job because he went to school and learned how to break windows and slam desks.' "
A few giggles broke the tension. Marva walked over to Freddie, pushed his desk into the row, and put her arm around him.
"I love you," she told him. "I love you all, and I am going to continue to love you and care about you and worry about you. Sometimes things happen in life that we can't do anything about. We don't let them get us down, do we? We go on doing the best we can, making something of our lives. If you stop learning, if you stop building your minds, then everything I have been teaching you is wasted. Then you will make me a failure as a teacher."

★ ★ ★

When the children had gone home, I rolled up some of my posters and packed up a few of my books and plants. I decided I'd come back for the rest or send Clarence to pick them up. Relief was beginning to wash over me.
I had seen it all. Children coming to school so dirty I had to

take them into the bathroom and scrub their arms and elbows with alcohol. A parent barging into the school with an extension cord to beat a child. I had worked hard, worked until I was exhausted, trying to change it, trying to give the children something more to look forward to in life than they could see in Garfield Park. If I was as strong as I thought, then I was strong enough to admit defeat.

A student's mother walked into the room. She told me that parents had already heard about the principal switching the children around. One of the teacher's aides had gotten the word and started making phone calls. There was a group of angry parents downstairs in the office. They were angry at the idea of disrupting two classes and sixty children just to find a place for one teacher.

While she talked, she kept her eye on the box of plants on my desk. She said, "Mrs. Collins, when you start packing up your plants, I know you're ready to go. But we want you to stay." The other parents were downstairs with the principal insisting on it.

I didn't answer. I tried to imagine the shouting and fussing in the office. The thought of the principal being swarmed over by those parents made me smile. Poor man, he never expected it. He probably figured the parents would ignore things as they usually did—not so much because they didn't care but because so many of them were easily intimidated by teachers and school administrators. They were afraid of not knowing what to say, afraid of looking dumb, embarrassed by their own lack of education. Too often they were self-conscious about the way they talked, about the way they looked or dressed, expecting the teacher to laugh at them. I was glad the parents were taking a stand. However, I was no longer going to be involved. I had settled the matter for myself and had started to feel comfortable with my decision.

I put on my coat, turned off the lights, and closed the door of the classroom. Downstairs I heard the commotion. Hoping no one would see me, I turned and ran out of the building. I needed serenity so badly. The last thing I could have endured at that moment was fighting and arguing. What I had to do at that point was hold on to my reason, my dignity. My sense of personal identity depended on it.

That night Clarence and I talked it over, and I told him I had made up my mind to resign from Delano. He said I had to do what I thought was best, but I suspect he was more relieved than he let on. I went to bed thinking everything was finally resolved, and for the first time in weeks I slept soundly.

The next morning several parents telephoned to ask about the rumor that I was leaving. They told me if I didn't come back to school, they weren't going to send their children back either. They would boycott the school and keep their children home.

Whether or not they meant it, I was alarmed. Things could get out of hand in a place like Garfield Park, and I was afraid a boycott would prove dangerous. Not that I doubted the parents' intentions, but I was worried that some of the older boys in the neighborhood might use it as an excuse to start trouble. I did not wish to be the cause of anything.

On Monday I returned to Delano. The principal gave me back my class and I resumed teaching. Neither the children nor I mentioned what had happened.

For me that was the end. All I wanted to do was make it through to June. I couldn't fight any longer. As the weeks and months passed, I became steadily more depressed. It got to the point that I dreaded walking into the school building. On Friday evening I was already worrying about Monday. By Sunday I was tearing through my house like a whirlwind, cleaning and scrubbing and polishing. Or I fell silent. My family had to put up with a lot of moodiness from me. I alternated between shouting, complaining, and crying. I was holding on for June.

Those last few months of the school year were the most difficult. Relief was so close, I could see it ahead. But each day was so long and painful. I gave all my remaining energy to my students. There was nothing left for me. I didn't fix my hair and often went without washing it. I stopped caring what I wore and forgot about makeup. Mornings, I would grab anything, even a pair of blue jeans. And there were times I wore the same clothes two days in a row, something I had never done before.

Naturally my students saw the change. I didn't hide my feelings from them. I told them that sometimes I hurt inside and felt like crying but it wasn't because of anything they had done. It was important that they understood because children, especially young ones, are quick to assume they are responsible

for whatever might be troubling the adults around them. Sometimes the class was a kind of group therapy session. They
shared their experiences, and I was open in talking about mine.
I never believed a teacher should pretend to be perfect. A
teacher who never displays any human weaknesses makes children self-conscious about admitting their own. A perfect
teacher, like a perfect parent, is an impossible model for a child
to live up to.

Yet my students were learning, learning to read, to do
math, and to exercise their minds. In September my second-
graders had started out with the first book in the Open Court
series; in June they finished up in the middle of the fifth grade
reader. They knew of Aristotle, Aesop, Tolstoy, Shakespeare,
Poe, Frost, and Dickinson. If I had changed, my teaching
methods had not.

On the last day of school I hugged and kissed each of the
children goodbye. I gave them a list of books to read over the
summer. "You are the brightest children in the whole world," I
reminded them one last time, "and you must never forget that.
Remember, no one can take your knowledge from you. You are
the only ones who will determine whether you succeed or fail in
life. You must never give up. Always try to fly."

It was past noon when I gathered my things together and
walked out of Delano. The children milling around in the front
of the building ran up to me, tugging at me. "I love you," I
called to them, crossing the street. That was the truth; they
were the only reason I had held on for those last months. But I
promised myself I was never going back. As long as I lived, I
would never set foot in that building again.

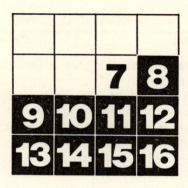

My departure from Delano was no great gesture of protest. I was almost thirty-nine years old. I wasn't some young upstart out to prove something to myself and to the world. I still liked teaching, but it had to be in a place where I could be comfortable. I was willing to stay in the public schools and try to make the system work, as a lot of teachers do. But I no longer had the energy to do that and take on my colleagues too.

After spending the past fourteen years learning how, I wasn't about to give up on teaching. I figured I would take the summer to unwind, and then I'd consider the other possibilities. I had a feeling things would work out.

In July a group of neighborhood women organizing a community school came to see me. Dissatisfied with the public schools, they wanted to start a private elementary school for children in the Garfield Park area. They asked me to be director. It sounded wonderful. I had some strong opinions about what a school should be, and here was the chance to apply those ideas. I accepted their offer immediately, without even considering what it took to get a school started. It seemed to me that all I needed were students, some books, and a blackboard.

None of the women knew much more about setting up a school than I did, but the president of a community college on the West Side, Daniel Hale Williams University, offered some assistance. He agreed to provide our new school with a basement classroom rent-free, and he let us use some typewriters and mimeograph machines.

Next we met with the director of the Alternative Schools Network, an organization of community-participation schools in and around Chicago. Unlike the free schools that grew out of the antiestablishment mood of the late sixties, the ASN schools evolved in the early seventies as part of the back-to-basics movement. The government-funded Alternative Schools Network paid my salary as director and curriculum developer, and their staff showed us how to open a private school.

During the last weeks of August I raced around trying to collect books. I bought some in secondhand bookstores and borrowed others. One day when I was passing the Delano schoolyard, I noticed the trash bins were filled with books, the very books I had used with my students, the Open Court readers. None of the other teachers had any use for them. I rescued the phonics-first series from the garbage, confident that I could use them to save children from a similar fate.

On September 8, 1975 Daniel Hale Williams Westside Preparatory School opened its doors. Though we had spread the word around the neighborhood, enrollment was not overwhelming. Parents were leery of chancing a new school. Many were put off by the $60 a month tuition. I wasn't discouraged. Aristotle said, "The heights of great men were not attained by sudden flight." I would work with what I had. I had only four students, ranging from second grade to fourth grade. One of them was my daughter Cindy. If the school was going to be good enough for other children, it had to be good enough for my own.

I had thought about the effects of teaching my own children, and I decided that whatever difficulty there might be in having your mother for a teacher, it was certainly no greater than the problems Cindy would face trying to learn in some other school. As for my sons, Eric would stay where he was because he was in eighth grade and due to graduate at the end of the year. Patrick was enrolled in a private school near Lincoln Park. I felt he would benefit by being on his own, out of the shadow of his older brother and his younger sister.

I didn't know very much about my other three students and didn't really want to know their backgrounds. Knowing a child's previous record can sway a teacher's expectations. Each child came to me with a clean slate. Still, from the initial interviews I had with the children and their parents, I could tell that each had had a problem of one kind or another.

Gary Love was angry and defensive at nine years old. He talked back to his mother and to me during the interview and made it very clear he hated school.

Eight-year-old Allen Pratt was being raised by a father who was a member of a motorcycle gang. I didn't know why Mr. Pratt enrolled his son in the school. He never told me. I suspected it may have been because he didn't have a permanent address, which might have posed a problem in registering Allen in a public school. When I asked Allen to read a sentence in the reader, he didn't even know the words *and* or *the*. On top of everything else, Allen was the dirtiest child I had ever seen. His hair was matted down; he had dried food on his mouth and chin and streaks of grease on his arms. The boy looked as though no one had washed his clothes in months.

My third student, Tracy Shanklin, was seven years old and had been passed into second grade at Delano. She couldn't read a sentence like "Sam sat at a mat," and she didn't know how to do simple addition. She was a quiet girl, very submissive and downcast. Everything about her seemed to say "I'm a nobody." Mrs. Shanklin was impatient with her daughter's progress at Delano. She enrolled Tracy in Daniel Hale Williams Westside Preparatory after hearing about it from a woman who lived in her apartment building.

From one point of view, having so few students was an ideal teaching situation. Any teacher who had to keep track of thirty or forty children would have gladly traded places with me. But the size also presented a problem. How would I turn four students and one classroom into a real school? I decided to use the same style of teaching I had developed at Delano. To me the four students sitting in the classroom that first morning might just as well have been forty. I was ready to teach.

★　★　★

Cindy was already sitting in the front row opposite Marva when the other children started to arrive. Tracy Shanklin, holding her mother's hand, was the first. Her mother stood in the doorway and gave Tracy a gentle nudge to go inside. The girl looked up hesitatingly, then dropped her eyes to the floor and walked into the room, heading slowly for the last seat in the last row. Mrs. Shanklin whispered to Marva that at Delano her daughter had been seated in the back of every classroom she was in, overlooked by teachers because she was such a quiet child. It was a pattern Marva recognized repeatedly in slow learners. She hurried over to Tracy, catching her before she settled into the chair. Hugging the child close to her, Marva led her to a desk beside Cindy.

"I love you too much to have you so far away from me," Marva said. "I will be lonesome if you sit in the back of the room."

Marva was introducing Tracy to Cindy when Gary Love, big for his age, bounded into the room, swaggering and snapping his fingers behind his back, jiving to some imagined music.

"Sweetheart, is your hip broken? If it isn't, there's no reason to come in here walking that way, slopping and popping your fingers. Why don't you come sit over here?" Marva patted the back of one of the front seats.

Gary plopped into a desk in the middle of the room. "You make me."

Marva shrugged. "I don't make children do anything. You make yourself what you are. You must decide for yourself what you want to do in here, peach. You have the right to learn. You also have the right to fail, if you choose."

Marva stopped, letting him think the matter over, and went to usher Allen Pratt to a desk. She was about to put her arm around Allen when a wave of sweat hit her nose.

Turning to the others, she said, "Children, look through the books on your desk. I will be right back." She took Allen's hand, whispering, "Come with me, darling," and she led him down the hall to the women's washroom. Embarrassed, Allen refused to go inside. Marva shoved open the door, shouted hello, and waited for a response. When no one answered, she said, "It's all right, sweetheart. No one is there. You're such a handsome young man, but we can't see just how good looking you are beneath all that dirt. Let's scrub you down and find the real you."

Coaxing him over to the basin, Marva wet some paper towels, rubbing the grease and sweat off the child's neck and arms. He pulled away. She kept talking to him, asking him about his summer, about his former school, about his father's motorcycle, anything and everything she could think of to make him relax.

When she had finished, Marva handed the boy a dry towel. "All right, tomorrow I'm going to bring you some clean clothes. Starting today and for the rest of your life, you're going to have to wash your own face."

She hugged him as they walked back to the classroom. Allen scooted into a chair. Cindy and Tracy were talking quietly and seemed to be getting along well. Gary had shunted himself off to the far left corner. From the look of the zig-zagged rows of desks, it seemed he had tried out every chair in the room before settling there. Gary's eyes were closed as his head swayed and his fingers snapped, keeping beat to a tune playing silently inside him.

"Darling, no one is going to be handing out the good jobs to someone who sits there popping his fingers," Marva said, ruffling Gary's hair. He recoiled, turning his body to the wall. "You have a right to sit there all day staring at the wall if you want. You'll never become a millionaire that way, but you can stare away if it pleases you. However, you cannot sit here snapping and tapping because you are interfering with everyone else's right to learn."

She walked up to the front of the room to commence her customary first-day-of-school pep talk. In her tailored suit, hoop earrings, and high-heeled shoes, she was as imposing a figure as she had been at Delano. Daniel Hale Williams Westside Preparatory may have been a makeshift school, but there was nothing informal about the teacher or her classroom. Perhaps as a consequence of her southern background, Marva subscribed to the idea that formality established a tone and decorum that encouraged her students to see a school, regardless of its setting, as hallowed ground, a place of learning.

"You are the best and brightest children in the world and there is nothing you can't do," she began. She rated their former schools for failing them, promised that she would not let any of them fail, sympathized with their fears and frustrations in school, told them she loved them, and then "tossed the ball into their court"—they had the choice of learning or sitting on the sidelines. Her speech was peppered with such similes as "Life is like a football game: you have to hit the line hard." She piled up aphorisms, partly out of habit but mostly because they helped children remember ideas.

"No one is going to hand you anything on a platter, not in this classroom. Not in this life," she said, revving up her students. "You determine what you will be, what you will make of yourselves. I am here to help you, but you must help me to do that. You can all win if you do not spend too much time trying to fail.

"In your other schools you probably started out each day saying the Pledge of Allegiance. Here we are going to start each day making a pledge to ourselves."

It was something Marva had composed herself. She asked the children to listen closely and repeat each line after her. "This day has been given to me fresh and clear . . ." Marva waited. Cindy belted out the words. Tracy followed, mumbling softly. Allen's voice picked up the word *clear,* but Gary was close-mouthed, sitting in a defiant posture with his back against the wall.

"I can either use it or throw it away," Marva continued. "I promise I shall use this day to its fullest, realizing it can never come back again." Except for Gary, the class repeated in voices that were getting stronger. "I realize this is my life to use or to throw away."

When the children finished their refrain, Marva took a sweeping step over to Allen's desk, positioned her hands solidly on each side of it, and hunched over to look the child squarely in the eye.

"Are you going to throw away your life?" she asked.

Allen crouched in his seat and giggled.

"This is not funny. What you do with your life is not a joke. Are you going to throw your life away?"

Allen sat upright with a frightened look. He rapidly shook his head no. Sometimes Marva came on too forcefully. Sometimes, she knew, there was too much anger in her teaching—

anger not at the children but at the desolation in their lives. She smiled, flicked her finger ticklishly under his chin, and slid over to Tracy, making the same inquiry. Sheepishly Tracy whispered no. Then Marva asked Cindy, who responded dutifully. Weaving among the desks, she approached Gary.

"Sweetheart, what are you going to do? Use your life or throw it away?"

Gary sat stonefaced, his arms across his chest.

"Of course it's your life to do with as you please," Marva reminded, "but there is a whole world out there calling you. If you throw away your life, you're just letting society have its way." She spun around to face the other children. "You know, boys and girls, there are some people who look at places like this, neighborhoods like Garfield Park, and they say 'Oh, children from there are not very smart. They aren't going to grow up to be anyone or do anything special.' If you decide to waste your lives, you are letting all those people be right. No one can tell you what you will be. Only you have the power to decide that for yourselves."

From that point Marva pushed on to Emerson and "Self Reliance." As before, she spent most of the first morning trying to convince her students that they wanted to learn. Her approach was to make the children see the link between an education and a job, a way out of the ghetto. She seldom missed a chance to draw the connection, because it was a reason they already understood.

When Tracy rummaged through her lunch sack a half hour before noon, Marva reminded, "Don't worry so much about feeding your stomach. Feed your brain first and you'll always find a way to get food for your stomach.

"Children, you are not in school for your parents, for your teachers, or for anyone else. You are here for yourselves. Your education is going to help you, not me." She swung over to the bookshelf and reached for a Bible that was nestled among *Plato's Republic, The Odyssey of Homer, Little Women, Candide, Charlotte's Web, The Brothers Karamazov,* and *Charlie and the Chocolate Factory.* Opening the text to the underlined passages, Marva quoted: "Proverbs, Chapter 3, verse 35 says 'Honor is the portion of wise men, but fools inherit shame.'

Chapter 6, verse 6: 'Go to the ant, O sluggard, study her ways and learn wisdom.' Chapter 10, verse 4: 'The slack hand impoverishes, but the hand of the diligent enriches.' "

Marva paused and looked out at the children. "What do you think those proverbs mean?" She knew there would be no flurry of hands waving. Not yet. These children had never had a dialogue with a teacher before. They were not accustomed to anyone asking them what their thoughts were. "All right, Cindy, would you please tell us what they mean?"

"A lazy person will be poor and won't have anything," Cindy blurted out quickly, repeating one of her mother's pet phrases.

"Very good." Marva sat on the edge of Tracy's desk. It was an intimate pose, suggesting that she might be about to share a secret. "The proverbs tell us that the wise man will advance in learning and will be able to take care of himself. But the fool destroys himself. A people without vision—without knowledge, without education—will perish.

"Children, that is why you are here. You must have an education to live a good life. To survive. You may not believe what I am telling you. And you may not believe what your parents and other adults tell you. But surely you believe what the Bible tells you."

For a few moments the children sat in awed silence. Even Gary was having some difficulty trying to look cool and aloof. Marva said it was time for lunch. The pensive mood lost out to the rustling of brown paper lunch bags and voices bartering Twinkies for potato chips.

Except for Cindy, the children were not reading at the level appropriate for their age. Marva started them with the most basic lesson, going over the alphabet, pronouncing the vowel and consonant sounds. Next Marva selected two consonants and one vowel, writing them on the board and saying their sounds.

"Consonant *m,*" she said. "Mmm is the sound you make when something tastes delicious. Vowel sound *e.* In this case we have two *e*'s, so we put a macron over the first *e* to show that it says its name, and we put a slash through the second *e* to show it is silent. Next we have consonant *t,* which makes the sound of a clock ticking."

The children repeated each sound as Marva watched their pronunciation, showing them that with the sound of *m* their lips had to be pressed together, with *e* their mouths had to be open, and with *t* their tongues had to hit the roofs of their mouths.

She wrote *Meet me.* Allen, Tracy, and Cindy each took a turn reading the words aloud. Gary refused. He was busy twisting a pencil between his fingers, as though he were winding the propeller of a model airplane. Marva didn't force him. She said, "If you pay attention and learn, you will have choices in life."

Turning her attention to the other children, she asked them all to go up to the blackboard to take dictation. Her technique was to teach reading, writing, and spelling concurrently.

Still reveling in the novelty of having her mommy for a teacher, still not certain whether she was playing school or going to school for real, Cindy raced up to the blackboard. Allen gave a shrug, as if to say "Oh, why not," and found a spot for himself. Tracy squeezed in next to Cindy. With a piece of chalk in her hand, Tracy began to whimper. She couldn't do it, she said.

"I love you," Marva told her. "You have no reason for crying in here. We don't shed tears, we just go ahead and try to do it. No one is going to shout at you or laugh at you for making a mistake."

Tracy said she would try. Marva decided it was time to invite Gary into the lesson. She walked over to him, placed a hand on each shoulder, and whispered, "I'm not going to leave you alone. I care about you. Let's try to do some work."

"I'm not gonna do any damn work!" he shot back.

"You are too important to be left all alone. You are the most important child in this world, and people have left you alone for too long already. The Lord gave you a head to use, and if you care about yourself at all, and I know you do, then you will use it. I am not going to give up on you. I am not going to let you give up on yourself. If you sit there leaning against this wall

all day, you are going to end up leaning on something or someone all your life. And all that brilliance bottled up inside you will go to waste."

Marva took his arm and led him to the blackboard. He stood there, still determined to do nothing. She considered it a victory. He had not run back to his seat or, worse, out the door.

"All right, children," she began, "let's first make a capital letter *M*, mmm. Why a capital? Because we are beginning a sentence. Vowel sound *e*, then vowel *e* again, then consonant *t.*" As she spoke, Marva moved from child to child, guiding their hands with her own, helping them to form the letters. "Now you have written the word *Meet*. Put your finger down on the board so you can leave a space for the next word. All right, finger space, then consonant *m, mmm, vowel sound e,* and period because it is the end of a sentence."

When she finished, Marva glanced back at Gary, who was still standing in place with his hands in his pockets. Though she preferred to win her students with affection, she was no pushover. She felt that children needed and wanted discipline. Towering beside Gary, she spoke matter-of-factly, carefully measuring her voice so he would not mistake her firmness for hostility.

"There is no one on this earth who is going to make me a poor teacher," she said. "If you do not want to participate, go to the telephone and tell your mother, 'Mother, in this school we have to learn, and Mrs. Collins says I cannot fool around, so will you please pick me up.' "

Gary considered her statement for a moment, broke off some chalk, and scribbled *Meet me*. He returned to his seat, deliberately bumping into other desks along the way. Marva squelched the desire to reprimand him, asking him instead if he hurt himself. Her question was the last thing Gary expected to hear from his teacher. There was even some disappointment in his voice as he muttered, "I'm okay." He sat down.

On that first afternoon the quartet of students got their first taste of literature, *Aesop's Fables*. Before Marva began reading aloud, she prepared her students for the story. She explained the Latin origin of the word *fable* and defined the term, pointing out the difference from a fairy tale.

"Aesop," she continued, "was a Greek slave who lived on Samos, which is an island that belongs to the country of Greece. Some people think Aesop was black, or at least dark-skinned. He had a heavy nose and thick lips, and he was rather homely looking. When we describe a person's facial features and the way a person looks, we are describing physiognomy." Marva printed the word *physiognomy* on the board and placed the diacritical marks over the vowels.

"Now, Aesop is said to have lived about 600 years before Christ, which means he lived more than 2,500 years ago." She paused. Allen was staring at the clock, his head propped up against his hand.

"We don't sit in here daydreaming our lives away." She took his hand from the side of his face and held it in her own as she continued. "Even though Aesop was a slave, he was a very wise man. The story goes that Aesop was standing with two other slaves while a master was choosing which one of them to buy. The master asked the slaves what they could do. One slave said, 'I can do anything.' The next said, 'I can do everything.' When it was Aesop's turn, he said, 'I can do nothing.' The master asked why not. Aesop replied, 'If this one can do anything, and that one can do everything, then that leaves nothing for me.' "

The children giggled. Gary grinned also, but when he caught Marva watching him, he immediately assumed a deadpan look.

"The master thought Aesop was the most clever man he had met, so he bought Aesop. After a while the master set Aesop free because he was so impressed by Aesop's wit and wisdom."

Marva let the last line sink in for a moment. It was a good example of making the most of your abilities. "At the time Aesop lived, people were very *disgruntled*—they were very upset—with the government and the politicians. Let's try to use as many new words as we can, children. Let's expand our vocabularies. What does *disgruntled* mean? It means upset. Even though the people were disgruntled with the government, they were afraid to complain. Instead of complaining, Aesop poked fun at the government through his stories, using the animals in his fables to describe the behavior of people. Now, a story that pokes fun at something is called a *satire*. What is it called?"

"Satire," answered Cindy.

"Very good. There is another word to describe how we make fun of something, either by our language or by the tone of our voice, and that word is *sarcasm*. When we see a fat man stuffing a piece of cake in his mouth, we might say, 'He really *needs* that piece of cake, doesn't he?' That is using sarcasm. We are making a sarcastic remark."

By the time Marva's students were ready to hear the fable of "The Frogs Asking for a King" they had already been exposed to a smattering of etymology, vocabulary, literary terminology, and Greek history. The fable itself was not much longer than half the printed page, but Marva's telling of it took almost twenty minutes. She stopped at words to explain their meaning, dissecting prefixes, asking for synonyms. She broke off after certain phrases to check for comprehension or add more background, roving into the knowledge of related studies.

"Who did the frogs ask to find them a king?" she asked.

"Zeus," Allen answered, looking at the floor as he spoke.

"That's right, but don't talk to the floor, talk to me. No one trusts a person who can't look you in the eye. They asked Zeus because he was the most important Greek god. The ancient Greeks believed in many gods. They had a god of the sun and a different god for the moon. A god of love and a god of war. We are going to learn all about these gods when we study Greek mythology. Zeus was the king of all the other gods. He ruled over them and he ruled over humankind. The Greeks built beautiful temples and shrines to honor Zeus. The most famous statue of Zeus was considered one of the Seven Wonders of the World."

Marva continued with the fable, interrupting and starting again, asking questions and prying up responses: "Do you think it was a good idea to give the frogs a log for a king? What could that log do for them? Could it hear their complaints? Give them advice or tell them what to do? No, it could only sit there, couldn't it? Sometimes the people running our government act like logs, don't they? They don't always seem to hear what we are saying. Did you ever hear the expression *like a bump on a log?* What does that mean? It means a person is lazy, or *indolent,* doesn't it? And what does that new word *indolent* mean? It means lazy, doesn't it?"

Marva followed the Socratic method, in which a teacher asks a series of easily answered questions that lead the student to a logical conclusion. To the philosopher's method she added her own brand of energy, pacing up and down the aisles, patting a head, touching an arm, rattling off questions, complimenting answers, and employing grand histrionics. The lesson did not end with the last line of the fable. It was time to strike the moral.

"What do we learn from this fable, children? What is Aesop trying to tell us?" There was silence. "Well, what about the two kinds of kings in this story? First we had a log that did what, Tracy?"

"Nothing," the girl whispered.

"Darling, you have to speak much louder than that. If you don't, I'm going to have to climb on top of a desk and stretch all the way to the ceiling so you can practice shouting up that high."

The children laughed and Marva laughed with them. "All right, all right, let's finish up this story. So we had a log that did nothing, and then we had a stork who came to be king but ended up doing what?"

"Eating the frogs," said Allen.

"One ruler was too lazy and the other was———."

"Evil," shouted Cindy.

"It didn't do the frogs any good to wish for a king, did it?" All but Gary shook their heads no.

"Wouldn't the frogs have been better off learning how to take care of themselves? The fable shows us we have to lead ourselves instead of looking for others to lead us. If we don't think for ourselves, others will do what? They will do our thinking for us. We must each be the captain of our fate and the master of our soul."

From that day forward everything the students read or wrote would bear upon that theme, the keystone of Marva's teaching. Whether it was vocabulary, reading, mathematics, or literature, from Aeschylus to Zola, Marva's highest aim as a teacher was to endow her students with the will to learn for themselves.

By the end of the first day she knew exactly where each child was. Before she dismissed them that afternoon, she passed out sheets of math homework and phonics exercises, tailored to each child's needs. Allen was the first to catch the discrepancy.

Leaning over to look at Tracy's papers, he said, "I don't have those things. How come I don't have the same papers she does?"

Marva narrowed her eyes, furrowing her brow. "You don't look like her, do you? What makes you think you should do the same work she does?"

Making her way over to Gary, she placed three sheets of homework on his desk. He examined one of them curiously. "You got to be kidding," he said, throwing all of his wallop into the word *got*. "You want both sides of the paper for homework?" His voice cracked in disbelief midway through the question.

"Both sides?" Marva said, affecting a throaty drawl. "When your mother gives you dinner, do you want only half a chop? When someone hires you for a job, are you going to get only half the work done?"

Gary didn't answer. After the children had filed out the door, Marva found his homework papers on the floor under his desk. This boy had to change his priorities, but she wasn't going to force him. Eventually, with lots of praise and lots of hugging, his defensiveness would melt. The one thing all children finally wanted was the chance to be accepted for themselves, to feel some self-worth. Once they felt it, children became addicted to learning, and they had the desire to learn forever.

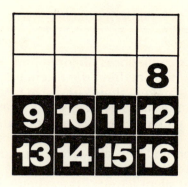

In my view the main thing is to get children reading. A child who doesn't know how to read can't do anything. But children do not learn to read by osmosis. It requires work— hard boring work without any shortcuts. It is drill and more drill. Repetition and memorization. Children must learn how to use key sounds to unlock words and they must recite long lists of words that have the same *a* sound as in *apple*, the same short *i* sound as *Indian* and *it*, the short sound of *u* as in *umbrella*, the short sound of *o* as in *ostrich*, or the sound of short *e* as in *eskimo*.

On the first day of school the children learned to read, write, and spell *Meet me*. On the second day I used the same method to introduce a new initial consonant, the letter *s*. The children pronounced the consonant and vowel sounds in *See me*, and then they went to the board and wrote the words as I dictated. Having learned the *ee* spelling for the vowel sound *e*, the class went on to learn that *ea* also says *e*. I wrote *e* on the board, putting a macron over the *e* and a slash through the silent letter. And the children read and wrote *See me eat*.

Day three, the children progressed to reading and writing *See me eat meat*. Day four, I taught them the consonant *h* and the children read and wrote *See me heat meat*. On the fifth day I reviewed everything, pretending I didn't know the sounds myself. By pretending that it was just as difficult for me to learn I was able to bait the children into reciting the sounds on their own. It was a way of informally testing them and at the same time building their confidence. Children jump at the chance to show that they know something the teacher doesn't.

"Children, as many times as I have gone over these sounds, I keep forgetting them. My old brain isn't working right. I think the sentence says *see-ee me ee-ate me-ate.* Is that right?"

Of course the children all started laughing. "You mean that's not right? Well, what did I do wrong?"

"You said the silent letters," they shouted.

"I did?" I said surprised. "You mean I forgot the rule that when two vowels go walking, the first one does the ———.' "

"Talking and says its name," they bellowed.

By the beginning of the second week of school the children advanced from pronouncing initial consonants to consonant blends. I explained what a blend was with an easily visualized image: "When Mommy bakes a cake, she doesn't just plop the eggs and the sugar and the flour into the bowl, does she? She stirs everything together, she blends the ingredients to make a cake. We are blending two letters, putting two letters together to make one sound."

I started them off with *th,* showing them how to put their tongues between their teeth to say the sound. We practiced putting our tongues between our teeth: thirty, thirteen, three, that, they, the. I wrote the word *the* on the board, underlining the blend *th.* The next step was to have the children incorporate this lesson into one they had already learned. At the board they wrote *See me heat the meat.*

From there we went on to the *igh* spelling of the vowel sound *i.* Following the same method I had used with *ee* and *ea,* I put a macron over the *i* and a slash through the silent letters *g* and *h.* So that the children could identify the sound with something concrete, I had them all take a deep sigh. I put an *s* in front of *igh* and had the children say the word *sigh.* Next I added the final consonant *t* so that the word was *sight.*

The children learned the family of words in which *igh* says *i*: night, right, might, tight, light, fight. Building on the previous sounds, they were able to write *See the night light.*

I told the children that now they were on their way to reading. They would want to learn another consonant blend, *fl.*

To show how the blend *fl* changes a word, I had the children say *fat* and *flat*, *fight* and *flight*. I reviewed *th* once again and then had the children combine everything they had learned thus far by saying and writing *See the night flight*.

The third blend was *br*, and the children read and wrote *See the bright light*. After that it was back to the vowel sounds to learn the long *i*, as in mine and kite, and the long *a*, as in gale. I explained that these vowels become long when they are followed by a consonant and an *e*, formulating this as the *i blank e* rule and the *a blank e* rule. Putting it all together, the children read and wrote *I might take a night flight*.

These lessons were the kernels of reading. The children progressed through the entire alphabet in the same way. They learned all the long vowel sounds and the short vowel sounds through compounding and repetition. They learned all the beginning consonant blends and then word endings like *ble, gle, tch, nk, ng, dge,* and *tion*.

They studied all the vowel and consonant rules and the exceptions to the rules. They knew, for example, that the letter *c* says *s* when it comes before *e, i,* or *y* and that in all other instances it says *k*. They knew that at the beginning of a word the letter *x* says *z*, at the end of a word *x* says *ks*, and after the letter *e* it says *gz* or *ks*, as in textile and exist.

The children had the sounds and the rules coming out of their ears. They were starting to wriggle in their seats at the routine, but I kept coaxing them on. "This is not baby work. These are the tools of language. How are you going to build anything without the right tools? Every word you will read in Shakespeare or Cicero or Dante is made up of sounds like these. You have a choice. You can learn these sounds and become literate lifters of mankind, or you can be lazy leaners all your life, turning to the next person to help you get by."

The expressions "literate lifter" and "lazy leaner" usually brought out a chuckle. Children like alliteration. I often have my students practice their initial consonant sounds by reciting tongue twisters like "Peter Piper picked a peck of pickled peppers" and "Betty Botter bought butter." I used the phrases "literate lifter" and "lazy leaner" so many times that the children began saying them on their own. More than once I heard Cindy and Allen teasing back and forth, asking one another, "Are you gonna be a literate lifter or a lazy leaner?"

After a month I started all four children on the second grade reader in the Open Court series, *A Trip Through Wonderland*. They read aloud every day as I checked their pronunciation and comprehension. Cindy, as I expected, breezed through the reader. I had worked with her from the time she was three years old, reading aloud to her, playing word games, and going over the sounds of the alphabet. She had started to read at age five, but her teacher at the Lutheran school discouraged her, making her self-conscious because none of the other kindergarteners knew how to read. Reading wasn't part of the kindergarten curriculum. When she passed into first grade, Cindy was still so far ahead of her classmates who were learning to read with the look-say books that she just lost interest. My big job with her was to awaken her enthusiasm.

Allen also caught on quickly. He was a very bright child, but he had been ignored and allowed to daydream. The sad truth is that children who are dirty or physically unattractive are often passed over in a classroom. I had to keep after Allen about his grooming, sending him to the bathroom to wash his face and scrub under his fingernails. I brought him some clean clothes—pants and shirts my son Patrick had outgrown—and I took his own soiled things home to wash. Little by little he seemed to take more care to keep himself clean. One morning I saw him in front of the drinking fountain trying to wash the stains off his pants.

Tracy and Gary, however, were both a problem. Tracy didn't want to read. She cried and complained of headaches. I saw that the reader was too difficult for her, but when I tried to give her the easier first grade book, she wouldn't take it. She and Cindy had taken to one another immediately and become fast friends; Tracy wanted to do the same work Cindy was doing. I reasoned it might be better for her to start at the higher level and build up her self-esteem than to feel she was behind her newfound friend.

Still it was a struggle to get her to read. She kept saying, "I can't do it, I can't do it." And I kept telling her how pretty and bright she was and reminded her of the story "The Little Engine that Could." When it was her turn to read, I put my arms around her and praised her for each word she read. As soon as Tracy finished three or four words in a row correctly, I had her stop, lest the fifth word prove too difficult. I did not want Tracy discouraged. Until she had a better opinion of herself, Tracy had to be insulated from failure.

Where Tracy became weepy, Gary would get angry. He'd take one look at the exercises or homework papers, shake his head, and shove them under his desk. I didn't make a big deal about it. I handed him the same paper along with the new one on the next day. It took about five days for Gary to see he was getting nowhere. He wasn't getting rid of the papers and he wasn't getting me upset. I wanted Gary and the other children to know I was always in control of the classroom. When Gary threw a batch of papers on the floor, I saw an opportunity to set things straight.

"I know children are always testing their limits," I said, "because when I was a child, I was always testing mine, always trying to see what I could get away with. There isn't a trick you can pull on me that I don't know. I probably did it myself when I was your age because I was full of mischief and always getting ideas in my head. My mind was always clicking, but it wasn't always to my advantage."

Stretching the facts a bit, I told them how I dumped a bushel of plums down a neighbor's well. Hiding behind a berry hedge giggling, I watched as an old woman pulled up a bucket of purple water and ran screaming into the house crying Jesus had given her a sign. The children laughed uproariously, including Gary. I described how I would occasionally turn back my parents' living room clock so I could have an hour longer to play outdoors. And I told them how I hated to go to Sunday chapel when I was in college. To avoid going I would put my coat on over my nightclothes, march out the front door of the dormitory, and sneak back inside when the housemother wasn't looking.

"But one morning the housemother caught me and I had to sit through the entire chapel service on a hot Sunday morning with my overcoat buttoned up to my neck, hiding my nightclothes. You see, I wasn't so smart after all, was I? I was the same as all children, always testing adults, always testing my teachers. The teachers who didn't know what they were doing had a hard time with me. And when a teacher would let me get by, I did just that. I remember handing in the same paper ten times to the same teacher, who never knew the difference.

"In elementary school I used to keep steel marbles in the pocket of my dress, and when the teacher's back was turned, I would rattle them making all sorts of noise. I also kept half a dozen Mr. Goodbar candybars in my desk. I would take all the wrappers off the candy beforehand so they wouldn't make any noise, and when the teacher wasn't looking, I would pass out pieces of melted chocolate to the other children.

"Now, I am not going to let you be so bored that you have time for that kind of foolishness. You will never turn in a paper that I do not read. You will never be asked to read something that I have not also read. So don't try to fake the characters or the story. No one will try to put anything over on anyone in here. That is not what we are here for. You are here only to learn, so you can make something of your lives."

I didn't expect my speech to have an instantaneous effect on Gary. I knew that for him to keep his pride intact, any initiative would have to appear to be strictly his own doing. To save face, he couldn't allow me to think that anything I said or did had changed his mind about school. The rest of that afternoon went much as usual. I handed him papers and he tossed them on the floor. I called on him to read and he sat there silently. I said, "That's your right, Gary."

It was the same the next day. But the day after, when I called on him to read, Gary decided to give it a try. He made it through the first few words. As soon as he had trouble, he flung the book across the room.

"You have to take stumbles before you can learn to walk," I told him. "It's all right to make mistakes. I make mistakes. I'm only a poor mortal and I don't have all the answers. I don't always understand things. I'm counting on you to help me with my mistakes and I'll help you with yours. However, I do not have all the money in the world to spend on books, and you have no right to destroy the ones we have. If you do not wish to use them, then someone else will, but you have no right to ruin them for others."

He picked up the book. When he settled down, I leaned over him, rubbed his arm, and pronounced the words aloud with him as he read.

As the weeks passed, Gary found it difficult to remain hostile. No matter how many times he shouted to me, "I hate you and I'm not going to do the damn work," I always answered, "I love you all the time, even when you behave like this." I guess it took the fun out of fighting. A fair fight was one thing; taking swipes at someone who wasn't fighting back was quite another. Gradually Gary began to do the work. He still had an attitude. And he didn't get along with the other children.

★ ★ ★

On October 16, 1975 Daniel Hale Williams Westside Preparatory School accepted its fifth student, Erika McCoy. In a way it was Erika who brought Gary into line—not because of anything she did but because of what she was. She was in awful shape. A chubby girl of not quite six years, Erika seemed intent on destroying herself, and everything else in sight.

The moment the other children saw her in the doorway, licking the mucus that was running from her nose, they broke into laughter. For Gary it was a moment of reckoning. A look at Erika gave him a quick shot of confidence. Until then he hadn't known how well off he was. If he wasn't a wiz like Cindy or even as good as Allen, he sure was ahead of this new girl. He got up from his desk at the back of the room, climbed into a seat next to Allen, and joined in the giggling and shaking of heads.

"You may know where you're going now, but that doesn't mean you forget where you came from." Marva gave the four students a hard look. Of course she understood their laughter—she was aghast herself—but she couldn't allow it. "Are some of you forgetting the problems you had?" She directed her look at Allen. "Did you like it when people in other schools laughed at you? We don't laugh at each other in here. We support each other and help each other. We are all part of the same family in this school. And people in a family help each other all the time."

As she walked into the room, Erika deliberately bumped

right into a wall. She had been dressed up prettily in a velveteen jumper, white knee socks, and patent leather Mary Jane shoes. Her mother had braided her hair with ribbons, but Erika looked completely disheveled. Her socks were hanging down around her ankles, and her feet were half out of her shoes as she broke their backs with her heels. One hair ribbon had been loosened. She was chewing on the other.

She staggered into the classroom, knocking desks and turning over chairs. She was behaving like a severely disturbed or retarded child. Clinically she was neither. Somehow she had been made to feel that she was supposed to act like that.

Erika McCoy had spent most of her nearly six years living with her grandmother in Mississippi. She had moved to Chicago over the summer to live with her mother. Ella McCoy did not know her daughter very well. As a public school teacher she thought she knew children, but she didn't have the slightest inkling of a problem when she enrolled Erika in the first grade at a nearby Lutheran school. She had chosen a parochial school because she had no faith in the Chicago school system.

Each afternoon when Mrs. McCoy picked up her daughter at the parochial school, she would faithfully ask the teacher how Erika was doing and whether there was anything she needed to help her daughter with at home. Each day, just as faithfully, the teacher told Mrs. McCoy, "No, everything is fine." Then came the phone call. The teacher was requesting a conference to discuss "Erika's problem."

Mrs. McCoy was beside herself. It was only three weeks into the semester. What could be wrong? She drove to the school that evening. The teacher said, "Erika cannot read and she will probably never learn to read. We are taking her out of first grade and putting her into a special class."

Mrs. McCoy didn't hear another word. Her daughter was only five and a half years old and already these people were writing her off. Dazed, Mrs. McCoy went home to work with Erika. Erika shook her head, "No, I can't do that. My teacher said I can't learn how to do that." No matter how much Mrs. McCoy tried to coax her daughter, bribing her with ice cream, candy, and a new toy, Erika would only repeat, "Oh no, Mommy, my teacher said I can't do that. I can't learn that."

Mrs. McCoy spent three sleepless nights worrying about her daughter. On Sunday evening she happened to watch a local television program on alternative schools. Part of the show dealt with the school Marva was running in a basement classroom at Daniel Hale Williams University. Mrs. McCoy looked up Marva's phone number and called. Marva told her to bring Erika to the school.

The following morning Marva settled Erika at a desk and told her, "Don't you worry about a thing. You are a very smart girl. You will soon be doing what everyone else in here does. Right now they have a little head start because they have been here longer. I will work with you and teach you. Soon you will be reading and adding and subtracting numbers, too."

The class began with arithmetic.

"What is arithmetic? It is a Greek word meaning what?" Marva asked.

"Skilled in numbers," came a chorus of four voices. Gary was joining in for the first time, and his participation certainly did not go unnoticed.

"My goodness, Gary, we've come a long way. You see how well you can do when you try?" Marva smiled and Gary too looked pleased with himself.

Marva wrote 2+3=5 on the board.

"Which number is the sum, children?"

"Five," they answered.

"And two and three are called what, Allen?"

"Addends," he said.

"Très bien." Marva printed *addends* on the board and placed the diacritical marks over the vowels. Phonics was incorporated into everything from math to science.

"An addend is a number that is added to another number. You must remember the words *sum* and *addend* because they are used on all the standardized tests. Those words trip up many students. If the question was 'Find the sum of the addends two and three,' what would your answer be?"

"Five," they responded.

"Very good." Marva handed out math worksheets.

The children were working at different levels in math.

Cindy was doing two-digit addition, learning to carry tens. Tracy was still having a difficult time with simple addition. Gary and Allen were both on multiplication. Marva moved from child to child, teaching each one individually.

Tracy was drawing sticks beside each problem, counting up the sticks to find the answer.

"You are not going to count sticks or blocks or circles or rabbits in here," Marva said, bending over Tracy's desk. "Look, sweetheart, six and seven cannot possibly make eight. Eight is only one more than seven. You want to add six to seven. Count out loud with me: eight, nine, ten, eleven, twelve, thirteen. Six and seven make thirteen."

Tracy began erasing her wrong answer.

"No, darling. Remember, we draw a circle around the error and put the correct answer above it. We proofread mistakes, we don't erase them. When you erase a mistake from the paper, you erase it from your mind, too, and you will make the same mistake over again."

Marva looked up and saw Erika had taken off her socks and was chewing on them instead of the hair ribbon.

"That's not how the brightest child in the world behaves," Marva said, taking the socks out of Erika's mouth. Handing her a pencil, Marva asked Erika if she could print her name at the top of the math paper. Erika shook her head and said she couldn't. "Don't say 'I can't,' " Marva told her. "Say, 'I'll try.' If you say, 'I'll try,' then we'll get it done together." Erika grabbed the paper, crumpled it into a ball, and threw it on the floor.

"I love you and I know you can do it," Marva said, taking out a fresh sheet.

"No!" Erika shouted, punching holes through the paper with her pencil.

At lunch Erika took the cap off her thermos and let the juice dribble all over her dress. She took apart her sandwich, licking the mayonnaise from the bread and getting it all over her face. The other children giggled and whispered among themselves.

"She's crazy," Gary said.

"I don't want to hear any name-calling," Marva told him. "God made us all special. If you don't like someone, then you write a letter to the Lord and say, 'Lord, you goofed on so-and-so.' "

Suddenly Erika looked straight at the group, a dab of mayonnaise smeared on the tip of her nose. "My teacher said I can't read."

"If you don't forget what that teacher told you, I'm going to get terribly angry," Marva shot back. Before her lay weeks of deprogramming, telling Erika over and over, "You are not a bad girl, you are not a stupid child." It wasn't going to be easy for either of them.

★ ★ ★

I estimated it would take Erika a month, about the same time it took most children to get started reading. Usually it took a month for the lessons on sounds to jell and for students to become comfortable expressing their thoughts in class. Erika was the most difficult child I had ever encountered. I couldn't seem to reach her. I had always been sure of my ability to move children, but my approach wasn't working with Erika. All the affection, the praise, and the encouragement seemed to hit deaf ears. By Christmas vacation, nearly two months after she had come to the school, Erika was no different than on the first day she arrived.

In the middle of a lesson she would get out of her seat, sit down on the floor, and scoot around the room on her behind. Often I had to hold her on my lap to keep her still while the other children read aloud. Erika rubbed against the board, covering her backside with chalk dust. If she wasn't stuffing socks into her mouth, then she was biting a pencil. She wrote all over her reader with crayola, and when I gave the children their first novel, *Little Women,* Erika chewed the edges of the pages. I told her to stop. She snapped, "I can if I want!" She tossed her head defiantly.

Mrs. McCoy told me her daughter was just as diabolical out of school. While riding in the car Erika would grab the steering wheel or throw a sweater over her mother's head. She would tear up people's houses wherever she went visiting. One time she replaced the assorted chocolates in a box of candy with rocks, to the dismay of an elderly neighbor woman. Mrs. McCoy had no control over her daughter and absolutely no idea how to handle her. Neither did I.

I wasn't upset with Erika but with myself for not being able to get through to her. Several evenings I burst into tears just thinking about that child. Clarence tried to console me, telling me to forget about it, but I couldn't forget. I was not going to let any child fall victim to a label of failure.

A few days after we returned from the Christmas holidays, Erika ran out of the classroom, up the stairs, and out of the building. I chased after her, grabbing her arms tightly. Holding her close, I said that was not the way to behave; children couldn't run out of school any time they wanted to. She pushed away from me and shouted, "I can do what I want! My mommy lets me. I say, 'Please, please,' and she lets me do what I want."

I realized then how blind I had been. I should have recognized the problem before. All the signs had been there, laid out before me in a pattern like the numbered drawings in a coloring book. I recalled that Mrs. McCoy had brought a pot of spaghetti for the whole class on Erika's second day in school. I recalled hearing that she took Erika to the movies or to an amusement park on weekday afternoons. No wonder endearments and praise hadn't worked. The child was used to hearing them all the time, indiscriminately, indulgently. In that moment I saw that Erika had been begging not only for attention but for discipline.

I took her by the hand, led her back inside the classroom, and sat her down at her desk. I distributed reading comprehension worksheets mimeographed from old editions of the California Achievement Tests. I frequently gave my students the old tests for practice, even at Delano. I didn't put much stock in standardized tests myself, but as long as so many other educators did, my students would probably have to take these tests at one time or another, when they transferred out of my school or went on to high school. Thus it was important for them to know how to take tests.

"I don't need any tests to show me how much you know. I see it every day by what you do in here. But we learn how to take tests because we live in a world that often judges us by how we perform on tests."

I was guiding the children through the first few examples when I heard paper tearing. Erika was ripping her sheet into long shreds.

"I saw a man yesterday giving a million dollars to anyone who could tear up paper. Employers pay a lot of money for someone to do that, don't they? You'll get the best job in the world knowing how to tear paper, won't you?" The other children shook their heads no. I took away the paper and gave Erika a new one. "I want you to circle the synonyms on this paper, right now."

"I won't!" she screamed.

I saw a lot of myself in Erika, the same strong will and determination. I had to show her that I was more determined than she. The four other children had forgotten about their own work and were watching. If I didn't do something fast, I was going to lose all of them. I whirled around, grabbing the first object that came to hand, an extension pipe from a vacuum cleaner left by the maintenance crew. Clutching the pipe in my hand, I stood over Erika and stared her dead in the eye.

"I'm going to kill you today if you don't finish your paper," I shouted. No sooner were the words out of my mouth than I was stunned at having spoken them. Still dazed by my rage, I heard one of the children gasp. They were all listening with large-eyed disbelief. There was a loud throbbing deep in my own throat and my whole body was quivering.

I didn't know what had come over me. I could never hit a child. Never. I had never in my life threatened a child. I wondered whether this desperation was for Erika or for myself. I wished I could drop the pipe to the floor and go on with the lesson as if nothing had happened. But once I had begun this thing, I had to see it through. The big question was whether the child would call my bluff.

Holding back the quaver in my voice, I told her, "Everyone says you are crazy. I don't believe that. But if you don't finish that paper, then I'll know you're crazy. You might as well be dead if you are going to go through life the way you are."

Erika's eyes were riveted on the paper. Her hands were planted firmly on it, palms flat and fingers pressed together. Her right hand jerked slightly, tipping the pencil off the desk. She leaned over, picked it up, and held it pinched between her thumb and forefinger. She hastily circled the word *throw* as a synonym for *pitch*. Moving on to the second question, she matched *silly* with *foolish*.

I wanted to laugh. Erika had been listening all along! All the time she had been acting up, all the time she had been tearing her papers and chewing her books, seeming not to pay attention, she had been listening and learning. I stood there until she finished the page. After the last question, Erika tilted her round face upward. "Am I in first grade or was I put back?"

I gaped at her. She understood perfectly about the label that had been put on her. I said that of course she was in first grade. "We don't ever go backwards in here. What is past is past. We only move forward."

Reassured, she handed me her paper, then pulled the ribbon from her pigtail and chewed on it. I decided to take care of one problem at a time.

Erika joined the other children in the reading group. Over the next few days she seemed to become a different child. Of course her change had really not come about suddenly. All those weeks Erika had probably been working things out in her own head, taking note of herself and the other students. And she had been sizing me up, testing my attitude, my trustworthiness, and my acceptance of her. It wasn't my threat that made her alter her behavior for the long run. What sustained the change in Erika was her own decision to settle down, a decision contingent on whether I came through for her. I did my best.

After a while Erika's seeming lack of interest was replaced by active curiosity, her lethargy turned into ambition, and her obstreperousness gave way to a measure of self-control. The potential had always been there. It exists in all children. The challenge for a teacher is to bring the potential out. There is no such thing as *the* way to reach a student. Any way is *the* way as long as it works for the individual child.

Some children, like Allen and Tracy, respond easily to affection and warmth. Others, like Gary, hide their fears and frustrations behind a wall of defensiveness; they have something to prove to themselves and everyone else. Erika seemed convinced that there was something wrong with her, that no one would accept her. Through her actions she issued a challenge: "Are you going to believe in me and accept me no matter what I do?"

I discovered that Erika was a pleaser. She did what people expected her to do; she became what they expected her to become. According to her mother, a previous teacher had told Erika that she was dumb, and that was exactly what Erika tried to be. She didn't try to prove her teacher wrong. I laid before her a different set of expectations. And Erika responded. Children rise to the level their teachers set, as numerous studies have shown.

Erika still had a thirst for attention, but she sought it now through precocity. Erika became a zealous student, sometimes overly zealous. Every time I asked a question, her hand would shoot up, waving frantically. "Me, Mrs. Collins, call on me, please!" When I had my students memorize a poem a week, Erika memorized three or four. She would turn in a paper and then ask to do it over again because it wasn't neat enough.

Once she began reading and saw what fun it was, there was no stopping her. She became addicted to books. If she wasn't reading one of the Judy Blume books or one from the Laura Ingalls Wilder series, then she was trying out *The Fables of La Fontaine* or *The Song of Roland.* One day, as I went around the class asking each child what new bit of knowledge he or she had learned that day, Erika said, "I'm like Socrates. The only thing I know is how much I don't know. I'm learning something new every day." As much as I praised her, though, I still had to keep after her.

Erika pulled up academically first. Socially she dragged behind. She didn't know how to talk to the other children, how to mingle, and her frantic enthusiasm put them off almost as much as her previous antics had done. It didn't matter to Erika. She knew I was determined to teach her and prove she wasn't stupid. For the time being, that was enough.

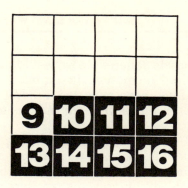

By January 1976, a little more than four months after the school started, the size of my class had almost tripled as a result of word of mouth and publicity from the television news feature and from an article in *The Chicago Defender,* a black-owned newspaper. Teaching became more complicated. I was running a one-room schoolhouse. In contrast to my teaching at Delano, where all the students had been in the same grade and around the same age, I now had boys and girls of all ages and abilities with an odd assortment of problems.

The new children were crammed together in the front half of the room. Theodore was the oldest, a beefy twelve year old who looked like the tackle on a football team. I had one year to build up his third grade reading level and get him ready to pass the high school entry exams. Next to him George Beecher slumped nonchalantly in his seat most of the time. A round-faced eleven year old, he walked with a waddle and could barely write his name. He could not add four plus one or read "bat" or "cat," even though his previous teachers at a Catholic school had promoted him to sixth grade with a report of "making fair progress." His five years in parochial school had been a waste. He gave the teachers no trouble and they left him alone. For five years he sat in the back of the room and listened to other students perform. I had seen that pattern before. Fat children, quiet children, dirty children, and children with unappealing or perhaps scarred features were hidden away in the back of a classroom and forgotten.

Frail six-year-old Janette Moore wouldn't talk. She sat and stared. No feeling. No emotion. Just a blank look. Her mother told me the child had been molested. I didn't talk about the incident with Janette. It took me four months to get her to smile when she was tickled.

Theodore, George, and Janette were representative of the thirteen new students. Not one was reading at the level appropriate for his or her age. Some had been labeled "unteachable" or "learning disabled" by previous teachers and psychologists and had been placed in or recommended for special learning programs. These children arrived at the school with satchels full of official memoranda documenting their behavior disorders and their emotional, psychological, or psychosocial problems. They were a band of misfits and discards, and nobody else seemed to want them. I needed students. I felt I could help them.

Most of their parents knew very little about me or the school. I don't think they were coming to me because of the curriculum or educational philosophy of the school. They came because we had an open door and empty desks. I was just one more alternative to be tried, probably not much different from the ones they had tried before or the ones they would have to try later, when I too gave up on their children.

Some of the parents came to me in a more desperate mood. For them our school was a last resort. Their children had been turned out of school, in some cases illegally, and they had nowhere else to go. I had the feeling that some of these parents were less concerned with what I could do for their children than with finding a place to dump their problems.

The first thing I did was toss aside all the reports and cumulative records. My experience had shown me that those reports were wrong more often than they were right. I had seen too many children with their personalities ink-blotted, their IQs probed, and their every move analyzed—children written off as losers.

One of the things I hated most about the public schools was how quickly teachers "blue-slipped" children for psychological referral. Every time they came across a child who was too hard to deal with, out came the blue slip, a convenient excuse. The private and parochial schools were just as quick to label a child. Erika McCoy was one example, one of many who came to our school. One mother told me her son's Catholic school principal recommended that the boy transfer to the Beacon School for emotionally disturbed and learning-disabled children. A teacher at Beacon told her, "Your son doesn't belong here. He is not emotionally disturbed. When a child misbehaves in the Catholic schools, they are quick to ascribe it to mental problems."

Too often teachers, school psychologists, and social workers have preconceived notions about children and pigeonhole them accordingly. Children with divorced parents run a high risk of being stereotyped, as do children from wealthy families, or those with working mothers, and black children living in neighborhoods like Garfield Park. Tell some people where these children live, and right away they assume that the children are abused or neglected, that they come to school hungry, have no clothes, and have never lived with a father. Some teachers assume that these children can never learn anything.

Over the years I've heard all the arguments from people in and out of education. What good is it to teach a ghetto child Shakespeare? Why bother teaching literature and philosophy? Just give them some vocational training, if they can handle that much.

We live in a label-conscious society where people are forever trying to categorize and classify each other. We tend to overuse terms like "learning disability," "developmental disabilities," "behavior disorder," and "hyperactive," bandying them about until they are stretched beyond validity. A child who fidgets in his seat isn't necessarily hyperactive. Maybe that child is bored. Maybe that child doesn't know how to do the work and is afraid to ask for help. Or maybe that child is just active. One boy's kindergarten teacher claimed he was hyperactive because he wouldn't put his head down during morning rest period. The child's mother, a pediatric nurse, argued that her son had twelve hours of sleep every night and simply wasn't tired during the day. Another teacher advised a mother not to feed her seven-year-old son sugar-coated breakfast cereal because the boy showed signs of hyperactivity. When the mother asked what the symptoms were—did her son have any trouble learning or was he a behavior problem?—the teacher replied no, the child was very bright but he had too much energy and she couldn't keep up with him.

Often a problem in the classroom lies not with the child but in the relationship between the child and the teacher. A teacher's assessment of a child is necessarily based on that teacher's life experience. That means certain children trigger a positive or negative reaction because of the teacher's past, a reaction having little to do with the children's abilities or personalities. For example, a child might remind a teacher of someone, perhaps a sibling or a classmate he or she didn't get along with.

Teachers are, after all, people, and there are times when they respond to situations not as teachers but as unhappy people. Occasionally a child gets stuck with a label because the teacher overreacts in frustration over behavior that might be nothing more than normal childish antics. Sometimes a teacher is just angry with a child and wants to retaliate. And all too frequently a teacher's personality, attitudes, and preferences color his or her response to a child.

A teacher can make or break a child, favor or stigmatize him. Just as there are teachers who are inspiring, who can spark interest and turn students on to learning, there are teachers who can turn a student off, not only to school but to himself. Not that it is done consciously. But a teacher has to be sensitive to all things at all times. Even such offhand remarks as "Your older brother was a brilliant student" or "You're the biggest one in class so you stand in the back row for the assembly program" can alienate a child.

I was aware of these issues as an educator and as a parent. Around the time my thirteen new students enrolled in the school, my son Patrick, who was ten, was having difficulty with one of the teachers at his new private school. For some reason Patrick's teacher didn't like him. She would display every child's paper but his. She kept him inside during recess taking tests, and she criticized him in front of the others, turning him into the class dummy. Eventually the other children supported the teacher's characterization, poking fun at Patty in the gym or in the lunchroom.

I knew Patrick could do the work. I sat with him at night as he read Chaucer's "Knight's Tale" aloud without any trouble. I couldn't understand why that teacher was riding the boy so hard. Clarence and I both wanted to pull Patty out of the school, but Patty kept insisting he didn't want to be a quitter and he didn't want to be pampered like a sissy. So I mistakenly gave in and let him stay, hoping the situation would ease itself and the teacher would have a change of heart. Meanwhile Patty began stuttering, and I'd have to say, "Take your time, baby, Mommy's here."

Several nights I got out of bed and found Patty sleeping fitfully, gnashing his teeth and mumbling, "Oh no, I can do it." I felt angry and guilty and desperate—the same feelings many of my students' parents had experienced. And like those other parents, I didn't know what to do. Since Patty was so determined to stick it out at that school, at least until the end of the year, how could I undercut his resolve? And if I did take him out, I didn't know where I would put him. Over the years I had pretty well exhausted the list of private schools in the city, and I thought the worst thing I could do would be to put him in school with me. He would surely feel like a defeated baby running back to his mother.

All I could do was comfort him and reassure him, trying to rebuild his shattered confidence each day. The whole family gave him all their love and encouragement and support. I hated Patty's teacher, more than I had ever hated anyone before. I wondered, if they are doing that to my child, how many others are suffering the same or worse?

For students the vast pool of teachers is like an educational lottery. A child is lucky to draw a good teacher and get off to a winning start, but there is no guarantee that another teacher the next year will keep the child on track.

My attitude toward teachers' evaluations—of my own children and those in my class—kept me from taking anybody else's word for what a child was or was not. I didn't have faith in aptitude tests either. Some children become confused and disoriented and can't perform when taking those tests. Patrick was one of them. Sometimes a child, worried about doing well and living up to a parent's expectations (set perhaps by an older brother or sister), freezes during a test.

And I didn't believe psychological tests were any more conclusive, especially since the results often depended on interpretation. For example, one of my students, a seven-year-old girl, had undergone a "mental status examination." Asked to draw a picture of her own choice, she drew a park scene—a yellow sun, two blue clouds, a green lawn, a big brown and green tree, and three flowers surrounding a figure of a child throwing something in a garbage can. According to the psychiatrist's evaluation, the "theme of the garbage can indicated perhaps preoccupation with being abandoned, thrown away." Yet another psychologist said the drawing could indicate a preoccupation with neatness and cleanliness. Who was the parent to believe?

Because of all the problems my son Patrick was having with his teacher, the school psychologist put him through a battery of tests, which included a human figure drawing. Because he had drawn the feet first, the psychologist concluded Patrick had a problem. However, I thought that was perfectly natural since Patty has big feet, his brother Eric has big feet, and I have big feet.

Knowing all the things that can contaminate an expert's judgment of a child, I refused to view any child as unteachable. I didn't know whether my new students had clinical dysfunctions. Maybe some did. But I was never going to teach them as though they did. I was not going to narrow my expectations. I was convinced that somehow, and in some way, I would be able to reach each child.

Like so many other children I had taught over the years, my thirteen new students all seemed to have the same feelings of worthlessness and insecurity. Whatever their individual problems, the one thing they all had in common was too much failure. I knew I would have to implant new success messages. I had to condition them to think positively, as I had done with all of my previous students.

There was one big difference with the entry of these new

children. Mine was not the only voice of encouragement; it was now backed by a chorus of support from my five original students. By now they were old hands at Emerson. They knew all the proverbs and quotations about believing in oneself. And they were rooting for the newcomers.

Before, I had been the only one saying "I won't let you fail." Now it was "We are not going to let you fail. We are going to be right there to help you along."

Turning to Cindy and Tracy and Erika and Gary and Allen, I asked, "There was a time in here when all of you did not what?"

"Did not know," they answered.

"And now you must do what? You must help whom?"

"Another child," they shouted.

Learning was to be a group effort. Everyone in the school was part of the team, and like any team, the school would only work if everyone pulled together. This was the first time I was dealing with so many different age groups and achievement levels. Without the all-for-one-and-one-for-all spirit, there was no way to get a twelve year old to feel good about sitting in the same room with children five, six, and seven years old.

More important, each child needed to feel loved and wanted. Each child needed the sense of belonging. Most were still suffering the stigma of being the outcasts and oddballs in their previous school. Our class had to be a support group, urging one another along and delighting in each other's small accomplishments, much the way a group of Weight Watchers rallies around a new dieter or an Alcoholics Anonymous meeting takes a new member under wing. I didn't want any of the children to feel that they were on their own. Therefore, I tried to turn the age discrepancies into an advantage, creating a climate where students would tutor and help one another.

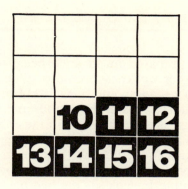

By the end of February 1976, one month after they had entered the school, all thirteen of the new students were reading. Some were reading better than others of course, but all of them had a hold on the roots of phonics. I thought I would die when I had to go back to the very beginning all over again and teach the new children that sounds make up words and words stand for thoughts. But I did it, as I would continue to do with each new child, starting right in with the drills, the chanting, and the sing-song recitation of the vowel and consonant sounds. I was tired of the routine, but I never let it show. A good teacher has to be a ham. I always tried to appear as fresh and energetic as if I were teaching the exercises for the first time.

"What I do here is no miracle," I would tell my students. "It's simply hard work. My feet are killing me. My throat hurts from talking, and when you are asleep at night, I am up preparing your lessons."

Each child at the school got the work he or she needed. That was the only way I could effectively teach such an assortment of students. I would say, "We don't all wear the same size shoe, do we? When we go to the doctor, we don't all get the same kind of medicine, do we?" If a child was having difficulty with homonyms such as *to* and *too,* the appropriate worksheet would be on the desk the next morning. If a child was having difficulty adding dollars and cents or working out story problems, there were other worksheets. None of the individualized lessons could be prepared in advance because I never knew what specific need or weakness would surface each day.

The children's reading ability evolved from the embryo of phonics. Once children master the sounds and learn how to syllabicate, they progress rapidly. A first grade child who is taught intensive phonics can read four-syllable words within four to five months. Studies show that with phonics a first-grader can have a reading vocabulary of 24,000 words by the end of the year. A child learning the look-say method has a reading vocabulary of 1,500 words at the end of the fourth grade. The look-say vocabulary does not include such common words as *boil, brain, copy, pain, pity, pray, pride, puff, root, spare, stir, sum, tax, thirty, twelve, vote.* With phonics a first-grader can read those words after a few weeks.

Phonics enables a child to decipher words and so allows better reading comprehension. When a child understands the relationship between a series of spoken sounds and the printed word, the child will read for meaning. Comprehension is hampered with the look-say method because a child has to guess at words. Busy trying to identify each word from memory, the child can't concentrate on what a sentence means. With look-say there is a tendency to displace words and meanings. A child who has to rely on memory and context clues to recognize whole words is prone to misread words and make word substitutions. A study of misreading errors made by high school students—including students who had passed college entrance aptitude tests—showed that instead of reading *Solomon,* the students read *salami.* They misread *delicacy* as *delinquency, hurricane* as *hammer, groceryman* as *clergyman, inert* as *inherent,* and *imbecility* as *implicitly.* In total the study recorded approximately 100,000 similar misreading errors made by students ranging from first grade to college.

As soon as my students learned the sounds of words, they also learned homonyms, synonyms, antonyms, and spelling. The moment they were introduced to a vowel sound, the children put it to work, using the spellings for that vowel to form words. For example, using the spellings for the *a* and *e* sounds, they completed such words as .... t (a number),

_ _ t (we do this with food), h _ _ (we feed this to horses), f _ _ t (we walk on these), th _ _ (a plural pronoun), pl _ _ n (not fancy), and str _ _ _ _ t (a line that is not crooked).

Later the children progressed to transcribing words from the phonetic spelling. What might have looked like a foreign language to some students was perfectly clear to my brood. They knew that ə-noi is annoy, ə-myōōz is amuse, kāk is cake, frīt is fright, frē-kwənt is frequent, i-rā-sər is eraser, myōō-zik is music, and ik-splō-zhən is explosion. I kept their reading and writing skills working in tandem. My students were never going to think by the mile and write by the inch.

Critics of the phonics method claim it can't teach children to read well because there are too many irregular sounds and spellings in the English language. The German schwa sound, for instance, has some thirty different spellings, including: _a_ in _tidal, e_ in _sicken, i_ in _charity, o_ in _come, u_ in _typhus, ion_ in _vacation, le_ in _sickle, m_ in _prism._

I dealt with the irregularities by spotlighting representative words. When I taught a sound, I brought in all the spelling patterns for that sound. To teach the sound of _z_, I used words like _music, zebra, has,_ and _treasure._ The three _f_ spellings, as in _fight, phone,_ and _cough,_ were taught together. _Ck_ and _ch_ words were taught together when they both made the hard _k_ sound as in _tack_ and _ache._ Words like _sugar, tuition, permission, special,_ and _ocean_ were taught along with _sh_ words like _ship, shall,_ and _shelf_ and words having the French _ch_ sound, as in _challis_ and _charlatan._ The soft _ch_ sound, as in chime or cheese was taught separately.

In order for the children to practice distinguishing the sounds, I composed chanteys that they recited aloud in cadence, clapping twice at the end of each refrain:

Change and chord, change and chord
Change says _chuh_ and chord says _ck._

Chin and chagrin, chin and chagrin.
Chin says _chuh_ and chagrin says _sh._

Go and edge, go and edge
The vowel signal *e* changes *g* to *j*.
Beg and beige, gap and revenge.

Cap and rice, or can and nice
The vowel signal *e* changes *c* to *s*.

Sweater and pleasure, sweater and pleasure
The vowel *ea* now says *eh*.

Sit and site, sit and site
The vowel signal *e* hits the vowel before it
and makes it say its name, and makes it say its name.

Bread and knead, bread and knead
Bread says *eh* and knead says *e*.

Accumulate and quotient, accumulate and quotient
Accumulate says *q* and quotient says *kw*.

There are 180 rules for consonant and vowel sounds. We were constantly repeating drills and reviewing phonics. And we continued over the years, even when the children had progressed to reading things like *The Brothers Karamazov*. The phonics review allowed their spelling to keep pace with their reading.

I started off Theodore and George, my oldest students, in the sixth grade reader. The only way to motivate children is to make them stretch. Both these boys belonged in the third or fourth grade books, but there would have been no incentive for them to learn if they felt they were doing the same work as the younger children.

Cindy, Erika, Allen, and Gary pushed on to the third grade book by the middle of the year. So did Tracy. I had worked with her alone, tutoring her before and after school until I brought her up to where Cindy was. In class I continued to guard her reading, stopping her after a few sentences so she wouldn't make a mistake. Months went by with Tracy experiencing these small, controlled spurts of success. One day when I cut short her turn, she looked up at me doe-eyed and asked, "Please, Mrs. Collins, can I try more? Can I read one more sentence?" I was thrilled. She wasn't merely trying to please me. She had finally reached the point where she felt competent. Of course I let her

go on reading aloud. When she came to the end of the paragraph, the rest of the class, led by Cindy and Allen, burst into
applause. The support of her classmates sealed Tracy's confidence. From that day on she was out of her shell.

Meanwhile Janette and some of the other newcomers were
working with the second grade book. As soon as they were able
to read the material, I skipped them on to the more advanced
reader. As a motivating technique I always told the children the
grade level of the book they were reading. If they were reading
well, I'd say they were not going to finish the book they were on,
they were going to move ahead to the third, fourth, or fifth
grade book. Little children always want to be like the big children. The incentive for the older children was to read at or
above their grade level so they could be role models for their
younger classmates to look up to. Somehow there was no competitive atmosphere.

By loving and touching and talking to each child, I tried to
create an atmosphere of mutual caring. The children cheered
one another when they recited or read aloud, and occasionally
they even applauded me. And when a younger child moved up
to a higher level, the older students offered congratulations.
They were proud of their classmate's accomplishment. Allen,
for example, proved to be such an excellent reader that by May
I felt he could handle the sixth grade reader. Theodore and
George took him under wing like big brothers.

We all shared in each other's success. No one laughed at
or called attention to another child's shortcomings. And anyone
who dared to try was immediately reminded of Coleridge's line
from *The Ancient Mariner:* "All things both great and small . . .
He made and loveth all." If a student tried to score points by
tattling on a classmate, I immediately said, "If God had meant
for you to see for me, he would have stuck our heads together."

★　★　★

Every two weeks the children had to report on a book they
read outside class. Marva was accumulating a stockpile of
books, some donated and some purchased at charity book fairs
or used bookstores. The inventory was a literary mulligan stew,

classical authors mixed in with writers of popular children's fiction. E. M. Forster, Somerset Maugham, and William Faulkner shared the shelves with Judy Blume, Roald Dahl, and Shel Silverstein.

On the second and fourth Fridays of the month Marva chose a book for each child, handing out copies of *The Jungle, Pride and Prejudice, O'Henry's Tales, Mysterious Island, Spring Is Here, Tales of a Fourth Grade Nothing, Lord of the Flies, 1984, The Fall of the House of Usher,* and *Great Expectations,* among others. Marva seemed to dispense the books arbitrarily. However, her policy was the older a child, the more difficult the book, even if the child's reading level was not quite high enough. Children used to failure needed goals if they were going to succeed. That was her rationale for giving Theodore, her twelve year old with the third grade reading ability, one of the thickest books on the shelf, *Moby Dick.*

"Hey, Mrs. Collins, I got the wrong book."

"No, sweetheart, I gave you the right book, *Moby Dick.*"

"But it's got so many pages and so many words on a page. It's got no pictures. This is a book for big kids."

"I think you're big enough."

"Naw, in the old school I always got easy books."

"Well, in this school we don't give young men like you easy books. We don't expect you to do the same work the little children do. Give this book a try. You don't have to understand everything in it, but see what you can do. It's made up of words and words are made up of what?"

"Sounds," Theodore grinned.

"That's right. And as long as you remember your sounds and know how to use a dictionary, you'll do fine."

At the end of the day Theodore left the school clasping the copy of *Moby Dick* so that everyone could see the title and the thickness. Marva wanted him to show it off. As far as she was concerned, all he had to do at the end of the two weeks was tell her the book was about a big fish. As it turned out, he told her Moby Dick was a big, white, man-eating whale.

It was through Operation Read, the forty-five minutes of free reading right after lunch, that Marva stimulated her students' interest in books, exposing them to a vast range of stories, topics, and authors. Each child read a chapter or two from a book or a short story or some poetry or a masterplot summary from *Digests of World Literature*. It was the only silent reading the children did in class. After the reading there was a period in which the children told about their individual reading.

They read and Marva read along, encouraging them to try new authors. She stocked her shelves with the very best stories possible, such as Ovid's *Metamorphoses* ("Don't get hung up on the long word; the book is nothing but the Greek myths all over again," she reassured the children), the *Satyricon,* Guy de Maupassant's stories, Greek drama, *Candide,* and *Crime and Punishment.* Marva knew the children would return to these books years later like lifelong friends.

After the quiet reading time, Marva would take the first turn at telling what she read. She would dramatize the stories, sometimes putting in things that weren't there to make the telling more vivid. Pacing across the front of the room, she explained how Raskolnikov carefully counted the number of steps from his house to the pawnbroker's apartment as he prepared for his crime.

"*Crime and Punishment* is a psychological novel," she said. "*Psychology,* which is the study of why people think and behave the way they do, comes from the Greek word *psyche,* meaning the human soul or mind. Now this is a story of guilt. No one knows for sure that Raskolnikov murdered the old woman and her sister, but he thinks they know, so he gives himself away. If you do something wrong, your guilty conscience makes you think everybody knows about it. Raskolnikov is poor and unhappy, and he doesn't have many friends. Children, is that a good excuse for getting bad thoughts in his head and committing murder?"

Another time she dramatized the sufferings of Candide, telling how he was expelled from the Baron's castle, captured and tortured by the Bulgarians, shipwrecked, caught in an earthquake, and flogged—all within the first few chapters. She told her students about *The Happy Prince* by Oscar Wilde, pointing up the lesson that a generous heart is rewarded. By way of contrast, she outlined the gloomier view taken in *Lord of the Flies.*

"You see what happens when you don't care about your

fellow man. All children like to be free of restrictions. You all think it would be ideal not to have adults around to tell you what to do. But we need restrictions; we all need order and discipline. Without them we would all be destroyed. Society would be chaos."

When Marva finished summarizing what she had read, some child would invariably say, "Oh, can I read that next?" And then a classmate would ask, "Can I have it after you?"

Her synopses were not confined to literature. Sometimes she told the children the stories behind operas such as *La Bohème* or *The Marriage of Figaro* or narrated ballets such as *Giselle, The Nutcracker,* and *Petrouchka.* The making of educated young men and women, she believed, required exposure to the full breadth of culture. How else would children from an inner-city ghetto learn about opera or ballet?

Then Marva went from child to child, asking what he or she had read that day. It was during one of these oral periods after Operation Read that George Beecher, the overweight and sullen eleven year old, finally opened up. George had been ignored for so long in his previous school that he found it hard to break the habit of not participating in discussions. Marva encouraged him but didn't push. When children were ready to come around, they would. She asked him what he had read, and suddenly he rose to the occasion.

"I read part of *The Pearl* by John Steinbeck," he mumbled. The children had to state the title and the author before they began explaining anything else.

"Speak up, darling," Marva told him. "Don't let someone else steal your thunder or you'll always be just a little raincloud."

"This guy Kino," he continued, "found the biggest and greatest pearl in the world. He was poor, and then he found the pearl and everyone wanted to be his friend. The doctor wouldn't take care of his sick baby before, but now he came to take care of it and be Kino's friend."

"Why wouldn't the doctor take care of the baby?" The question came from a classmate.

" 'Cause the doctor only wanted to take care of rich people," George said, pleased by the other student's interest and confident of his answer. "Rich people had money and the poor people only had fish to give him."

"Yeah, I know a lady who got sick and the doctor didn't want to take care of her 'cause she was on public aid," chimed in Theodore.

"Everyone's always pushing poor people around," said Allen.

"When you're poor, the landlord turns off the heat and he don't care if you freeze," added Gary.

"Let's not cry about what's wrong with this world," Marva told them. "Complaining isn't going to change things. Learn all you can so you will become the doctors, the lawyers, the politicians, and the thinkers. Then you can change things yourself."

"Aw, politicians don't change things," said Cindy. "They have those picnics every year in the park and pass out free hotdogs, but they don't do a thing."

"Then you will have to be the ones to come back to neighborhoods like Garfield Park and rebuild them," answered Marva. "Now, George, go on with your story."

"Well, first everyone acted like they was Kino's friends, but it was fake 'cause they really wanted to get that pearl. And then someone went sneaking around Kino's house at night looking for the pearl and Kino had to fight him off and Kino's wife started to think the pearl was bad."

"Sweetheart, what do you think Steinbeck is telling us in this book?" Marva asked him.

"That people always want money and want to get the rich things someone else got."

"Very, very good. And what else is Steinbeck saying? He's showing us that having valuable things doesn't necessarily make us happy."

"Nope. When you got something good, it can turn out bad. It's like you always tell us, Mrs. Collins, life's not perfect."

George's philosophizing won him an ovation from his classmates. After that he became even more talkative in class, continually waving his hand to be called upon. He followed Marva around like a puppy, telling her about his latest book. One day he was shadowing her so closely that she jumped when he burst into a description of King Arthur and the Knights of the Round Table. Marva laughed and hugged him. Only months before, if that child had been sneaking up behind someone, it surely would not have been to discuss a book.

Some days there was no question that the children were learning. Other times I felt as though I wasn't really getting through to them. I invested all my energy and effort in trying to make my students special, trying to separate them from the others out on the street. Yet they seemed to backslide so easily.

Gary Love pouted and lapsed back into a defeatist attitude the minute something looked difficult. And Tracy Shanklin seemed to forget more than she remembered. She was trying to do the work, but it took me nearly four months to teach her how to subtract twenty-seven from thirty. Once in a while Allen came to class smelling so bad that no one wanted to sit next to him. Erika had come far with her academic skills, but she still lacked social presence. She still walked on the backs of her shoes, let her nose run, barked at the other children, and fought for the limelight in every discussion.

I had to keep reminding myself where these children had been; they had all taken giant steps forward. I could measure their progress in the small daily victories, as when Gary took homework papers home and returned them the next day or Tracy read aloud excitedly and enthusiastically. However, I needed more. Since I was running a one-room school without official accreditation (Illinois law did not require private schools to be registered or recognized by the state), I needed some traditional proof that my students were learning—in the form of test scores. If my experience at Delano had done anything, it had made me cynical enough to know that their achievement had to be documented in some way. Of course, what test could measure a change in their attitudes, their priorities, their philosophy about life?

Toward the end of May I led my students through practice runs of the Stanford-Binet and the Iowa Achievement Tests, just as older students study for college boards or the bar exam. I made sure my children knew how to follow directions. I reviewed the language used in test questions, words like *integer, inversion, transformation, obtuse angle,* and *acute angle.* And I went over the symbols for *greater than, less than, congruent, parallel, perpendicular, equal to, not equal to, equilateral,* and so on. I knew my children had the knowledge, and I wanted to make sure they would not be stumped by the phrasing of a test question.

When the day came for official testing, I administered the Stanford-Binet series. First I reassured the children that the tests were not going to show who was smarter than someone else. They were only a tool for me to use in determining which subjects needed more of our attention in class. When the results were tabulated, I was delighted.

I had not expected miracles, only solid improvement, and there was plenty of that. Even the children who had entered the school in January had increased their reading and math comprehension substantially in a matter of months. George Beecher, for example, who was at a third grade, fifth month (3.5) level when he arrived, jumped up to 4.2. Tracy and Erika showed even more dramatic gains. Neither had been able to read a word back in September. By the end of our first school year Tracy, at age seven, scored 3.7 and first-grader Erika tested at 4.2. The biggest surprise, however, was eight-year-old Allen, who tested at a seventh grade level.

It had been a wonderful year for the children. They had achieved in our one-room school as they could not have in schools with large budgets, resource centers, and all sorts of teaching aids and audio-visual equipment. The most important reason was that their attitude about school had changed.

On the last day of the school year I couldn't get the children out the door.

"What is this?" I laughed. "Don't you know that children are supposed to be excited about vacation? You're supposed to be happy about being out of school. Don't you know that?"

"No!" they sang out.

"What have I done to you? Lord, what have I created?" I teased, throwing my hands up in mock despair. "I love you all, but I need to get off my feet. And I've worked you so hard all year long, you deserve a rest, too. But remember, a rest from school is not a rest from what?"

"From learning," they chorused.

"And what are you going to do over the summer?"

"Read ten books."

"And I am going to read all twenty books on the list, because I won't know which ten you choose. At this school you can never what?"

"You can never fool Mrs. Collins," they roared.

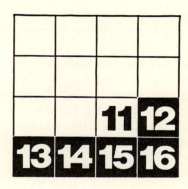

At the end of that year I decided to take the school out of Daniel Hale Williams University. I appreciated the free space they had given us to get the school going, but I wanted to be independent. The university was involved too much in politics, and I thought it best to separate the school from that environment. The group of women who had helped organize the school said that since I had been running the school, I had their permission to take it over as my own. They told me I could take the students with me, some books and supplies, and even the name of the school.

When I first told Clarence what I wanted to do, he didn't say that I was crazy or even that having my own school was a crazy idea. I spent nights talking to him, discussing the finances of operating a school, the physical space requirements, and above all my purpose. After a few weeks of considering the project, I launched into the paper shuffling. First off, I shortened the name to Westside Preparatory School. I had to incorporate as a not-for-profit organization to get tax-exempt status. Then Clarence and I began hunting for a location. We drove around Garfield Park checking for space in day-care centers and churches, but we found the same dead end wherever we looked. Either the rent was too high or people didn't want the kind of children my school would have. They had visions of rowdy disruptive children stealing and vandalizing.

By the middle of July I had exhausted all the possibilities. I decided to use what I had—the vacant upstairs apartment in my two-flat house. Clarence did all the work. He pulled out kitchen cabinets and plumbing, removed the sink, stove, and refrigerator, knocked down walls and rebuilt new ones, and installed new lighting fixtures. He hammered and sawed long into each night and all through the weekends. By the end of summer I had my school—a classroom fashioned out of a kitchen and the adjacent family room.

For seed money to get the school started, I had planned on using the $5,000 I had withdrawn from my pension upon leaving Delano. However, the construction materials and the attorney's fees for incorporating the school had eaten up most of the money. There wasn't enough left for desks and blackboards and teaching materials.

Still, if the odds were against me in starting a school, luck was in my favor. In late August I received a call from a friend telling me about a suburban school district that was getting rid of desks and blackboards. This friend, who owned a chain of hardware stores and served on his local school board, bought up some of the desks and blackboards as well as a duplicating machine, a record player, and a set of children's encyclopedias. He sent them to me in the store delivery trucks. With this windfall and the books I had accumulated the previous year, Westside Preparatory School was nearly ready.

Taking my household money, I bought fifteen more desks. Then I began a letter-writing campaign to neighborhood banks and businesses, telling them about the school and its objective: to help the children in Garfield Park make something of themselves. I asked for whatever support they could give—not money but office supplies, an old typewriter, or perhaps a water cooler. The response was poor. All I received were reams of scrap paper, much of it from the probate court of Cook County. I used all that paper and more in mimeographing math problems, reading lists, word definitions, phonics exercises, and short stories (in lieu of textbooks). Still, the absence of any substantial public backing was a disappointment. From then on, whatever I had to do I would do myself. The school was going to make it. I would see to that.

In September I had an enrollment of eighteen children. Tracy, Erika, George, and Theodore returned, as did most of my previous students. Naturally my daughter Cindy was also there. I had lost Allen. His father refused to send him to a school in someone's house. Janette had moved to another part of the city, and so had another of my girls, nine-year-old Patricia Washington. Her new house was beautiful, her school was big and sprawling, but, as she told me in a phone call, "They don't hug and touch in the school out here."

There were three new children to take their places. One was an eleven year old named Laura Brown who spelled every word with jumbled letters. Then I had a pre-schooler, four-year-old Calvin Graham. And the third new student was my son Patrick.

I had begun to feel that Patty needed someone to challenge him more, to light a fire under him. Recently he had been doing well enough in a "progressive" private school, but I was convinced he could realize more of his potential in an environment where the educational aims were more clearly defined. Not every child benefits from a "progressive" education; some children need more direction and prodding than others. A child who is a self-starter, already ambitious and motivated, may do well in a situation where students have the freedom to set their own goals. For the child who isn't as well motivated, that freedom may result in goals that are set too low.

Over the years, I have come to believe that some of the problems plaguing modern education are the result of the emphasis placed on "progressive" teaching methods. In an effort to follow John Dewey's notion of a student-centered rather than subject-centered approach to learning, schools have too often sacrificed subject matter, being more concerned with how they taught rather than what they taught. During the late 1960s and the 1970s, when our society was becoming fascinated with pop psychology, many young men and women entered the teaching profession thinking "As long as I can relate to a child, what difference does it make if he or she can't spell *cat*?"

Dewey's philosophy has been misconstrued, misapplied, and frequently seized upon as a convenient rationale for not teaching fundamental material. When parents and school boards have challenged the subject competency of teachers and accused schools of not teaching basic skills, administrators and teaching theorists have rushed to the defense, claiming that "humanistic" education is more important than knowledge.

The problem is that some schools cannot strike a balance between "progressive" and "traditional" teaching methods. People wrongly assume that it has to be one or the other. If you teach the basics in a classical curriculum, you can still pay attention to a child's feelings and attitudes. Moreover, it is a mistake to assume that in order to stimulate creativity and critical thinking you must rule out any learning by rote. Memorization is the only way to teach such things as phonics, grammar, spelling, and multiplication tables.

There is a tendency in education to reject arbitrarily a method of teaching simply because it's old-fashioned. The fact is a teacher can combine both progressive and traditional approaches to learning, each enhancing the other. There is no reason why a teacher can't be sensitive to a child's needs and at the same time teach the child subject matter and skills. That blend has always been the basis of Westside Preparatory School.

School was scheduled to begin at nine o'clock. That held true only on the first day. By the second day, and always after that, school started as soon as the first child arrived, as early as 7:30. The first child would come into the kitchen with my family, and I would begin a review of whatever subject he or she was weak in. While I cleared off the table, combed my hair, and put on lipstick, the child would linger for a few minutes, sipping a glass of juice or eating leftover bacon or flapjacks. As I was finishing my morning household routine, we would begin the drills on math, questions about the readings, or working out the sounds of letters. Which *a* in cake? Which *o* in boat? Which *i* in light? I fired off the questions as I darted from the kitchen to the bathroom to the bedroom. And between bites of breakfast the child responded. Then we would move upstairs and write words on the board, putting in the diacritical markings, of course. I would look over the homework papers so that I could see whether the child was ready to move ahead to something new.

I gave homework every day, though never in massive doses. A child should not have to do thirty math problems overnight. Five or ten problems are enough to see if a child knows what he is doing. I didn't give homework as busy work, but to reinforce a lesson. And I never gave homework until I was certain that the child could do it successfully. I didn't want parents to have to help. Homework was for the benefit of the child, not the parents.

When I saw a child ready to leave at the end of the day without his or her papers, my standard comment was: "Unless you are a genius or your daddy is a millionaire, you cannot afford to leave your books here and not do your homework."

I never punished or reprimanded a child for not turning in homework. I simply reminded all my students that they would not receive their report cards (written evaluations instead of grades) if they did not turn in their daily homework. It was one more way of teaching them about what would be expected of them in the adult world, where rewards are based on performance.

"If you don't do your job, your employer will not give you a paycheck," I reminded them. "No one is going to pay you for something you don't do. Remember what Kahlil Gibran said: 'If this is your day of harvest, in which fields have you sown your seeds?' For now, going to school is your job, and doing homework is one of the responsibilities of that job. I don't want to hear 'The dog ate my paper' or 'My baby brother tore up my report.' We can't go through life giving excuses for what we don't do."

★   ★   ★

At Westside Preparatory School there was nowhere to escape learning. Even the bathrooms had phonics charts tacked on the walls. Marva's classroom was organized and efficient, yet it had the friendly comfortable clutter of a house. Thirty desks were squeezed into the cramped space. Paperbacks and worn hardcover classics were piled in teetering stacks on the floor and on the shelves of an old bookcase.

As in any one-room schoolhouse, different activities were going on all at once. During mathematics some children might be doing addition and subtraction, others multiplication, others long division, while still others might be learning to reduce fractions. Marva walked the aisles, reading over the children's shoulders as they worked. She didn't wait for them to ask for help. She made herself always accessible, for she knew that children are usually hesitant to walk the long mile to the front of the classroom and announce that they do not understand. Often the confused child stayed in his seat and forgot about solving problems until he fell so far behind that he gave up completely.

"Six times five can't be eleven," Marva said, spotting an error on one of the girls' papers. "Sweetheart, remember you are adding six *five* times. We're going to cheat you out of all your money if you can't multiply."

She glanced up and saw another girl chewing gum.

"Get the gum out of your mouth, sweetheart," she said firmly. Then lovingly, "Put it in the garbage and not in your pretty hands."

On her way to Laura Brown's desk she stooped to pick up some papers scattered on the floor beside George. She handed them to him. "I think we're just going to have to get you a secretary," she teased, "because you can't seem to keep your things in order." Mussing his hair, she moved to Laura, the girl who scrambled her letters like alphabet soup and made backward twos, fours, and nines.

"Peach, didn't anyone ever tell you not to go over the margin of the paper? You begin to the right of the red line, like this." She picked up the girl's pencil and printed Laura's name on the page. "See, we print our letters and numbers neatly on the paper. We don't make scratch marks all over it going every which way."

Looking up, she saw Calvin sitting with his index finger in his mouth. "Sweetheart, take your finger out of your mouth. You're a big boy now."

As she turned back to Laura, there was a loud scraping noise. Gary had scooted forward in his desk. "You did a good job of pushing that desk," she told him. "Mommy told you to get up this morning and go to school so you could push a desk, didn't she? You get good jobs pushing desks, don't you?"

Nothing escaped her. She was aware of all things at all times, and without losing her focus, she could address every one of them. She could tell a girl to stop combing her hair, tell a boy to tuck in his shirt, or another to blow his nose, without once losing the attention or concentration of the particular child she was working with. Marva just squeezed Laura's shoulder to remind her that the teacher was still there for her.

Reading lessons were in groups. While Marva worked with one group, pointing out words to watch and giving background on a story, the other students busied themselves with comprehension exercises, theme writing, researching an author or topic in the encyclopedia, composing sentences, and doing analogies ("Photograph is to caricature as fact is to exaggeration").

One morning during reading Gary announced, "I'm finished." He slammed his book shut on his paper, a letter to Robinson Crusoe offering encouragement and survival tips. He stood beside his desk with his hands in his pockets, looking as though he was about to take off for a leisurely stroll around the classroom.

Marva had been working with Theodore, tutoring him from a high school literature book so that he would be ready for the high school placement exam. She shot Gary a disapproving glare.

"Don't give me that 'I'm finished' business," she said. "We are never finished in life. We don't ever stand around idly or sit with our hands folded, acquiescing. God isn't finished with you and I'm not either."

"Okay, okay, don't have a coronary," Gary said, sitting down and holding up his palms in surrender.

Marva laughed. "I love your spunk. Don't ever let anyone break your will. Since you are finished, why don't you read us your theme?"

Gary withdrew the paper from his book and began to read aloud: "Dear Mr. Crusoe, You will feel better if you have courage, strength, and patience. You need tenacity."

"Tenacity!" Marva exclaimed. "Gary, that is terrific. Since you have done such a wonderful job of helping Mr. Crusoe, why don't you take one of the younger children out on the stairs and help him with his sounds. You help him the way I helped you."

The buddy system was an integral part of life at Westside Prep. It helped the new children feel more comfortable and adjust faster, and it offered the seasoned students a review of the material and developed their sense of responsibility. The buddy system was invaluable for Gary, who tended to become wrapped up in himself, and especially beneficial for Erika, who still didn't get along well with the other children.

The first time Marva solicited her help, Erika was leaning against the wall, rubbing her head up and down against it, and chewing on a pencil.

"We eat our food, not our pencils," Marva told her. Erika removed the pencil from her mouth but continued to rub her head against the wall. Marva handed her a copy of *Professor Phonics Gives Sound Advice* and asked her to go over the word lists with Calvin.

"Huh?" Erika wiped her nose on her sleeve.

"If you have a question, say 'What, Mrs. Collins?' And don't wipe your nose on your dress. Take a tissue. Do you see me wiping my nose on my dress? Do what you see me do. Now, I want you to help Calvin the same way I helped you. We have to pass on what we learn in here. We are all responsible for one another."

Erika shook her head. "I can't."

"By now you know we don't ever say 'I can't' in here. A year ago you said you couldn't read and now look at you. You are so bright and you learn so fast. I need you to help me with a new student."

Thinking it over for a moment, Erika led the boy to the stairs and did a perfect imitation of Marva as she coached Calvin through the long and short vowel sounds. Her voice was too loud but there was a reassuring, patient quality to it. Marva overheard her telling Calvin, "You can do it."

Ultimately, tutoring the other students drew Erika out. When Marva added more pre-schoolers to the class roster, Erika teamed up with Cindy and taught them beginning sounds, read them fairy tales, and pointed out the moral in such verses as:

There once was a boy named Pierre

Who would only say "I don't care."

His mother said, "Stop pouring syrup on your hair."

Pierre said, "I don't care."

In her desire to emulate Marva, Erika proved to be a natural teacher herself. And being responsible for other students seemed to make her more responsible for herself. She slowly became more fastidious about her appearance. Perhaps she reasoned that as a teacher she had to set an example, as Mrs. Collins did.

Four years after she arrived at Westside Preparatory School as a defeated, backward, asocial child, Erika McCoy wrote:

> If Fredrick Douglass can, so can I. If Fredrick Douglass could learn when learning seemed almost impossible for a black man, so can I. If Fredrick Douglass could free our people from the bondage of slavery, surely I can free my people from the bondage of ignorance. If Fredrick Douglass could conquer the impossible, surely I can conquer ignorance. If Fredrick Douglass could deliver speeches to thousands of people, surely I can deliver a speech to the few. If Fredrick Douglass could scale the high walk of success, surely I can too.

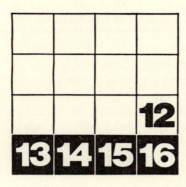

Throughout the year, as in every year of my teaching, my main goal was to motivate the students to make something worthwhile of their lives. Everything we said or did in class was directed toward that aim. More than anything I wanted to supplant apathy and defeatism with positive expectations. I didn't want my children to feel stigmatized by where they lived. I didn't want them to succumb to a ghetto mentality. If I had my way, they would dream and hope and strive and *obtain* success.

I was forever compiling lists of positive, motivating slogans:

> You are unique—there is no one else like you
> The world moves aside to let you pass only if you know where you are going
> Character is what you know you are and not what others think you are
> You know you better than anyone else in this world
> People's ideas actually tell you how they feel about themselves

And I was constantly reminding the children that some of the greatest people in history—Socrates, Milton, Galileo, Einstein, Edison, and Columbus—were ridiculed and told they would never amount to anything.

Every day I put a different quotation on the board:

> What I do concerns me, not what others think of me
> Hitch your wagon to a star (Emerson)

Vivere est cogitare (Cicero)
Speak the speech trippingly on the tongue (*Hamlet*)
Cowards die many times before their deaths; The valiant never taste of death but once (*Julius Caesar*)
The mass of men lead lives of quiet desperation (Thoreau)
He who eats my bread does my will

I felt it was as important to deal with attitudes as with any of the academic subjects. In fact it is probably more important. Without the right attitude, everything else is wasted.

I told the girls not to walk around with their socks falling down like a scrubwoman's or with their nail polish chipped. My eleven- and twelve-year-old girls were instructed not to wear plunging necklines or walk around looking like dimestore floozies. Everyone knew there would be no gum chewing, nail biting, unbuttoned shirts, loose shirt tails, jazzy walks, jive talk, or finger snapping.

I'd ask the children, "How are you going to run a corporation if you can't run yourself? Are you going to sit behind a conference table in an executive suite popping gum or sticking your fingers in your mouth? How are you going to keep your life in order if you can't keep your appearance or your desk or your notebook in order?"

My approach is to address a fault without ever attacking a child's character. Who they were was always separate and distinct from what they did. The gum chewing was displeasing, not the child. I might tell a child, "You are acting like a fool. Why? You are not a fool." With that difference clearly established, the children could open themselves to my comments and criticisms. A child could give up the behavior without giving up any dignity or self-worth. I tried to show the children that I wasn't sticking them with an arbitrary list of do's and don'ts. These were the rules of etiquette observed in the adult world.

"Do not ever mouth off to an adult," I warned. "I don't care how wrong the adult is, just say 'yes' or 'no.' I don't care what the rest of society is doing, I don't care how many people tell you not to take anything from anyone, I want you to know when to do and say the right thing.

"There is a time to talk and a time to shut up. A time to be proud and a time to be humble. When a policeman says stop, he means stop and not go. Black children get in more trouble because they mouth off. Why get beaten up or even killed because you didn't know when to keep your mouth shut? If I teach you Shakespeare and Cicero and Dostoevsky, what good is it going to do you if you don't live to tell it?"

I prepared my children for life. And I didn't mince any words in doing it. I didn't hesitate to discuss crime in the ghetto, drugs, prison, or teenage pregnancy. I told them welfare is just another form of slavery. I warned them not to hang out on street corners or places they didn't belong, because they could easily be picked up and arrested for something they didn't do. And I bluntly told them to face the fact that no one was going to hire them for a job if they walked into an office wearing picks in their hair, if they slinked into a room as though their hips were broken, or if the boys wore earrings or high-heeled shoes or wide-brimmed hats.

I think it's foolish and hypocritical that many people allow black youths to take on extreme styles and mannerisms under the guise of finding their black identity—without pointing out the social and economic consequences. I reminded my students that blacks don't go to work only for blacks. I encouraged them to become universal people, citizens of the world.

I did not teach black history as a subject apart from American history, emphasize black heroes over white, or preach black consciousness rather than a sense of the larger society. My refusal to do so was a sore spot between me and some members of the black community. As far as I was concerned, it was a waste of precious class time to teach a child that he or she was black.

I'd say to my students, "Is there anyone in here who doesn't know he's black?" And the children would shake their heads and laugh. Then I'd ask, "Is there any black child in here who plans on turning white?" Again there would be laughter. "In that case let's get on with the business of learning."

I'm opposed to teaching black English because it separates black children from the rest of society; it also implies they are too inferior to learn standard language usage. How many black youths are cut off from the job market because they do not have a command of the English language? I was convinced black English was another barrier confining my students to the ghetto, and I had no intention of letting them be confined. I cautioned my children, "When you don't know the language, people are always going to take advantage of you. It's like being a visitor in a foreign country."

Instead of teaching black pride I taught my children self-pride. All I wanted was for them to accept themselves. I pointed out that in many ways the ghetto is a state of mind. If you have a positive attitude about yourself, then no one can put you down for who you are or where you live.

The concept of self-determination goes hand in hand with self-discipline. The general rule in my class was that behavior contributing to the learning process or benefiting another child was acceptable. Anything that took away another child's right to learn was not. Talking in the classroom, for example, was not prohibited per se; my response depended on the nature of the conversation and when it was taking place. Certainly no one was free to interrupt me or anyone else who was speaking or reciting. If a child was talking about lunch or any other personal business, then the next child did not need to hear it. If the talk was about how to put together a car engine or about a character in a story, then it was helping me teach.

Fighting upset me more than anything else, and my students knew it. I told them that when they fought they didn't hurt each other, they hurt me. It meant I failed to teach them what values were important in life. I never took sides in a student scuffle, and I refused to hear who threw the first punch. Instead of listening to any feeble excuse about who did what to whom, I had the two culprits embrace and say "I love you" to one another. It was a fairly good peace-keeping technique—most of the time.

One morning in the beginning of November eleven-year-old Sonya walked into the classroom with fresh scratches across her face. She looked like a cat had attacked her.

"What happened?" I asked, putting cocoa butter on the wounds.

"Lynette did it," Sonya mumbled. "She did it on the bus."

"On the bus? You mean the two of you were fighting on the city bus?"

Sonya nodded.

"Didn't the passengers stop you? What did the bus driver do?"

"Nothing."

I was furious. The moment Lynette sauntered into the room, I called both girls over to me. "Wherever you girls go, you represent me," I told them. "Imagine, someone on the bus could have said, 'Those girls go to Westside Preparatory School.' I bet no one on that bus knew you girls read Shakespeare or Socrates or Emerson. All they saw were two wild cats clawing at each other in public. So all I have done, all that I have taught you has been for nothing."

"I didn't start it. She did," Lynette insisted.

"I don't want to hear that," I said. "I don't care who started it or who finished it. How much are you worth to yourself? Are you willing to destroy yourself to get back at someone? Do you have to prove to the crowd that you take nothing from no one? Do you have to prove you're tough? Don't throw away your life."

I was angry and the girls knew it. I made them apologize. They did it begrudgingly and quickly went to their seats. The scratching incident disturbed me because it was different from the usual sort of classroom skirmishes, where one child mischievously shoves another or sticks a foot in the aisle to trip a classmate. Theirs was a real fight, presenting something more hateful, more violent. I couldn't let the matter drop.

"Children," I said to the entire class, "when you're willing to destroy one another, how can you complain about society being racist? Until you learn to help and love each other, don't talk about what other people are doing to you.

"I don't believe in saying 'Oh, he's just a child' or 'She's just a child.' The way you act as children will determine what kind of adults you become. School is a miniature society where we learn and practice to become useful adults. You must use your time wisely. We can't begin to make something of our lives when we are filled with hate. It's not an easy thing, but you've got to learn to walk away from your enemies. If you don't, they will drag you down."

The children were all listening silently. I didn't think I was getting through to them. Suddenly I felt ineffectual.

I was shaken once again by the fear that I had made no real change in the lives of my students. Of course they were memorizing poetry and quoting the classics. Was it all mimicry? What I so desperately wanted to give them was the substance, not the trappings, of an education. The fighting episode was a painful indication that I might not have succeeded. It nagged at me all day. By evening it provoked me to compose a "school creed":

> Society will draw a circle that shuts me out, but my superior thoughts will draw me in. I was born to win if I do not spend too much time trying to fail. I will ignore the tags and names given me by society since only I know what I have the ability to become.

> Failure is just as easy to combat as success is to obtain. Education is painful and not gained by playing games. Yet it is my privilege to destroy myself if that is what I choose to do. I have the right to fail, but I do not have the right to take other people with me. God made me the captain of only one life—my own.

> It is my right to care nothing about myself, but I must be willing to accept the consequences for that failure, and I must never think that those who have chosen to work, while I played, rested, and slept, will share their bounties with me.

> My success and my education can be companions that no misfortune can depress, no crime can destroy, and no enemy can alienate. Without education, man is a slave, a savage wandering from here to there believing whatever he is told.

> Time and chance come to us all. I can be either hesitant or courageous. I can swiftly stand up and shout:

"This is my time and my place. I will accept the challenge."

I had said all this before in many different ways. These maxims were the cornerstone of my teaching. Now they were solidified into something whole. The next morning I told the children they would recite the creed every day until they knew it by heart.

"My hope," I explained, "is not that you will *look* literate but that you will *be* literate. Remember the story of the emperor's new clothes? I don't want to turn you into a bunch of emperors running around without any clothes. I don't want you to pretend you are educated. I want you to act and *think* like educated people all the time."

Then I reminded the children of the lessons in Tolstoy's tale "The Three Questions."

"Who is the most important person?" I asked.

"I am," the children shouted.

"What is the most important thing?"

"To do good."

"And what is the most important time?"

"Now!"

A few months were sufficient to dispel all my romantic visions about starting up a school of my own. It was one thing to teach, another to be also principal, secretary, janitor, and pencil sharpener. The roughest part was keeping the school afloat financially. Though the school was in my house, the income from tuition was barely enough to cover the operating expenses. Only half my students were paying the full $70 per month tuition. Some paid what they could afford; others didn't pay anything at all. When the money came in, it was in dribs and drabs. Meanwhile there were monthly bills for utilities, insurance, and supplies.

Clarence gave me his full support. He never spoke a word of resentment about the eighteen hours a day I frequently put into my teaching. Only when he judged my enthusiasm had gone too far afield would he ask, "Whose children are you talking about? The ones in the school or our own?" It was his way of reminding me there was more to life than school.

Without him there would have been no Westside Preparatory School. He was the strong silent partner. I had one kind of strength, Clarence had another. When the bills added up and our money ran out, he rolled up his sleeves and took on part-time carpentry and construction jobs.

I found weekend work typing medical reports, as I had done before, but the financial pressures didn't ease. Besides the school costs, Clarence and I were having a difficult time managing our household budget. For the past year I had been receiving a small salary as a curriculum developer for the Alternative Schools Network, but it was $10,000 less than what I had earned at Delano.

On top of the monetary problems, I had to contend with a relentless parade of city inspectors knocking at the door with their building and fire codes. Despite the fact that Clarence had complied with the city's specifications when building the one-room school, the inspectors continued to badger me. I couldn't understand why they seemed so intent on making Westside Prep into the model for building standards when there were schools in the Chicago system that were downright hazardous. Several public schools long slated for demolition or structural renovation were still making do with falling ceiling plaster and rickety fourth-floor staircases. In some schools students were meeting in makeshift basement classrooms with exposed steam pipes sweating overhead.

I telephoned City Hall and complained. I said I wanted to be allowed to teach. I preferred to do it peacefully in my own school, but if I had to I'd teach on the steps of City Hall. I explained that my students were not costing the taxpayers any money; by educating these children I was in fact keeping them off welfare rolls in the future.

For months the inspections continued and so did my complaints. Eventually the inspectors stopped hounding the school. Maybe they had just tired of *my* persistence.

Between the bills and the city bureaucracy, each day was a contest for survival. I had to do whatever I could to keep the school going. I knew the school would work only if I made it work. And the children worked because I did.

My goal is to have my students know a little about everything. "The knowledge you put in your heads is like money in the bank," I told them. "You may not need it today, but it is there to use when you need it. You may not always remember everything you are reading and learning, but you are storing it in your minds for the future. Someday when someone mentions Dostoyevsky, you won't have to stand there looking surprised and thinking it's the name of a Russian dance."

Once children learn how to learn, nothing is going to narrow their minds. The essence of teaching is to make learning contagious, to have one idea spark another. A discussion of *Little Women* included everything from a lesson on the Civil War to an explanation of the allegory in *The Pilgrim's Progress,* which the little women in Alcott's novel loved to act out. When the children studied Aristotle, they learned the principles of logical thinking. Plato's *Republic* led to de Tocqueville's *Democracy in America,* which led to a discussion of different political systems, which brought in Orwell's *Animal Farm,* which touched off a discussion of Machiavelli, which led to a look at Chicago's city council.

Through the riddle of the Sphinx, which appeared in the second grade reader, the children were also introduced to Sophocles' *Oedipus Rex,* the Greek theater, and other heroes and legends of ancient Greece. Mention of the Roman deity Jupiter, lord of heaven and prince of light, triggered a science lesson on the solar system, which brought in the ancient geographer and astronomer Ptolemy, then Copernicus, then Isaac Asimov, Carl Sagan, and the U.S. space program. Archimedes' discovery of water displacement and specific gravity tied in to Sir Isaac Newton's work with gravity and light, which in turn spurred an introduction to Einstein's theory of relativity. When I taught Voltaire's *Candide,* I pulled in Pope's "Essay on Man" and Leibnitz and the "optimistic" school of philosophy. If I was teaching Chaucer, I introduced Boccaccio, telling the children how Chaucer drew his "Clerk's Tale" from Boccaccio's "Patient Grisel."

In one of the most unlikely progressions of learning I began talking once about triangles and ended up with Hinduism. The children learned that Pythagoras figured out how to measure the side of a right triangle, that Pythagoras was a philosopher who believed the human soul was immortal, and that his idea of the transmigration of souls was part of the Hindu religion.

For every story the children read in their basal readers, I brought supplementary material. I also pointed out every allusion in a story, not ignoring a single footnote at the bottom of a page. I blitzed the children with facts, but I did not go into all subjects in detail. Mostly, I hit upon them in a generalized way. I wanted to get my students to see the flow of knowledge.

★ ★ ★

Each day there were frenzied classroom exchanges between Marva and the children as she tested their memories and pushed them to draw analogies.

"What drug takes its name from Morpheus, the god of dreams?"

"Morphine," the children called out in unison.

"From where do we get the words *geography* and *geology?*"

"The goddess Ge," they answered.

"Who was Ge?"

"Greek goddess of the earth."

"The word *choreography* comes from which of the nine muses?"

"Terpsichore."

"Sacred hymns are inspired by which muse?"

"Polyhymnia."

"Which breakfast food do we get from the grain goddess Ceres?"

"Cereal."

"What does *museum* mean?"

"Temple of the muses."

"And what is a muse?"

"A Greek goddess."

"How many muses were there?"

"Nine."

"What else does the word *muse* mean, Laura?"

"To think about something," she answered.

"Let's give her a hand," Marva said. And the class applauded. Then Marva went on. "Which of King Priam's sons has a name that means to bully?"

"Hector," the class responded.

"And who killed Hector?"

"Achilles."

"How did Achilles die?"

"Paris shot him with an arrow in the heel," Gary shouted, before anyone else could put together a complete sentence.

"And when we use the phrase 'Achilles' heel,' what do we mean, Tracy?"

"A weak spot," Tracy said.

"When we have a weak spot, we are what?"

"Vulnerable," replied Erika.

"Which one of Ovid's stories is similar to Shakespeare's *Romeo and Juliet?*"

"Pyramus and Thisbe," the children chorused.

"George, which Bible story is like the story of Orpheus and Eurydice?"

"The story of Lot and his wife," he answered.

Theodore shouted, "Hey, Mrs. Collins, that's cool. Everything links into something else, doesn't it?"

Marva beamed. "Now you've got it. Every scholar, every writer, every thinker learned from those who came before. You are all becoming so erudite, we are going to have to dub you MGM—"Mentally Gifted Minors.""

★　★　★

I read constantly in order to tie together fragments of information and interweave subjects. As a business major in college I had not taken many courses in the arts and sciences. My education was about the same as that of the average grammar school teacher, merely a sampling of some basic courses. I had to teach myself more. I read with an urgency so I could teach my students what they needed to know. I believe a teacher has to keep polishing his or her skills. You can't take the attitude "I know how to teach," and resist learning anything new.

I was always on the lookout for a new book to spark my children's interest. Teaching children to read was one thing; keeping them interested in reading was something else. I was forever reading up on new children's books in *The New York Times Book Review,* the local Sunday newspapers, and *The Library Journal.* I searched through *Masterplots* and *Children's Treasury for the Taking.* And I stalked bookstores and libraries on a regular basis.

I feel that to be a good elementary school teacher one needs to have a general knowledge about all fields of study. The best training a teacher can have is a solid liberal arts education. Instead of emphasizing methods courses, training institutions should require education majors to have a broad background in literature, science, art, music, and philosophy. The object of teaching is to impart as much knowledge as possible. Students can only give back what a teacher gives out.

Eventually my children began to recognize parallels and relationships on their own. Sometimes when they recited their compositions, they would summon forth a plethora of citations. Laura Brown, the girl who had written word salads when she first arrived at Westside Prep, wrote the following theme a year later:

> Pascal said, "A man without a thought is a stone or a brute. A man is a reed, but a thinking reed." Cicero was right—"Vivere est cogitare." To think is to live. Let us stand up and shout this is my time. We are fools to depend upon society to make us into what we refuse to mold ourselves into. Confused aliens are Hecate's delight.

A few days after we had read about Patrick Henry and our nation's founding fathers, one of my eight-year-old boys turned in the following book report on Maya Angelou's *I Know Why the Caged Bird Sings:*

> The caged bird sings because it wants to be free. It wants to sing like the other birds. It wants to swing on the limbs like the other birds. Give the caged bird freedom or give it death.

Drawing analogies and tossing off literary allusions became second nature to the children, appearing even in their jokes. Four-year-old Calvin accidentally wet his pants one day, and as I took him to the bathroom to clean him off, six-year-old Lewis shouted, "Out, out, damned spot!" Then there was the time George and Theodore were arguing. Reaching her arms beseechingly to the ceiling, Tracy called out, "Wherefore art thou, Themis, goddess of justice. We need your help, quick." One day the group was discussing how Medea tore her sons to pieces and got revenge after Jason left her and took a new bride. "Well, you know what they say," Erika wisecracked, "Hell hath no fury like a woman scorned."

Such learned extracts were applied as readily outside class. While Cindy and I were shopping in a department store, we saw a boy of about five crying and clinging to his mother's skirt as she tried to purchase some cosmetics. Cindy turned to me, shook her head, and coolly remarked, "Mommy, I think that boy has an Oedipus complex."

The children were showing off their newfound knowledge like a new toy. In the middle of the semester I took them to see the movie *The Man Who Would Be King,* based on the short story by Rudyard Kipling. Schools had been invited to attend a special screening of the film and hear a lecture on Kipling. My children were already well acquainted with the author. They knew his *Just So Stories* and *The Jungle Book,* and some had memorized "If" for their weekly poetry recitation.

As the children filed into the theater, the guest lecturer came running up to me. "Oh, there must be some mistake," he said. "Your children won't understand or appreciate this."

Looking around the auditorium, I saw that most of the audience was of high school age. "You just lecture the way you normally would to the older students. Don't worry about my children."

When the movie was over, the speaker began talking about Kipling's life, his schooling in Britain and his return to India at the age of eighteen. George began shaking his head vehemently. Suddenly his hand shot up. Squinting out into the audience, the man motioned for George to stand up. "Yes, young man, do you have a question?" he asked.

George shook his head no.

"Then what can I do for you?"

"I read in the encyclopedia that Kipling was seventeen

when he went back to India," George stated, taking his seat.

Applause mixed with laughter rang out from the audience. A few of the high school boys sitting with their feet propped up flashed a victory salute and shouted, "That's the way, kid, right on!"

In any other circumstances I would not have encouraged such pedantry. With the lecturer assuming that my children wouldn't understand, I made an exception and allowed them the spotlight. Cindy asked why Kipling was so British-oriented. And George, bolstered by the earlier success, took the floor a second time. "In whose memory was the Taj Mahal built?" he asked the speaker.

"It was built by the Shah Jahan in memory of his favorite wife, Mumtaz Mahal."

"That's right." George nodded, satisfied with the man's answer.

In late January there were a few changes. Two new students arrived and three others left. Theodore, who had come to the school the year before reading at a third grade level, passed the high school entrance exam and was admitted to a parochial high school. One father took his seven-year-old daughter out of Westside Prep because he could not afford the tuition. I offered to have the girl stay on a scholarship, but the father refused, saying, "I'm as proud as you are, Mrs. Collins. I don't believe in handouts any more than you do."

Another parent withdrew her five-year-old son because she was displeased that her child wasn't doing enough "creative things"—cutting out valentines and snowflakes and making paper bag puppets. She seemed to think that white children were doing that sort of thing in their progressive schools. I had no intention of having my students cut and paste and finger paint or march around with rhythm bands. Black children from inner-city neighborhoods cannot afford to spend time finger painting in school. When these children enter kindergarten, they are in most cases already behind socially and academically. Statistics show that they fall even further behind while in elementary school, so that by the sixth grade they are reading at a 2.2 level. The only way to combat that trend is to give the four and five year olds a strong start reading and writing.

That's not to say I stifle creative expression. My students were exposed to art, drama, and music but within the context of the basic curriculum, not as separate subjects. The children acted out fables and stories, wrote their own poetry and plays, and drew illustrations for the stories they read. Their reading selections included biographies of Mozart, Beethoven, Leonardo da Vinci, and Michelangelo. Our class discussions ranged from symphonies and sonatas to frescos and miniatures.

When I lost a student to coloring and cut-outs, I didn't try to dissuade his mother. Parents set their own expectations for their children, and they have to decide whether a particular school or teaching method suits their needs. Not all parents like the Montessori approach. Not all parents favor the Suzuki method of teaching children a musical instrument. So I didn't expect every parent to be satisfied with Westside Prep. I couldn't be all things to all people, and I didn't try to be.

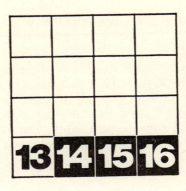

Since my first year of teaching, my students have always learned to love Shakespeare. Even the boys who picked their teeth with switchblades and dared other teachers to make it safely to their cars in the afternoon always begged for more. At Delano I had to sneak in the lessons on Shakespeare, because they were never included in the curriculum prescribed by the Board of Education.

Many educators and textbook publishers seemed to think that children should not be reading Shakespeare or, for that matter, any other great works of literature. The prevailing thought among the curriculum experts was that the best way to teach inner-city children to read was through "realistic" story content: the recommended material for teaching reading skills included stories about stealing, sex, drugs, running away from home, alcoholic fathers, know-nothing mothers, children who lied and conned adults, and children who committed crimes.

For years, the textbook companies had published readers that were totally unrealistic. Parents never argued, Father always looked neat and tidy, Mother never worked and was always baking cookies, the house was always spick-and-span, and brothers and sisters never disagreed. Little Jane's hair was always perfect, and her shoes were never scuffed.

Then the publishers and experts tried to make readers more lifelike. But in the process they have gone to the opposite extreme. A selection from one popular textbook reads:

I found a piece of rope, made a noose, slipped it about the kitten's neck, pulled it over a nail, then jerked the animal clear of the ground. It gasped, sloppered, spun, doubled, clawed the air frantically; finally its mouth gaped and its pink-white tongue shot out stiffly. I tied the rope to a nail and went to find my brother.

I don't believe in sheltering children or limiting their reading to stories with a Pollyanna vision of the world. Life is chaotic and imperfect, and children should be taught to understand that. Topics like death, greed, and violence are not taboo. They are often themes of great literature. However, some of today's textbooks smack of educational hucksterism: offer children anything; just get them to read!

According to the curriculum experts, everything has to be "relevant." One mathematics textbook has a chapter on probability that asks students to determine: What are the odds that a cabdriver will get a counterfeit $10 bill? What is the probability that a girl will become pregnant if she is taking birth control pills that are 97 percent effective? What is the probability that a person living in a certain community has either syphilis or gonorrhea?

All that "relevance" undermines the very purpose of an education. It doesn't expand the children's horizons or encourage inventiveness and curiosity. Instead it limits perspective to the grim scenes they see every day of their lives. Children do not need to read stories that teach "street smarts." They learn enough on their own. What they need are character-building stories. They need to read for values, morality, and universal truths. That was my reason for teaching classical literature.

It is senseless to hand children prepackaged, specially designed reading material when there are so many relevant lessons to be plucked from the writings of great authors. But it takes a creative, hard-working teacher to ferret out those things, to focus on the content, not the mechanics of reading.

★   ★   ★

William Shakespeare's plays were a gold mine of meaningful themes, and the students at Westside Preparatory School loved reading them. *Macbeth* was a special treat. The children were intrigued by the action of the play, the witches, the ghosts, and the idea of a cold, calculated murder. They came away from the play fully aware that crime exacts a price.

Students of every age level were treated to *Macbeth*. For the younger children, ages four and five, Marva gave a digest of the story: "Now the witches can only hurt people if those people are already evil, and since Macbeth was already inclined to do evil, the three witches persuaded him to murder King Duncan while he was a guest at Macbeth's home . . ." Sitting cross-legged on the floor, their eyes glued to the storyteller, the children heard how the ghost of King Duncan haunted Macbeth and how Lady Macbeth tried to rub the imaginary bloodstains from her hands, crying, "Out, damned spot, out I say."

The students reading at a first, second, or third grade level received a narrative adaptation of *Macbeth* from *Favorite Tales from Shakespeare* by Bernard Miles. As always, the children read aloud, and periodically Marva asked each student to define a word, supply a synonym or antonym, or discuss the meaning of a paragraph.

"Did the witches make Macbeth do evil?"

"No," replied the children.

"The witches only predicted that he would do evil. Macbeth himself made the evil happen. Others can predict, but the individual determines his own life. Society predicts that you will fail. But you what?"

"Determine our own life," said Laura.

"Very, very good. Why do you think Macbeth is so depressed, so troubled?" Marva asked.

" 'Cause he thinks people are going to find out how he murdered King Duncan," answered Maria, who had joined the school in January.

"He has a guilty conscience," added one of the boys.

"That's right," Marva said. "The murder ends up destroying him. That's what happens in life. People may offer us glorious things, but they don't tell us the price we have to pay for them. After the deed is done, the weird sisters say, 'Macbeth shall sleep no more.' There is always a penalty to pay. If someone doesn't catch you, then your own conscience will. We don't like ourselves very much when we do something bad, do we?''

In Marva's hands Shakespeare became a vehicle for positive attitudes. The children reading the adaptation learned the themes by following the action of the play. The students reading at or above the fourth grade level pulled out meaning line by line from the original text.

"What does Duncan mean when he says, 'The love that follows us is sometimes our trouble?' ''

"Sometimes we trust people and think they love us, but they turn against us," said Gary.

"Very good. And when Macbeth has second thoughts about killing Duncan, what does Lady Macbeth do?''

"She calls him a coward," said Cindy.

"She makes fun of him for not being man enough to do it," added Patrick.

"How many of you have had that happen to you?" asked Marva. "Did you ever have your friends call you a coward or a baby or a chicken because you didn't want to go along with something?''

A few of the boys looked around the room before they reluctantly nodded.

"So what does Macbeth do? What does he tell Lady Macbeth?''

"He gets her off his back by saying he's going to be a bigger man than anyone else," George said.

"So you see what happens, children? Macbeth ends up committing murder to prove he is tough. His wife ridicules him, she makes fun of his manhood, so he feels he has to go out and murder Duncan to prove he is a man. If he liked himself, if he had self-respect, he would not have had to prove anything, would he? It's the people who don't like themselves very much who make trouble for the others.

"The mess society is in today starts with people who don't like themselves. And when that's the case, nothing is going to help you, is it? Not drugs, not alcohol. Those things don't make life any better. You have to get your head on straight. Could the doctor give Lady Macbeth anything to cure her mind? Could he 'minister to a mind diseased?' "

The children shook their heads.

"What did the doctor tell Macbeth?" Marva asked.

The children ran their fingers up and down the page looking for the line. Erika blurted out, "I've got it, Mrs. Collins. He says, 'the patient must minister to himself.' "

"It's sort of like what Socrates says, isn't it, Mrs. Collins?" Gary said. "Macbeth should have known that 'Straight thinking leads to straight living.' " Gary sat back, evidently pleased with himself.

All the children were proud of themselves. Reading Shakespeare gave them an enormous sense of self-worth. Some days Marva wished the whole world could hear them, especially the experts with theories about what inner-city children should not and could not read.

The children's acquaintance with Shakespeare didn't end with *Macbeth*. Eventually they went on to read *Twelfth Night*, *A Midsummer Night's Dream*, *Hamlet*, *Romeo and Juliet*, *Merchant of Venice*, *Julius Caesar*, and *King Lear*. In the meantime Marva made sure Shakespeare remained in the children's minds. Sentences such as "Shakespeare lived in England" and "The three witches in *Macbeth* were evil" were given as dictation exercises, and Marc Anthony's funeral oration became part of a lesson on rhetoric and propaganda. Several of the children memorized the funeral oration or Hamlet's soliloquy for their weekly poetry recitation. Lines from the plays and sonnets became topics for daily writing assignments.

William Shakespeare had already become an old friend to the students at Westside Prep when, one morning in the spring of 1977, Marva read a story in the *Chicago Sun-Times* about high school students in the suburbs who did not know who Shakespeare was, when and where he lived, or what he wrote. For example, one student wrote that "the global theater was a three-sided octagon." She clipped the article and brought it to class for her students to see. It was a great ego booster. The children shouted exultant cheers, drummed victory rolls on their desks, and clasped their hands overhead, hailing themselves champions. None of their day to day small triumphs in the classroom could match their first thrill of seeing how they compared to the outside world.

"Shoot, you mean those rich high school kids in the suburbs don't know Shakespeare was born in 1564 and died in 1616?" Gary's hubris might have been the fatal flaw in many of Shakespeare's heroes, but in Marva's students it was a hard-earned and welcome virtue.

"You see," Marva said, breaking through the noise. "You make your own success. Children can go to expensive schools, but it doesn't mean they learn any more or any better. Buildings don't teach, people teach. Everything works in here because we make it work. All the money in the world isn't going to make a difference."

That afternoon Marva gave in to some pride of her own. She wrote a letter to *Sun-Times* columnist Zay Smith, telling him that she had read his story and that she had students from "the allegedly fetid ghetto" who had a reading acquaintance with Shakespeare. She explained a little about her school. Marva followed up the letter with a telephone call several days later, inviting Smith to visit the school any time. "I'd match these students now with students anywhere in the suburbs," she added.

Unannounced, Smith dropped in on Westside Prep at nine o'clock the next morning. As he later wrote in his *Sun-Times* column, "I wasn't expecting any miracles. So I wasn't prepared for what I saw." Sitting quietly in the back of the classroom, Smith observed a typical day at Marva's school. He watched "four year olds writing sentences like 'See the physician' and 'Aesop wrote fables,' and discussing diphthongs and diacritical marks—calling them correctly by name." He heard "second-graders reciting passages from Shakespeare, Longfellow and Kipling," and "third-graders learning about Tolstoi, Sophocles and Chaucer."

Amazed at a teacher working such wonders, Smith interviewed some of the children. One girl said, "When I went to my old school I didn't learn anything. My teacher used to go around pinching our ears. Here somebody believed in me." And another girl told him, "We do hard things here. They fill your brain."

Smith's story on Westside Prep, along with a sampling of student writing (compositions on Michelangelo, Leonardo da Vinci, Aesop, and Hinduism), appeared on the third page of the Sunday edition of the *Sun-Times* on May 8, 1977. It went out on the *Sun-Times* wire service and was picked up by other newspapers around the country. Readers were touched by the story of children who had been discarded as "unteachable" climbing to superior achievement in a school that was always short of books, paper, pencils, and even chalk. And Marva was catapulted into an unexpected, though not entirely unsought, spotlight.

★   ★   ★

What pleased me the most about the publicity was having people see the kinds of knowledge my students were attaining, because it had become a common assumption that the liberal arts curriculum was beyond the capacity of black children. The public response to the newspaper article was overwhelming. People started sending me ten, twenty, and thirty dollar donations. One man sent me a check with a note saying that he had read the story aboard a plane on his way to Nevada. He was so moved by the work I was doing that he mailed the check the minute he landed at the Las Vegas airport.

The story struck different chords in different people. For some the contributions represented an endorsement of alternative education. I suspect other people responded to the portrayal of an underdog, a risk-taker, and educational maverick. Whatever the reasons, I was glad to get the contributions. I put every dollar into the school, buying such things as a set of *The Great Books* and dictionaries for every child in the class.

I had always had very strong opinions about education, and suddenly I had a public forum to air my views. Shortly after the story appeared in the newspaper, I received an invitation to speak before a gathering of educators in the Dade County, Florida public schools. They were even paying a $500 honorarium. A bit uncertain about the kind of response I would receive from my audience of teachers, I talked about phonics, recommended reading lists, and explained the methods I used to teach literature and writing skills. I discussed the importance of a positive attitude and stressed that any child could learn if a teacher cared enough to teach.

The audience reaction was mixed. Some of the teachers came up to me afterwards eager to share ideas. Others were antagonistic or just plain rude. They probably resented an ordinary classroom teacher standing up there telling them about *her* methods. It wasn't as though I were an expert from the Department of Education or a university professor who had researched countless learning theories. Sometimes teachers depend too much on the experts—some of whom have never taught in a classroom—instead of looking toward their colleagues for techniques and advice. Perhaps that's one of the problems with education today. There is often a reluctance among teachers to pool information and learn from one another.

The Monday morning after my first public speaking engagement, I walked into the class with my $500 check in hand and passed it up and down the rows of desks for the children to see.

"You see," I told them, waving the check, "people will pay you for the ideas you have in your head."

"You mean you got all that money just for talking?" Gary asked.

"That's right. I talked all about phonics and the dictation I give you and the quotations I put on the board and the poetry you recite . . ."

"Heck, *I* could've told them all that," he said.

"You mean those people *paid* you just to tell them what we do in here every day?" Tracy sounded incredulous. Listening to me preach about the value of an education was one thing; seeing the proof was quite another.

"Yes, they did," I said, recognizing a chance to expand on my major theme. "If you have the knowledge, if you have the skills, people will come to you. You will find work. You don't need to steal or wait for someone to give you something for nothing. A free ride is never worth very much anyway. If I give you some of my clothes, I don't give you my favorite dress, do I?

I'll give you something that's old and worn out, won't I? Just how much is that going to be worth to you?"

"But how come those people want to know what we do?" George asked. He and the others were still in awe of the $500.

"Because a lot of people are surprised at the kinds of things you children are learning," I told him. "Black America has been led to believe that we are supposed to fail. When we do fail, people look down on us, and that leads to a lot of hate. Things do not have to be that way. We can make them better. You were not born to fail. You were born to succeed. You were born to be millionaires! But you are going to have to learn. No one owes you a thing in this life. I don't want anyone to give you children anything—except your dignity."

By then the school year was nearly over, so the children were used to my sermonizing. Most of them had sat through two years of it, and it was taking hold. Children who had come to me lacking all confidence, convinced they couldn't do anything, were now talking about becoming doctors, judges, scientists, and teachers. Sonya, one of the girls who had been fighting on the bus six months before, insisted she was going to be the first black woman president of the United States. She and the other children walked around quoting from what they had read and boasting about what they knew. They'd come to me and say, "I know this big kid in high school, and he never even heard of Dante Alighieri." To some outsiders my children may have appeared to be little know-it-alls. I loved their spirit.

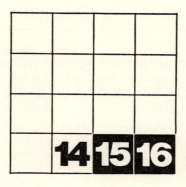

Despite the financial strain, the new Westside Prep had survived its first year, and every one of my children had made progress. Now nine, Tracy was long rid of her headaches and crying and was comfortable reading more than a year above her grade level. She was even writing themes on such subjects as "The Four Major Religions of the World," with lines like: "It is not possible, the Hindus believe, to achieve perfection in one lifetime. Therefore a man is born on earth again and again."

Laura Brown, the sixth-grader who had once written every word with jumbled letters, was reading from an eighth grade book at the end of the year. George was in a twelfth grade literature book, and four-year-old Calvin was reading at a second grade level. Erika McCoy was still having trouble keeping the shoes on her feet, and the other children seemed to tolerate her more than they liked her, but at seven and a half years old she was an insatiable reader, headed into a summer vacation with Dickens, Melville, and the Bronte sisters. And Gary Love, who once resisted learning anything, had become an ambitious writer:

> Somnus, god of sleep, please awaken us. While we sleep, ignorance takes over the world.... Take your spell off us. We don't have long before ignorance makes a coup d'état of the world.

That kind of success with my students made me push ahead with an almost maniacal fervor. Now, I had come to recognize, I *was* trying to challenge the system. And it was an inexorably demanding task. At times I felt exhausted and frustrated, I was afraid I had taken on too much. I worried about losing the school, about letting the children down, and about failing myself.

The summer offered little rest. After the Zay Smith article and my few speaking engagements, there was a steady stream of mail from people seeking my advice on educational matters. There were more offers to speak, reporters requesting interviews, and inquiries from parents who wanted to enroll their children in my school. By September 1977 Westside Prep had an enrollment of thirty students and a waiting list of almost the same number.

All the parents had stories to tell. Some of them came to me because they refused to accept the judgment of school officials who had said their children were mentally retarded, emotionally disturbed, or learning-disabled. Others came because their children had been expelled from school as behavior problems. One mother cried as she told me that her son had been suspended from school so often that he spent more time on the streets than in a classroom. She was sure Westside Prep was the only chance standing between him and reform school.

All the parents were frustrated and worried; some were desperate. One of the most distraught was Cathy Mullins' mother, who had heard about Westside Prep from a woman who happened to sit next to her on a city bus. She told me her eleven-year-old daughter, after falling far behind in school, had given up on herself. The child walked around crying all the time and had worked herself into such a nervous condition that her hair was falling out.

I took in Cathy Mullins. Ironically, I had an easier time with Cathy than with her father. He had disagreed with his wife over enrolling their daughter in the school and he objected to my methods.

"What are you doing to our girl?" he said one afternoon during the second month of school, bursting into the room just as the children were leaving. "She's messed up enough without you giving her all these big words to learn and the Latin and the poetry. She's a slow child. Don't you know she can't do that kind of work?"

"Any child can learn if she is not taught too thoroughly that she can't," I answered curtly. I believed in every one of my students. Why didn't their parents? Criticism from parents—even when it is unintentional—tends to lodge in a child's mind, particularly if that child already has self-doubts.

"The kind of work you want Cathy to do puts too much pressure on her," Mr. Mullins said.

"Did Cathy tell you that?" I asked him. Cathy was doing well. In two months' time her reading ability had gone from a second grade level to the fourth grade.

"Well, no. But going by what those other teachers used to say, I just figured . . ."

"Life is pressure, Mr. Mullins. There's no sense isolating these children or keeping them so sheltered that they won't ever be able to cope with anything. Other schools don't teach a child to push, to achieve. I do."

Some parents had the opposite complaint. They felt that I wasn't pushing their children hard enough and that the children weren't progressing fast enough. It amazed me that these parents could allow their children to get behind in school and then assume I could bring the children's skills up to the right grade level in only a few months. With some children it was possible, but others learned more slowly and needed more time to adjust and become motivated. A few times parents demanded to know why I had their child reading from an easier book or doing simpler math than the other children.

Others seemed to want to turn over all responsibility for their children to me. I believe it is the parents who must be strong and set the tone. Yet some parents don't spend time reading, don't read to their children, and don't have books around the house. Somehow they expect teachers to make their children into competent and eager readers. There are parents who don't set rules and limitations for their children, yet they expect the teacher to maintain discipline and order in the classroom. And some parents wonder why their children don't do homework, yet at home these same children are never given responsibilities or chores.

If I wasn't battling the parents' criticisms, then I was fighting their apathy. Some of the very same parents who had pleaded with me to rescue their children washed their hands of any further involvement once the children were in my school. Some even avoided paying the tuition. When there was real hardship, when a parent was out of work or ill, I accepted a child on scholarship. A few parents paid whatever they could afford each month. In lieu of tuition a few mothers helped out answering the telephone, opening mail, and copying selections from textbooks. The increased enrollment meant more work of all kinds, not just more teaching.

What infuriated me though, was that parents who seemed to have money to spend on other things, didn't seem to feel that paying for their children's education was a priority; they wanted an education for their children for nothing, without lifting a finger to help themselves. To a great degree, they too had to be educated.

In the meantime, I still had the burden of supporting my cash-starved school. I continually had to remind parents of their overdue payments. They responded by saying they had no money to give. I told them, if you are not willing to work for your child, please do not lean on the rest of us. Not all of my students had "caring parents." Some of them didn't give a damn about what happened to their children, though I struggled every step of the way to teach them. Yet, finally, when many of my students were reading and learning material well beyond their age level, there were parents who declared there had never been a learning problem in the first place.

However, I was determined not to let my students grow up having such short memories. What upset me was the idea of people forgetting where they had come from. So I repeatedly warned my students, "Don't you ever forget what you started from when you first came to this school. Don't forget how envious and ashamed you were because you couldn't read as well as some of your classmates. Don't forget, because when you grow up and finish college, you are the ones who are going to have to come back here to neighborhoods like Garfield Park and turn them into places people want to live in and not run away from."

The number of students really didn't make a difference.

Even with thirty children I ran the classroom the same way I had done the previous year. I struggled to parcel out individualized attention, while keeping up the momentum of the class as a whole. I moved from child to child, correcting mistakes on the spot and giving instant feedback on every paper as soon as it was completed. And still I tried to catch sight of everything: a child talking or throwing a paper clip, resting his head on his desk or even copying—"Your understanding must be your understanding and not your neighbor's, unless you plan on taking him with you every place you go."

As always, the emphasis for the new students was on phonics. Returning students worked in various reading groups. One group read legends, fables, Greek myths, and American tall tales; another studied selections from classics by Voltaire, Nietzsche, Goethe, Emerson, Thackeray, Dickens, Chaucer, Tolstoy, Flaubert, Swift, Dostoyevsky, Colette, Boccaccio, and Petrarch; a third group delved into biographies of Helen Keller, Harriet Tubman, Abraham Lincoln, and Frederick Douglass.

Math lessons ranged from algebra and geometry for the eleven and twelve year olds to numeration and telling time for the kindergarteners. In science some children were studying the planets and the galaxy; others learned about the earth and its history; still others worked on plant and animal life, biological adaptations, and classification. And social studies lessons were just as diverse, with kindergarteners learning about building strong communities, first-graders studying citizenship and national heroes, second-graders exploring the seven continents, third-graders looking at Chicago history and politics, fourth-graders learning about state and federal government, and fifth-through eighth-graders studying various periods of American and European history.

Running a multi-level one-room school was a constant juggling act. Yet it wasn't as complicated as it might seem. Whenever possible I tried to teach subjects not in isolation but as part of a central curriculum. Language arts (reading, writing, grammar, and vocabulary) were correlated with social studies and science. For example, when the children learned about the seven continents, they read a story from one of the countries under discussion. When they studied the solar system, they read about the lives of Galileo and Copernicus, compared Aristotle's theories to Galileo's, wrote reports about them, and analyzed the parts of speech in such sentences as *Copernicus showed that the planets revolve around the sun.*

I had always stressed vocabulary, encouraging the children to look for synonyms in the dictionary and thesaurus, teaching Latin and Greek derivations, and explaining the meaning of prefixes such as *ab* (away), *ad* (to), *com* (with), *dis* (opposite), *re* (again), and so on. That fall I discovered a secret weapon for building vocabulary, a book called *Vocabulary for the College-Bound Student.* As it happened, my son Eric, who was then a sophomore in high school, was using the book in his English class. I frequently perused my children's textbooks—it's important for parents to know what their children are learning—and this one turned out to be a gem. I ordered copies for all the students in Westside Prep.

"Words are ideas. They make up thoughts. If our words are limited, our thoughts are limited," I said, holding up the book and pointing to its title. "You see what this says? It says for the college-bound student, not the failure-bound student. To succeed in life, you must be a thinker, and to be a thinker, you must have vocabulary."

For their first homework assignment from this book the children studied and memorized five words and definitions. I said I wanted them to learn the words, but I didn't want them to write the words ten times and then say "Hallelujah, I'm finished!"

The next day the children were all flagging their hands, eager to shout out the definitions.

"What does *blithe* mean?" I asked.

"Happy and cheerful," blurted out Erika, jumping the gun on everyone else.

"Laura, what's *buoyant?*" I asked.

"Cheerful," she answered.

"Very good. Look how far you've come. Now who can tell me another word that means cheerful?"

Calvin, who had come to the school the previous January at the age of four, was waving and shouting, "Call on me, call on me."

"All right, Calvin, what's a synonym for cheerful?"

"Jocund," he said proudly. Everyone clapped. I couldn't help beaming. I told him he was probably the only four and a half year old in the world who knew that word.

I have always believed young children can grasp complicated words, as long as they know how to syllabicate and decode sounds. No word is too difficult if a child has the right phonics tools. The only thing standing between a young child and a difficult word is the child's fear of it. By exposing them to the complexities of language, I made sure my children were not intimidated by words.

I reinforced phonics by having my students repeat the pronunciation of words like *charlatan, bronchitis, Andromache, Petrarch,* and even *adiadochokinesis*—a medical term (describing a muscular disorder) some of my boys discovered on their own while playing a dictionary game which involved trying to stump one another over pronunciations. Every day I gave the children dictation, using such sentences as "The politician was accused of malfeasance" or "The president was lionized by the people." Whenever I spoke, I tried to supplement their vocabulary by serving up new words. And I urged them to incorporate the new words into class discussion and into their compositions.

Very often the children strung together the new words the same way they did quotations. When a few of the children were reading *Uncle Tom's Cabin,* the assignment I gave was to compose the kind of letter Eliza might have written to her son Harry when she overheard he was going to be sold. One paper read:

My frolicsome, jocund son,
This is a time of tribulation, not jubilation. I am disconsolate over your plight, but I do not want you to be glum, doleful, and dejected because you have nostalgia. You must be brave. I love you.

In November, spurred by a suggestion from its Chicago bureau, *Time* magazine ran a story about the school in its education section. The response was unbelievable. A television producer from Los Angeles donated a check for $5,000. Another $2,000 came in from a movie star who wrote that he was sending the money on the advice of his psychiatrist. There was a gust of $10 to $100 checks stapled to letters. In all, the windfall came to nearly $10,000. To me it was like the Irish Sweepstakes. The expansion of the school from eighteen to thirty students had sunk us into a financial hole. Clarence was working more part-time jobs than I could keep track of. We poured all of our savings into the school, ignored the upkeep of our house, and let our life insurance policies lapse. But these contributions enabled me to pay off some bills.

The aftermath of the *Time* article set the pattern for what would happen every time Westside Prep was featured in the mass media. Teachers wrote me asking my advice on how to teach a child to read or how to get a child to love learning. Some told me of their own frustrations with the educational system and with apathetic colleagues who criticized them for being "too optimistic" or ridiculed them for "wasting time caring about students." I also heard from corporate executives who complained about the illiteracy of employees and from college administrators appalled at the poor reading skills of incoming freshmen.

More than 2,000 letters came from parents—frightened, worried parents all calling for help. They told the same kinds of stories I had heard so many times before—only now I was hearing them from people all across the country, not just from black parents living in the inner-city. A mother from California wanted to know what to do for her son, who had been diagnosed in the usual way by his teachers: "hyperactive, brain damaged, bright but a poor achiever, immature, and not properly motivated." There was a letter from a woman in a small Michigan town, saying her teenaged daughter was "a casualty of our failing public school system—an A and B student who can't read and comprehend, think independently and has no clear understanding of our world and how it works."

There were pleas from parents who believed their children were wrongly categorized as retarded or learning disabled. Others wanted to know how they could pull their sons and daughters out of public schools and teach them at home. A St. Louis mother complained that her two boys "entered school

open and receptive" but "the school discouraged these qualities." Another woman, from Maryland, said her teenage son
was being wasted in a learning disabilities class where all he did
was play and paint, doing nothing that could be described as academic all year.

I knew the poor shape education was in, but I had never
realized the extent of the public's desperation. One letter, written by a woman from upstate New York, seemed to sum it up:

> My son is in first grade. Already he dislikes school,
> which is causing him to be a discipline problem to his
> teacher. I know he does not receive her love and en-
> couragement. His teacher informed me she did not
> have the time with 28 other active youngsters in her
> room and besides he is 'too old' for this kind of treat-
> ment. It scares me and is tearing me apart. The sys-
> tem is losing him and as a result I am afraid I may
> also.

People were crying out for help, yet there was so little I
could do. What kind of remedy could I offer parents in a letter
or a long-distance phone call? Everyone was looking for a cure-
all, hoping for some quick-fix for a chronic problem. Parents
were so desperate that I sometimes got the feeling they'd buy
a snake-oil potion if it promised to turn their children into
readers.

Meanwhile, with thirty students my enrollment was nearly
up to the limit imposed by the city's building code. I could only
accept a handful of new students, squeezing in a few more
seats and having some of the four year olds sit on the floor. I
wanted to move the school into larger quarters, but I didn't
have enough money or a steady enough income from the school
to guarantee rent, and many landlords wanted the rent paid
months in advance.

Following the *Time* article, other publications did stories
on our school, including educational journals, the *Chicago Tri-
bune Magazine, People* magazine, and *Good Housekeeping.* The
publicity brought still more parents, teachers, school administrators, and more press filing into my classroom. The director of

the Free Schools in Europe read about Westside Prep in the European edition of *Time* and came all the way from Germany to observe my children.

Over the next two years the children and I were the subjects of articles in newspapers and magazines all over the country. We were also featured on local and national television. I appeared on ABC's *Good Morning America,* and in November 1979 CBS's *60 Minutes* aired a segment on Westside Prep. As a result of the *60 Minutes* broadcast I received more than 6,000 letters from desperate parents.

★ ★ ★

Marva's students reveled in the excitement of being neighborhood celebrities and seeing their pictures in newspapers and magazines. A few of the children had been interviewed by reporters. One boy gleefully told the class that his relatives in the South had read about the school. And two of the girls told how they had been walking to the playground one day when a woman stopped them on the street to ask: "Aren't you some of those Marva Collins children?"

Marva decided she had better set her students' priorities straight about all the attention they were receiving.

"People are always reading about the bad things that go on in Garfield Park, and it is our obligation to show a different side of our community. Everyone is coming to see you because you're so bright, but we can't afford to go sticking out our chests. We can't get too carried away with this publicity. We can't run around bragging and forget what we are here for, or we'll all end up like a bunch of Petunias. Who remembers the story of Petunia?"

"Petunia was the hen who went around telling all the other barnyard animals she knew how to read when she didn't," Cathy Mullins said. After seven months in the school Cathy had pulled up to reading at her age level. Her nervousness had disappeared, her hair stopped falling out, and she no longer shuddered and whimpered when someone looked at her. She had developed such confidence that months later, when the school year was over, she would take charge of organizing the year-end class party.

"And what happened to Petunia and the rest of the animals?" Marva asked.

"They all got blown up and ended up in the hospital or walking around on crutches," George answered. " 'Cause when the mailman brought a package to the barnyard, the other animals asked Petunia to read what was in it. And since she really didn't know how to read, she pretended it said candy."

"What did the package really have in it?"

"Explosives," the children chortled.

"Now we're not going to be Petunias sticking out our chests and bragging about how much we know, not without putting in the effort to learn it," said Marva. "Your picture appearing in the paper today is not going to make you happy for the rest of your life. Getting your picture in the paper or in every magazine in this country is not going to pay your bills. It's not going to put food on your table or keep you warm in the winter. People are impressed by what you have learned so far, but that doesn't mean you can sit back and congratulate yourselves and do nothing. The more successful a person becomes, the harder he or she has to work to stay there. Let's not worry about what people *write* about us. Let's just worry about getting things *right* ourselves."

Things settled back to a kind of normalcy, and in the weeks that followed, the children attended to their work, Marva raced and bounced around the classroom, and everyone tried their best to ignore the visitors who filed into the room and sat on the folding chairs in the back corner. When the children gave in to their curiosity and turned their heads to stare at a stranger or look over a reporter's shoulder as he was jotting notes, Marva quickly reminded them what they were in school for.

"You won't know that man ten years from now," she'd say. "His name isn't going to be on your paycheck." Her caveat was enough to spring all eyes face front. Never mind that their ministers were forever telling them "God will provide." Marva had taught them her own corollary: God will provide if you first have the brain to provide for yourself.

★　★　★

My children were drawing on everything they learned. One Monday morning twelve-year-old Renee Williams came to class with an observation inspired the previous day at church.

"Mrs. Collins," she said. "You know how Jesus in his Sermon on the Mount said, 'I come to fulfill you, not harm you'? Well, I bet that's where Shakespeare got the idea for the line 'I come to bury Caesar, not to praise him.' "

During a discussion of Euripides' tragedy *Andromache* I asked them how they thought the heroine felt when she went from being a queen to being a slave.

"She probably wanted to kill herself like Cleopatra did," Cindy said.

"And when a person kills himself, what is that called?" I asked.

"Suicide," the class answered.

"When Orestes killed his mother Clytemnestra, that was matricide," Gary added.

"And when you kill your father, that's patricide," Patrick said taking his cue from Gary.

"So killing infants is infanticide," Erika chimed in.

"Yeah, and killing pests is pesticide," said another voice, followed by a guffaw.

Aside from the children's academic progress there were changes far more subtle. They had a discernible pride not only in their work but in their school as well. The school, they felt, belonged to them and they displayed a proprietary sense about its upkeep. I was determined to instill a *we* mentality in my students and make them realize the school would only work if all of us stuck together to make it work.

I had told them that everything they tore up or lost would have to be replaced, then tuition would have to go up, and soon only the rich would be able to go to school at Westside Prep. To illustrate my point I brought the utility bills and invoices for school supplies to class. It was a simple but compelling economics lesson. Everything has a cost. As long as they were learning, the investment was well worth it. "See the bill from People's Gas Company? I want that much learning out of you today."

Despite all the attention I was getting from the media, my priority was still my students. Once I entered the classroom the rest of the world didn't exist. My students knew and understood me better than anyone else. They certainly knew me better than the media that was calling me "super teacher" and "miracle worker." I hated those epithets. I resented the way they made it all sound so easy.

There was no miracle or magic in what went on in our school. If it were that simple, then teaching would not have been such hard work for me, and learning would not have been so demanding for the children. It was because of all the effort and difficulty that the children savored every accomplishment. And once they started to succeed they wanted to succeed even more. They didn't ever want to turn around again.

Before the 1977–1978 school year was over George and Laura were both accepted by high schools, and Cindy and Erika won commendations in a statewide student writing contest. Both had written essays on the subject of violence, drawing upon the *Iliad* to make the point that violence has always been around. They were invited by the Illinois State Superintendent of Schools to read their papers at the Illinois Young Authors Conference.

Sitting in the auditorium as the girls presented their papers, I kept picturing Erika as she had been nearly three years before. The same child who had been called retarded was now expressing her thoughts before an audience.

Like every teacher I had days when I was impatient with my students' progress. There were times when I could not seem to break through to a child. And there were some lessons that fell on deaf ears no matter how much I banged on desks or waved my arms to get the point across. Yet I made certain that I never underestimated by children's intelligence or their ability to learn. I kept in mind the countless schools across the country that mislabeled children, simplified textbooks, diluted curricula, and created special curricula for "underprivileged" children. How many are victimized by an educational philosophy which presupposes that background and environment limit a child's capacity to learn? How many children are discouraged from pursuing an education because teachers have taken it upon themselves to judge who can achieve and who cannot? I wasn't there to judge my students. My job as a teacher was to get their talents working. And that's what I tried to do.

The following year the school had a waiting list of several hundred students. Otherwise life at Westside Prep continued much the same. New students replaced those who left, and like their predecessors these children had to be brought up to level. Some of them were real hellions. One boy, Derrin, couldn't sit next to someone without kicking him. After a while, as their brains began to click, the children's hands and feet became still. Order seems to evolve naturally once children realize why they are in school. Six months after Derrin came to the school, a reporter who was talking to him a bit too long heard the boy say, "I don't mean to be rude, but you are taking away my skills."

The children who had been with me for several years were like sponges soaking up everything I could give them. Just as I used to drill them, they now began to push me, constantly asking what does this mean and what does that mean. They were fascinated with words, and they hunted through the dictionary for the sheer joy of finding polysyllabic words to try out on one another.

The great books were their greatest teacher. While there are critics who claim the classics are too difficult for younger students to read—that an eleven year old, for example, can't understand something as complicated as *The Brothers Karamazov*—I have found that great literature not only teaches students to read but makes them thirsty for more and more knowledge. These books *are* over the head of the student reader; that is the purpose of reading them. We read to stretch the mind, to seek, to strive, to wonder, and then reread. We discuss the ideas contained in those books with others, and we temper our own thoughts. The great books are great teachers because they demand the attention of the reader. The mundane content of second-rate literature turns students off from reading forever.

However, I did not leave the children to read these books by themselves. They read a chapter aloud each day in class and a chapter each night at home. We went over these books paragraph by paragraph, often line by line, discussing the ideas and following the characters, action, and movement of the story. The literature they read became part of them. The more I worked with them and the older they got, they began to communicate with each other through the things they learned. Their street lingo began to disappear sometimes to be replaced with lines they had read.

To me they were beginning to sound like Rhodes Scholars—even when they were insulting one another. Once when a student told a lie in class, someone said, "Speak the speech trippingly on thy tongue," and another chimed in, "The false face does hide what the false heart does know." If a girl was acting too flirty, the other girls would accuse her of acting like the Wife of Bath. One day my son Patrick had a pimple on his face and his sister Cindy told him he looked like the Summoner in *Canterbury Tales*. Another time when a rubberband shot across the room, I asked Michael whether he had done it. He said no and blamed it on Phillip, who said, "Et tu, Michael? This was the most unkindest cut of all."

When the 1978–1979 school year ended, several students, including Cathy Mullins, passed into high school, skipping from seventh to ninth grade. Upon finishing fifth grade, Tracy Shanklin was reading two years above her grade level. Erika and Cindy, in fourth grade, were reading high school books.

That year I had sent all my students aged eight and above to be tested independently at a nearby Catholic school. They took the California Achievement Test, Form 18-C, which was valid for students between seventh and ninth grades. Ordinarily only my older students took that test, but I felt it was also a good experience for the children below seventh grade, whose scores were adjusted upward in accordance with their age.

The results of those tests showed that most of the children had made extraordinary improvement in vocabulary, spelling, reading comprehension, and math. In a few instances a student's test score jumped four years after one year at Westside Prep. Not all my students were reading above grade level. Some were still quite far behind. However, all showed significant improvement from where they had been. There were sixth-graders reading at a fourth or fifth grade level, but those students had started the year struggling with second and third grade material. They had made wonderful progress. I was pleased.

★ ★ ★

The Catholic school admissions director, Harvey Gross, who administered the California Achievement Test to students from more than seventy Chicago area schools, noted that Marva's Westside Prep students scored higher and showed greater progress than any other group he tested. Yet he was quick to say that test scores alone didn't tell the whole story. One had to watch Marva's students in the classroom to see the full effect of her energy and her conviction that children can learn.

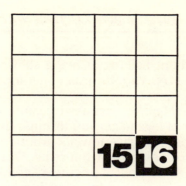

15 16

The one question that ought to be asked on a teaching application is: do you love children? To me that's the most important criterion for a teacher, more important than credentials or college degrees. A devotion to children was the quality I looked for in all the people who applied for teaching jobs at Westside Prep. Often I didn't sense it in the most seasoned teachers, long-time veterans of public, private, or parochial schools. Others without any formal training or teaching experience sometimes struck me as having the personality and enthusiasm that made an effective teacher: one of those was Lillian Vaughn, a CETA (Comprehensive Employment Training Act) worker placed with me for training by the Alternative Schools Network.

At the time I was anxious to have an assistant to help me with the four and five year olds, who naturally worked at a slower pace than the older students. The job was made to order for Mrs. Vaughn. A short, quiet, rather shy woman of thirty-eight, she was eager to work with the children, which was reason enough for me to try her out. It didn't matter that Mrs. Vaughn had only had a year of college or that her only previous experience was as a teacher's aide, going from school to school to assist in the administering of standardized tests. It was all the better. There would be no bad habits to contend with, no professional ego to bruise.

Lillian Vaughn seemed to love children; she was gentle and patient with them. Further she was receptive to learning my methods without balking at being shown what to do. The first thing I told Mrs. Vaughn was to get a pair of comfortable shoes.

"To be a good teacher you need a comfortable pair of shoes and a strong pair of legs to get you through the day. No teacher sits in this school. You have to walk around to each and every child, not just the ones in the front seats. You have to check for errors in the back as well. Remember, children only want to finish their work. They couldn't care less whether they get it right. They don't want to be bothered. They will tell you they understand when they really don't."

I gave Mrs. Vaughn explicit directions that every child had to be praised and patted, hugged and touched each day. Slower children needed to be praised for something daily just as much as the brighter child. I told her to think of something positive to say before going over a child's errors. Then I started Mrs. Vaughn the same way I started with any new student, teaching her the phonics drills. I gave her guidelines on how to draw morals and analogies from fables, fairy tales, and poetry. I wrote out elaborate lesson plans and then led her through each step from beginning to end.

The first few months Mrs. Vaughn stayed in the classroom with me, following my moves and tutoring the children. I watched her like a hawk, the same way I watched my students. Once when she was reading a fairy tale to the little children, I heard four-year-old Andy cry and say he was afraid of the witch in the story. Mrs. Vaughn told him not to act like a silly baby.

I left the reading group I was working with and called her aside. "Never make children feel that their fears or questions are silly," I told her. "The fears are real to them. And try not to embarrass a child in front of the other children. They don't like to be ridiculed in front of others any more than we do."

"But I never meant to embarrass him," she apologized.

"I'm sure you didn't, but we have to be conscious of everything we say to children. You have to make yourself aware of how they might interpret something that we say very innocently."

Another time Jimmy Tucker and Donald Ellis were fighting over a pencil and I overheard Mrs. Vaughn tell them she was going to send notes home to their mothers. I interceded. First I scolded the boys, "Don't go on about 'This is mine and This is yours.' If you spend your time learning instead of fighting over a pencil, then someday you'll each be able to own your own pencil factories."

Later I explained to Mrs. Vaughn that as a teacher she had to take care of problems herself. "Remember, if you take the problems to the parent, you and the child will not learn to trust each other and work together. Children respect teachers who do not always send notes home to parents."

I went on for weeks overseeing everything Mrs. Vaughn said and did. I stressed that phonics had to be taught daily; no religious fervor for just one day. When I felt she wasn't putting enough expression into the reading of a story, I urged her not to be afraid to become a good actress. A teacher must excite the students about learning.

After a while I felt that Mrs. Vaughn was ready to take charge of the youngest group, the pre-schoolers and kindergarteners. I set up space for her class in what had been the living room of the second-floor apartment, down the hall from my classroom. There were no desks and chairs. The youngsters sat on the carpet, surrounded by piles of books and papers, and Mrs. Vaughn kneeled beside them, inching from child to child, helping each to print the upper and lower case letters and to sound out words.

"You have to get down to a child's eye level and talk directly to that child," I insisted. As tall as I was, I was forever stooping and bending down when I talked to a student. "Children, especially the little ones, are easily intimidated by someone towering above them and speaking from on high."

Teacher training was a new area for me. The simplest part was explaining my curriculum. It was far more difficult to show someone how to understand children, how to be sensitive to their needs. Just as a teacher knows his or her own family members, he or she must know the students, their needs and their interests. Each child is unique.

My methods were a far cry from those endorsed in most teacher training institutions, where the emphasis is mostly on abstract theory and professional jargon. To this day I don't understand how hearing about "learning interference due to retroactive and proactive inhibition" will ever help a teacher get through to the freckle-nosed boy with the crooked teeth and make him feel confident and motivated. Many teachers who are honestly looking for ways to improve their techniques walk away from the in-service training sessions overwhelmed with information but without any answers. It's like asking directions to the bus stop and getting a lecture on mass transit systems.

The fancy dressing of "education-speak" has even spread to job titles. Every profession has its lexicon of fancy job descriptions, and education is no exception. There are curriculum facilitators, master teachers, test administrators, LMC (Learning Materials Center) supervisors, TESL (Teaching English as a Second Language) instructors, LD (learning disability) specialists, and EMH (Educable Mentally Handicapped) coordinators. The serious side of it is that while everyone is closely guarding his or her own title, the children are left to fend for themselves.

When teachers turn to the education experts for help, they rarely seem to offer any practical advice. The experts are busy trying to build professional reputations based on some new gimmick. Each has had its fling: new math, teaching machines, continuous progress and non-graded classrooms, open classrooms, team teaching, core curriculum, back-to-basics, black English, and bilingual instruction. One school superintendent had his local community declare an annual "Teachers Day" to improve teacher morale and enthusiasm. What about student morale and enthusiasm? Another superintendent's favorite gimmick was getting businesses to sponsor schools.

That is typical of the American approach to problem-solving. People seem to think that if they throw a few more dollars at a problem it will go away. It is like putting a band-aid on a hemorrhage. When the Chicago public schools were in the throes of a financial crisis, the Chicago School Finance Authority, charged with overseeing school funds and expenditures, hired a consulting firm to make a $33,000 study on cost-saving recommendations. Then, the next year, after the school board failed to do anything about the recommendations, the city allocated another $200,000 for a second study on how to cut school costs.

I remember a time, years back, when schools and teachers tried to deal with their own problems. Then federal dollars became available and suddenly everyone had a problem he couldn't solve and was writing grant proposals. People got billions of dollars to study problems, and when those studies didn't work out, people got more government money to do a new study to find out what went wrong with the first one.

Countless studies have been done on how to teach inner-city students. To me it seems perfectly plain that inner-city children should be taught the same way other children are taught, because all children want the same things out of life. A ghetto child learns in the same way as any other child and is equally capable of reading Dante, Homer, Pascal, or Chaucer. A child—any child—may not go on to college or become a great scholar, but there is no reason he or she can't gain some appreciation for literature or get something worthwhile out of discussing the great books.

I don't hold with a "ghetto approach" to teaching. The experts claim that correcting an inner-city child's grammar will damage his or her identity. I believe that not correcting grammar will damage that child's whole life. While others lowered their standards for inner-city students, I made mine higher.

Busing is another example of a self-defeating approach to black education. It only makes minority children ashamed of themselves and their neighborhoods, as though only schools in white neighborhoods can teach. My goal is to make my students proud and to involve them in improving their community.

Busing doesn't accomplish anything useful. It is merely another way of side-stepping the real problem—ineffective teachers are everywhere. Statistics clearly show that many white, middle-class children are graduating as functional illiterates. In 1976 a Hudson Institute study reported that the most precipitous decline in student achievement was among the brightest and most advantaged children—those from middle-class families. Miseducation is not a function of a child's race or neighborhood but of the teaching methods he or she is exposed to from kindergarten on.

New methods and theories are not the solution. In fact they have been the primary cause of miseducation. In the mid-1960s many educators supported a trend away from the use of books towards "experiential learning activities." They said students needed to experience concepts and ideas instead of just reading about them. One educational psychology textbook used in teacher training courses stated: "Today's schools probably depend far too much upon reading as a data gathering technique." Why then were educators surprised when students went all the way through school without being able to read? And why was everyone surprised when those same non-readers became teachers themselves and spawned a whole new crop of miseducated students?

No amount of money or theory or gimmickry will cure what is wrong with education. Teachers need to stop looking for excuses and teach. They have to read and prepare and learn what they do not know, and then they have to bring that knowledge to their students, taking as much time as necessary to make sure every child learns. Any teacher who leaves a child as she found him negates her duty as a teacher.

I trained Mrs. Vaughn and eventually other teachers by giving them the same advice I gave my students. "You can't weep or talk your way through a mess," I said. "When you come up against a problem, you have to work your way through it."

★ ★ ★

Ella McCoy came to the school for a few days as a parent volunteer, helping to answer the phone and sort the mail. She ended up staying on as a teacher, becoming Marva's protégée. She quit her job after six years of teaching in the public schools. The last straw was overhearing the principal call to a student, "Hey, you fool, come here!"

Having witnessed the transformation of her daughter Erika from a six year old who had been considered retarded to a ten year old who read twenty-three books over the summer, including *Tale of Two Cities* and *Jane Eyre,* Ella resolved to stick with Marva to repay that debt. She wanted to give other children the same hope that had been given to her child.

Ella did not know where to begin. Although she had graduated from a midwestern teachers' college, she did not know how to syllabicate words. She knew nothing about literature or poetry. Like any one of Marva's students and like Lillian Vaughn, Ella needed to start out with the basics—the phonics, the drills and memorization, the vocabulary, the spelling and grammar rules. She studied the fables, mythology, and classics as though she were cramming for an introductory course in English Lit.

Ella trained in the classroom with Marva, trying to help with the children. "I couldn't really help them," she confessed later, "because I didn't know the material myself." When the school day was over, Ella became Marva's pupil. Marva taught her when a vowel sound was long and when it was short, when to double a consonant and when not to. Before, it had all been a matter of guesswork for Ella: she had never had a method for determining whether the word was *hoping* or *hopping*.

More than the fundamentals of language, Ella felt she was learning how to teach for the first time—how to motivate children and get them going. "Everything works when the teacher works," Marva told her. "It's as easy as that, and as hard. It's your duty to find a way to reach each child. If the child doesn't move, it's the teacher's fault."

Ella watched Marva and did what she did. Ella praised the children, patted them, scolded them, hugged them, prodded them, joked with them, was firm with them, held their hands, and pumped them full of confidence and love. Her rapport with the children came naturally. All she could think about was reading and studying and finding ways to move each child. She had never realized teaching was so demanding.

"Each teacher must prepare, prepare, prepare, and prepare some more," Marva had told her. "We never assign to children what we do not understand ourselves. Never assign children books that you haven't read. Remember, written book reports are often copied. The child copies the front of the book, the middle, and the end. Have the child describe the book orally, and be ready for the child to test you to see if you have read the book."

Because she had not read many of the classics herself, Ella became a steady customer at the library. Marva encouraged her to "look through old anthologies, the kind that kept children interested in school before the publishers watered them down and choked so many children on boredom."

After the first day she taught on her own, taking over half of Lillian Vaughn's class, Ella was exhausted. Her legs weren't used to walking up and down all day. However, she knew she couldn't be a teacher at Westside Prep and sit behind a desk, wondering what the child in the back was doing. She had to get up and see for herself. In Marva's school errors had to be checked immediately or a child would fall behind. Ella found energy she never thought she had and she trusted her legs would get stronger and the ache in her lower back would eventually go away. The children needed her full attention now.

A new student, Arnold Rogers, reminded Ella of Erika as she had been before. The child's previous teachers had disposed of him as a lost cause at eight years old. If ever there was a child who had been trampled by armies of specialists clashing over diagnoses, it was Arnold. He had gone through the educational system like a lab rat in a maze, scrutinized by psychologists, audiologists, ophthalmologists, speech pathologists, and social workers. Arnold did have a physiological problem: surgical correction of a cleft palate had left him with speech and hearing difficulties. No one was certain whether these difficulties prevented Arnold from learning.

His principal and teachers saw Arnold merely as a child with "severe behavior disorders," and they wanted him placed in a special school for emotionally disturbed and retarded youngsters. When a psychologist from the Chicago Board of Education examined Arnold, he kept asking her, "Why are you so *obese?*" The psychologist later said to his mother, "So many of our black boys end up in jail . . ."

To his public school teachers Arnold was a clear-cut case, which they had chronicled for months:

11/10/78 Playing with cough drops. Passing them all around to classmates instead of doing seatwork.

When told his work was not finished he scribbled everything black.

Grabbed Michael Lane in lunch line and tried to lift him up.

Put his lunch tray in Michael Lane's face.

Playing with spider ring of Derrick's.

During math, Arnold was imitating everything I said. He was playing with his pencil and flipped it onto the floor.

Pushing Beverly's desk back.

11/14/78 Arnold began his A.M. work with little difficulty. He did come up to ask me words 3 times, however.

11/15/78 While walking to lunch, Arnold stopped at water fountain and turned on faucet.

2:30 P.M.—Pushed down all the boys in line while standing at the door, for no apparent reason.

2/16/79 During Black History assembly, Arnold seemed confused as to where he was to stand and what he was supposed to say. While on stage, he was looking around—somewhat detached and disinterested in the program.

Note that Arnold needs constant reminding to complete one entire task. During a regular class day he must be spoken to often.

2/21/79 During assembly program, Arnold was holding his hands over his ears. When asked whether the music was too loud—said yes. Several times got out of seat to walk away. Had to be reminded to sit quietly.

3/26/79 Arnold had 2 hours to do three papers. He played with his ink pen and ball for those 2 hrs. instead of working.

Miriam Rogers didn't care what kind of "evidence" the teachers had against her son. She was determined to prove he did not have a behavior disorder. She couldn't understand how a teacher could allow a child to dawdle at his desk for two hours playing with a ball. Why didn't the teacher simply take the ball away and tell Arnold to get busy? As Arnold's father told the principal: "My son understands what you are trying to do to him. He is not crazy, but you are trying to make him crazy."

Arnold's parents got a lawyer from the Legal Assistance Foundation to fight having their son placed in a special school for emotionally disturbed children. They argued their case before representatives from the Board of Education at a special due-process hearing. They won. The hearings officer ruled that there was insufficient proof of a behavior disorder, although there was ample evidence that Arnold had "serious learning disabilities in the areas of visual-motor perception, visual processing and eye-hand coordination."

Arnold remained in school with the same teacher and received speech and visual therapy from the school clinician. Two months after the hearing there were problems once again. Arnold was suspended for throwing food and fighting in the lunchroom. Having had her fill of the public schools, Miriam Rogers tried to enroll Arnold in Westside Prep.

Marva was out of town. Ella, who had been working at the school for seven months, met privately with Mrs. Rogers and surprised her by showing little interest in Arnold's history of misbehavior: "As far as I'm concerned, your son is an eight-year-old child who *will* learn." When Marva telephoned, Ella said, "Please, Mrs. Collins, let's squeeze Arnold in. We'll find the space somehow." With only three weeks left before the school closed for the summer, Marva agreed to take Arnold until the end of the term without any fee.

Marva met Arnold and his mother at the door. "Why were you suspended from your other school?"

"For fighting and throwing food." His mother spoke for him. Arnold was too ashamed of his speech impediment to attempt more than a one-word answer to any question.

Marva nodded. "Arnold, sweetheart, you already know

how to fight. If you want to spend your time throwing around food and garbage, if you want to be a garbageman all your life, then you don't need an education."

"Huh?" Arnold looked up at Marva, confused.

"I beg your pardon. We don't say 'huh' in here. We speak in sentences." Marva kneeled next to him, her eyes level with his, her hands on his shoulders. "Your mother can't be with you your whole life and neither can I. You must make it on your own. Love, you are going to learn in here every day starting today."

Arnold stared in amazement.

"Now, sweetheart, can you spell *cat* for me?" Marva asked.

"C-a-t," he answered hesitantly.

"Very, very good. You're so bright," Marva said. Then she turned to Mrs. Rogers. "There is nothing wrong with your son that time and patience can't take care of."

Arnold became one of Ella's students. She sat him down and said, "Arnold, sweetheart, from now on you're going to learn. Children don't fail in here because I don't let them fail. You will learn to read so you can have choices in life."

The other children were reading *Aesop's Fables*. Arnold refused to open the book. He bolted out of his seat and into the bathroom where Cindy and Tracy were sitting on the edge of the bathtub reading. Cindy looked up from her book. "Do you want to use the bathroom?" she asked.

He shook his head. He spied a hammer that Clarence had left on the floor beside the toilet. He grabbed it and took a swing at Cindy, hitting her on her arm. She screamed and ran out of the room with Arnold chasing after her.

"I'll take that hammer, Arnold," Marva said. What surprised Arnold even more than the suddenness of her appearance was her tone. She spoke calmly and softly, yet something told him she meant business. He shoved the hammer at her and started to turn away. Marva held him by his arm while she consoled Cindy and checked for injuries. Satisfied that Cindy wasn't hurt, Marva turned back to Arnold. "In this school we put our energy in our brains, not our fists and certainly not in hitting others with hammers or sticks or anything else."

Arnold raised his head to look at her, wondering if she was crazy.

"This is your last school, darling," she continued. "You are here to stay. No one is putting you out. But you are going to produce, you are going to read, because if you can't read, then you can't do anything in life." She tucked in his shirt and started to walk him back to Ella's classroom. "I know there's a good you locked up inside that angry you. It's just waiting to come out if you will only let it.

"There once was a famous sculptor named Michelangelo. Do you know what a sculptor is?" Arnold shook his head without lifting his eyes. "Well, a sculptor is someone who carves and chisels statues out of blocks of wood or stone. Michelangelo liked to make things out of marble. And he would walk around the streets of Florence, Italy, where he lived, and every time he saw a piece of marble he would think of the beautiful angels he could carve from it. Just as Michelangelo thought there was an angel locked inside every piece of marble, I think there is a brilliant child locked inside every student in this school."

Marva sat Arnold down at his spot in the second classroom. Ella was giving dictation. Ella paused and held his shoulder: "You can do it. You can do it." She printed his name at the top of a paper and wrote out the last sentence of dictation: *Aesop wrote fables.* Taking Arnold's chin in her hand, she said, "Now let's say the first word together. The *a* is silent so we begin with the *e* sound. Say *ee.* You have to open your mouth in a smile."

Arnold repeated the vowel.

"Oh, that's good. Now *sss,* make the sound come through your teeth. Then *ah,* open your mouth wide. And *puh,* make a popping sound with your lips. Now put all the sounds together and say *Aesop.*"

"Aesop," Arnold said.

"Very good. Aesop, Aesop," Ella repeated.

"I know it's Aesop. How many times ya gonna tell me? Wads duh nex' word?"

Ella laughed and mussed his hair. "You're going to do just fine."

Marva was watching this scene from a distance, looking on with pride in both the child and the teacher.

At the end of the first day Ella sent Arnold home with a sheet of math problems for homework. She didn't expect him to do them all. If he did one, it would have been something. But he finished the page. By the end of the week Arnold was starting to read. He was taking dictation and writing on the lines of the paper, which he had never done before. He came in scrubbed and with his shirt tucked in. Once he discovered that no one made fun of the way he talked, he began to answer questions and read aloud—drawing cheers and applause from his classmates.

His mother didn't know what to make of it. Arnold had always been such a frustrated and angry child. He used to say he couldn't wait until he got to be sixteen years old so he could drop out of school. Now he woke up in the morning excited about going to class, telling his father to drive faster. He didn't mind staying late in the afternoon to finish work. Sometimes Ella would drive him home and stop for a hotdog or milkshake. He looked forward to Ella's tutoring him over the summer; as he told his mother, "I got to learn 'cause I'm going to go to college and do a lot of things when I grow up."

One morning the bubble burst. Arnold came to school upset. The sparkle was gone, replaced by his old belligerence.

"What happened, baby?" Marva asked.

Arnold told her he forgot his homework and his father had yelled at him in the car for it.

"Who runs this school, your dad or Mrs. Collins?" Arnold had never seen her so angry—not even the time he hit Cindy with the hammer.

"Mrs. Collins," he answered.

"That's right. And you know what we say in here: if you can't make a mistake, you can't what?"

"Make anything."

"Good. Now get a smile on that face. I can't stand to be around sad children."

That afternoon, Marva telephoned Arnold's father. "Mrs. McCoy and I are trying so hard to build confidence in Arnold," she told him, "but by shouting at the boy you are going to undo everything we have done so far. Arnold has been called every name in the book and now he needs praise and plenty of it—from everyone."

A few days later came the end of another school year. It had been five years since Marva left Delano to begin an alternative school. The students who had first come to her as ornery, scared, bored, underachieving children were now stepping into adolescence as confident and determined young men and women. Erika left for the summer handing Marva a copy of a newly published biography of Sacajawea. "Mrs. Collins, you've got to read this book. It's terrific."

Gary Love said his last goodbyes to Marva and Westside Prep. Gary, who used to insist he couldn't do anything, had won a scholarship to a private academy in the northern suburbs. Marva's son Patrick was also going to high school in the fall.

There were other changes afoot for September. Clarence was leaving his job at Sunbeam to help Marva manage the school's business affairs. Westside Prep had grown into a full-fledged educational institution, and Marva was finally moving it out of her house. The 60 Minutes feature had opened a financial spigot that allowed her to make plans for accommodating some of the children on the waiting list, which had swelled to about 700 students. Almost $50,000 in contributions had rolled into Westside Prep, including a $10,000 check from an anonymous donor whom Marva jokingly called J. Beausfoot Tipton from the TV series The Millionaire. Another $75,000 came from a film production company that bought the rights to make a movie about Marva and the school. The contributions, the movie money, plus the income from her workshops and speeches enabled Marva to rent space on the second floor of the old, and practically vacant, National Bank of Commerce Building, a few blocks away on Madison Street.

In September 1980 Westside Prep would have an enrollment of 200 students. Marva had said all along that Westside Prep was not the "one-room fairy tale" some of the press had labeled it. She was going to prove that good education could happen on any scale.

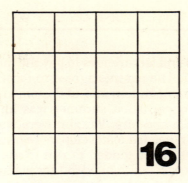

16

I had dreamed of expanding the school for nearly three years, ever since I had to draw up that first waiting list with thirty names. Yet when it finally came about, the expansion happened so fast I felt as though I were whirling on a merry-go-round and couldn't catch my breath. The school didn't just grow. It seemed to explode. We jumped from 34 students in June to an estimated fall enrollment of 200, with a waiting list of over 500 more.

The summer was chaos. Everyone was swept up in moving the school. Clarence, Eric, and Patrick worked frantically, painting, building bookshelves, hanging blackboards, and carrying all the desks, books, and filing cabinets from the upstairs of our house to the second floor of the bank building. Cindy, Tracy, and Erika unpacked cartons of new textbooks and supplies. Ella, Mrs. Vaughn, and I made class lists, wrote up lessons, mimeographed worksheets, arranged desks, and put up posters and phonics charts. Some of the parents pitched in too, helping out with registration, phone calls, and office work.

Expansion on this scale made it necessary that I do something about the other sort of parents, those who remained uninvolved in the education of their children, to the point of never paying tuition. One father seemed to typify their attitude when he said, "I know you won't put my child out if I don't pay tuition. You like children too much." I flatly informed the parents we would have to change that policy in the fall. Tuition was the only reliable source of income for the school. I couldn't count on contributions and lecture fees to pay the monthly rent or salaries for my staff. The parents agreed to form an association to deal with delinquent tuition and to do some fund raising.

My chief concern that summer was hiring and training new teachers. Ella and Mrs. Vaughn were working out beautifully, though both needed to develop more initiative in handling student problems. They tended to run to me with everything, from a child who needed a band-aid for a scratch to a student who was disrupting the class, but they were hard-working, dedicated teachers. Most important, they believed in the children. I wanted to find two other teachers just like them.

I had a stack of resumés from people all over the country, even a few inquiries from Europe. Resumés and letters couldn't tell me what I wanted to know. I was interested in attitudes, not credentials. I didn't want people who pitied poor little black children. Nor did I want teachers who had limited expectations of what children could achieve.

Since August had to be set aside for training new teachers, I didn't have time to go through a long interviewing process. Fortunately I didn't have to. I hired one teacher, Patricia Jurgens, on a referral and recommendation from a friend of mine. The other teacher I decided on was Marcella Winters, the mother of one of my students. She had gone back to school and had just completed her degree in education. I knew and liked her as a person before I ever knew her as a teacher. She was outgoing and high spirited, a bundle of energy. The main reason I hired her was that she had an interest in the school and believed in what we were doing. Her daughter had been enrolled in Westside Prep for two years.

I drilled the new teachers in my methodology. "The teacher who can only work with the well-motivated child and the well-behaved child has no place at Westside Preparatory School," I told them. "I want teachers who will make the slow student become good and the good student become superior."

★　★　★

A wig emporium and a Frederick's of Hollywood-style lingerie shop flanked the entrance to Marva's new school in the National Bank of Commerce Building. In the lobby an elderly security guard sat at his post by the iron-gated doorway to the empty bank. The bank had closed nearly twenty years ago, when everything else in Garfield Park shut down.

The building's only tenant was Westside Prep, installed in the mezzanine overlooking the unused teller cages. Marva paid $2,400 a month to rent the windowless, musty space that was too hot in the fall and spring and too cold in the winter. It was a stiff price, but that was a fact of life in that neighborhood.

By 2:30 in the afternoon, when the children filed out of school, hawkers had set up their wares on card tables in the outer vestibule, hustling parents to buy rhinestone rings and gold-plated chains. Outside, car exhaust mixed with the smells from the fried chicken franchise across the street, and customers were already seeking out the taverns around the corner.

It was an improbable setting for a school, perhaps even more improbable than the apartment above Marva's house. Yet Westside Prep was drawing students from all parts of the city and even from Chicago's western and far-southern suburbs. Many parents now felt that the only place their children could get a high-quality education was in the heart of a ghetto.

One student commuted by train from Elgin, Illinois, thirty-five miles away. Eighth-grader Sandra Parsons—a former junior high school student who performed at a fourth grade level in both reading and math—made the daily sixty-mile round trip from East Chicago, Indiana. And nine-year-old Brian Shoemaker came from the Lincoln Park area, a neighborhood of lakefront condominiums and $250,000 Victorian rowhouses, whose residents included the likes of Governor James Thompson. Brian had attended the Lincoln School, one of the highest rated of the city's public schools, where he had been a fourth-grader reading at a first grade level.

Westside Prep's 200 students were divided among five classes. Some classes had more than forty pupils—ten to fifteen more than the Chicago Teachers' Union allowed in the public schools. Lillian Vaughn, Patricia Jurgens, and Marcella Winters took charge of the pre-schoolers, kindergarteners, and first-graders—about half of the school's enrollment. Most of these younger children did not have any difficulty learning; their parents were sending them to Westside Prep in the hope that they never would. The few who had problems had drastic ones. Mrs.

Vaughn had a six-year-old student who showed signs of being autistic. According to his grandfather, who raised him, Charles had never talked. All he did was grunt.

Marva and Ella taught the older students, the hard-core problem children. Besides not having academic skills, some of these youngsters had enough emotional disorders to fill the glossary of a psychology textbook. One boy had been in and out of thirteen schools in four years. Another youngster, who had a penchant for stabbing other children with pencils, had been thrown out of the Drusso Mental Health Center. Then there was "The Slasher," an eight year old who would remove the blade from pencil sharpeners and run around cutting up his classmates' coats, hats, gloves, and scarves.

Tommy, at twelve, was in a constant depression, hating himself, hating his brother, hating everyone for not liking him; he even hated his last name, which he refused to use. The word *kill* nearly always came up when he spoke. If Marva said, "How do you feel today?" Tommy would say, "I feel like killing myself." When Marva said, "Have a nice weekend," he'd answer, "If I don't kill myself falling off my bike" or "If I don't kill myself getting hit in the head with a soccer ball."

Marva kept a straight face and praised him, saying he was handsome or she liked something he was wearing. She believed that he was not really self-destructive; he wanted attention. Marva resolved to show him there were more positive ways of getting it. Their exchanges began to sound like a cross between a Burns and Allen sketch and *Waiting for Godot*.

"I *don't* like myself. I want to kill myself."

"My, what a beautiful shirt you have."

Tommy would shrug and try again. "My brother hates me. I'd like to kill myself."

"Oh, what lovely eyes you have." Marva replied.

It went on for months. Then one afternoon Marva wished him a good evening.

"I . . ." Tommy paused.

What was it going to be this time? Marva wondered.

"I . . . I love you, Mrs. Collins," Tommy shouted, throwing his arms around her in a bearhug.

★　★　★

That first breakthrough was a joy to me, but it was only a beginning. Tommy inched into learning, still elusive, still testing and feeling his way. He spent part of the day in Ella's class, working on phonics and math and then came to mine for social studies and science. During one of the social studies lessons, while the students were taking turns reading aloud, I called on Tommy to read a short passage that I had selected especially for him. It contained eleven words that I was sure he could sound out. As he read, I stood beside him squeezing his shoulder. And when he finished, the whole class applauded.

"I gotta see Mrs. McCoy. Can I go see Mrs. McCoy?" he said excitedly, already half-standing. When I gave the okay, he bounded out the door and rushed into Ella's room. "I knocked 'em dead in Mrs. Collins' class. I sure knocked 'em dead!"

Seeing Westside Prep's *wunderkinden* splashed across the TV screen and featured in newspapers and magazines led some skeptics to accuse me of hand-picking only the brightest students. They saw only how far the children had come, not where they had been.

In a way I did hand-pick the students. Often the severity of a child's problem speeded up admission to Westside Prep. An older student took precedence over a pre-schooler or kindergartener for two reasons. First, the older child needed more immediate attention, sometimes having only four or five months to develop his or her skills to qualify for high school. Second, the pre-school and kindergarten enrollment had ballooned, and I didn't want my teachers to have more students than they felt they could handle.

Sometimes I gave priority to a child who wasn't even on the waiting list, and that selection policy brought on a barrage of complaints from parents who had long-standing applications on file. I also drew fire from some parents and members of the black community when I accepted some white students to Westside Prep. I tried to be fair, but I couldn't please everyone. It was up to me to make the decision on each new enrollment.

It was my school and I felt the public had no right to tell me how to run it. That especially meant government bureaucrats and special interest groups pushing minority rights. I live in the middle of Garfield Park, they do not. They do not know what works here, I do. People who have never set foot in this neighborhood always seem to think they know exactly what is good for it. All the do-gooders come in and criticize what is wrong. But do they ever come up with better alternatives?

Some people criticized my kind of "tough love," but I did not need any outsiders telling me I was too firm with my students. I felt just as sorry as they did for those children. No one knew better than I what kinds of homes some of them came from. But I was doing something constructive about it. I wasn't just passing out candy, rubbing the children's heads, and telling them how cute they were. I was trying to give them the skills to survive, forever telling them that each person must decide what he or she is going to leave to society for the privilege of living here. It was through the children in my school that I hoped to change the attitude of future generations.

The school itself represented the kind of determination, perseverance, stick-to-it-iveness, and pride I wanted the children to have. Sometimes, as I walked through the classrooms or when I overheard four and five year olds running around saying, "I'm a universal citizen," I was amazed at what we had accomplished in five years.

Westside Preparatory School had come full circle. With an enrollment of 200, operating a school that size became complex and demanding. I suddenly had an enormous overhead, a payroll, and all kinds of administrative duties. I had to deal with the newly formed Parents Association, occasionally being the referee at their meetings. One father simply could not get along with the other parents, and finally I had to ask him to withdraw his two children from the school. Once or twice I even had to put an end to bickering and resentment among my staff—the same kind of dissension as at Delano. I had to remind my teachers that they were not the important ones, that only the children mattered.

The 1980–1981 school year was a period of transition. I found myself pulled in a dozen directions. I had to oversee what my staff was doing, but I couldn't be in every classroom every minute of the day. I had to run the school as a whole, in addition to teaching my classes. I kept reminding myself that people were sending their children to this school because they wanted the kind of education demonstrated in the one-room school on Adams Street.

Of course the school lost some of the intimacy of a one-room setting, but I made sure I knew every one of the 200 children. I was determined not to lose sight of the philosophy on which the school was founded—we were there to serve the individual needs of each child. I kept telling my teachers that they should be the ones sharpening pencils and washing the blackboards. The children were there to learn, and learning was a full-time job.

I also had to remind my staff that whatever a child should have learned in a previous school didn't matter. Their duty was to start that child up from where he or she was. There were times when I had to caution my teachers not to write a child's name on the board for talking. Most of all I stressed the importance of praise and positive reinforcement.

I didn't want to be a principal. I fought the remoteness of being an administrator. The hours I spent in the classroom teaching were all the more precious because they kept me from losing touch with the children. Yet I had to be a principal. One of the newer teachers proved to be reluctant to follow my methodology, though I hoped she would eventually come around. I was especially anxious not to dismiss her in the middle of the year because children need continuity in their education. Schools have always moved black children around like pawns on a playing board, and I was not going to do that. If the other aspects of their lives were in chaos, then it was up to me to give my children the stability they needed. Unfortunately the teacher did not work out and she left the following year.

By January the school was operating with a certain momentum of its own. For the most part the teachers were carrying on my methods—especially Ella, who had a strong enough personality to take charge when I had to be away. The children themselves were the best indication that the school was working. At eight years old Calvin Graham, who had started at Westside Prep four years before, was reading at a ninth grade level. The older children had adopted him as a sort of class mascot, and I could barely keep a straight face at some of the things that came out of his mouth. One afternoon I was going around the class asking the children to give me a thought for the day. In turn they recited quotations from Emerson, Shakespeare, and Socrates. When I came to Calvin, he said, "To associate with fools is like going to bed with a razor." Surprised, I told him I wasn't familiar with that line. He said he made it up himself.

Arnold Rogers, the child Ella had worked so closely with, blossomed during that year. His mother said he hated to miss school, even when he was sick. Once he had the stomach flu but refused to stay home. In class he had an unfortunate accident, and when I took him to the washroom, he said to me, "Oh, Mrs. Collins, I'm so chagrined. I'm so humiliated." I told him that any eight-year-old boy who had the word *chagrin* in his vocabulary had no reason to be humiliated about anything. Several months later that same child, who had struggled to overcome a severe learning disability associated with a speech impediment, stood before an auditorium filled with people and recited the poem "Invictus."

I was proud of all the children. Their accomplishments spoke for themselves. Sandra Parsons, for example, the thirteen year old who had arrived in September doing fourth grade work, tested a few months later at a tenth grade level and was admitted to the freshman class at a private high school in Indiana. Another girl, who came to me in the fall from one of the city's most acclaimed public schools, where she was scheduled to repeat seventh grade, scored at a tenth grade level in vocabulary and at an eleventh grade level in reading comprehension when she took the California Achievement Test in January. And in June 1981 Tracy Shanklin, who had started with me six years before, was accepted into a parochial high school—a year above her age level—and was slated for advanced algebra and sophomore biology classes.

Former students of mine were now attending a variety of private, parochial, and public high schools, where most of them were holding their own. Some did only average work. A few had a difficult time adjusting and had to work hard to pull up their grades. Still, considering all these students had been so far below average when they first came to Westside Prep, the progress they had made was remarkable.

Somehow people have a hard time accepting the fact that inner-city children can achieve on a higher plane than most schools require. It was precisely that myth that I wanted to shatter. With that in mind, I took on children from the Cabrini-Green housing projects in the summer of 1981.

★　★　★

Cabrini-Green is the essence of Chicago's mean streets, a graffiti-scrawled stretch of high-rise public housing where murder, rape, and gang terror are daily events. In March 1981 Cabrini-Green caught nationwide media attention when Mayor Jane Byrne moved into one of the apartments in an effort to curtail the violence and pacify frightened residents.

Trying to keep things cool over the summer, city officials stepped up the police patrols, built a new baseball field to get the children off the streets, and also sponsored a tuition-free Summertime Institute for 140 Cabrini-Green area youngsters, kindergarten through sixth grade.

Mayor Byrne asked Marva to organize the eight-week summer school program. She accepted without hesitation, asking specifically for students who had behavior problems or were reading at least two grades below their age level. This time critics would hardly be able to accuse her of selecting the brightest students.

Marva used the same textbooks and teaching materials she used at her school, not the ones the city school system wanted to provide. She set up the curriculum, prepared the lesson plans, and hired the teachers. There was one catch: her staff had to include five teachers from the public schools, a concession to the Chicago Teachers' Union.

More than two dozen applied. Some of the interviews were brief. One applicant demanded a classroom with windows. Another was dismayed that the Byrd Elementary School, where the program was being held, was not air-conditioned. A third wanted to know how many aides she would have. Others balked when Marva told them they would not be able to sit behind a desk. Needless to say, those teachers weren't hired.

Organizational details were taken care of the day before

the program started, much to the irritation of some teachers who didn't want to show up before the children. Marva refused to waste any class time passing out books and papers. By 8:30 on the first morning Marva and her staff were ready to begin teaching.

Marva was to supervise the seven classrooms. During the first week she spent most of the three-hour daily session with the sixth-graders, the oldest students and the by now chronic non-learners. To see her then was to see the quintessential Marva at work—preacher, flatterer, aphorist, quipster, booster, parent, and teacher.

"Good morning, I love you," Marva greeted the students. "You are all very special students and you are going to learn here . . ." Beginning with an introduction to phonics, she raced excitedly around the room, urging the children to an enthusiasm that matched her own. "Show me a teacher who is dragging," she reminded her staff, "and I'll show you a listless class."

Though it was summer, no one in class was ever allowed to sleep or daydream. "Wait a minute," Marva said, stopping in the middle of an explanation of the vowel reversals in *diary* and *dairy*. "Sit up everybody. Sit up and look alive."

One boy was leaning over his desk, his head resting on his arm. Marva went over to him and gently lifted his head. Nudged out of his nap, he angrily pushed Marva away.

"If you touch me again, I'm gonna kill you!"

"Good, I've lived too long anyway." Marva remained calm.

"Why don't you beat him? His teacher last year always hit him with a stick," a child called from across the room.

"Because that is not the way human beings should treat each other. I am a teacher. I wasn't trained to be a jailer or a disciplinarian. School is not a place where we beat people. It's where we go to learn to have a better life. Beating someone doesn't do any good. When you are finished beating someone, how much better off are you? How much richer are you?"

Marva turned back to the boy. "What's your name, darling?"

He didn't answer.

"Sam, he's Sam," a classmate said.

"Now look, Sam," Marva continued, "you are going to sit up if I have to spray you with cold water. I will not have you drooping and wilting on me. I do not droop and wilt on you. You will learn here. You have no choice."

Standing beside Sam, her hand on his shoulder, she turned to address the whole class. "Some of you are in sixth grade and you can't even read at a first grade level. I'm not saying that to put you down. I'm telling you the facts as they are. When you go back to your regular schools in September, you will be the brightest children in your class."

Marva walked to the front of the room, handing one boy a tissue as she passed him and reminding another to take the pick out of his hair. Pointing to the words she had printed in long lists on the board, Marva explained that the letter *e* at the end of a word makes a middle vowel long. She recited the words and the children echoed: "Rod and rode, pin and pine, cut and cute, sit and site, dim and dime, cub and cube, man and mane, kit and kite, mad and made, pal and pale, fin and fine."

A boy wearing a gold Superman tee-shirt started making faces and laughing and whispering to the child next to him. Both of them giggled. Marva stopped.

"Is it funny when we fail?" she asked. "Is it funny when we have no food? Is it funny when we have no money to go to the doctor?"

Marva glowered at the student who created the distraction. "Is it funny when we haven't got a dollar?" she repeated. The boy shook his head. "Well, then, stop clowning because this is money up here," Marva said, pointing to the vowel sounds on the board.

Moving to the second boy, she asked, "Why are you paying attention to him? Don't grin at him. He's sad. Get on your knees and pray for him. Children who keep clowning do it because they can't do anything else.

"Children, you are foolish to spend school time clowning and grinning. Teachers come in here wearing nice clothes, and they drive away from here in nice cars. They get all that from you, from the public paying their salaries. You pay them to teach. If you just sit there grinning and not learning, you are paying them for nothing."

Taking the arm of the boy in the gold tee-shirt, Marva eased him out of his seat. "Now, let's go to the board, and we'll do these vowel sounds together."

Slowly the boy followed, and with Marva helping him he sounded out the list of words. He strutted back to his desk with an air of success.

Marva told the class to open their readers to the story of *Peter Rabbit* by Beatrix Potter.

"Do we copy the whole story?" asked a girl.

"Copy the story?" Marva was puzzled.

"Sure, we always copy the story and do the questions in the back."

"You don't copy anything from a book. You learn what the book has to teach you. If you are used to copying, you are not used to thinking. You are going to think in here. You are not going to be looking at a picture and filling in a word. You are going to do things that require brains."

Marva gave the children background on the author, telling them that Beatrix Potter grew up in England. "England is in the British Isles. 'England, Ireland, Scotland, and Wales, four little dogs without any tails.' That's how you remember the British Isles." Continuing, Marva told about the author's lonely childhood, reflected in the point of view of her stories. "And what is point of view? It's the attitude an author shows in a story."

Marva highlighted words to watch, giving the pronunciation and the definition. "*Implored* means begged. What did I do if I implored you?"

"You begged," the class said in unison.

"Exert. The *ex* has the sound of *eg*. The *ert* sounds like *zurt*. *Exert* means to try very hard. What does it mean?"

"To try very hard."

"Oh, you are so smart. Now we are going to read a story about a rabbit who was naughty. What happens to people who do bad things?"

"They come to no good," answered a thin girl wearing a long-sleeved blouse.

"So it is better to stop a bad thing before it gets started, isn't it?" As she spoke, Marva walked over to the girl and began rolling up the sleeves of the child's blouse. Leaning down to her ear, Marva whispered that it was too hot to have on long sleeves.

"I want all eyes on the books. Don't lose your place reading. You will get lost in the world that way."

She called on a child to begin the reading of *Peter Rabbit:* "Once upon a time. . . ." When he finished the first few sentences, Marva stopped him to check for comprehension. "Who is this story about?" she asked.

"Rabbits," a chubby boy in the front seat answered.

"There are lots of rabbits. What are these rabbits' names?"

"Aw, this story is taking too long," complained a boy as he banged his book shut.

"All year you have been copying a story out. That is why you have problems with reading. I have read this story at least sixty times. I have been using this book for fourteen years. It's easy for me as a teacher to sit behind a desk and ask you to answer the questions at the end. It is much easier than standing here and asking what everything means. If the story is too long, life is too long. How many of you want to die this minute? You need to take time to learn. How many of you would tell me to stop if I were putting $20 bills on your desk? Well, don't tell me to stop teaching you either. Everything I teach you is like money in the bank."

The children read half the story. Sensing their interest flagging, Marva told them to close their readers and take out Bernard Miles' *Favorite Tales From Shakespeare.* She launched into an introduction to *Macbeth.*

"The witches predict but people determine," Marva said. "Everyone said, 'Oh, Cabrini-Green,' when I told them I was coming here to teach. They tried to predict something. They tried to predict that I would find trouble here. But you determine. You determine what you are going to be and what you are going to make of Cabrini-Green. You can be as great as you want to be. And this neighborhood can be as good or as bad as you want it to be."

A child in the back let out a groan. "If you have a headache or a stomachache, go home. No one pays you for aches and pains. People will only pay you to do work."

"Is it almost lunchtime?" blurted another child.

"Are you children worried about getting one free carton of milk and one free sandwich from the city, when I am teaching you so that you can get your own milk and food your whole life?"

Marva stood beside the child who had asked about lunch. "I love you," she told him, "and I am not going to go home and talk about you behind your back. I am going to tell you the way it is right to your face. See the torn shirt you are wearing? Without an education you will always have a torn shirt. I am going to bring you a shirt tomorrow, and I expect you to act like someone who wears good clothes, starting now. Right now."

The class read part of *Macbeth*, saving the rest for the next day. They went on to work on synonyms. At a quarter of twelve Marva began passing out homework sheets.

"I already got one," said the boy with the Superman shirt, clowning again.

"Do not say 'I already got one.' Say 'I have one.' But don't tell me to stop giving you homework. I asked you before would you tell me to stop giving you money? You know, you are a handsome boy. You don't have to stretch your mouth back like that in a grin. You were born to win, so don't make yourself a loser."

Hearing papers rustling, Marva looked up and saw some of the boys folding their homework and shoving it into their back pockets.

"Don't crumple your papers into little pieces," Marva said. "Big people take their papers home flat. How would it look if some lawyer or executive brought important papers home looking like that? All of you sit down and straighten those papers. You all have such a poor image of yourselves. Be proud of your work. Be proud of what you do."

As the children were leaving the room, Marva intercepted the boy in the Superman shirt. Putting her arms on his shoulders, she said, "You are in sixth grade and your reading score is 1.1. I don't hide your scores in a folder. I tell them to you so you know what you have to do. Now your clowning days are over. You haven't done a thing to me. You've done it to you. If I have to love you more than you love yourself, I'll do that."

Marva's biggest problem at Cabrini-Green was not the children but some of the teachers. Some had no enthusiasm. They watched the clock, let children fall asleep, and acted as though it was killing them to move. One woman quit after four days, telling Marva it was just too difficult: she was too tired and uncomfortable standing all morning. Marva had to replace a second teacher, a woman who claimed to be a reading specialist. As it turned out, she didn't know a thing about phonics. Marva discovered she was giving her students busy-work instead. On one occasion Marva walked into this woman's classroom and found her assigning a composition on "My Trip To A Foreign Country." She expected the students to write about traveling to a foreign country when some of them had never traveled more than a few miles beyond Cabrini-Green. Worse than inappropriate, the topic was boring. It was standard who-cares fare, like the traditional "How I Spent My Summer Vacation."

Marva wasn't about to let the project fail because of poor teachers, so she brought in reinforcements. Ella McCoy came in to help supervise. Even Erika did some tutoring. She walked up and down the aisles supplying a synonym or an antonym, assisting a younger child to read aloud and offering encouragement. One of the eight-year-old boys said the work was too hard and he couldn't do it; Erika looked at him sternly and said, "Yes, you can. There isn't anything you can't do if you try. You're the brightest child in the world."

Over the course of the summer a lot of children dropped out of the Summertime Institute. But by the end of eight weeks the children who had remained in the program improved their skills. They had been given a test of vocabulary, spelling, and reading comprehension at the beginning of the session, and their post-program scores all showed increases. In a matter of weeks some of the students had jumped to readers a grade level higher.

On the last day of the program the assembly hall at Byrd School was crowded with media and city officials as Mayor Byrne presided over the awards ceremony, passing out certificates of achievement to eighty-seven students. Later the press surrounded several children.

"What did you learn?" a TV correspondent asked.

"Norse gods and Greek gods," answered one boy.

"I learned Shakespeare, *Macbeth,* reading comprehension, and dictation," said another. "Learning was fun."

"I'm going to keep on studying and learning words," eight-year-old Dorian Hudson told a newspaper reporter. And an eleven-year-old girl said, "I want to take some of what I learned back to my own school and teach it to others."

When the reporter asked the girl what her name was, the child answered, "Chatapne Calvin. There is a long mark over the vowel *e.*"

Epilogue

In September 1981, Westside Preparatory School moved into its own permanent facilities—two adjoining one-story brick office buildings that blended in with the factories, warehouses, and storefront churches along Chicago Avenue on the outskirts of Garfield Park. From its facade, no one could tell it was a school. But everyone knew it was there just the same.

It was Marva's school, but it seemed to belong to the whole neighborhood. People saw it as a beacon of hope on the West Side, a stand against the transience and waste that had plagued the area for nearly two decades. And they were proud of it. How many schools in the middle of a ghetto had ever been a model for achievement? In Marva, the children of the neighborhood had someone to look up to who was not a hustler, entertainer, or sports figure. She and Westside Prep were abiding proof that a person didn't have to be a Dr. J. or a Lena Horne to make it.

Not everyone saw her that way. Marva had her share of scoffers and detractors. Most of her critics were within the teaching profession. Her visibility and her incriminations against the educational system understandably made her a prime target. From Albert Shanker, President of the United Federation of Teachers, to her former colleagues at Delano, critics took issue with Marva and with the "success claims" of her students. They accused Marva of exaggerating her students' accomplishments, of fixing her pupils' test scores, and of raising her school's average test scores by getting rid of poor achievers. There were also charges that she was running an educational sweatshop, and that her students were not learning to read, think, and discuss the great works of literature, but that they were merely memorizing passages by rote.

The more the press and the public extolled Marva, the more vocal her critics became. Both the praise and the criticism built to a crescendo following the airing of a television docudrama about Marva in December 1981. *The Marva Collins Story* touched off a backlash from some Chicago public school teachers who felt the movie was an affront to them and to public education in general. In defense, they set out to discredit her.

Two months later, a newspaper published by an organization of substitute teachers printed an exposé charging that all the publicity surrounding Marva and Westside Prep was the result of a "carefully constructed" five-year "media hoax" that was "aimed at further crippling public education here and around the country." The article alleged that press coverage of Marva had been inflated and misleading. It claimed that Marva's school was not taking the rejects of the public school system but that Westside Prep's student body was made up of middle-class children handpicked for high ability. At the same time, it questioned Marva's acceptance of CETA money when all along she had been an outspoken critic of federal aid.

A few of the local media jumped on the story, attacking Marva with the same hyperbole they had used in praising her. They went after her personality—depicting her as egotistical vindictive, and quick-tempered—and they began looking for the proverbial skeletons in her closet, treating her as if she were a high-profile politician. In an interview, one newscaster went so far as to ask whether Marva was "a sinister woman." Another columnist, angered by Marva's statements that "money isn't the answer to educational problems" and by her endorsement of publicly funded tuition vouchers, accused Marva of "playing into the hands of the right wing" and allowing herself to be used by politicians to support school funding cuts.

Two radio and television reporters hit the hardest with a litany of allegations. Quoting a handful of disgruntled parents and a former Westside Prep teacher, they contended that Marva had misrepresented her credentials; that she had plagiarized another educator's ideas for an opinion column she wrote for the *Sun-Times;* that Westside Prep teachers mistreated students; that Marva refused to release her students' test scores for verification; and that she pressured parents for tuition and barred from the school pupils whose parents had not paid the monthly fees.

Because of Marva's enormous reputation, the controversy became a national story covered by *The New York Times, The Washington Post, The Wall Street Journal,* and *Newsweek.* But all of the news reports were not negative. In fact some journalists defended Marva. Chicago *Sun-Times* columnist Mike Royko called the complaints against Marva "nitpicking—the kinds of gripes that might be kicked around during a teachers' coffee break. But nothing worth screaming headlines." He added that the "complaints didn't alter the basic fact that Collins was and is getting the kinds of results in her school that would delight most public school principals."

Correspondent Morley Safer, who did the *60 Minutes* report on Marva in 1979, stood by his original reporting. He told *Newsweek* the critical stories aired on the Chicago outlet of his own network were "outrageous" and "loaded with inaccuracies" and he said, "I'm convinced that Marva Collins is one hell of a teacher."

The Wall Street Journal saw the controversy as "a story about the politics of education in this country, especially education in the inner city, where the public schools have failed miserably. Mrs. Collins's private success invited reaction because it became a reproach to that failure." The article concluded that "it's clear her critics have more on their minds than her personal foibles. They know that her success showed that poor black children can learn outside the public schools—with little money and without the bureaucracy."

Newsweek summed it up by stating that perhaps Marva had taught the nation at least two lessons. "The trivial one is that not even the heroes of television docu-dramas are guaranteed to be free of human flaws. The important one is how much trust, faith, and hope the nation will invest in a teacher who holds out the simple promise, once taken for granted, of teaching kids to read."

Initially, Marva refused to respond to the charges. She told reporters, "My best defense is what I do. These children can read." But friends and supporters urged her to answer her critics and eventually she did so on a special two-part *Phil Donahue Show*. Meanwhile, Westside Prep parents and community supporters held rallies for Marva, and newspapers received letters to the editor calling the criticism "a witchhunt."

The controversy only lasted a few weeks. When it was over, Marva was battle-fatigued, yet she and Westside Prep were unscathed. The school still had a full enrollment and a long, growing waiting list. She still had enormous public support and legions of admirers. As far as most people were concerned, the only thing the uproar had proven was that Marva was human and not a superwoman—which was what she had maintained all along. In an interview with *The New York Times* she said: "I've never said I'm a superteacher, a miracle worker, all those names they gave me. It's unfair to expect me to live up to it. I'm just a teacher."

For all their attempts to tear down Marva's image, her critics had never once questioned her commitment to teaching. And it was only through that commitment that she cared to be judged. The sneers and insinuations would never diminish her real achievement: Children who were educated, motivated, confident, and determined to make their own way in the world. They were her legacy.

Recommended Phonics Books

Foltzer, Monica. *Professor Phonics Gives Sound Advice.* Cincinnati: St. Ursula Academy, 1965, 6th ed., 1976.
————. *A Sound Track to Reading.* Cincinnati: St. Ursula Academy, 1976.

For information on phonics programs and materials, contact:
The Reading Reform Foundation
7054 E. Indian School Rd.
Scottsdale, AZ 85251

Reading List
for Children Ages Four,
Five, and Six

Title	Author
Pierre	Maurice Sendak
Chicken Soup and Rice	Maurice Sendak
Tales from Shakespeare	Charles Lamb and Mary Lamb
You Will Go to the Moon	Ira Freeman
Twenty-Three Tales by Leo Tolstoy	Leo Tolstoy
Fairy Tales and Fables by Leo Tolstoy	Leo Tolstoy
Grimm's Fairy Tales	Wilhelm and Jacob Grimm
Russian Fairy Tales	Pantheon Books (publisher)
The Wonderful Story of Henry Sugar and Six More	Roald Dahl
The Silver Pony	Lynd Ward
Cricket Magazine	Open Court Pub. (publisher)
The Marvelous Misadventures of Sabastian	Lloyd Alexander
The Prince and the Pauper	Mark Twain
Hitty: Her First One Hundred Years	Rachel Field
The Royal Book of Ballet	Shirley Goulden
Stories of India	Dolch Series (publisher)
Stories of England	Dolch Series (publisher)
The Secret Garden	Frances H. Burnett
Famous Poems of Henry Wadsworth Longfellow	Doubleday (publisher)
Charlotte's Web	E. B. White

Title	Author
The Arbuthnot Anthology Children's Literature	Zena Sutherland
The Firebird	Viking Press (publisher)
Castles and Dragons	Crowell (publisher)
Pilgrim's Progress Retold for Children	Laurence Morris
The Water Buffalo	Pearl S. Buck
Mike's House	Julia Sauer
Rain Drop Splash	Alvin R. Tresselt
Hi, Mr. Robin	Alvin R. Tresselt
Spring is Here	Lois Lenski
Summer Day	Lois Lenski
I Like Winter	Lois Lenski
The Wonderful Egg	Dahlov Ipcar
Against Time	Roderic Jefferies
The Animal	Abingdon Books (publisher)
Among the Dolls	William Sleator
Animals You Will Never Forget	Readers Digest Press (publisher)
The Bad Times of Irma Baumlien	Carol Ryrie Brink
Baker's Hawk	Jack Bickham
Benjamin the True	Claudia Paley
The Best Christmas Present	Barbara Robinson
The Cay	Theodore Taylor
The Crack in the Wall	Karl H. Meyer
The Fiddler on High Lonesome	Brinton Turkle

Reading List
for Westside
Preparatory School

Adams, Russell L., *Great Negroes, Past & Present,* Golden Press.

Adler, Irving, *Mathematics,* Golden Press.

Aldington, Richard, *The Portable Oscar Wilde,* Viking Press.

Alexander, Lloyd, *The Marvelous Misadventures of Sebastian,* Dutton.

Alighieri, Dante, *Divine Comedy.*

Aristophanes, *The Plays of Aristophanes.*

Armstrong, Sperry, *Call of Courage.*

Asimov, Isaac, *Inside the Atom,* Harper & Row.

Aurelius, Marcus, *Meditations.*

Austen, Jane, *Pride and Prejudice.*

Bach, Richard, *Jonathan Livingston Seagull.*

Bamberger, Richard, *Physics Through Experiment,* Sterling.

Barr, George, *Research Ideas for Young Scientists,* McGraw-Hill.

Bendick, Jeanne, *The First Book of Time,* Franklin Watts.

Blackwood, Paul, *Push and Pull: The Story of Energy,* McGraw-Hill.

Bleeker, Sonia, *The Masai; Herdes of East Africa,* William Morrow.

Bond, Michael, *A Bear Called Paddington,* Houghton Mifflin.

Bontemps, Arna, *Frederick Douglass: Slave-Fighter-Freeman,* Alfred A. Knopf.

Bowie, Walter, *Bible Stories for Boys & Girls.*

Brent, Robert, *The Golden Book of Chemistry Experiments,* Western Publishers.

Braidwood, Robert J., *Archeologists and What They Do*, Franklin Watts.

Bronouski, Jacob & Selsam, *Biography of an Atom*, Harper & Row.

Bronte, Emily, *Wuthering Heights.*

Buehr, Walter, *The First Book of Machines*, Franklin Watts.

Bulfinch, Thomas, *Book of Myths.*

Bunyon, John, *Pilgrim's Progress.*

Carson, Rachel, *The Sea Around Us*, Golden Press.

Chaucer, Geoffrey, *The Canterbury Tales.*

Chekhov, Anton.

Clarke, Arthur, *The Challenge of the Sea*, Holt, Rinehart & Winston.

Cleary, Beverly, *The Mouse & The Motorcycle*, William Morrow.

Cleator, P. E., *Exploring the World of Archeology*, Children's Press.

Clymer, Eleanor, *The Second Greatest Invention; The Search for the First Farmers*, Holt, Rinehart & Winston.

Colum, Padraic, *The Children of Odin.*

Cottrell, Leonard, *Land of The Pharaohs*, World Publishers.

Cousteau, Jacques & Dumas, Frederic, *The Silent World*, Harper & Row.

De LaFontaine, Jean, *Fables of LaFontaine.*

Dickens, Charles, *Great Expectations; The Old Curiosity Shop; David Copperfield; Bleak House.*

Dickinson, Alice, *The First Book of Plants*, Franklin Watts.

Dostoyevsky, Fyodor, *The Brothers Karamasov; Crime and Punishment.*

Drisko, Clark, *Unfinished March.*

Dunbar, Paul L., *Poetry of Paul L. Dunbar.*

Eaton, Jeanette, *Marcus and Narcissa Whitman,* Harcourt Brace Jovanovich.

Edel, Abraham, *Aristotle.*

Emerson, Ralph Waldo, *The Portable Emerson.*

Epstein, Sam & Beryl, *Harriet Tubman, Guide to Freedom*, Garrard.

Faulkner, William, *Light in August.*

Felton, Harold W., *Nat Love, Negro Cowboy,* Dodd, Mead.

Field, Rachel, *Hitty, Her First Hundred Years.*

Flauber, *Life of Thoreau.*

Fleming, Ian, *Chitty, Chitty, Bang, Bang; The Magical Car,* Random House.

Foster, G. Allen, *Communication,* Criterion Books.

Foster, Genevieve, *Augustus Caesar's World 44 B.C. to A.D. 14,* Charles Scribner's Sons.

Franklin, Benjamin, *The Autobiography of Benjamin Franklin.*

Freeman, Ira & Mae, *The Story of Chemistry,* Random House.

Golding, William, *Lord of the Flies.*

Gallant, Roy A., *Exploring the Universe,* Doubleday.

Goldsmith, Ilse, *Anatomy for Children,* Sterling.

Goldston, Robert C., *Legend of the Cid.*

Gregor, Arthur S., *The Adventures of Man: His Evolution from Prehistory to Civilization,* Macmillan.

Gunther, John, *Death Be Not Proud.*

Harte, Bret, *The Luck of the Roaring Camp.*

Harrison, George Russell, *The First Book of Light,* Franklin Watts.

Haviland, Virginia, *Favorite Fairy Tales Told in Czechoslovakia,* Little, Brown.

Henry, O., *The Gift of the Magi.*

Hardy, Thomas, *The Return of the Native.*

Hogben, Lancelot, *The Wonderful Book of Energy,* Doubleday.

Homer, *The Odyssey* (do background on Homer first; explain the term *odyssey,* which now means long voyage)

Hugo, Victor, *Les Miserables.*

Huxley, Aldous, *Brave New World.*

Heyerdahl, Thor, *Kon-Tiki,* Books, Inc.

Irving, Washington, *Rip Van Winkle; The Legend of Sleepy Hollow.*

Jacobs, Joseph, *The Fables of Aesop,* Macmillan.

Jones, Vernon, *The Most Delectable History of Reynard the Fox.*
Judson, Clara Ingram, *Andrew Carnegie.*
Juster, Norton, *The Phantom Tollboth,* Random House.

Kosinski, Jerzy, *The Painted Bird.*
Knight, David C., *The First Book of Air,* Franklin Watts.
Knight, Eric, *Lassie, Come Home.*
Kohn, Bernice, *The Peaceful Atom,* Prentice-Hall.
Kredel, Fritz (illustrator), *Aesop's Fables,* Grosset & Dunlap.
Krylov, Ivan, *Fifteen Fables of Krylov,* Macmillan.

Lamb, Charles, *Tales from Shakespeare.*
Lee, Harper, *To Kill a Mockingbird.*
Leonard, William E., *Aesop & Hyssop* (Fables in verse), Open Court.
Lindgren, Astrid, *Pippi Longstocking; Pippi Goes on Board,* Viking
    Press.
London, Jack, *White Fang and Other Stories.*
Lowie, Robert H., *Indians of the Plains,* Natural History Press.

Malcolmson, Anne, *Selections from the Tales of Chaucer.*
Mandell, Muriel, *Physics Experiments for Children,* Dover.
Marlowe, Christopher, *Dr. Faustus.*
Morgan, Alfred, *First Chemistry Book for Boys & Girls,* Charles
    Scribner's Sons.
Mead, Margaret, *Anthropologists and What They Do,* Franklin Watts.
McCloskey, Robert, *Why They Wrote: The Canterbury Tales.*
Mullin, Virginia L., *Chemistry Experiments for Children,* Dover.
McKendry, John J., *Aesop, Five Centuries of Illustrated Fables,* Metro-
    politan Museum of Art.
McLeod, Mary, *King Arthur & His Knights.*
Murasaki, Lady, *The Tales of Genji.*

North, Sterling, *The Wolfing.*

Orwell, George, *Animal Farm; 1984.*
Olbracht, Ivan, *Indian Fables,* Paul Hamlyn.

Peare, Catherine Owens, *Mary McLeod Bethune,* Vanguard Press.

Plato, *Five Great Dialogues.*

Plutarch, *Plutarch's Lives.*

Poe, Edgar Allan, *Ligeia.*

Potok, Chaim, *My Name Is Asher; Lev.*

Preston, Edward, *Martin Luther King: Fighter for Freedom.*

Rabelais, Francois, *The Portable Rabelais* (including the adventures of Gargantua & Pantagruel).

Rawlings, Marjorie, *The Yearling,* Henry Z. Walck.

Reeves, James, *Fables from Aesop,* Henry Z. Walck.

Rogers, J. A., *World's Great Men of Color,* volumes I, II, Collier Macmillan.

Rollins, Charlemae H., *They Showed the Way: Forty Negro Leaders,* Thomas Y. Crowell.

Scott, Walter, *Quentin Durward; Ivanhoe.*

Seides, George, *The Great Quotations.*

Spenser, Edmund, *Saint George & the Dragon.*

Serwer, Blauche, *Jewish Tales: Let's Steal the Moon.*

Serrailler, *Beowulf.*

Sophocles, *Oedipus the King.*

Starkie, Walter, *Don Quixote Cervantes.*

Stevenson, Robert Louis, *Treasure Island.*

Scherman, Katherine, *The Slave Who Freed Haiti: The Story of Toussaint Louverture,* Random House.

Sere Dy, Kae, *Singing Tree.*

Tennyson, Alfred, *Poems of Tennyson,* Houghton Mifflin.

Thoreau, Henry David, *The Portable Thoreau* (Essays); *Walden.*

Tolstoy, Leo, *Fables & Fairy Tales* (Ann Dunnigan, translator), New American Library.

Tolstoy, Leo, *War and Peace.*

Townsend, George, *Aesop's Fables,* Parents Magazine Press.

Twain, Mark, *Puddin Head Wilson; The Prince & the Pauper; A Connecticut Yankee in King Arthur's Court* (explain the word *pseu-*

donym and that Mark Twain, George Eliot, and others wrote under a pseudonym).

Untermeyer, Louis (editor), *Aesop's Fables*, Parents Magazine Press.

Von Loon, Hendrich Willem, *The Story of Mankind*, Liveright.

Vivian, Charles, *Science Experiments & Amusements for Children*, Dover.

Voltaire, Francois, *Candide and Memnon*.

Williams, Beryl & Samuel, *Plant Explorer: David Fairchild*, Julian Messner.

Williams, Jay, *Song of Roland*.

Wilson, Mitchell, *The Human Body*, Golden Press.

Wise, William, *The Two Reigns of Tutankhamen*, G. P. Putnam's Sons.

Wohlrabe, Raymond, *Crystals*, J. B. Lippincott.

Wolck, Henry Z., *The Adventures of Don Quixote*.

Wyatt, Edgar, *Chief Geronimo*.

Wyler, Rose, *First Book of Weather*.

Poetry: Children should be encouraged to memorize famous poems of their choice, for example: "Abou Ben Adhem" by James Henry Leigh Hunt, "House by the Side of the Road" by Sam W. Foss, "If" by Rudyard Kipling, "Invictus" by William Ernest Henley, "Keep a-Going" by Frank Slanton. These poems can be found in *101 Famous Poems*.

Title	Author
101 Famous Poems (These should be used as daily readings just as basics readers. Far too many schools deprive children of the opportunity for reading good poetry.)	Roy J. Cook (ed.)
Library of World Poetry	William Cullen Bryant (ed.)

Story Poems: The Golden Treasury of Poetry	Louis Untermeyer (ed.)
Edgar Allan Poe's Selected Stories & Poems	Edgar Allan Poe
Poems of William Shakespeare	William Shakespeare
Selected Poems	Langston Hughes
Poems of Emily Dickinson	Emily Dickinson
Poems for Young People	Paul L. Dunbar

Epics: Introduce epics and that all epics begin in medias res (Latin for "in the middle of things"). That is, when all epics begin, much of the action has already taken place. This is a good time to introduce a little of Milton's *Paradise Lost.*

Title	**Author**
The Epic of Gilamesh	N. K. Sandars (ed.)
Mideaval Epics	(Published by Modern Library, Random House)
The Story of Roland	James Baldwin (ed.)

Biography:

Title	**Author**
Pocahontas and Her World	Frances Carpenter
The Story of George Washington Carver	Arna Bontemps
Frederick Douglass, Slave-Fighter-Freeman	Arna Bontemps
Nat Love, Negro Cowboy	Harold W. Flenton
Thurgood Marshall, Fighter for Justice	Lewis H. Fenderson
City Neighbor: The Story of Jane Addams	Clara Ingram Judson
Amelia Earhart	Jerry Seibert

The Story of My Life	Helen Keller
Gandhi, Fighter Without a Sword	Jeannette Eaton
Mary, Queen of Scots	Emily Hahn
Peter the Great	Nina Brown Baker
Drake, the Man They Called a Pirate	Jean Lee Latham
The World of Marco Polo	Walter Buehr
The Plays of Aristophanes	Aristophanes
Plutarch's Lives	Plutarch

Acknowledgments

I would like to thank my husband Clarence, my children Eric, Patrick, and Cynthia for being so patient with me during the months while I worked with Civia on this book. I am grateful to the students and parents of Westside Preparatory School, who enabled me to realize my dream, and to my own personal class who gave me much of the background for this book. Particular thanks to Lorraine Shanklin, Eileen Wells, and Patricia DeBonnett. I am grateful to the numerous visitors who came to the school, liked what they saw, and spread the word about what I was trying to do. To my mother, Bessie Maye Johnson, who always insisted I do everything the right way. To Robert and Nancy Soukup, who have followed my teaching career from the time of Delano until now. To Louise Godbold, who saved me thousands of dollars in psychiatric care. To Lillian Vaughn, who saw the school from its humble beginnings to the present and never missed a day of work. To Ella McCoy, who has taken on half the burden of running the school. And to my entire staff, who are patient and energetic enough to do without a desk and chair all day. Finally, I would like to thank all the wonderful people throughout the nation who have sent me letters of support.

Marva N. Collins